902

Fundamental Microsoft Publisher 97

About the Author . . .

June Kanai Reeder has been teaching and writing about desktop publishing products for more than ten years. She is the author of *Inside Corel Ventura 5.0* and *Teach Yourself Word Pro 96*, and has coauthored and contributed to numerous other books and publications. She is the owner of Ideas to Images, a software training and consulting firm in Houston that specializes in graphics and desktop publishing.

Fundamental Microsoft Publisher 97

June Kanai Reeder

Osborne **McGraw-Hill**

Berkeley   New York   St. Louis   San Francisco
Auckland   Bogotá   Hamburg   London   Madrid
Mexico City   Milan   Montreal   New Delhi   Panama City
Paris   São Paulo   Singapore   Sydney
Tokyo   Toronto

Osborne/**McGraw-Hill**
2600 Tenth Street
Berkeley, California 94710
U.S.A.

For information on translations or book distributors outside the U.S.A., or to arrange
bulk purchase discounts for sales promotions, premiums, or fundraisers, please
contact Osborne/**McGraw-Hill** at the above address.

Fundamental Microsoft Publisher 97

1234567890 DOC 9987

ISBN 0-07-882347-1

Publisher: Brandon A. Nordin
Editor-in-Chief: Scott Rogers
Acquisitions Editor: Joanne Cuthbertson
Project Editors: Janet Walden, Cynthia Douglas
Editorial Assistant: Gordon Hurd
Technical Editors: Eric and Deborah Ray
Copy Editor: Jan Jue
Proofreader: Pat Mannion
Indexer: David Heiret
Computer Designer: Jani Beckwith
Illustrator: Lance Ravella

This book is dedicated to my mom and dad

CONTENTS AT A GLANCE

PART I

BEFORE YOU BEGIN

CONTENTS

PART II

THE BASICS

PART III

ADVANCED OPTIONS

PART IV
CASE STUDIES

ACKNOWLEDGMENTS

I wish to thank everyone who helped put this book together; Joanne Cuthbertson, acquisitions editor, and her assistant, Gordon Hurd; Eric and Deborah Ray, technical editors; Janet Walden, senior project editor and Cynthia Douglas, associate project editor; Jan Jue, copy editor, Pat Mannion, proofreader, and David Heiret, indexer; and all of the people in production who did such a fine job laying out the pages: Roberta Steele, Marcela Hancik, Peter Hancik, Mason Fong, Jani Beckwith, Dennis Weikel, Lance Ravella, Sylvia Brown, and Leslee Bassin.

Welcome to Microsoft Publisher 97! Using Publisher, you can produce sales brochures certain to dazzle your clients, web pages to catch the eye of any surfer, and business forms to simplify your workload. You will find this book an indispensable aid in discovering how to operate Microsoft Publisher quickly and easily.

Why You Need This Book

Learning a new software application is a bit like learning a foreign language. First, you learn the basics, such as saying hello and good-bye. Next, you progress to more complicated phrases and concepts. When learning software, it also works well to get comfortable with the basics and then focus on advanced options and features. The first part of this book is organized to provide you with the basics of creating publications. The goal here is to quickly get you using Microsoft Publisher. Advanced features are discussed in later chapters to help you develop more complicated and complex publications.

This book provides detailed coverage of the many features and options in Microsoft Publisher. In case you haven't noticed, the documentation provided with the Publisher software offers more of an introduction to design, as opposed to step-by-step instructions on using the software. While the design tips are handy, you also need a book that provides the actual steps for operating the software—this book gives you both.

What's in This Book

In addition to thorough examination of the features of Publisher, this book is loaded with tips, tricks, and shortcuts guaranteed to make your job (and, therefore, your life) easier.

Easy-to-Follow Instructions

Step-by-step instructions for building documents and using the many features of Publisher appear throughout the book. All you have to do is open the book, cozy up with the computer, and get to work.

Timesavers, Tips, and Shortcuts

When learning software, it's always fun to discover ways to streamline your work. In every chapter throughout this book, you'll find lots of timesaving features, useful tips, and handy shortcuts.

Design Tips

There's a reason why graphic artists and designers make money—they know the rules of their business and they know how to catch a reader's attention and communicate information. Tips for designing publications are sprinkled throughout the pages in this book. No, these tips won't make you a professional designer, but they will help prevent you from making costly design and page layout mistakes.

How This Book Is Organized

This book is divided into four main parts, each intended to introduce and explain the features of Microsoft Publisher.

Part I: Before You Begin

Producing professional publications requires more than knowing how to operate Publisher. The first part of the book introduces the concept of desktop publishing—what it is and how it works. This part also covers important issues to consider before you begin designing, such as your budget and how the document will be printed. A chapter on design do's and don'ts is provided to let you in designers' "tricks of the trade."

Part II: The Basics

Part II familiarizes you with fundamental Publisher concepts such as using PageWizards to start new publications, add text and pictures to your publications, and proofing and printing your work. Everything in this section is integral to operating Publisher!

Part III: Advanced Options

Part III discusses advanced features of Publisher such as adding tables, WordArt, and sound to publications. You'll also discover how to build a web page, and work with background pages and advanced text formatting options to build more complicated publications.

Part IV: Case Studies

To provide you with an opportunity to build a publication from the ground up, three case study/exercise chapters are included in the last part of the book. Step-by-step instructions are provided to help you understand the process for building a publication from concept to printed product.

How to Use This Book

Fundamental Microsoft Publisher 97 is part tutorial and part reference in nature. If you are new to the software, you will find this book an indispensable teaching tool. As you sit at your computer with Microsoft Publisher 97, use the book to work through various features and steps. After you gain basic proficiency with the software, this book will become an invaluable reference tool. If you are already familiar with Publisher, you will appreciate how the book is logically organized and thoroughly indexed and referenced to help you quickly locate portions of the software you need to review. Now, you're ready to dig in!

PART

I

Before You Begin

1

What Is Desktop Publishing?

Simply defined, *desktop publishing* is the process of using a personal computer and printer to combine text and graphics on a page. Desktop publishing allows you to enter and format text as you write, scale graphics on-the-fly, and then piece it all together on the computer screen. Even the casual user can create postcards, brochures, newsletters, and web pages quickly and easily on a personal computer.

This chapter introduces the concept of desktop publishing and how it revolutionized printing and publishing. It then focuses on how Microsoft Publisher works to help you create professional-looking publications. You'll learn about the elements Publisher uses to compose documents. The chapter ends with a look at how Publisher can use other software applications to help you build and design publications.

The Desktop Publishing Revolution

The advent of desktop publishing in 1985 caused quite a stir in the graphic design and printing industry. Before desktop publishing, the design and production of printed publications was the exclusive domain of publishing companies and design professionals. By simplifying the publishing process, desktop publishing brought the power of publishing into the office and home. Now when you need a slick brochure to attract a new client, you can just sit down and design it. If you need a quick flyer for a garage sale, just type in the text, print some copies, and voilà!—it's ready to be posted. Desktop publishing has revolutionized the way people communicate.

 **NOTE:** *In 1985 Aldus Corporation released PageMaker for Macintosh computers. It's ironic that at the time many experts in the printing and publishing business declared desktop publishing "a passing fad."*

Before the Revolution: Publishing in the Old Days

Desktop publishing has all but done away with the days of fitting copy and setting type, using a proportion wheel and a cropping tool to size and position graphics, and cutting and pasting everything together to produce the page layout. Gone also is much of the waiting that accompanied the traditional print process. To produce a print project mechanically, you waited for the type to be reset because it was needed in 11 point type size instead of 10 point, waited for a graphic to be enlarged 112 percent not 110 percent, and waited for your thumb to heal after you stabbed it with the Exacto knife while cutting and pasting. With desktop publishing, you can change typefaces and type sizes in a few seconds, scale and move text and graphics around the page quickly, even totally redesign the project. And through it all, you can take comfort in the fact that it's pretty tough to stab yourself with a mouse.

Why Desktop Publishing Is Hot

Control is high on the list of reasons to produce your own publications. With desktop publishing, *you* are the designer—it is up to you to create a publication that exactly fits your needs. You write the text, pick the colors, and determine which types of graphics to use. You control the tone and look of the publication.

In addition to satisfying control freaks, desktop publishing also makes it easy to change your mind or fix mistakes. Rather use blue than green? No problem, one click and it's changed. Misspell the company name? Delete the wrong text, enter the correct text, and you're ready to go.

You can also save a lot of money with desktop publishing. Imagine you need 20 posters created for an upcoming sales event. With a computer and a printer, you can do it yourself. You don't have to hire a graphic professional to design the document, or hire a publishing company to print it.

The need for speed is another reason why desktop publishing is so popular. In these busy times, you'll be able to enter and format text, add a few graphics, and then print ten copies in time for a noon meeting.

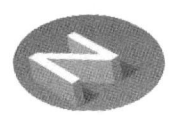 **NOTE:** *Although desktop publishing allows everyone with a computer and the right software to produce publications, not everyone is a graphic designer. Chapter 3 is devoted entirely to design "do's and don'ts."*

What Microsoft Publisher Can Do

The creators of Publisher built the software to meet the demands of small business owners, entrepreneurs, community leaders, and other professionals. They recognized that many people need newsletters, invoices, brochures, sales receipts, and other publications to communicate information and conduct business. However, they also realized not everyone is trained in page design, and it can get expensive to pay a graphic artist every time a document is needed. The creators of Publisher built a software application that's easy to learn and that creates publications quickly.

Publisher does not have all the bells and whistles associated with higher-end desktop publishing applications, but it does have many features to help you simplify and streamline your work. For instance, with Publisher you can easily insert page numbers, add the current date and time, rotate text, and apply decorative borders around pictures. Imagine trying to do all that by hand.

In contrast to some desktop publishing programs, you'll find Microsoft Publisher very easy to use. Many commands can be activated with a single mouse click or keyboard shortcut. Information in the menus and dialog boxes is straightforward, written in layperson's terms, so you don't have to be a graphic designer to understand them. You can operate Publisher without knowing what "kerning," "leading," or "tracking" means.

Predesigned Documents Guarantee Success

Although desktop publishing revolutionized the way publications are created, it hasn't changed the fact that many people don't know how to design a document. Knowing design rules and techniques is not a prerequisite for purchasing desktop publishing software (although in many designers' minds, it should be). Alas, untrained page designers frequently end up creating unreadable junk. Too many fonts, too much text, too many boxes are all surefire signs that *someone* didn't know what he or she was doing. So, while you may be saving money, you're sending out junk, which eventually turns people off and loses you money.

Publisher helps untrained page designers by providing a wide variety of predesigned publications, all designed by professional page layout artists. To help you set up the publication, Publisher uses *PageWizards*—a set of steps where you choose the style of the publication and then customize it to fit your needs. To keep everybody happy, Publisher provides PageWizards for all kinds of publications, such as greeting cards, resumes, invoices, and fax sheets. (When you need to zone out, try the paper airplane PageWizard.) Within each category of PageWizard, you will find several different styles and designs. For instance, as displayed in Figure 1-1, you can choose from a jazzy, fun, decorative, industrial, modern, or influential business card. With so many choices, it's tempting to create cards for your spouse, your kids, your dog, your cat…

 **NOTE:**   *For a detailed look at the types of PageWizards available and how to use them, refer to Chapter 5.*

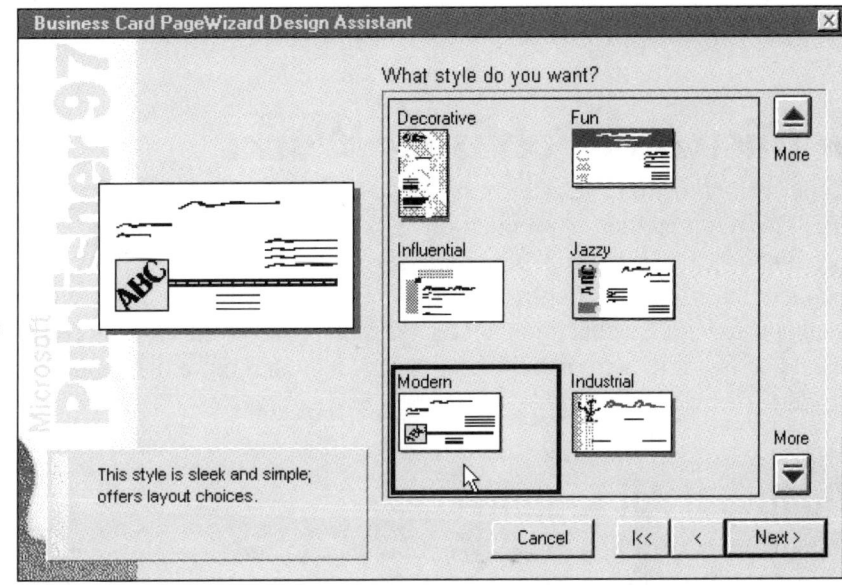

For business cards and other publications, PageWizards give you several style choices ranging from jazzy to formal

FIGURE 1-1

For adventurous types, Publisher makes it easy to alter the predesigned publications. It's simple to change the size of a graphic or move it somewhere else on the page. You may want to have more graphics and less text—whatever—you're in charge.

To prevent you from making a major design faux pas, Publisher provides a Design Checker to check the overall layout and design of your publication. So, when you're finished designing, you can activate the Design Checker and see how you fared. You'll learn more about the Design Checker in Chapter 10.

You Provide the Information, Publisher Does the Work

When you select a PageWizard, Publisher asks you a series of questions to help in the production of the publication. PageWizards are great for getting started with the design of the publication. Do you want two or three columns for text? Do you want to print on both the front and back of the pages? Each PageWizard asks questions specific to the type of document you are producing. For instance, the calendar PageWizard asks if you want room for a picture on the calendar, if you want room to write on the calendar, and how you want the names of the days to appear (see Figure 1-2). You simply click the desired options and Publisher goes to work.

How Microsoft Publisher Works

Look at any brochure, newsletter, or magazine spread, and notice all of the elements used to put together a publication. Photographs, charts, logos, illustrations, headlines, text, lines, and boxes are essential components of a well-designed publication. Microsoft Publisher allows you to quickly and easily combine these elements to build a publication. Of course, placing all of the elements on every page would be overkill, but it is important to have a good mix, so the publication attracts readers to your publication.

Putting It All Together

Publisher works with five main types of *objects* to build a publication. As shown in Figure 1-3, they are text, picture, table, WordArt, and drawn objects. Each object is

PageWizards prompt you through a series of steps to help build and customize the publication

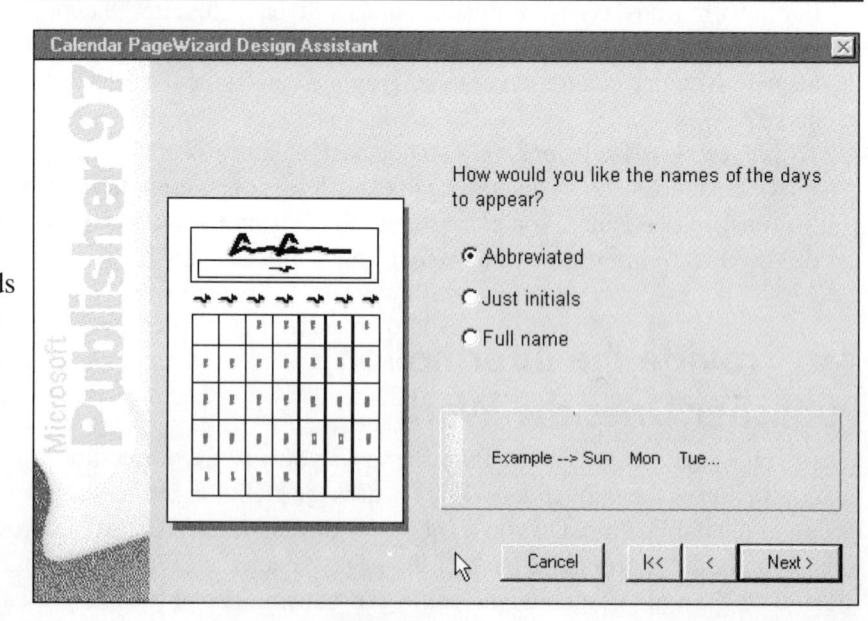

FIGURE 1-2

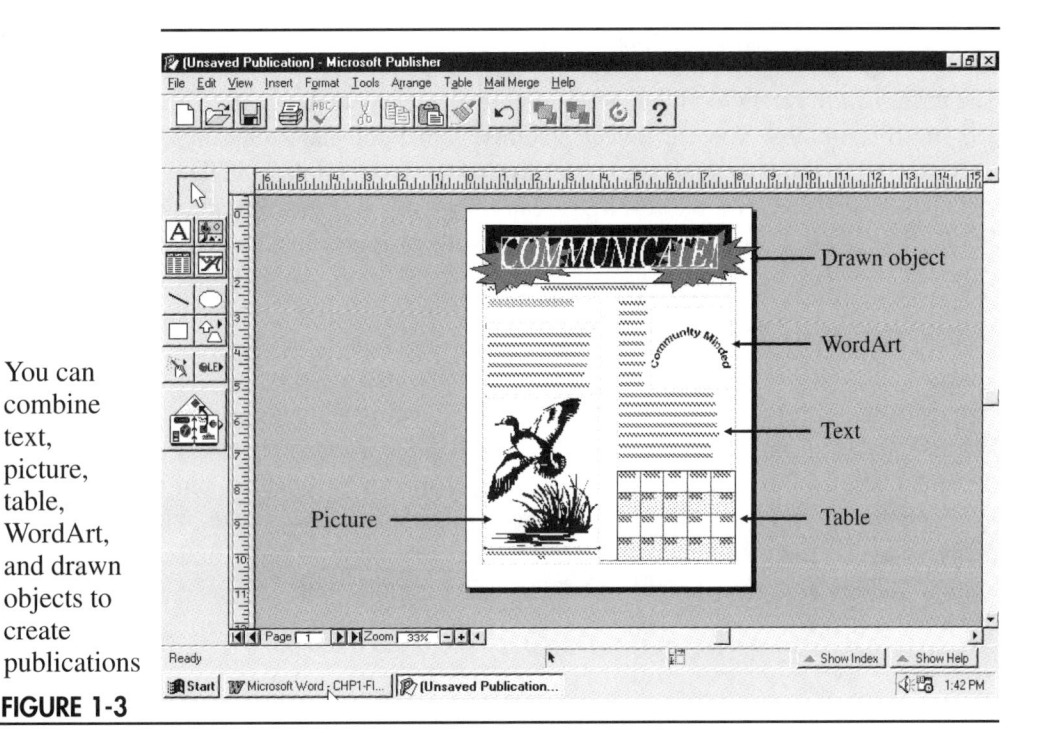

You can combine text, picture, table, WordArt, and drawn objects to create publications

FIGURE 1-3

stored in a box or *frame*. The frames can be easily moved and sized. As containers for objects on the page, frames are an important part of working with Publisher. You'll discover more about frames in Chapter 7.

Working with Text Objects

Text is the principal component of any publication. You can enter text directly into Publisher, or import text created in a word processing application such as Microsoft Word. When working with text, remember the goal of any publication is to communicate information. Always consider readability as you format and place text. For instance, before using 8 point type in an effort to squeeze more on the page, consider how it will affect the readability. You may end up creating something that no one wants to read.

Text can also be an important graphic design element. Enticing headings and fancy first-letter effects lure your reader into text. For more information on working with text, refer to Chapter 8.

Working with Picture Objects

The term *picture* refers to all kinds of graphic elements, such as photographs, clip art, and illustrations. You can select pictures from Publisher's clip-art gallery or create them in a drawing application such as CorelDRAW. Photos and line drawings can also be scanned, and the resulting scan image can be placed in a publication. For more information on working with picture objects, refer to Chapter 9.

Working with Table Objects

Tables help you present information in a concise and orderly way. Tables are frequently used in proposals and reports to add weight to arguments and conclusions. For instance, you can state "Sales have increased in the last year," but as Figure 1-4 demonstrates, a table supports the statement by displaying the actual numbers.

Publisher provides a table editor for creating and formatting tables. You'll find many powerful features for creating tables, such as merging cells, and adjusting column width and row height. You can also import tables created in other

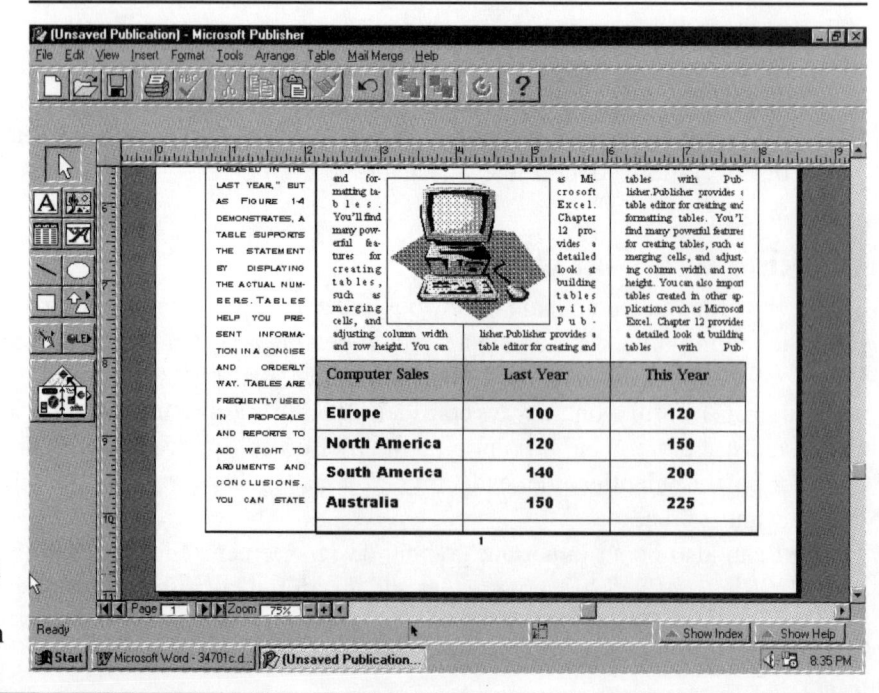

You can easily create tables to display and condense information

FIGURE 1-4

applications such as Microsoft Excel. Chapter 12 provides a detailed look at building tables with Publisher.

Working with WordArt Objects

WordArt objects are part text and part picture. You can think of WordArt objects as text objects that have been slanted, warped, or curved, and thus turned into picture objects. As mentioned earlier, text can be a major graphic design element; WordArt helps you design with text. For instance, in Figure 1-5, the text was created in WordArt so a wavy effect could be applied.

WordArt objects are created in a separate OLE server program—the next section of this chapter examines OLE applications. You'll find more on using WordArt in Chapter 13.

Working with Drawn Objects

Similar to picture objects, drawn objects are graphic shapes created with the drawing tools in Publisher. For instance, you can draw a box around text, or draw an arrow

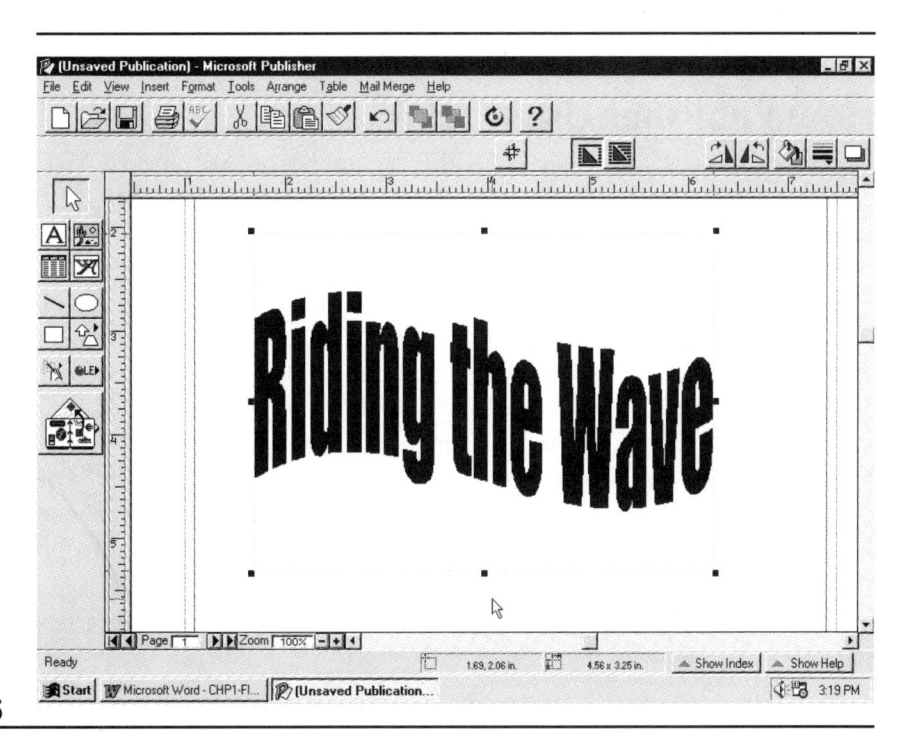

Use WordArt objects to spice up text with graphic effects

FIGURE 1-5

that leads the reader's eye across the page. To learn more about drawing with Publisher, refer to Chapter 11.

Using Your Favorite Programs

No one computer program can do it all. It generally takes the power of several types of applications to build a publication. For example, while Publisher provides some drawing tools, it certainly is no match for a drawing application such as CorelDRAW. Further, although you can enter text and build tables in Publisher, you may wish to use your favorite word processing or spreadsheet application instead. WordArt, discussed earlier, is another good example. WordArt can apply special effects to text, something Publisher cannot do. Publisher allows you to access the features of other applications through a process called *object linking and embedding* or OLE (pronounced "olé"—like in bullfighting).

Basically, object linking and embedding provides special options for placing objects created in other applications in your Publisher document. *Object* is a generic term that encompasses any kind of computer-generated text or graphic. For instance, with OLE you can place a graphic object created in CorelDRAW into a Publisher document.

How Publisher Uses OLE

One of the ways Publisher uses OLE is to build WordArt objects. You start the WordArt application, create the text object, and exit WordArt. The OLE/WordArt object appears on the page.

Another way to create OLE objects is to cut and paste. If you cut or copy an object from an application that supports OLE and then paste this object into Publisher (which also supports OLE), you have created an OLE object. For example, you can copy a graphic from CorelDRAW and paste it into Publisher. The pasted graphic is an embedded object.

 **NOTE:** *Microsoft applications such as Word, Excel, and PowerPoint heavily use object linking and embedding. Check the software documentation if you're unsure whether your favorite application supports OLE.*

Summary

This chapter introduced you to desktop publishing and to how Publisher helps you build quality publications. You're probably ready to get to work. But wait, there are several key issues to be determined before any text or graphics hit the page. Read Chapter 2 to help you get started on the right track.

2

What to Consider Before You Design the Page

Designing and printing publications can be a timely and costly undertaking. It's easy to make mistakes, such as choosing the wrong colors or adding so much text the main message gets buried. You wouldn't be the first if you produced a flyer announcing a grand opening and forgot to include the date. One of the keys to creating effective, compelling publications is preparation. The prep work you put into a publication before you design can save you hours of redo work and pockets full of money.

Consider this chapter a kind of thinking cap for building publications. The goal is to get you thinking about issues affecting the design of a publication before you start putting it together. The chapter begins by looking at the purpose and target audience of the publication. It also helps you consider how much money can be spent on the publication. For instance, can you spring for full color? The chapter ends with a look at why it's important to consider how the publication will be printed before you start designing.

What Should the Publication Accomplish?

First, you have to get the readers' attention. Today's readers decide very quickly whether to read a publication or toss it. You must make sure the primary message of your publication is easy to see. Once you've got their attention, the goal becomes communicating information.

The information to be communicated varies greatly among different types of publications. For instance, the goal of a sales catalog is to let customers know about merchandise and sales prices. The goal of a business card is to identify a person and company, as well as supplying an address and phone number. The goal of an invoice is to state the fee for the specified products or services. Sounds simple enough, but thinking about what *needs* to be in a publication is a big step in eliminating what *doesn't* need to be in a publication.

Creating a Mock-up

You can save a lot of time by writing down what elements are necessary to convey your message. Ask yourself: What text information is needed? What graphics are important to illustrate the information? Will tables be useful to condense numerical data? If you're building a publication with multiple pages, create a paper mock-up of the publication, and jot down what goes where (see Figure 2-1). Consider what needs to go on the first page, and what can appear on secondary pages. You'll be surprised at how quickly the mock publication fills up.

Ranking the objects in order of importance can also be helpful. If you run out of room, simply start cutting items from the bottom of the list. Ranking can also help you determine what items need to be dominant on the page. For instance, on a postcard announcing computer training classes you want to feature the dates of the classes.

Deciding first what needs to be in the publication makes it easier to design. You can then focus on arranging text and pictures, text formatting, and color selections, rather than debating whether you even want to include an item.

Are You Selling, Training, or Just Doing Business?

Readers are savvy. If a publication doesn't look right, sound right, or even feel right, they won't read it. Think about your own habits regarding brochures and other publications. You expect an elegant, glossy advertisement for luxury cars but a more simple, basic look for used cars. In fact, if an ad for used cars is too elegant and

Before designing, create a paper mock-up of a publication to help you visualize how text and other elements will fit on the page

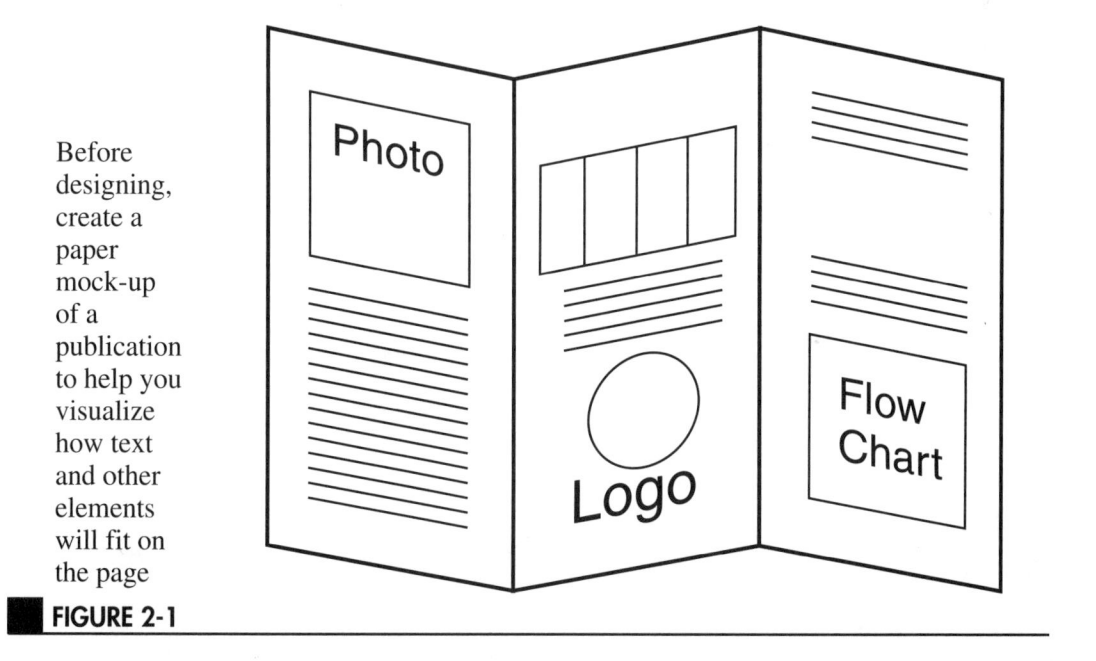

FIGURE 2-1

expensive looking, you might think the prices are inflated to pay for such fancy ads. Psychology plays a role in advertising. Put yourself on the couch and analyze your own expectations to gain some insight into publication design.

When you're selling a product or service, readers expect some flash. You have to get their attention. Scan other sales publications to discover what works. Consider what made you want to look at the publication in the first place.

However, when producing training materials, give readers clear, straightforward instructions. No flashy graphics are necessary. Don't put too much on a page. In Figure 2-2, which page looks more inviting? Readers like to move through training materials quickly—it makes them feel as if they're really progressing.

Business materials such as fax sheets, invoices, expense reports, and time sheets generally work best if you supply only the necessary information. For business documents, Microsoft Publisher's predesigned publications alone are worth the price of the software. As displayed in Figure 2-3, the PageWizard for business forms make it easy to quickly build all kinds of forms.

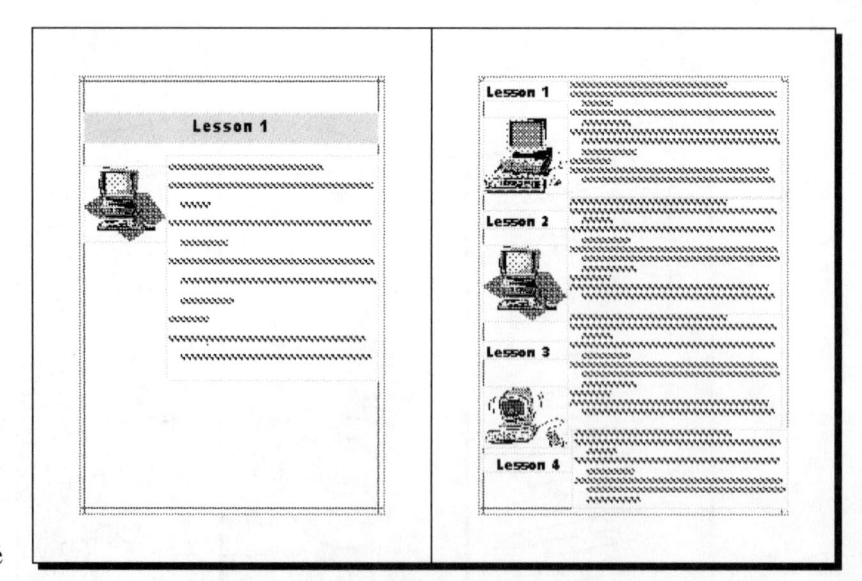

Cramming a lot on the page just to save on printing costs can be a mistake

FIGURE 2-2

Black-Tie or Blue Collar: Designing with Your Audience in Mind

Successful publications are designed with the target audience in mind. It's imperative that you consider the taste and style of the people you want to read your document. Close your eyes and imagine an advertisement displaying clothing for Generation X'ers. It has a certain look, doesn't it? Now imagine an ad for expensive timepieces—it has a completely different style. Creating publications that meet the expectations and demands of a target audience doesn't happen by accident. Designers work hard at finding a look that appeals to a certain group of people.

 **TIP:** *For more information on identifying your target audience, visit a library or bookstore for books on advertising and marketing.*

In addition to the design of a publication, your target audience should also influence which paper stock is used for printing, how the publication is folded or bound, and the printing process. These elements work together to produce the look and feel of a publication.

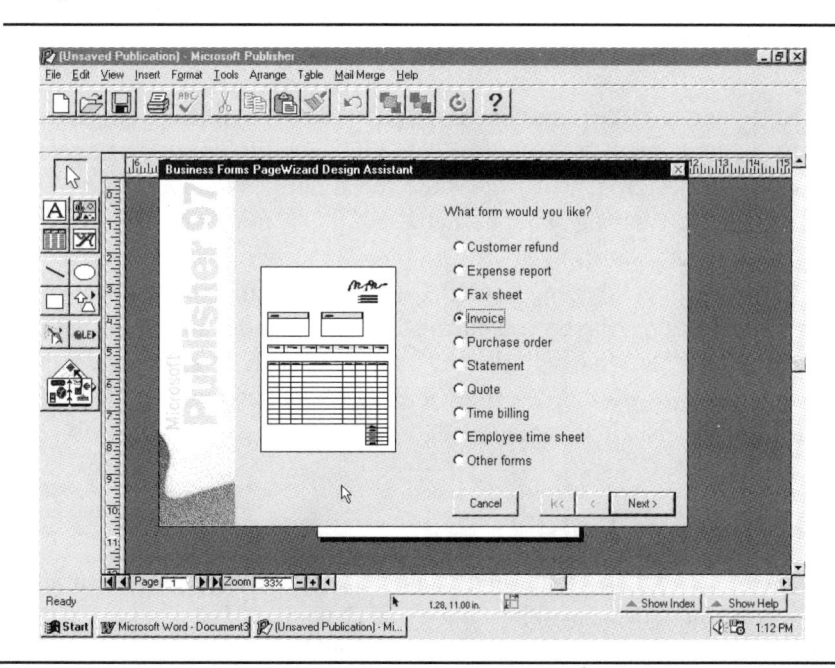

Use Publisher's predesigned business forms to build documents quickly

FIGURE 2-3

Don't forget to consider writing style when building publications. Once you've got the readers enticed by the page design, don't turn them off with inappropriate dialect and jargon. For instance, writing that reads like a legal brief is too rigid for sales materials. It can be tough to alter your writing style. Sometimes it helps to study the writing in similar publications. Here's a trick—after writing the copy for a publication, put it away for a couple of days. You'll be able to look at it more objectively, fix mistakes, and tighten up sentences. Try to look at it through the eyes of your customer.

Take a Tip from the Professionals

Professional page designers have "idea boxes," where they stash appealing and attractive publications and packaging. Many corporations urge their professional designers to go on scavenger hunts for new and trendy ideas they might adapt. Idea boxes include everything from magazine covers to Christmas ornament packaging. When the time comes to design a new publication, designers rummage through the box looking for something to catch their eye and get the creative juices flowing.

 **NOTE:** *Hallmark Cards, Inc. routinely invites designers to attend screenings of newly released movies with artistic merit so the designers can keep up with new looks.*

Start your own idea box. Focus on publications aimed at your target audience. Throw in junk mail, business cards, annual reports, and newsletters. If you're preparing to design a web page, take the time to surf competitors' web pages. Magazines focusing on the Internet usually list new web sites and those with award-winning designs.

When you begin digging through the idea box, remember it's okay to borrow an idea here and there. Maybe you like a color from one document and a typeface from another. Make sure that you do not copy too much from anyone's design when making your own work. You cannot and should not copy an entire design or image from someone else. It's illegal.

Typecasting Publications

Typeface—the design of the text characters—influences the appearance of your publication more than any other single visual element. The typeface you choose can help or hinder the reader's ability to understand your message. Typefaces seem to have a personality of their own. Notice in Figure 2-4 that although the text is the same, the change in typefaces produces very different looks.

Publisher provides a good selection of typefaces. You can choose your own typefaces, mixing and matching them to create a certain look. If you're not feeling particularly creative or just want to save time, rely on the typefaces used in Publisher's predesigned publications. A brochure classified as "casual" will use informal, friendly typefaces. The newsletter in Figure 2-5 was classified "art deco" and uses trendy, modish typefaces.

If you decide to buy additional typefaces, look for typeface packages designed for specific uses. Typeface catalogs describe the best use for many typefaces and also suggest typefaces that work well together.

Consider Your Budget

Before placing any text or graphics on the page, consider the amount of money you can spend producing the publication. In addition to printing costs (discussed in the next section), consider costs you may incur in the development of the publication.

Carefully select typefaces that fit the tone of your publication

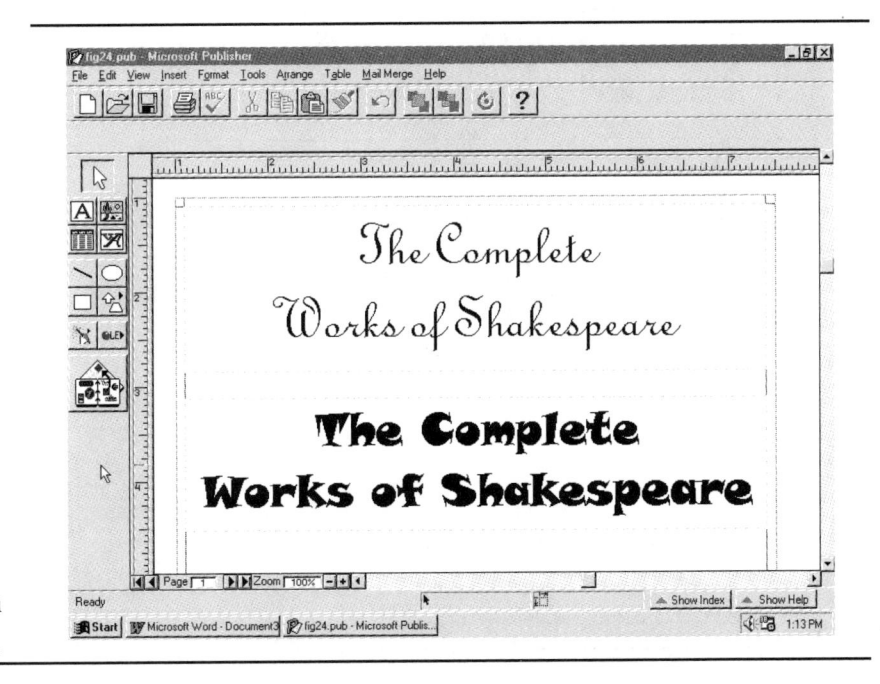

FIGURE 2-4

For instance, will you need to hire a professional designer? If you're new to page design and in charge of producing the annual report for a Fortune 500 company, it wouldn't be a bad idea. The designer doesn't necessarily have to create the whole publication. Maybe the designer just helps you develop the publication's theme, or sketches a snazzy corporate logo. The designer can also recommend typefaces, paper stock, and printing options.

Will you need to purchase any photographs? Hiring a photographer can get pricey, but sometimes a photograph of a particular product or site is a must for a publication. Once you get your hands on the photograph, remember it will have to be scanned—this also costs money, unless you have a scanner. What about clip art? Finding a specific type of clip art is usually a little easier than locating a photograph. Check the shelves of computer stores to find clip art sorted by professions and interests, such as medical, legal, real estate, sports, and travel.

Don't Put the Cart Before the Horse

Desktop publishing programs such as Publisher make using color and other special effects so simple, it's easy to forget that these things cost money to print. You can

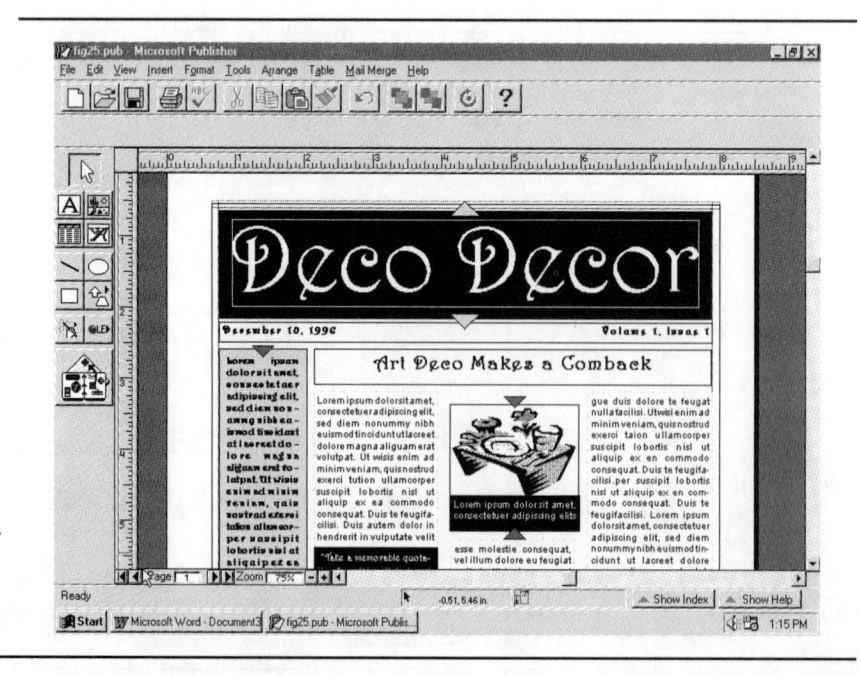

The PageWizard for newsletters includes an "art deco" style with complementary typefaces

FIGURE 2-5

2

add color photographs, use color in graphics and text, and create tri-fold brochures with a couple of mouse clicks. However, commercial printers charge more for color printing than black and white, and they charge more to fold publications. Make sure you can afford to print these elements before you use them in your design, so you don't end up with a publication that looks great on the computer screen, but is too expensive to print.

Consider Printing Before You Design

Printing is generally the biggest cost of producing a publication. However, printing costs depend largely on how you will output the publication. Are you printing to a color printer sitting on your desk? This is great if you've got the printer and only need a few copies. Are you sending the job to a commercial printer? This is where money becomes an issue; nonetheless, if you desire a certain look and numerous copies, commercial printing is the only way to go.

 **NOTE:**   *Chapter 10 provides more information on color printing and on working with commercial printers.*

Consider printing costs before you begin designing, so you'll know what you can and cannot afford. For instance, cost may force you to stick with black-and-white printing and avoid color. Knowing this certainly helps in the design process. From the start, you know to shoot black-and-white photos. (Color photos printed in black and white lose some contrast and definition.) You know to avoid color clip art, or at least to modify it to black and white. As you create the page, you can use black and white on text elements such as headings and on fancy first letters or graphic elements such as lines and borders.

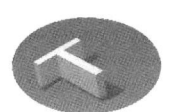 **TIP:**   *Don't design in color if your output will be black and white. You won't get a good screen representation of how the publication is going to look after it is printed.*

Determining beforehand what color and special effects are within your budget can help you avoid a lot of redo work. For example, imagine you placed a graphic that *bleeds*—runs all the way to the edge of one of the pages in your publication. Then you learn that the printer charges for these bleed effects. So you have to go back and resize the graphic and maybe even rework the whole publication design.

Before you design, talk to the printer, show them samples of what you like, and get familiar with what will and won't inflate the cost of your publication.

Alternatives to Color

Sure, people like color. But there are other ways to enhance the look of a publication. Consider a nice paper stock. Heavy, glossy paper can add a formal feel to business reports and brochures. Recycled paper provides a casual, more contemporary experience. Visit a paper supply store and rub your fingers through some paper. There's an amazing number of choices.

While you're at the paper supply store, look into preprinted paper to add a little color. Especially useful for printing on a black-and-white printer in your home or office, preprinted paper is great for spicing up invitations, announcements, and flyers.

Rather than eliminating color completely, check out pricing for *spot colors*. Spot color is the addition of one color to the printing process. Technically, spot color printing prints black and the selected spot color. Rummage through your idea box for good ideas on working with spot color.

Summary

This chapter discussed important issues to be considered before you design a publication in Publisher. Elements such as the target audience greatly affect the style of a publication, and factors such as printing costs affect what color and other special effects you can use in the design. Chapter 3, the last chapter of this part, covers design do's and don'ts—rules and techniques to help you avoid some common pitfalls of page design.

3

Design Do's and Don'ts

There's nothing like designing a publication to make you appreciate the skill and talent of professional graphic artists. Years of education and experience have taught them to create publications that look clean and organized. If you don't have such training, your publications may look messy and cluttered. Before you decide to sign up for a course in page design at your local night school, read through this chapter to discover a few tricks of the trade.

The information in this chapter will not make you a professional page designer. However, it will help you avoid some common mistakes in publication design. With Publisher's predesigned publications and the following list of do's and don'ts you should be able to sail through the design process.

This chapter covers basic page design rules and techniques. The rules are not inflexible—in fact, you may come across publications that very effectively break the rules. But if you're a newbie to desktop publishing, stick with the basics to ensure creation of professional-looking publications. You may want to read through this chapter before and after designing a publication. Going through the information again after laying out a publication helps you locate mistakes that may have been overlooked.

Do Use White Space Effectively

White space is the part of the page where nothing is printed. You'll find white space in the margins around the page, between columns of text, and around text and graphics. To a designer, white space is as much a design element as pictures and text. Blocks of white space draw attention to type and graphics. Notice how the white space in Figure 3-1 draws the eye to the ad copy and graphic.

White space helps the reader's eye to relax. White space makes the message more appealing and easier to read. In general, formal publications, such as annual stockholders reports, benefit from generous use of white space.

 **TIP:**   *The center of the page is the first place the reader looks; place your most important elements there.*

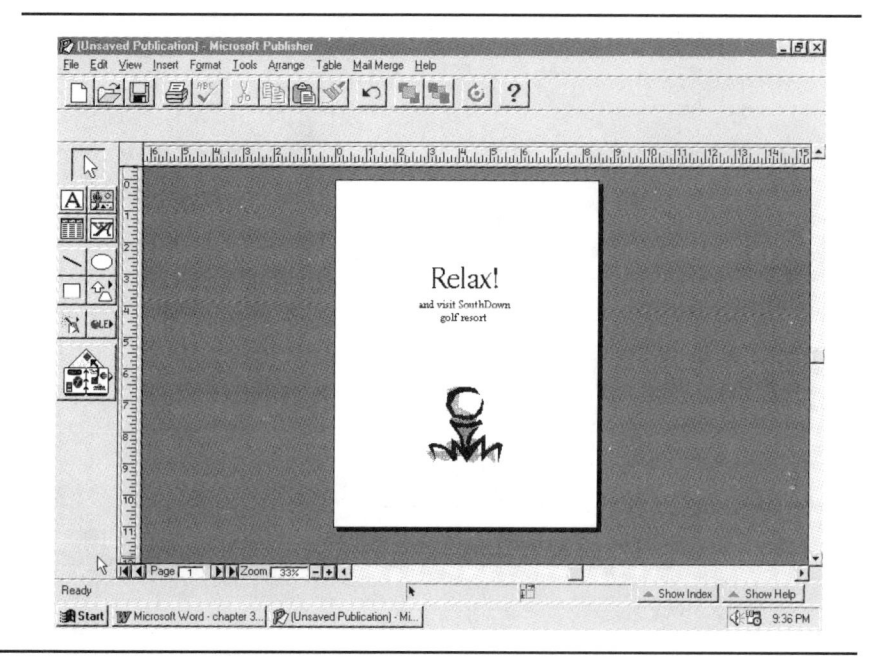

In this ad, white space is a design element to lead the reader's eye to the main text

FIGURE 3-1

Don't Try to Fill Every Inch of the Page

A common mistake in publication design is to jam as much as possible on every page. Readers look for one main element, such as a photo or heading, to draw them into a page. When there are too many things on a page, nothing dominates. Rather than enticing readers, overcrowded pages confuse them, often causing them not to look at a publication at all. Too many elements appear on the left page in Figure 3-2. On the right page, some of the elements were removed, adding white space to emphasize the remaining text and graphics.

The left page in Figure 3-2 also has a patch of white space stuck in the middle of the page. Although white space is generally good, when it appears in the middle of a page, it can look unprofessional. Eliminating white space in the middle of the page is usually as simple as enlarging a graphic or increasing the size of headings to fill in the white space.

TIP: *To eliminate white space in the middle of a page, enlarge a graphic or increase the size of headings.*

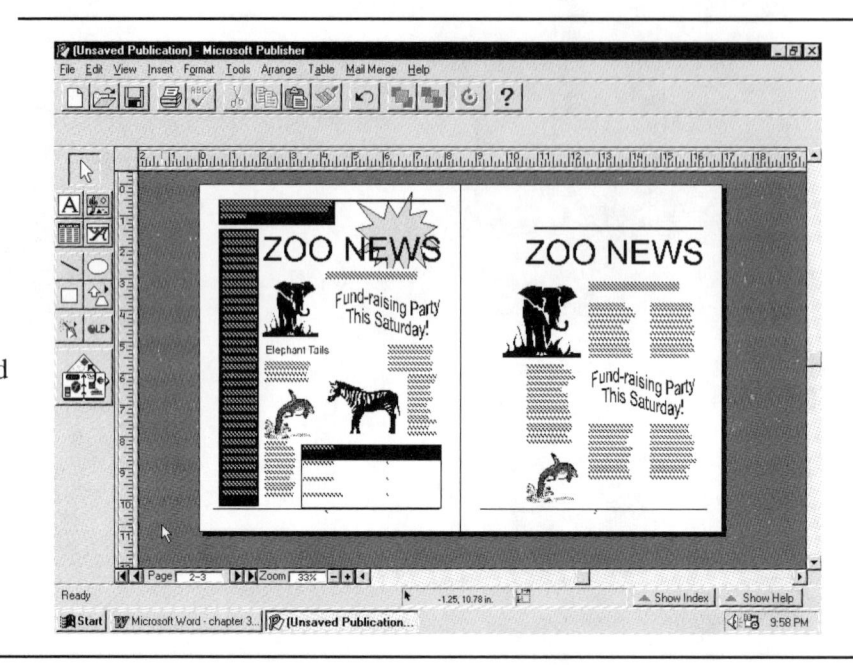

By uncluttering an overcrowded page (left), you can focus attention on the text and graphics (right)

 **FIGURE 3-2**

Don't Place Too Much Space Between Columns of Text

Wide spaces between columns of text break up the flow of a story or article. In Figure 3-3, the $\frac{3}{4}$ inch spacing between columns of the left page creates white "stripes" running vertically down the page. Notice how simply decreasing the column spacing to $\frac{1}{4}$ inch (as on the right page) and forcing the extra white space to the outside margins enhances the look of the publication.

The space between columns should not be as wide as the margins around the page. In general, larger type sizes require larger column spacing. For instance, try $\frac{1}{4}$ inch column spacing for 10 to 12 point type, and perhaps $\frac{1}{2}$ inch column spacing for 24 point and larger type.

TIP: *In general, stick with two or three columns across the width of the page. Page designs with too many columns look cluttered. In addition, the narrow width of the columns makes text hard to read.*

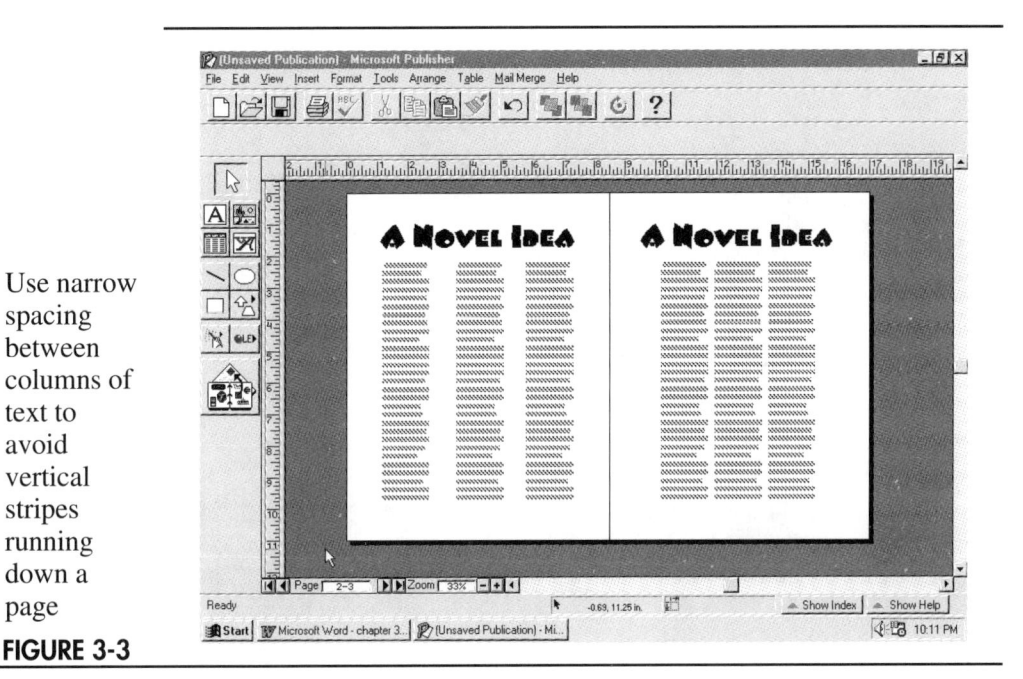

Use narrow spacing between columns of text to avoid vertical stripes running down a page

FIGURE 3-3

Don't Scrimp on Margins

Margins work as picture frames around a publication. The white space in margins increases the appeal of other elements on a page. In addition, don't forget that margins allow a reader room to hold your publication. You don't want the reader's thumb hiding important information. The left page in Figure 3-4 uses a ¼ inch margin. (There's also too much spacing between columns and graphics.) Notice how much more readable the document looks when white space is pushed to the outside in a 1 inch margin.

As a general rule, margins should be at least twice the width of the space between columns of text. Many designers add extra margin spacing at the top and bottom of a page to reduce the length of text columns and encourage reading.

 **TIP:** *Generally, make margins at least twice as wide as the space between columns of text.*

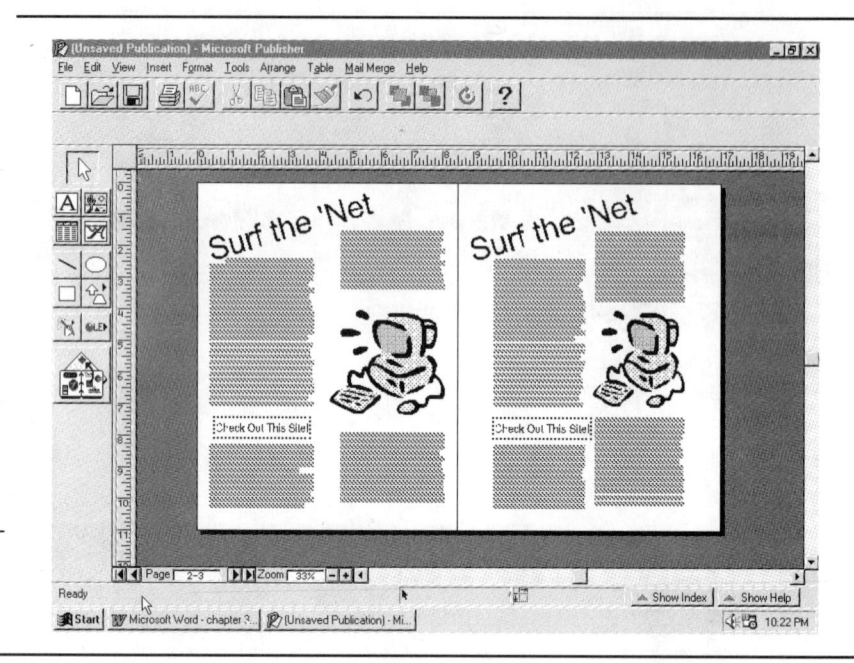

Adequate margin spacing is a sign of a professional-looking publication

FIGURE 3-4

Do Select Fonts Carefully

Technically, a *font* is a specific typeface in a specific type size. For instance, Times New Roman in 12 point is one font. Times New Roman in 14 point is another. In fact, Times New Roman in 12 point bold is yet another. To many designers, the fonts used to design a publication are the most important design element. Typefaces set the tone for the publication, and type size determines how dominant text appears on the page.

NOTE: *Refer to Chapter 8 for more information on formatting text characters in Publisher.*

You may already have a fairly good idea about typeface selection. For instance, most people wouldn't use a typeface with little animals in the letters on a wedding invitation. If you're not sure about a font—for instance, you think it might be a little too fancy—it might be best to stick to a basic font such as Times New Roman or Arial. Typefaces can be classified into three broad categories. *Serif* typefaces have small strokes at the ends of the characters. These strokes (serifs) help guide the reader's eye from letter to letter. Popular serif typefaces are Times New Roman, Century Schoolbook, and Swiss. As displayed in Figure 3-5, serif typefaces can look friendly or formal. Serif fonts are generally considered the best choice for body text.

As the name implies, *sans serif* typefaces do not have the strokes. Popular sans serif typefaces include Arial, Avant Garde, and Century Gothic. As shown in Figure 3-6, sans serif type has a simple, clean look suited to signs and flyers. Sans serif type is considered ideal for headings and other short text blocks. However, avoid using sans serif fonts in long text blocks, since it can be difficult to read.

Script and *decorative* typefaces commonly have distinct characteristics that elicit certain responses from a reader. For instance, in Figure 3-7, the first typeface has an elegant appeal, the second, a casual style. Because of their distinct looks, script and decorative fonts work well in logos and advertising. Popular script and decorative typefaces include Brush Script, Hobo, Stencil, and Freestyle. Script and decorative typefaces would not work well in body text.

Don't Use More Than Two Fonts

A common design mistake is using too many typefaces on a page. The result is a publication that's confusing and amateurish (see Figure 3-8). On the other hand,

Some typefaces have small extensions, called *serifs,* which increase their readability

FIGURE 3-5

Sans serif type looks great in large headlines and titles

FIGURE 3-6

Use script or decorative typefaces to elicit a strong response from your reader

FIGURE 3-7

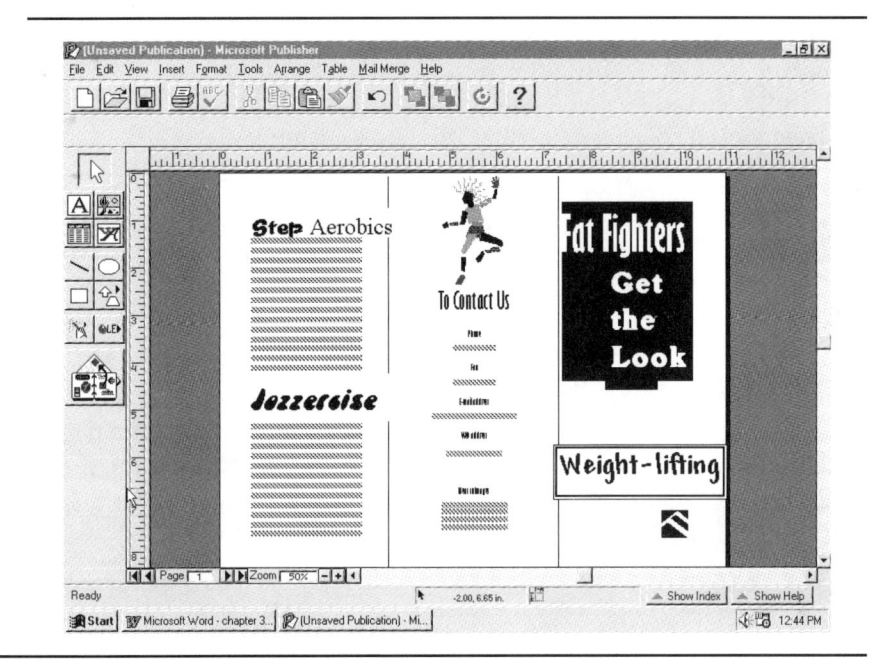

Use of too many typefaces adds confusion to a publication

 **FIGURE 3-8**

using one typeface throughout a publication looks weak and bland. As a general rule, stick with two fonts in a publication. Select a serif typeface for the body text and a sans serif for headings.

TIP: *Generally, use only two fonts in a publication—a serif typeface for body text and a sans serif typeface for headings.*

Two typefaces provide a lot of size and style options. For instance, headings can be in 36 point Arial bold, and subheadings in 20 point Arial. You could use Times New Roman in 12 point for body text, and Times New Roman 12 point italics for captions.

Don't Underline Headings or Body Text

Many moons ago, when people used typewriters, underlining was the only way to emphasize a word. However, underlining cuts off *descenders* (the part of letters such as *y, g,* and *q* that descends below the normal line of text), making words hard to read (see Figure 3-9).

In desktop publishing, you have an alternative to underlining. Use the bold and italic type style options to draw attention to headings and specific words in body text. However, use bold and italics sparingly. Too much bold and italics can make the page looked spotted, detracting from its readability.

 **CAUTION:** *Heavy use of bold and italics can detract from a page's readability.*

Don't Use Tiny Text

It's tempting to reduce the size of body text to cram more on the page. This can backfire though, because text gets so small no one wants to read it. For maximum readability, body text should not get smaller than 10 point. Rather than using tiny text, edit it to take less space.

Use bold and italics rather than underlining to emphasize words and headings

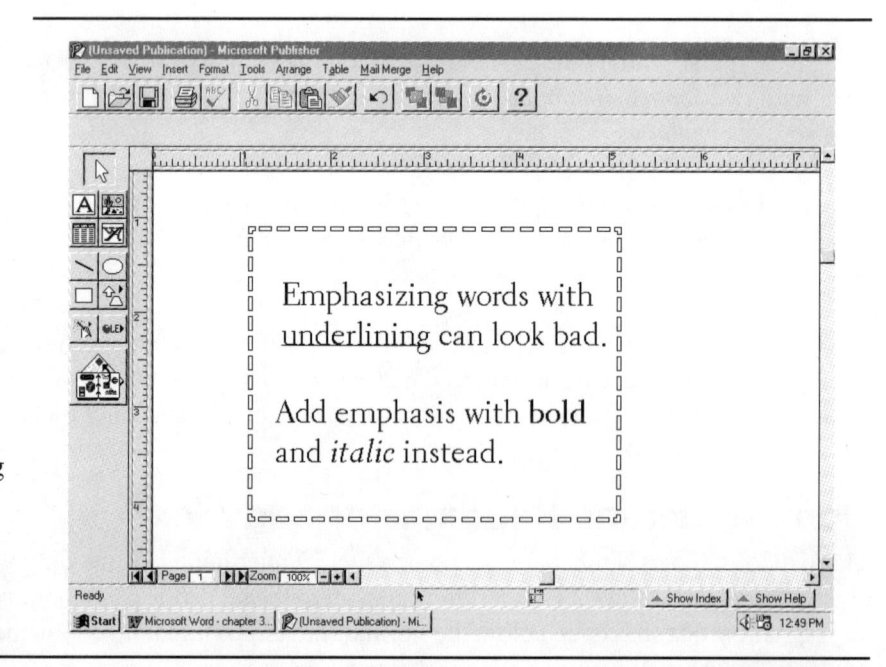

FIGURE 3-9

Don't Use Justified Text

Justified text, where both margins of a text block are aligned (straight), can be difficult to read. In a justified text block, extra spacing appears between words, creating what many designers call *rivers* of white space (see Figure 3-10). To stop the flow of the rivers, use flush left/ragged right text alignment.

Don't justify heading text either. The extra spacing between the words can ruin the cohesiveness of a headline.

Do Aim for Consistency

Elements on a page should be repeated in appropriate places. Repetition of certain elements is a good sign that a publication was designed by someone with know-how. Consistency is particularly important in longer publications such as books and reports. Consistency ties together information on the separate pages, creating a cohesive, organized publication. Look through various publications to distinguish what elements need to be consistent across the pages. Generally, page margins,

The excessive white space in justified text can make it hard to read. Use flush left/ragged right text alignment instead

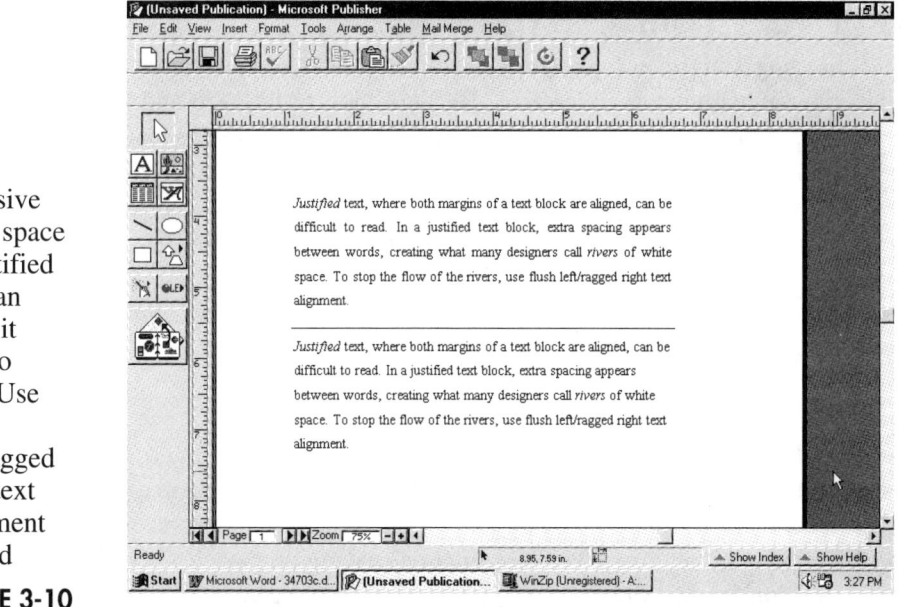

FIGURE 3-10

number of columns, text formatting, colors, and header and footer information are repeated from page to page.

 **NOTE:** *Refer to Chapter 16 for timesaving information about creating header and footer text.*

Lines, logos, fancy first letters, and other graphic elements are a great way to achieve cohesiveness. The repetition of these objects adds consistency to the publication. For instance, adding a thin line along the top and bottom of every page helps bring the publication together.

Don't Vary Color Across Pages

Avoid switching colors within the pages of a publication. Use of blue graphic accents on one page and red on the next breaks up the publication rather than uniting it. It's much more appealing to use both colors on every page consistently. For instance, a red logo and blue lines displayed on every page would tie a publication together.

Don't Vary Fonts Across Pages

Avoid changing fonts on every page in a publication. Consistency in text formatting for headings is particularly important. Readers look to the size and format of a heading to provide cues to the significance of information. In this book, all main headings appear in a specific typeface and type size. Likewise, all second and third level headings use consistent formatting. The reader can look through the book and quickly identify a new section by the formatting of a main heading.

 **TIP:** *Aim for consistency in your page design by using the same fonts and colors on all pages of a publication.*

Publisher provides tools for adjusting line and character spacing of text blocks. For best results, keep line and character spacing consistent throughout a publication. For instance, some novice page designers might increase the line spacing on page 1 to fill up the page, and then decrease the line spacing on page 2 to cram in more text. Such inconsistency would be a sign of an inexperienced designer.

Don't Vary Margins Across Pages

Avoid fluctuating margin spacing throughout the pages of a publication. Going back and forth between 1 inch and $\frac{1}{2}$ inch margins looks disorganized. It's okay to be creative with margin spacing, but keep it consistent throughout. For a different look, try using wide outside margins (see Figure 3-11) or wide top margins.

Do Select Graphic Elements Carefully

Graphics are key elements of good page design. Although words are the meat of a publication, the pictures and graphics are the sizzle. The photographs, technical drawings, charts, and illustrations included in your publications are attention-grabbers. They are designed to explain technical concepts, emphasize sales growth, and provide visual support to your text. Designers often spend a great deal of time selecting graphics for a publication.

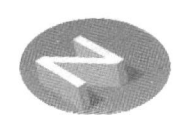 **NOTE:** *Refer to Chapter 9 for more information on inserting clip art and other graphics into your Publisher publications.*

No matter what margin style you choose, repeat it throughout the pages in a publication

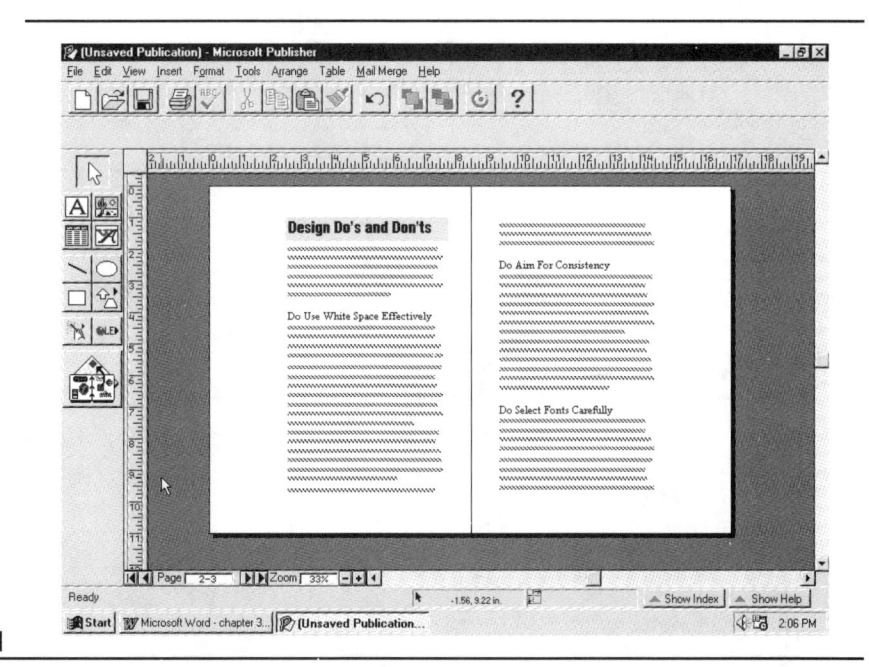

■ **FIGURE 3-11**

Don't Use Too Much Clip Art

Avoid placing too much clip art on the page just because you have room. Remember, white space is not your enemy. Use clip art only to increase interest or understanding of accompanying text. If there's no apparent reason to include clip art, don't. It's often better to use one strong, contributing piece of clip art rather than several weak ones.

 **CAUTION:** *Too much clip art lessens the impact of everything on the page.*

Avoid using *bitmapped* clip art that prints with "jagged" edges (see Figure 3-12). Bitmapped graphics are composed of dots and generally do not retain their quality when enlarged. Anything that has been scanned is bitmapped. Keep in mind that bitmapped images may not print well. Do a test run on scanned photographs, drawings, maps, and logos before including them in a publication. Bitmapped clip art and graphics generally have the filename extension .BMP,

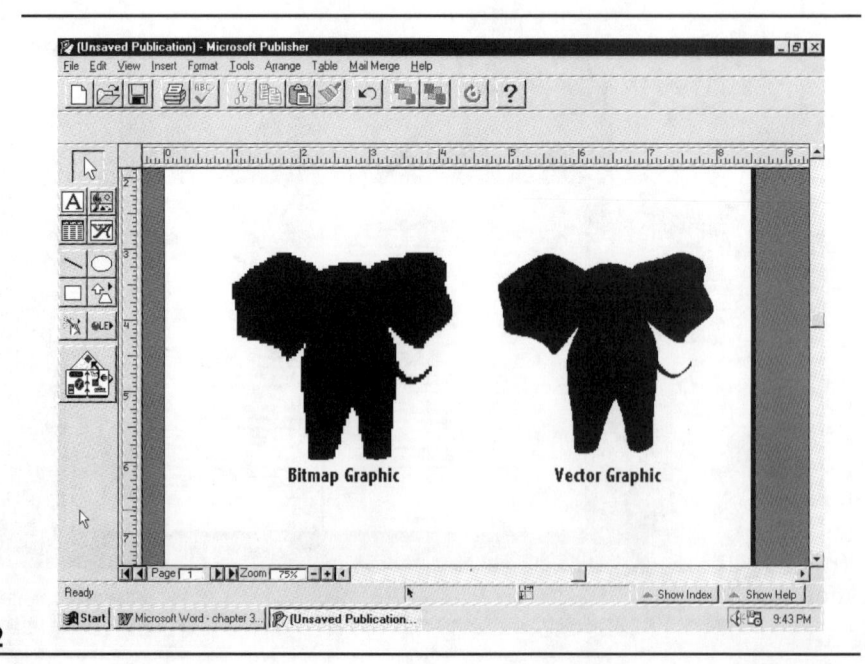

Bitmapped graphics print with jagged edges; vector graphics have smooth edges

FIGURE 3-12

.TIF, or .PCX. Graphics on web pages are bitmapped; they use the filename extensions .GIF and .JPG.

When shopping for clip art, look for artwork saved in a vector format. *Vector* graphics are composed of lines and curves, and can be enlarged without creating jagged edges. Vectored clip art and graphics have filename extensions such as .EPS, .CGM, and .WMF.

Don't Place Borders Around Everything

Borders work as graphic elements in capturing the reader's attention. When too many borders are placed on the page, they lessen the impact of the page. Professional page designers use borders to *separate* and *unite* text and graphics. For instance, in Figure 3-13, the border around the newsletter's table of contents separates it from the rest of the text. The border around the employee photo and accompanying text unites the section. The border around the photograph prevents the edges from looking washed out.

Publisher provides a big selection of artwork for creating borders. This "border art" includes everything from simple borders, such as lines and dashes, to cartoonish

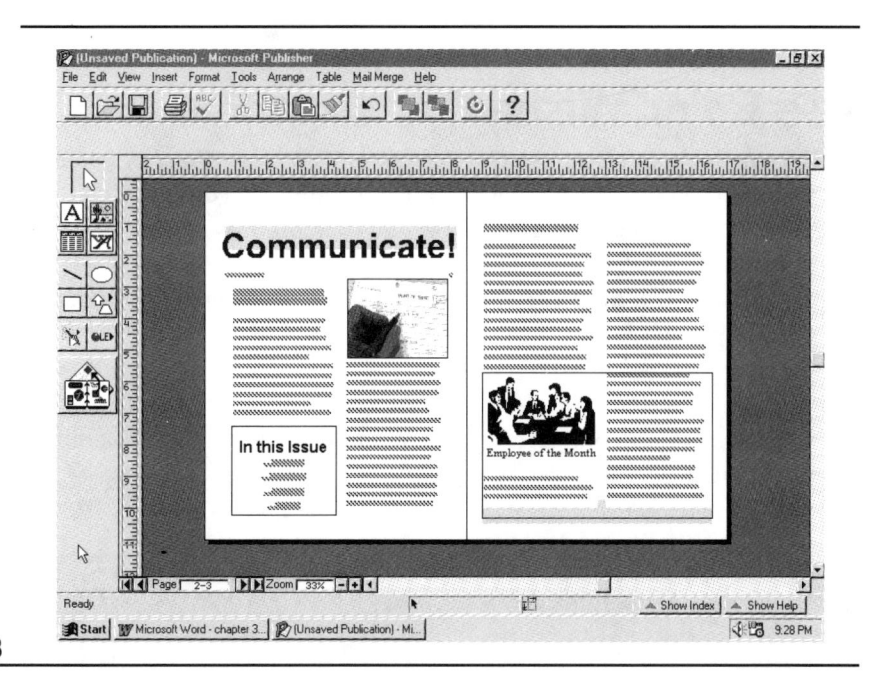

Use borders to unite and separate, not just to decorate

■ FIGURE 3-13

borders, such as baby bottles and apples. Save cartoon borders for nonbusiness publications, such as party invitations and garage sale flyers.

Don't Place Too Many Charts and Graphs on a Single Page

Use of too many charts and graphs on a page intimidates readers. If the charts are clear and straightforward, you can probably put two on a page. However, with complex charts, stick with one per page. If necessary, consider adding additional pages to a publication rather than cramming several charts on one page. Increase the comfort level of a page with charts by adding explanatory text and lots of white space.

Don't Use Too Many Photographs

Avoid the temptation to use every photograph you've got. A single, large, story-telling photograph is more effective than a bunch of small, uninspiring photos. In addition, don't make all photographs in a publication the same size. As displayed in Figure 3-14, a group of photos is more attractive and easier to view when one photograph is sized noticeably larger than the rest.

Do Use Color Wisely

Color is an inspirational, powerful design tool. Color has a strong emotional pull that makes the proper use of color essential in publication design. Color is classified as warm or cool, light or dark, vivid or dull, tranquil or exciting.

 **TIP:** *Consider the emotional and cultural implications of color when designing.*

Many of color's emotional effects are culturally determined. Generally speaking, people experience

- Black as evil, chic, cold, elegant, expensive
- White as pure, innocent, peaceful

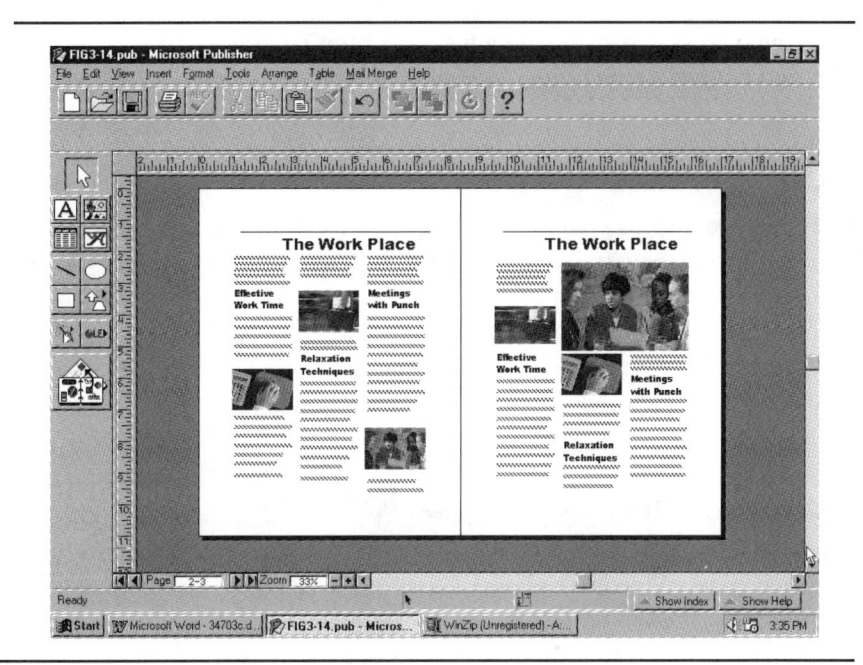

Add a little variety to a publication by grouping photographs

FIGURE 3-14

- Red as passionate, intense

- Yellow as sunshine, uplifting

- Green as nature, but also with a shade of envy (green is frequently considered bad luck)

- Blue as light, breezy, dignified, sedate

- Purple as royalty, both sophisticated and whimsical

- Brown as rustic, earthy, natural

Check out a Pantone Matching System (PMS) swatch book for inspiration on selecting colors. Similar to a paint swatch book you'd find at a hardware store, a PMS book displays a series of premixed printing inks called *spot colors.* Many art supply stores and commercial printers sell PMS books. Chapter 10 provides more information on working with spot colors in the printing process.

The combination of colors you choose creates a color scheme that should be repeated throughout the publication. As mentioned earlier in this section, color can be an important element in tying together a publication. One of the best bets for selecting colors is checking out what colors similar publications are using. You can also find books focusing on marketing and color choices.

Don't Overdo Color

Use color sparingly; too much color distracts from the message. It's great if you can afford full color, but don't add color to every element on the page. Full color makes a strong statement. Color photographs combined with colored lines, borders, shading, and text gives a carnival-like feel to a publication.

Color works well in photographs, lines, and other graphics. Before adding color to text, consider how the color will affect readability.

Don't Use the Wrong Color

When selecting colors for a publication, consider what a color means to your target audience. To accountants, red is negative, associated with losing money. To medical professionals, red symbolizes blood. If the publication will be distributed in a foreign country, make sure your color choices don't have negative connotations there.

Combining colors can be tricky, too. Combine black and orange on the page and what do you get? A Halloween publication. The colors pink and light blue might be considered too "babyish" for a business publication.

Don't Add Color to Body Text

Although desktop publishing applications make it easy to do, avoid adding color to body text, captions, and small headings. The color detracts from the readability of the text. The contrast of the black ink against the white page makes long blocks of small text readable. But it's hard to read black text set against a darkly colored background—for instance, black text on a red background. Although black text on a light tan background would be okay, the reverse, tan text on a black background, would be unreadable.

Summary

Now, with a few design tips and tricks under your belt, you're ready to begin creating publications with Publisher. Before you start the next section of the book, "The

Basics," which begins with an orientation to Microsoft Publisher, here's a quick review of the do's and don'ts presented in this chapter.

Do Use White Space Effectively

- Don't try to fill every inch of the page
- Don't place too much space between columns of text
- Don't scrimp on margins

Do Select Fonts Carefully

- Don't use more than two fonts
- Don't underline headings or body text
- Don't use tiny text
- Don't use justified text

Do Aim for Consistency

- Don't vary color across pages
- Don't vary fonts across pages
- Don't vary margins across pages

Do Select Graphic Elements Carefully

- Don't use too much clip art
- Don't place borders around everything
- Don't place too many charts and graphs on a single page
- Don't use too many photographs

Do Use Color Wisely

- Don't overdo color
- Don't use the wrong color
- Don't add color to body text

PART

II

The Basics

4

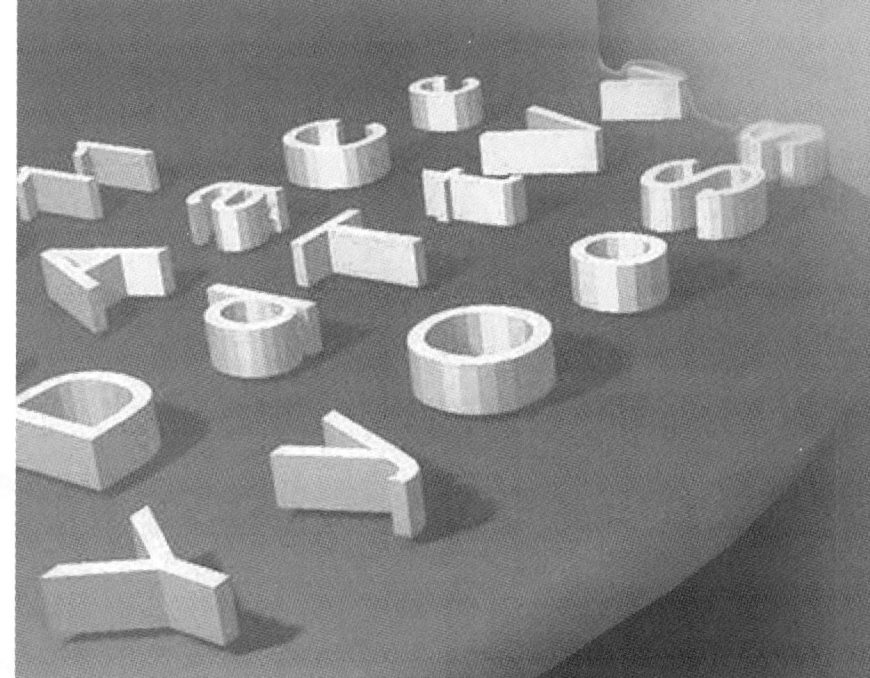

Getting Familiar with Microsoft Publisher

Microsoft Publisher provides all the tools you'll need to produce any type of publication. You'll find features for creating newsletters, catalogs, and web pages. To produce long documents, such as manuals and reports, Publisher provides options for building tables and automatic page numbering. Plus, Publisher provides lots of handy keyboard shortcuts to speed up your work.

This chapter introduces you to Publisher. First, the chapter discusses how to start Publisher and then tours the available screen tools. You'll see how to use Publisher's rulers, toolbars, and status line. The chapter ends by reviewing Publisher's Help system, which offers quick demos and searching tools.

Starting Microsoft Publisher

Microsoft Publisher 97 was designed to work with the Windows 95 operating system. To start Publisher, click on the Start button and point to Programs. A submenu appears listing the applications loaded on your system. Click on Microsoft Publisher to start the program (see Figure 4-1).

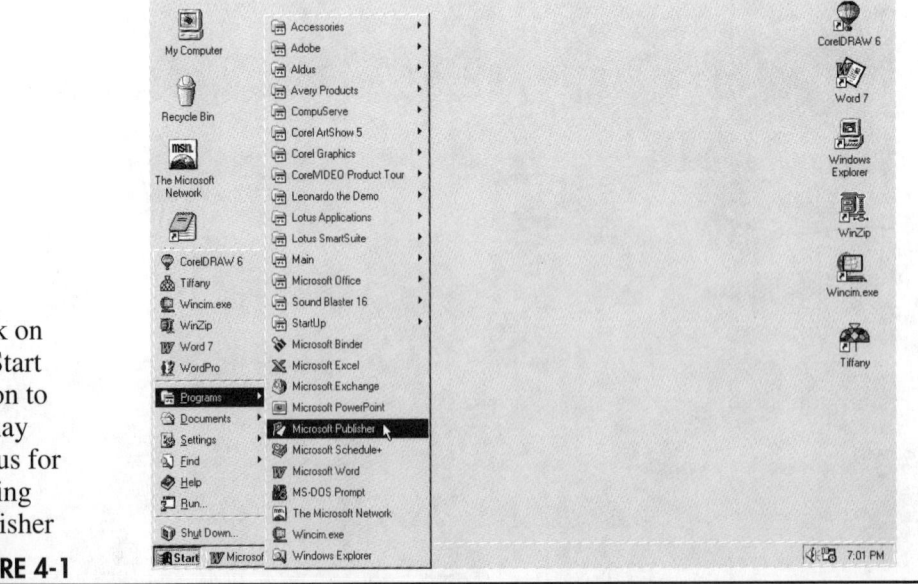

Click on the Start button to display menus for starting Publisher

FIGURE 4-1

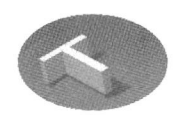 **TIP:** *You can also press CTRL-ESC to access the Start button.*

Publisher is installed in the Programs folder, unless specified otherwise. If you do not find Publisher in the Start menus, use the Windows Explorer to find the mspub.exe file. Double-click on the file to start Publisher. For information on options available when installing Publisher, refer to the section "Installing Microsoft Publisher" in Appendix A.

Adding a Publisher Shortcut to Your Windows 95 Desktop

You can add shortcuts to the Windows 95 desktop to make it easier to start an application. To add a shortcut for starting Microsoft Publisher:

1. Place the mouse on a blank spot on the Windows 95 desktop, and click the right mouse button. From the pop-up menu select New, then Shortcut. The Create Shortcut dialog box appears.

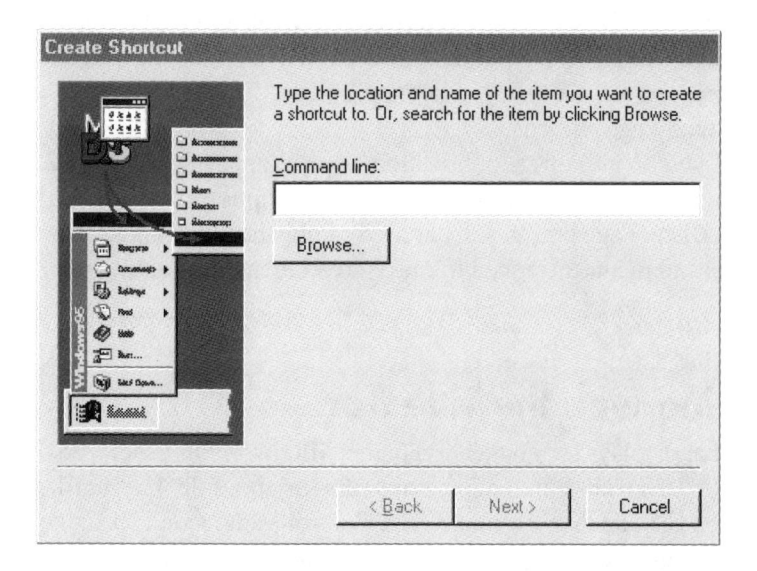

2. Click on the Browse button. In the Browse dialog box, change to the drive and folder where the file mspub.exe is located. Unless specified otherwise during installation, Publisher is located in the Publisher folder.

3. Select the mspub.exe file. Click the Open button to add the filename to the Create Shortcut dialog box. Click on the Next button.

4. The shortcut name appears as "mspub.exe" unless you enter another name. For instance, you might enter "Publisher" or "desktop publishing." Click the Finish button. When the shortcut appears, drag it to a convenient location on your desktop.

Follow these same steps to add shortcuts for other applications to your desktop. For more information on creating and editing shortcuts, refer to your Windows 95 documentation.

Touring the Publisher Screen

A good understanding of the screen tools is essential to becoming efficient in any program. In this section, you'll learn about the page area, menus, toolbars, and other screen tools that make up the Publisher screen.

When you first start Publisher, a dialog box appears displaying PageWizards and other options for creating a new publication (see Figure 4-2). PageWizards give you a head start in creating and formatting publications. For instance, when you create a calendar with a PageWizard, the days of the week and the numbers of the days are automatically added to the publication. You will also see this dialog box displayed every time you start a new publication or file. Chapter 5 takes a closer look at working with PageWizards.

After you create a new publication, a page appears. Figure 4-3 shows a new document created by selecting the Blank Page option (you will learn more about using the Blank Page option in Chapter 5). Publisher surrounds the new publication with tools and menus designed to make creating and formatting publications quick and easy.

Working with the Title Bar

The title bar displays the application name, Microsoft Publisher, and the publication filename. "Unsaved Publication" appears in the title bar until you save the publication file and give it a name. The Control Menu icon appears to the left of the application name; click on it to reveal commands for moving, sizing, restoring, and closing the Publisher window.

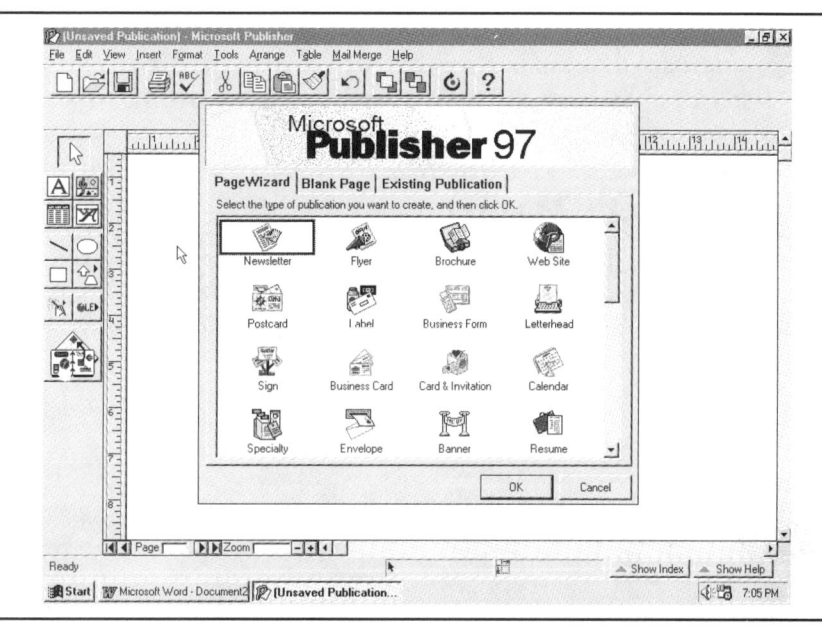

When you first start Publisher, a dialog box appears displaying PageWizards available for creating new publications

FIGURE 4-2

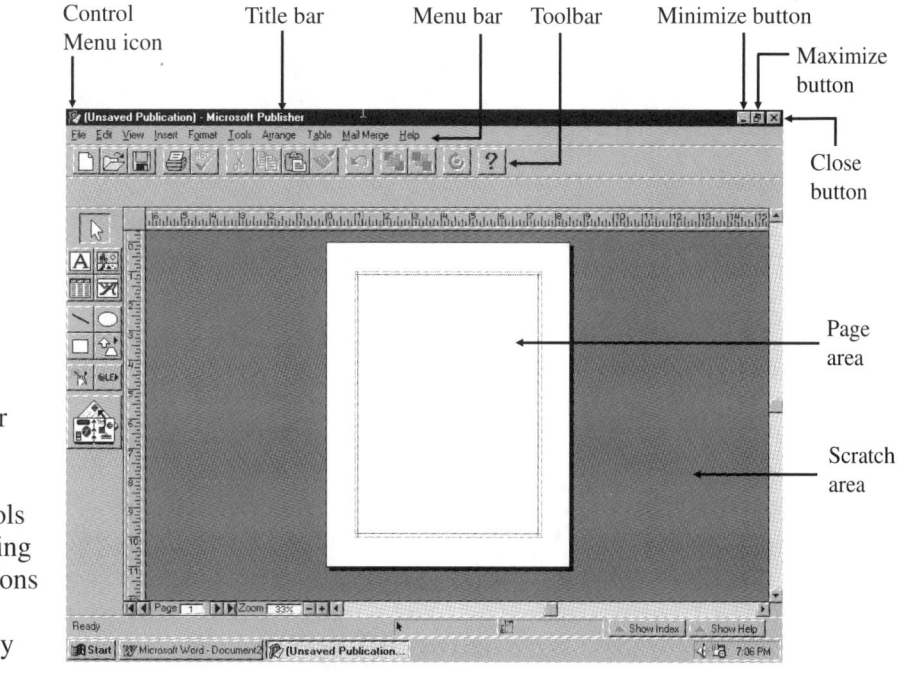

The Publisher screen includes many tools for creating publications quickly and easily

FIGURE 4-3

 **CAUTION:** *In Windows 95, the Close button is on the right side of the title bar. In Windows 3.1, it was on the left. Watch out—it's easy to accidentally click the Close button when you really meant to click the Maximize button.*

Working with Menus

The menu bar provides access to commands that help you edit and format your publications. Click the mouse button on a menu name to display a drop-down menu. Several menu commands include a right-pointing arrow that leads to a submenu with additional choices, as shown here:

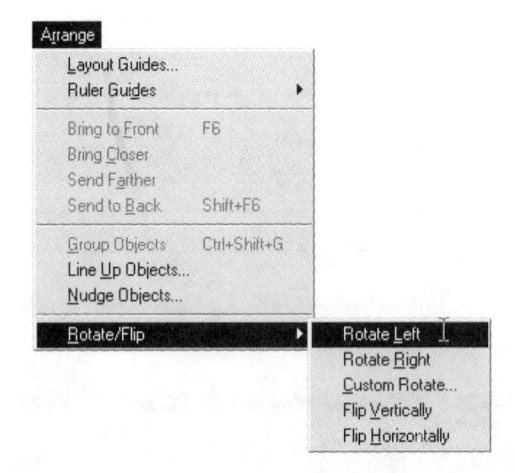

Some menu commands also have keyboard shortcuts that appear to the right of the command. For example, the keyboard shortcut for Send To Back is SHIFT-F6.

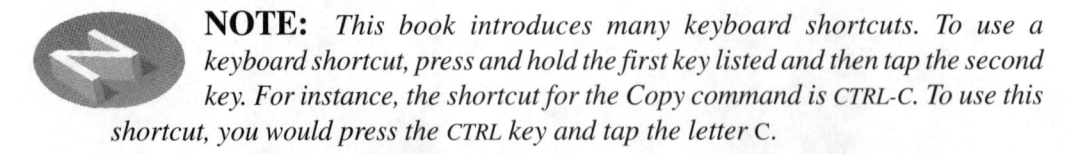 **NOTE:** *This book introduces many keyboard shortcuts. To use a keyboard shortcut, press and hold the first key listed and then tap the second key. For instance, the shortcut for the Copy command is CTRL-C. To use this shortcut, you would press the CTRL key and tap the letter C.*

Menus can also be accessed by holding the ALT key and typing the letter underlined in the menu name. For instance, pressing and holding ALT while you tap the letter *F* drops down the File menu. Pressing ALT and tapping *T* drops down the Tools menu. Once a menu appears, you only need to press the letter underlined in the desired command (not ALT). For instance, in the Tools menu, you can press *N* to activate the Design Checker.

Clicking the right mouse button reveals a pop-up menu with context-sensitive commands. The pop-up menus display commands available for the page area or object that you clicked on. For instance, Figure 4-4 shows the pop-up menu that appears when the right mouse button is clicked on the page or desktop. The pop-up menu contains different commands when the right mouse button is clicked on a selected text block or graphic. For instance, clicking the right mouse button on a selected graphic displays a pop-up menu with commands such as Copy Graphic and Fill Color.

Examining the Page Area

The white rectangle in the middle of the screen represents the first page of a publication. In Figure 4-3, the page area is vertical, using a *portrait* page orientation. (A horizontal orientation is called *landscape* page orientation.) Chapter 6 looks at the features for adjusting page orientation and size.

The gray area surrounding the page is the *scratch area.* Think of the scratch area as a desktop where you can place objects, such as graphics and text blocks (see Figure 4-5). For instance, when beginning a new publication, many designers like

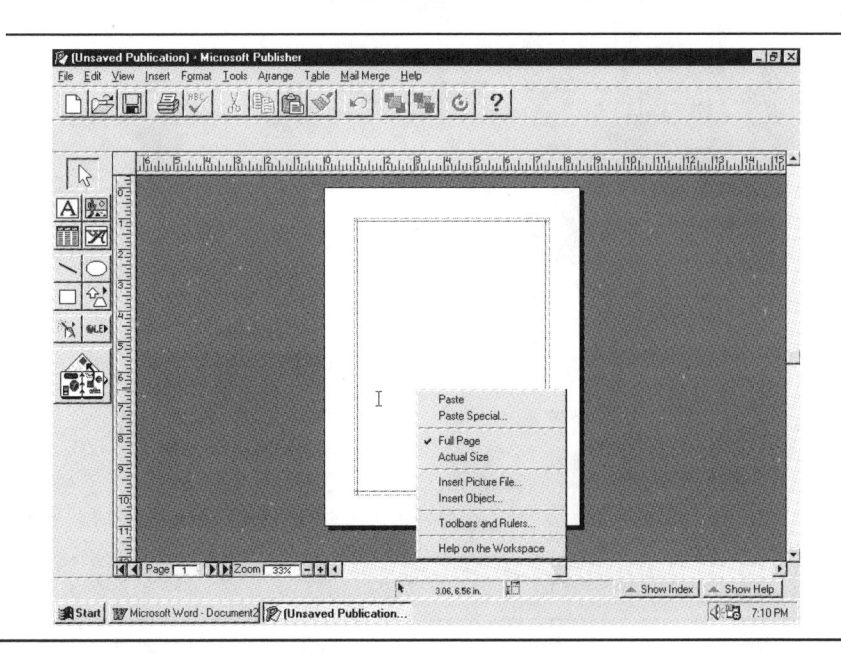

Use the
pop-up
menus to
access
frequently
used
commands

FIGURE 4-4

to place all the elements that will appear in a publication on the screen. Then they arrange and size the elements to build the page layout.

Working with Margin and Column Guides

Pink and blue lines appear on the page area representing the margin and column guides. When you adjust the page margins and columns, the guides change to reflect the latest measurements. In Figure 4-6, the top margin was set to 2 inches, and the left, right, and bottom margins were set at 1 inch. The guides also indicate the page is set up for two columns. These guides do not print.

Working with Snap To Guides

Publisher's guides have a "magnetic pull" called *snap to* that forces objects to align to the guides. The snap to feature makes it easy to use the margin and column guides for sizing and aligning objects on a page. For example, you could use Snap To Guides

You can use the scratch area surrounding the page area to place objects as you build a publication

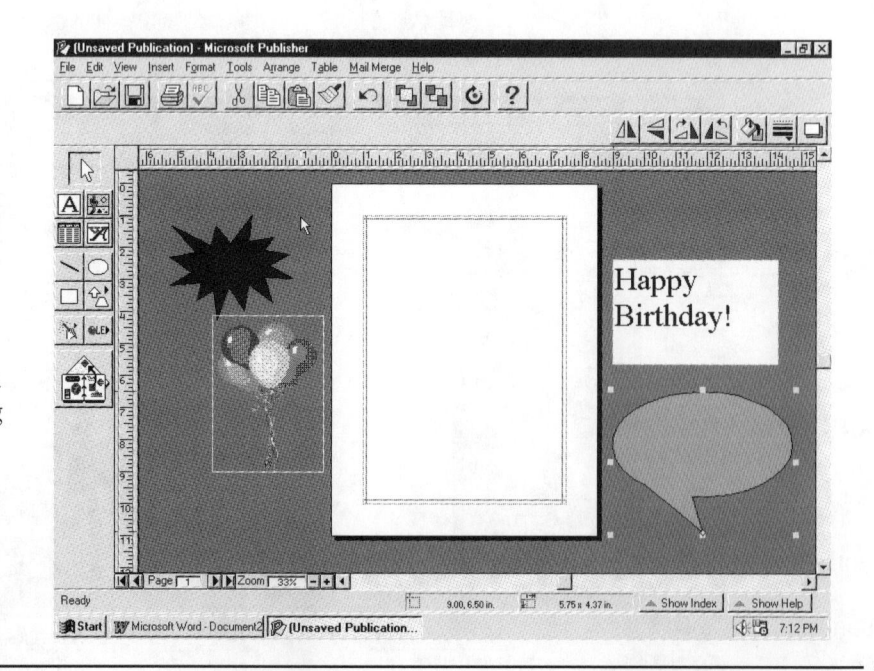

FIGURE 4-5

Margin and column guides

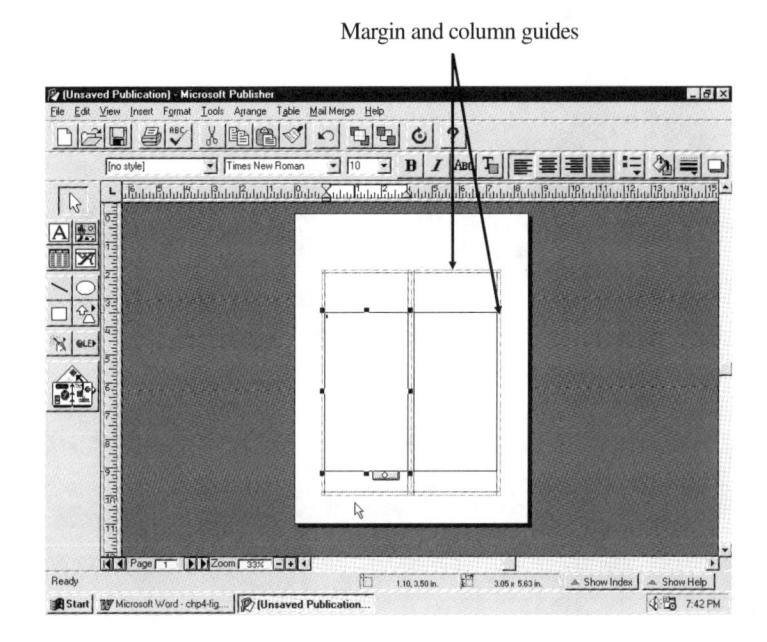

Guides appear on the page area to help you align objects on a page

FIGURE 4-6

when drawing text frames in a two-column layout to ensure both columns are the same width. You will learn more about drawing, moving, and sizing frames with Snap To Guides in Chapter 7.

By default, Snap To Guides is turned on. To turn it off, click on the Tools menu and select Snap To Guides. Repeat the steps again to turn Snap To Guides back on. You can also use the keyboard shortcut CTRL-W to turn Snap To Guides on and off.

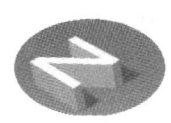

NOTE: *When a check mark appears by a command, it is turned on. When no check mark appears, it is turned off.*

Hiding and Displaying Guides

As mentioned, the margin and column guides do not print—they are just visible on the screen. As shown in Figure 4-7, you can hide the guides. Before printing, it's a good idea to hide the guides and get a clear look at how the page will appear when printed. To hide the guides, select Hide Boundaries And Guides from the View menu. To redisplay the guides, select Show Boundaries And Guides from the View menu.

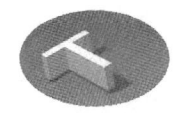

TIP: *You can also use the keyboard shortcut, CTRL-SHIFT-O, to toggle between hiding and displaying boundaries and guides.*

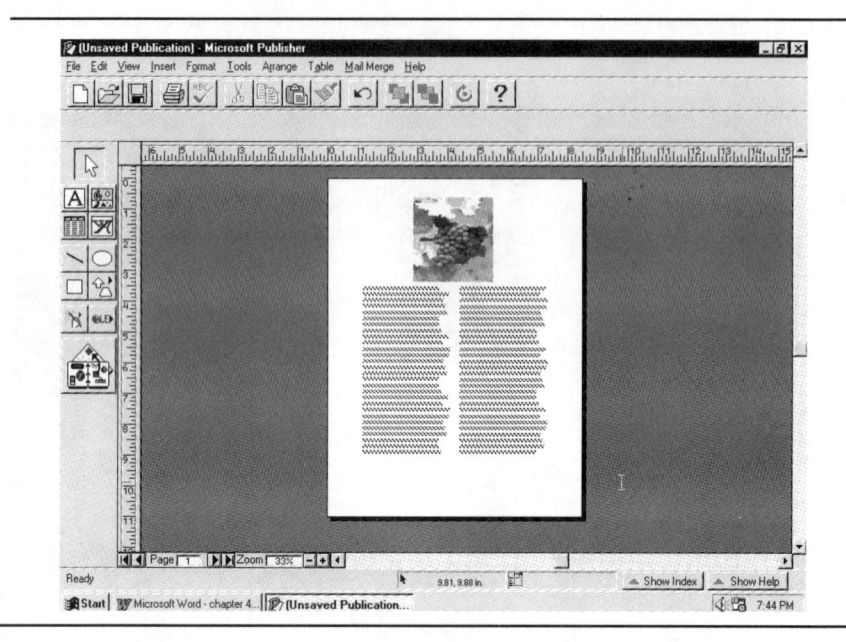

Hide the margin and column guides to see how the page will look when printed

FIGURE 4-7

Overview of Publisher's Toolbars

When you first start the application, Publisher displays the Standard toolbar and Graphic toolbox loaded with tools for accessing frequently used commands. For instance, you can click on the Save tool to quickly save a file and the Spelling tool to begin spell-checking a publication. To see the function of each tool, place your mouse on the tool to display an instant description called a *tooltip* (see Figure 4-8). If you are familiar with other Microsoft applications, such as Word and Excel, you'll recognize many of the tools. For example, the Cut, Copy, and Paste tools are the same in all Microsoft products.

At the top of the screen, the Standard toolbar stores tools for general tasks such as opening, saving, and printing files. Table 4-1 gives a brief overview of the function of the tools in the Standard toolbar. The table also references where to find more information in this book about using a tool.

The Graphic toolbox provides tools for drawing frames and graphics, and for working with the Design Gallery. Table 4-2 gives a brief overview of the function of the tools in the Graphic toolbox. As before, the table references where to find more information in the book about using a tool.

Tooltip   Standard toolbar

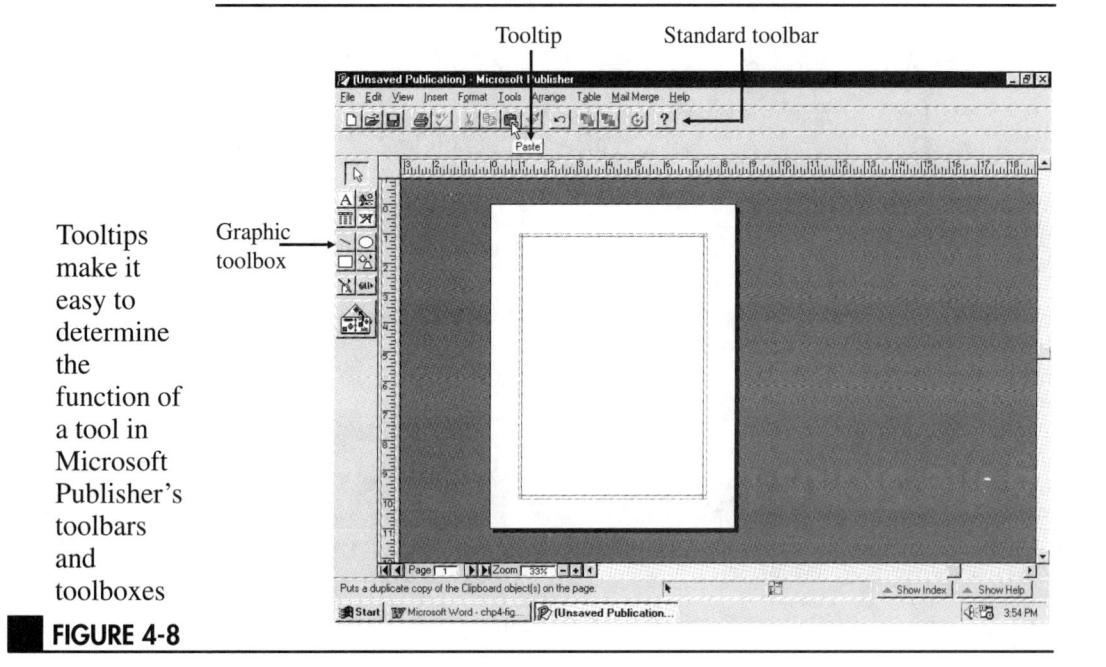

Tooltips make it easy to determine the function of a tool in Microsoft Publisher's toolbars and toolboxes

FIGURE 4-8

Graphic toolbox

Tool	Name	Function
New	New	Creates a new publication (Chapter 5)
Open	Open	Displays the Open Publication dialog box so you can open an existing publication (Chapter 6)
Save	Save	Saves the publication file
Print	Print	Prints one copy of the publication with the current print settings (Chapter 10)
ABC	Spelling	Begins spell-checking the publication

Overview of the Standard Toolbar

TABLE 4-1

Tool	Name	Function
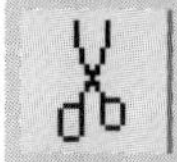	Cut	Removes selected text or object and places it on the Clipboard (Chapter 8)
	Copy	Places a copy of selected text or object on the Clipboard (Chapter 8)
	Paste	Places a copy of Clipboard contents on the page (Chapter 8)
	Format Painter	Copies the formatting of the selected object to another object (Chapter 8)
	Undo/Redo	Reverses the last change you made
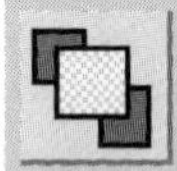	Bring To Front	Brings the selected object to the front (Chapter 11)
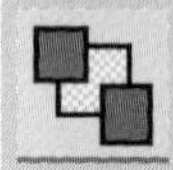	Send To Back	Sends the selected object to the back (Chapter 11)
	Rotate	Rotates the selected text or object
	Help	Shows Help screens

Overview
of the
Standard
Toolbar
(continued)

TABLE 4-1

Publisher also provides a Formatting toolbar, which appears when an object is selected on the page. You will notice the Formatting toolbar change automatically depending on what you are doing. For instance, in Figure 4-9, a text frame is selected, and the Formatting toolbar provides tools for editing and formatting text. When a picture frame is selected, the Formatting toolbar displays tools for formatting picture frames, such as text wrap and object color.

Tool	Name	Function
	Pointer	Used to select, size, and move text and objects
	Text	Creates frames for entering text (Chapters 7 and 8)
	Picture	Creates frames for holding graphics (Chapters 7 and 9)
	Table	Creates frames for building tables (Chapter 12)
	WordArt	Creates frames for creating WordArt (Chapter 13)
	Line	Draws lines on the page (Chapter 11)
	Oval	Draws ovals and circles on the page (Chapter 11)
	Box	Draws rectangles and squares on the page (Chapter 11)
	Custom Shapes	Draws a variety of shapes on the page (Chapter 11)
	PageWizards	Inserts a calendar, ad, coupon, or logo on a page (Chapter 5)
	Insert Object	Creates object linking and embedding (OLE) objects
	Design Gallery	Adds predesigned objects to a page (Chapter 9)

Overview of the Graphic Toolbar

TABLE 4-2

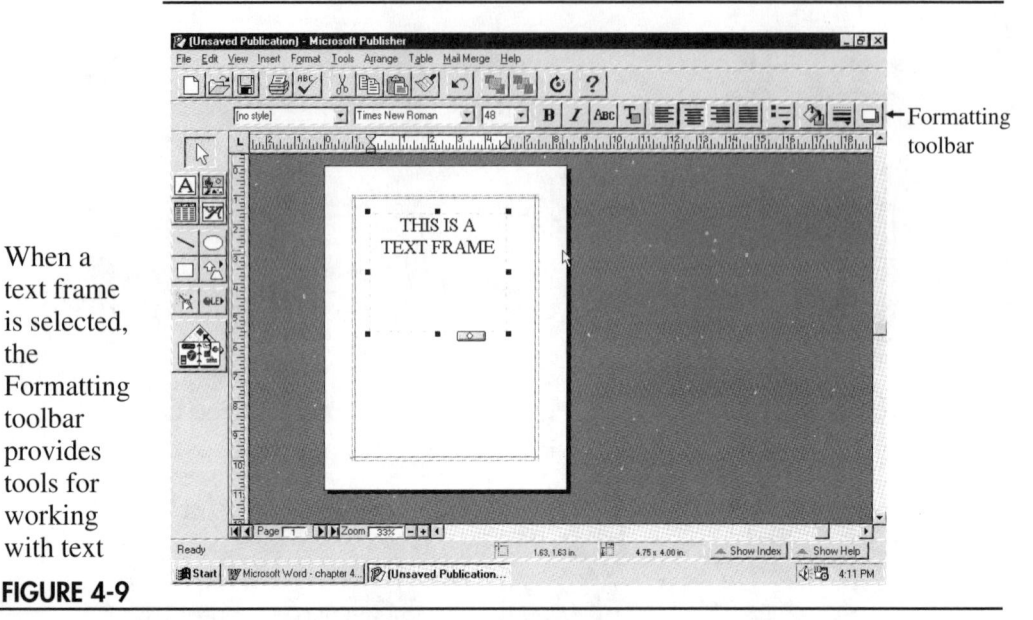

← Formatting toolbar

When a text frame is selected, the Formatting toolbar provides tools for working with text

FIGURE 4-9

Hiding and Displaying Toolbars

With Publisher, you can customize the look of the screen by hiding and displaying the toolbars. You can also adjust the size and color of the toolbars. To see the options available for working with toolbars:

1. From the View menu, select Toolbars And Rulers.

2. In the Toolbars And Rulers dialog box, a check mark indicates an option is turned on or active.

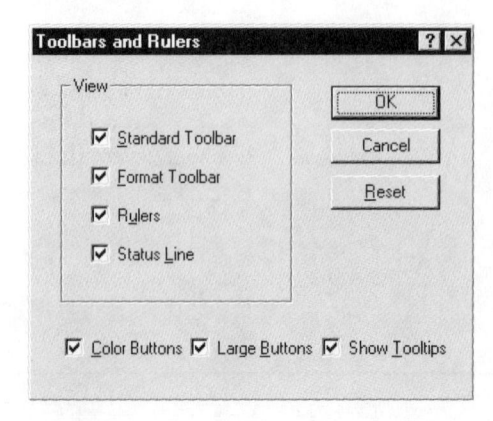

- To hide the Standard or Formatting toolbar, click to remove the check mark by that option. You cannot hide the Graphic toolbox.

- To display the tools on the toolbars in black and white (not color), click to remove the check mark by Color Buttons.

- To decrease the size of the tools on the toolbars (making more room for the page area), click to remove the check mark by Large Buttons.

- To not display tooltips (discussed earlier in this section), click to remove the check mark by Show Tooltips.

3. Click OK to accept any changes you made.

Repeat the preceding steps to redisplay a toolbar or turn on an option.

 **TIP:** *When working with dialog boxes, you can usually press ENTER as an alternative to clicking on the OK button.*

You can also place the cursor on a toolbar (or ruler) and then click the right mouse button to display a pop-up menu, shown here, for displaying/hiding toolbars:

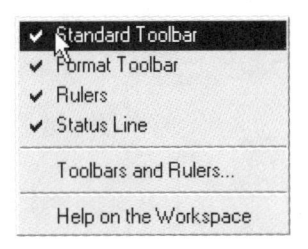

A check mark will appear next to the name of each toolbar that is displayed. To hide the toolbar, just uncheck it by clicking on its name. If you need to access the Toolbars And Rulers dialog box (illustrated in the previous steps), click on the Toolbars And Rulers command on this shortcut menu.

Working with Rulers

Rulers appear along the top and left side of the scratch area. You'll find rulers helpful for sizing and positioning elements in your publications. Notice as you move the mouse, small hairlines appear in the rulers to indicate the exact position of the mouse on a page. The hairlines are helpful for aligning elements to specific points on a page.

You can also use the rulers to set tabs and change paragraph indents. As shown in Figure 4-10, when a text frame is selected, the top ruler indicates the width of the frame. Chapter 17 discusses the use of rulers to add tabs and indents.

You can hide the ruler by choosing Toolbars And Rulers from the View menu. In the Toolbars And Rulers dialog box, click to remove the check mark by Rulers and click OK. Repeat the steps to redisplay the ruler.

Working with Snap To Ruler Marks

Publisher provides a Snap To Ruler Marks feature that helps you align text and objects based on the marks in the rulers. Snap To Ruler Marks gives the increment marks in the ruler a "magnetic pull" that forces objects to align to the marks. As you

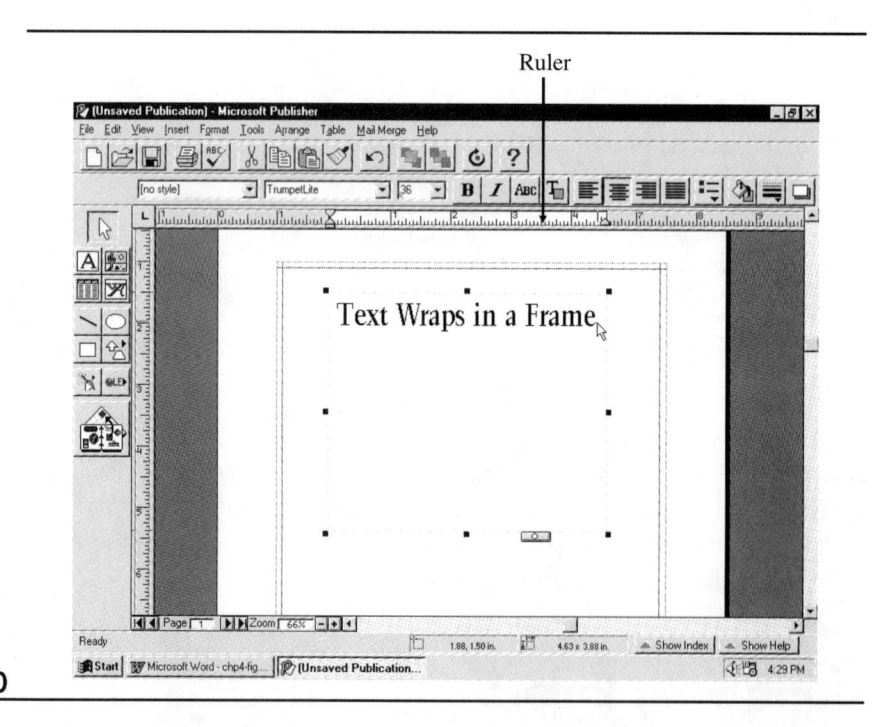

The ruler indicates the width of a selected text frame

FIGURE 4-10

move objects, the object "jumps" to the closest ruler mark. While Snap To Guides (discussed earlier in this chapter) is good for aligning large page elements, Snap To Ruler Marks is helpful when you're aligning small objects on a page.

By default, Snap To Ruler Marks is turned on. To turn it off, click on the Tools menu, and select Snap To Ruler Marks. Repeat the steps to turn Snap To Ruler Marks back on.

Moving Rulers and Zero Points

In the days before desktop publishing, page designers used T-squares to size and align objects. You can use Publisher's rulers as a T-square. Just as a T-square can be picked up and moved around the page, so can the rulers. In Figure 4-11, the rulers were moved to help align the photographs.

To move a ruler, position the mouse pointer over the ruler until you see a two-headed arrow. Press and hold the mouse button, and drag the ruler down into the page. Release when the ruler is at the desired location. To move both rulers at

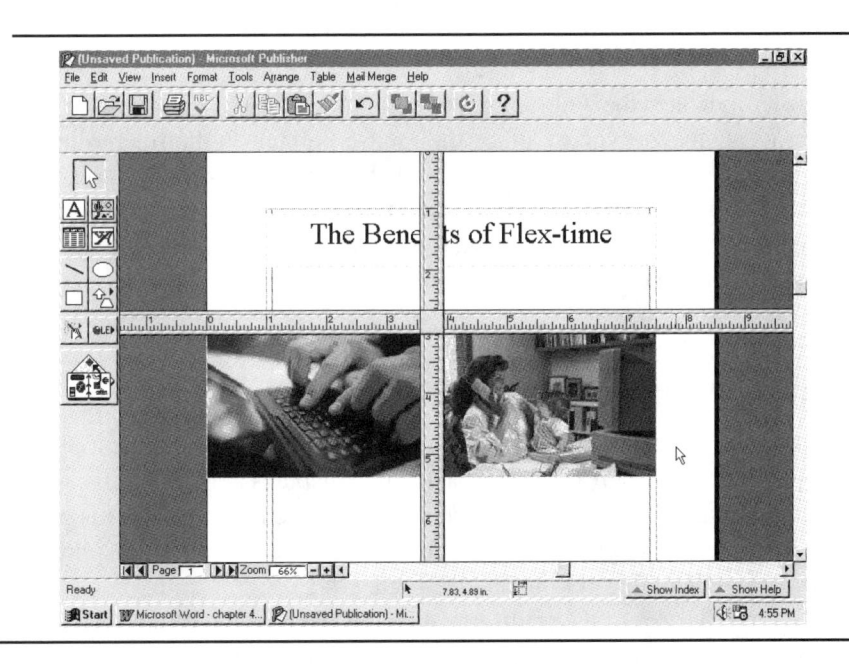

Move the rulers to help align and size text and objects on a page

FIGURE 4-11

the same time, position the mouse pointer on the box in the upper-left corner where the two rulers intersect, as shown here:

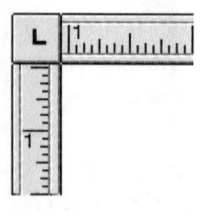

When you see the two-headed arrow, drag both rulers to the desired location.

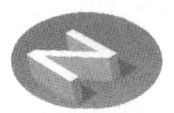

NOTE: *In addition to moving the rulers, you can create* ruler guides *for aligning objects. Refer to Chapter 7 for more information.*

The *zero point* in rulers can also be adjusted. The zero point is the position of zero on the horizontal and vertical rulers. Normally, the zero point corresponds to the upper-left corner of the page area. You can move the zero points to make it easier to measure the size of an object or the distance between two objects. In Figure 4-12, the zero point on the horizontal ruler was moved to line up with the column guide. The ruler indicates the width of the column guide is about 2 inches.

To move the zero point, place the mouse pointer on the ruler where you want zero to appear. Press and hold SHIFT, and click the right mouse button. To move the zero point for both rulers, position the mouse pointer on the box in the upper-left corner where the two rulers intersect. Press and hold SHIFT. Using the right mouse button, drag to where you want the zero points to appear.

Using the Status Line

Publisher's *status line* along the bottom of the screen is a valuable tool for learning the application. The left side of the status line displays helpful tips for working with menu commands and tools—for instance, when the mouse pointer is placed on the Two-Page Spread command in the View menu, the status line displays additional information about that command (see Figure 4-13).

The middle area of the status line displays the position of the selected object. In Figure 4-13, the status line displays how far the selected frame is from the left edge of the page (1.75 inches) and how far the frame is from the top of the page (3.09

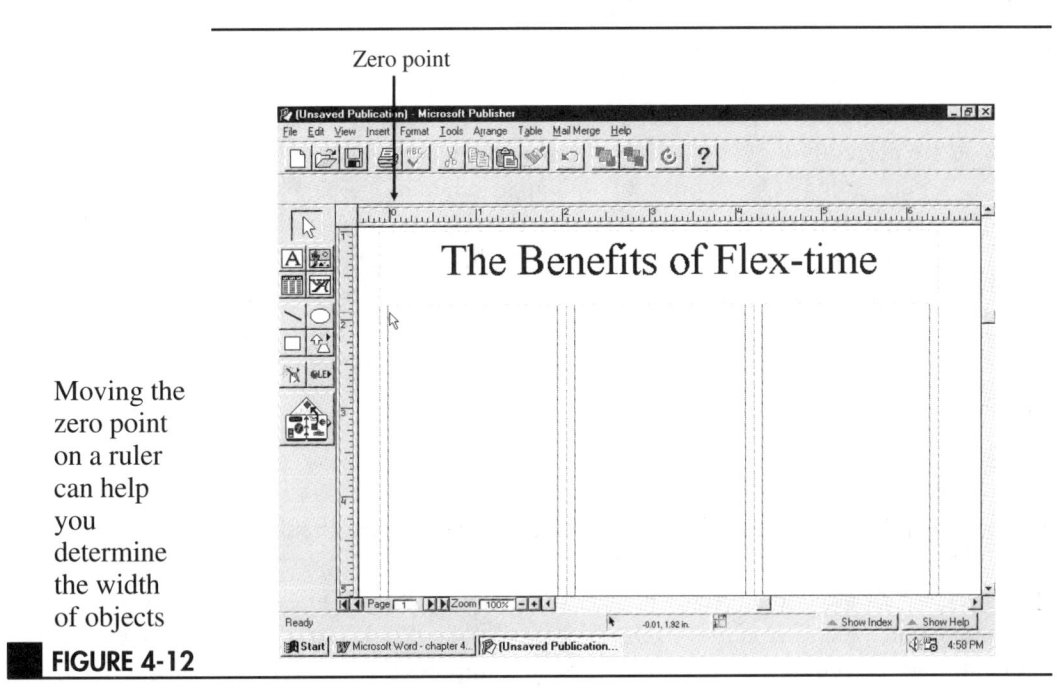

Moving the zero point on a ruler can help you determine the width of objects

FIGURE 4-12

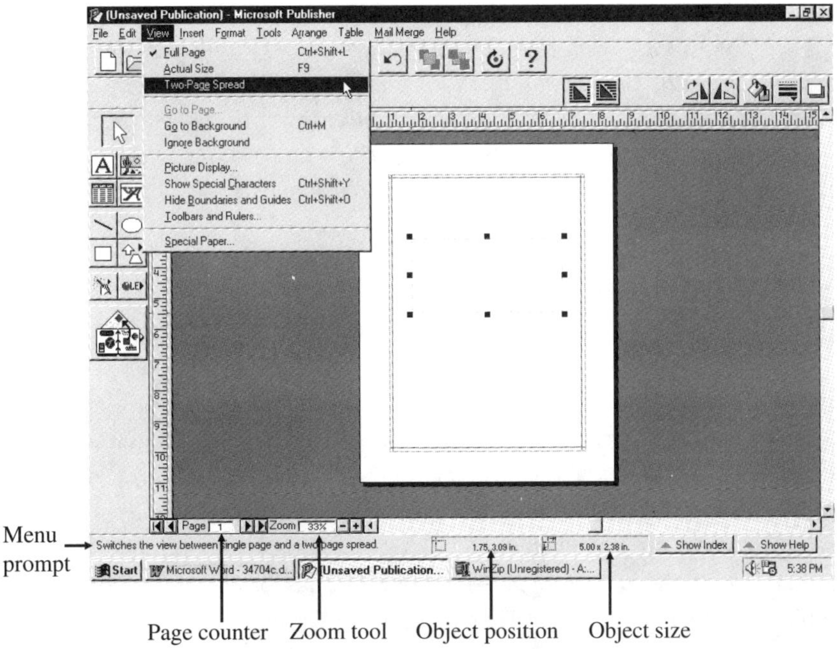

Watch the status line to quickly determine a selected object's position and size

FIGURE 4-13

inches). The area next to the object position shows the object size. The frame inFigure 4-13 is 5 inches wide by 2.38 inches tall.

Right above the status line is the page counter, which displays the number of the page you are currently looking at. You also use the page counter to move between pages in a publication. The Zoom tool also appears above the status line—this is used to zoom in for a close-up of the page and zoom out for an overall look. Chapter 6 provides more information about working with the page counter and Zoom tool.

You can hide the status line by choosing Toolbars And Rulers from the View menu. In the Toolbars And Rulers dialog box, click to remove the check mark by Status Line and click OK. Repeat the steps to redisplay the status line.

Working with Help

The documentation provided with Microsoft Publisher does not really get into the specific commands and steps used to format and build publications. The *Microsoft Publisher 97 Companion* discusses general topics such as "Designing Like a Designer" and "Choosing the Right Pictures." The Publisher documentation frequently refers you to the Help system, so it's important to get familiar with it. This section discusses using Publisher's Help system effectively.

NOTE: *Although the information in the* Publisher Companion *is useful, knowing the actual methods and processes Publisher uses to create a publication is essential. The information in this book is designed to help you in both respects. You'll find lots of design tips and printing information as well as step-by-step instructions for building publications.*

Showing Help Screens

Unlike other Microsoft Help systems, Publisher's help is always available on the screen. Click on the Show Help button in the bottom right corner of the screen to reveal the Help screen (see Figure 4-14). Position the mouse pointer on a topic (the pointer changes to a hand shape), and click to see more information. For instance, clicking on the topic, "Create or open a newsletter" takes you to a new screen of information. Click on the small left-pointing arrow at the bottom of the Help screen to return to the previous screen. Click on the Hide Help button in the bottom right corner to hide the Help screen. You can also click on the Help tool in the Standard toolbar to show and hide the Help screen.

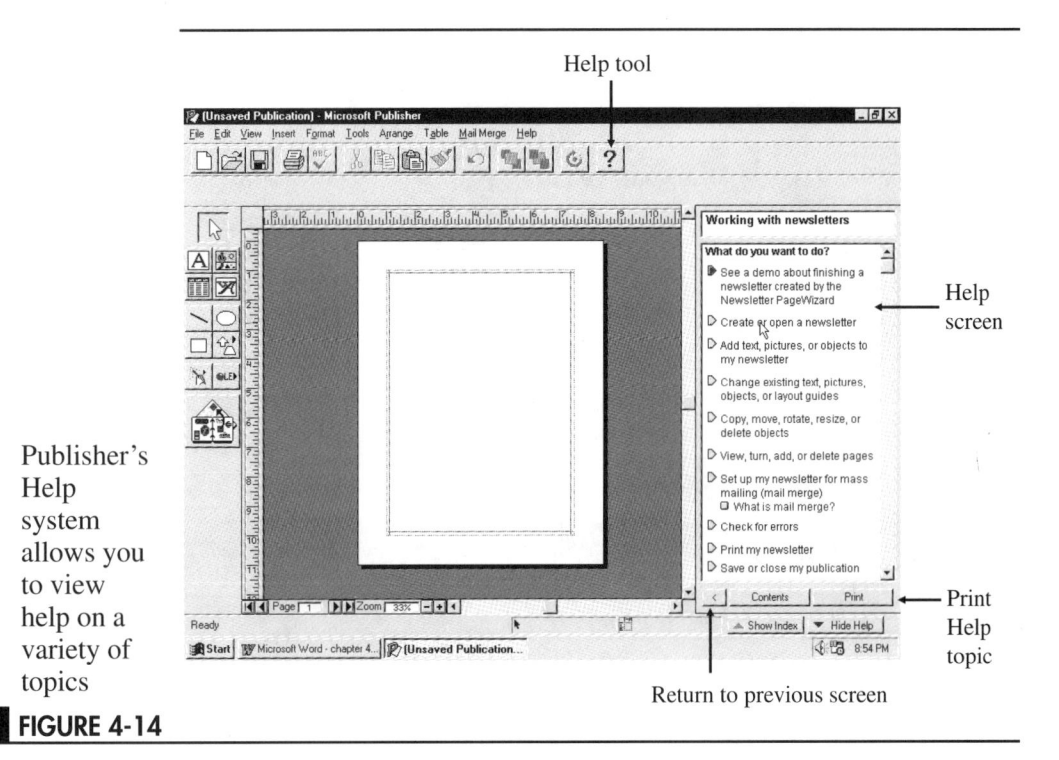

Publisher's Help system allows you to view help on a variety of topics

FIGURE 4-14

To print the information on the Help screen, simply click the Print button at the bottom. This prints one copy of the information to your default printer.

Showing Index Screens

Using the index to search through help topics makes it easier to find information about a specific topic. To display the Index, click on the Show Index button in the bottom right corner of the screen. As shown in Figure 4-15, the Help screen is also displayed when you turn on the Index screen.

At the top of the Index screen, enter the topic on which you want to find information. Publisher searches through the index for the topic and displays the appropriate information in the Help screen. Click on the Hide Index button to hide the Index screen. You can also use the Show Index/Hide Index commands in the Help menu to work with the Index.

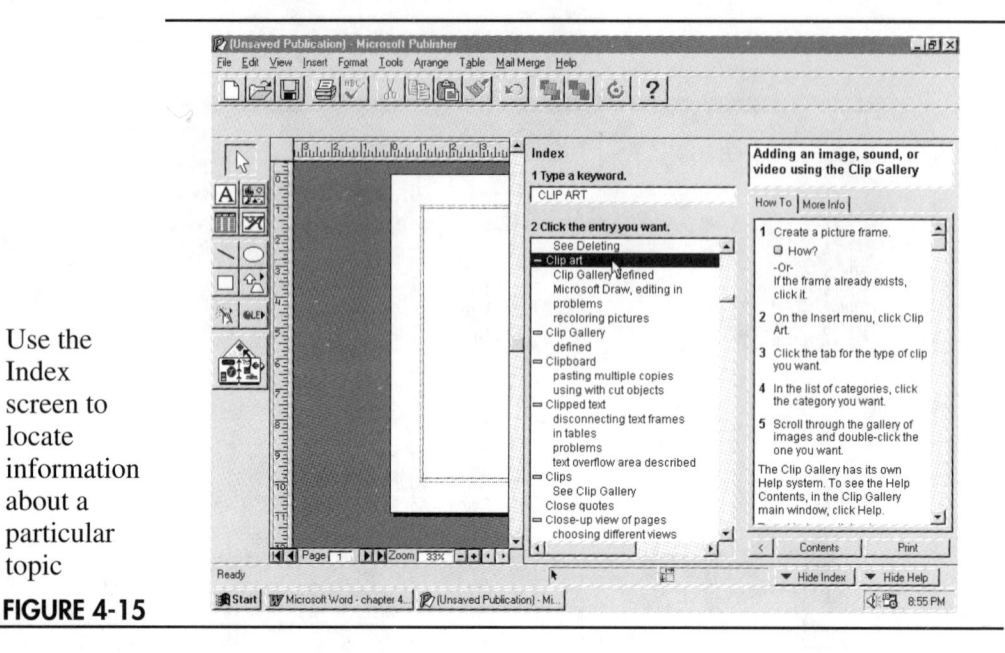

Use the Index screen to locate information about a particular topic

FIGURE 4-15

Running a Demo

Publisher provides a series of online demos to help you understand the whys and hows of various features. The demos are short presentations focusing on a specific topic. To run a demo, select Quick Demos from the Help menu. From the Publisher Demos dialog box, select the demo you wish to view and click OK. After a few seconds, the first screen of the demo appears. The bottom left corner of the screen indicates how many screens make up the demonstration. For instance, in Figure 4-16, the demo on backgrounds consists of six screens of information. To move to the next screen, click on the Next button. To close the demo, click on the Cancel button.

Exiting Publisher

When you are ready to shut down Publisher, select Exit Publisher from the File menu. You are prompted to save any unsaved publication files. To quickly close Publisher with the mouse, click on the Close button (the *X*) in the top right corner of the screen.

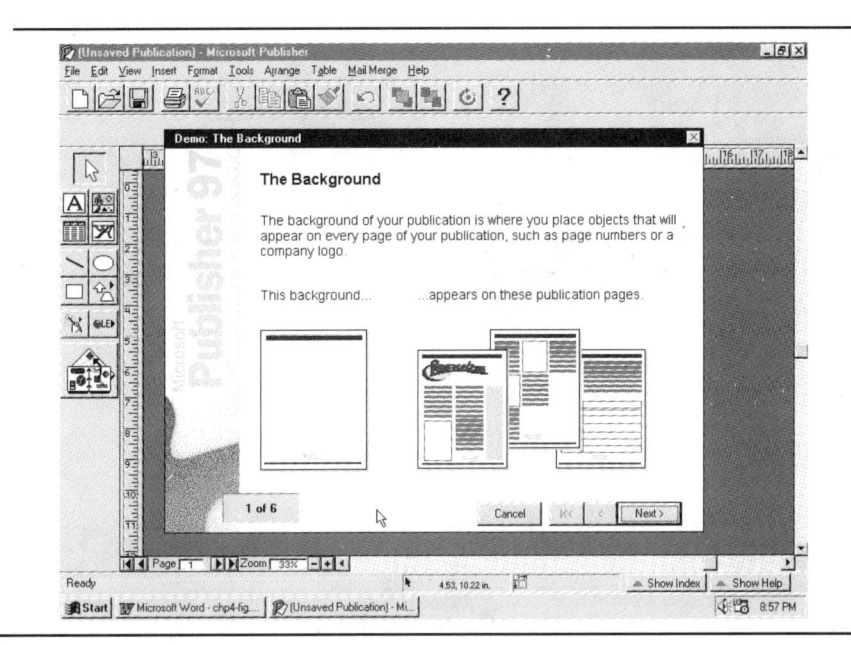

Check out Publisher's online demos for a quick overview of software features

FIGURE 4-16

TIP: *Use the keyboard shortcut ALT-F4 to exit Publisher.*

Summary

The goal of this chapter was to acquaint you with the Publisher's menus and other tools. Being familiar with the tools available on the Publisher screen is important when you begin creating publications. The Standard toolbar and the Graphic toolbox were examined, as well as the ruler and status line.

Now that you're familiar with the screen tools and Help system in Microsoft Publisher, you're ready to begin creating publications. The next chapter discusses starting new publications using PageWizards, blank pages, or existing publications. You'll also find information about opening, saving, and closing files.

5

Creating and Saving Publications

Creating publications is easy with Microsoft Publisher's wide assortment of predesigned publications. You'll find help for creating every type of publication, ranging from booklets to balance sheets to business cards. You can also start with nothing more than a blank page if you prefer to design the page yourself.

This chapter first looks at working with PageWizards, the quickest way to create professional-looking documents. PageWizards are an important part of Publisher, so you'll find a thorough discussion of using them in this chapter. An example of creating a sign and newsletter with PageWizards is included to help explain the process. This chapter also discusses additional ways you can create new publications, such as starting with a blank page or using an existing publication as a guideline (template) for a new one.

The next part of the chapter discusses the importance of selecting a printer before you begin designing. Don't skip this section—it can help you avoid a lot of repair work later. The chapter ends with information about opening, saving, and closing publication files.

We're Off to See the Wizards

Publisher simplifies the whole publication production process with the use of *PageWizard Design Assistants*. (It'll seem like magic when a wizard helps you create a publication in five minutes!) PageWizards provide access to predesigned documents for all kinds of publications, such as "Help Wanted" signs and birthday cards. After you select a specific type of PageWizard, such as the Newsletter PageWizard, various styles for that type of publication are available. You pick the desired look, and then the PageWizard continues by asking questions about your document. For instance, the Newsletter PageWizard asks if you want one or two stories on the first page of the newsletter. PageWizards ask the name of your company or organization and other kinds of information related to a specific type of publication. In a nutshell, PageWizards do much of the work for you.

NOTE: *Other Microsoft applications such as Word and Excel also use wizards to help with the production of charts and tables.*

If you are new to page design, you may just want to let Publisher take over. All you'll need to do is enter some text, maybe change some graphics, and print. If you want the help of a PageWizard but crave more control, don't worry. You can modify every aspect of a publication set up by PageWizards. If you don't like the clip art, typeface, or color, for example, you can change it. PageWizards are designed to enhance and speed up your work, not make you feel tied to a particular page layout.

PageWizards Make It Easy

In many ways, PageWizards remove some of the anxiety and uncertainty of publication production. Some desktop publishing applications, after creating a new publication, leave you staring at a blank page. Not so in Publisher. PageWizards build the layout for you, creating text and picture frames. Think of frames as boxes that float above the page. You will learn more about frames in Chapter 7.

Since the predesigned publications available with PageWizards were designed by professional page designers, you don't have to fret about clashing typefaces, conflicting colors, and unreadable text. You can take the predesigned publication as is, or you can customize the design by selecting new typefaces and graphics, and adding and sizing pictures.

PageWizards for Every Type of Document

There are 18 PageWizards in Publisher. Each PageWizard offers different styles of personal and business publications. Table 5-1 provides an overview of available PageWizards. Refer to this when you begin a new publication.

PageWizard	Description
Newsletter	Twenty newsletter styles with options for entering a newsletter title, date, and for controlling story flow.
Flyer	Multiple styles for each type of flyer—personal, business, or community.
Brochure	Fifteen brochure styles, from programs to price lists for two- and three-fold brochures.
Web Site	Web page designs for business, personal, and community web pages. You have options for placing text and graphic hyperlinks (links connecting web pages).

Publisher's
Page-
Wizards

TABLE 5-1

PageWizard	Description
Postcard	Business, personal, and community postcard styles, such as grand openings and sales. You'll also find options for entering company names and addresses.
Label	Labels for bulk mailing, CD cases, and videocassettes.
Business Form	Page designs for expense reports, fax sheets, quote sheets, employee time sheets, and more.
Letterhead	Thirteen letterhead styles with options for entering company names and addresses.
Sign	Sign styles for business, public information, and personal signs, such as garage sales and picnics.
Business Card	Twelve business card styles ranging from modern to industrial. A phone index card is also included.
Card & Invitation	Options for creating Christmas and birthday cards, as well as invitations.
Calendar	To create monthly or yearly calendars. You can also add a picture and leave room for text in the calendar days.
Specialty	To create everything from bookmarks, certificates, and gift tags to itineraries, menus, even an emergency phone list.
Envelope	Six envelope styles. The wizard will place your company name on the envelope.
Banner	Five banner styles with looks ranging from formal to wild.
Resume	To create chronological, entry-level, or curriculum vitae resumes. You can also choose from several resume styles.
Paper Airplane	Four paper airplane styles such as "stubby" and "wing-tip wonder."
Origami	To create a cup, boat, parrot, and crane from folded paper.

Publisher's Page-Wizards (*continued*)

TABLE 5-1

Once you start looking through the PageWizards, you'll probably think of a bunch of new publications you want to produce. Many of them, such as an "Open for Business" sign, can be produced in five minutes. Others, such as newsletters, take a little more time. The next section discusses the steps for starting new publications by use of PageWizards.

Creating Publications with PageWizards

When you're ready to create a new publication using a PageWizard, select Create New Publication from the File menu. The dialog box that appears when you first start Publisher is displayed here:

Make sure the PageWizard tab is selected at the top of the dialog box. Click on the desired PageWizard (you may have to scroll down to see them all), and click OK. After a few seconds, the first screen of the selected PageWizard appears. Because PageWizards vary in content and complexity, the next section provides two step-by-step examples of working with PageWizards.

PageWizards at Work

Basically, all PageWizards work the same. Looking at a simple and then a more complex PageWizard will give you a good idea of the features and options available with PageWizards.

Example: Using a Simple PageWizard

The following steps illustrate using the relatively simple Sign PageWizard to create a "Help Wanted" sign:

1. From the File menu, select Create New Publication (or use the keyboard shortcut and press CTRL-N). On the PageWizards tab in the dialog box, select Sign PageWizard, and click OK. (You can also double-click on Sign PageWizard.)

2. The first screen of the Sign PageWizard appears and shows the four types of signs you can create—Business, Personal, Public Information, and Other. Select Business and click on the Next button in the bottom right corner of the screen.

3. The next screen displays the available sign types. A description of the selected sign appears in the lower-left corner. Use the up and down arrow buttons on the right to move through the sign choices. Select the "Help Wanted" sign and click Next.

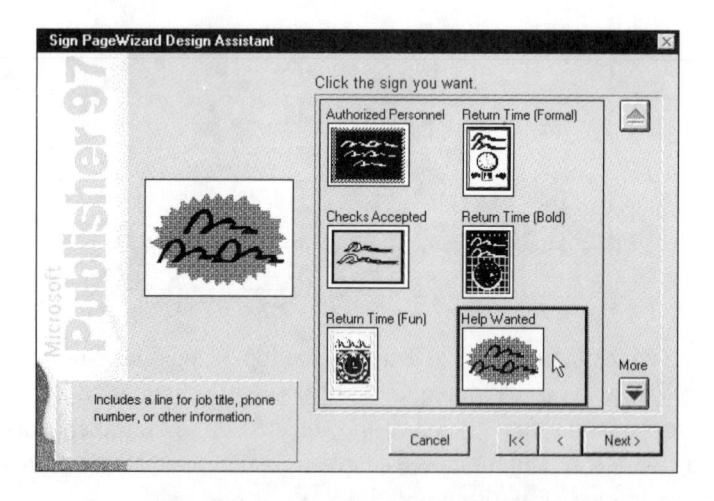

4. The third screen tells you the layout of the publication is complete. Because it is a relatively simple wizard, it does not offer any layout choices for you to work through. Click on the Create It button. The sign is created.

5. Publisher displays a final screen informing you the PageWizard has finished its work. You can also display help messages as you complete the sign. Click Yes to see the help messages and No to not see them. Click OK to close the PageWizard, and view the new publication.

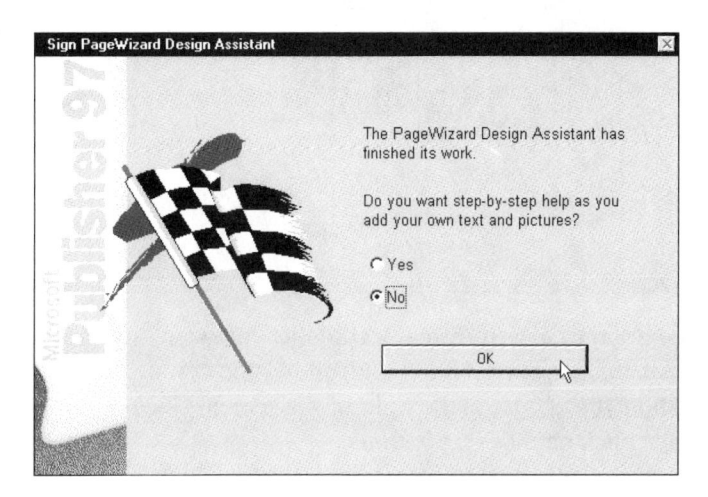

A text frame reading "Your Text Here" appears at the bottom of the screen. Click on the text to select it. Now you can type in your own text, such as "Part-time Cashier." The new text replaces the selected text in the frame (see Figure 5-1, next page). When finished editing the sign, save the file if you wish (saving is discussed later in this chapter in "Saving Documents"), and choose Close from the File menu.

Example: Using a Complex PageWizard

Newsletters, by design, are more complicated publications than signs. The Newsletter PageWizard therefore provides more options, such as number of columns. Keep in mind that these options can be changed after the PageWizard has created the publication. The following steps illustrate using the Newsletter PageWizard to create a three-column newsletter.

1. From the File menu, select Create New Publication (or press CTRL-N).

2. On the PageWizards tab in the dialog box, double-click on the Newsletter PageWizard. The first screen of the Newsletter PageWizard asks you to select a style for the newsletter, and its left side shows you a preview of each one. Select Classic and click on the Next button.

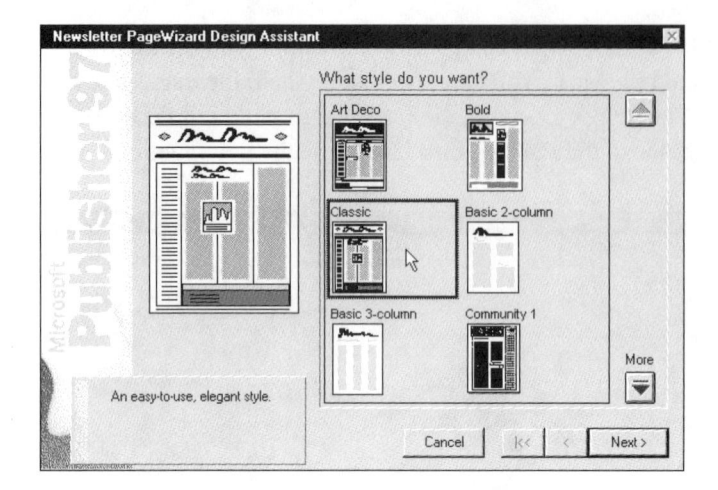

3. The next screen asks how many columns you want—one, two, three, or four. Again, the preview on the left shows the newsletter layout based on the option you choose at the right of the screen. Click on Three Columns and then click on the Next button.

Simply click on the text frame, and begin typing to place your information on the sign

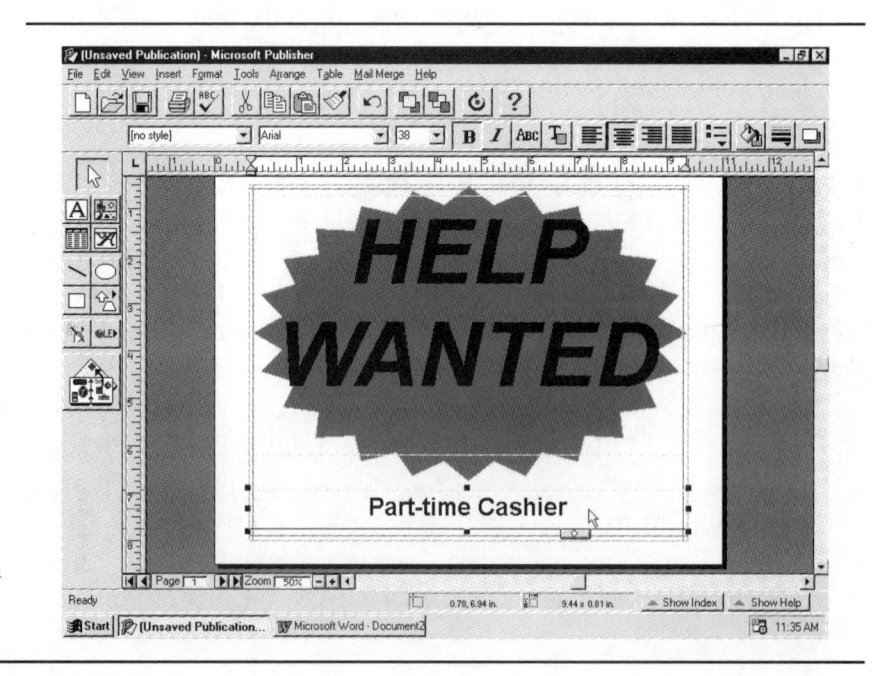

FIGURE 5-1

4. The next screen asks how many stories you want to appear on the first page. Placing several stories on the first page enhances reader interest. If the whole story doesn't fit, it can be continued on later pages. Select Two Stories and click on the Next button.

5. The next screen asks you to enter a title for the newsletter. Type in **Communicate!** and click on the Next button.

6. The next screen asks if you want to include a table of contents, date, and volume and issue numbers. Leave all the options on, and click on the Next button.

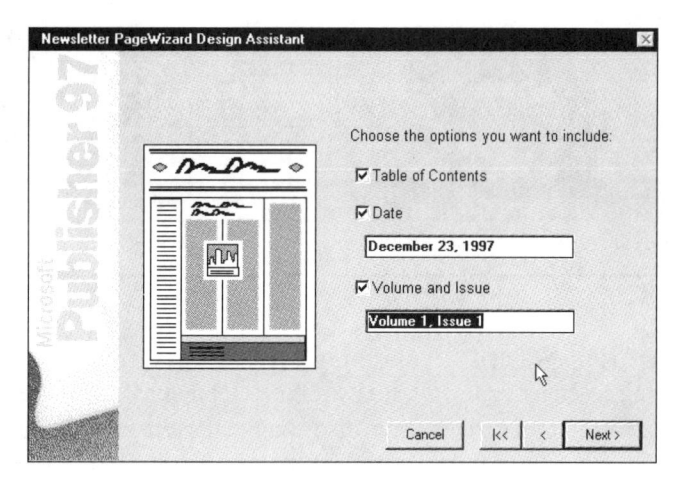

7. The next screen asks how many pages you want; stick with four. Click on the Next button.

8. The next screen asks if you want to leave room for a mailing label, select No. Click on the Next button.

9. The next screen asks if you will be printing on both sides of the paper. Select Yes and click on the Next button.

10. Click on the Create It button on the final screen of the Newsletter PageWizard to build the newsletter. A message appears as the newsletter is built, indicating the progress of the job.

11. When finished, you are asked if you want to display help as you complete the newsletter. Make your choice and click OK. The newsletter appears on screen, as shown in Figure 5-2 (notice the newsletter title, "Communicate!").

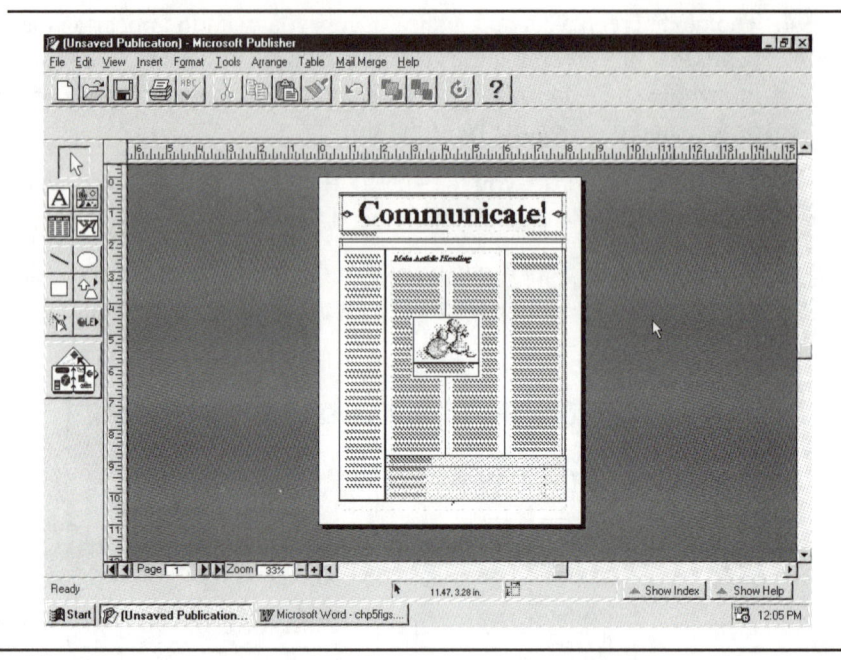

With the help of PageWizards you can quickly design professional publications, such as newsletters

FIGURE 5-2

As with the "Help Wanted" sign, simply click on a text frame in the newsletter and begin typing to enter your own text. Refer to Chapter 8 for more information on entering and formatting text. You can also change the clip art in the picture frame. Double-click on the picture frame to reveal the Microsoft Clip Art Gallery. Here, you can select a new image. Refer to Chapter 9 for more information on working with clip art and graphics.

Starting with a Blank Page

Publisher also allows you to build new publications from the ground up, without help from a PageWizard. You'll find the Blank Page option useful when you are comfortable with working with Publisher and want to design the page yourself. There are several types of blank pages to choose from, such as web pages, side-fold cards, and business cards. You can even set up custom-size blank pages.

Remember, when you use the Blank Page option to start a new publication, nothing more than a blank page appears on screen—it is up to you to build the page layout with text and picture frames.

To start a new publication using the Blank Page option:

1. From the File menu, select Create New Publication, or press CTRL-N. In the dialog box, click on the Blank Page tab.

2. Select the type of blank page you want to build and click OK. The blank page appears.

If you do not see an option for the blank page style you want, click on the Custom Page button in the lower-left corner of the dialog box to get to the Page Setup dialog box. The following section discusses the options available for custom pages.

Setting Up a Custom Page

Publisher provides four layout categories—Normal, Special Fold, Special Size, and Labels. The options are available in the Page Setup dialog box (see Figure 5-3) and can also be applied after a document is created. However, to help you get the publication right the first time, the options are discussed in-depth here.

Working with Normal Layouts

Normal layouts are pages that match the size of the paper they are printed on, such as newsletters and flyers. Normal layouts do not require folding. As described in the previous section, clicking on the Custom Page button displays the Page Setup dialog box. As shown in Figure 5-3, Normal is the default layout style. At the bottom of the dialog box, you can choose from Portrait (tall) or Landscape (wide) orientation. To change the paper size for a normal layout, click on the Print Setup button. In the

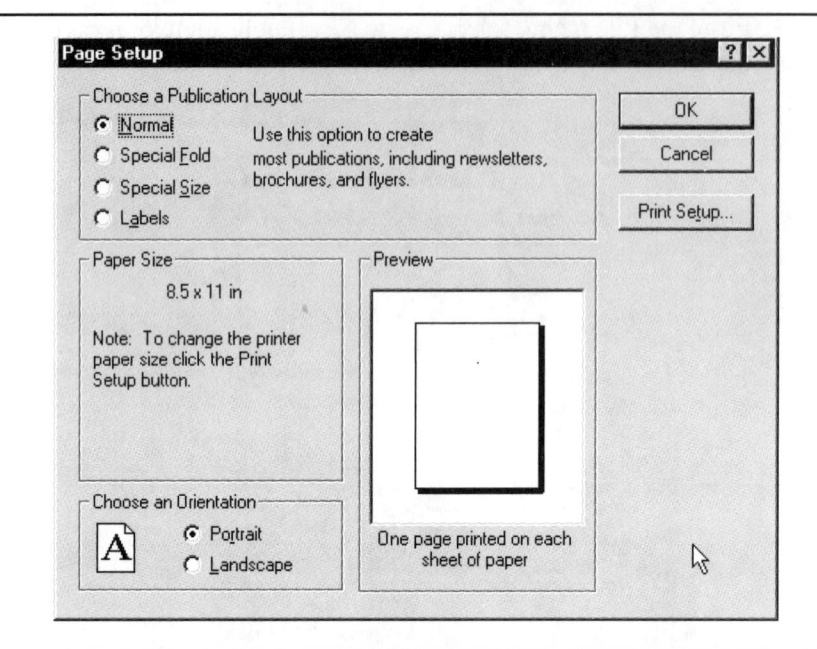

Use the Page Setup dialog box to choose a publication layout

FIGURE 5-3

Print Setup dialog box choose a paper size that the selected printer can output. When finished, click OK to return to the Page Setup dialog box. Click OK again to create the new blank publication.

NOTE: *As you work with the different layouts, keep in mind that many of the options available depend on the selected printer. Refer to the section "Selecting a Printer" later in this chapter for more information.*

Working with Special Fold Layouts

Use Special Fold layouts to create publications that require folding a single sheet of paper once or twice to create the individual pages in the publication. For instance, with the Tent Card layout, the front and back are actually printed on one side of the paper. After printing, the publication is folded, creating the "front" and "back" of the card.

To use a special fold layout, select Special Fold in the Publication Layout section of the Page Setup dialog box. As shown in Figure 5-4, click on the Choose A Special Fold drop-down arrow, and select the desired fold from the list. You can also enter new measurements for the width and height of the paper and change the orientation.

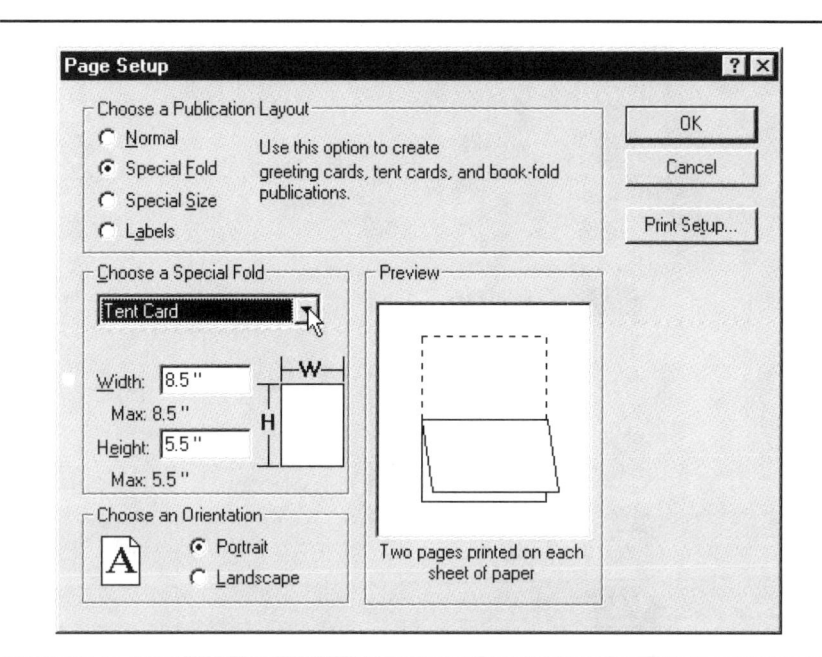

When you select a special fold, a preview of the fold appears on the right

FIGURE 5-4

Notice the maximum height and width—this is determined by the size of paper the selected printer can print. When finished, click OK to create the new blank publication.

Working with Special Size Layouts

The Special Size layout option is for publications whose pages are either larger or smaller than the paper they will be printed on. Publications larger than the paper they're printed on include banners and posters. To create the final publication, you have to attach several sheets of paper. (Some printers can output to large sheets of paper. This is another reason for selecting the right printer early in the production process.) Publications smaller than the paper they're printed on include business and index cards. To create the final publication, you trim off the parts of the paper you don't need.

To use a special size layout, select Special Size in the Publication Layout section of the Page Setup dialog box. As shown in Figure 5-5, click on the Choose A Publication Size drop-down arrow, and select the desired size from the list. You can also enter new measurements for the width and height of the paper and change the orientation. When finished, click OK to create the new blank publication.

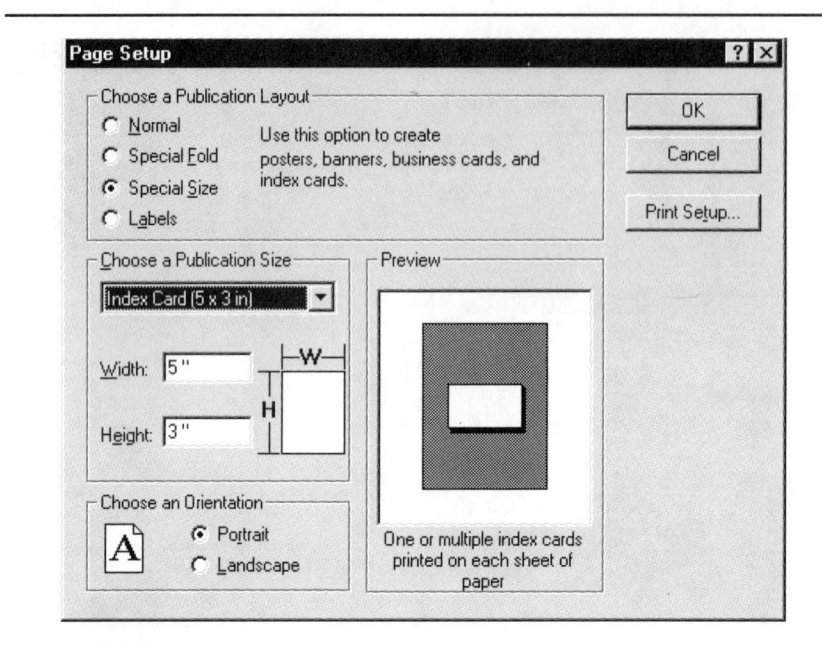

When you select a special size, a preview of the size appears on the right

FIGURE 5-5

Working with Labels Layouts

The Labels layouts allow you to choose a label type from a listing of the standard Avery labels. To use a Labels layout, select Labels from the Publication Layout section of the Page Setup dialog box. As shown in Figure 5-6, scroll through the list of labels to select the desired style. When finished, click OK to create the new blank page of labels.

Modifying Web Page Layouts

The bottom of the Create New Publication dialog box (shown earlier in "Starting with a Blank Page") includes a button for customizing web pages. Click on the Custom Web Page button to display the Web Page Setup dialog box shown in Figure 5-7. Under Page Width, select the Standard option to create web pages that fit all video displays. Select Wide to create web pages that fit high-resolution video displays such as SVGA. Select Custom to enter your own width and height for the web page. Click OK to create the new blank web page. Refer to Chapter 15 for more information on designing a web page.

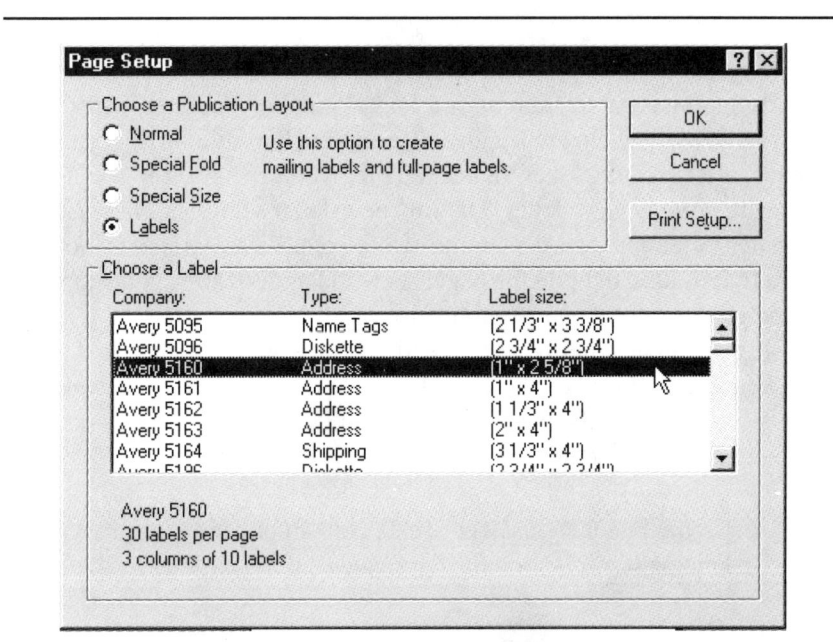

When you select a label type, a description of the label appears below

FIGURE 5-6

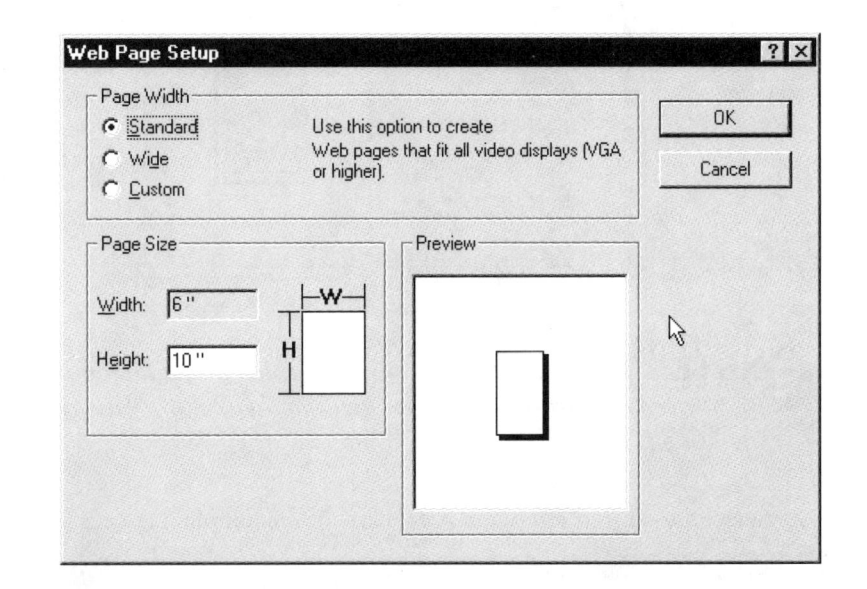

You can specify the size of a web page with the Web Page Setup dialog box

FIGURE 5-7

Creating Publications Based on Templates

After designing a publication with a PageWizard or building it from scratch, you may want to use it again and again as a guideline for building new publications. For instance, after creating a newsletter for July, you can save it to use as the basis for creating the August newsletter. The July newsletter serves as a *template* for the new newsletter. A template works similarly to a PageWizard in that it includes text and picture frames used to build the page. As with PageWizards, you simply replace the text and graphics for the new publication.

Using templates helps you speed up production and also helps establish consistency in design. By using the template to start the new newsletter, you can easily follow some of the basic structure and design of a previous newsletter.

To create a new publication based on a template:

1. From the File menu, select Create New Publication, or press CTRL-N. In the dialog box, click on the Templates tab.

 **NOTE:**   *The Templates tab will not display in the dialog box until you have saved at least one template. Refer to the section "Saving Templates" later in this chapter for more information.*

2. Select the desired template. A preview of the template appears on the right.

3. If you can't find the template you want, click on the Click Here To Open A Template Not Listed Above button at the bottom left corner of the dialog box. Change the drive and folders as necessary to locate the template file.

4. With the correct template selected, click OK.

When you create a new publication based on a template, notice the title bar displays "Unsaved Publication." Basically, you have opened a copy of the template file, and it needs to be saved as any other new publication. Don't hesitate to make changes to the new publication—since you are working with a copy, you are not altering the original template file.

5

Selecting a Printer

The whole reason for building publications is so you can print them. If you create a publication with one printer selected and then switch to another one to print, the printed publication may look different from what you see on the screen. Changing printers can cause discrepancies in the fonts, character formatting, the paper size you can use, the area of the page that will print, and the quality of the printed publication.

To avoid discrepancies between what you see on the screen and what you get when you print, set up the printer *before you begin designing.* Select the printer that will be used to output the final copy of the publication. If the final copy (not just rough drafts) will be printed by the LaserJet on your desk, make sure the LaserJet is the selected printer. If the final copy will be printed by an outside printing service, such as a commercial printer or copy shop, select the printer they will be using to output the publication. It doesn't matter whether you have the actual printer—all you need is the *printer driver,* the file that tells Publisher how to compose your publication for that printer. Ask the outside printing service what printer driver you should use. For instance, a service bureau may tell customers to select the QMS Colorscript 100 printer driver. If you do not have the printer driver file (chances are that you do—with your Windows 95 software), the commercial printer will usually give you a copy.

NOTE: *As discussed in Chapter 2, you should have already determined the printing process and what (if any) colors you'll be using.*

As a safety precaution, Publisher provides generic printer drivers that work with most printers. The MS Publisher Imagesetter driver is for black-and-white printing, and the MS Publisher Color Printer driver is for color printing. These drivers can be installed during the Publisher installation. In most cases, selecting one of these printer drivers will provide good results. As mentioned earlier, call the printer or copy shop to determine the best printer driver for your publication.

 **NOTE:** *The steps for installing printer drivers, from a commercial printer or Publisher's generic printer drivers, are outlined in Chapter 10.*

Once you have the correct printer driver installed, use the following steps to select it immediately after starting a new publication:

1. From the File menu, select Print Setup. The Print Setup dialog box, shown here, appears.

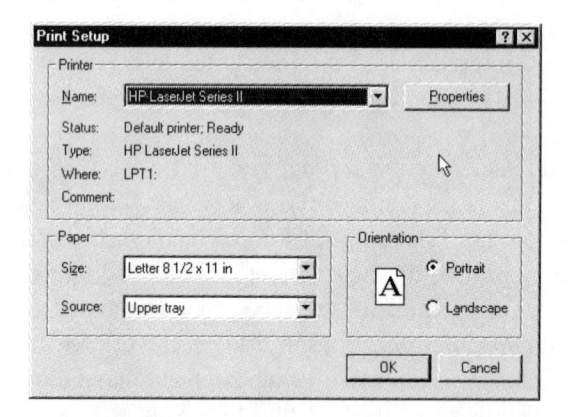

2. Click on the Name drop-down arrow, and choose the desired printer driver. Information about the selected printer, such as the status of the printer, appears below the Name box.

3. Click on the Properties button to display the properties for the selected printer. Figure 5-8 displays properties for the MS Publisher Imagesetter. In this dialog box you can change the page size and orientation. Click OK to return to the Print Setup dialog box.

The
selected
printer has
properties
that can be
adjusted

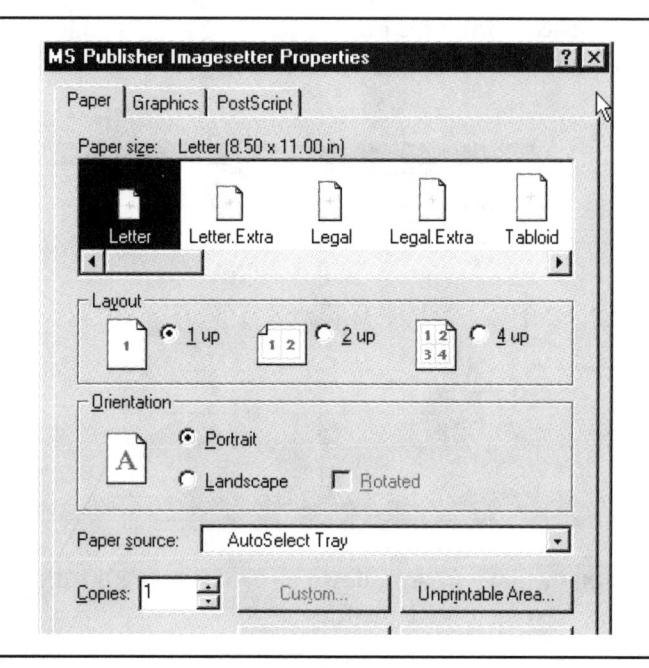

5

FIGURE 5-8

4. Click OK again to set up the selected printer for your new publication.

The properties of a printer can get rather technical. As a general rule, if you don't know what an option means, leave it alone. In some cases, your printing service may instruct you to change an option. For instance, the service may ask you to change the page size to Letter Extra if you plan on placing elements close to the edge of a letter-size page.

NOTE: *If you do change printers after designing but before printing, take time to review the publication. Look for changes in font, text placement, and page setup.*

Saving Documents

After you start a publication and select the printer, it's time to save the publication file. Don't put off saving too long—it's no fun to lose hours of work due to a power outage or application error. To save files for the first time:

1. Select Save As from the File menu. The Save As dialog box appears, as shown here. By default, Publisher saves files in the Publisher folder.

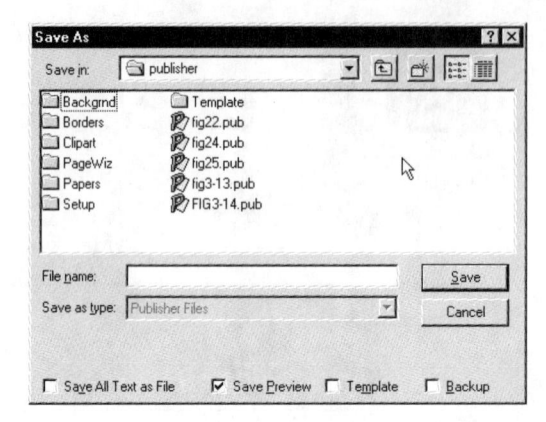

2. Click on the Save In drop-down arrow to choose the drive and folder where you want to save the file.

3. Enter a filename in the File Name box. Don't worry about adding a filename extension; Publisher automatically adds the extension .PUB. You can use spaces and enter up to 255 characters (including the drive letter and folder names) for a filename in Windows 95.

4. Click OK to save the file. The new filename appears in the title bar at the top of the screen.

Publisher also enables you to create a backup copy of your documents. This comes in handy when you accidentally delete a file, because you still have the backup. The backup file has the same name as the original publication file but has the extension .BAK. To create a backup file, click on the Backup option in the Save As dialog box.

Saving Templates

To save a template, click on the Template option when saving a publication file in the Save As dialog box. Templates use the .PUB filename extension and by default are stored in the Publisher folder's Template subfolder. However, you can store them anywhere. After saving a template, you can use it to build new publications as discussed previously in the section "Creating Publications Based on Templates."

Saving Changes

If, after saving, you make changes to a file, select Save from the File menu to update the file and save the changes. You can also click on the Save tool in the Standard toolbar. With the Save command Publisher assumes you want to overwrite the previously saved version, so a dialog box does not appear asking where to save the file.

 **TIP:**   *Get into the habit of using the keyboard shortcut CTRL-S to save the publication file frequently.*

5

If you need to change the location where the file is saved, use the Save As command in the File menu, and specify the new location in the Save As dialog box.

Adjusting the Reminder-to-Save Message

By default, Publisher asks you to save a publication file every 15 minutes. That is, if you have not saved, Publisher displays a reminder message. You can adjust how often the reminder message appears or turn it off altogether. From the Tools menu, select Options. The Options dialog box appears, as shown in Figure 5-9. Click on the Editing And User Assistance tab at the top of the dialog box. To turn off the reminder feature, click to remove the check mark by Remind To Save Publications at the bottom of the dialog box. If you wish to increase or decrease the timing for the reminder feature, enter a new number in the minutes box.

Closing Documents

When you're finished working on a publication, select the Close Publication command from the File menu. If you have not saved the latest changes, Publisher asks you to save before closing. Click Yes to save and then close the file, click

At the bottom of the Editing and User Assistance tab in the Options dialog box you can adjust how often the reminder-to-save message appears

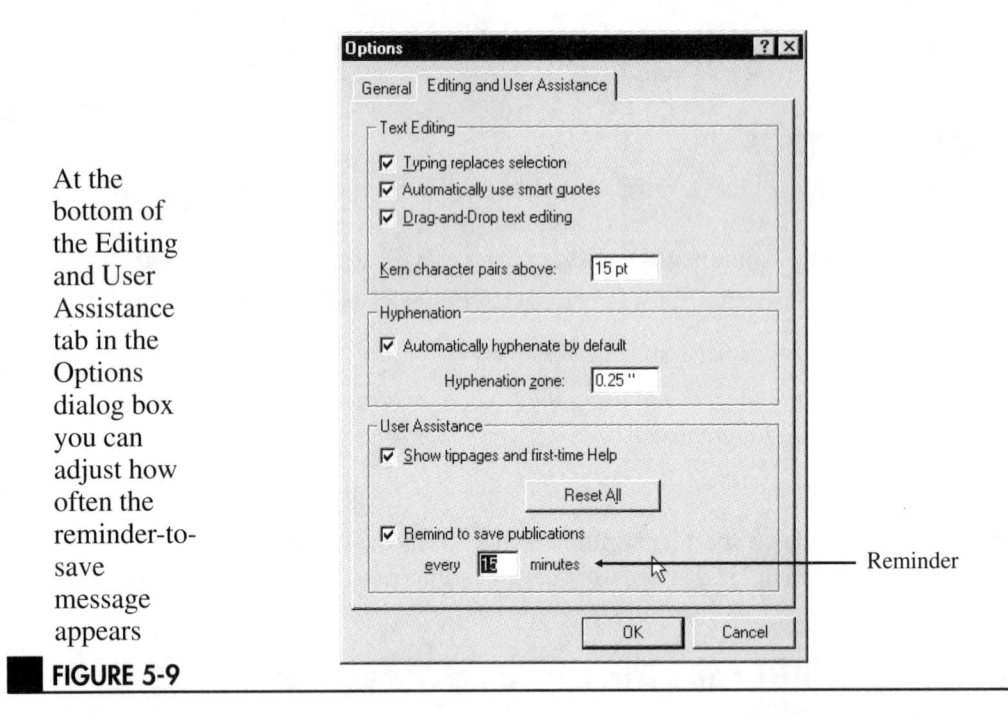

Reminder

FIGURE 5-9

No to close the file without saving, or click Cancel to return to the publication without closing.

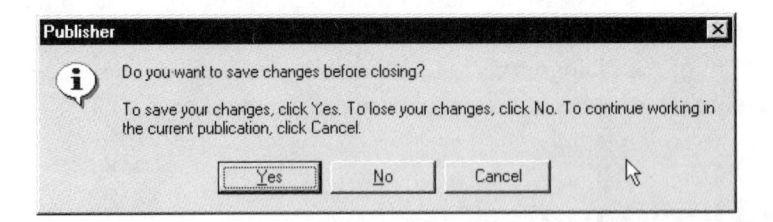

You may not need to use the Close command. Keep in mind that opening a new publication also closes the current publication, and exiting Publisher also closes the publication.

Opening Documents

After creating, saving, and closing a publication, you may need to retrieve it. Publisher uses the filename extension .PUB. To open a file:

1. Select Open Existing Publication from the File menu. The Existing Publication tab of the Create New Publication dialog box will be displayed.

2. In the list on the left, select the filename you want to open. A preview of the publication appears on the right. Click OK to open the file.

3. If you do not see the publication file you want to open, click on the Open A Publication Not Listed Above button at the bottom of the dialog box. The Open Publication dialog box appears.

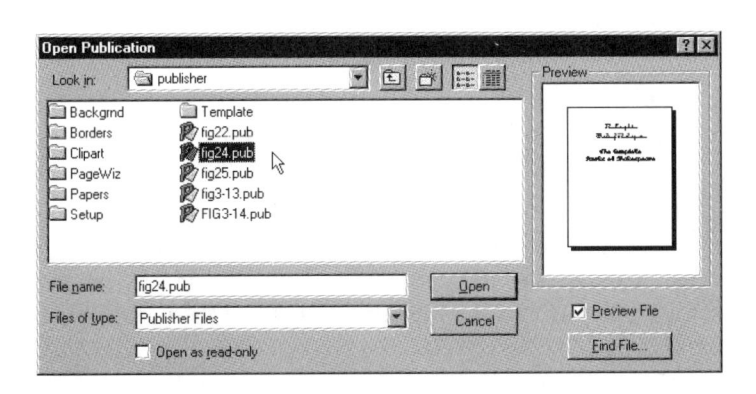

4. Click on the Look In drop-down arrow, and select the drive where the file is stored. The folders stored on that drive appear in the dialog box.

5. Double-click on the folder and subfolders containing the file to be opened. An icon of a *P* appears next to the Publisher filenames.

6. Select the filename and click OK to open the file.

You can only open one file at a time in Publisher. This means when you open a file, any publication that was already opened will be closed. If you have not saved the currently open publication, a message appears prompting you to save it.

 **TIP:** *You'll find the names of the most recently opened files displayed at the bottom of the File menu. Click on the filename to quickly open a file.*

Opening Files from Other Applications

If you are switching to Publisher after using a word processing application or you plan on opening files created in another application, you're in luck. Publisher can open files created with popular word processing programs such as Word for Windows and WordPerfect. You don't have to worry about reformatting the whole thing, because the typefaces, sizes, and styles such as bold and italic remain intact.

Generic text file formats, such as ASCII and RTF, can also be opened. And Publisher can open Microsoft Excel files. Spreadsheet data is opened as a table in Publisher. Refer to Chapter 12 for more information on working with tables.

 **NOTE:** *When you open a file with graphics, the graphics will be placed in a Publisher picture frame. You may have to adjust the location and size.*

Opening a file created in another application is basically the same as opening a Publisher file. Click on the Open tool in the Standard toolbar. In the Open Publication dialog box, change to the drive and folder where the file is located. Now, click on the Files Of Type drop-down arrow to reveal a listing of file formats that Publisher can open (see Figure 5-10). Choose the file type, such as "Word 6.0/95 For Windows&Macintosh" or "WordPerfect 6.x." The files in the specified file type appear in the dialog box. Select the filename and click OK to open the file.

Publisher
can open
files
created in
word
processing
and
spreadsheet
applications,
such as
Word for
Windows
and Excel

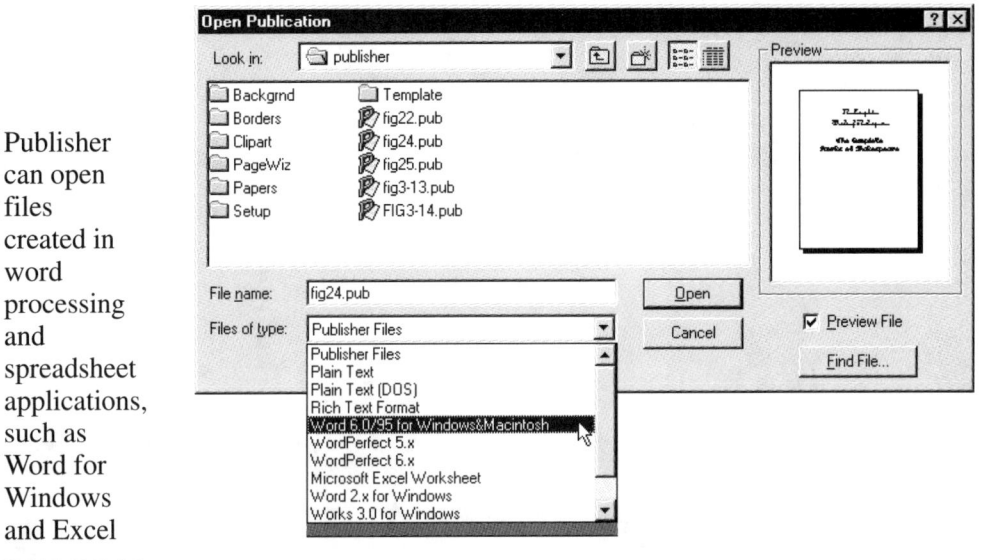

FIGURE 5-10

5

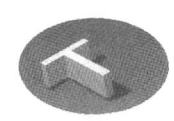 **TIP:** *Press* CTRL-O *to display the Open Publication dialog box.*

Remember, when you are ready to shut down Publisher, select Exit Publisher from the File menu. To quickly close Publisher with the mouse, click on the Close button. The keyboard shortcut to exit Publisher is ALT-F4.

Summary

This chapter looked at the many options you have for creating new publications. You can use one of Publisher's PageWizards to help you build a publication, start one from scratch, or use an existing publication as a template to build a new one. This chapter also stressed the importance of selecting the right printer *before* you begin designing a publication.

Now that you know how to start new publications, you ready to begin working with them. Chapter 6 discusses moving through pages, inserting pages, zooming in and out of the page, and working with page views.

Working with Publications

You've started the publication (with a little help from PageWizards) and selected the printer. Now you're ready to build and modify your publication. You can enter text, add pictures, and tinker with the page layout. But before you jump in, there are a few more basics you should know.

This chapter discusses the mechanics of working with a publication, for example, using the page controls and Zoom indicator. You'll also learn how to insert and delete pages in a publication. The Undo feature, common to most Windows applications, is then discussed. This chapter also covers page views, which make it easier to see different aspects of your work. The chapter ends with options for adjusting the page setup, setting margin spacing, and changing the column layout.

Moving Between Pages in a Document

After creating a publication, you'll need to move back and forth through the pages of the document to add and delete text, move and size pictures, and otherwise proof your work. Publisher's *page controls* provide the easiest way to move through a document.

As displayed in Figure 6-1, the page controls appear in the bottom left corner of the screen. The *page counter* displays the number of the page you are looking at. To move to the next page, click on the right-pointing arrow immediately right of the page number. To move to the previous page, click on the left-pointing arrow immediately left of the page number. Click on the left-pointing arrow with a line to move to the first page of a publication. Click on the right-pointing arrow with a line to move to the last page of a publication.

In longer publications, it can be tedious to click on the page control arrows ten times just to move from page 5 to page 15. When you need to skip several pages quickly, select Go To Page from the View menu. In the Go To Page dialog box, shown here, enter the number of the page you want to see and click on OK. You can also click on the page number in the page controls to quickly display the Go To Page dialog box.

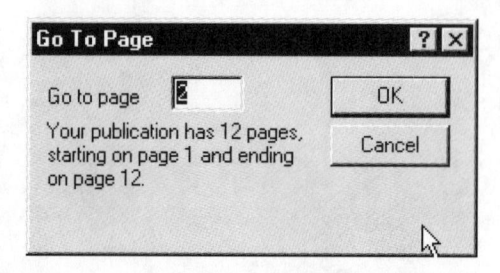

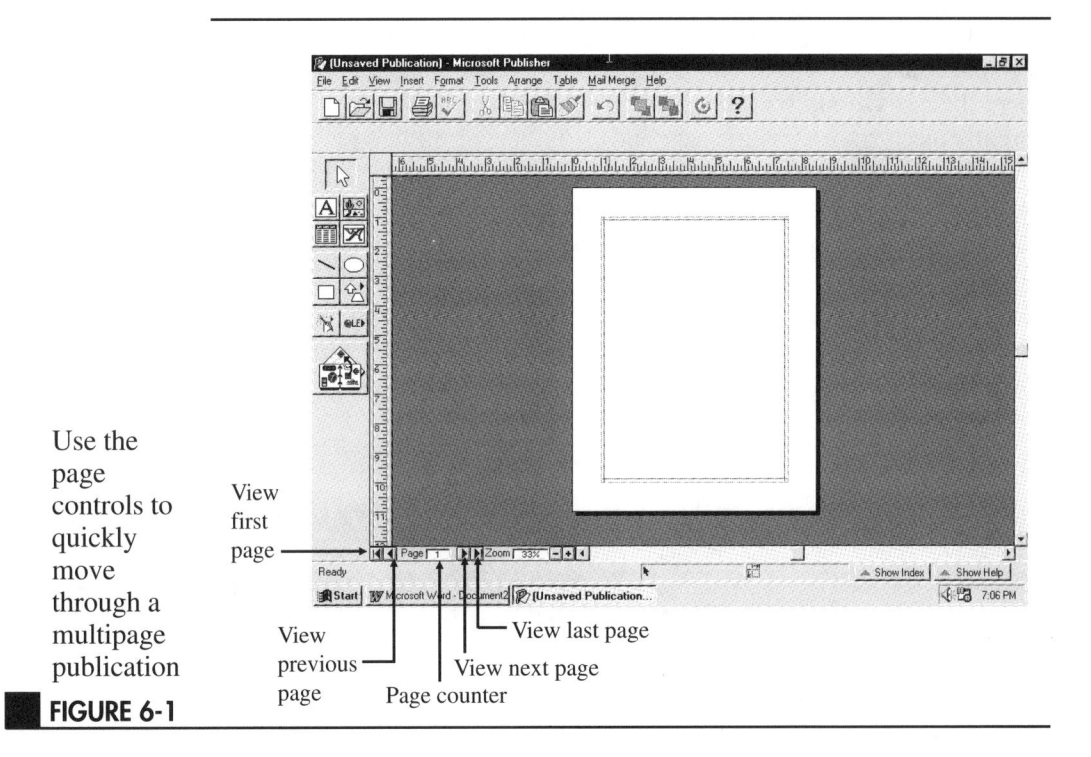

Use the page controls to quickly move through a multipage publication

View first page →

View previous page —

Page counter

View next page

View last page

FIGURE 6-1

TIP: *Press SHIFT-F5 to go to the next page, and press CTRL-F5 to go to the previous page.*

Inserting Pages

With Publisher, you can insert pages at any time. Each page you add will have the margin and column guides you've already set. (Adjusting margin and column settings is covered later in the section "Setting Margins and Columns.") In addition, any objects placed on the background will be visible on the newly inserted page(s). Refer to Chapter 16 for more information on viewing and placing objects on the background.

When inserting pages, you have the option to insert them before or after the currently displayed page. For instance, when viewing page 2, you can insert a page *before* page 2 (the original page 2 then becomes page 3). Or you can insert a page, which would become page 3, *after* page 2. Any subsequent pages are renumbered to accommodate the new pages.

You can also choose to insert a text frame on the new pages. The text frame is sized according to the margin guides. This is handy for creating books or reports where there may only be text on the page. Publisher also gives you the option to copy all objects from a specific page and place them on the new page(s). For instance, suppose you were doing two flyers, one for a company picnic and one for a neighborhood picnic. You could design the company picnic flyer, and then copy everything from that page onto the new page. After a few minor adjustments, your neighborhood picnic flyer would be complete.

To insert one or more pages in a publication:

1. Go to the page where you want to insert the new page.

2. From the Insert menu, select Page. The Insert Page dialog box appears.

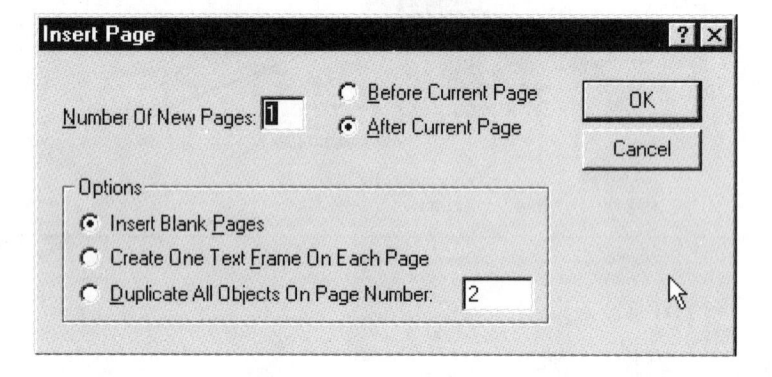

3. Enter the number of pages you want to add. Select Before Current Page to add pages before the page you are viewing. Select After Current Page to add pages after the page you are viewing. By default, Publisher inserts blank pages.

   ■ To add a text frame to the new pages, select Create One Text Frame On Each Page.

   ■ To copy objects from a page, select Duplicate All Objects On Page Number. In the box, enter the number of the page you want to copy.

4. When finished, click OK.

The first of the newly inserted pages is displayed. Use the page counter to move through the pages.

TIP: *Use the keyboard shortcut CTRL-SHIFT-N to quickly add one page after the current page.*

Deleting Pages

If you add too many pages or later need to reduce the size of a document, you can delete unwanted pages. For example, suppose you use the Newsletter PageWizard to build a four-page newsletter, and then discover you need only three pages. To delete a page from a publication:

1. Go to the page you want to delete.

2. From the Edit menu, choose Delete Page. If there are any objects on the page, Publisher displays a message informing you that all objects on the page will also be deleted. Click OK to delete the page and objects. Click Cancel to not delete the page and objects.

In Publisher, you can only delete one page at a time. Repeat the preceding steps to delete additional pages. If you want to delete a page but not the objects on the page, move them to another page before deleting. Moving and copying frames is covered in Chapter 7.

TIP: *If you accidentally delete a page, select Undo Delete Page from the Edit menu immediately.*

Undoing Commands

You may wonder, "what happens if I make a mistake?" As anybody who uses computers to build publications can tell you, you *will* make mistakes. You will accidentally delete a page, or erase some text, or demolish a frame.

Fortunately, there is a way to reverse your actions. The Undo command undoes your last step. For instance, imagine you accidentally delete a page with a paragraph that took you forever to write. Rather than trying to re-create the material, simply select Undo from the Edit menu. Or click on the Undo/Redo tool in the Standard toolbar. The deleted page (and text) is returned to the publication.

NOTE: *Because so many commands can be undone, Undo is a powerful tool for those who are learning an application. With Undo, you can experiment with commands to see if they do what you wanted, knowing you can always reverse them if necessary.*

Undo also undoes commands such as setting margins, changing typefaces, and moving text. When you select Undo from the Edit menu, the command indicates what will be undone. For instance, when the Undo command indicates Undo Text Deletion, you know deleted text will be placed back into the document. Unlike some other Windows applications, Publisher has only *one* level of Undo. This means when you make a mistake, you need to Undo it *immediately,* before executing another command.

Working with Page Views

Producing publications in Publisher requires that you perform a variety of tasks. One big job is entering, editing, and formatting text. Another is building the page layout with picture frames and tables.

In producing your Publisher publications, you will find yourself jumping back and forth between these tasks. Sometimes you will need to get in close for fine-tuning, and other times you will want to step back from your work for a big-picture view. That's why Publisher provides three ways to view your documents. These page views are called *Full Page, Actual Size,* and *Two-Page Spread.*

To determine which view is currently being used to display a publication, select the View menu. The three view options appear at the top of the menu list, as shown here. A check mark appears by the current page view.

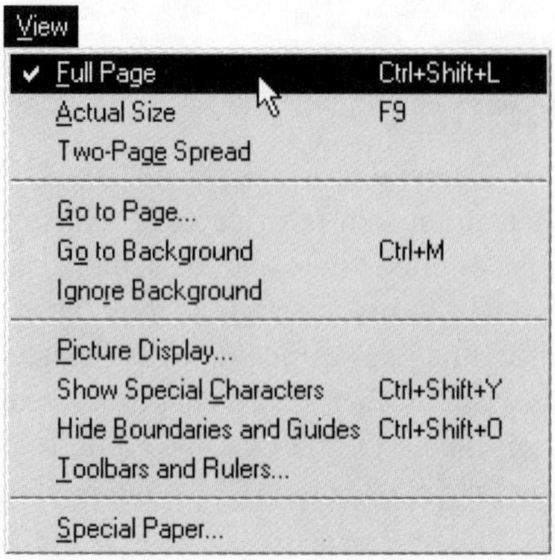

View	
✓ Full Page	Ctrl+Shift+L
Actual Size	F9
Two-Page Spread	
Go to Page...	
Go to Background	Ctrl+M
Ignore Background	
Picture Display...	
Show Special Characters	Ctrl+Shift+Y
Hide Boundaries and Guides	Ctrl+Shift+O
Toolbars and Rulers...	
Special Paper...	

Using Full Page View

As the name implies, Full Page view provides a view of the full page. When you start a new publication, Publisher displays the first page in Full Page view (refer back to Figure 6-1). To switch to Full Page view, select Full Page from the View menu.

NOTE: *The margin and column guides affect the page view. As discussed in Chapter 4, use the keyboard shortcut CTRL-SHIFT-O to hide and display the margin and column guides.*

Full Page view is great when you're drawing frames on the page to add text and graphics. After the frames are in place, use Full Page view to move and size frames to adjust the page layout. When you're adjusting margins and columns, Full Page view makes it easy to see how the change affected the whole page. Although body text is not readable in Full Page view, you can see large headings and titles.

Using Actual Size View

Actual Size view zooms in to display the text and graphics in approximately the size they will print (see Figure 6-2). To switch to Actual Size view, select Actual Size from the View menu.

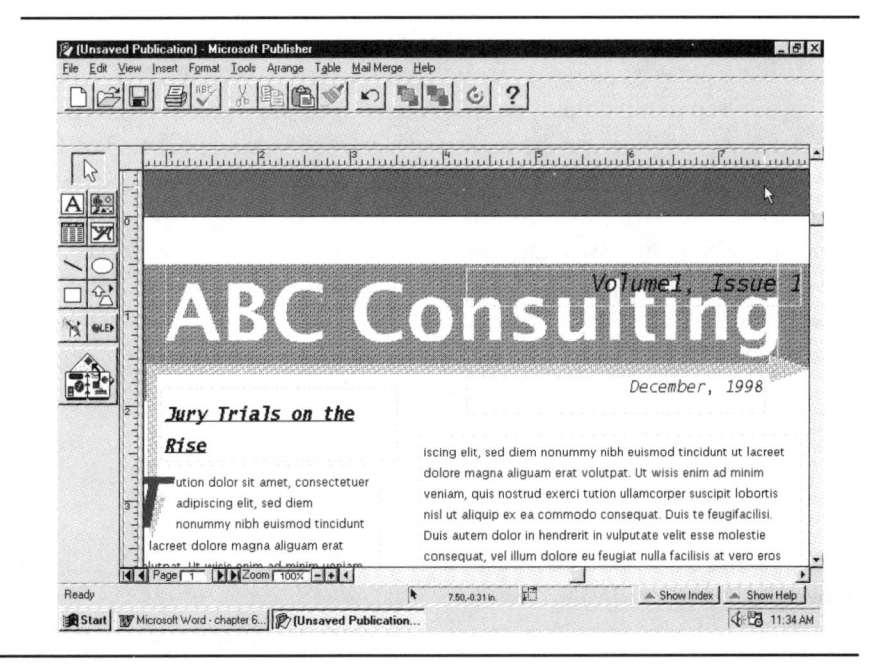

Actual Size view enables you to see the page elements at the size they will print

FIGURE 6-2

 **TIP:** *Press the F9 key to quickly toggle back and forth between full page and actual size views.*

Obviously, Actual Size view is essential when entering, editing, and formatting text. When you're modifying clip art, use of Actual Size to view the art up close is also handy. Switch to Actual Size view when you're building tables and creating WordArt.

Using Two-Page Spread View

Two-Page Spread view allows you to view both the left and right pages of a publication at the same time. To understand the concept of left and right pages, think of a four-page book, as shown here.

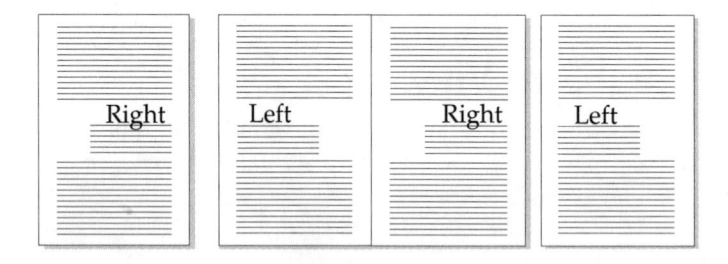

Page 1 is a right page, page 2 is a left page, page 3 is a right page, and page 4 is a left page. Keep in mind that you will only see one page at a time when viewing the first and last page, because the first page is a right page and has no left-facing page, and the last page is a left page with no right-facing page.

To switch to Two-Page Spread view, select Two-Page Spread from the View menu. The ability to view facing pages at the same time lets you create page layouts that consider facing pages as a single unit called a *double-page spread* (see Figure 6-3). When a publication is printed and bound, your reader sees two facing pages at once—not a left page, then a right. Designing facing pages as a double-page spread gives your publication a more professional look. To return to single page view, select Full Page from the View menu.

Hiding and Displaying Pictures

After placing pictures (especially large photographs) in a publication, you may notice that *screen redraw* (how long it takes the screen to display the image) is significantly slower. Publisher provides two options for speeding up screen redraw.

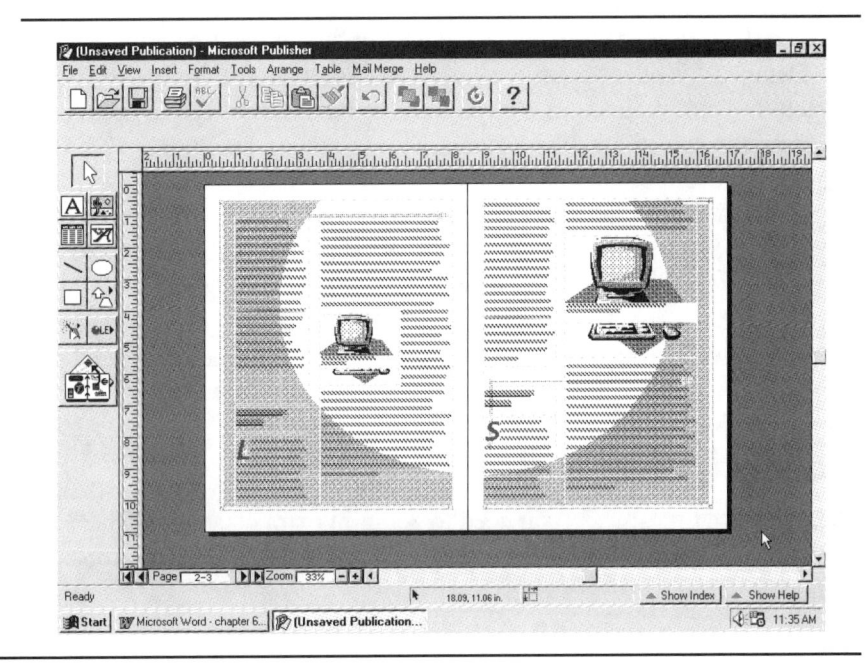

Two-Page Spread view lets you view the left and right pages of a document at one time

FIGURE 6-3

You can display the pictures at a lower resolution, or hide the pictures entirely. How pictures are displayed on screen has no effect on printing. The pictures print at the resolution of the output device.

To change how pictures are displayed, select Picture Display from the Edit menu. The Picture Display dialog box, shown here, appears.

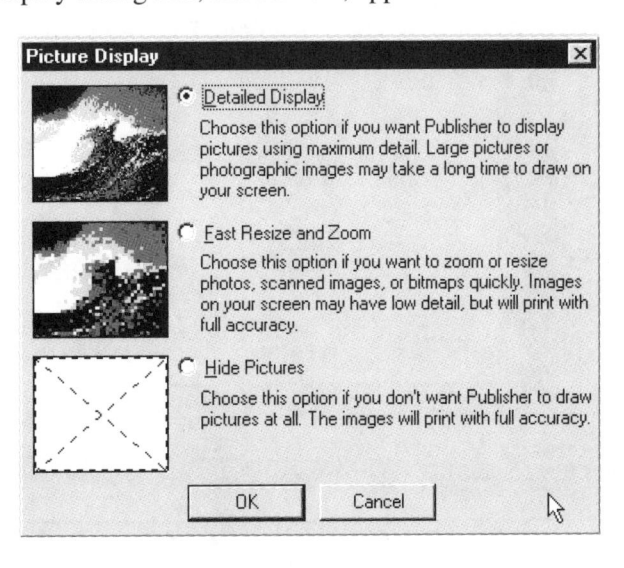

By default, Publisher displays pictures in high resolution with detailed display. The Detailed Display option provides the best look at the photographs and other pictures in your publication. Select the Fast Resize And Zoom option to speed up screen redraw but still see the pictures. This is a lower-resolution screen view where some of the detail of the pictures may be lost.

Hiding pictures is the best way to speed up screen redraw. Select the Hide Pictures option in the Picture Display dialog box to not show the pictures on the screen. Instead, boxes appear on the screen representing the pictures (see Figure 6-4).

Although hidden pictures cannot be viewed, you can still move and size them as you would a visible picture. Sizing and moving picture frames is covered in Chapter 7.

Zooming In for a Better Look

There may be times when you need to zoom in extra close to a page. For instance, suppose you are creating a flowchart with Publisher's drawing tools. To get the

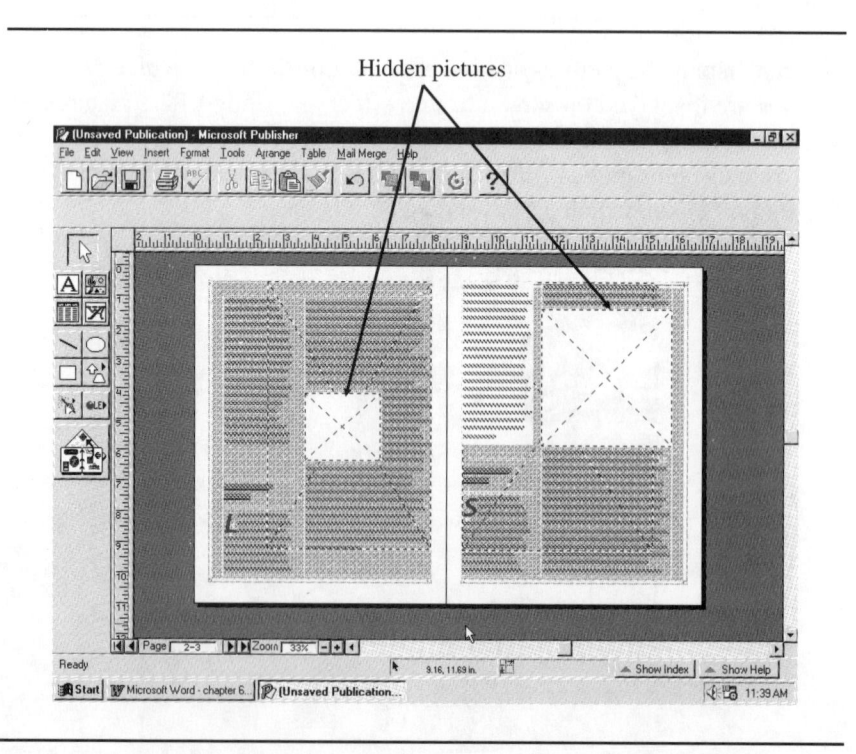

Boxes represent the hidden pictures on a page

FIGURE 6-4

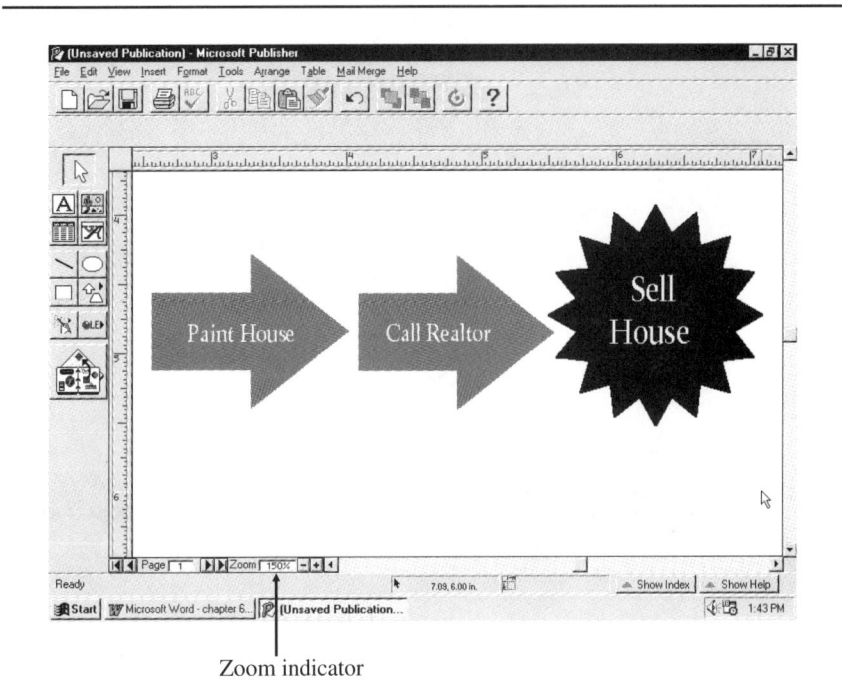

The Zoom indicator displays the level or percentage of zoom

Zoom indicator

FIGURE 6-5

arrows and other shapes lined up perfectly, you need to see the objects up close (see Figure 6-5). The *Zoom indicator* at the bottom of the screen provides a quick way to zoom in for close-up work and zoom out for an overall page view.

To zoom into the page, click on the + (plus) sign on the Zoom indicator. To zoom out of the page, click on the - (minus) sign on the Zoom indicator. The percentage of zoom appears in the Zoom indicator as you click on the + and - buttons. In Figure 6-5, the zoom level is 150 percent.

You can also click on the percentage in the Zoom indicator to display a pop-up menu. In the menu, simply click on the desired zoom level. If an object on the page is selected, the Zoom To Selection option appears on the pop-up menu shown here. Select this option to zoom in as closely as possible to the selected object.

Full Page
Actual Size
Zoom to Selection
10%
25%
33%
50%
66%
75%
100%
150%
200%
400%

TIP: *You can also use the Zoom indicator to move back and forth between Full Page and Actual Size views.*

Scrolling Across Pages

Once you've zoomed into a page, you may want to stay at that zoom level but just move up or down the page a little. Use the *scroll bars* on the bottom and right-hand side of the screen to adjust the position of the page (see Figure 6-6). Click on the up and down *scroll arrows* to move vertically up and down the page. Click on the left and right scroll arrows to move horizontally across the document. You can also drag the scroll box in the scroll bars to quickly move around the page.

If you like keyboard shortcuts, press the PAGEUP key to move up the page, and press PAGEDOWN to move down the page. Use CTRL-PAGEUP to move to the left of the page. Press CTRL-PAGEDOWN to move to the right.

Adjusting the Page Layout

When using PageWizards to build publications, you may be asked to choose the page orientation (whether the page is portrait or landscape), and the page size. Likewise, when using the Blank Page option to create a new publication, you choose the desired page size. As explained in Chapter 5, when working with the Blank Page option, you click on the Custom Page button (on the Blank Page tab of the initial Microsoft Publisher 97 dialog box) to display the Page Setup dialog box (see Figure 6-7). Here, you can adjust the page orientation and layout of the new publication.

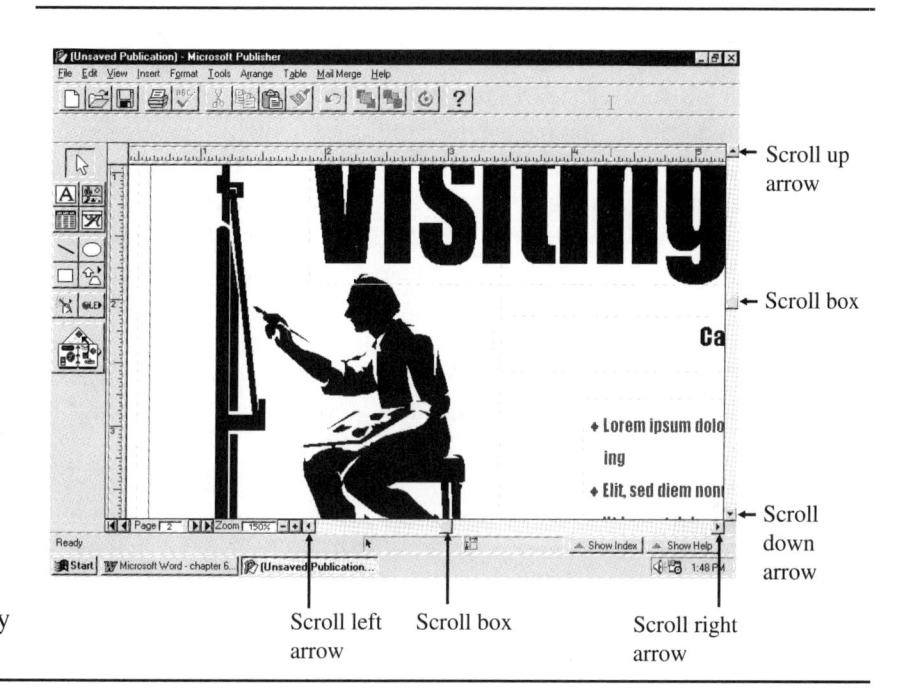

When you have zoomed in, use the scroll bars to move vertically and horizontally

Scroll up arrow

Scroll box

Scroll down arrow

Scroll left arrow

Scroll box

Scroll right arrow

FIGURE 6-6

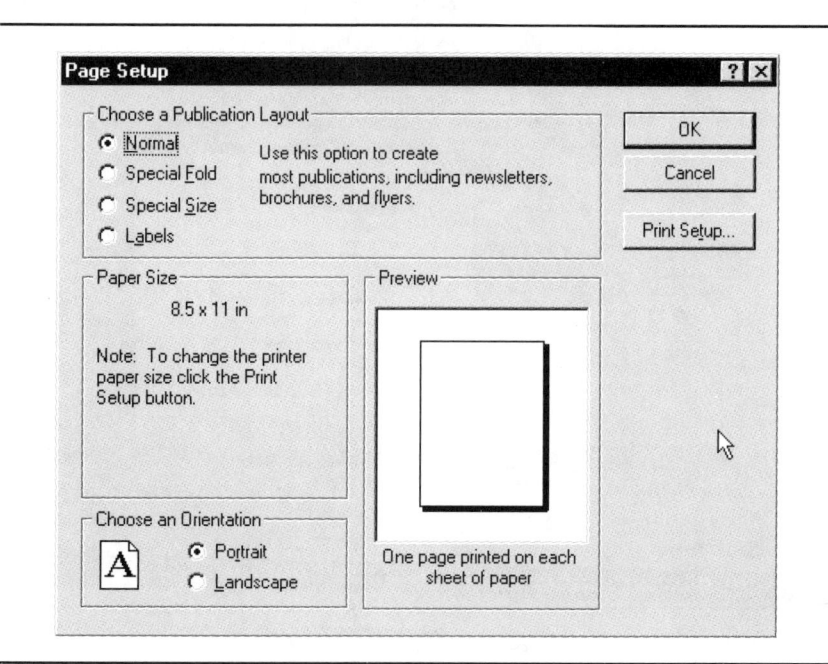

The Page Setup dialog box offers options for adjusting paper size and orientation

FIGURE 6-7

Although it is best to select the correct page settings from the start, there may be times when you need to adjust the page layout after the publication is started. For instance, imagine you selected Blank Page | Full Page to create a certificate. After creating the publication, you realize the certificate should use landscape, not portrait, page orientation. To change the orientation to landscape, select Page Setup from the File menu. Select Landscape in the bottom left corner of the Page Setup dialog box (see Figure 6-7). Chapter 5 provides an in-depth look at the layout and paper size options.

When a PageWizard is used to create a publication, text and pictures are automatically placed on the page. Be aware that text and objects will *not* be adjusted to fit the new page settings. For instance, the Flyer PageWizard was used to create the flyer in Figure 6-8. After the flyer was created, the orientation was changed to landscape. Notice the elements did not adjust to fit the new orientation. Objects *you* added to the page will not be adjusted to fit new page settings either.

 **NOTE:**   *Since any existing text and objects on the page are not adjusted, it's important to get the page setup nailed down early.*

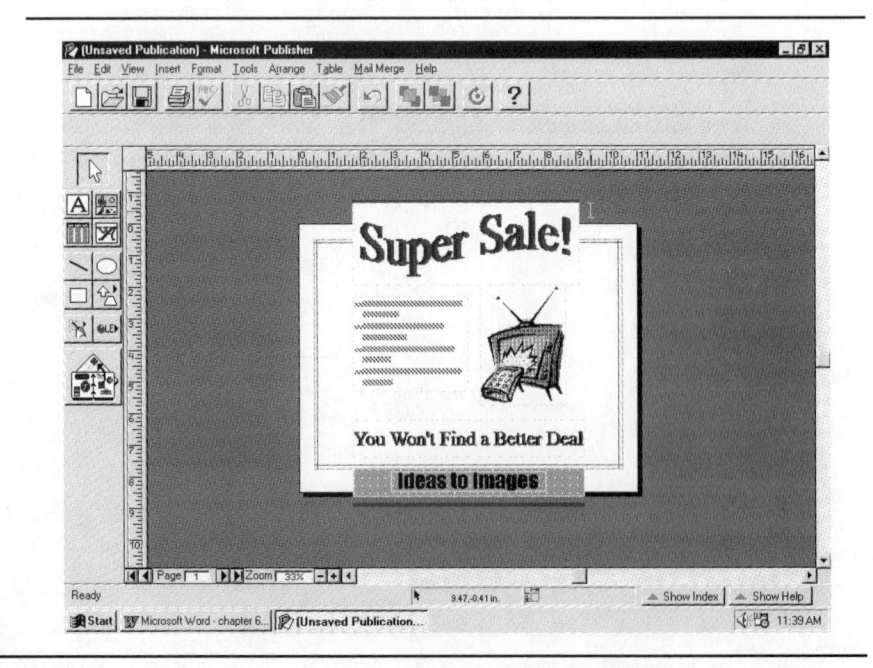

Publisher adjusts only the page, not existing objects, when you change the page settings

FIGURE 6-8

Changing the orientation of a page changes the orientation of all pages in a publication. For instance, you cannot have portrait orientation on one page and landscape on another. This is also true for paper size and layout. Start a new publication when you need a different page setting.

Setting Margins and Columns

Page margins act as a kind of frame around your document, providing visual starting and stopping places for each line of text. Adding columns to a page is a great way to enhance the look of a publication. Both margins and the space between columns add much-needed white space to a publication. Recall from the design do's and don'ts in Chapter 3 that white space gives the readers' eyes a chance to rest.

As with page settings described in the previous section, existing objects on a page are not moved when margin and column settings are adjusted. For instance, the Newsletter PageWizard was used to create the three-column newsletter in Figure 6-9. Afterward, the column guidelines were changed to two columns. (You can see the guideline running through the middle column.) The text objects did not move.

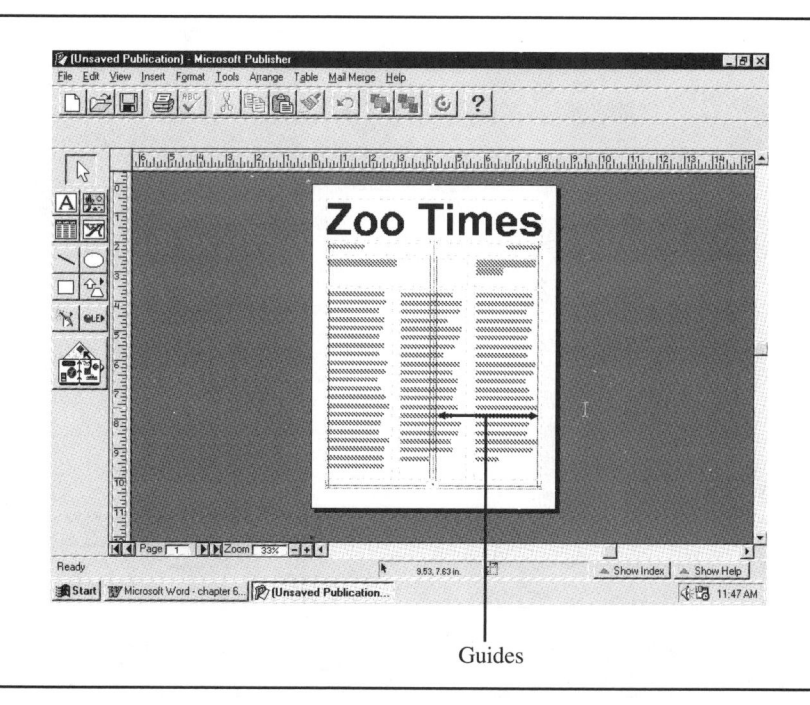

Changing margin and column guides does not affect any existing objects on the page

FIGURE 6-9

Guides

NOTE: *Press CTRL-SHIFT-O if your margin and column guides are not visible.*

The margin and column settings are best used when you are creating a publication from a blank page. As discussed in Chapter 4, margin and column guidelines have a snap-to feature that helps you align objects to the guidelines.

Setting Margins

You can adjust the margins around the top, bottom, left, and right edges of the page. Publisher provides additional options for producing double-sided publications. In a double-sided publication, the front and back of the pages are printed, creating left and right pages. Brochures and newsletters are often double-sided.

By default, Publisher places identical margins on the left and right pages of double-sided publications. However, you can *mirror* the margin settings across the left and right pages. For example, in Figure 6-10, the left page margins are mirrored

Mirroring margins allows for wider inside margins if the publication will be bound

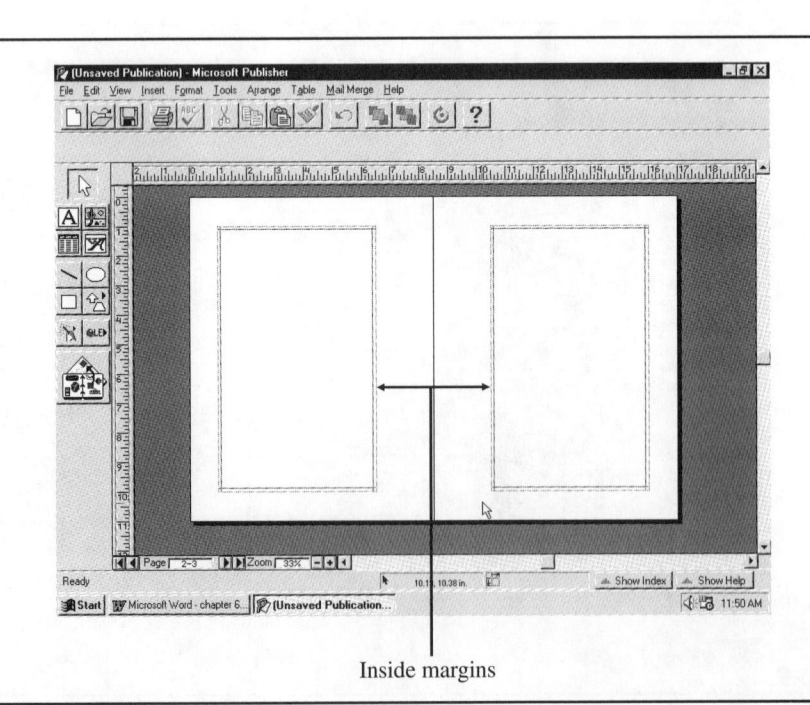

Inside margins

FIGURE 6-10

(flipped) on the right page. Notice the inside margins on both the left and right pages are wider than the outside margins.

The following steps illustrate setting page margins. A blank page is used.

1. From the Arrange menu, select Layout Guides.

2. The Layout Guides dialog box that appears provides settings for the left, right, top, and bottom margins. To adjust these settings, click the up or down arrow to increase or decrease the margin size. Each click increases or decreases by a 0.10-inch increment. You can adjust the margin size manually by simply typing the desired number in the accompanying box.

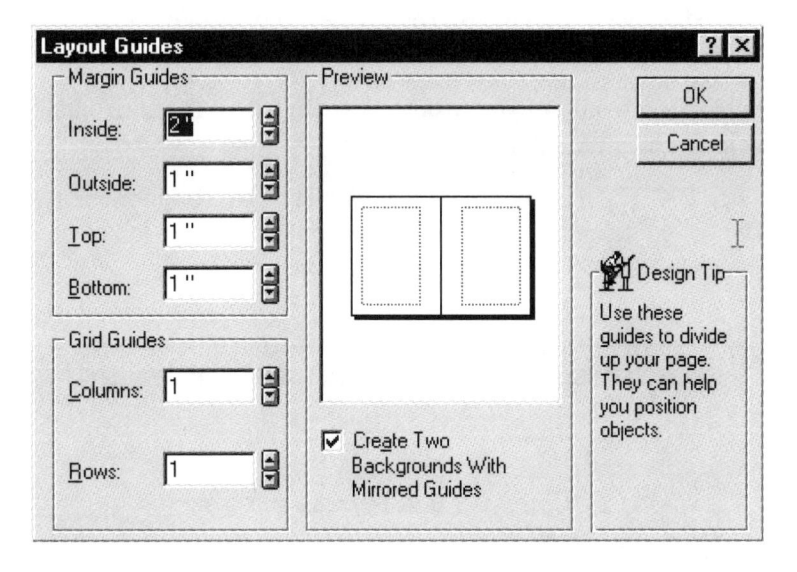

3. Click on Create Two Backgrounds With Mirrored Guides to mirror the margin settings on the left and right pages. When this option is selected, notice the margin guides read "Inside" and "Outside" as opposed to "Left" and "Right."

4. Click OK to apply the margin settings.

Recall that you need to switch to Two-Page Spread view to see both the left and right pages in a publication. Page views were discussed earlier in this chapter. Keep in mind that any objects on the page before you changed the margins are not repositioned to match the new settings.

Setting Columns

Several PageWizards ask you to select the number of columns as the publication is being created. For instance, the Newsletter PageWizard lets you choose one, two, three, or four columns. The objects placed on the page by the PageWizard are aligned to the selected number of columns.

However, if you start with a blank page, Publisher defaults to one column. To adjust the number of columns:

1. From the Arrange menu, select Layout Guides.

2. In the bottom left corner of the Layout Guides dialog box, enter the desired number of columns. The Preview box displays the selected number of columns.

3. Publisher also allows you to enter row guidelines for horizontally aligning objects. Enter the desired number of rows in the Rows box.

4. Click OK. The page in Figure 6-11 displays two columns and two rows. Use the guidelines to align objects as you build the page layout.

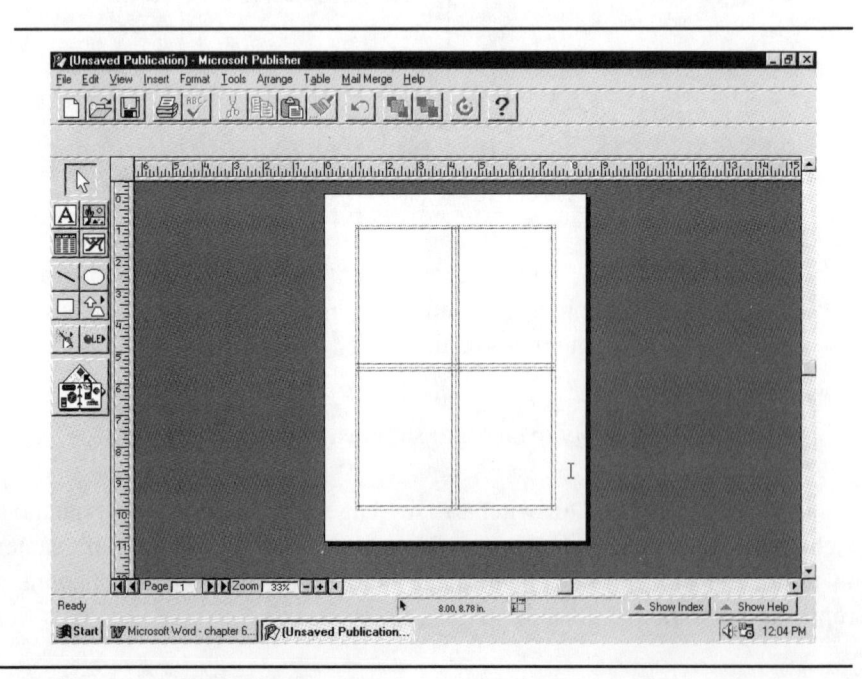

You can add guidelines for columns and rows

FIGURE 6-11

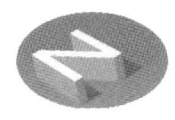 **NOTE:** *Using too many columns detracts from the readability of your publication.*

It's important to note that unlike other desktop publishing applications, you cannot place text on the page without first creating a text frame to hold the text. The guides are there to help you size and align text and picture frames.

Summary

The features discussed in this chapter make it easier to create and build publications. Inserting pages, switching page views, adjusting the page layout, and setting margins and columns are important parts of page layout. They affect the readability of a publication as well as give it a little flair.

The next chapter focuses on working with frames to hold the text, pictures, tables, and other elements in a publication.

6

7

Framing Publications

In Publisher, frames play an integral role in page design. Page layouts are built by adding frames, into which text and pictures are loaded. Imagine a page from a magazine with several different design elements such as text, photographs, and illustrations. If the page were designed in Publisher, each element on the page would be placed in a frame. The frames determine where the text and pictures appear on the page.

Designing with frames makes it easy to build your page layout. When you want a picture to appear at the top of the page, simply draw a picture frame at the top and add the picture. Designing with frames also makes it easy to change your mind. If you want to move a picture on the page, just drag the frame to the desired location. The flexibility of working with frames makes it easy to experiment with different page layouts until you find just the right look.

This chapter focuses on using frames to build page layouts. First, the chapter explores the different types of frames, such as picture and text frames, that are used to build Publisher publications. Drawing, sizing, moving, grouping, and aligning frames are covered next. The rest of the chapter deals with formatting frames by setting margins and adding color, borders, and shadows.

Building-Blocks of Page Design

Frames are the building-blocks of page design in Publisher. Text, pictures, tables, and WordArt are placed into frames and then arranged on the page to create a pleasing layout. Think of frames as rectangular boxes that "float" on top of the page. The size of the frame determines how big a picture will appear on the page, or how much text fits in a frame. Frames containing text can have different column settings, so you can quickly and easily create multicolumn layouts.

 **NOTE:** *The rest of this book assumes you understand the basics of working with frames. Following chapters discuss placing text, pictures, and other elements into frames.*

If you use a PageWizard or template to create a new publication, frames are automatically placed on the page to hold the text and pictures. If you use the Blank Page option to create a new publication, you will have to draw the frames yourself.

However, whether you are drawing them yourself or working with existing frames, you will need to know how to move, size, and otherwise manipulate frames.

Exploring Publisher's Frames

Publisher uses four types of frames to build a page layout. As displayed in Figure 7-1, you can use a combination of these frames to create your own custom layout. Each frame has *properties,* which are attributes applied to the frame. These attributes vary according to frame type. For instance, text frames can have columns, but picture frames cannot. The following section examines the different types of frames.

Text Frames

Text must be placed in a text frame (or a WordArt frame—more on that later). The size of the frame determines how much text can fit in it.

The Text frame tool is used to create text frames. Text can be flowed from frame to frame. You can also set margins and columns within individual text frames. For

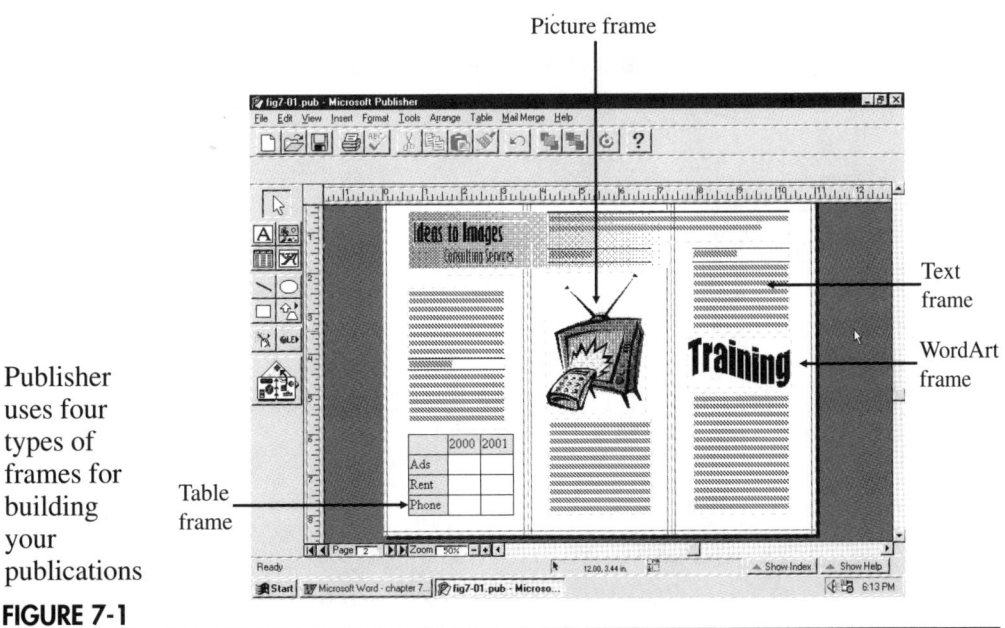

Publisher uses four types of frames for building your publications

FIGURE 7-1

instance, in Figure 7-2, the left text frame has one column of text, and the right frame has two. Chapter 8 provides more information about working with text.

Picture Frames

Pictures—this includes photographs, clip art, drawings, and logos—are placed in picture frames. You can wrap text around picture frames and place margins inside them (see Figure 7-3). As with other types of frames, you can add borders around the frame. The Picture frame tool is used to create picture frames. Chapter 9 provides more information about working with pictures.

Table Frames

Tables are built with table frames. As shown in Figure 7-4, a selected table displays column and row markers, and gridlines. Data is entered in the table and formatted. As with other applications that create tables, you can merge cells, add and delete rows, and adjust column width.

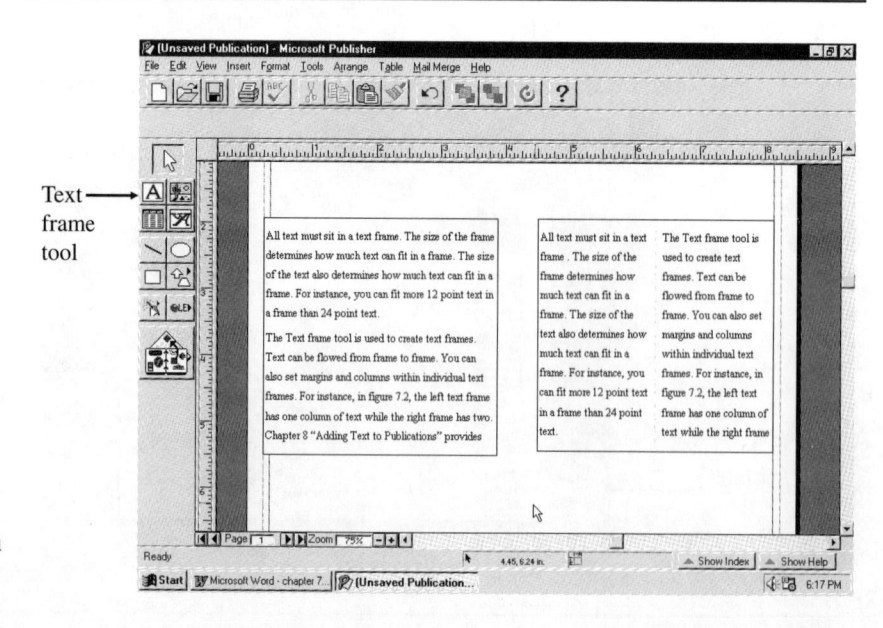

Text frame tool

Publisher uses text frames to hold text on the page

FIGURE 7-2

Picture frame tool

Publisher uses picture frames to hold pictures on the page

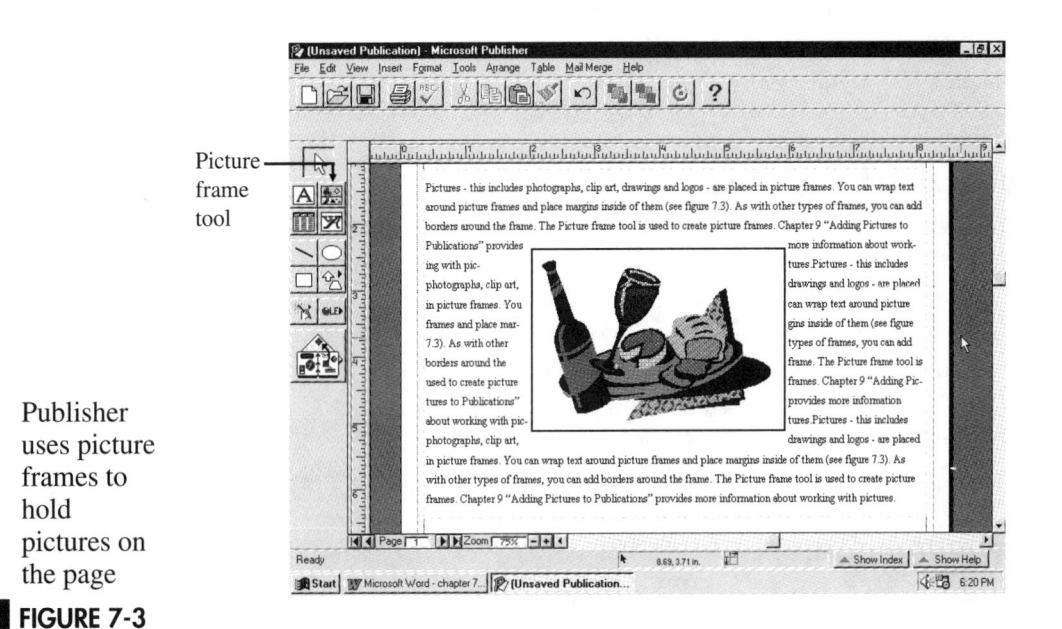

FIGURE 7-3

7

Column and row markers

Table frame tool

Publisher uses table frames to hold tables on the page

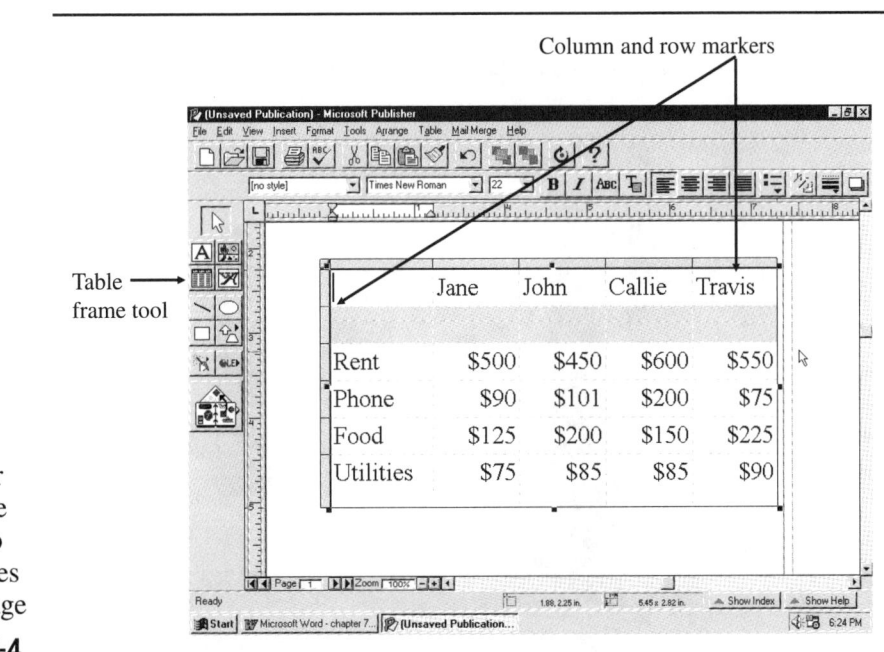

FIGURE 7-4

The Table frame tool is used to draw table frames. When a table frame is created, Publisher displays a dialog box asking you to select the number of rows and columns. Chapter 12 provides more information on working with tables.

WordArt Frames

WordArt text is different from regular text in that you can tilt, slant, rotate, or warp it (see Figure 7-5). WordArt is great for titles, logos, and other large text where you want to add extra punch. WordArt is actually a small application that works in conjunction with Publisher.

The WordArt frame tool is used to create WordArt. When a WordArt frame is created, a dialog box appears asking you to enter your text. Chapter 13 provides more information on creating WordArt.

Frame Basics

Although Publisher uses different types of frames to build layouts, they work basically the same when it comes to drawing, moving, and sizing. What you put in

WordArt
frame tool

Publisher
uses
WordArt
frames to
hold
WordArt
text on the
page

FIGURE 7-5

the frame may vary, but how you add the frame and then manipulate it is the same for all frame types. This section discusses the basics of working with frames.

 **NOTE:** *Give yourself time to practice working with frames. Start with a blank page and begin drawing!*

Before adding frames, take a moment to consider your page layout. If frames already appear on the page, you'll need to know how to move, size, and delete them. If your page is blank, you'll need to draw frames and then adjust them to fit.

 **NOTE:** *You'll notice Publisher displays yellow pop-up notes with help or shortcut information when you perform some of the commands discussed in this chapter. Reading these is a great way to learn the program.*

Many of the features discussed in this section also apply to boxes and other graphic shapes drawn with Publisher's drawing tools. Chapter 11 provides more information.

Drawing Frames

As discussed, there are four frame tools—Text, Picture, Table, and WordArt. After determining the type of frame you want to draw, select the appropriate tool by clicking on it with your mouse. The tool is "pushed in," indicating it is selected. Drawing frames in Publisher is similar to creating rectangles in applications such as CorelDRAW. The following steps illustrate drawing a frame:

1. Select the desired frame tool. Move the mouse cursor into the page area. Notice the mouse cursor shape changes to a cross hair.

2. Position the mouse where you want the top left corner of the frame to start. Hold the mouse button and drag diagonally. An outline of the frame appears as you drag.

3. When the outline of the frame is the desired size and shape, release the mouse button. The frame is created (a picture frame is shown in Figure 7-6). Notice the frame tool is no longer selected—the Pointer tool is now selected.

Selection handles appear around a text or picture frame after it is drawn. The WordArt dialog box appears after a WordArt frame is drawn, and the Create Table dialog box appears after a table frame is drawn.

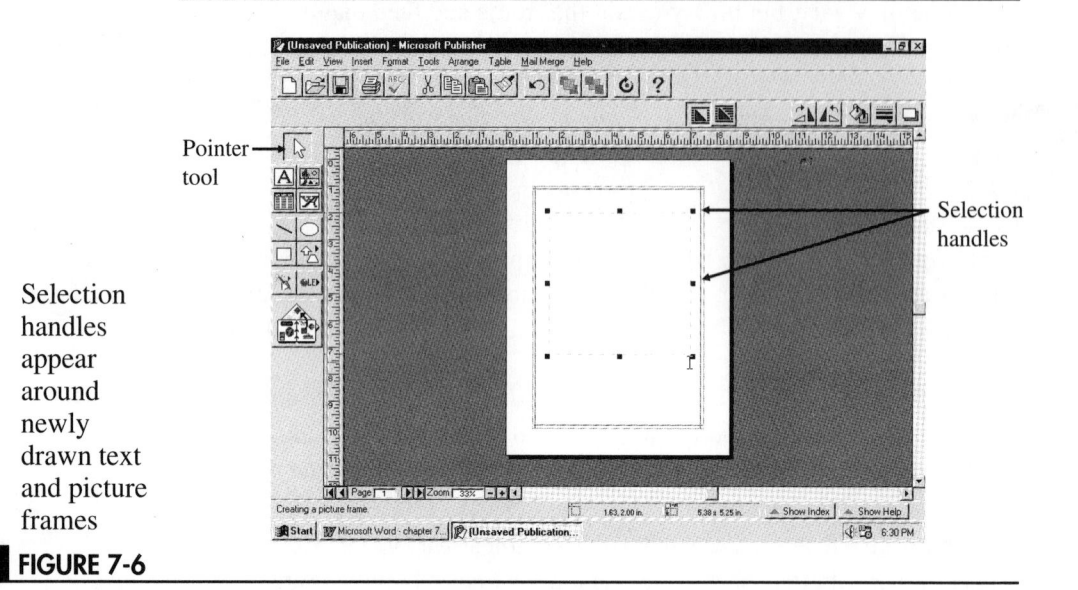

Pointer tool

Selection handles

Selection handles appear around newly drawn text and picture frames

FIGURE 7-6

 **TIP:** To draw a perfectly square frame, press and hold *SHIFT as you draw the frame. To draw a frame from the center out, as opposed to corner to corner, hold CTRL as you draw the frame. To draw a square frame from the center out, hold CTRL and SHIFT as you draw the frame.*

Selecting Frames

Before you can modify a frame in any way, it must be selected. As mentioned, a frame is automatically selected immediately after it is drawn. To select a previously drawn frame, simply position the mouse cursor in the frame and click. Selection handles appear around the frame indicating it is selected. In addition to the selection handles, column and row markers appear around table frames.

Selecting Multiple Objects

By default, only one frame is selected at a time. If you want to select several frames, hold SHIFT while clicking on other frames. If you want to move two frames, for example, select the first frame and then select the second while pressing SHIFT. Gray selection handles appear around both frames, indicating both are selected (see Figure 7-7). You can then move both frames together, as the "Moving Frames" section later in this chapter will explain.

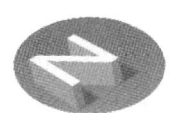

NOTE: *A Group Objects icon appears when several frames are selected. You'll learn more about grouping later in this chapter in "Grouping Frames."*

Deleting Frames

After drawing frames on the page, you might decide you added a few too many. To delete a text frame, select it and choose Delete Text Frame from the Edit menu. To delete a picture frame, select it and choose Delete Picture Frame from the Edit menu. To delete a table frame, select it and choose Delete Table from the Edit menu. To delete a WordArt frame, select it and choose Delete Object from the Edit menu. The contents of the frame are also deleted when you delete a frame.

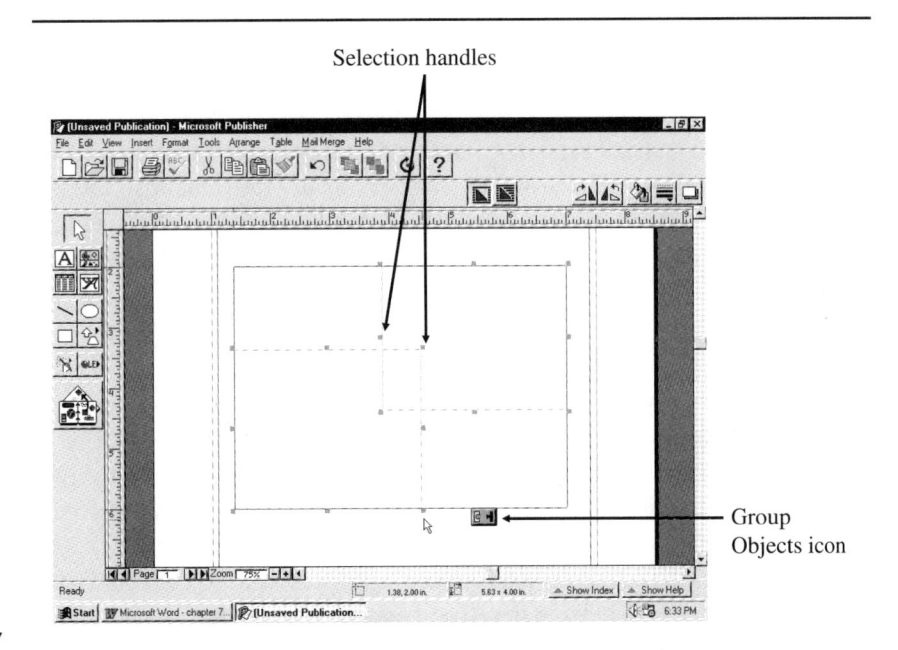

Selection handles

The selection handles turn gray when multiple objects are selected

Group Objects icon

FIGURE 7-7

TIP: *In most cases, to delete a frame, you can also just press* DELETE. *However, if the frame contains text or table data, pressing* DELETE *will only delete information inside the frame. To delete the frame and the text or table information inside, press* CTRL-DELETE.

Moving Frames

You can move frames anywhere on the page (even off the page onto the scratch area). If you have several frames selected, they will move together as a group. The following steps outline how to move frames:

1. Select the frame you want to move. Selection handles appear when a frame is selected.

2. Position the mouse cursor on the outside edge of the frame (not on a selection handle). The shape of the mouse cursor changes to the Mover cursor (a moving van).

3. Press and hold the mouse, and drag the frame to a new place on the page. An outline of the frame appears as you move the frame. When the frame is in the desired location, release the mouse button.

Hold SHIFT as you move the frame to limit its movement to up and down or left and right. For instance, to move a frame straight up or down, hold SHIFT and drag the frame up or down. The SHIFT key constrains the movement so the frame does not move to the left or right. If you hold SHIFT and drag to the left or right, the SHIFT key constrains the movement so the frame does not move up or down.

Nudging Frames

Nudging is perfect when you need to move a frame a small distance—perhaps to line it up with other frames. (More methods for aligning frames will be presented later in the chapter in "Aligning Frames.") To nudge a selected frame, hold ALT and tap one of the directional arrow keys on your keyboard. The frame moves one pixel each time you press an arrow key.

Publisher also has a dialog box for nudging—select the object you want to nudge, and choose Nudge Object from the Arrange menu to get to the Nudge Objects dialog box, shown here.

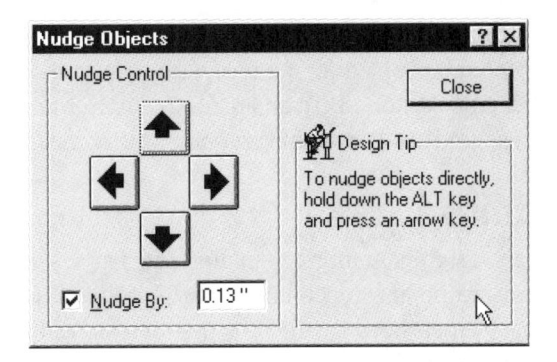

Click on the arrows in the Nudge Objects dialog box to move the object. To change the nudge distance, click in the Nudge By box and enter a new amount. For instance, you might enter **.25** to have frames move $\frac{1}{4}$ inch whenever you nudge. The nudge amount in the dialog box also affects nudging done with the arrow keys.

Sizing Frames

You can use the selection handles to change the size of a frame. Use the corner handles to adjust both the width and height of the frame at the same time. Use the middle selection handles to size the frame in one direction only. For instance, sizing with the bottom middle selection handle adjusts the height of the frame.

The following steps outline sizing a frame:

1. Select the frame and position the mouse cursor over one of the selection handles. The mouse cursor changes to the Resizer cursor.

2. To enlarge the frame, drag away from the frame's center. To reduce the frame, drag toward the frame's center.

3. When the frame outline is the desired size, release the mouse button.

When a picture or WordArt frame is sized, the picture or WordArt sizes along with the frame. For instance, if you reduce the frame size, the picture in the frame is also reduced. When a text or table frame is sized, the size of the text is not affected. For instance, if you were to double the size of a text frame, the type size would not increase. Instead, sizing a text or table frame affects the amount of text that is displayed in the frame. If the frame is too small, some of the text or table will get cut off. In this case you would need to enlarge the frame or flow the remaining text to another frame. Chapter 8 deals with text reflow.

Pictures and WordArt can become distorted as you adjust the size. For instance, if you widen a frame containing a picture of a face without also increasing the height of the frame, the face becomes distorted. To enlarge or reduce a frame while maintaining its original proportions, hold SHIFT as you drag one of the corner handles.

Rotating Frames

To enhance your page design, you might want to rotate frames to display at an angle (see Figure 7-8). Any frame and its contents can be rotated. However, be careful rotating text and table frames, because the information can become unreadable. You can rotate one frame or several frames at one time.

To rotate just a single frame:

1. Select it and place the mouse cursor over one of the corner selection handles.

2. Press and hold ALT to display the Rotator icon.

3. Hold the mouse button and drag clockwise or counterclockwise to rotate the frame.

4. Release the mouse button and ALT when the outline of the frame is in the desired position. You cannot rotate more than one frame at a time this way.

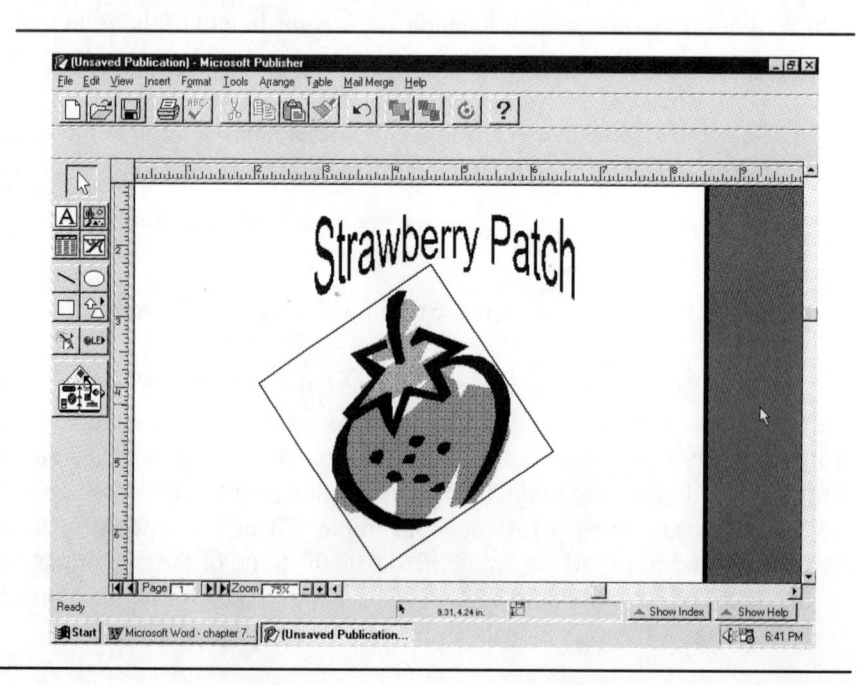

Hold ALT and drag a corner handle to rotate a frame

FIGURE 7-8

TIP: *Hold CTRL-ALT and press LEFT ARROW to rotate a frame counterclockwise in increments of 5 degrees. Hold CTRL-ALT and press RIGHT ARROW to rotate a frame clockwise in increments of 5 degrees.*

As outlined in the following steps, the Arrange menu provides another way to rotate frames. You can rotate one or several frames at a time with this method:

1. Select the frame (or frames) you want to rotate. From the Arrange menu, select Rotate/Flip.

2. To rotate the frame 90 degrees to the left, select Rotate Left from the submenu. Select Rotate Right to rotate the selected frame 90 degrees to the right.

3. Select Custom Rotate to display the Rotate Objects dialog box, shown here. Enter the desired rotation angle in the Angle box, and click on the arrow buttons to rotate the frame. When finished, click on the Close button to close the dialog box.

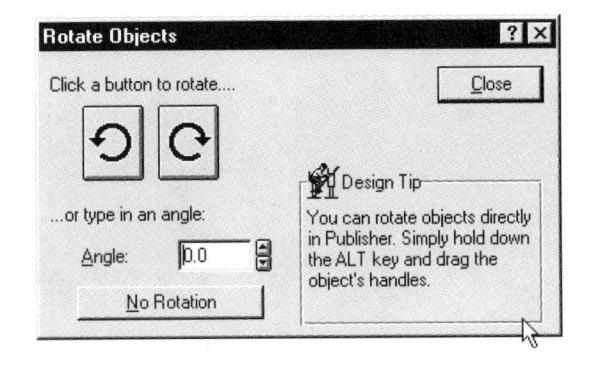

Generally, you would not want to rotate more than one element on a page. Rotating is a strong design element; use it sparingly. If you do need to rotate several frames, it will look better if they are all rotated at the same angle.

Grouping Frames

Multiple frames can be grouped or locked together so they can be manipulated more easily. For instance, instead of moving three frames one at a time, you could group the three frames and then move the group. Grouping allows you to treat multiple frames as one frame.

To group several frames, select them. Remember, hold SHIFT to select more than one frame at a time. Gray selection handles appear around each selected object. As shown in Figure 7-9, a Group Objects icon also appears. Click on the Group Objects icon to group the frames together. Now, whenever you click on any part of the group, all of the frames are selected. You can move, size, and rotate the group as one object.

As you may have noticed, the Group Objects icon changes when objects are grouped. The shapes in the icon become interlocked like puzzle pieces. When the shapes are interlocked, the icon becomes the Ungroup Objects icon, used to ungroup the frames. If you click on the Ungroup Objects icon the frames are ungrouped and become separate again.

NOTE: *Grouped frames can still be formatted individually. This will be covered later in the chapter under "Formatting Frames."*

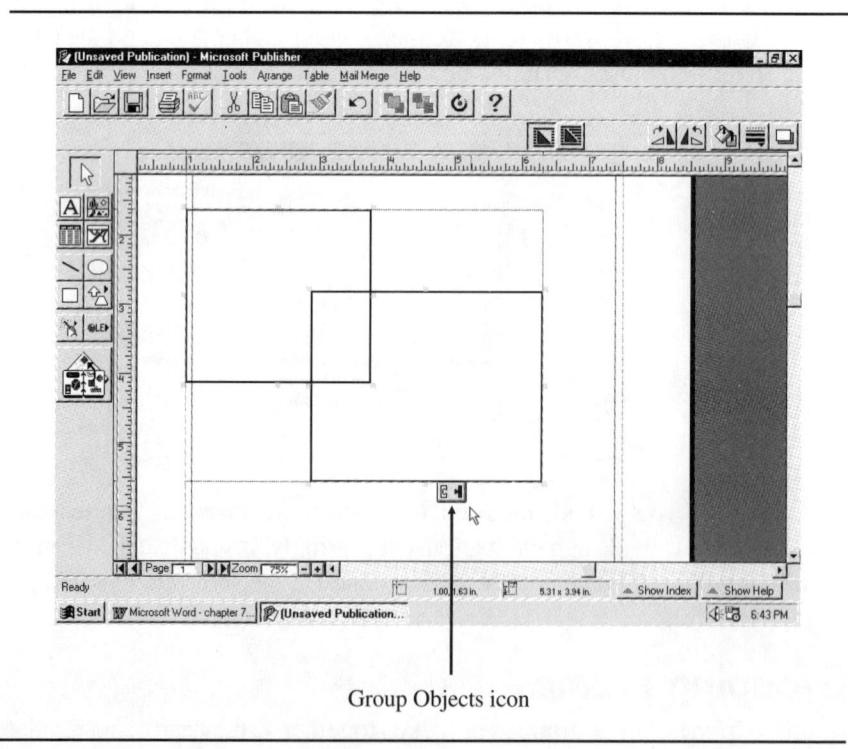

Use the Group Objects icon to quickly group several frames

Group Objects icon

FIGURE 7-9

Moving and Copying Frames to Other Pages

As a designer, you'll want to be able to experiment with the page layout and to move frames around freely. For instance, you may want to see how the picture frame sitting on page 1 would look on page 2. Or you may decide to place the frame containing the company logo on pages 1 and 3 of a publication. Publisher makes it easy to move and copy frames to other pages.

Text can also be moved and copied in a publication. Refer to Chapter 8 for a detailed look at working with the Windows Clipboard to move and copy text.

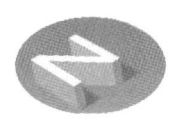 **NOTE:** *Whenever you want a text or picture element to appear on every page of the publication, place it on the background. Chapter 16 discusses placing objects on background pages.*

Moving Frames

To move a frame from one page to another, move the frame to the scratch area. Recall from Chapter 4, the scratch area is the gray area surrounding the page. When a frame is moved to the scratch area, it is visible as you move to other pages in the publication. As an example, suppose you moved a frame from page 1 to the scratch area. Now, when you move to other pages, the frame appears in the scratch area. To place the frame on page 3, display page 3 and move the frame onto page 3.

It's important to note that the frame must be moved completely off the page and onto the scratch area. If any part of the frame is still on the page, you will not be able to see the frame when you display another page.

Copying Frames

To make a copy of a frame on the same page, hold CTRL and move the frame to another location. When you release, the original frame stays in its original position, and a copy of the frame appears in the new location on the page. (Make sure you let go of the mouse button before releasing CTRL.)

To move the copy to another page, place it in the scratch area. Display the page you want to put the copied frame on, and move the frame onto that page.

Moving and Copying Frames to Other Publications

Once you've set up a frame with the desired text, table, picture, or WordArt, you may decide it looks so good you want to use it in other publications. Publisher uses the Cut, Copy, and Paste commands to move and copy frames to other publications. The Standard toolbar provides tools, shown here, for these commands, which are also found under the Edit menu.

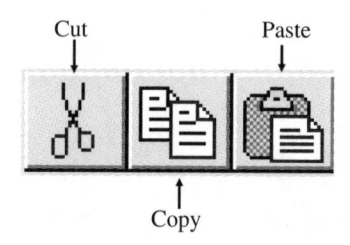

When you cut, copy, and paste picture or WordArt frames, the picture and WordArt are also moved or copied. It's a little more complicated with text and table frames. If any text or table information is highlighted, only that information will be cut or copied. To cut or copy the entire frame, click in the text to make sure no text is highlighted before cutting or copying.

Using the Cut Command to Move Frames

As with other Windows applications, Publisher uses the Cut and Paste commands to move frames and their contents from one publication to another. The following exercise illustrates how to move a frame to another publication:

1. Select the frame you want to move. Click on the Cut button in the Standard toolbar. The frame is removed from the page. Save the publication if desired.

2. Open the publication and display the page where you want to place the frame. Click on the Paste button in the Standard toolbar. The frame is pasted in the same position from which it was cut. For instance, if you cut the frame from the bottom-left corner of the first publication, the frame is pasted in the bottom-left corner of the second publication. You can move and size it as necessary.

Copying Frames

When you want to place a copy of a frame in another publication, use the Copy and Paste commands. The copied frame is not linked to the original frame, so you can modify either frame without affecting the other. The following steps illustrate placing a copy of a frame in another publication:

1. Select the frame you want to copy. Click on the Copy button in the Standard toolbar.

2. Open the publication and display the page where you want to place the frame. Click on the Paste button in the Standard toolbar. The frame is pasted in the same position from which it was copied. You can move and size it as necessary.

Aligning Frames

In some page designs, you might want the frames to line up vertically or horizontally. In addition to nudging, Publisher offers you more efficient techniques for accurate allignment. For instance, in the catalog displayed in Figure 7-10, the frames on the first page are horizontally aligned across the top. The frames on the second page are vertically left-aligned. With Publisher, you can line up frames with column guides or use the Line Up Objects command.

7

Aligning Frames to Column Guides

The margin and column guides on the page can have a "magnetic" pull that forces the sides of frames to snap to the nearest column guide. In Figure 7-11, the Snap To Guides feature was used to ensure that the frames are the same width as the column guides. When you move or size a frame close to a column guide, the frame *snaps to* or aligns itself with the guide. By default, Snap To Guides in the Tools menu displays a check mark indicating the feature is turned on. Click on Snap To Guides again to disable this feature.

Publisher makes it easy to align frames vertically or horizontally for a professional look

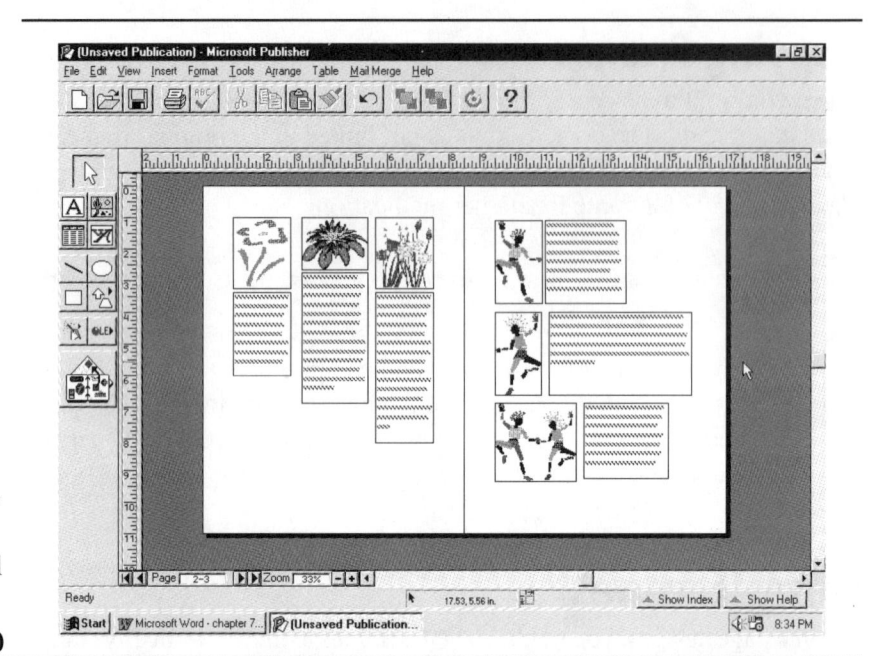

FIGURE 7-10

Enabling Snap To Guides makes it easy to align frames with the column guides

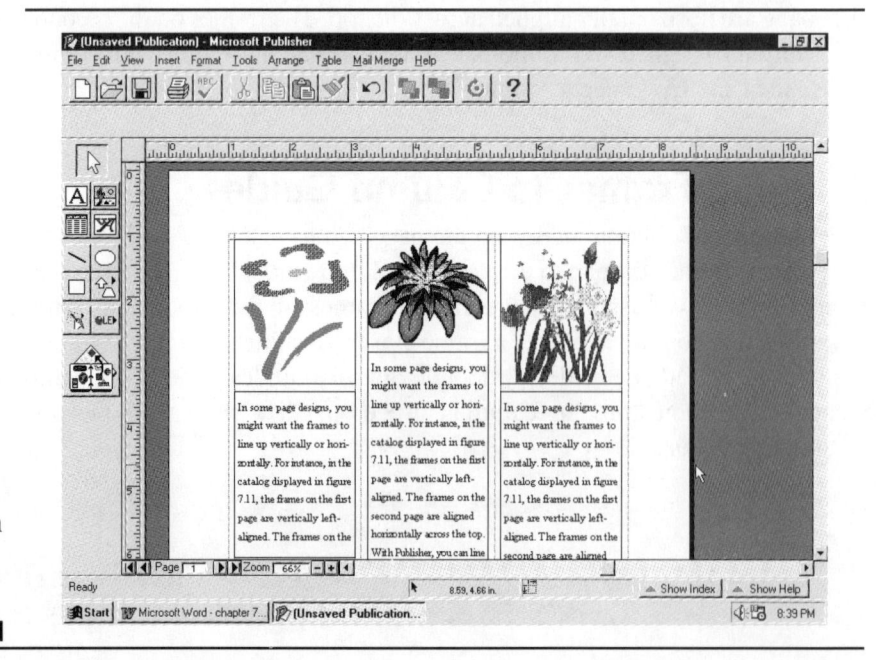

FIGURE 7-11

Aligning Frames with the Line Up Objects Command

Rather than just eyeballing it when arranging frames vertically or horizontally, use the Line Up Objects command. Frames can be aligned with other frames or to the center of the page.

The following describes how to align frames with other frames:

1. Select the frames you want to align with each other. Remember, use the SHIFT key to select multiple frames. From the Arrange menu, select Line Up Objects. The Line Up Objects dialog opens.

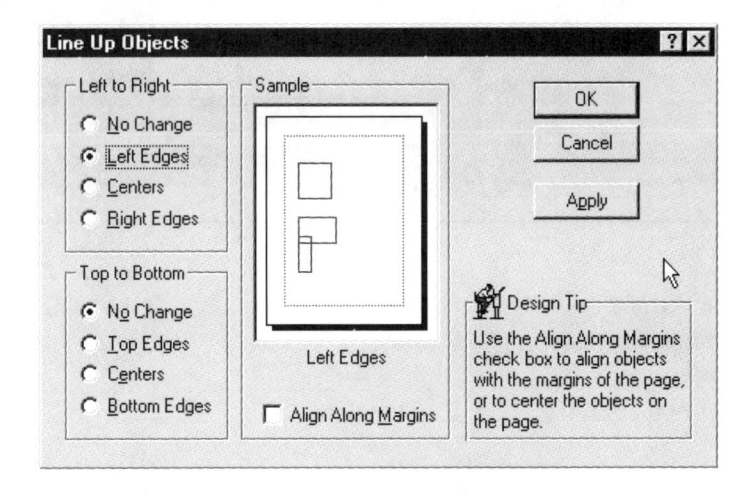

2. Choose the desired alignment options under Left To Right and Top To Bottom. For instance, choose Left Edges to left-align the frames. A sample of the alignment appears. Click OK.

Aligning Frames to the Center of the Page

The Line Up Objects command also provides an option for placing one or several frames in the center of the page. Use of this command is an easy and precise way to center frames in the page. If several frames are selected, the frames will all be moved to the center of the page and will overlap each other.

Frames can be aligned to the horizontal and vertical center of the page. Or, as shown in Figure 7-12, frames can be aligned to the horizontal center of the page,

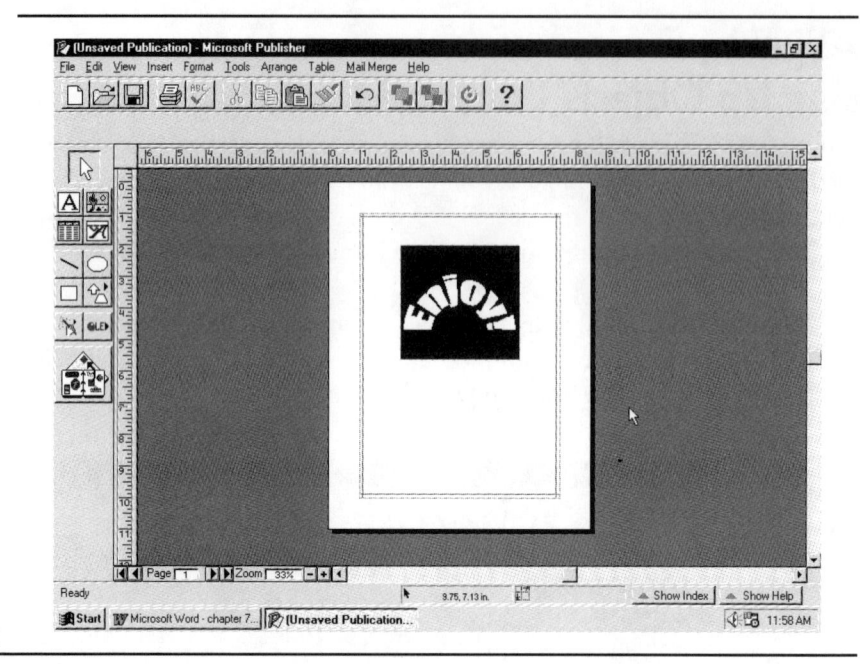

Frames can
be aligned
to the
vertical or
horizontal
center of
the page

FIGURE 7-12

but not the vertical (and vice versa). The following steps describe aligning frames
to the center of the page:

1. Select the frame(s) you want to align.

2. From the Arrange menu, select Line Up Objects. Below the sample in the
   Line Up Objects dialog box, click on Align Along Margins.

3. To horizontally align the frames, click on Centers under Left To Right. To
   vertically align the frames, click on Centers under Top To Bottom. Click
   OK to align the frames.

NOTE: *If you don't want the frames to overlap each other when moved
to the center of the page, group the frames first.*

Formatting Frames

Every frame has individual formatting specifications, which make it possible to design a multitude of page designs. Imagine the page designs you can create by formatting one text frame in a two-column layout, and a picture frame with a shadow and borders. Take a moment to thumb through newsletters, brochures, and other publications to analyze different page designs.

By default, no lines or margins are applied to new frames. It is up to you to format the frame to meet your specifications. When you need several frames set up with the same formatting, apply the formatting and then (with the CTRL key as discussed earlier) make copies of the frame. The frame attributes are copied to the duplicated frames. The Format Painter is another way to create several frames with the same formatting—use of the Format Painter is covered at the end of this chapter in "Saving Time with the Format Painter."

Adding Margins to Frames

When a picture is loaded into a frame, the picture fills the entire frame area, touching the edges of the frame (see Figure 7-13). The same is true for WordArt frames. However, text and table frames have 0.04-inch margins, acting like a cushion of white space, added to the top, bottom, left, and right sides of the frame. There will be times when you will want to add margins or increase the margin spacing. For instance, when two text frames are placed side-by-side, it's a good idea to increase the margin spacing (try .25 inch), so there is enough white space between the text in the two frames. If a border appears around a frame, text or table information can become especially hard to read because the text and table information is so close to the edges of the frame. As you can see in Figure 7-13, margins help give text or pictures room to breathe in a frame.

Generally, margins are added to all four sides of a frame. With pictures, however, you might not need to add all those margins. If a picture is wider than it is tall, for instance, it might touch only the left and right sides of the frame, and you would need to add only left and right margins.

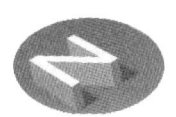 **NOTE:** *Tables also have margins for individual cells within the table. Refer to Chapter 12 for more information on working with tables.*

Frame margins prevent text and pictures from touching the edges of a frame

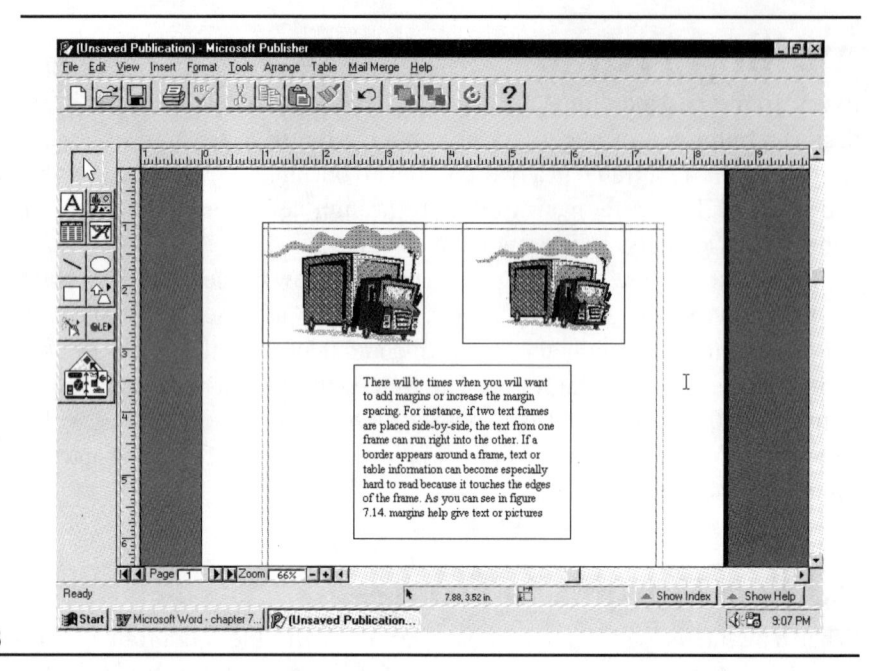

FIGURE 7-13

Use the following steps to add or adjust margin settings in a frame:

1. Select the frame where you want to add margins. For text frames, choose Text Frame Properties from the Format menu. For picture frames, choose Picture Frame Properties from the Format menu. For WordArt frames, choose Object Frame Properties from the Format menu. For table frames, choose Table Cell Properties from the Format menu.

2. In the Frame Properties dialog box (the Picture Frame Properties dialog box is used as the example in the illustration here), enter the desired amount of margin spacing in the Left, Right, Top, and Bottom boxes. You can also click on the up or down arrow by the margin spacing boxes to increase or decrease the amount.

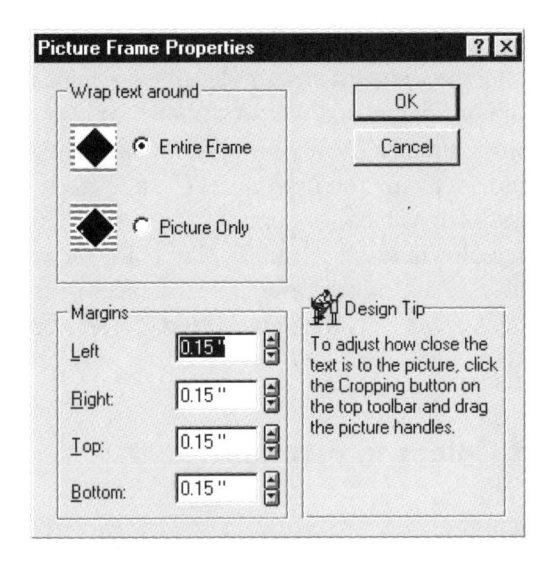

3. Click OK.

Margins are added to the selected frame. You will not see the margin boundaries in the frame until you have loaded text or graphics into the frame.

7

Adding Color to Frames

Color can be added to the background of frames to spice up the text or picture in the frame. When selecting colors, remember the process you will be using to print the publication. If you will be printing in black and white, stick with black, white, and shades of gray. If you are printing one spot color, select the color and stick with it (and black and shades of gray) as you design. Remember to talk with the people who will be printing the publication if you are working with an outside printing company. If you are outputting to a full-color printer, you can select any color.

 **NOTE:** *Many of the steps for adding color to frames also apply to adding color to shapes drawn with Publisher's drawing tools. Refer to Chapter 11 for more information.*

The background of text and table frames is "filled" with white by default. As displayed in Figure 7-14, the white fill prevents any underlying color or elements from showing through the frame. Picture and WordArt frames are clear by default—you can see through these frames. Frames filled with white or another color become opaque, and you cannot see through them. You must select Clear to create a transparent frame.

Publisher displays RGB values for some of the colors. "RGB" stands for red, green, and blue—the color model used to display color on monitors. The values indicate how much of a certain color is used. For instance, with the color RGB 102, 255, 15, the first number represents the value of red, the second the value of green, and the third the value of blue.

Applying Solid Colors to Frames

The following steps illustrate adding color to frames. The option of selecting Clear for creating transparent frames is also covered.

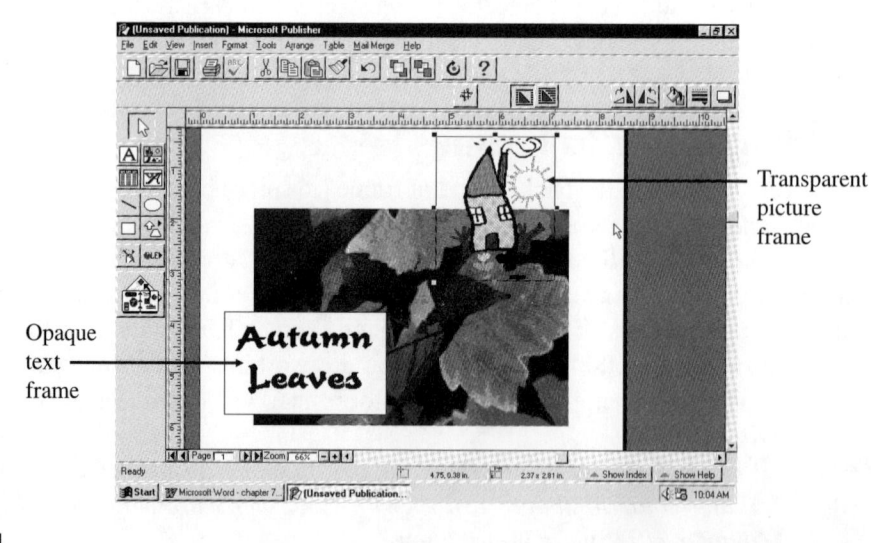

You can adjust frames to be opaque or transparent

Opaque text frame

Transparent picture frame

FIGURE 7-14

1. Select the frame(s) to which you want to apply color.

2. From the Format menu, choose Fill Color. The Colors dialog box appears.

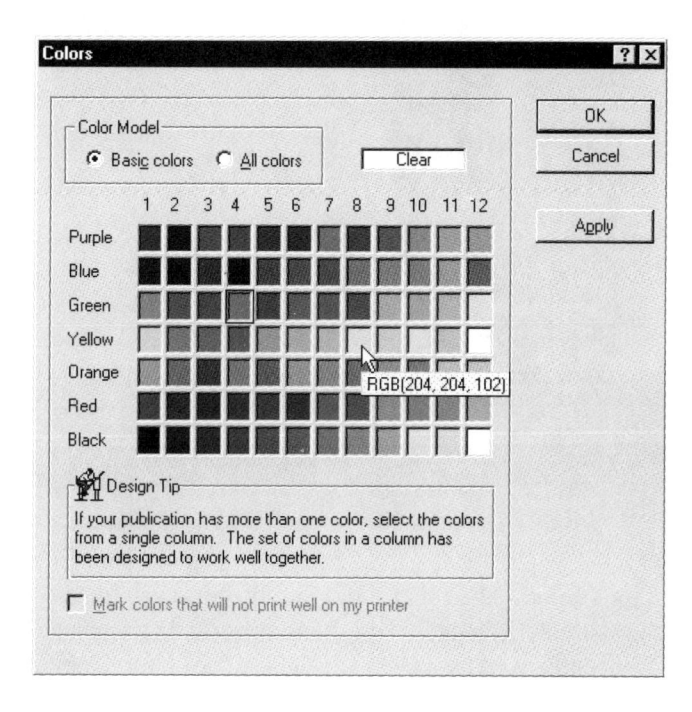

3. Place your mouse over a color to display a pop-up menu with the color name or RGB values.

4. Click on a color to select it. To create a transparent frame, click on Clear at the top of the dialog box. Click OK to apply the color.

For more color choices, click on the All Colors option in the Color dialog box. Another dialog box appears with a spectrum of colors.

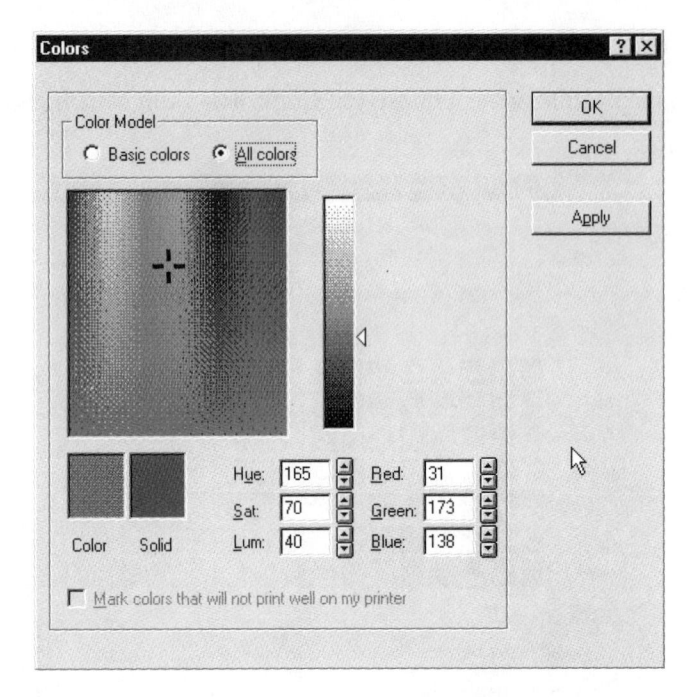

You can click on a color in the spectrum or build your own colors by entering RGB values. You can also enter values for Hue, Saturation, and Luminance. This is another color model frequently used by graphic designers for building colors.

 You can click on the Object Color tool in the Formatting toolbar to display a drop-down list of colors. Click on the desired color to apply the frame color. Click on the Clear option to create a transparent frame.

 **TIP:** *Use the keyboard shortcut CTRL-T to toggle back and forth between transparent and white-filled frames.*

Working with Tints

Publisher provides the option of changing the tint or shading of a color. A *tint* reduces the color and adds white in place of the removed color. For example, a 50 percent tint of red reduces the density of the red by half, allowing more of the white of the page to show through, therefore printing a light red. A *shade* reduces the color but adds black in place of the removed color. A 50 percent shade of red would print as a dark red with some definite black overtones.

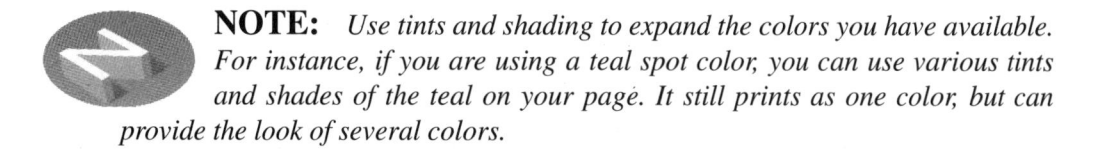

NOTE: *Use tints and shading to expand the colors you have available. For instance, if you are using a teal spot color, you can use various tints and shades of the teal on your page. It still prints as one color, but can provide the look of several colors.*

Use the following steps to apply a tint or shade to a frame color:

1. Select the frame you want to color. From the Format menu, choose Fill Patterns And Shading.

2. In the middle of the dialog box, click on the down arrow by Color 1 and choose a color.

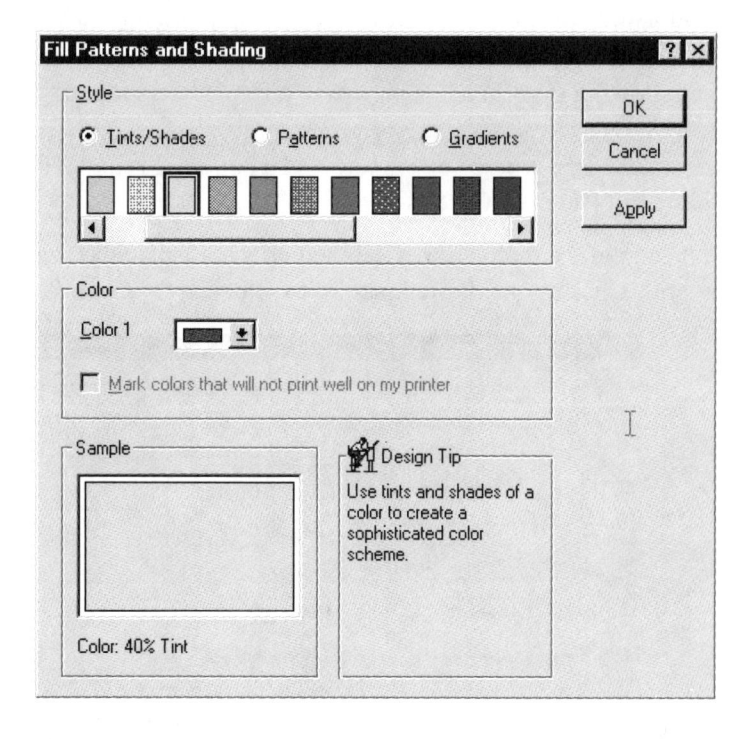

3. At the top of the dialog box, the available tints and shades for the color appear. Use the scroll bar to see all of the choices.

4. Click on the desired tint or shade. The preview shows the color and the percentage of tinting or shading that you chose. Click OK.

Light tints are good for drawing attention to sidebars and pull-quotes. Dark shades can be applied to text and clip art. Don't go overboard with tints and shades. For professional-looking publications, use one shade (maybe two) or one tint on a publication. For instance, if your colors are red and black, you might use the 20% red tint. Don't mix shades and tints on one publication. Too many shades and tints make the page look spotty.

Do some test print runs with the tints and shades. The shades, especially, can get rather dark looking on the page—looking more like black than any other color. The tints can print with a "dot pattern" look. Find the ones that work for you.

Working with Fill Patterns

Publisher also enables you to fill frames with two-color patterns. The patterns are comprised of simple patterns, such as polka dots and crosshatches. You select the foreground and background colors for the patterns.

Use the following steps to add a pattern to a frame background:

1. Select the frame where you want to add a pattern. From the Format menu, choose Fill Patterns And Shading.

2. At the top of the dialog box, select Patterns to display the available patterns. Click on the desired pattern to select it.

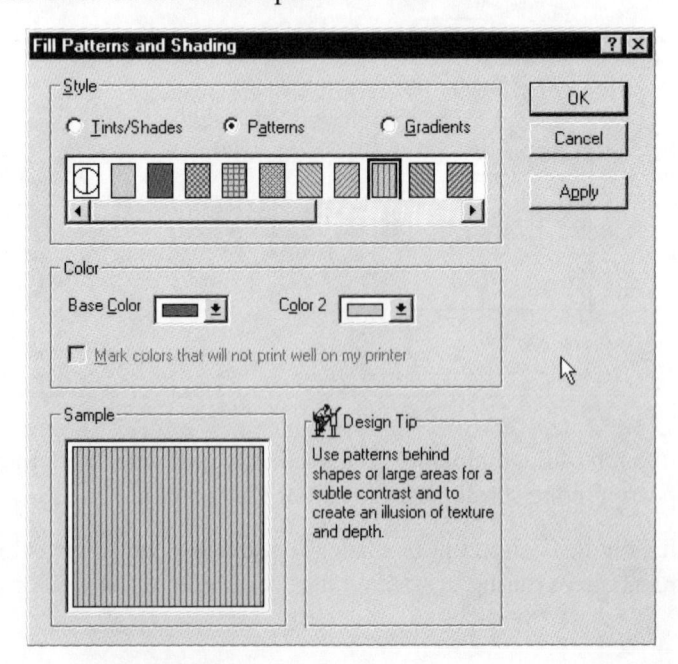

3. In the middle of the dialog box, click on the down arrow by Base Color and choose the foreground color. Click on the down arrow by Color 2 and choose the background color.

4. Review the sample and click OK.

Applying Gradient Fills to Frames

Gradient fills blend one color into another (see Figure 7-15). For example, a gradient fill might blend blue into green. Gradient fills are great for creating three-dimensional shading and highlighting effects. Publisher provides a variety of gradient styles.

The following steps outline adding gradient fills to frames:

1. Select the frame where you want to add a gradient. From the Format menu, choose Fill Patterns And Shading.

2. At the top of the dialog box select Gradients to see the available gradient styles. Use the scroll bar to see all of the choices.

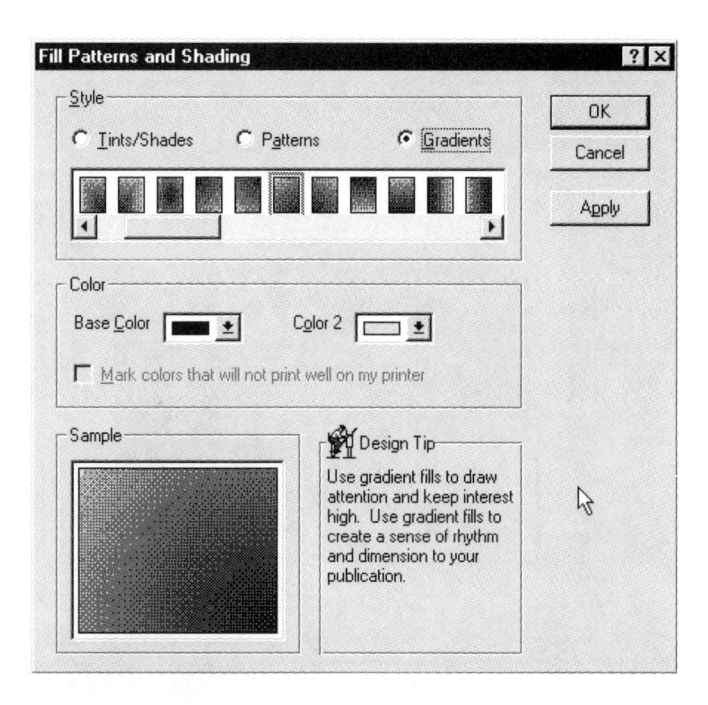

3. In the middle of the dialog box, click on the Base Color down arrow and choose a color. Click on the Color 2 down arrow and choose the second color.

4. Review the sample and click OK.

For best results, create gradient fills by use of similar colors. For instance, a gradient fill might blend from yellow to orange, or yellow to light green. These blends also look more realistic. Blending from opposite colors, such as red to green or yellow to purple, can create a brownish, muddy-looking section in the middle of the blend—and the muddy-looking stuff will print!

Adding Shadows to Frames

Shadows create the appearance of an element floating above the page. Generally, one or two elements with shadows is plenty (see Figure 7-16)—you don't want to overdo the effect. Adding shadows is easy. Simply select the frame where you want to add a shadow, and click on the Add/Remove Shadow tool in the Formatting toolbar.

Gradient fills allow you to blend one color to another

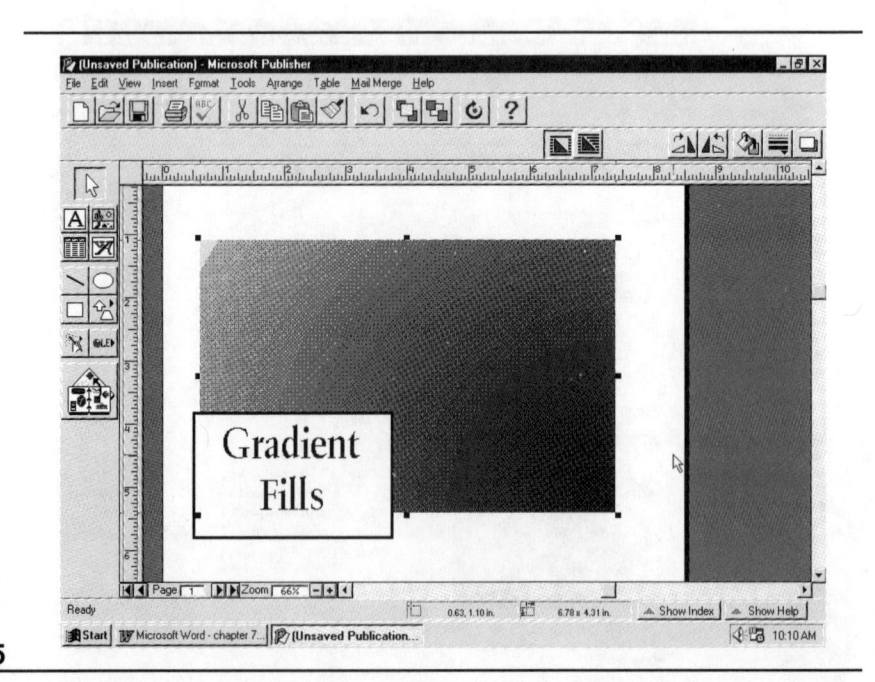

FIGURE 7-15

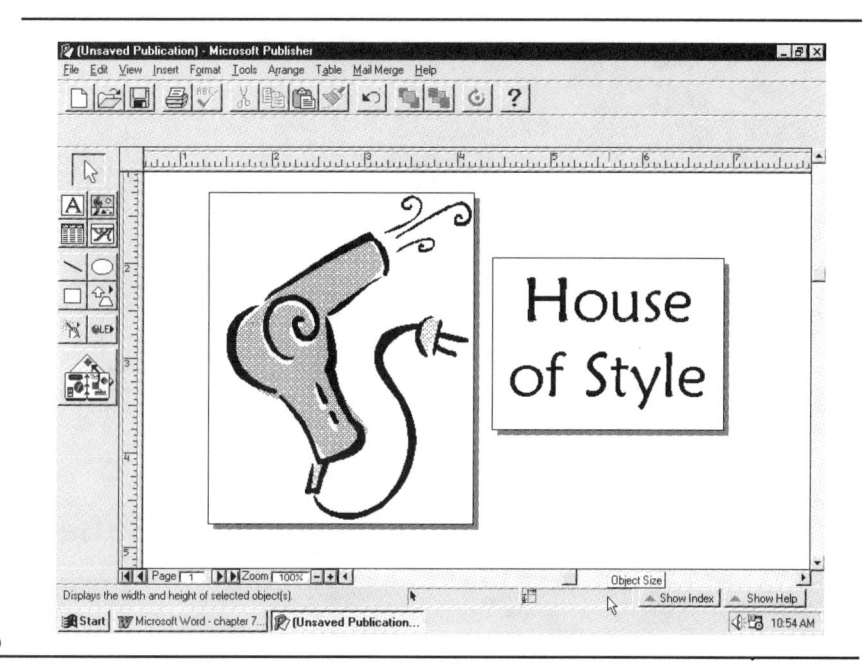

Use
shadows
to draw
attention to
frames in a
publication

FIGURE 7-16

Adding Borders to Frames

The boundaries of the frames you see on the page do not actually print. If you draw a frame on a page, then print the page, the frame is not visible. Only the text and pictures loaded into the frame actually print. You can apply borders to frames to create a printable box around the frame. In Figure 7-17, borders are placed around the frames containing text. As you can see, borders are a good way to visually separate several text frames on a page.

To give you real design flexibility, Publisher allows you to control the color, style, and thickness of the borders.

Applying Line Borders

Lines used as borders for frames are probably the most effective, because they keep the page design simple and clean. You can choose from a preset line thickness, or enter a custom line thickness. In most cases, stick with a relatively thin line for bordering frames. Thick lines draw too much attention to the border instead of what's in the frame.

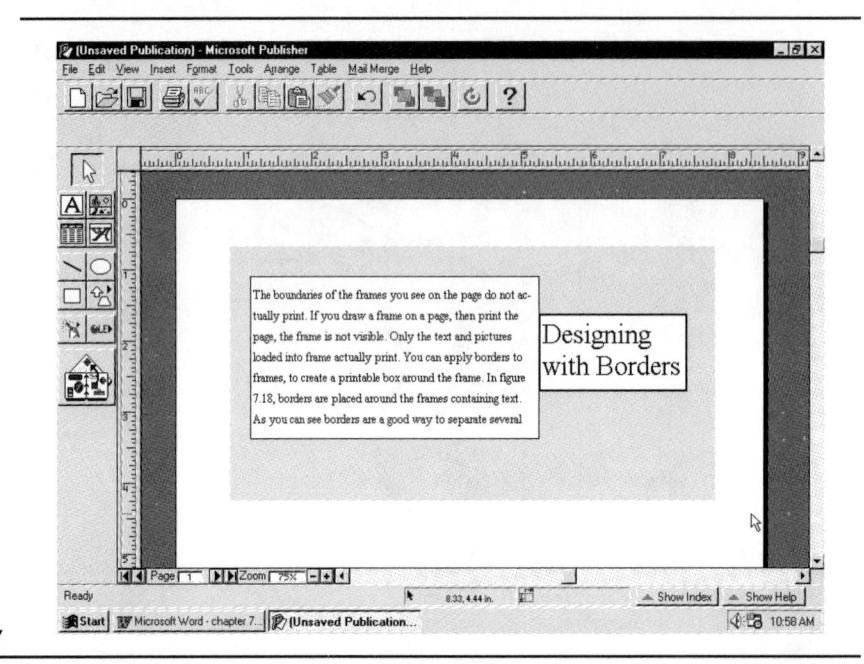

Applying
borders to
frames is a
good way
to separate
elements
on a page

FIGURE 7-17

The thickness of line borders is measured in *points*. Points are a printer's term of measurement. Type is also measured in points. There are 72 points per inch. The following steps illustrate applying line borders to frames:

1. Select the frame(s) to which you want to apply a border. From the Format menu, select Border.

2. Make sure the Line Border tab is selected at the top of the BorderArt dialog box. Click on a preset thickness, such as 2 pt, or enter your own custom thickness in the last box.

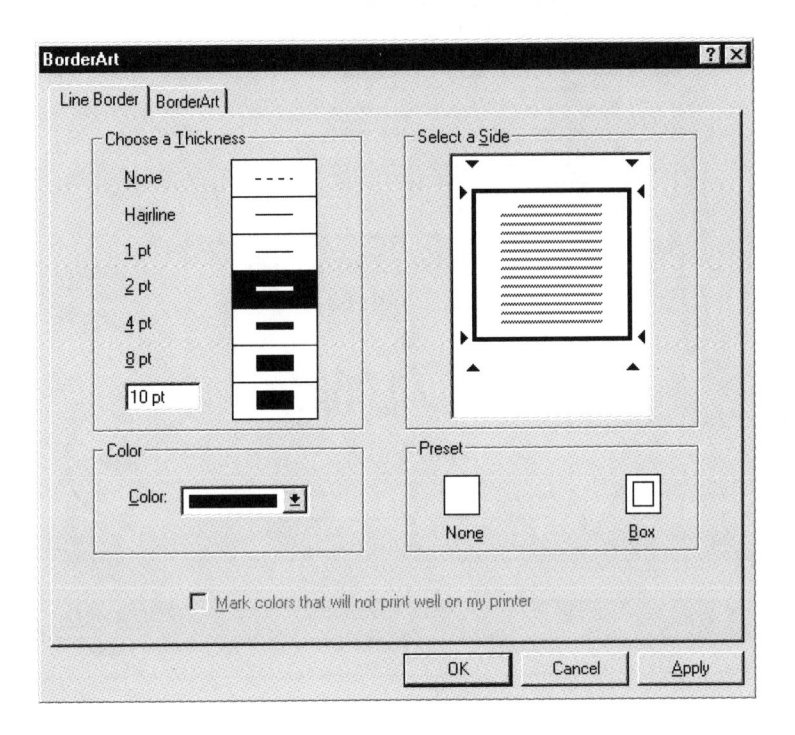

3. Click on the Color down arrow to pick a color for the line border. Click OK to apply the border.

 **TIP:**   *You can also click on the Borders tool in the Formatting toolbar to quickly apply line borders and BorderArt.*

Applying BorderArt

Publisher provides a wide selection of artwork for use as borders around frames. BorderArt ranges from subtle dashed lines to rather gaudy borders involving baby rattles and ladybugs. Some, such as the coupon-cutout dashes shown in Figure 7-18, could be very useful in postcards and brochures.

Consider Publisher's BorderArt when applying borders around frames

FIGURE 7-18

You can adjust the size and color of the BorderArt. Use the following steps to apply BorderArt to frames:

1. Select the frame(s) to which you want to apply a border. From the Format menu, select Border (or click on the Borders tool in the Formatting toolbar).

2. Click on the BorderArt tab at the top of the BorderArt dialog box to display the border designs. Use the scroll bar to view all the choices.

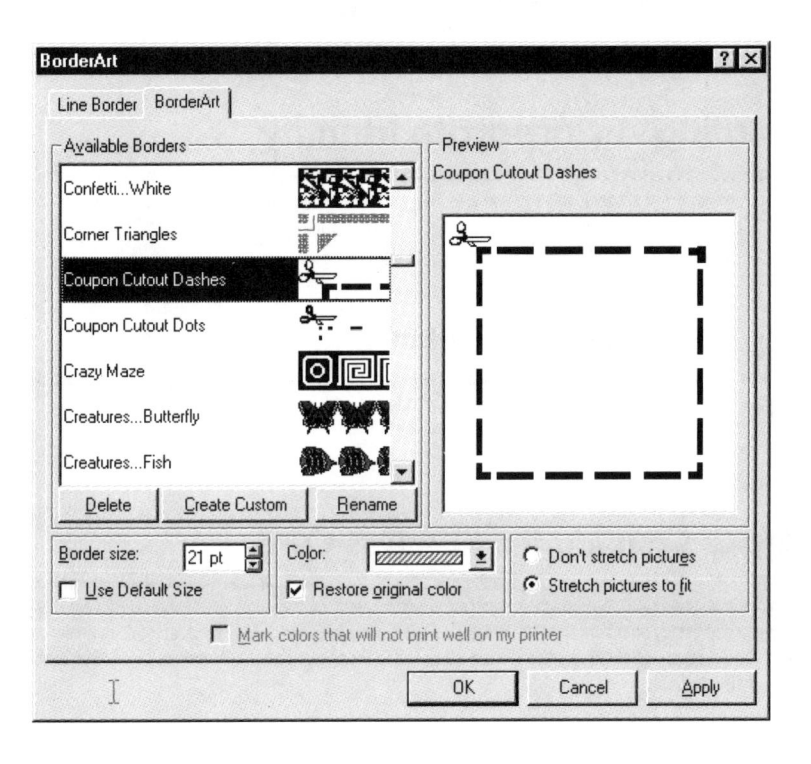

3. Select the desired BorderArt—a preview of the border appears. Enter a new value in the Border Size box to adjust the thickness of the border. Click on the Use Default Size option to return the border to its original size.

4. Click on the Color down arrow to pick another color for the BorderArt. Click on the Restore Original Color option to return the border to its original colors. Click OK to apply the BorderArt.

Saving Time with the Format Painter

When designing a page, you may want several frames to use the same formatting attributes. In addition, once you get a frame that looks good, you may want to use

Creating a Corporate Identity

Establishing a clean, professional look for your corporate communication materials is a must. Here, repeating color and graphics on a letterhead, business card, and envelope ties these pieces together for a great first impression!

Step 1: Creating the Letterhead

The "drop cap" letterhead style was selected as the look for all the pieces. The Letterhead PageWizard built the design by asking for the company name, phone number, and address.

Step 2: Creating the Business Card

The business card was created with the Blank Page option. The default card orientation was landscape, so the Page Setup command was used to change it to portrait. The graphics and company information were copied from the letterhead and pasted onto the card. The graphics were moved to the top of the card, and the company information was moved to the bottom. Slight adjustments were made to the frames containing the graphics and text so they would fit better on the card.

Step 3: Creating the Envelope

Since there is no blank page option for envelopes, the Envelope PageWizard was used to create the envelope. The Classic style was selected, and then the elements from the Classic style envelope were deleted. Next, the graphics and company information from the letterhead were pasted on the envelope. The frames containing the graphics and text were moved to the top left corner. The phone number was not included on the envelope.

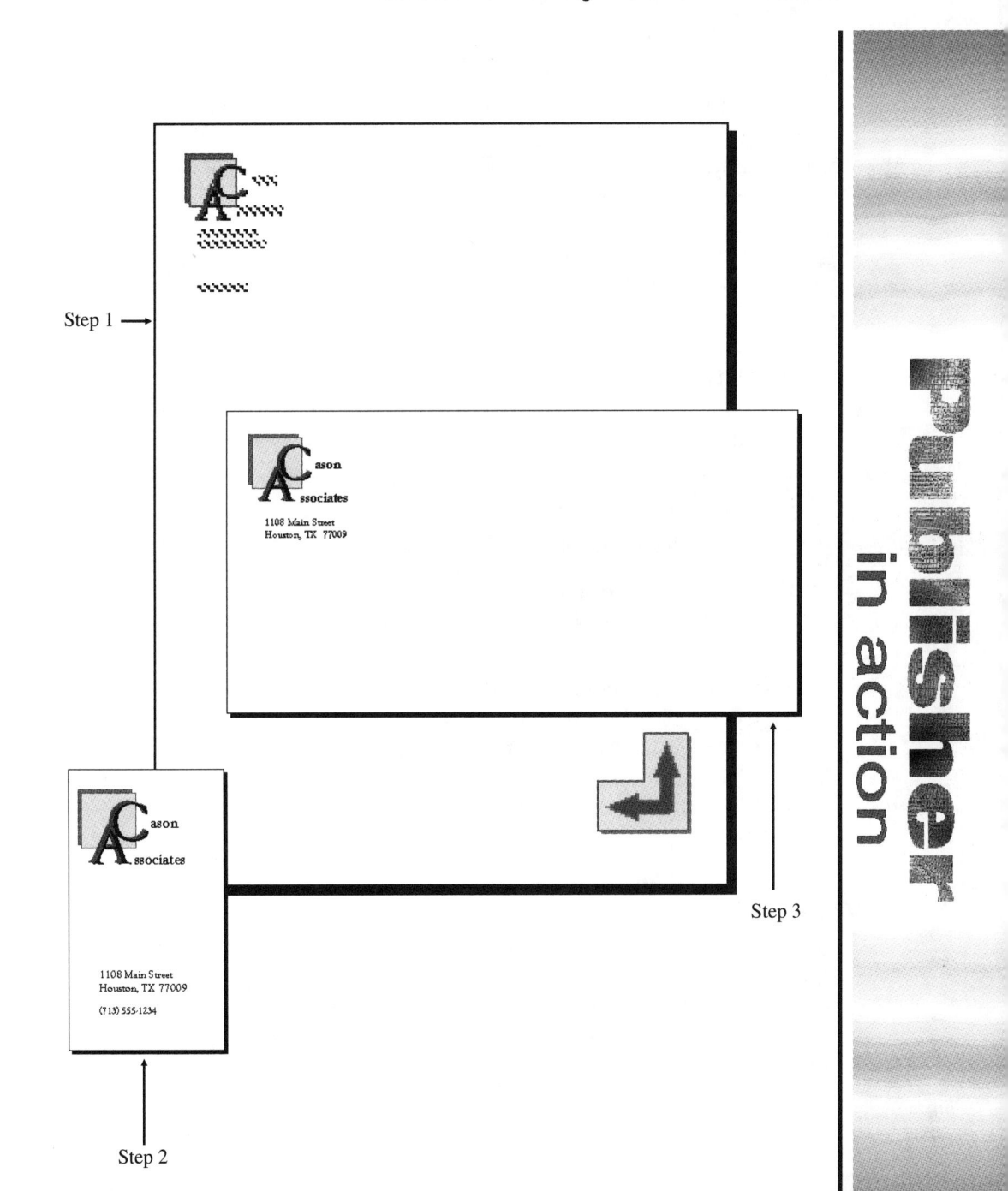

Step 1 →

Step 3

Step 2

Publisher
in action

those attributes in other frames. Rather than applying the same color, pattern, borders, and margins to several frames, use the Format Painter to quickly copy formatting from one frame to another. The Format Painter can copy attributes between different types of frames. For instance, you can copy formatting from a picture frame to a text frame.

 **NOTE:** *The Format Painter can also be used with text and table information. You'll learn more about the Format Painter in later chapters.*

 The Format Painter appears on the Standard toolbar. To use the Format Painter:

1. Select the frame displaying the attributes that you want to copy to another frame.

2. Click on the Format Painter tool—the mouse cursor changes to display a Paintbrush cursor.

3. Click the Paintbrush cursor on the frame where you want to place or "paint" the formatting attributes.

As an example, imagine you had a picture frame with a line border, 0.50-inch margins, and a gradient fill. You can use the Format Painter to apply those same attributes to a text frame. First, select the formatted picture frame. Click on the Format Painter. Now, click the Paintbrush cursor on the text frame. The attributes, border, margins, and gradient fill are copied to the text frame. What a great time-saver!

Summary

Publisher uses frames to hold text, pictures, tables, and WordArt in publications. This chapter focused on the basics of working with frames to prepare you for editing publications built with PageWizards and for building publications from scratch.

Chapter 8 discusses entering, editing, and formatting text.

8

Adding Text to Publications

Text can be entered directly into frames with Publisher. In fact, Publisher's tools for text-handling rival many word processors. Text can also be imported into the frames from applications such as Microsoft Word. Regardless of how the text gets into the frame, chances are good it will need to be modified and formatted. Being familiar with the text editing and formatting tools in Publisher will make working with text much simpler.

First, this chapter examines getting text into a publication—by typing it in directly or by importing it from another application. Since you may import more text than can fit in a frame, flowing text across frames is covered here. Next, the chapter discusses selecting text, moving and copying text, and inserting special characters, such as fractions. The chapter then looks at formatting text—everything from applying color to aligning paragraphs is discussed. The last section of the chapter examines use of the Format Painter and spell checking of publications.

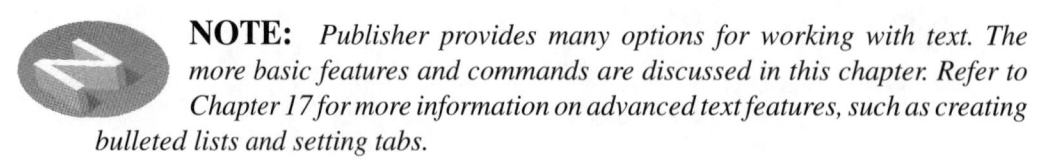 **NOTE:** *Publisher provides many options for working with text. The more basic features and commands are discussed in this chapter. Refer to Chapter 17 for more information on advanced text features, such as creating bulleted lists and setting tabs.*

Working with Text Frames

As discussed in Chapter 7, Publisher uses text frames to hold and position text on a page. Text frames can be moved, sized, and rotated. Each text frame has individual frame settings for margins, columns, color, and borders. The capability to establish separate settings for each frame provides a lot of options and flexibility in page design. You can apply the frame settings before or after entering text in the frame.

 **NOTE:** *Text frames can be rotated, as discussed in Chapter 7. Highlighted text within a frame cannot be rotated.*

The size of the text frame determines how much text shows. Obviously, a text frame covering $\frac{1}{4}$ of a page cannot display or hold as much text as a text frame covering a whole page. Formatting also dictates how much text appears in a frame. Certainly more 12-point text can fit in a frame than 36-point text.

 **REMEMBER:** *As mentioned in Chapter 7, points are a printer's term of measurement. There are 72 points in an inch. Points are usually used to size type and lines.*

When you use PageWizards to build publications, text frames are already positioned on the page, and the text in the frames is already formatted. Of course, you can change it as desired. When you draw text frames on the page yourself, they will be empty until you enter text.

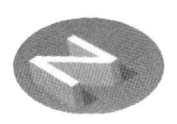 **NOTE:** *Text is also used in WordArt frames. Refer to Chapter 13 for more information on working with WordArt.*

Entering Text into Frames

When PageWizards are used to build publications, text frames display sample text that is meant to be replaced by your text. To enter text, you simply click on the text in the text frame and begin typing. The sample text is highlighted and replaced with your text. The formatting, typeface, and type size of the sample text is applied to your new text.

It's a little different when you draw new text frames on a page. After the frame is drawn, or whenever it is selected, an insertion point appears in the top left corner of the frame (see Figure 8-1). The insertion point indicates where new text will be entered in the frame. As you begin typing, the text displays in a default typeface and type size, such as Times New Roman 10 point. Unless you have adjusted the formatting, text is left-aligned and set at single line spacing. You'll see how to adjust text formatting later in this chapter.

Note that you may need to zoom in on the text frame to actually see the text you are entering. Remember, to zoom in, you simply click on the + sign on the Zoom indicator in the bottom left corner of the screen. When you are working with text, the Formatting toolbar automatically becomes the Text Formatting toolbar. You'll find yourself using several of these tools as you edit and format text.

8

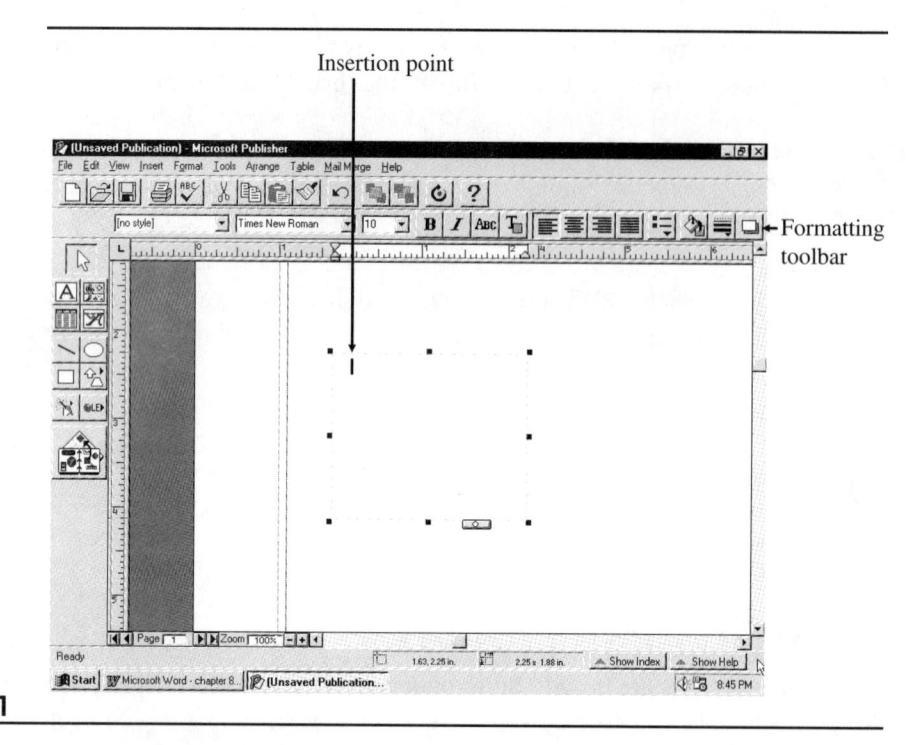

Insertion point

Formatting toolbar

New text appears at the insertion point

FIGURE 8-1

Tips for Entering Text

As you know, typing with a computer is different from typing with a typewriter. Here are a few suggestions to keep in mind when entering text in Publisher:

- You only need to type one space after punctuation at the end of sentences. Two spaces were added in the days of typewriters. Now with proportional fonts, extra spacing is automatically added after sentences, so you only need to enter one space.

- Do not press ENTER at the end of every line; text will automatically move to the next line when it reaches the edge of the frame.

- Instead of pressing ENTER twice to leave space between paragraphs, consider using the line and paragraph spacing options discussed in Chapter 17.

- Don't press SPACEBAR to line up text vertically. It may look okay on the monitor, but it probably won't print right.

- Instead of pressing SPACEBAR or TAB to indent the lines of a paragraph, consider using the paragraph indent options covered in Chapter 17. You might also try the numbered and bullet list options available for text. These are also discussed in Chapter 17.

- Consider creating a table instead of using tabs to create columns of text. Tables are covered in Chapter 12.

The trick to effectively entering and formatting text is to know the commands and features available in Publisher. Take time to get comfortable with the program.

Importing Text from Other Applications

In addition to entering text directly into a Publisher frame, you can also add text created in a word processing application such as Microsoft Word. Inserting a file created in another application is called *importing*. Although you may enter the bulk of your text directly into Publisher, don't rule out the need for importing text from a word processor. You may be in charge of laying out the publication, for example, and want to incorporate text written by someone else. The writer might have used a word processing application to create the text. If you don't import the text, you would have to reenter it into Publisher.

Spreadsheet data created by Microsoft Excel or Microsoft Works can also be imported into a text frame. Since Publisher doesn't provide tools such as formulas and functions for creating spreadsheets, importing spreadsheets allows you to place this type of information into your Publisher publications. The imported data will become a table in Publisher. Refer to Chapter 12 for more information on working with tables.

After text or a spreadsheet is imported, you can use Publisher's text-editing tools to make changes. Once the text or spreadsheet data is placed in Publisher, you can work with it as you would text entered in Publisher. In most cases, Publisher can preserve the text formatting. However, text and spreadsheet information will lose its formatting when it's imported unless the file format supports RTF (Rich Text Format). Applications that support RTF include Excel, Works, Word, and other Windows-based word processing applications.

File Formats Supported by Publisher

Publisher can import various word processing and spreadsheet file formats into text frames. If you use an application not listed in Table 8-1, see if your application can save information in one of these file formats and then insert the data into a text frame.

File Format	Filename Extension
Microsoft Word for Windows, versions 2.0, 6.0, and 7.0	.DOC
Microsoft Works for Windows version 3.0 and Microsoft Works for Windows 95 word processing files	.WPS
Microsoft Write for Windows 3.1 and Windows 95	.WRI
WordPerfect for DOS and Windows, versions 5.0, 5.1, and 6.0	You can use any filename extension with WordPerfect files.
Plain text or ASCII text. Almost all word processing applications can save files in this format.	.TXT. In most cases, formatting will be lost.
Rich Text Format. Most Windows-based word processing and spreadsheet applications can save files in this format.	.RTF. Formatting will be preserved.

File Formats Imported by Publisher and Their Filename Extensions

TABLE 8-1

Text or spreadsheet data from Windows 95 applications, such as Word and Excel, can also be copied and pasted through the Windows Clipboard. You'll learn more about moving and copying data later in this chapter.

Inserting Text and Spreadsheet Files into Text Frames

Use the following steps to import a text or spreadsheet file into a text frame:

1. Select the text frame into which you want to insert the text or spreadsheet file. The insertion point appears in the top left corner of the frame.

2. From the Insert menu, choose Insert Text File. (Use this command to insert spreadsheet files also.) The Insert Text File dialog box appears.

3. Change to the drive and folders where the file you want to import is located.

4. All Files (*.*) appears in the Files Of Type list box; this means Publisher is ready to import any accepted file format. To see a listing of file formats, click on the Files Of Type down arrow to display a list of supported file formats. If desired, you can select the specific format of the text or spreadsheet information you are importing.

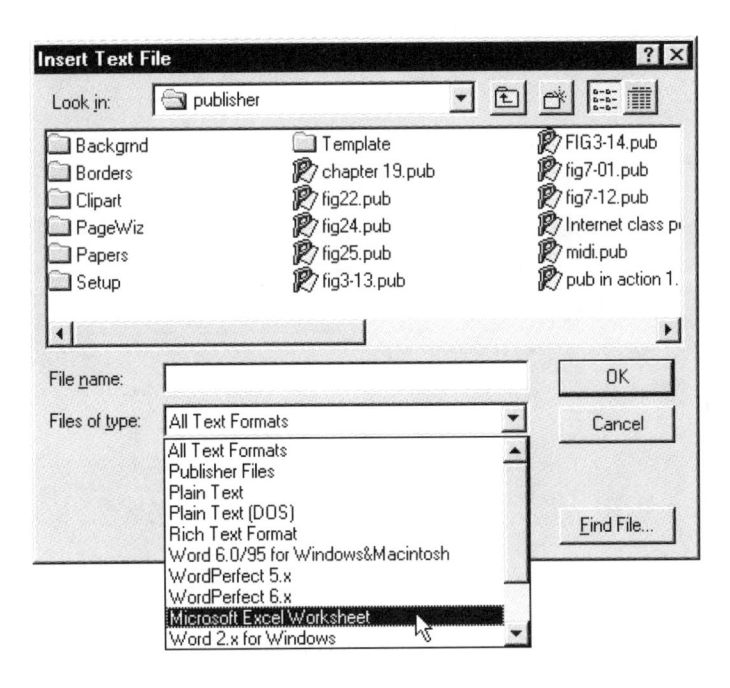

5. The files in the specified format appear in the File Name list box.

6. Select the file you want and click OK.

The text or spreadsheet data appears in the frame. Keep in mind that the frame may not be large enough to display all of the text. If it isn't, Publisher displays a message asking if you want to use autoflow. To have Publisher automatically flow the text to another frame, click Yes. Click No if you wish to control the flow of the text yourself. Publisher then displays another message indicating it will create a new text frame on a new page for the remaining text. Click Yes if you wish Publisher to continue the text into a new text frame on a new page, or No to cancel the autoflow. The next section examines flowing text from frame to frame.

Flowing Text Across Several Frames

Rather than displaying an entire text file in one text frame, you might decide to flow text across several frames. When designing a newsletter, for example, you might want to flow an article from a text frame on page 1 to a text frame on page 2.

When a text frame is selected, a Connect icon appears in the bottom right corner. As shown in Figure 8-2, if the frame has more text than it can display, the Connect icon appears as three black dots (like an ellipsis). If the frame contains all of the text, the Connect icon appears as a white diamond.

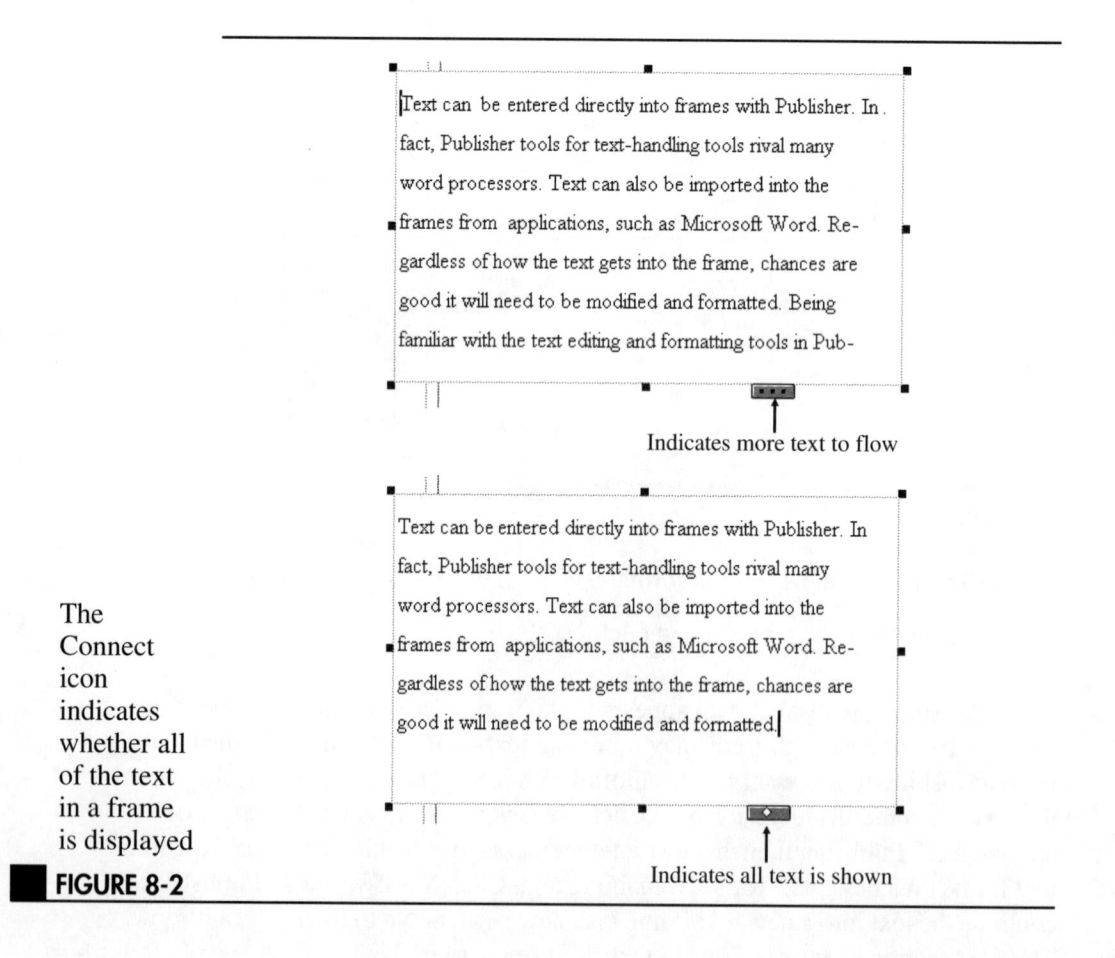

Indicates more text to flow

The
Connect
icon
indicates
whether all
of the text
in a frame
is displayed

Indicates all text is shown

FIGURE 8-2

Before flowing text, draw all of the frames that the text will be placed into. The following steps illustrate flowing text across two frames:

1. Select the text frame containing more text than it can display.

2. Click on the Connect icon—the mouse pointer changes to a Pitcher cursor.

3. Click the Pitcher cursor in the frame where you want to flow the remaining text. (You may have to move to another page.) The text is "poured" into the selected frame. If the Connect icon indicates there is still more text to be flowed, repeat the steps until all of the text is placed.

When text is flowed across several frames, icons appear on the frames, allowing you to move back and forth between the frames (see Figure 8-3). When you click

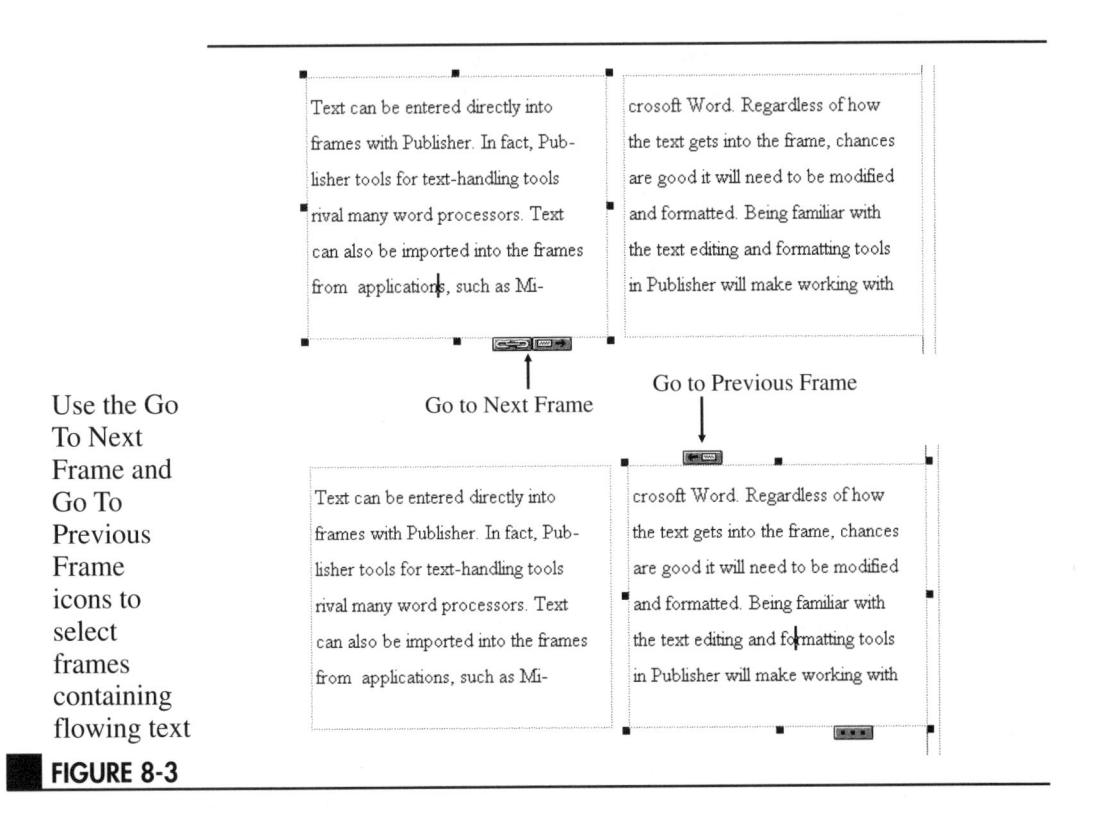

Use the Go To Next Frame and Go To Previous Frame icons to select frames containing flowing text

FIGURE 8-3

on the Go To Next Frame icon on the first frame, the next frame where the text is flowed is selected. When you click on the Go To Previous Frame icon, the previous frame where the text is flowed is selected.

Changing the frame size affects the flow of the text. Suppose that you have a text file flowing in a frame on page 1 to a frame on page 2. Reducing the size of the first frame means that less text can be displayed in the frame. The text that no longer fits in the first frame is flowed into the second frame. Because more text is added to the second frame, watch for the Connect icon to indicate if all of the text is displayed in the second frame.

Editing Text

When producing publications, you're bound to want to add or delete text. In fact, most of us are adding and deleting text up to the very last moment. If you are new to word processing, this section will provide you lots of valuable information for editing text. Even if you're a pro, take a minute to browse through the section to discover some new features and shortcuts. Everyone can use a few good tricks.

Showing Special Characters

As you edit documents, you may find it convenient to see where the ENTER and TAB keys were used. Select the Show Special Characters option from the View menu to display symbols representing where the ENTER key, TAB key, and SPACEBAR were pressed. A symbol also appears indicating line breaks. These special characters do not print.

NOTE: *Working with line breaks is covered in Chapter 17.*

As shown in Figure 8-4, a paragraph mark (¶) appears where ENTER was pressed. A right arrow appears where TAB was pressed. A dot appears where the SPACEBAR was pressed. A ↵ appears where a line break was created. To hide the symbols, select Hide Special Characters from the View menu.

Showing special characters is handy when you edit publications created by someone else. In Figure 8-4, the symbols in the text frame indicate the TAB key was used to indent text. If there were no tab symbols, you could assume the indents were added by use of text-formatting options.

Showing special characters makes it easier to see what keys were used to enter text

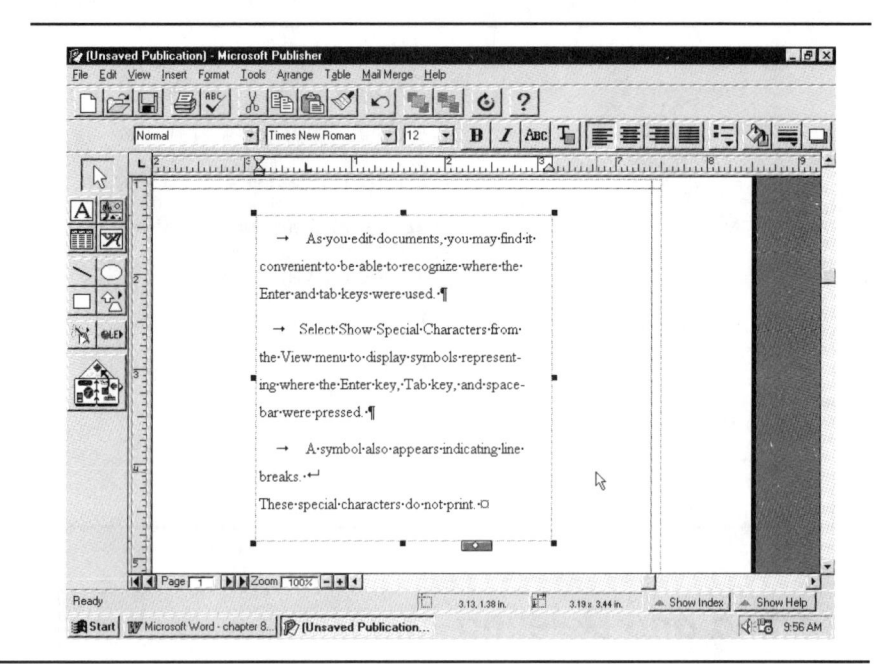

FIGURE 8-4

Moving the Insertion Point

Before editing text, you need to move the insertion point to the exact spot where you want to add or delete text. You can move the insertion point with the keyboard or with the mouse.

Moving the Insertion Point with the Keyboard

You can press keys to move the insertion point through the text in a text frame. Table 8-2 discusses the keyboard shortcuts for moving the insertion point.

Moving the Insertion Point with the Mouse

It is often quicker to use the mouse rather than the keyboard to move the insertion point. When the mouse is placed in the text frame, the cursor turns into an *I-beam,* which looks like the letter *I.* Move the I-beam to where you want to begin editing, and click to place the insertion point. With this method, you can quickly move the insertion point as you edit several paragraphs.

Press	To Move the Insertion Point
CTRL-HOME	To the top of the text frame
CTRL-END	To the bottom of the text frame
HOME	To the beginning of the line
END	To the end of the line
UP or DOWN ARROW	Up or down one line
LEFT or RIGHT ARROW	Left or right one character
CTRL-LEFT ARROW	To the left one word
CTRL-RIGHT ARROW	To the right one word

Keyboard Shortcuts for Moving Through Text

TABLE 8-2

Inserting and Deleting Text

When new text is inserted, existing text automatically moves over to make room. To insert text, click to place the insertion point where you want to enter new text and start typing.

NOTE: *When editing text, don't forget about using the Undo command to retrieve accidentally deleted text. Chapter 6 discusses use of the Undo feature.*

Publisher provides several methods for deleting text. This section discusses deleting text one character at a time. You'll find more on deleting in the following section, "Highlighting Text."

To delete text, click to place the insertion point in the text you want to delete. Then use either of these options:

- Press BACKSPACE to delete the text character to the left of the insertion point.

- Press DELETE to delete the text character to the right of the insertion point.

Pressing BACKSPACE and DELETE can also delete tabs, line breaks (where SHIFT-ENTER was pressed), and paragraph breaks (where the ENTER key was pressed).

Highlighting Text

When you need to delete large amounts of text, such as sentences or paragraphs, highlight the text before pressing DELETE or BACKSPACE. Highlighting enables you to delete all of the selected text with one keystroke. Text must also be highlighted before you can apply formatting such as bold or italic.

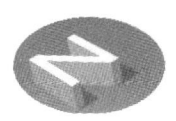 **NOTE:** *Highlighting text may also be referred to as* selecting *text.*

To highlight text, position the I-beam in front of the text to be highlighted. Press and hold the mouse and drag to the right. (You can also place the I-beam after the text to be highlighted and drag to the left.) The text is highlighted as you drag. When the desired text is highlighted, release the mouse. To highlight several lines of text, move the mouse up or down slightly as you drag. To quickly highlight a single word, double-click with the mouse on the word.

> To highlight text, position the I-beam in front of the text to be highlighted. Press and hold the mouse and drag to the right. The text is highlighted as you drag.

You can also use the keyboard to highlight text. Click to place the insertion point in front of the text to be highlighted. Now, hold down SHIFT and press RIGHT ARROW several times. The text characters to the right are highlighted as you press the arrow key. You can also hold SHIFT and press LEFT ARROW to highlight text to the left. Hold CTRL-SHIFT as you press RIGHT or LEFT ARROW to highlight a word.

 **TIP:** *To highlight all of the text in a flow, click anywhere in the text flow and press CTRL-A.*

Replacing Highlighted Text

When text is highlighted, any new text that you enter replaces the selected text. *Replacing* means you don't have to press DELETE or BACKSPACE; you just highlight the text to be deleted and start typing. Suppose you're producing a report and need to replace one sentence with another. Just highlight the old sentence and start typing the new one.

By default, Publisher is set up to replace highlighted text with new text. If, however, this is not happening, select Options from the Tools menu. Click on the Editing And User Assistance tab, and turn on the Typing Replaces Selection option.

Moving and Copying Text

Remember when you would spend all day producing a report on a typewriter, bottle of correction fluid by your side, and when you finished, your editor/boss/client decided to make a *few* changes? "Move these paragraphs, move this sentence, copy this paragraph to pages 3 and 4, and place the company name on these pages." You basically had to start all over. Luckily, those days are gone. Producing a report on a PC with Publisher makes moving and copying text easy. All it takes are a few mouse clicks or keystrokes to make those last-minute editing changes.

Understanding the Clipboard

The Windows Clipboard is a temporary storage area that holds text and other data as it is transferred to a new location. Text can be either moved or copied to a new location. When it's moved, text is cut from its original location and then pasted into another. When it's copied, a duplicate of the text is placed on the Clipboard and then pasted elsewhere. The Clipboard works behind the scenes, meaning you won't see any windows or dialog box representing the Clipboard as you move and copy text.

Highlighted text is sent to the Clipboard by use of the Cut and Copy commands. The Clipboard stores this text, which may be a character, word, sentence, or several paragraphs. The Paste command is used to paste the Clipboard contents back into the document. As discussed in Chapter 7, the Standard toolbar provides tools for cutting, copying, and pasting.

Two important notes: first, the contents of the Clipboard are replaced when another selection of text is cut or copied. For instance, if you copy one paragraph to the Clipboard and then copy another, only the last paragraph is stored on the

Clipboard. The first paragraph is gone. To prevent accidental loss of text, it's a good idea to paste right away when you're cutting and copying text.

The second thing to remember: text stays on the Clipboard even after pasting. For instance, if you cut a paragraph and paste it on page 2, the paragraph stays on the Clipboard, so you can continue pasting the text on pages 3 and 4. As mentioned, the Clipboard contents are not replaced until you cut or copy a new selection. The Clipboard is also emptied when you exit Windows 95.

NOTE: *If you're interested in seeing the contents of the Clipboard, double-click on the Clipboard Viewer in the Accessories folder. The Clipboard Viewer is optional during Windows 95 installation, so if you don't find it, you may have to add it.*

Other frames, such as table and picture frames, can also be moved and copied in a publication. Chapter 7 discussed the steps for moving and copying frames. The Clipboard also allows you to cut, copy, and paste data from other applications. Refer to the section "Transferring Data from Other Applications" in Chapter 17 for more information.

The following sections examine cutting, copying, and pasting text within one publication or among several publications.

Moving Text: Cutting and Pasting

When editing, you might need to move text within a text frame or from one text frame to another. For instance, in a report, you may decide that a paragraph would read better at the end of a text frame or perhaps in the next frame into which the rest of the text is flowed.

Use the following steps to move text:

1. Highlight the text you want to move. Remember to highlight everything you want moved, such as punctuation marks and tabs.

2. From the Edit menu choose Cut Text, or click on the Cut tool in the Standard toolbar. The text is removed from the frame.

3. Position the insertion point where you want to paste the text. This might be in the same text frame or in another text frame on another page.

4. From the Edit menu, select Paste or click on the Paste tool. The text is pasted at the insertion point.

After highlighting text, you can also click the right mouse button to display a context-sensitive pop-up menu. *Context sensitive* means the menu displays commands based on what you have highlighted or selected. For instance, when text is highlighted, the context-sensitive menu displays Cut Text and Copy Text. If a frame is selected, the menu displays Cut Frame or Copy Frame.

 **TIP:** *The keyboard shortcut for Cut is CTRL-X. The shortcut for copy is CTRL-C. The shortcut for paste is CTRL-V.*

Copying Text: Copying and Pasting

Copying lets you place the same text several times in a publication. When designing a brochure, you may want the company name, address, and phone number to appear frequently in the publication. Rather than typing the same information again and again, copy the text and then paste it in the desired locations.

The steps for copying text are very similar to those for moving, except that you use the Copy command instead of the Cut command. Use the following steps to copy text and paste it elsewhere in a publication:

1. Highlight the text you want to copy.

2. From the Edit menu choose Copy Text, or click on the Copy tool in the Standard toolbar. A copy of the highlighted text is sent to the Clipboard.

3. Position the insertion point where you want to paste the text. This might be in the same text frame or in another text frame on another page.

4. From the Edit menu select Paste, or click on the Paste tool. The text is pasted at the insertion point.

If you want to move or copy all the text in a frame, select all of the text and then use the Cut or Copy command. Selecting just the frame and cutting or copying will not cut or copy the text—only the frame.

Moving and Copying Text Between Documents

You may wish to cut, copy, and paste text between publications. For instance, you want to use several paragraphs written for a sales brochure in a new proposal. Rather than retyping the text for the proposal, you can copy it from the brochure. Cutting or copying text between publications is basically the same as cutting and copying text within publications.

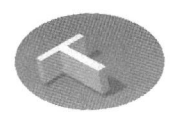

TIP: *When transferring data between publications, it's a good idea to copy rather than cut text from the original publication. This way you are not removing text from the original publication.*

Use the following steps to cut or copy text from one publication to another publication:

1. Highlight the text you want to cut or copy.

2. Select Cut Text or Copy Text from the Edit menu, or click on the Cut or Copy tool to place the text on the Clipboard.

3. Open the publication in which you want to paste the text. You may be asked to save the current publication before you can open the second publication.

4. Position the insertion point in the text frame where you want to place the cut or copied text. Select Paste Text from the Edit menu, or click on the Paste tool. The text is pasted from the Clipboard.

Unlike other Windows applications, in Publisher you can have only one publication file open at a time. This means the current publication is closed when you open the new publication to paste the text.

Using Drag-and-Drop

Just as the name implies, you can drag selected text and drop it in a new location. Drag-and-drop is probably the easiest way to move text. (In fact, it's easy to do this by accident.) Drag-and-drop is also fast—one quick mouse drag as opposed to the two steps involved when cutting or copying and pasting text. Text moved or copied with drag-and-drop is not sent to the Clipboard. Text or other data currently in the Clipboard is not replaced when you drag-and-drop text.

Drag-and-drop is great when you're moving and copying text short distances, such as switching the order of two paragraphs, or changing the order of words in a list. You can also drag text from one text frame to another. You cannot, however, drag and drop text from one page to another. When you're moving and copying text over several pages, use the Cut, Copy, and Paste commands.

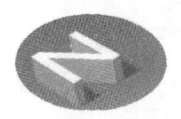 **NOTE:** *You can disable drag-and-drop. From the Tools menu, select Options. Click on the Editing And User Assistance tab, and turn off the Drag-and-Drop text-editing option.*

Moving Text with Drag-and-Drop

Dragging and dropping require that you be pretty handy with the mouse. It may take several attempts before you get good at it.

1. Highlight the text you want to move.

2. Place the mouse cursor over the highlighted text, and hold down the mouse button. The cursor displays "Drag" when placed over the highlighted text.

3. Drag the cursor to where you want to insert the highlighted text. The cursor displays "Move" when it is where text can be placed.

4. Release the mouse button to drop the text.

Notice the text is selected after you drop it. If you begin typing, the new text replaces what is highlighted. Be careful to remove the highlighting by clicking elsewhere in the text.

Copying Text with Drag-and-Drop

By default, drag-and-drop moves text. You can copy and drop by holding down CTRL as you do a normal drag-and-drop. To copy and drop:

1. Highlight the text and place the mouse cursor on the text to display the Drag cursor.

2. Hold down CTRL and drag the text to the new location. The cursor displays "Copy," indicating the text will be copied.

3. When ready to drop the copy, release the mouse button and CTRL.

Inserting Symbols

Many publications, such as marketing reports and sales brochures, require the insertion of copyright marks and registered trademarks. Technical manuals might use fractions and other mathematical symbols to define concepts and theories. In addition, publications produced for international audiences might use accented letters and a variety of currency symbols such as yen and deutsche mark.

NOTE: *It looks more professional to use the fractions symbols, rather than just typing the number, a slash, and the next number. If the fraction you need doesn't appear among Publisher's symbols, you can create it. Use the superscript and subscript type styles referred to later in the chapter in "Dressed for Success: Formatting Text."*

The symbols are available in almost every typeface. This means you can find accented letters in Times New Roman and Arial. Some fonts, such as Wingdings, are a collection of symbols, not text characters. In these symbol fonts you will find everything from smiley faces to airplanes.

The following steps illustrate inserting symbols into a text frame:

1. Click to place the insertion point in the text where you want the symbol to appear.

2. From the Insert menu, select Symbol. The Insert Symbol dialog box appears.

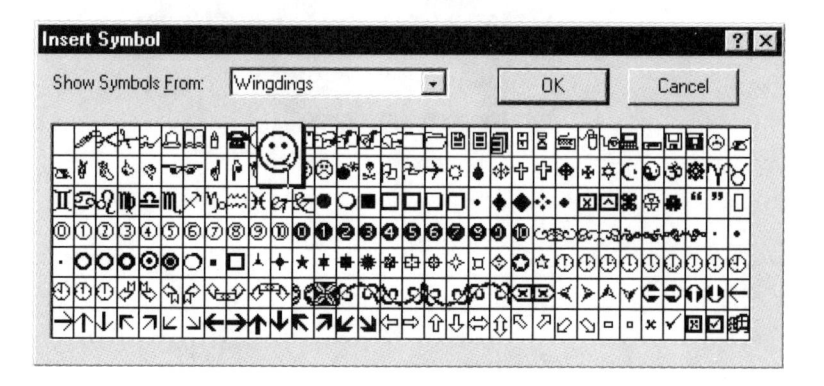

3. Click on the Show Symbols From down arrow and select the desired typeface. The special characters in the selected font appear.

4. To see an enlarged view of a character, press and hold the mouse on a symbol. Double-click on a character to insert it into the text.

The symbols can be formatted as regular text characters. Formatting options are discussed later in this chapter. Use DELETE and BACKSPACE to remove symbols.

Inserting the Date and Time

Publisher makes it easy to insert the date and time into your publications. By default, the date and time are entered as codes that automatically update whenever you open the publication file. For instance, suppose you insert the date January 1, 2000. When you open the file the next day, the date will read "January 2, 2000." You can also choose to display the date and time as plain text. In this case, the date and time are not updated. Use this feature when you want the specific date or time not to be changed.

To insert a date or time:

1. Select the text frame where you want the information to appear. If there is already text in the frame, click to place the insertion point exactly where you want the date or time to appear.

2. From the Insert menu, choose Date Or Time. The Date And Time dialog box appears.

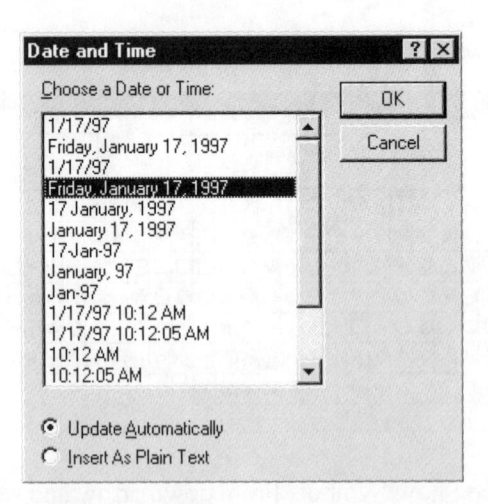

3. Select the desired date or time format. At the bottom of the dialog box, make sure the Update Automatically option is selected if you want the date or time to update automatically. Click on the Insert As Plain Text option to insert information that will not be changed or updated.

Dressed for Success: Formatting Text

After entering and editing text, you're probably eager to begin *formatting*—choosing typefaces, type sizes, type styles, and color for the text in your publications. You can draw attention to headings in a brochure by applying a large, bold typeface. Adding color to titles and bullets on overheads adds visual interest. Good text formatting catches the eye and draws the reader into the page. Inadequate formatting can result in bland pages or overdone layouts that diminish the readability of your publication.

Before applying the text formatting discussed in this section, you will need to highlight text. For example, if you want to make a word bold, you need to highlight the word first. To change the typeface of a headline, you need to highlight the headline. For a quick review of highlighting text, refer back to the section "Highlighting Text" earlier in this chapter.

Applying Typefaces and Type Sizes

The typeface you choose greatly influences the tone of the publication. Some typefaces add a casual feel—great for a company picnic flyer. Other typefaces are more serious; these work well for business reports and other formal documents. Type size is also a major consideration. Size helps convey the importance of the message.

The fonts to choose from will vary depending on the other applications you have installed in addition to Publisher, the type of printer you are using, and whether you have added any other fonts. The following steps illustrate selecting fonts:

1. Select the text you want to modify. For example, you might select a headline or title.

2. Choose Character from the Format menu. The Character dialog box appears.

3. Click on the Font down arrow to display a list of available fonts. Click on the font name to select it. A preview of the font appears in the Sample window of the dialog box.

8

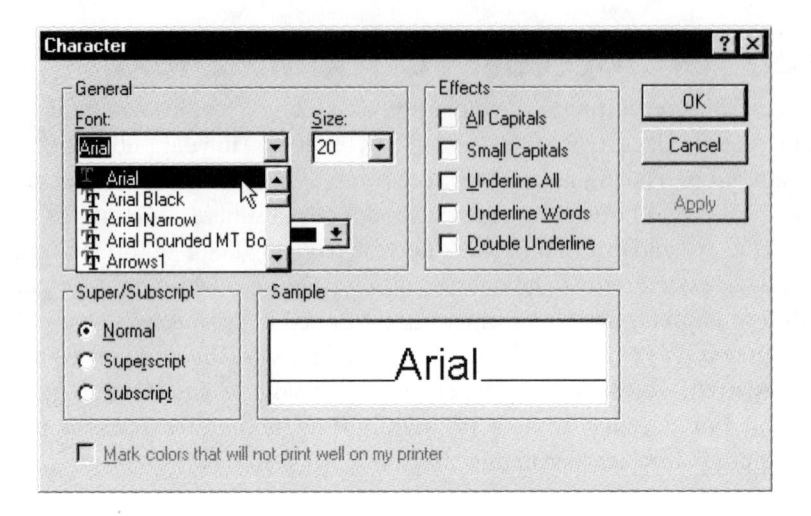

4. Click on the Size down arrow and select the desired size.

5. Click OK to apply the formatting to the highlighted text.

You can also select a typeface and size by clicking on the Font and Size tools in the Formatting toolbar. After highlighting text, click on the down arrow by the Font tool to see a list of available fonts. As shown in Figure 8-5, the font names appear in the actual font, giving you a handy preview. Click on a font name to select it.

 **NOTE:** *It can be difficult to select a specific symbol font from the Font tool drop-down list since the symbols are displayed and not the font name. Use the Character dialog box described earlier to select symbol fonts.*

To adjust the type size, highlight the text and click on the down arrow by the Size tool. Select the desired size from the list. When selecting type sizes, you can also manually enter type sizes that do not appear in the list. For instance, you can enter 100 in the Size box and click OK. Publisher also allows you to enter point sizes such as 9.5 or 10.2. This can be done in the Character dialog box or in the Size tool on the Formatting toolbar.

TIP: *After clicking on the down arrow to display the list of fonts, you can press the first letter of the font name to quickly jump to the fonts beginning with that letter. For instance, pressing* A *would move you to the fonts beginning with* A, *such as Arial.*

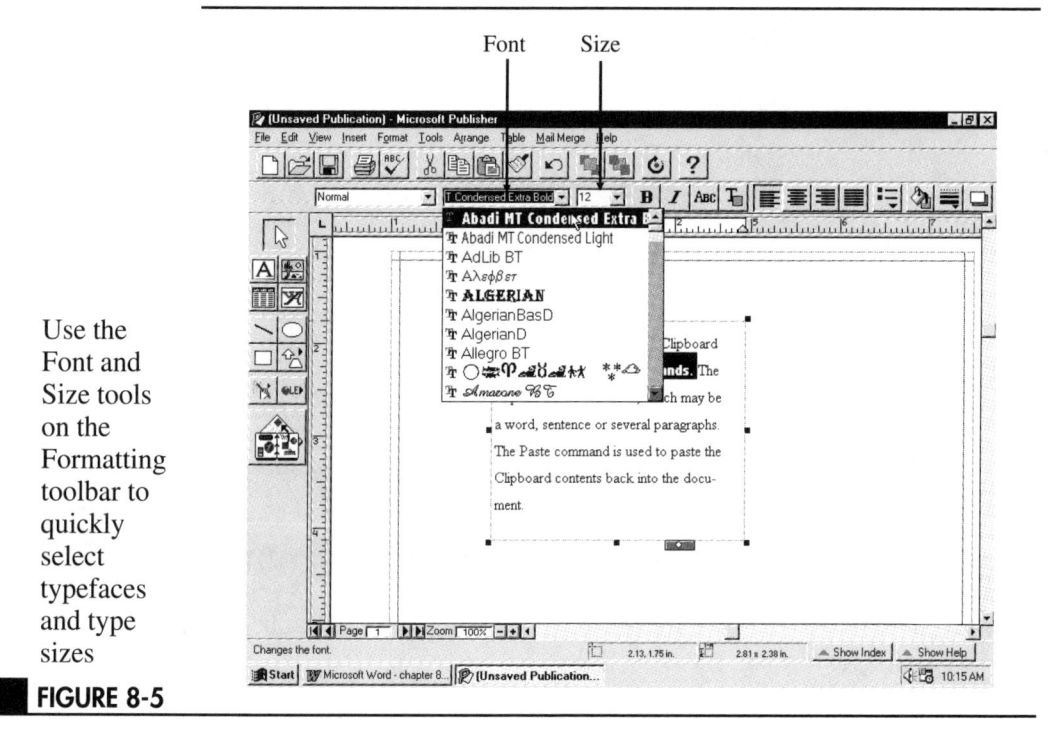

Use the Font and Size tools on the Formatting toolbar to quickly select typefaces and type sizes

FIGURE 8-5

Applying Type Styles

Type styles, such as bold and italic, lend emphasis to text. Publisher offers a wide selection of type styles, as shown in Table 8-3. The table also includes shortcuts when available.

The following steps illustrate applying type styles:

1. Highlight the text you want to modify. Select Character from the Format menu.

2. To apply bold, italic, or both, click on the down arrow by Font Style and select the desired style. The Sample window displays the selected style.

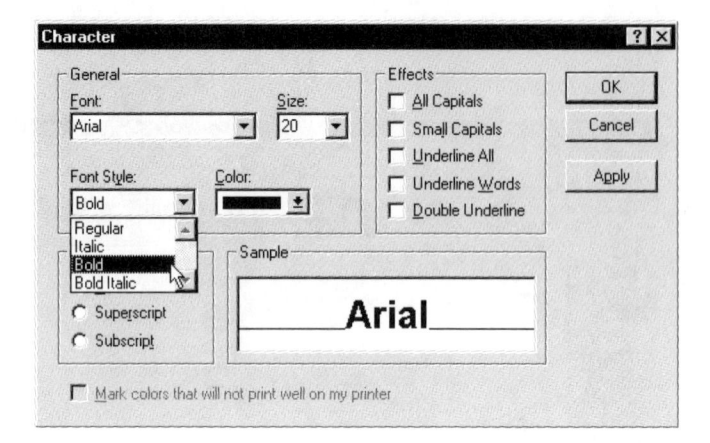

3. Click on the Superscript or Subscript option in the Super/Subscript section of the dialog box to apply this formatting to the text.

4. In the Effects section, click on the check box by the desired type style. (Only one type of underlining can be selected at a time.) If you change your mind about a style in the Effects section, click on the check box again to remove the check mark.

5. When finished, click on the OK button to apply the text styles.

Style Name	Example	Keyboard Shortcut
Bold	This is **bold**	CTRL-B
Italic	This is *italic*	CTRL-I
Superscript	This is ^{superscript}	
Subscript	This is $_{subscript}$	
All Capitals	THIS IS ALL CAPITALS	
Small Capitals	THIS IS SMALL CAPITALS	CTRL-SHIFT-K
Underline All	This is underline	CTRL-U
Underline Words	This is word underline	
Double Underline	This is double underline	

Type Styles in Publisher

TABLE 8-3

Bold, italic, and small capitals can also be applied with tools on the Formatting toolbar, as shown here:

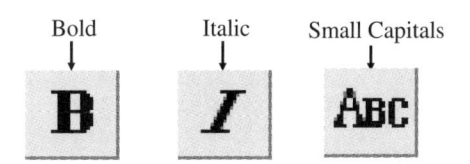

After highlighting text, simply click the mouse on the desired tool. The tool appears to be pushed in. To remove the type style, highlight the text again, and click again to deselect the tool.

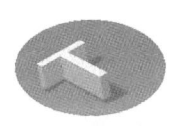

TIP: *Avoid underlining headings. Underlines separate the heading from the text it's supposed to introduce.*

Adding Color to Text

When budget allows, more and more people are incorporating color into their publications. Color catches the reader's eye, drawing him or her into the page. When producing a sales brochure, you might add color to the company name and other title text. When creating overheads, you can use color to draw attention to bulleted text. Be careful when adding color to text; light colors on a light background make text impossible to read. In addition, adding color to small text, such as 12-point text, makes the text harder to read.

NOTE: *As discussed in Chapter 7, you can add color to frame backgrounds. Be careful when coloring text and the frame background. For instance, yellow text on a red background would not be readable. For the most part, it's probably best to place text, whether black or another color, against a white background.*

Use the following steps to add color to text in a publication:

1. Highlight the text you want to color. Choose Character from the Format menu.

2. Click on the Color down arrow and select the desired color. You can click on More Colors to view additional colors and a color spectrum, and click

on Patterns & Shading to apply a tint or shade of a color to text. (Refer to the section "Adding Color to Frames" in Chapter 7 for more information on working with color spectrums, tints, and shades.)

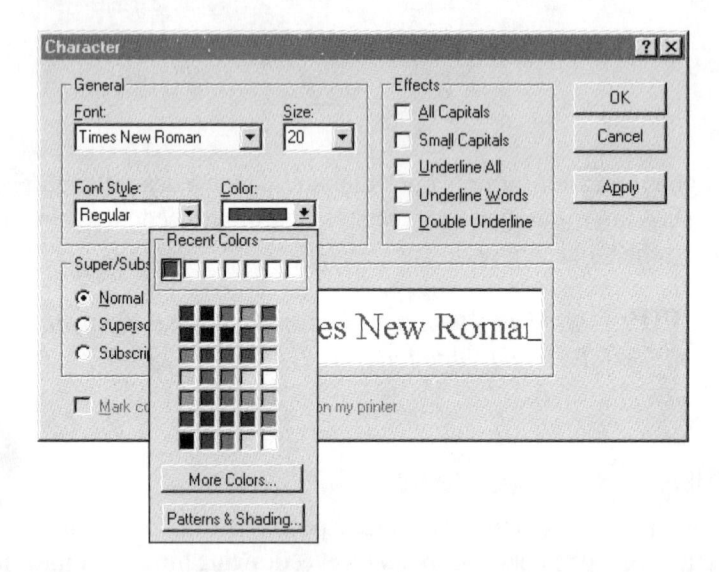

3. The sample text is displayed in the selected color. Click OK to apply the color.

You can also apply color to text by clicking on the Font Color tool in the Formatting toolbar. As displayed in Figure 8-6, the most recently used colors appear at the top of the drop-down menu when the Font Color tool is selected.

NOTE: *You cannot apply patterns or gradients to text. Refer to Chapter 7 for information on applying patterns and gradients to frames.*

Aligning Paragraphs

Publisher enables you to control the horizontal alignment of paragraphs. In Figure 8-7, the first paragraph is left-aligned, the second is centered, the third is right-aligned, and the fourth is justified. (*Justified* means both the left and right sides of the text are aligned—as in newspapers.) Generally, body text is left-aligned, while titles and other headings may be centered. By default, Publisher left-aligns text.

Font Color

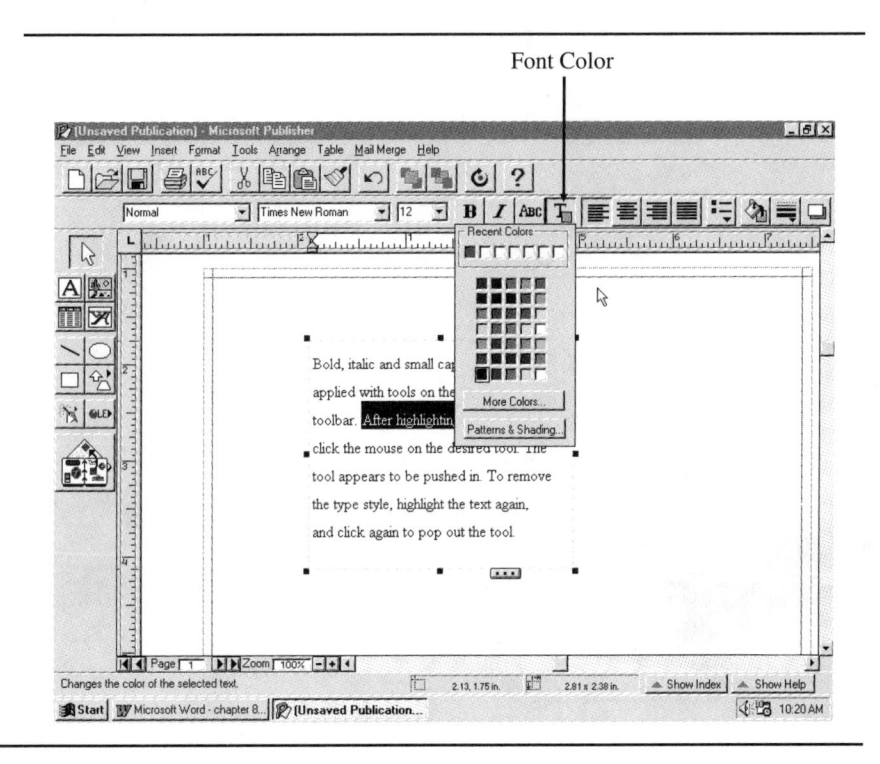

Use the Font Color tool to quickly apply color to highlighted text

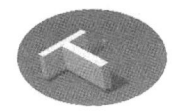
FIGURE 8-6

8

NOTE: *A paragraph is defined by where you press ENTER. For example, when you press ENTER, everything you type until you press ENTER again is a single paragraph. Paragraphs range in size from a single character to many sentences.*

To change the alignment of a paragraph, click to place the insertion point in the paragraph you want to align. You do not need to highlight the entire paragraph. Now click on the Left, Center, Right, or Justified tool in the Formatting toolbar to apply the desired alignment.

TIP: *As discussed in Chapter 3, studies indicate left-aligned paragraphs provide the best readability. Justified text is considered harder to read because more words are hyphenated and large gaps can appear between the words.*

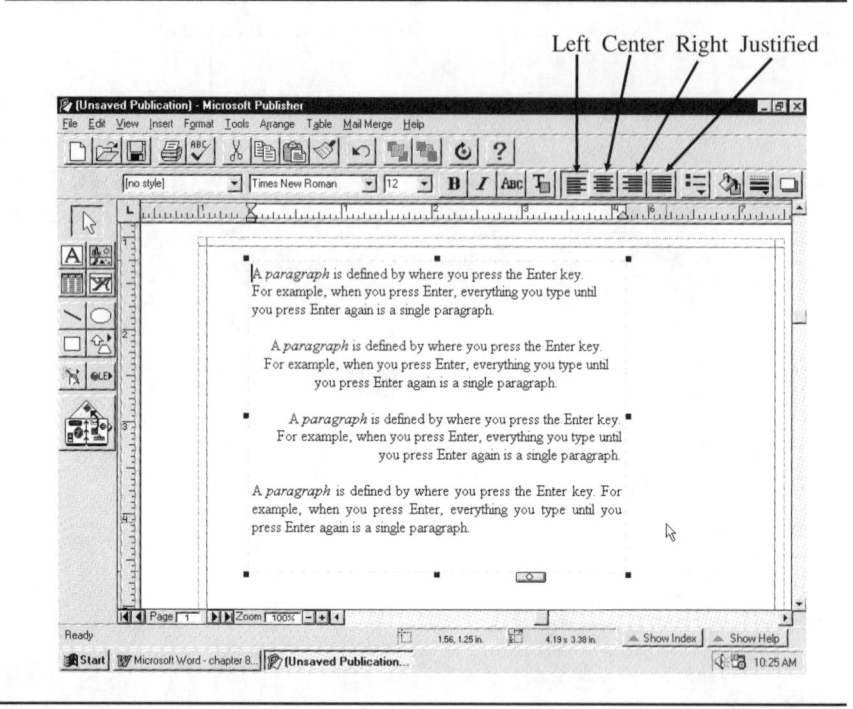

Left Center Right Justified

Paragraphs can be left-aligned, centered, right-aligned, or justified

FIGURE 8-7

Adding Columns to Text Frames

Adding columns to text frames is a great way to enhance the look of a page design. The columns control the flow of text in the frame. By default, text frames are set up for a one-column layout. You can design individual column layouts for each text frame as shown in Figure 8-8. One article is placed in a frame set up for two columns; the other article appears in a frame set up for three columns. Setting different columns for each text frame is great when you're designing newsletters.

With Publisher, you control the number of columns as well as the spacing between the columns. Keep in mind that the more columns you specify, the narrower each column of text appears. Flowing text into extra-narrow columns forces the reader's eye to jump from line to line. Stick with two, three, or four columns for best results.

Use the following steps to add columns to text frames:

1. Select the text frame where you want to add columns, and choose Text Frame Properties from the Format menu.

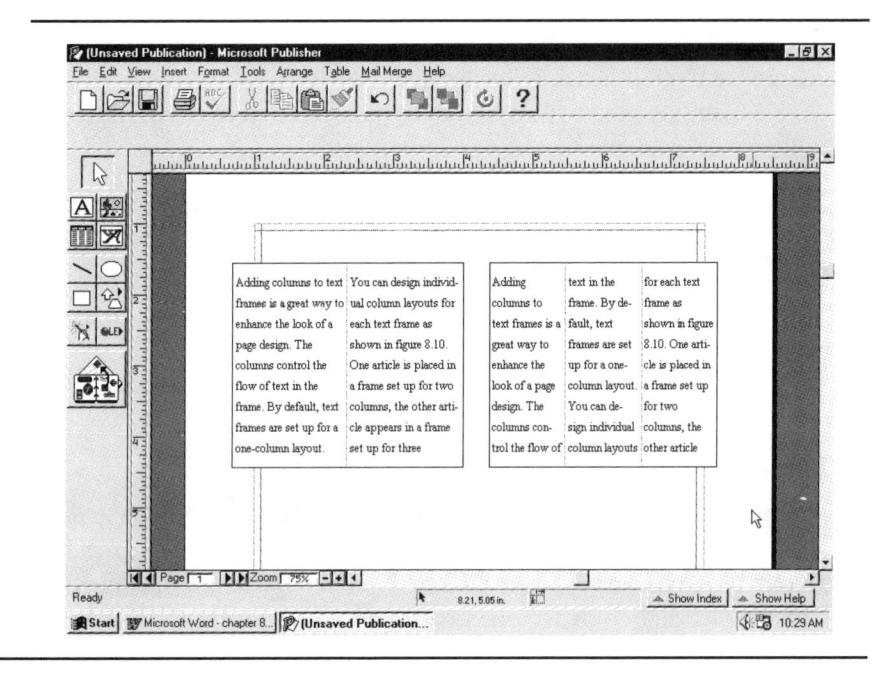

You can apply columns to text frames to control the flow of text

FIGURE 8-8

2. In the Text Frame Properties dialog box, enter the desired number of columns in the Number box.

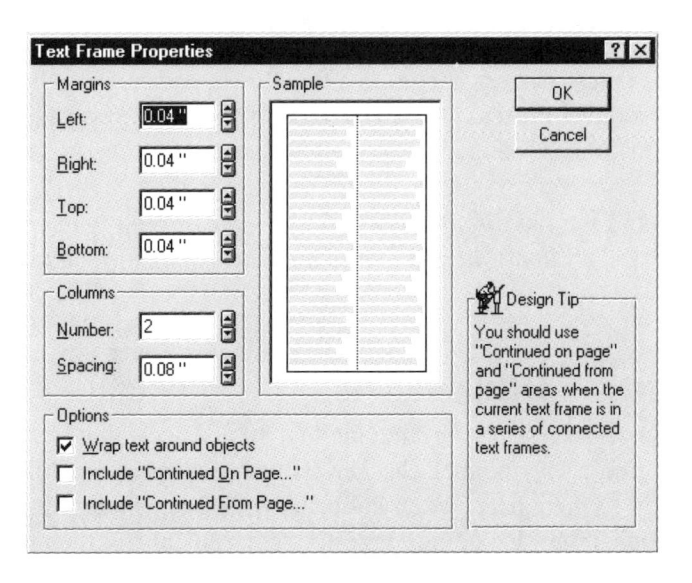

3. Publisher puts 0.08 inch as the default spacing between columns. Enter a new amount if desired. Spacing between columns is often called a *gutter.* Keep in mind that with a two-column layout, there is one gutter; with a three-column layout, there are two gutters; and so on.

4. A preview of the selected number of columns appears. Click OK.

Nonprinting lines indicating the columns appear in the frame. If text was already in the frame, it is wrapped in the columns. New text entered in the frame will be placed in the columns.

Using the Format Painter with Text

In Chapter 7, you learned how to use the Format Painter (on the Standard toolbar) to copy formatting from frame to frame. The Format Painter also is great for applying formatting from one set of text to another. For example, after selecting the typeface, size, type style, and color for one heading, you could use the Format Painter to quickly apply the same formatting to another heading. This is much easier than formatting the headings one at a time.

The following steps illustrate use of the Format Painter with text:

1. Highlight the text with the formatting you want to copy, and click on the Format Painter tool in the Standard toolbar.

2. The mouse cursor changes to a Paintbrush cursor. Drag the Paintbrush cursor over the text where you want to apply the formatting. The formatting is "painted" onto the new text.

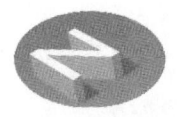 **NOTE:** *As discussed in Chapter 7, the Format Painter can also be used to quickly apply the formatting attributes of one frame to another.*

Using Spell Check

Publisher provides a spell-checking facility, Spell Check, that identifies misspelled words. When you start the spell checker, Publisher scans your publication to identify words not in its dictionary. When Publisher finds such a word, it provides a series of correction options, including suggested replacements for the misspelling.

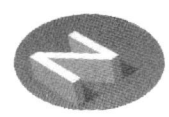

NOTE: *Always run Spell Check on your publications. Even if you're a great typist and an excellent speller, everyone makes mistakes. It's best to find those mistakes before others do.*

Publisher checks the spelling in text and table frames. You can spell-check a single text frame, or all text and table frames in a publication.

CAUTION: *Publisher does not check the spelling of text in WordArt frames.*

Publisher will not recognize many last names, company names, technical terms, and locale names. To prevent these from constantly being found during a spell check, you can add them to Publisher's dictionary. (Adding items to the dictionary is discussed next in the steps for running a spell check.)

Use the following steps to spell-check a publication:

1. Select the text or table frame you want to spell-check.

2. Choose Check Spelling from the Tools menu, or click on the Spelling tool in the Standard toolbar.

3. If nothing is misspelled, no dialog box appears. If Publisher does find a misspelling, the Check Spelling dialog box appears.

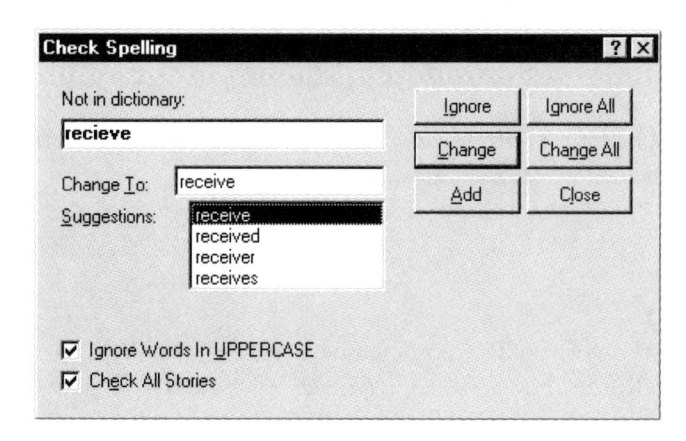

4. When a word is found that Publisher does not recognize, it is displayed in the Not In Dictionary box on the left. If available, suggested spellings appear. You have several options:

- Select the correct spelling and click the Change button to place the correct spelling in your publication. To change any additional occurrences of the same word, click the Change All button.

- If none of the suggested spellings are correct, you can type the correct spelling in the Change To box and click Change or Change All.

- When Publisher stops at a word that you want to leave as is, click the Ignore button. Click the Ignore All button to ignore the word throughout the publication.

- Click the Add button to add the word to Publisher's dictionary. Once added, the word will no longer be found during spell checks.

5. After checking the selected text frame, Publisher asks if you want the rest of the publication checked. Click Yes to check the spelling in other text and table frames, click No to cancel the spell check.

6. When the check is finished, the Check Spelling dialog box automatically closes. You can also click on the Close button to stop the spell check.

Turn on the Ignore Words In Uppercase option to have the spell check ignore words appearing in all capital letters. For instance, an organization might enter acronyms related to their business in all capitals. Turning this option on tells Publisher to ignore these words.

 **NOTE:** *Publisher does not check for irregular capitalization and repeated words as some applications do.*

Summary

Formatting text is one of the most creative aspects of producing publications. In this chapter you learned how to select typefaces, sizes, and type styles, as well as other features for controlling the look of text. With the text looking good, you're ready to begin working with the pictures on your pages. Chapter 9 examines features such as selecting clip art and using Publisher's Design Gallery.

Adding Pictures to Publications

A publication gains instant visual impact with the use of pictures. Effectively used pictures favorably predispose people to accept your product, service, or point of view. Pictures combined with well-designed pages create positive first impressions that can greatly affect how you or your organization is perceived.

This chapter begins with a look at different types of visual material that can be placed in a Publisher publication. An overview of bitmapped and vector graphics is also provided. Next, the chapter examines placing clip art and photographs from Publisher's Clip Gallery into frames. As discussed in this chapter, you can modify clip art by changing the colors and cropping any unnecessary parts of the image. Inserting pictures and graphics from other applications is discussed, including a list of file formats accepted by Publisher. The chapter ends with a look at using the Design Gallery for special text and graphic effects.

Defining Pictures

Picture is the word Publisher uses to describe the visual elements that can be added to publications. A better word would be *graphic*. To many graphic designers, "picture" means a photograph; whereas "graphic" means drawings, logos, clip art, charts, and more. In this chapter, graphic is used unless a more specific term such as "photograph" or "chart" applies. The word "picture" is often used in the instructions, such as when Publisher uses "picture" in the menu commands or tool name.

Graphics: A Smorgasbord of Choices

Graphics enhance the look of a publication. Selecting the right graphics to appear in your publication is one of the most important aspects of publication design. Consider the many types of graphics that are available. Obviously, photographs are one of the most compelling, eye-catching visual elements you can add to a page.

Illustrations and drawings created in graphic software applications such as CorelDRAW can be placed in publications. You can design the graphic yourself, or use the clip art included with the software. Graphic applications enable you to create logos, which can be placed in business cards and brochures. You can create diagrams of equipment and floor plans for placement in technical manuals. Maps, depicting everything from oil wells to store locations, can be placed in marketing and sales reports to improve the attractiveness and clarity of the publications.

9

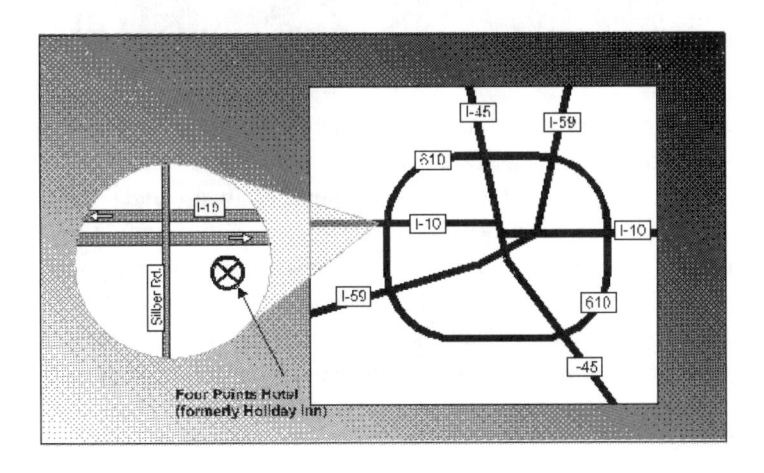

 **NOTE:** *Publisher includes several tools for drawing basic shapes such as circles, lines, and squares. Refer to Chapter 11 for more information.*

Bar, line, and pie charts created in applications such as Microsoft PowerPoint are another popular form of graphic. Charts quickly communicate comparisons, relationships, and trends. Organization charts depicting "who reports to whom" are important in internal publications such as departmental newsletters. Flowcharts display a sequence of events—what is done first, what is done second, and so on.

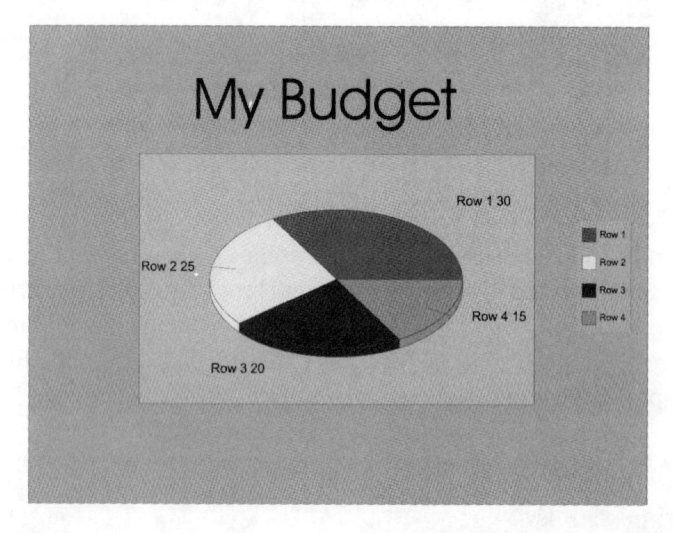

As discussed in Chapter 3, consider the relevancy of a graphic before placing it in a publication. Keep digging to find the right graphic. You can buy Photo CDs and clip-art packages in stores specializing in computer hardware and software. Look in the phone book under "Photographs" to locate companies that sell stock photographs. If you're on the Internet, there are several FTP and gopher sites you can visit to download photographs. Check out one of the Internet "yellow pages" books for URL information. You can also do a search for "clip art" in a search engine such as Yahoo! (www.yahoo.com) or AltaVista (www.altavista.com). You might discover some interesting sources of graphics.

Understanding Bitmapped and Vector Graphics

All graphic images fall into one of two basic categories: bitmapped or vector. *Bitmapped* graphics are composed of dots that are arranged in a specific order to create the image. The key in Figure 9-1 is a bitmapped drawing. When the image is small, the dots defining the image are undetectable. When the image is enlarged, however, the dots that compose the image can be seen. Images created in applications such as Photoshop and Windows Paintbrush are bitmapped images. In addition, you are creating bitmapped images when you scan artwork or photographs. As a general rule, bitmapped graphics do not size well. The quality of the image will suffer if you enlarge or reduce the bitmap graphics. You may be able to enlarge or reduce the image slightly without much quality loss, but any major resizing will make a noticeable difference in how your bitmaps look.

NOTE: *Table 9-1 (in the section "Graphic File Formats Supported by Publisher" later in this chapter) lists the graphic file formats that can be placed in Publisher. The table also notes whether a file format is bitmapped or vector.*

Vector graphics are composed of lines and curves. When a vector graphic is resized, the lines and curves adjust, and the image remains smooth. Applications

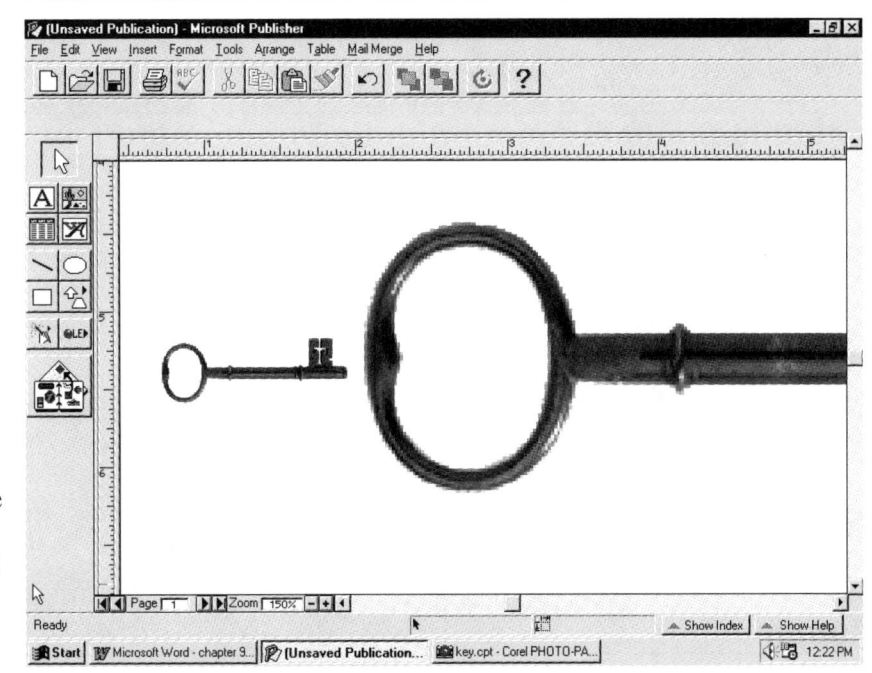

Bitmapped images are composed of dots. The image can be distorted when resized

FIGURE 9-1

such as CorelDRAW, PowerPoint, Illustrator, and Freehand create vector graphics. In Figure 9-2, the Statue of Liberty is a vector graphic. When the graphic is enlarged, the lines remain clean and smooth.

Because you can adjust the size of vector graphics without the image deteriorating, they are the optimal option for illustrations that will be placed in Publisher. When shopping for clip art or hiring a professional artist to design graphics, make sure the graphics are in the vector format. Although vector graphics are more flexible, there are times when you will need to use bitmapped graphics. Remember, for instance, that photographs are bitmapped.

Working with Picture Frames

Publisher uses picture frames to position graphics on a page. As discussed in Chapter 7, these frames can be moved, sized, and rotated. Each picture frame can be

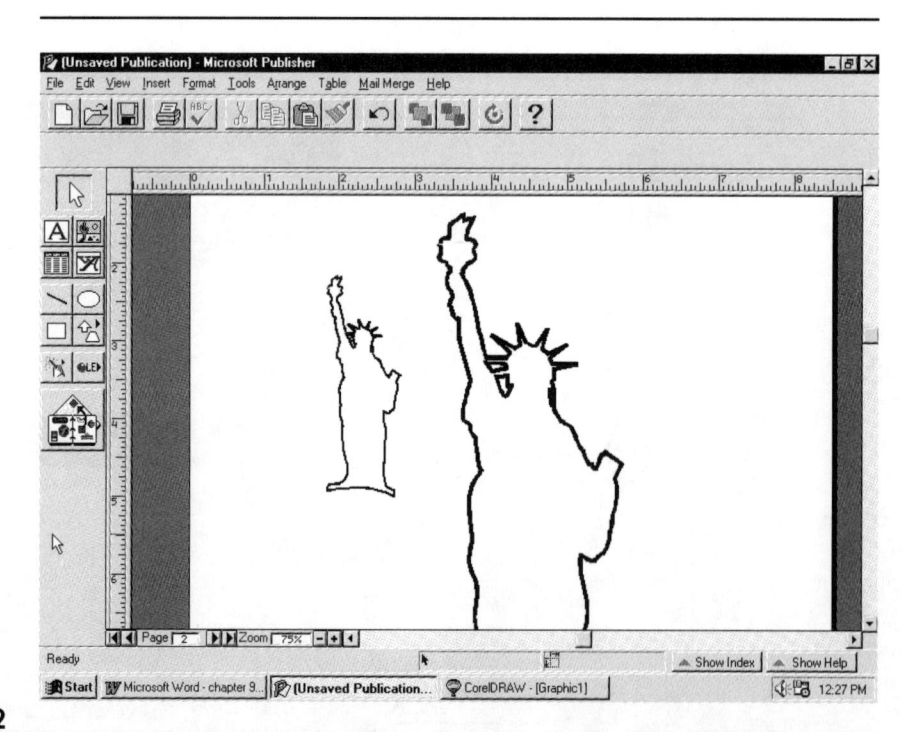

You can resize vector graphics without distorting the image

FIGURE 9-2

formatted to display different margins, colors, and borders. Frames can be formatted before or after placing graphics in the frame.

When you need to move a graphic from one page to another, or copy a graphic to several pages, use the steps in Chapter 7 for moving and copying frames. Graphics placed in picture frames are automatically moved and copied with the picture frame.

When you use PageWizards to build publications, picture frames are already positioned on the page, with clip-art drawings or photographs in place. Of course, you can select new clip art if desired. When you draw picture frames on the page yourself, the frames are empty until you insert a graphic.

Working with Publisher Clip Art

Clip art is predesigned artwork. There is clip art for everything from computers to food to airplanes to state maps. Clip art can enhance the appeal of a publication as well as help to communicate a message. When you can't draw and don't want to hire someone to draw for you, clip art is a real lifesaver.

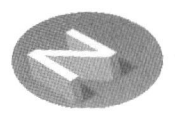 **NOTE:** *The term "clip art" comes from the large books full of predesigned artwork that artists used to have to clip out with scissors. Now clip art comes on computer disks, so no more clipping is required.*

Publisher provides an extensive selection of drawings, photographs, sounds, and video clips. Publisher uses the Clip Gallery to display the available clip art. More clip art can be located through a web site set up specifically for Microsoft Publisher users. This is covered later in this chapter in the section "Using Clip Gallery Live."

The style of clip art you choose says a lot about a publication. Cartoonish drawings (as shown on the left here) lend a casual feel best used in picnic flyers and party invitations. Less animated, more realistic drawings (as shown on the right here) characterize a formal look good for financial and marketing reports.

Working with Frame Sizes and Clip-Art Proportions

When you place a graphic in a frame, the size of the frame determines the size of the graphic—the larger the frame, the larger the graphic. However, the *proportion* of the picture frame may not match the proportion of the graphic. For instance, a wide graphic may not fit well in a narrow frame. When you are placing a graphic in a frame, Publisher asks if the frame should adjust to the proportions of the graphic, or if the graphic should be adjusted to meet the dimensions of the frame. In most cases, you want the frame to adjust to the proportion of the incoming graphic. In the left frame in Figure 9-3, the frame was adjusted to fit the new graphic. In the second frame, the graphic was adjusted to fit the frame. You can see how this distorted the original shape and proportion of the graphic.

You can control whether the frame adjusts to the proportions of the new graphic, or the graphic adjusts to the frame's proportions

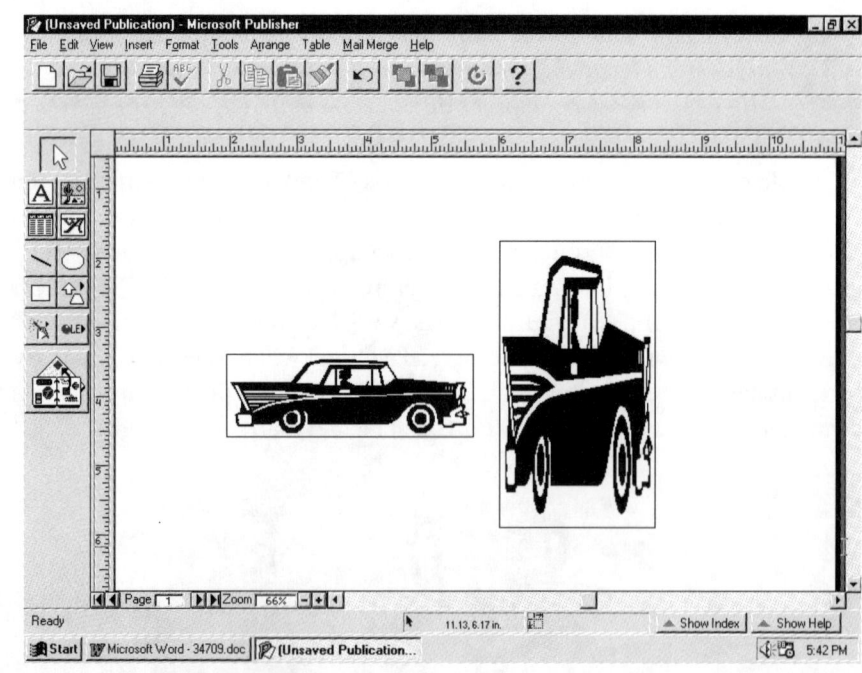

FIGURE 9-3

Placing Clip Art into Frames

When PageWizards are used to build publications, picture frames display sample clip-art images. These can be replaced with clip art of your choice. If you draw the picture frames yourself, they will be empty until you insert a clip-art image. Publisher uses the Clip Gallery to display available clip-art images. Publisher loads some of the clip art on your hard drive during installation. However, more clip art can be found on the Publisher CD. For access to all of the clip art displayed in the Clip Gallery, insert the Publisher CD into the CD-ROM drive before placing clip art.

Use the following steps to place clip art from the Clip Gallery:

1. If the picture frame already contains a clip-art image, double-click on it. If the picture frame is empty, click once on it and then choose Clip Art from the Insert menu. The Clip Gallery dialog box is displayed, as shown in Figure 9-4. At the top, click on the Clip Art tab to view clip-art drawings, or click on the Pictures tab to view photographs.

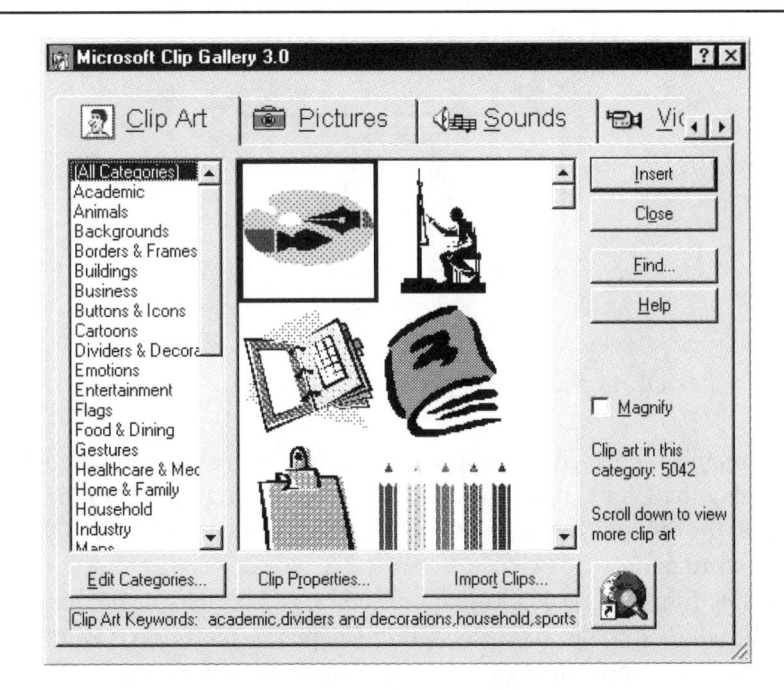

The Clip Gallery

FIGURE 9-4

 **NOTE:** *In the Clip Gallery, click on the Sounds or Video tab to insert sound files or video clips. Check out Chapter 14 for more information on adding sound and video to Publisher documents.*

2. Clip Art and Pictures are organized into categories. Click on a category name to display images relating to that topic. You may have to scroll to view all of the images.

3. Click on the desired clip art. For an enlarged view of the selected image, click on the Magnify check box on the right side of the dialog box.

4. Click on the Insert button. The Import Picture dialog box appears, shown here, asking if you want to adjust the size of the frame to match the proportions of the clip art, or to adjust the clip art to match the frame size. As discussed, to prevent distorting clip art, select the first option to adjust the frame to the proportions of the clip art.

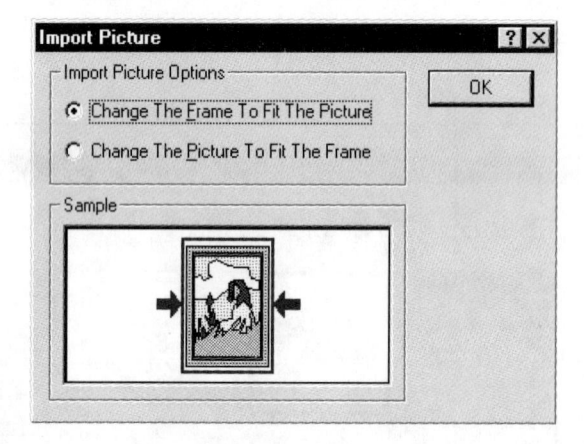

5. Click OK to place the clip art on the page.

Remember, once clip art appears in a frame, you can simply double-click on it to display the Clip Gallery. You can add your own graphics to the Clip Gallery. Refer to the section "Importing Clips into the Clip Gallery" later in this chapter for more information.

Frame formatting, such as margins, color, and borders, is not altered when you add clip art to a frame. As discussed in Chapter 7, the Format Painter can also be used to quickly apply the formatting attributes of one frame to another.

Working with Clip Properties

After selecting an image in the Clip Gallery, click on the Clip Properties button to display the filename, file type, and file size of the clip art. The Clip Properties dialog box, shown in Figure 9-5, also displays the drive and folders where the clip-art file and the file containing the preview of the clip art are located.

Working with Keywords

Clip properties also include *keywords*. A keyword is a descriptive term that helps you locate a specific clip in the Clip Gallery. For example, suppose you were looking for an alarm clock. You could use "alarm clock" as a keyword for locating all of the alarm clocks in the Clip Gallery. Although you won't know every keyword, you can enter basic words, such as "transportation," "people," "football," and "flags." Keywords are assigned to clips in the gallery, either by Publisher or by you as you add new clips to the gallery. Each clip can have one or more keywords, or none.

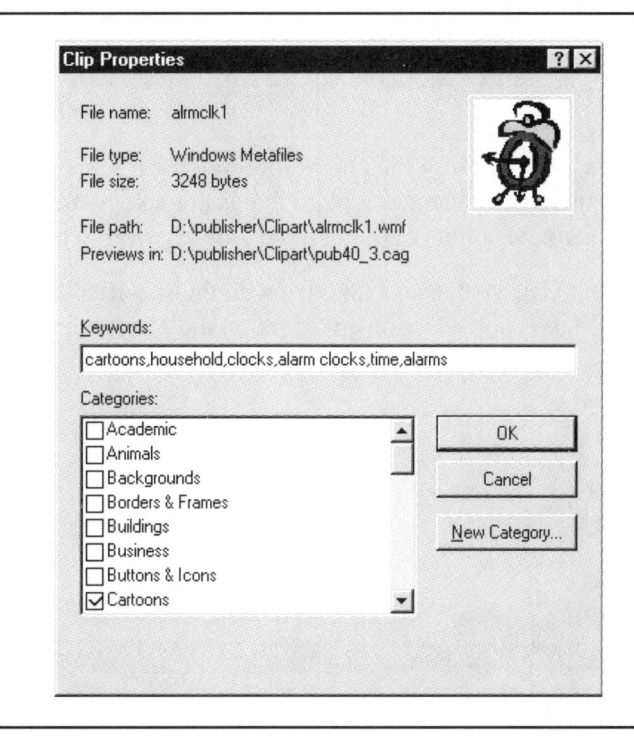

Use the
Clip
Properties
dialog
box to
determine
the size and
location of
the selected
clip art

FIGURE 9-5

The following steps illustrate searching for clip art by use of a keyword:

1. Click on the Find button in the Clip Gallery dialog box to display the Find Clip dialog box.

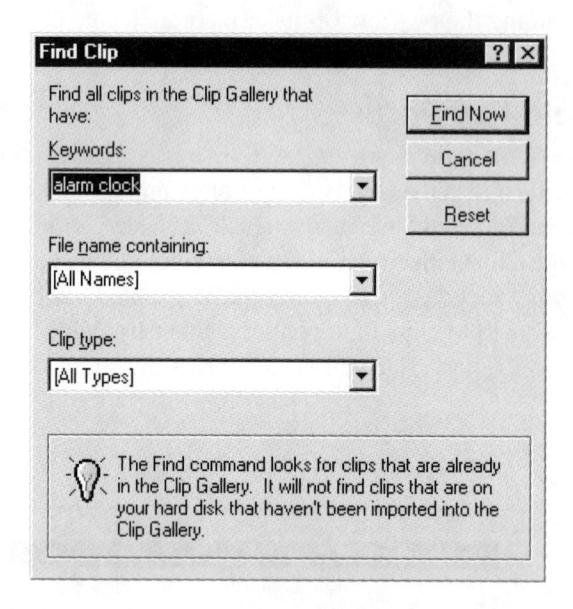

2. Type in a keyword for the clip you're looking for, and click on the Find Now button. (If you enter a word that is not a keyword for any clip art, Publisher tells you it could not match the keyword with a clip.)

3. The Clip Gallery displays all clips with the specified keyword assigned to them. Make your selection and click on the Insert button.

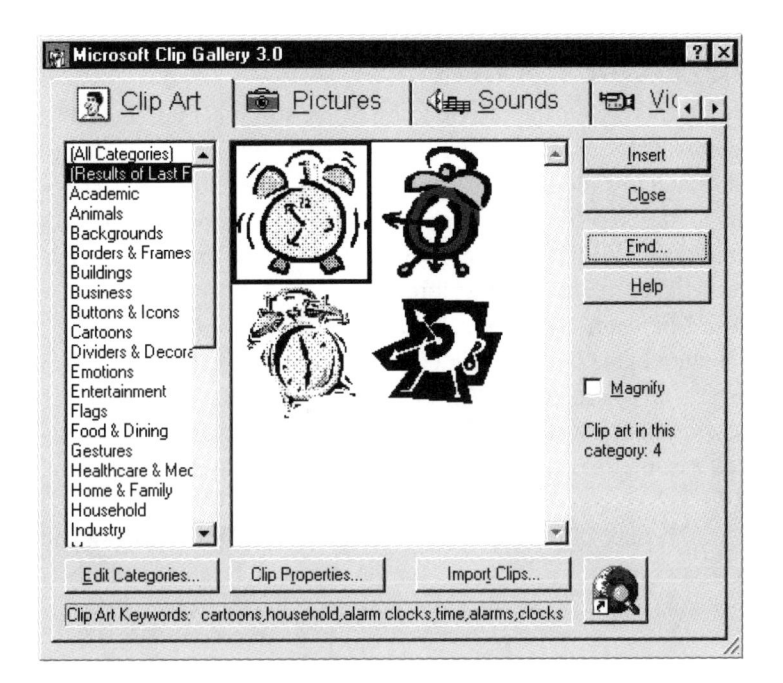

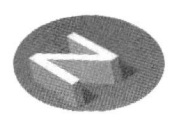

NOTE: *You can also see the keywords for a particular clip, by selecting it and referring to the bottom of the Clip Gallery window.*

You can change keywords or add your own by clicking on the Clip Properties button and editing the information in the Keywords box. This would come in handy if you plan on using several pieces of clip art frequently. For example, you could add the keyword "my favorites" to each frequently used piece of clip art. When it came time to select one of your favorites, you would simply enter the keyword "my favorites" in the Find Clip dialog box to quickly display the preferred clip art.

9

Using Clip Gallery Live

Clip Gallery Live is a web site provided by Microsoft that contains additional clips you can preview and download. If you download a clip file, it is added to your hard disk and automatically added to the Clip Gallery. To use Clip Gallery Live, you must have access to the World Wide Web (for example, through a provider such as Microsoft Network, Prodigy, or CompuServe) and a web browser (such as Netscape Navigator or Microsoft Internet Explorer).

If you use Microsoft Network as your Internet service provider, you can simply click on the button in the bottom right corner of the Clip Gallery (it looks like a world map). This starts up Microsoft Network and takes you to the Microsoft web site.

If you use another service provider, such as CompuServe or Prodigy, enter the URL http://www.microsoft.com/clipgallerylive to display the web page, as shown in Figure 9-6.

Once you're connected to Clip Gallery Live, you can find, preview, and download clips, as shown in Figure 9-7. Previews for the clips will be automatically added to the Clip Gallery.

Log onto the World Wide Web to access all kinds of clip art through Microsoft's Clip Gallery Live

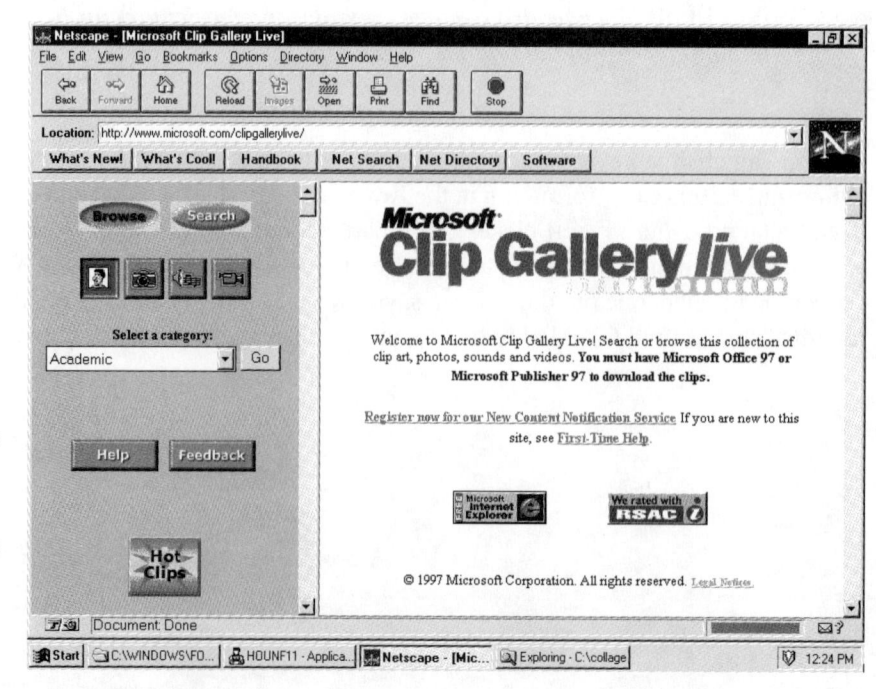

FIGURE 9-6

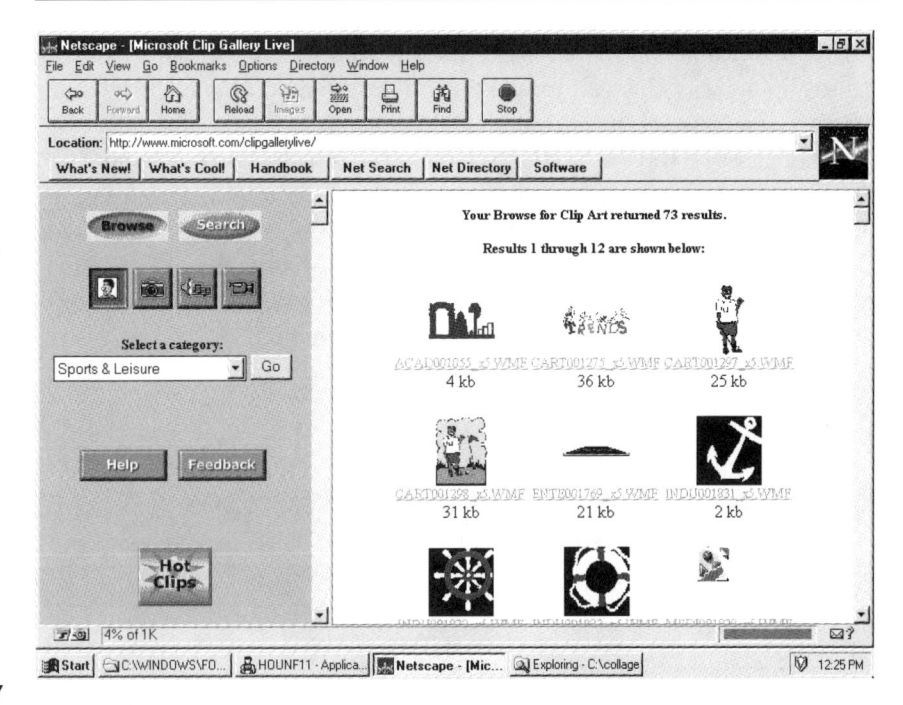

Clip Gallery Live lets you easily find, preview, and download clip art

FIGURE 9-7

NOTE: *Microsoft web pages are constantly being changed and updated, so you may find the web page looks different when you log on.*

Recoloring Graphics

The colors in clip art and other graphics can be replaced with colors that better fit the needs of your publication. For instance, a clip art's colors may not work with your color scheme—you are using mostly blue and green, and the clip art is full of orange and yellow. Or, several colors appear in the clip art, but you're limited to one spot color and black. Graphics created in other drawing applications such as CorelDRAW can also be recolored.

NOTE: *As discussed in Chapter 7, you can add color to frame backgrounds. Make sure the color used in the frame background works with the colors in the graphic. If you're not sure, stick with a white background for the graphic.*

Recoloring clip art enables you to create special looks. The image on the left in Figure 9-8 displays how one piece of clip art appears without modification. The same clip art was changed to white and the frame color was changed to black to create a new look for the clip art.

There are two ways to recolor graphics. The first method is a feature in Publisher; the second method requires you to use another program, Microsoft Draw. Both are discussed in the following sections. Changing colors in photographs is a much more complicated task. It can be done by use of photo-manipulation or bitmap-editing applications, such as Adobe Photoshop and Microsoft Paint. Refer to the documentation in these programs for more information.

Recoloring Graphics in Publisher

You can recolor graphics in Publisher. However, with this option, all of the colors in the graphic are changed to shades of one color. For instance, suppose you have a clip-art image that uses red, blue, and yellow. If you recolor the image in Publisher,

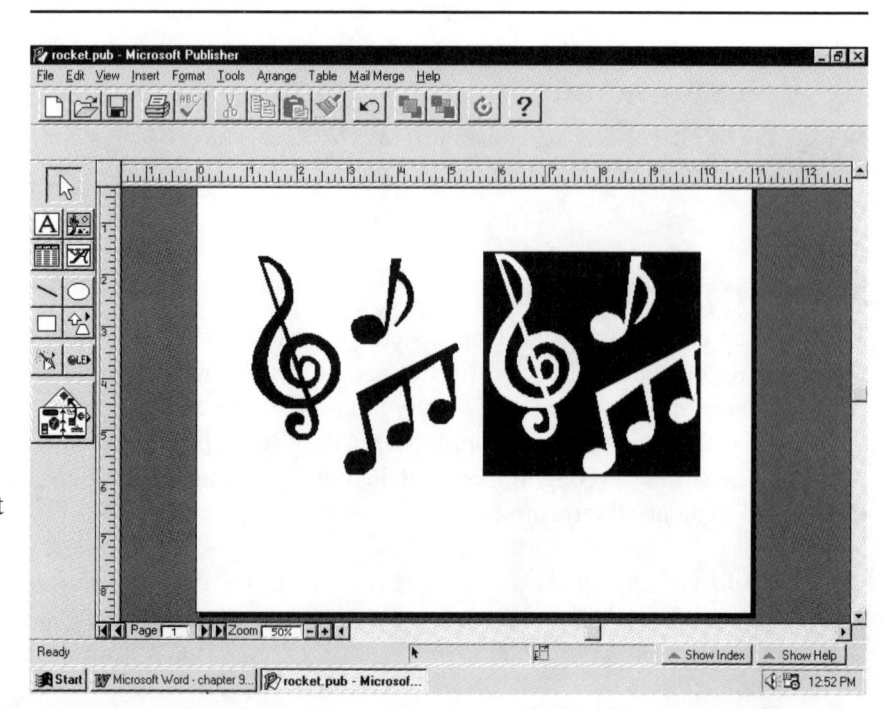

Experiment with colors in clip art to create interesting looks

FIGURE 9-8

the red, blue, and yellow are all replaced by shades of the new color you select. If you selected green, then the red, blue, and yellow are replaced with shades of green.

Use the following steps to recolor graphics in Publisher:

1. Select the picture frame containing the graphic you want to recolor.

2. From the Format menu, choose Recolor Object. The Recolor Object dialog box appears.

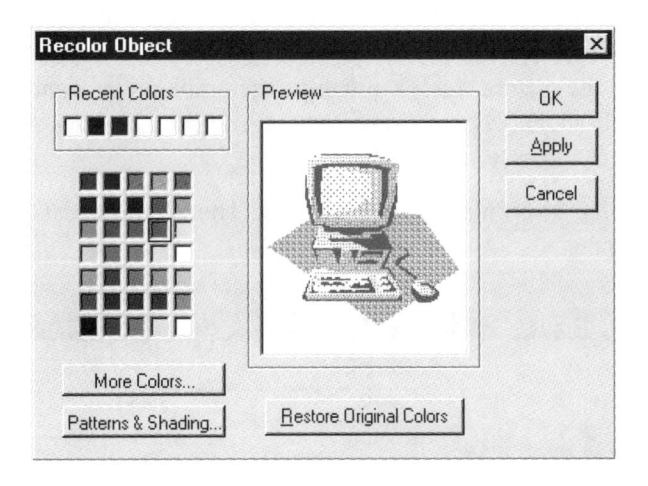

3. From the color palette on the left, click on the color you want used in the graphic. A preview of the graphic with the new color appears. Keep clicking on colors until you find the desired color. Click on More Colors to display a larger color palette.

4. You can click on the Restore Original Colors button whenever you wish to return to the original colors in the graphic.

5. Click OK to apply the change to the graphic on the page.

Changing all of the colors to one color is great when you are using one spot color in the design of the publication. A colorful graphic image can quickly be changed to shades of your spot color with this command.

Recoloring Graphics with Microsoft Draw

Microsoft Draw is a drawing program that comes with Publisher and is installed along with it. Use Microsoft Draw when you want to recolor graphics using more than one color. After you change the colors, the graphic with the new colors is placed back into your publication. This is great when you are printing from a color desktop printer or using a full-color printing process from an outside service.

 **NOTE:** *You can also import Publisher's clip art into other graphics applications, such as CorelDRAW, and change the colors there.*

Use the following steps to recolor graphics using more than one color:

1. Select the picture frame containing the graphic you want to recolor. From the Edit menu, choose Copy Picture. You can also click on the Copy tool in the Standard toolbar.

2. From the Insert menu, choose Object. The Insert Object dialog box appears.

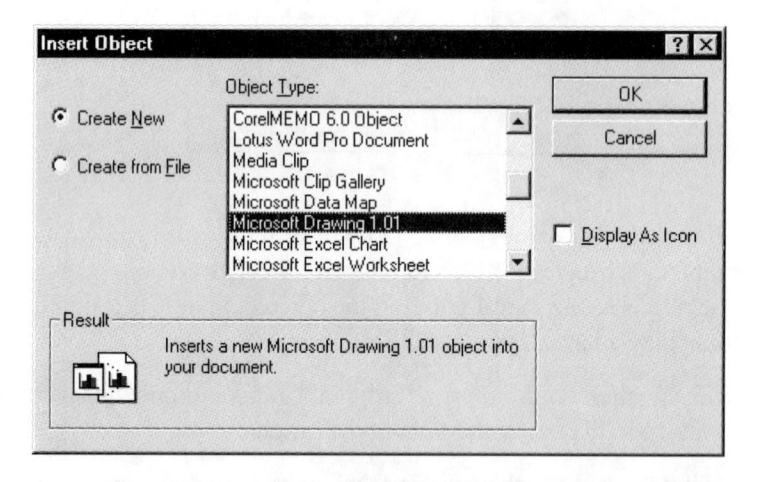

3. Make sure Create New is selected on the left. In the Object Type box, select Microsoft Draw 1.01 and click OK.

4. After a few seconds, the Microsoft Draw application is displayed. From the Edit menu (in Microsoft Draw), choose Paste to paste the graphic from Publisher in the drawing window.

5. To work with Microsoft Draw, select a portion of the graphic by clicking on it, and then choose a new color from the Fill color palette at the bottom of the screen. Refer to Microsoft Draw's online help for more information.

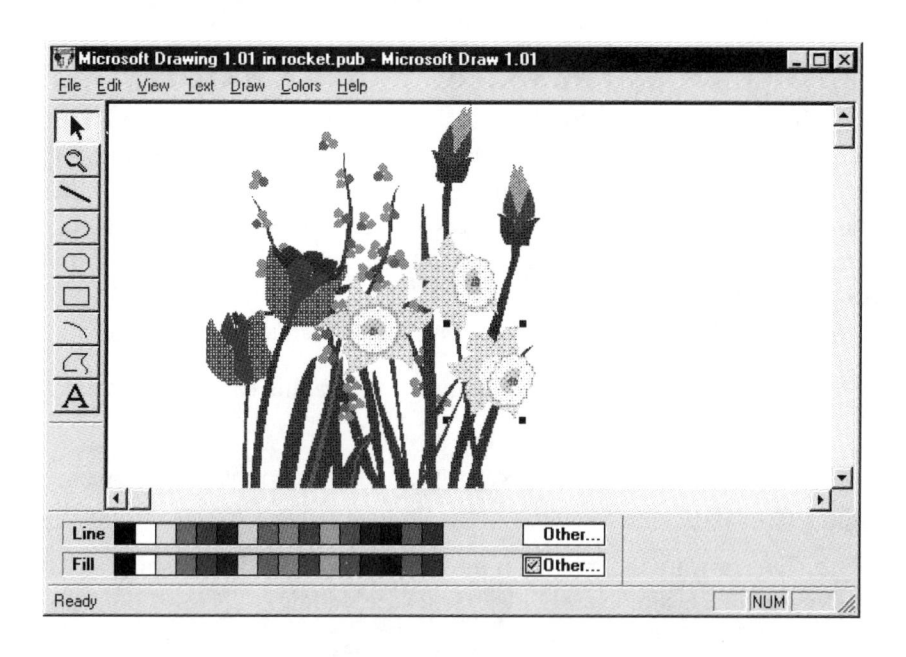

6. When finished, select Exit And Return from the File menu (in Microsoft Draw). A message appears asking if you want to save the changes made to the graphic in Publisher. Click Yes.

7. Microsoft Draw is closed and the newly recolored graphic appears on the page.

After a graphic is recolored with Microsoft Draw, it becomes a Microsoft Draw embedded object. This means if you double-click on the graphic, Microsoft Draw is automatically started.

NOTE: *The applications listed in the Insert Object dialog box all support object linking and embedding (OLE). Chapter 1 provides a brief overview of OLE. You can also refer to your Windows 95 documentation for more information. Which application names appear depends on the applications loaded on your computer.*

Cropping Graphics and Photographs

Sometimes clip art or photographs include elements you don't need. For instance, a clip art drawing might include a cat and a dog. If you want only the dog, you can *crop* or hide the portion with the cat. Cropping can be especially handy with photographs, since many photographers have a tendency to get too much extraneous detail in a shot. In Figure 9-9, the second photograph was cropped to show only two people talking instead of four.

Use the following steps to crop a graphic or scanned photograph:

1. Select the picture frame containing the graphic (photographs included) you want to crop.

2. Click on the Crop Picture tool in the Formatting toolbar. Place the mouse cursor over one of the selection handles—the mouse cursor becomes to a cropping icon.

3. Drag toward the middle of the image to crop it. To redisplay a portion of the image, simply drag away from the middle.

4. When finished, click on the Crop Picture tool again.

Cropping tool

Cropping can help you add emphasis to photos by removing unnecessary elements

FIGURE 9-9

When cropping, you don't lose the parts you've cropped out, you simply hide them. You can redisplay the parts that were hidden by uncropping the image. Besides clip art and other graphics, any type of scanned image can be cropped.

Working with Other Graphic Files

In addition to the clip art provided by Publisher, you can place scanned images and graphic files created in other applications in your publications. Drawing applications such as CorelDRAW are becoming more and more popular, and inserting graphics created in these programs can make your publication all the more appealing.

When you place a graphic in a publication, the graphic file becomes part of the Publisher file. For instance, if you add a photograph that has a file size of 4 megabytes, the Publisher publication file incorporates the photograph and is increased by 4 megabytes. It's important to realize that publication files with lots of graphics, especially photographs, get large quickly. Be aware that you might have to use file compression software (such as WinZip) or get a removable disk drive so you can transport the file to a printer or copying service.

Graphic File Formats Supported by Publisher

The graphics that can be placed in Publisher fall in the two categories discussed at the beginning of this chapter—bitmapped and vector. If you have a choice, vector graphics work better in publications, because they can be resized without compromising image quality. Vector graphics also tend to print better; you don't get the jagged edges associated with bitmapped graphics. Table 9-1 lists the graphic file formats recognized by Publisher.

When you scan a photograph or drawing, a bitmapped graphic generally is created in the .TIF file format. If you use an application not listed in Table 9-1, see if your application can save the graphic in one of the recognized file formats. For instance, files created in Freehand are not recognized by Publisher. However, in Freehand you can export the graphic to the .EPS format, which is recognized.

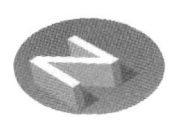 **NOTE:** *.GIF and .JPG files are used to develop web pages. Designing web pages is discussed in Chapter 15.*

Placing Graphics in Publications

It is important that, when placing graphics, you select the picture frame in which you want to load the graphic. If you do not select a frame, Publisher automatically

Graphic File Format	File Extension	Graphic Type
Computer Graphics Metafile	.CGM	Vector
CorelDRAW	.CDR	Vector
DrawPerfect	.WPG	Vector
Encapsulated Postscript	.EPS	Vector
Micrografx Designer/DRAW	.DRW	Vector
Windows Metafile	.WMF	Vector
Bitmap	.BMP	Bitmapped
Graphics Interchange Format	.GIF	Bitmapped
JPEG Picture Format	.JPG	Bitmapped
Kodak Photo CD	.PCD	Bitmapped
PC Paintbrush	.PCX	Bitmapped
Tagged Image Format	.TIF	Bitmapped

Graphic File Formats Recognized by Publisher

TABLE 9-1

creates one as it imports the graphic. The frame for the new graphic can be edited just like any other picture frame.

Use the following steps to place scanned images and graphics created in other applications in a publication:

1. Select the picture frame where you want to place the graphic.

2. From the Insert menu, choose Picture File. The Insert Picture File dialog box appears.

3. Change to the drive and folder where the graphic you want to place is located.

4. Click on the down arrow by Files Of Type to display a list of supported file formats. Select the format of graphic you are placing. For instance, choose CorelDRAW Picture to place a graphic created in CorelDRAW.

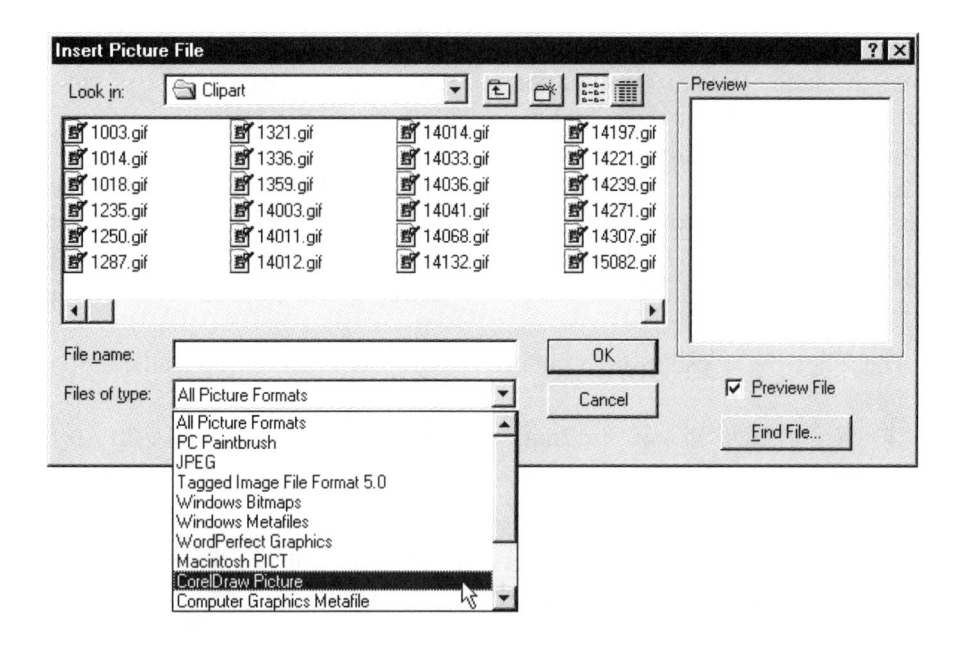

5. The files in the specified format appear in the File Name list box. Select the file you want. Turn on the Preview File option to preview a graphic before placing it on the page.

6. Click OK. The Import Picture dialog box appears. As discussed earlier, when you are placing clip art, the default option Change The Frame To Fit The Picture is usually the best choice. Click OK again to place the graphic.

When you are placing graphics, keep in mind that colors may look different once placed in Publisher. Text and graphic shapes appearing in a graphic cannot be edited in Publisher. For instance, you cannot change the typeface of text or the color of a square in a graphic. To alter the graphic, you need to return to the application used to create the graphic, make the changes, and then replace the graphic in Publisher.

Importing Clips into the Clip Gallery

Company logos and other graphics that you plan on using frequently can be added to the Clip Gallery. The main reason for adding clips to the Clip Gallery is to make them more accessible. As you scroll through the Gallery, you can see at a glance what's available. If you're looking for a specific clip-art image or type of clip art, you can zero in on it quickly by looking in a likely category. Or you can use the Find feature to search for a clip by keyword or filename.

The Clip Gallery supports vector file formats with the following filename extensions: .CGM, .WMF, .CDR, .EPS, .DRW, .WPG. The Clip Gallery supports bitmap file formats with the following filename extensions: .BMP, .TIF, .GIF, .JPG, .PCD, .PCX. Refer to Table 9-1 earlier in the chapter for more information about these file types.

The following steps illustrate importing a graphic into the Clip Gallery:

1. Double-click on a picture frame containing clip art, or choose Clip Art from the Insert menu. Click on the Clip Art tab to import a vector graphic; click on the Picture tab to import a bitmapped graphic.

2. At the bottom of the Clip Gallery, click Import Clips to display the Add Clip Art To Clip Gallery dialog box.

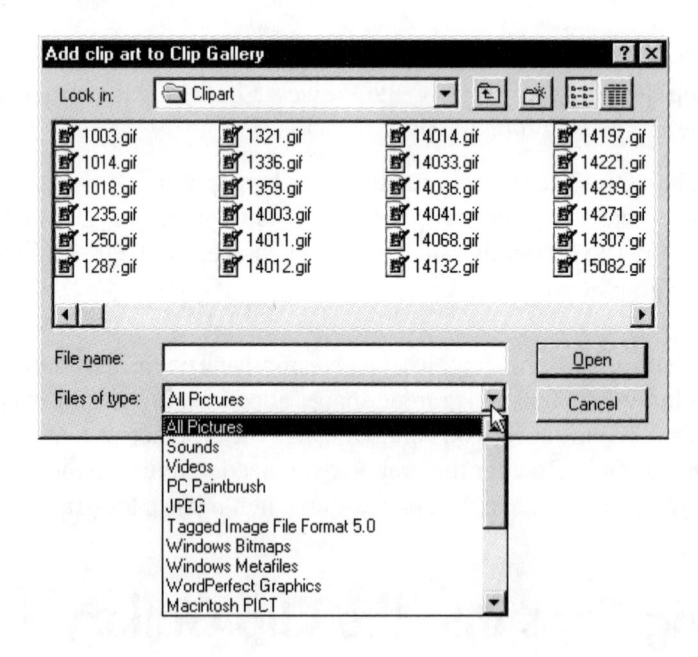

3. Change to the drive and folder where the graphic you want to place is located. Select the graphic file you want to place in the Gallery and click Open.

4. The Clip Properties dialog box appears (as was shown earlier in Figure 9-5). Under Categories, click as many categories for the graphic as you want. You can also type in keywords for describing the graphic. As discussed earlier, keywords can help you locate graphics.

5. Click OK to return to the Clip Gallery. The newly imported graphic is not displayed until you exit the Clip Gallery by clicking on Close and then redisplay the Clip Gallery.

Newly imported graphics appear at the top of the specified categories. You can work with them just as you would any other clip-art image.

Saving Time with the Design Gallery

Publisher's Design Gallery contains an assortment of design elements, such as calendars, pull-quotes, newsletter titles, and sidebars, that you can add to your publication (see Figure 9-10). These elements are a great way to give a publication a little pizzazz, especially when you aren't using color or many graphics. You can use the Design Gallery to insert a new design element in your publication, or to change the format of an existing one.

Inserting Design Elements

The design elements can be inserted as new elements in a publication. A new text or picture frame is created to hold the new element; you can then move or size it as necessary. For instance, you might want to add one of the "attention getters" from the Design Gallery to a postcard or flyer.

Use the following steps to insert an element from the Design Gallery:

1. Click in the gray scratch area surrounding the page to make sure nothing is selected.

Sidebar   Newsletter title

With the Design Gallery, you can quickly place a variety of design elements in your publication

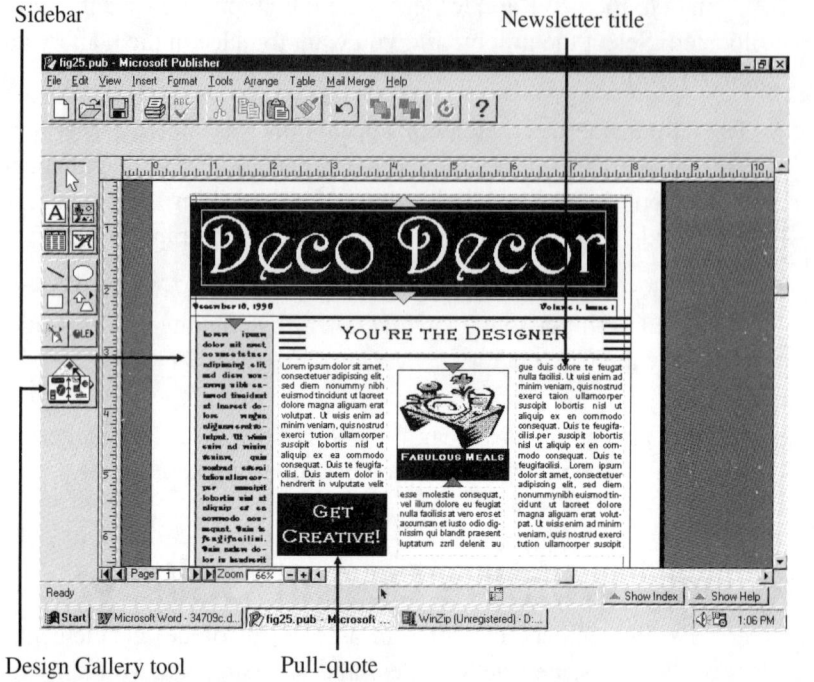

FIGURE 9-10   Design Gallery tool   Pull-quote

2. From the Tools menu, choose Design Gallery. You can also click on the Design Gallery tool. The Design Gallery is displayed.

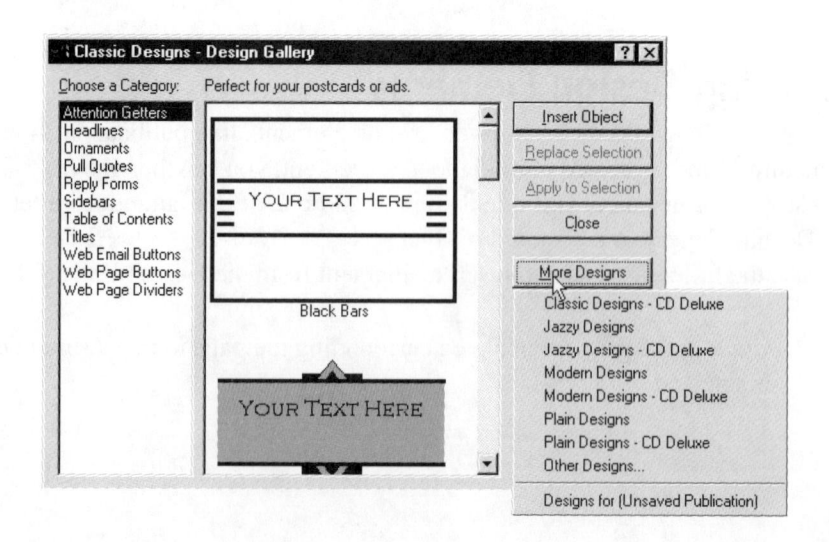

3. On the left, click the category that contains the type of design element you want to insert.

4. Select the desired design element—you may have to scroll to see them all. If you don't find one you like, try looking through another set of design elements. Click on the More Designs button, and choose a new design set.

5. After selecting the design element, click the Insert Object button to add it to your publication.

You can also drag the design element to your publication by pressing and holding the mouse button on the design element and then dragging it to the page area and releasing.

Replacing Existing Objects with New Design Elements

You can replace an existing text or graphic object on your page with a selection from the Design Gallery. For instance, you may have placed a graphic on the page, but then have decided to replace it with one of the "ornaments" available in the Design Gallery.

The steps are similar to inserting the elements as new objects. Use the following steps to insert an element from the Design Gallery:

1. Select the frame containing the text or graphic object you want to change.

2. From the Tools menu, choose Design Gallery. You can also click on the Design Gallery tool. The Design Gallery is displayed.

3. Click the category containing the type of design element you want to insert. Select the desired design element.

4. Click on the Replace Selection button to replace *both* the format and content (text in a frame or graphic in a frame) of the selected graphic with the new element.

5. Click on the Apply To Selection button to replace *only* the format (not the content) of the selected graphic with the new element. Only designs that are made up of one object (such as a text frame or a shape) can have their formats applied to the selection, so choose only a single-object design.

6. Click on the Close button to close the Design Gallery.

Designing a Social Event

Fund-raisers, charity balls, ribbon-cutting ceremonies, and other social events require elegant, formal publications. The look represents the glamour of the event and the worthiness of the cause. The Card And Invitation PageWizard in Publisher was used to design an elegant invitation. Complementing menus and table name cards were also designed. Clip-art images, typefaces, and colors were borrowed from the invitation and placed on the menus and name cards to create a connection among the publications.

Step 1: Designing the Invitation

The Card And Invitation PageWizard provides an invitation specifically set up for fund-raising events. The PageWizard asks the name of the organization sponsoring the event, as well as the date and time, so much of the information was automatically placed on the invitation. The clip art placed by the PageWizard displays a horn and musical notes, which work perfectly with the classical orchestra performing at the event. New text was entered to replace the sample text, which was formatted in the French Script typeface. A new picture frame was added to hold the organization's logo.

Publisher in action

Step 2: Designing the Menu

The Specialty PageWizard offers page designs for menus, but none of the designs worked with the look of the invitation. In addition, the menu will also be displayed as a table tent, so a folded publication was needed. To meet these needs, the menu was created from scratch by use of a blank page set up as a tent card. To achieve consistency between the publications, the musical notes from the inside of the invitation were copied and then slightly adjusted for the menu. Text frames were added to hold the menu items. The text was formatted by use of the same typeface (French Script) and same colors of the invitation. The organization's logo was also added to the menu. Once the text and graphic were in place, a copy of all of the elements was pasted on the other side of the tent card, creating a menu that could be viewed from both sides.

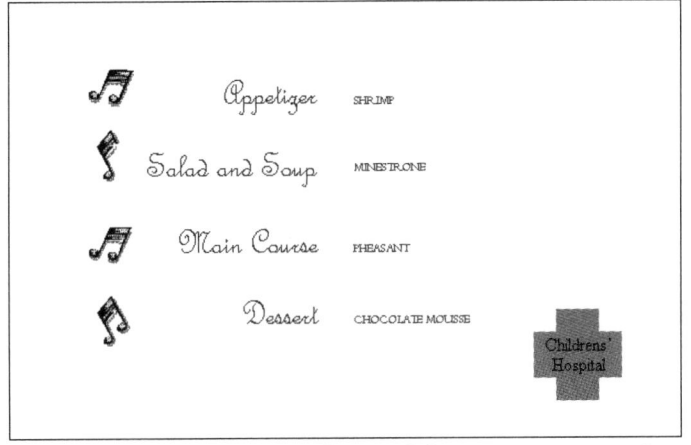

Step 3: Creating the Table Name Cards

The name cards were created by use of a blank page with a custom page size of 1 inch tall and 3 inches wide. The clip art of the horn was copied from the invitation and pasted onto the name card. The size was reduced to fit the dimensions of the name card. A text frame was drawn to add text announcing the name of the event. French Script, the typeface from the invitation and menu, was applied to the text. The guest's name will be written by hand, so a line was drawn with Publisher's line tool to designate where the name will be written.

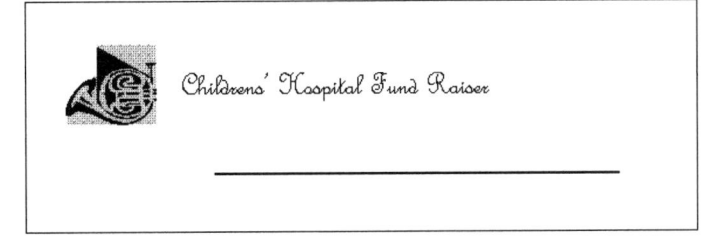

Remember, you can also use the Format Painter to copy the formatting attributes of one frame to another. This is discussed at the end of Chapter 7.

Summary

Publisher uses picture frames to hold graphics in a publication. The frames are moved and sized to build the page layout. In addition to using Publisher's extensive Clip Gallery, you can also place graphics created in other applications into publications.

The next chapter examines proofing and printing publications. Use of the Design Checker to proof the page layout is covered. However, the main part of the chapter focuses on the many aspects involved in printing publications.

10

Proofing and Printing

After all the editing and formatting it takes to build a professional-looking publication, you're probably anxious to print. (No matter how long you stare at a publication on the computer screen, it always looks different on paper!) However, it's important that what comes out of the printer looks as good as possible. That's where Publisher's Design Checker comes in—the Design Checker examines your publication for problems in the page design.

Use of the Design Checker to uncover page design problems is the first topic in this chapter. After that, the chapter focuses on the many aspects of printing publications. First, the chapter examines printing terminology such as "dpi," "PostScript," and "printer drivers." Following this is an overview of printing processes such as spot color and full color.

Since you are probably printing the publication (or at least proofs) in-house, the next part of the chapter examines options such as selecting the range of pages to print and the number of copies. Then, working with outside printing services is covered. You'll find tips on selecting a printing service and on setting up a publication for outside printing. The chapter ends with a look at special considerations when you're printing color, and tips on improving color output.

Proofing Your Page Layout

Nothing gets in the way of communicating a message like a poorly designed page. Too many fonts, too many colors, and too many special effects are just a few of the things that distract readers from the true message of the publication. However, not everyone's a professional page designer. Fortunately, Publisher provides the Design Checker to help you catch design mistakes.

Even if you feel confident about the page layout, it's worth the few minutes it takes to run the Design Checker. There may be a problem that's hard to spot. Running the Design Checker also can help you find solutions to problems you've already identified.

Working with the Design Checker

The Design Checker looks for specific problems in a publication. For instance, the Design Checker notifies you when a frame is placed on top of another frame.

If the "problem" is intended, you simply tell the Design Checker to ignore the problem. Following is a list of problems that may be found when you're running the Design Checker.

Problem	Description
Empty frames	Frames with nothing in them
Covered objects	Objects that are covered by other objects
Text in overflow area	Text frames not displaying all of the entered text
Objects in nonprinting region	Objects unprintable because they are placed too close to the edge of the page
Disproportional pictures	A graphic whose original dimensions have been distorted
Too many special effects	Pages with five or more graphics, WordArt, and BorderArt elements
Spacing between sentences	Multiple spaces after ending punctuation marks
Too many fonts	Publication using more than three fonts
Too many colors	Publication using more than three colors

NOTE: *Many of these issues are discussed in Chapter 3. There are also numerous good books on design available in bookstores. A useful one for nonartists is Roger C. Parker's* Looking Good in Print, *Ventana Press, 1990.*

By default, Publisher checks for all these problems. You can elect, however, to have Publisher check for only certain problems, such as too many fonts or colors.

Although the Design Checker can detect page layout problems, it does not find everything that may look askew in your document. Many designers wait a day or two, and then, with a fresh eye, look for problems they may have missed before.

Running the Design Checker

Use the following steps when you're ready to see how your publication stands up to the scrutiny of the Design Checker:

1. Select Design Checker from the Tools menu. In the Design Checker dialog box, click on All to check the page design of the whole publication. To check only certain pages, click on the Pages option, and enter the page number of the first page you want checked in the From box and the page number of the last page you want checked in the To box.

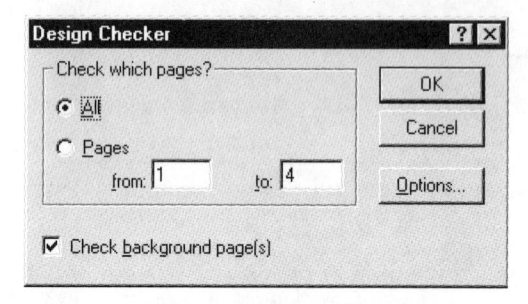

2. By default, the Design Checker also checks background pages. If you do not want background pages checked, turn off the Check Background Pages option. (Refer to Chapter 16 for more information on working with backgrounds.)

3. To control which problems the Design Checker will detect, click on the Options button. In the Options dialog box, click to remove the check mark by problems you do not want the Design Checker to look for. Click OK to return to the Design Checker.

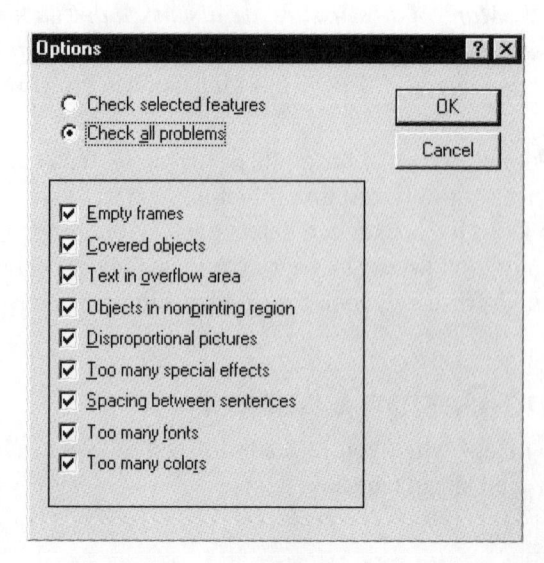

4. Click OK to begin checking the publication.

If a problem is found, the Design Checker displays a dialog box identifying the problem. For instance, in Figure 10-1, the problem is empty frames. (Empty frames can make it hard to select other frames, and they can add to page design clutter.) To ignore the problem and move on to the next problem, click on the Ignore button. Click on the Ignore All button to ignore any future instances of that particular problem. For example, if you know there are several empty frames, but you want to keep them, choose Ignore All so you are not notified about the empty frames each time.

When you want to correct a problem, click on the page. The Design Checker stays on screen, but you can use the tools to fix the problem. For instance, if you were notified of too many fonts, you can click on the page, highlight the text, and change the font. When you're ready to resume running the Design Checker, click on the Continue button.

Click on the Explain button when you want a little more information about a problem. The Help screen appears with topics about the specific problem. A message box appears when the design check is complete. Click OK.

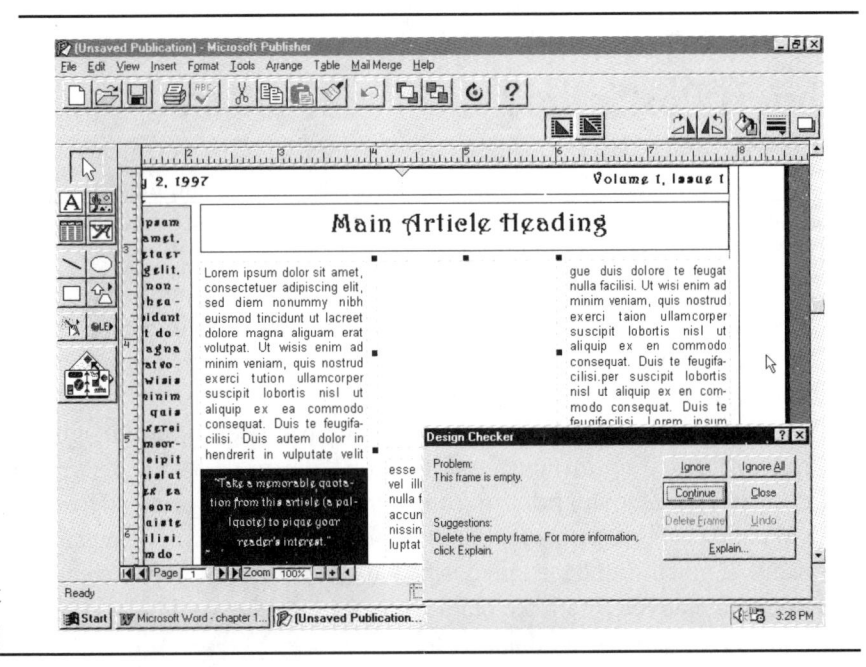

The Design Checker detects the problem with the page layout and offers suggestions for correcting it

FIGURE 10-1

Preparing for Printing

Whether you are a novice or an experienced page designer, printing always promises a little excitement. There's anticipation as a page glides out of the laser printer or as your latest full-color piece arrives hot off the press. Before you can experience this thrill, you have to consider many methods and procedures as you delve into the printing process. For instance, will the printing be done in-house, or are the files being sent to a service bureau or to a printer for high-resolution output? Are you using a spot-color or four-color printing process? All these questions and many more must be considered as you prepare to print your publications.

In this section, "desktop printer" refers to any printer you have in-house—a printer that you can directly operate. "Outside printing service" refers to the variety of organizations that work with the printing of publications.

Getting Familiar with Printing Terminology

As with most industries, publishing and printing have their own buzzwords and jargon. Getting familiar with the terminology helps you to understand processes used by your own desktop printer and to communicate your needs to an outside printing service. Here are some basic concepts and terminology.

What is PostScript?

PostScript is a page-description language that translates page elements such as fonts and the spatial arrangement of text and graphics into a language the printer can understand. Generally, a quick glance at the documentation provided with the printer will tell you whether you have PostScript.

PostScript is considered the industry standard by most publishing and graphic arts professionals. Its flexibility and sophisticated font-handling capabilities give it a clear advantage for the desktop publisher. Because of this, almost all outside printing services use PostScript printing devices.

You can experience problems if you switch page-description languages in the printing process. For instance, publications designed for a specific type of non-PostScript printer will print fine on that non-PostScript printer. However, when the publication is printed on a PostScript printer, problems in spacing and typefaces may occur. If you do not have PostScript and intend to work with an outside printer, it's important that you set up the publication for outside printing (with a PostScript printer) as discussed later in this chapter.

What Is dpi?

Dots per inch (dpi) is a measure of the output resolution produced by printers and image setters. The dpi varies according to the printer or output device. Generally, the higher the resolution, the higher the print quality.

Laser printers, such as an Apple LaserWriter or HP LaserJet, print at 300 to 600 dpi. Many letters, memos, and in-house newsletters are printed at this resolution. *Image setters* (such as a Linotronic 300 or Agfa 9000) can output at 1,270 or 2,540 dpi, providing higher resolution for professional-quality print jobs like magazines and posters.

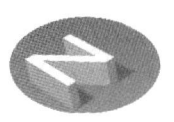

NOTE: *If your desktop printer prints at 300 dpi, consider taking the publication to a copy shop for printing at 600 dpi. At one time, 300 dpi was considered "business quality," that is, suitable for in-house newsletters and reports. However, with so many printers now outputting at 600 dpi, business quality has been upgraded to 600 dpi.*

If a commercial printer will be printing your publication, ask for advice on how to select resolution. The printer can provide valuable tips for determining the appropriate resolution, based on the printing process, paper stock, and cost.

Working with Printer Drivers

In the Windows 95 environment, all applications share the same printing services. Windows knows how to send information to a specific printer based on the printer driver for that device. A *printer driver* is a file that includes all the necessary information for controlling the printer, including a list of built-in fonts available in the printer's memory. Printer driver files have the filename extension .DRV.

10

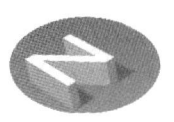

NOTE: *The steps for installing printers appear in the section "Selecting a Printer" later in this chapter.*

Many printer drivers are provided with the Windows 95 software. If the driver for your printer is not included, contact your printer dealer to obtain a driver file. Commercial printers may ask you to use a generic PostScript printer driver, or they may provide you with a copy of the printer driver file specifically set up for their equipment. Even if you don't have the printer or image setter, the printer driver tells

Publisher how to compose your publication for that device. Then you take the Publisher file to the printer for output.

Publisher's Printer Drivers

Publisher supplies two generic printer drivers designed to work with most printers and image setters. The MS Publisher Imagesetter printer driver is for black-and-white printing, and the MS Publisher Color Printer driver is for color printing. These drivers can be installed during Publisher installation. To be on the safe side, call the commercial printer to determine the best printer driver for your publication.

Printing With and Without Color

This section looks at three basic printing processes—*black-and-white printing, spot-color printing,* and *full-color printing.* Understanding the difference between these processes and knowing some of the associated terminology makes dealing with your desktop printer or an outside printing service a little easier.

Black-and-White Printing

Black-and-white printing is the most basic printing process. Eighty percent of all publications are printed in black and white. Black is printed on the page, and the white comes from the white of the page. To add depth and diversity to black-and-white publications, percentages of black are used to create what looks like gray.

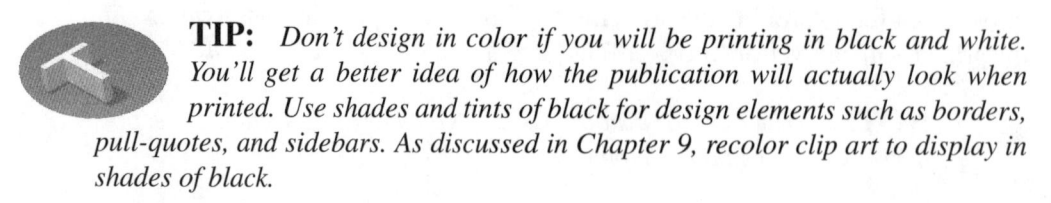

TIP: *Don't design in color if you will be printing in black and white. You'll get a better idea of how the publication will actually look when printed. Use shades and tints of black for design elements such as borders, pull-quotes, and sidebars. As discussed in Chapter 9, recolor clip art to display in shades of black.*

Spot-Color Printing

Spot color means the addition of one or two colors to the black. With spot color you can add some color to a publication, without the price tag of full color. Spot colors are premixed—like premixed paints at a hardware store. Spot colors assure consistency in color selection. They are numbered, so if someone in Missouri tells someone in Texas he or she likes Blue 218, they know they are talking about the same color.

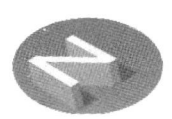 **NOTE:**   *Chapter 19 provides an example of selecting a spot color and using it to design and print a publication.*

The most popular type of spot colors is called *Pantone* or *PMS* (Pantone Matching System) colors. Swatch books, like paint color books, are used to show the color and its number. The Pantone swatch books are updated yearly. Make sure you're looking at a current copy, since the colors have a tendency to fade. Each color is shown on coated (glossy) or noncoated paper, to illustrate how paper stock affects the printed color. When you set up the print job, make sure the printing service knows the spot color you have selected. Keep in mind that a computer screen cannot display exactly how the PMS color will print. For instance, purple may look more blue on screen, red may appear pink. Remember that the printing service is using the color in the swatch book, so refer to the swatch book for a true version of the color, not to your screen.

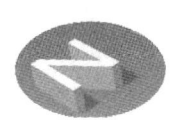 **NOTE:**   *Art supply stores often have Pantone swatch books for purchase. In addition, some printing services will provide one for you.*

Full-Color Printing

1 0

Full color is often referred to as four-color printing because of the four colors used. Combining percentages of four colors—cyan (light blue), magenta (bright pink), yellow, and black—produces the appearance of millions of colors, enough even to reproduce color photographs.

Full-color publications are becoming more and more popular. Resolution is an important issue with full color. Low resolution, 300 to 600 dpi, is fine for in-house publications such as overheads. But if you want your color to look really sharp, go with a higher resolution such as 1,270 or 2,450 dpi.

 **NOTE:**   *A great booklet for learning more about computers and printing is* An Introduction to Digital Color Prepress *distributed by Agfa Corporation. You can reach Agfa at (508) 657-7700.*

Know Your Printer

Before printing, take time to discover a few things about your printer by reading (or at least thumbing through) the printer manuals. If you're working with an outside printing service, it can also help to learn a little more about the printer. Use the following list to get acquainted.

- **Is the printer PostScript or non-PostScript?**   As mentioned earlier, PostScript printing devices are considered better for outputting publications with graphics. In fact, EPS (encapsulated PostScript) graphics will only print on PostScript printing devices.

- **What is the maximum page size? Can you print single- and double-sided?**   Knowing what sizes of paper a printer can work with helps when you're designing a publication. For instance, if your printer can print on tabloid size (11 x 17-inch) paper, you're ready to start designing posters.

- **What is the resolution—the dots per inch? Can the dpi be adjusted?** Knowing a printer's resolution helps you determine whether a publication can be printed in-house or needs to be done at an outside print shop. A resolution of 600 dpi is considered business quality, which means it's fine for in-house projects, sales reports, and newsletters. A resolution of 2,540 dpi is high quality, great for glossy magazine and brochures. Note that lowering the dpi when you print usually speeds up printing—a big time-saver when you need to proof a rough draft.

- **How much RAM does the printer have?**   The RAM (or memory) of your printer affects how fast the pages print, and how much graphic information the printer can handle. For instance, a printer with only 1 megabyte of RAM may not be able to print a page that uses multiple fonts and graphics.

- **What printers are installed?**   Refer to the Printers folder in Windows 95 to see what printer drivers have been installed on your system. Installing drivers is covered in the following section.

Selecting a Printer

As discussed in Chapter 5, it's important to select the printer that will be used to print the final (or master) copies of your publication *before* designing the publication. For instance, if the copy shop you are using to print a newsletter uses an Apple LaserWriter, select that printer before you begin designing the newsletter.

If you have already designed the publication, you can still select another printer. However, not all printers are created equal, and switching from one printer to another can cause problems in your page design. How text fits in a frame may be altered, fonts may be changed, and graphics may move slightly. Since problems can occur, make sure the right printer is selected before sending the publication to a printing service. It's better to fix problems yourself, rather than hoping the printing service will (because they probably won't).

NOTE: *Chapter 5 also addresses selecting printers. The important thing to remember is to select the printer* before *designing the publication.*

Installing Printers

Before you can select a printer, the printer driver must be installed. The following steps outline installing printers in Windows 95. If you are on a network, you might need to enlist the help of a network support person to help install a new printer. During this procedure you may be asked to insert your Windows 95 installation disks or CD-ROM, so have them handy.

1. Click on the Start button on the Windows 95 taskbar. Point to Settings and click on Printers.

2. Double-click on the Add Printer icon in the Printer window.

3. The Add Printer Wizard is displayed. Click on the Next button.

4. In the list box on the left, select the manufacturer of the printer. The list box on the right displays the printers produced by the selected manufacturer. Select the name of the printer you wish to add. Click on the Next button.

10

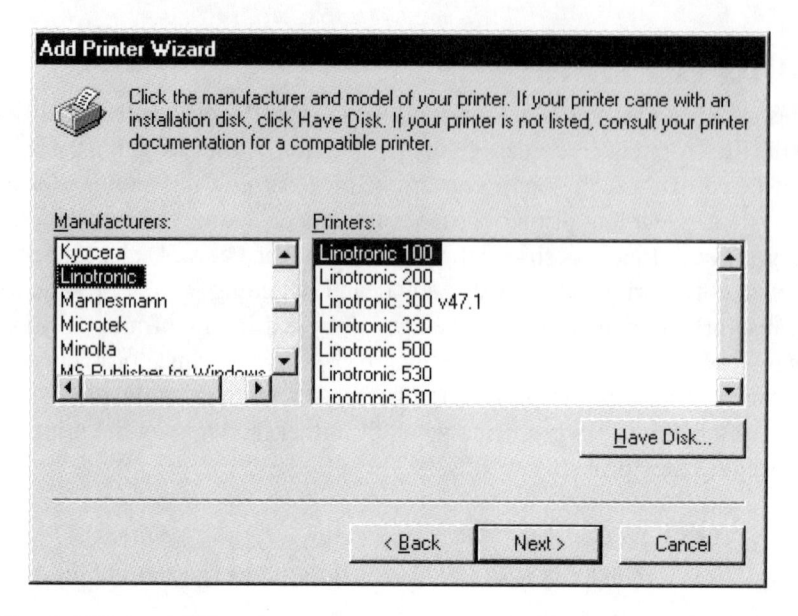

5. The Add Printer Wizard now wants you to identify the port you will be using for this printer. If you are selecting a desktop printer, select the port the printer hooks up to in the back of your computer—for instance, COM1 or LPT1. If you are selecting a printer to be used by an outside printing service, select FILE. Click on the Next button.

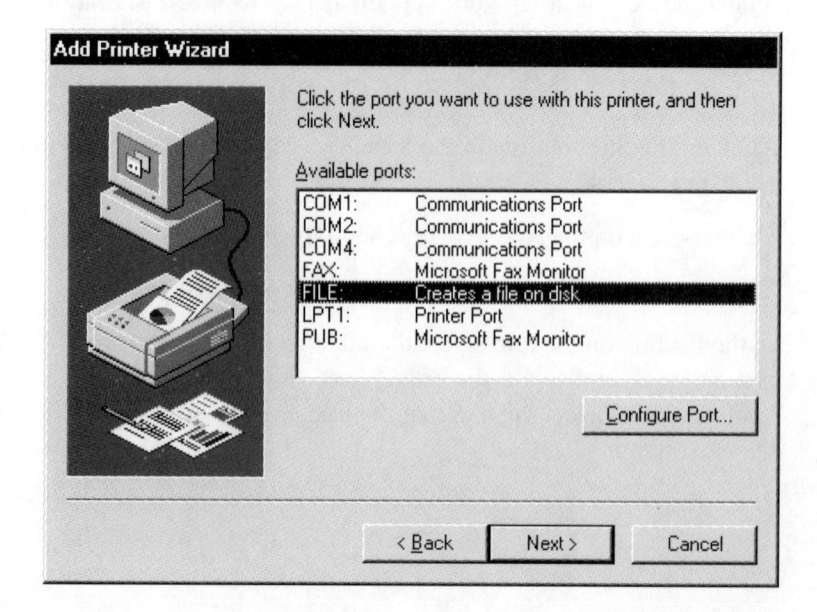

6. The next screen of the Add Printer Wizard tells you the name of the new printer and asks if you want it to become the default printer. Click Yes if you want all Windows applications to automatically use the new printer (unless told otherwise). Click No if you want the printer added but not to become the default printer. For outside printers, you probably want to choose No. Click on the Next button.

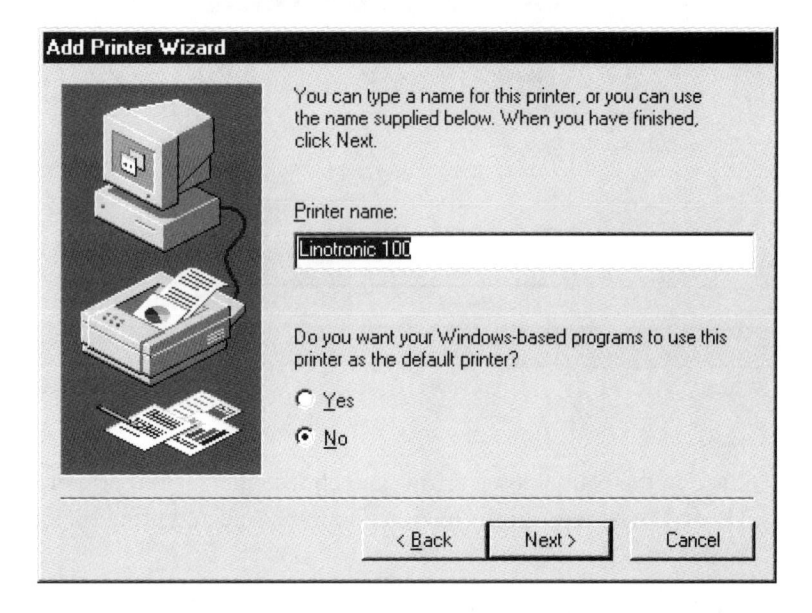

7. The next screen asks if you want to print a test page. If you added a desktop printer, it's a good idea to print a test page so you can make sure everything works. If you added an outside printer, choose No. Click on the Finish button.

8. A message appears indicating that Windows is loading the new printer driver file. If it cannot find it, another message appears asking you to insert your Windows disk or CD-ROM. Insert the disk and click OK. Windows will then locate the file and install the printer.

Selecting a Printer

After the driver is installed, use the following steps to select the printer in Publisher:

1. From the File menu, select Print Setup. The Print Setup dialog box appears.

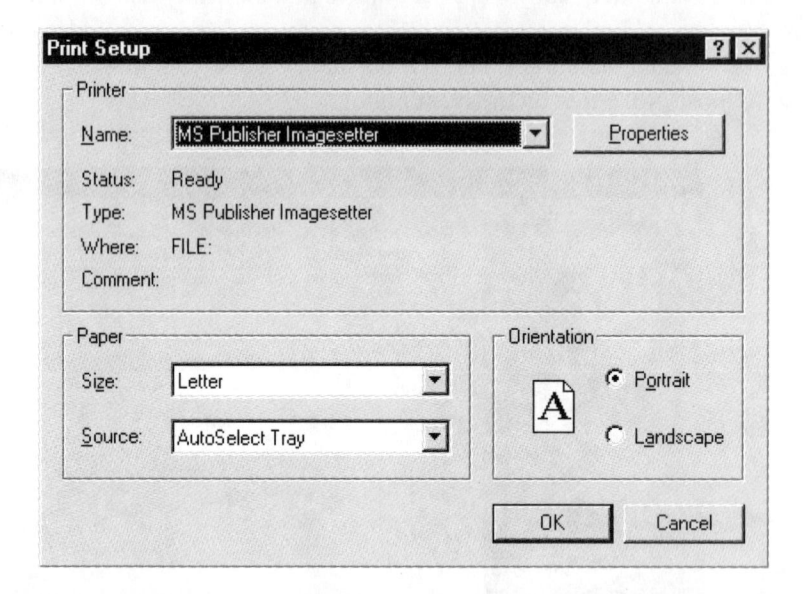

2. Click on the Name down arrow, and choose the desired printer driver. After a few seconds, information about the selected printer appears below the Name box.

3. Click on the Properties button to display the properties for the selected printer. Figure 10-2 displays properties for the MS Publisher Imagesetter. In this dialog box you can change the page size and orientation. Click OK to return to the Print Setup dialog box.

4. Click OK again to set up the selected printer for your new publication.

If you have already been working on the page design, examine the document to see if any changes were made when you selected the new printer.

Printing in Publisher

Whether printing the final copy or just rough drafts of a publication on your desktop (or in-house printer), it's necessary that you understand the printing options available in Publisher.

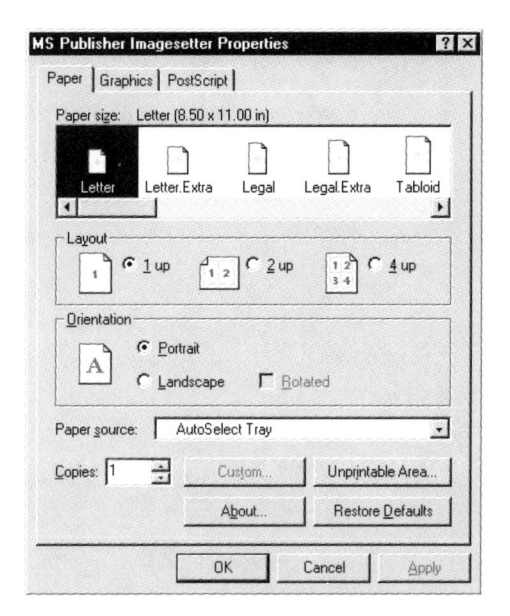

The selected printer has properties that can be adjusted

FIGURE 10-2

Publisher allows you to print an entire publication or just part of it. To print a publication, open the publication file and select Print from the File menu. The selected printer appears at the top of the Print dialog box, shown in Figure 10-3. Use the steps in the previous section to select another printer.

If the publication has already been set up for outside printing, the printing command will read "Print Proof" instead of "Print." When you select an outside printer as the main printer, your desktop printer becomes the *proof* (or rough-draft copy) *printer.* Setting up for outside printing is covered later in this chapter in the section "Preparing Publications for Outside Printing."

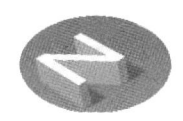

NOTE: *Just because your printer doesn't print color, doesn't mean you can't add some color to your publications. Check out preprinted paper designed to work with laser printers at computer shops and paper goods stores.*

Note that Publisher uses multiple sheets of paper to print publications that are larger than a sheet of $8\frac{1}{2}$ by 11-inch paper. You then put together the pieces of paper to create the publication. For instance, a poster designed at 24 x 36 inches is printed on several pieces of paper. You arrange the pages (perhaps even tape them together) to get a preview of the poster before sending it to the print shop.

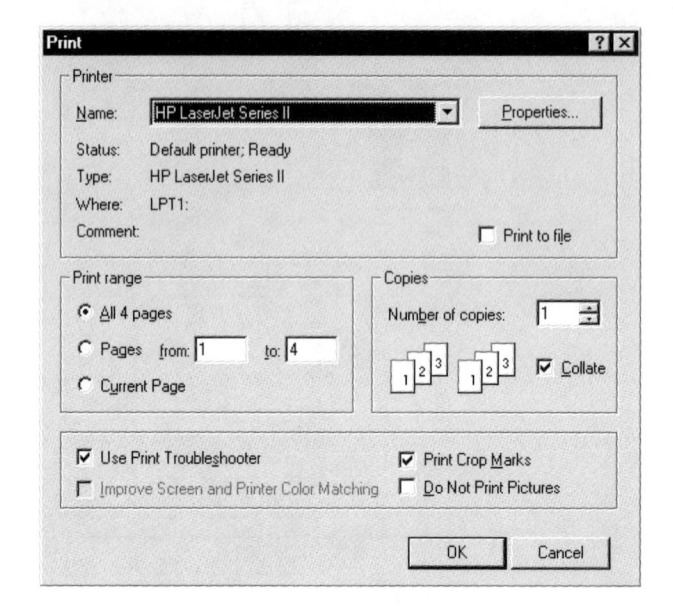

The Print dialog provides several options for printing publications

TIP: *Click on the Print tool in the Standard toolbar to quickly print one copy of the entire publication. No dialog box appears—it just prints automatically.*

Setting the Range of Pages to Print

The Print Range section of the Print dialog box allows you to select the pages you want to print. By default, All Pages (Publisher includes the total number of pages in this option) is selected—this prints the entire publication. To print a consecutive range of pages, click on the Pages option, and enter the first page number to print in the From box and the last page number to print in the To box. (The Pages option is grayed out in one-page publications.) To print the page currently displayed, click on the Current Page option.

TIP: *Press CTRL-P to quickly display the Print dialog box.*

Specifying the Number of Copies to Print

The Copies section of the Print dialog box enables you to specify the number of copies you want to print. Click on the up or down arrow by Number Of Copies to indicate the desired amount of copies. You can also type a number in the box.

If your publication has more than one page, the Collate box appears. It is on by default, so Publisher will automatically collate (that is, print the pages in consecutive order) the copies. When Publisher instructs your printer to collate the copies, it increases the print time. If you are in a hurry, turn off the Collate option, and then collate the copies by hand.

Printing Crop Marks

Publisher can print *crop marks*—fine lines that indicate the corners of the page. Suppose you were printing a postcard on letter-size paper ($8\frac{1}{2}$ by 11-inch)—printing crop marks would help you determine the edges of the postcard. You could use the crop marks to cut the postcard out of the larger paper.

Crop marks can only be printed when the publication size is no larger than half the size of the paper you're printing on. For example, crop marks would appear when printing a postcard on letter-size paper, because the publication is smaller than the paper. Crop marks also appear when the publication is larger than a letter-size page. For instance, crop marks appear when you print a large poster. In either case, if you do not want crop marks to print, turn off the Print Crop Marks option in the Print dialog box.

Printing Graphics

Graphics slow down printing. You can speed up printing by telling Publisher not to print the graphics. For instance, imagine you want to check the text formatting on a publication. You could print it without the graphics and speed up the print job. Turn on the Do Not Print Pictures option in the Print dialog box to get a printout with no graphics.

Working with the Print Troubleshooter

Publisher's Print Troubleshooter can help you identify and fix printing problems. By default, the Use Print Troubleshooter option is turned on in the Print dialog box. When it is enabled, the Print Troubleshooter displays a dialog box after each print job, asking if the publication printed successfully. If it didn't, the Print Troubleshooter helps you find solutions to your printing problems.

After an unsuccessful print job, Publisher displays the Print Troubleshooter Help screen (see Figure 10-4). You click on the problem to display additional Help screens with information about solving that type of problem. For instance, suppose you have a publication that never prints. In the Print Troubleshooter Help screen shown in Figure 10-4, you could click on the I'm Having General Printing Problems option. On the next Help screen, you could select My Publication Doesn't Print At All. The next screen displays a list of things to check (maybe the printer wasn't plugged in—that one always hurts). As you can see, the Print Troubleshooter tries to help you locate and solve printing problems.

As mentioned, the Print Troubleshooter is automatically turned on when you print. To turn it off, to remove the check mark by Use Print Troubleshooter in the Print dialog box.

Creating a Print File

The Print To File option in the Print dialog box creates a file that can be printed from another computer on which Publisher is not installed. This feature is normally used

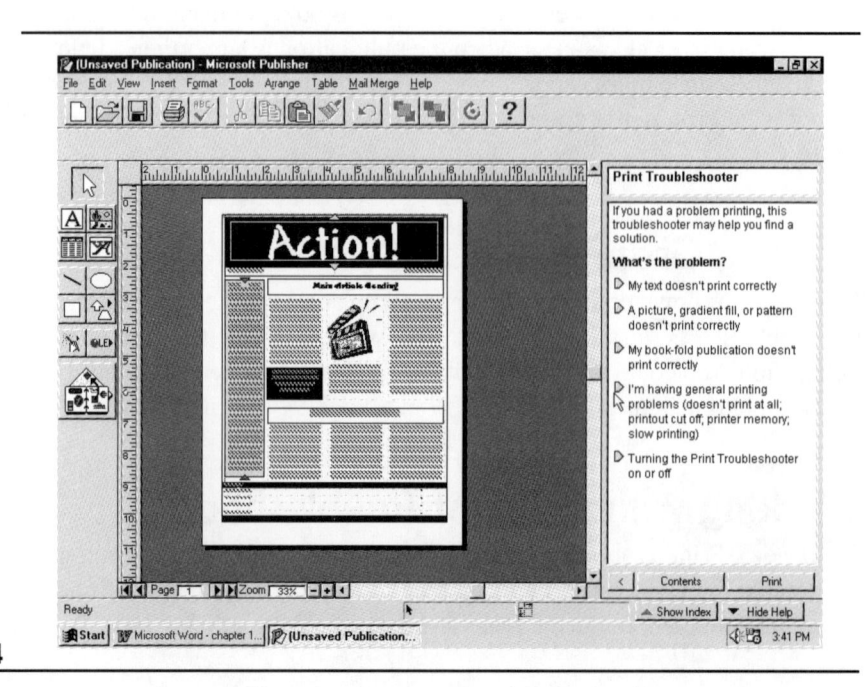

Use the Print Trouble-shooter to identify and correct printing problems

FIGURE 10-4

when you are sending a publication to an outside printing service. The outside printing service may not have Publisher installed on their systems, so you are sending them a file that can be printed without the Publisher software. It is important that the printer or output device used by the outside printer is selected before creating the print file. For instance, if the outside service uses an Agfa 9000, select this printer. As mentioned earlier, selecting another printer can cause discrepancies in the page design—you want to catch the discrepancies before they get to the printing service.

Keep in mind that when you *print to file,* you do not need the actual output device. You do not, for example, need to be hooked up to a Linotronic to install the printer driver. When you print to file, you are creating a print file set up with information for that particular device. Since most outside printing services use a PostScript printing device, many of them refer to print files as "PostScript print files."

Use the following steps to create a print file:

1. Open the publication file you want to print. Choose Print from the File menu. The Print dialog box appears (refer to Figure 10-3).

2. Make sure the correct printer is selected. Click on the Print To File option.

3. Select the other print options you want. (For instance, turn on Print Crop Marks.)

4. Click OK. The Print To File dialog box appears. Enter a filename; Publisher will automatically add the .PRN. If necessary, change to the drive and directory where you want to save the print file.

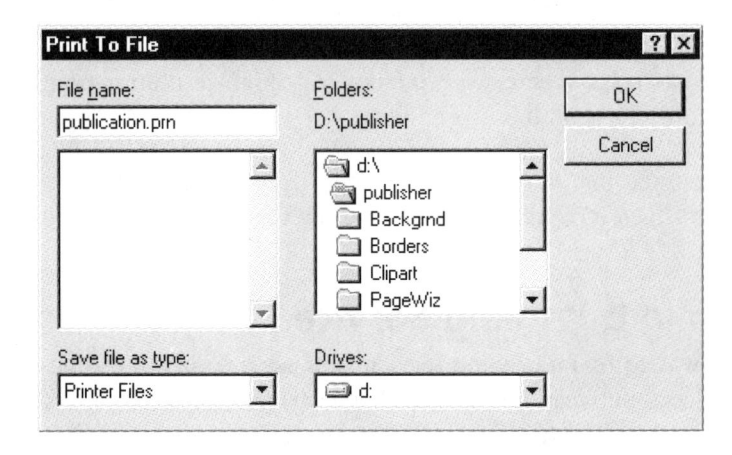

5. Click OK. A message box appears, displaying the status of the print job.

 **NOTE:**   *If you have set the printer port connection to FILE in Windows, you do not need to select the Print To File option to create a print file. The FILE port connection indicates a print file is to be created.*

Working with Commercial Printers

Different publications require different printing methods. When you want just a few invitations to a Super Bowl party, all you need is your easy-to-access desktop printer. But when you want 10,000 glossy sales brochures, you need an outside printing service.

There is a wide range of printing services out there—everything from copy shops to high-end commercial printers. Here's an overview of some printing services you'll come across as you begin your search:

- *Copy shops* work best for low-resolution output where you may need a few or a few thousand copies. You can get actual printed output from a copy shop, or take them the printed output and let them make the copies. Quick turnaround and low cost are advantages of working with copy shops.

- *Service bureaus* typically specialize in outputting film for high-end printing. The film is then taken to a commercial printer.

- *Low-run color houses,* as some printing services identify themselves, specialize in high- or low-resolution color print jobs under 5,000 copies. These places also focus on printing large publications.

- *High-end commercial printers* provide high-resolution printing, focusing mostly on print jobs over 5,000.

Of course, many printing services don't fit neatly into one of these categories—they mix and match their services based on customer demand.

Selecting a Printing Service

The best way to find a printing service is to ask a friend or business acquaintance who produces publications similar to what you have in mind. Ask what type of service they used. Who did they work with at the company? (Sales reps love referrals.) Were they happy with the service? Because you are new to printing, would those services be a good choice for you also? What companies have they used that they did *not* like? Get names and numbers, and then get on the phone and start asking questions. Tell them how you found them and what kind of printing services you need. Ask for general estimates on time and price. You'll discover a lot just by talking to the people at these services. Also important, you'll find out who's willing to take time to explain things to you.

Printing Services That Have Publisher

An important consideration when you're selecting a printing service is how they deal with Microsoft Publisher files. Generally, it's best if they have Publisher and print directly from it. When the service uses Publisher, you send in a copy of your publication file (always keep the original—just in case!). They open the file in Publisher and output it to their printer or image setter. A benefit of working with printing services using Publisher is that they can perform minor repair work. For instance, suppose after sending a file to a printing service you discover a technical term is misspelled. Since the printing service also has Publisher, they can open the file and correct the misspelling. (Watch out—they may charge for corrections.)

However, when a printing service uses Publisher to output your file, make sure they have the fonts you used in designing the publication. If your publication uses a font that the service does not have, a substitute font is printed. Substitute fonts rarely match what you intended, so ask the printing services for a list of the fonts they have and stick with those.

NOTE: *Although it may be preferable to find a printing service that uses Publisher, don't count on it. Publisher is relatively new to the desktop publishing arena, and most printing services will not take Publisher files. However, you may find that as Publisher becomes more popular, more printing services will start working with it directly.*

Printing Services That Do Not Have Publisher

If the printing service does not have Publisher, you will need to create a print file. The steps for creating a print file are covered earlier in this chapter. It's important that the printer driver used by the printing service (usually a PostScript device) is selected before creating the print file. The print file is sent to the printing service, where it is output from a computer without Publisher.

The disadvantage of sending print files is that they cannot be opened and edited. If you need to make a change or if the service finds a problem, you have to fix it in Publisher, create the print file again, and send it back to the printing service. It's important to take great care in preparing the publication file before creating the print file. The advantage of sending print files is that the fonts are part of the print file, so you don't have to worry whether the printing service has the fonts used in the publication.

Tips for Selecting a Printing Service

After determining whether the service works with Publisher, ask specific questions about your printing needs:

- Does the printing service output PC (not just Macintosh) files? You can better communicate your needs to the person in charge of printing if he or she has some knowledge of PC applications.

- Can you send files by modem? This cuts down on the time involved in transporting the publication to them.

- Will they let you know if there is a problem? At busy copy shops, this is not likely to happen. A sales representative from a printing company will probably work harder to keep your business. Let them know if you plan on doing *lots* of work with them. They love it!

- Find out the maximum and minimum number of copies that can be printed. Generally, copy and smaller print shops provide the best service and price on print jobs under 5,000. However, when the numbers get over 5,000, check out a large, commercial printer—the price per piece is often less than that of a smaller printing service.

- Find out what paper sizes they work with. Many copy shops cannot handle publications larger than 11 x 17 inches. Some printing companies specialize in outputting large publications—find one that does if you produce large publications.

- Find out if they provide trimming (trimming the page) and folding services. Many copy shops do not provide these services. Companies offering more specialized printing services will trim and fold publications.

- Find out if they scan photographs and drawings. Not everyone does and it can come in handy when you're nearing a deadline.

- Find out if they offer spot-color and full-color printing. Even if your current job does not require color, you may want to find a service with color capabilities for future publications.

- Find out if they have special paper stocks in-house or if they need to be ordered. Ordering slows down the turnaround time of a print job.

- Find out if they have spot-color inks in-house or if they need to be ordered. Again, ordering can add up to a week to the printing turnaround time.

Take a copy of your print piece and explain what you want. It helps to take sample publications that use colors, page sizes, and folds that you like.

Make it easy on yourself the first time you send a publication to an outside service. Start early on the publication, and allow time to make and fix mistakes. Send a sample of the publication (perhaps one page of a brochure) to the printing service so you get an idea of how your colors will look and if the fonts are printing as desired. Tell the printing service you want to print proofs of the publication, so you can fix any problems before all the copies are printed. Count on having a few printing mistakes—everyone does.

Preparing Publications for Outside Printing

Publisher can help you prepare a publication for outside printing. Set up a publication for outside printing immediately after creating it. As discussed earlier, page design can be slightly altered when a different printing process and printer are selected. After creating the publication and before designing it is the best time to set up a publication for outside printing. If you do set up the publication for outside printing after designing the publication, check it thoroughly to see if any changes occurred.

The procedure for setting up publications for outside printing involves three steps designed to get you thinking about the output process and to help you make some choices.

Step 1: Selecting a Printing Process

The first step helps you identify the printing process. You select whether the publication will be output in black and white, or by use of spot-color or full-color printing. Refer to the section "Printing with and Without Color" earlier in this chapter for more information.

Step 2: Selecting a Printer

The second step helps you select the right printer. If you do not have a printer driver for the printer used by the outside printing service, get a copy or ask if you can use one of the generic printer drivers supplied by Publisher. As mentioned earlier, the MS Publisher Imagesetter printer driver is for black-and-white printing, and the MS Publisher Color Printer driver is for color printing.

Step 3: Select Printing Features

The third step activates two features used by many outside printing services. The first feature lets you set up a publication for oversized or "extra" paper size. Generally, extra paper sizes are one inch larger than the actual image area. For instance, the extra paper size for $8\frac{1}{2}$ x 11 (letter-size paper) is $9\frac{1}{2}$ x 12. Outside printing services use oversized paper to print *bleeds* (printed objects that touch the edges of the page), and to print marks set up in the next option.

The second feature allows you to print crop marks, which indicate the page edges for trimming, and registration marks, which are used for aligning color. These marks will not print unless the page design area is smaller than the physical size of the paper. For instance, if your publication is designed for $8\frac{1}{2}$ x 11 and printed on $8\frac{1}{2}$ x 11, the marks will not print. However, if your publication is set up for extra paper size of $9\frac{1}{2}$ x 12, the marks will print. Call the printing service to determine which, if any, of these two features should be enabled.

Setting up Publications for Outside Printing

Use the following steps to set up a publication for outside printing:

1. From the File menu, select Outside Print Setup. The Outside Print Setup dialog box appears.

2. The dialog box asks you to select the type of printing you want:

   ■ Click on the Black, White, And Shades Of Gray, On Any Printer option to set up a black-and-white publication for outside printing. A preview of a black-and-white publication is displayed.

   ■ Click on the Full Color, On A Color Printer At Less Than 1200 dpi Resolution option to set up a publication for full-color printing. A preview of a full-color publication is displayed.

   ■ Click on the Spot Color(s) At Greater Than 1200 dpi Resolution option to set up a publication for printing with one or two spot colors. Once you click on the spot-color option, new options for selecting the spot color(s) appear in the dialog box. Click on the down arrow, and select a color that represents the spot color that will be used in the printing. As mentioned earlier, with spot-color printing, a color is generally selected from a swatch book. The color in the book is what will be printed on the publication. The color chosen in the Outside Print Setup dialog box is just a visual representation of the spot color.

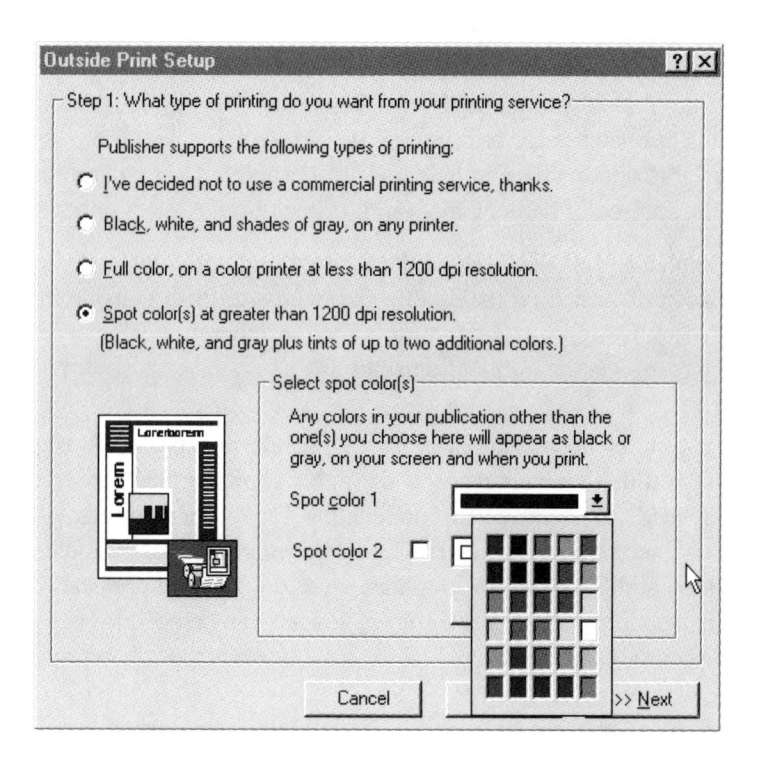

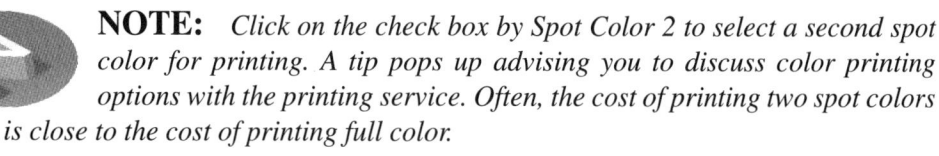

NOTE: *Click on the check box by Spot Color 2 to select a second spot color for printing. A tip pops up advising you to discuss color printing options with the printing service. Often, the cost of printing two spot colors is close to the cost of printing full color.*

3. Click on the Next button to move to the second screen in the Outside Print Setup dialog box. The second step asks you to select the printer used by the printing service.

■ Click on the first option, Use Publisher's Outside Printer Driver, to use the generic printer driver supplied by Publisher.

■ Click on the second option, Select A Specific Printer, to select a printer driver (perhaps one supplied by the printing service). Next, click on the double-arrow (>>) button in the dialog box to select the printer. The Print Setup dialog box appears. Click on the Name down arrow and choose the desired printer. (Refer to the section "Selecting a Printer" in this chapter for more information.)

4. Click on the Next button to move to the third screen in the Outside Print Setup dialog box. By default, both options are turned on. The Automatically Choose "Extra" Paper Sizes option tells Publisher to set up the publication for printing on oversized paper. The Show All Printer Marks option tells Publisher to print crop marks, registration marks, and the spot-color name. Click on the check box by each option to turn it off.

5. Publisher provides a checklist for working with outside printing services—click on the double arrow next to Print Outside Printing Checklist to print a copy of this list for yourself. Click on the Done button to complete the publication setup.

After you set up the publication for outside printing, a message may appear informing you that the properties of the publication's printer have changed and that Publisher needs to compose the publication for the new printer. It also says that embedded objects need to be updated. Embedded objects are elements, such as Excel spreadsheets and CorelDRAW graphics, created in another application and placed in the Publisher publication. Whether or not you have any embedded objects, click Yes to tell Publisher to compose the publication for the selected printing process and printer.

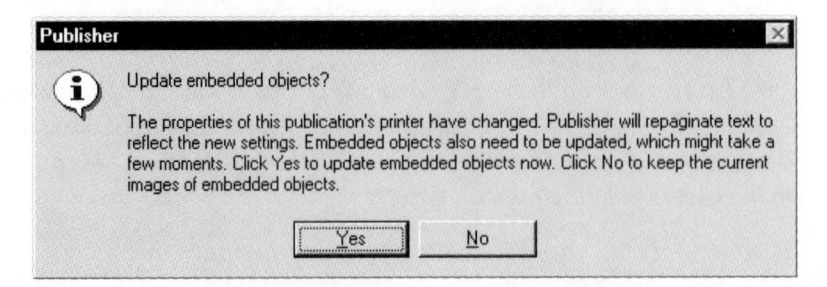

Setting up for outside printing affects what colors can be used to design a publication. After a publication is set up for black-and-white printing, tools and dialog boxes involving color selections only offer black, white, and percentages of black (gray). After a publication is set up for spot-color printing, the selected spot color(s), black, white, and percentages of black are displayed in tools and dialog boxes. All colors are available for publications set up for full-color printing. Publisher helps you design for a selected printing process by only offering colors available for that process.

Working with a Proof Printer

Once a publication is set up for outside printing, your in-house printer becomes what Publisher refers to as the *proof printer*. This means you can use your desktop printer to print a proof or rough-draft copy of the publication. The proof printer tries to print the page as the outside printer would—however, they are two different printers, so there might be some variations. Use the proof printer to check spelling and to get an overall idea of the page design.

 **NOTE:** *Depending on the cost and importance of the publication, you may also want to get a proof from the outside printer so you really know how the publication is going to look. It's better to catch mistakes before all the copies are printed.*

Printing Color

Color adds a lot to the design of a publication, but it can also add a lot of aggravation to the printing process. The problem is how the colors appear on the computer screen and how they look when printed. What looks dark blue on the screen may print purple, what looks red on the screen may appear bright pink when printed—it goes on and on. In addition, printers vary on how they output color—what prints blue on your printer may print dark green on the printer used at the outside printing service. Some outside printers will tell you that colors will print differently from day to day on the same printer!

The bottom line is that the color you see on your screen will not match what is printed. The problem is the way colors are generated. On the computer screen, red, green, and blue light (the RGB color model) are combined to create colors. For printing on paper, cyan, magenta, yellow, and black (the CMYK color model) are combined to create colors. The switch from one color model to another causes discrepancies in color design.

Here are a few suggestions for improving color printing:

- When you're printing spot color(s), select a color in Publisher that closely resembles the spot color you selected. Remember that this is not the real color. The real color will match the spot color you selected (perhaps from the Pantone spot-color book).

- When you're printing spot colors, find out if the printing service creates the spot color from process colors (cyan, magenta, yellow, and black) or uses the premixed spot color. A Pantone spot color book also shows spot colors created by mixing process colors, so you'll get a better idea of what will actually be printed.

- Get proofs. Ask to see a proof of the publication before all copies are printed. If the colors are off, you can change them.

- If a certain color is really important, say a company color, let the printing service know. They may be able to tweak the printer to help match the color.

- Find out if converting scanned images from RGB to CMYK before submission will help. You can use photo-manipulation software such as Photoshop to do this. The outside printer may provide this service for a fee.

The main thing you can do to improve color printing is to ask the printing service for tips and tricks that work with their specific printers.

Summary

This chapter focused on proofing and printing publications. The Design Checker is another way Publisher helps you create professional-looking publications. Publisher provides many features for setting up a publication for in-house printing or printing by an outside service. As discussed in this chapter, there are many things to learn when you begin working with outside printing services.

The rest of the book covers special features for designing Publisher publications. The next chapter discusses drawing objects, such as circles and squares, with Publisher's drawing tools.

III

Advanced Options

11

Drawing Graphics in Publisher

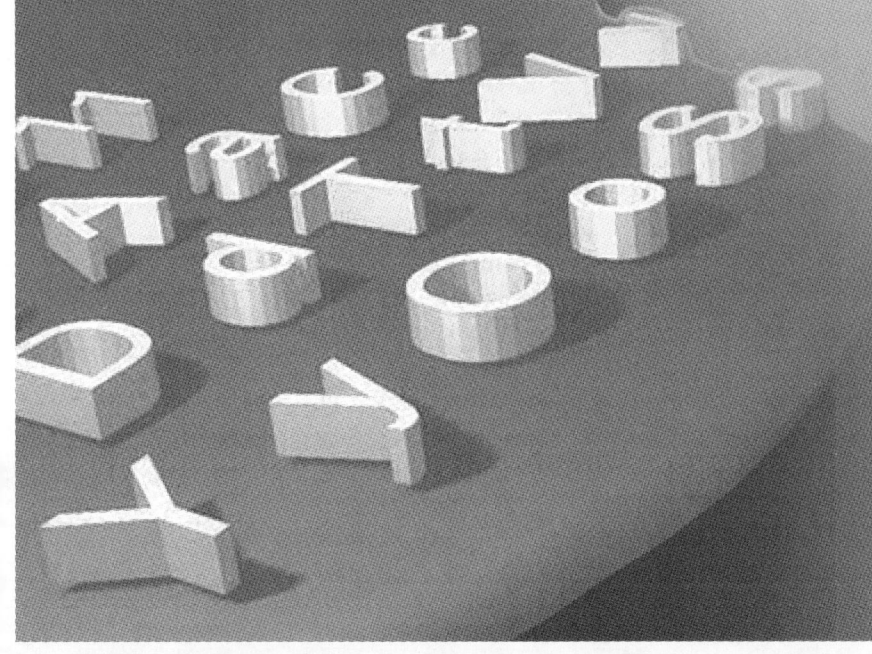

Graphics are a key element of good page design. Many graphics placed in publications are created in drawing applications such as CorelDRAW and Micrografx Designer. These applications provide the kind of high-power tools needed to design professional, eye-catching graphics. You don't always have to use a separate drawing program to create graphics, however. To enhance a page with simple graphics, such as lines, circles, and squares, you can put the drawing tools provided by Publisher to work.

This chapter examines drawing and editing with the drawing tools included in Publisher. First, you will learn how to use the line, oval, and box drawing tools. Using the Custom Shapes tool to draw other shapes such as stars, triangles, and diamonds is also covered. The chapter then discusses editing graphics by moving, sizing, and rotating them. The chapter ends with options for formatting graphics by adding color, borders, arrowheads, and shadows.

Drawing Graphics with Publisher

Publisher provides a set of drawing tools enabling you to create simple illustrations, graphs, maps, and logos. In fact, many publications, such as flyers and postcards, created with PageWizards already include graphics created with Publisher's drawing tools. Whether you drew the graphic or a PageWizard added it, graphics can be manipulated in many ways. For example, you can move a graphic, size it, or rotate it. You can also choose from a wide range of fill colors and border thicknesses to create even more enticing designs.

Unlike clip art and other graphics, graphic shapes created with Publisher's drawing tools are not placed in frames. Graphics are placed directly on the page. They can be drawn overlapping a frame, but they are not connected to the frame. For instance, if you delete a frame, any graphics overlapping the frame are *not* deleted.

NOTE: *Many commands for editing frames also apply to editing graphics created with Publisher's drawing tools. Because of this, you may find you are already familiar with some of the processes discussed in this chapter.*

Drawing Graphics

Publisher's drawing tools are stored in the Graphic toolbox on the left side of your screen. You must select the appropriate tool before drawing a shape. Click on a tool to select it—the tool appears to be "pushed in" when selected. As you move into the page area, notice that the shape of the mouse cursor changes to a cross hair.

Don't worry if the shapes are not in the exact position or size you need. The section "Editing Graphics" of this chapter discusses moving and sizing the shapes. When you begin drawing shapes, they will have a clear fill (or no fill) and a thin line outlining the shape. The steps for adding color and adjusting line thickness are covered later in this chapter.

 **NOTE:**   *You can change the default fill and line attributes of shapes. Refer to Publisher's online help for more information.*

Drawing Lines

 You use the Line tool to draw horizontal, vertical, and diagonal lines. Lines can be used to unite elements on a page, such as artwork and text frames.

It is easy to accidentally draw jagged lines. To create straight lines, press SHIFT while drawing the line. Use SHIFT to draw diagonal lines also; holding SHIFT forces the lines to draw in 45-degree increments.

The following steps illustrate drawing lines:

1. Click on the Line tool in the Graphic toolbox. Move into the page area, and place the cross hair where you want to begin the line.

2. If you want a straight line, press SHIFT. With your other hand, press and hold the mouse button, drag to where you want to end the line, and release the mouse button. Release SHIFT after releasing the mouse button.

To quickly add a diagonal line, select the Line tool and click on the page where you want the line to appear. You could then move and size the line as needed.

 **TIP:**   *A designers' maxim, "Lines should be used to unite or separate, not just to decorate," means don't add a line unless there is a reason for it. Is it uniting two elements? Is it separating one element from another? If the line serves no purpose, don't add it.*

Drawing Boxes

The Box tool is used to draw boxes or squares. Similar to lines, boxes can unite two elements, such as a photograph and text block. With the Box tool, you can draw rectangular-shaped boxes or perfectly square boxes. To draw square boxes, press SHIFT while drawing the box. Pressing SHIFT constrains the box to a perfect square shape.

The following steps illustrate drawing boxes:

1. Click on the Box tool in the Graphic toolbox. Move into the page area, and place the cross hair where you want the top left corner of the shape to appear.

2. If you want a perfectly square box, press SHIFT. With your other hand, press and hold the mouse button, and drag down and to the right. You'll see an outline of the box as you draw. Release the mouse button when the outline is the size you want. Release SHIFT after releasing the mouse button.

To quickly add a square box, select the Box tool and click on the page where you want the box to appear. You could then move and size the new box as needed.

TIP: *Avoid boxing every element on the page. More than one or two boxes per page can be distracting and looks unprofessional.*

Drawing Ovals

The Oval tool is used to draw ovals or circles. You can use ovals and circles to create a variety of logos and page designs.

With the Oval tool, you can draw ovals or perfect circles. The following steps illustrate drawing a perfect circle. The steps are very similar to those for drawing boxes.

1. Click on the Oval tool in the Graphic toolbox. Move into the page area, and place the cross hair where you want the top left corner of the shape to appear.

2. For a perfect circle, press SHIFT (this constrains the circle to a perfect circle shape). With your other hand, press and hold the mouse button, and drag down and to the right. You'll see an outline of the circle as you draw. Release the mouse button when the outline is the size you want. Release SHIFT after releasing the mouse button.

To quickly add a circle, select the Oval tool and click on the page where you want the circle to appear. You could then move and size the circle as needed.

Drawing Custom Shapes

Publisher provides the Custom Shapes drawing tool to help you quickly create stars, arrows, diamonds, and more. As shown in Figure 11-1, once you click on the tool, you have access to a submenu of different shapes. These shapes are great for creating flyers and overheads.

Similar to drawing squares and circles, you can hold down SHIFT while drawing a custom shape to constrain it to a perfect shape. For instance, hold SHIFT while drawing a star to create a perfectly proportioned star.

The following steps illustrate drawing custom shapes:

1. Click on the Custom Shapes tool in the Graphic toolbox. From the submenu, click on the shape you want to draw.

2. Move into the page area, and place the cross hair where you want the top left corner of the shape to appear.

3. If you want a perfect shape, press SHIFT. With your other hand, press and hold the mouse button, and drag down and to the right. You'll see an outline of the shape as you draw. Release the mouse button when the outline is the size you want. Release SHIFT after releasing the mouse button.

You can quickly add a shape to the page by selecting the Custom Shapes tool and clicking on the page where you want the shape. The shape can then be moved and sized as needed.

NOTE: *You can modify the shape of custom graphics. For more information, refer to the section "Adjusting the Shape of Custom Graphics" later in this chapter.*

Drawing Several Shapes at One Time

After you draw a shape, Publisher automatically selects the Pointer tool in the Graphic toolbox. After a circle is drawn, for example, the Oval tool is deselected and the Pointer tool is selected. If you want to draw another circle, you must reselect

11

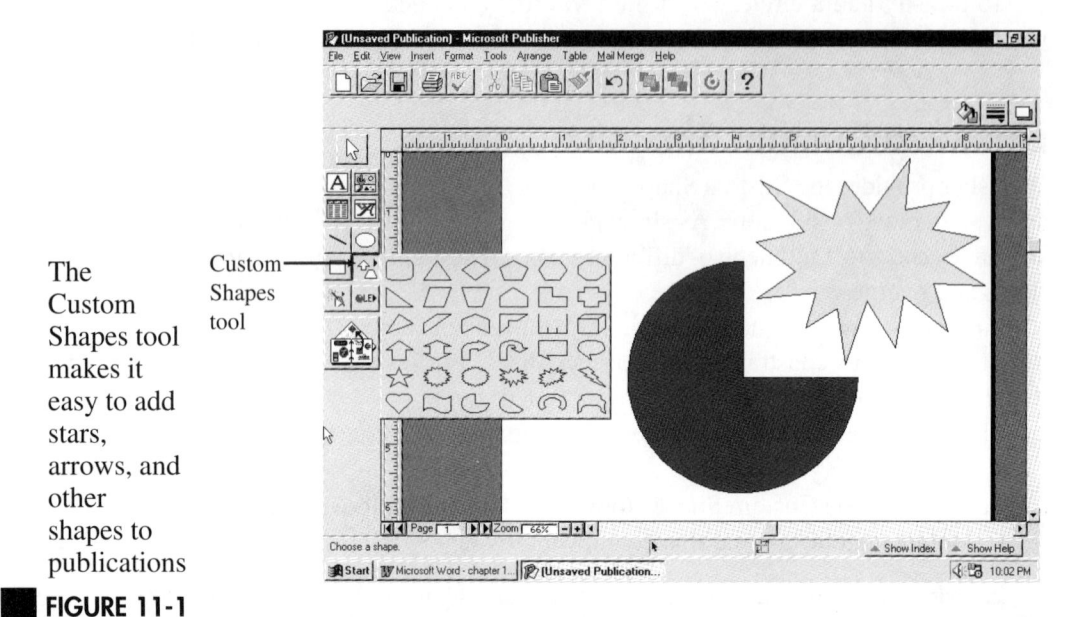

The Custom Shapes tool makes it easy to add stars, arrows, and other shapes to publications

FIGURE 11-1

the Oval tool. If you press CTRL as you select a drawing tool, however, the drawing tool stays selected, enabling you to draw multiple shapes. Pressing CTRL while selecting the Oval tool, for example, keeps the Oval tool selected so you can draw several circles or ovals at one time.

 **TIP:**   *You can also use the scratch area—the gray area surrounding the page area—as extra workspace for drawing objects. Objects in the scratch area do not print.*

Editing Graphics

Tinkering with a graphic's size and position or flipping and rotating it are all part of designing. This section focuses on selecting, deleting, moving, sizing, rotating, flipping, and stacking graphics created with Publisher's drawing tools.

Graphics, like frames and text, can be cut, copied, and pasted by use of the cut, copy, and paste commands in the edit menu, or by use of the Cut, Copy, and Paste tools in the Standard toolbar. Refer to the section "Moving and Copying Frames to Other Pages" in Chapter 7 for more information.

Selecting Graphics

Before moving, sizing, or formatting graphics, you must select the graphic to be edited. Selecting indicates to Publisher which graphic on the page you want the editing command to modify. Before deleting a circle, for example, you must select it. Before adding color to a box, you must select the box.

Selecting graphics is similar to selecting frames. Selection handles appear around a graphic immediately after it is drawn (see Figure 11-2). To select another graphic, position the mouse cursor on the shape and click. Selection handles appear around the graphic, indicating it is selected.

By default, only one graphic can be selected at a time. To select several graphics, press SHIFT while clicking on the other graphics. To select two graphics, for example, select the first graphic, press SHIFT, and click on the second graphic. Gray selection handles appear around both frames, indicating both are selected. Selecting several graphics at one time enables you to move or format all selected graphics at one time.

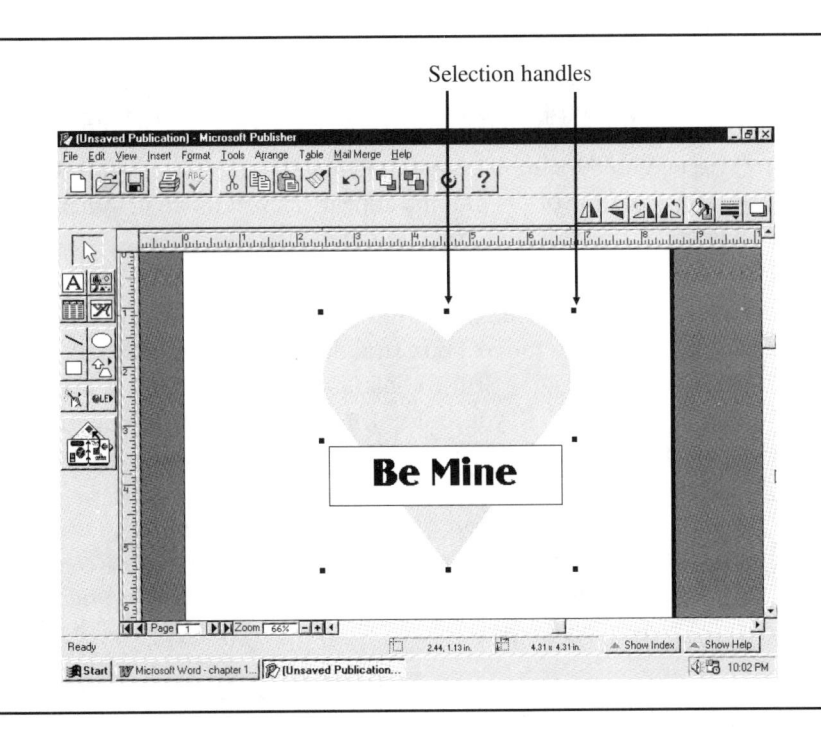

Selection
handles
appear
around
selected
graphics

FIGURE 11-2

 **TIP:** *You can also use the Pointer tool to draw a box around the graphics you want to select. All graphics in the box are selected when you release the mouse button. This is a great way to select a lot of graphics quickly.*

Deleting Objects

After drawing graphics on your page, you might decide you added a few too many. To delete a graphic, simply select it and press DELETE. To delete several graphics at one time, press SHIFT to select multiple graphics, and then press DELETE.

If you accidentally delete a graphic, immediately choose Undo from the Edit menu to retrieve it.

Moving Graphics

You can move graphics anywhere on the page (even off the page), giving you full control over the page design. If you have several frames selected, they will move together as a group. The following steps illustrate moving a graphic:

1. Select the graphic. Selection handles appear around the shape.

2. Position the mouse cursor on the graphic (not on a selection handle). The shape of the mouse cursor changes to the Mover (a moving van) cursor.

3. Press and hold the mouse, and drag the graphic to a new place on the page. An outline of the graphic appears as you move it. When the graphic is in the desired location, release the mouse button.

Hold SHIFT as you move a graphic to limit its movement to up and down or left and right. For instance, to move a box straight up or down, hold SHIFT as you drag the box up or down. Pressing SHIFT constrains the movement so the box does not move to the left or right. If you hold SHIFT and drag to the left or right, SHIFT constrains the movement so the box does not move up or down.

TIP: *The shortcut for quickly duplicating objects also applies to graphics. While dragging a selected graphic, hold CTRL. Release the mouse before releasing CTRL to create a duplicate of the graphic. The original graphic stays in the original position.*

Nudging Graphics

Sometimes it's hard to move a graphic a small distance with the mouse. Nudging is another way to move graphics. Nudging allows you to move graphics in one direction in small increments. To nudge a selected graphic, hold ALT and tap one of the directional arrow keys on your keyboard. The graphic moves one pixel each time you press an arrow key.

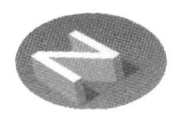 **NOTE:** *As with frames, you can also nudge graphics with the Nudge Object command in the Arrange menu. Refer to "Nudging Frames" in Chapter 7 for more information.*

Sizing Objects

It can be tricky to get the perfect size for a graphic on the first try. Rather then deleting the graphic and starting over, you can adjust the size of the graphic to meet your needs. As with sizing frames, the selection handles are used to size graphics:

- Use the corner handles to adjust both the width and height of the graphic.

- Use the middle selection handles to size the graphic in one direction only.

For example, when sizing a box, you would use the top middle selection handle to adjust the height of the box. You could use the left middle selection handle to adjust the width of the box. Use of one of the corner handles would adjust the height and width of the box.

The following steps illustrate sizing a graphic:

1. Select the graphic and position the mouse cursor over one of the selection handles. The mouse cursor changes to the Resizer cursor when placed on a selection handle.

2. To enlarge the graphic, drag away from its center. To reduce the graphic, drag toward its center.

3. An outline of the graphic appears as you size it. When the graphic is the desired size, release the mouse button.

11

Although sizing enlarges or reduces graphics, it can also change the proportion of a shape. For instance, when sizing, you can change a circle into an oval, or a square into a rectangle. If you want to maintain the original proportion of a shape, hold SHIFT as you size it. For instance, hold SHIFT while sizing a star to enlarge or reduce the star without distorting its original shape.

Adjusting the Shape of Custom Graphics

The shape of several custom graphics can be adjusted. For instance, in Figure 11-3, the top row of graphics shows them as they were originally created and the bottom row shows them after they were adjusted. As you can see, you can, for example, change the direction of the tip for cartoon balloons and the thickness of arrowheads in arrow shapes. The ability to fine-tune the shape of graphics is very handy when you are designing flowcharts and overheads.

As you know, selection handles appear around a custom shape immediately after it is drawn. Some custom shapes will also display a small white diamond. To adjust the shape, place your mouse on the white diamond. The mouse cursor changes to

If a white diamond appears when a graphic is selected, you can adjust the shape of the graphic

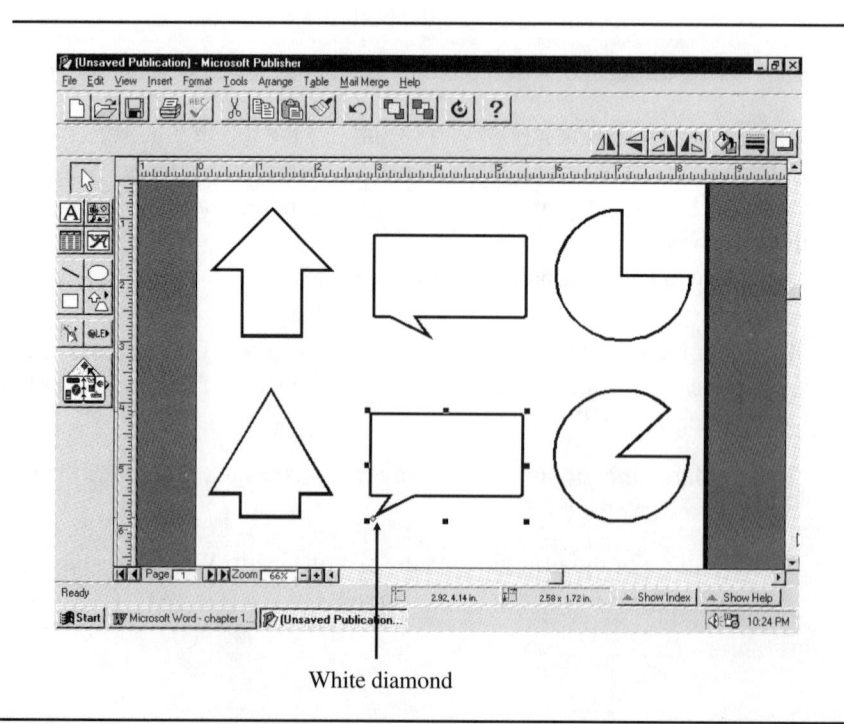

White diamond

FIGURE 11-3

display the Adjust icon—a double-sided arrow. Press and hold the mouse button, and drag the mouse to adjust the shape. An outline of the shape appears as you adjust it. When the graphic appears in the desired shape, release the mouse button.

Rotating Graphics

Graphics, similar to frames, can be rotated to add special emphasis. For instance, you may need to rotate an arrow so it points at a particular object. As shown in Figure 11-4, the Formatting toolbar provides tools for rotating graphics. After selecting a graphic, click on the Rotate Right tool to rotate the graphic 90 degrees to the right. Click on the Rotate Left tool to rotate the graphic 90 degrees to the left.

As described in the following steps, you can also use the mouse to quickly rotate a graphic:

1. Select the graphic and position the mouse cursor over one of the selection handles.

2. Press and hold ALT to display the Rotator icon. Hold the mouse button and drag clockwise or counterclockwise to rotate the graphic.

3. Release the mouse button and ALT when the outline of the graphic is in the desired position. You cannot rotate more than one graphic at a time this way.

As with frames, hold CTRL-ALT and press LEFT ARROW to rotate a graphic counterclockwise 5 degrees at a time. Hold CTRL-ALT and press RIGHT ARROW to rotate a graphic clockwise 5 degrees at a time.

 **NOTE:** *As discussed in the section "Rotating Frames" in Chapter 7, the Rotate/Flip and Custom Rotate commands are additional ways to rotate graphics. You can rotate one or several frames at a time with this method.*

11

Flipping Objects

Graphics can be flipped (or mirrored) vertically or horizontally. As shown in Figure 11-5, Publisher provides tools for flipping on the Formatting toolbar. Only graphics created with Publisher's drawing tools can be flipped. You cannot flip clip art and other graphics placed in frames.

Rotate Right tool   Rotate Left tool

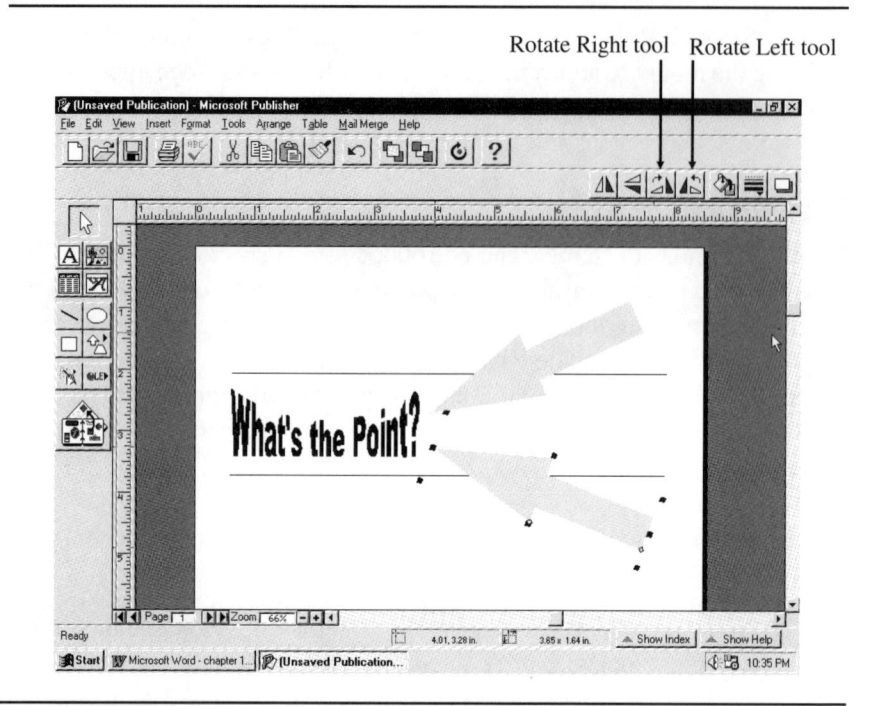

Use the Rotate Right and Rotate Left tools to quickly rotate graphics

FIGURE 11-4

Flip Horizontal tool   Flip Vertical tool

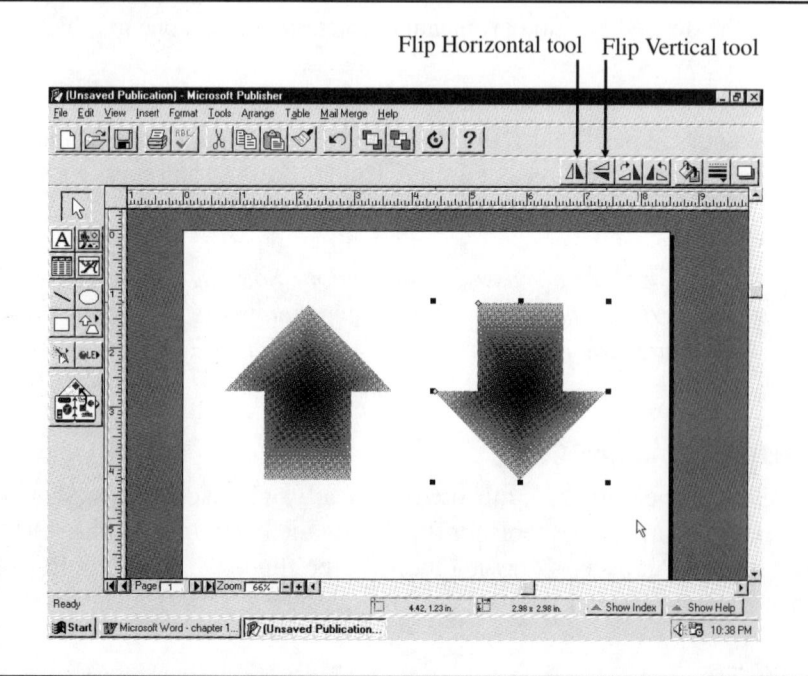

Flipping enables you to change the direction of a graphic

FIGURE 11-5

After selecting a graphic, click on the Flip Horizontal tool to flip the graphic along its horizontal axis. For example, you might want to horizontally flip a left-pointing arrow so it points to the right. Select the graphic and click on the Flip Vertical tool to flip the graphic along its vertical axis. For instance, you might want to vertically flip an arrow that points up so that it points down.

The Arrange menu provides another way to flip graphics. After selecting a graphic, choose Rotate/Flip from the Arrange menu. From the submenu, choose Flip Horizontal or Flip Vertical.

Layering Graphics

Graphics drawn with Publisher's drawing tools are placed on the page in the order they were drawn or pasted on the page. In the left set of graphics in Figure 11-6, a triangle was drawn first, then a star burst, and finally the half-circle shape. Because the triangle was drawn first, it is on the bottom, and because the half circle was drawn last, it is on top.

At times, you might want to change the layering order of graphics by moving a graphic in front of or behind other graphics. For example, in the right set of graphics in Figure 11-6, the triangle was moved to the front. Publisher allows you to bring

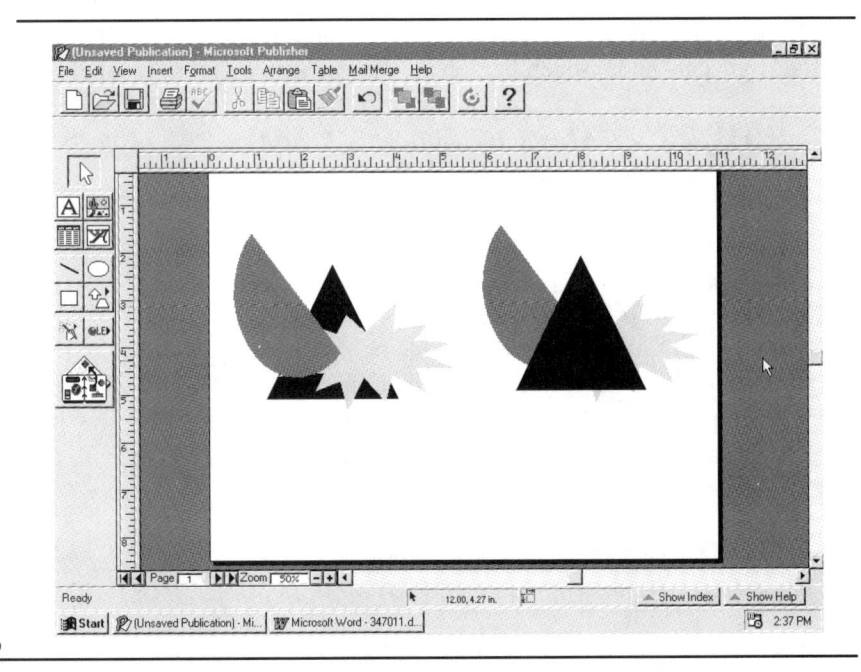

You can change the layering order of graphics

FIGURE 11-6

graphics all the way to the front or forward one graphic at a time. For instance, in the left set of graphics in Figure 11-6, moving the triangle forward one graphic would place it in front of the star burst—but not in front of the half circle. You can also send graphics all the way to the back, or back one graphic at a time.

The following steps illustrate adjusting the layering order of graphics:

1. Select the graphic you want to reposition.

2. From the Arrange menu, choose

   - *Bring To Front* to place the selected graphic on the top layer—in front of other graphics and frames

   - *Bring Closer* to place the selected graphic in front of the object directly above it

   - *Send To Back* to place the selected graphic on the bottom layer—behind other graphics and frames

   - *Send Farther* to place the selected graphic behind the object directly behind it

Frames are also affected when you are layering graphics. You can draw a graphic on top of a frame and then send the graphic behind the frame. As another example, if a frame appears under several graphics, you can move it to the front of the graphics.

TIP: *Use the keyboard shortcut F6 to bring selected objects to the front, and SHIFT-F6 to send selected objects to the back.*

Aligning Graphics

An internal part of page design is aligning or arranging page elements. For instance, the graphics in flowcharts need to be lined up horizontally and vertically. It looks unprofessional if graphics are just scattered everywhere on the page. Since alignment is an important issue, Publisher provides several methods for getting your page organized.

NOTE: *The alignment features discussed here also apply to aligning frames. Refer to Chapter 7 for more information about working with frames.*

Using the Ruler Guidelines

Publisher's ruler guidelines provide a quick, easy way to align graphics and other elements in your page designs. Ruler guidelines are nonprinting horizontal and vertical lines that you position on the page. The lines have a Snap To feature that works like a "magnet," pulling objects to the guidelines.

To place a ruler guideline on a page, place the cursor in the horizontal or vertical ruler. Hold SHIFT, press and hold the mouse button, and drag down into the page. A guideline appears—release the mouse button when the guideline is in the desired position. As shown in Figure 11-7, you can place several guidelines on the page.

Once the guidelines are on the page, you can move graphics close to the guidelines and they will "snap to" or align themselves to the guideline. In Figure 11-7, the guidelines are used to align the shapes in a flowchart.

The Snap To feature of the guidelines can be turned on and off. For instance, you may want Snap To turned on when placing graphics in a flowchart. However, you may want Snap To turned off when placing text, so text does not align to the guidelines. The Snap To Ruler Guides command is in the Tools menu. If a check mark appears by the command, it is turned on; click on the command to remove the

Make sure the Snap To Ruler Guides command is turned on when you are aligning graphics with ruler guidelines

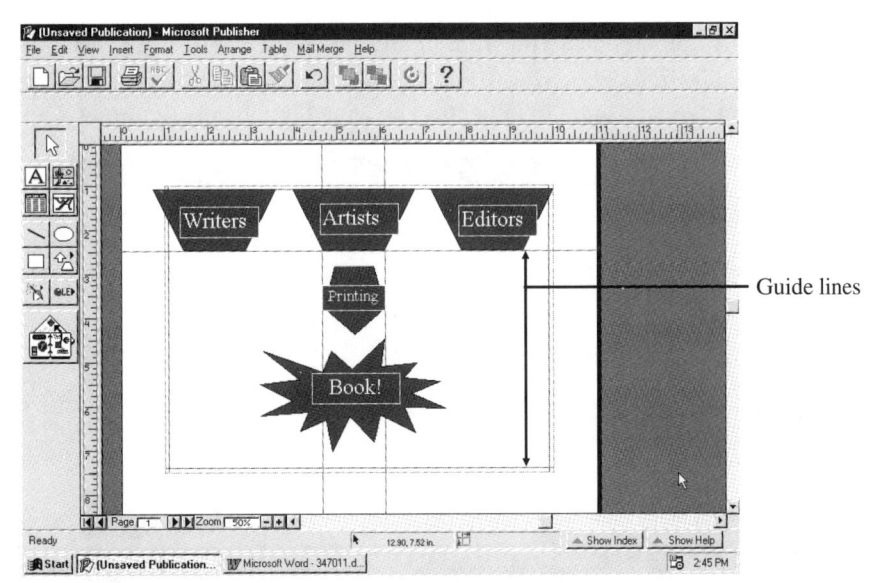

Guide lines

FIGURE 11-7

check mark and turn it off. Likewise, if there is no check mark, click on the command to add a check mark and activate Snap To.

TIP: *Press CTRL-W to quickly turn the Snap To Ruler Guides command on and off.*

To move a guideline, make sure the Pointer tool is selected. Place the cursor on the guide line and press SHIFT. Drag the guideline to a new location. To remove a guideline, use the same steps, but drag the guideline back to the ruler.

NOTE: *If you do not hold SHIFT when dragging on the ruler, the actual ruler will move. Moving the ruler can be useful when you are aligning graphics and other page elements. Refer to Chapter 4 for more information on moving rulers and zero points.*

Using the Line Up Objects Command

The Line Up Objects command provides another way to align graphics on the page. Graphics can be aligned with other graphics—for instance, in the organization chart in Figure 11-8, the tops of the rectangles were aligned.

The following steps describe aligning graphics with other graphics:

1. Select the graphics you want to align with each other. For instance, in an organization chart, you would select a row of boxes. From the Arrange menu, select Line Up Objects. The Line Up Objects dialog box appears.

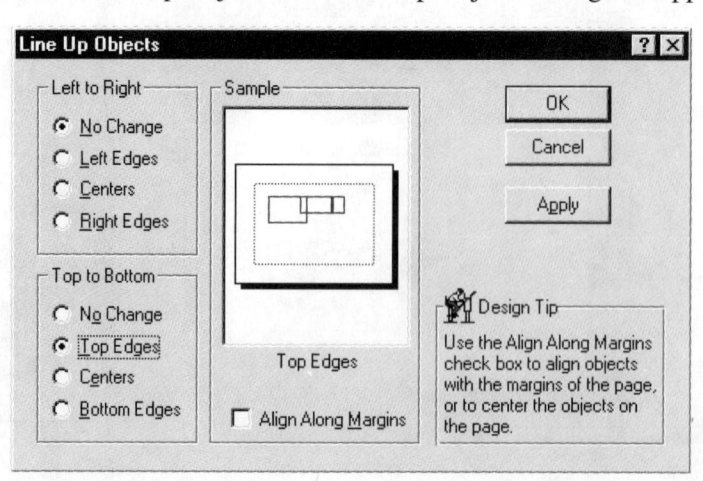

2. Choose the desired alignment options under Left To Right and Top To Bottom. For instance, in the organization chart, you could choose Top Edges to horizontally align the boxes. A sample of the alignment appears. Click OK.

The Line Up Objects command also provides an option for placing one or several graphics in the exact center of the page. For instance, after designing a logo with the drawing tools, you may want to move it to the center of the page. If several graphics are selected, the graphics are moved to the center of the page and overlap each other. Use the following steps to place graphics in the center of a page:

1. Select the graphic(s) you want to align.

2. From the Arrange menu, select Line Up Objects. Below the sample in the Line Up Objects dialog box, click on Align Along Margins.

3. Under Left To Right, click on Centers, and under Top To Bottom, click on Centers. Click OK to place the graphics in the center of the page.

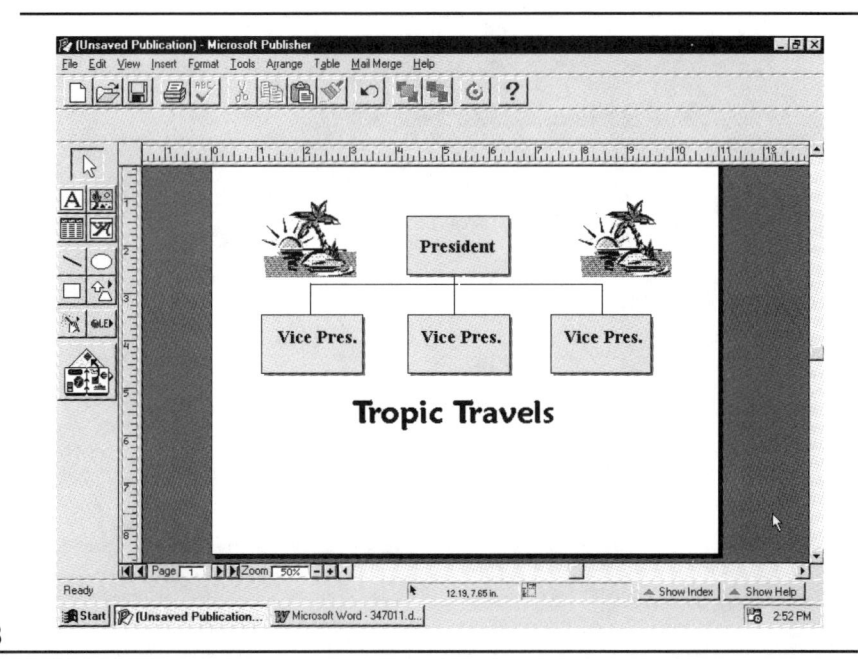

The Line Up Objects command allows you to align graphics with each other

FIGURE 11-8

If you don't want the graphics to overlap each other when moved to the center of the page, group the graphics first. Grouping is discussed in the next section.

Grouping Graphics

Graphics, like frames, can be grouped for easier manipulation. After arranging several graphics into a logo or chart, you could group the graphics to move them around the page as one element. Grouping also allows you to format several graphics at one time. For instance, in an organization chart, you might want all boxes to be filled with gray and to have a thick black border. Rather than formatting each box individually, you could group the boxes and then format all of them at once.

To group several graphics, select them. Remember, hold SHIFT to select more than one graphic at a time. Gray selection handles appear around each selected object. As displayed in Figure 11-9, the Group Objects icon also appears. Click on the Group Objects icon to group the graphics together. Now, whenever you click on any part of the group, all of the graphics are selected. You can move, size, and rotate the group as one object now.

Use the Group Objects icon to quickly group several graphics

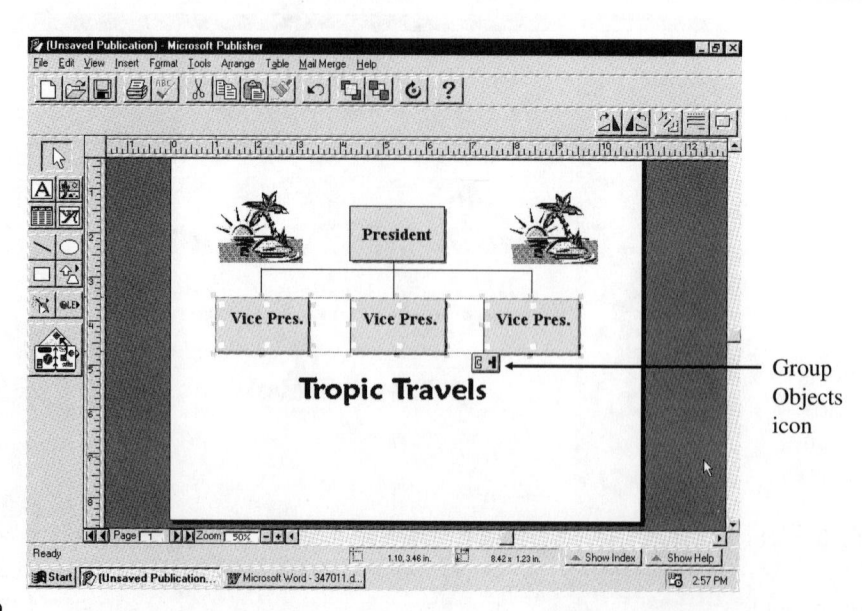

Group Objects icon

FIGURE 11-9

You can also combine graphics and frames into groups. For instance, you could group a text frame with a circle, or a picture frame with an arrow. To ungroup the frames, click on the Ungroup Objects icon. The graphics are ungrouped and become separate again.

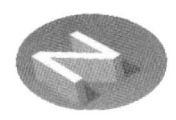 **NOTE:** *Some publications created by PageWizards use grouped objects; before manipulating these objects individually, you would have to ungroup them.*

Formatting Graphics

You can enhance graphics created in Publisher with color, borders, and shadows. Adding color to a logo or chart really makes it pop out on the page. Even if you can't afford color, special effects such as shadows and borders add pizzazz to a publication. If you're new to graphic design, take time to experiment with the effects available for graphics, such as gradient fills, that make page design fun and creative.

Many of the formatting options discussed here also apply to frames. For instance, the gradient and pattern fills discussed in this chapter can also be applied to frames. Refer to Chapter 7 for more information on working with frames.

Applying Fills to Graphics

You have several choices for adding fills to graphics created in Publisher. You can select a solid color, tints or shades, patterns, or gradient blends. When selecting colors, remember the process you will be using to print the publication. If you will be printing in black and white, stick with black, white, and shades of gray. If you are printing one spot color, select the color and stick with it (and black and shades of gray) as you design. If you are outputting to a full-color printer, you can select any color. Printing methods and color printing are discussed in Chapter 10.

11

 **NOTE:** *Use the Recolor Object command discussed in Chapter 9 to change the colors in clip art and graphics created in other drawing applications.*

When applying fills to graphics, keep in mind that only closed shapes, such as boxes, can hold a fill. A fill color cannot be added to open shapes, such as lines. When a fill is applied to a graphic, the fill prevents any underlying elements from showing through the graphic. For instance, in Figure 11-10, you cannot see through

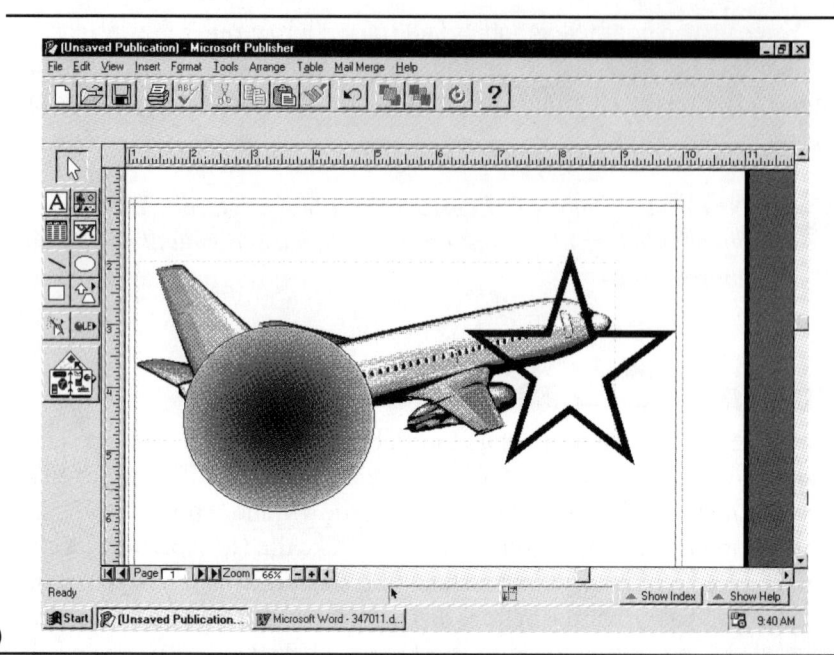

Use opaque and clear fills to create a variety of effects with graphics

FIGURE 11-10

the circle with a gradient fill. You can see through the star with a clear fill. A clear fill is different from a white fill—a clear fill is transparent, a white fill is opaque. Selecting a clear fill is discussed in the next section.

Applying Solid Fill Colors to Graphics

When you select a fill color, Publisher displays RGB values for some of the colors. (Recall from Chapter 7 that RGB stands for red, green, and blue—the color model used to display color on monitors.) The values indicate how much of a certain color is used. For instance, with the color RGB 102, 255, 15, the first number represents the value of red; the second, the value of green; and the third, the value of blue.

The following steps illustrate adding color to graphics. The option of selecting Clear for creating transparent frames is also noted.

1. Select the graphic(s) to which you want to apply color.

2. From the Format menu, choose Fill Color. The Colors dialog box appears.

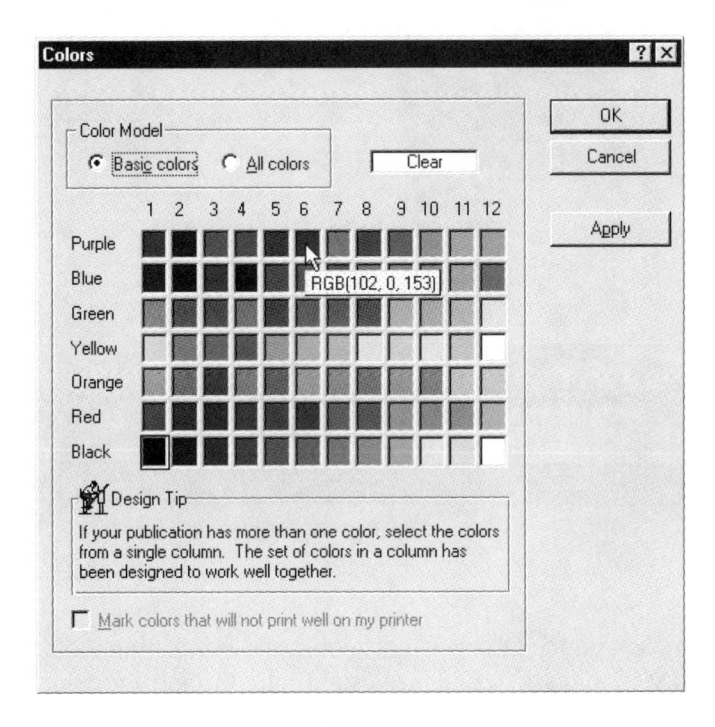

3. Place your mouse over a color to display the color name or RGB values.

4. Click on a color to select it. To create a transparent graphic, click on Clear at the top of the dialog box. Click OK to apply the color.

For more color choices, click on the All Colors option at the top of the Colors dialog box. A spectrum of colors is displayed. You can click on a color in the spectrum or build your own colors by entering RGB values. You can also enter HSL values for Hue, Saturation, and Luminance—another color model frequently used by graphic designers for building colors.

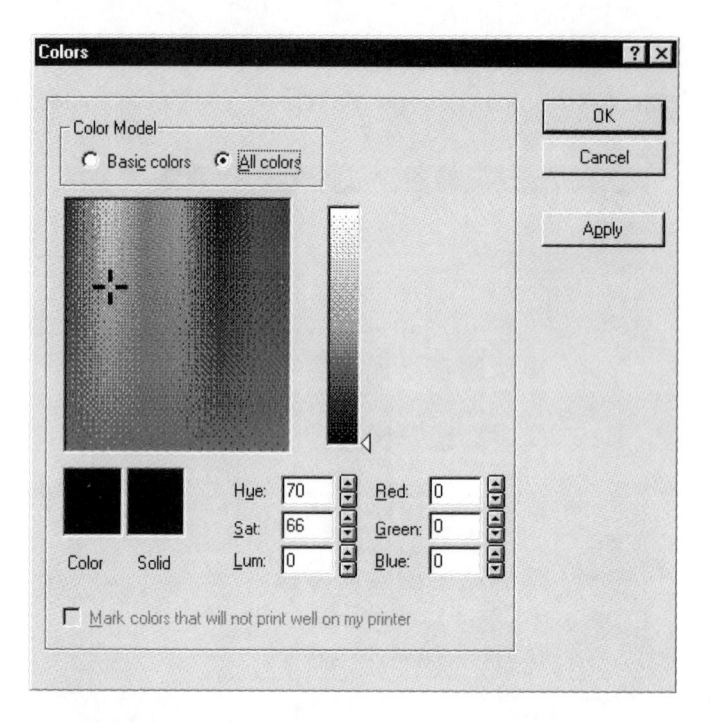

 You can click on the Object Color tool in the Formatting toolbar to display a drop-down list of colors. Click on the desired color to apply the color to the selected graphic(s). Click on the Clear option to create a transparent graphic.

 **TIP:** *Use the keyboard shortcut CTRL-T to toggle back and forth between transparent and white filled graphics.*

Working with Tints and Shades

For a little variety, try using tints or shades of colors to fill graphics. A tint reduces the density of the color—for instance, a 30 percent tint of green would print as light green. A shade reduces the color but adds black in place of the removed color. A 30 percent shade of green would print as a dark green with black overtones.

Tints and shades expand the colors you have available. For instance, if you are using a purple spot color, you can use various tints and shades of the purple on your page. It still prints as one color, but can provide the look of several colors.

Use the following steps to apply a tint or shade to graphics:

1. Select the graphic(s) you want to color. From the Format menu, choose Fill Patterns And Shading.

2. In the middle of the dialog box, click on the down arrow by Color 1 and choose a color.

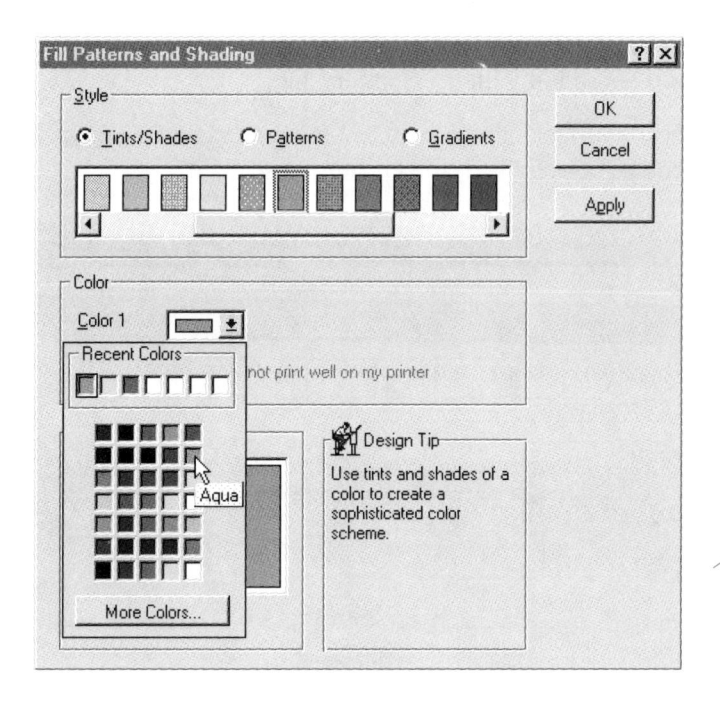

3. At the top of the dialog box, the available tints and shades for the color appear. Use the scroll bar to see all of the choices.

4. Click on the desired tint or shade. The sample shows the color and the percentage of tinting or shading that you've chosen. Click OK.

Study how other publications use tints and shades. In general you'll find that it's okay to apply the tints or shades to several objects—just don't use every shade and tint available on one page. Do some test print runs with the tints and shades. The shades can appear rather dark on the page—looking more like black than any other color. The tints can print with a "dot pattern" look. Find the ones that work for you.

Working with Fill Patterns

Publisher also enables you to fill graphics with two-color patterns. The patterns can be useful when you are creating charts and other design elements. The patterns are composed of simple patterns, such as polka dots and cross hatches. You select the foreground and background colors for the patterns.

Use the following steps to add a pattern to graphic(s):

1. Select the graphic where you want to add a pattern. From the Format menu, choose Fill Patterns And Shading.

2. At the top of the dialog box, select Patterns to display the available patterns. Click on the desired pattern to select it.

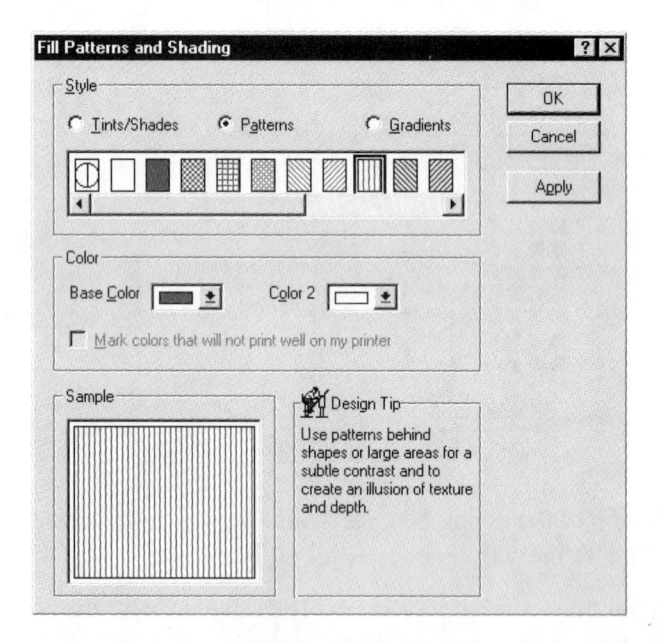

3. In the middle of the dialog box, click on the down arrow by Base Color and choose the foreground color. Click on the down arrow by Color 2 and choose the background color.

4. Review the sample and click OK.

Patterns can increase the time it takes to print a publication. If this is an issue, use patterns sparingly and in small areas on the page.

Applying Gradient Fills to Graphics

Gradient fills blend one color into another. For example, a gradient fill might blend red into orange. Gradient fills are great for adding shading and highlighting effects and Publisher provides a variety of gradient styles.

The following steps outline adding gradient fills to graphics:

1. Select the graphic(s) where you want to add a gradient. From the Format menu, choose Fill Patterns And Shading.

2. At the top of the dialog box, select Gradients to see the available gradient styles. Use the scroll bar to see all of the choices.

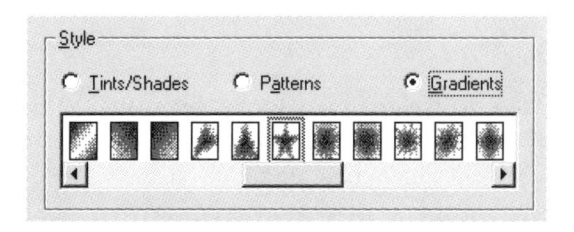

3. In the middle of the dialog box, click on the down arrow by Base Color and choose a color. Click on the down arrow by Color 2 and choose the second color.

4. Review the sample and click OK.

For best results, create gradient fills that use similar colors. For instance, a gradient fill might blend from yellow to orange, or yellow to light green. These blends also look more realistic. Blending from opposite colors, such as red to green, or yellow to purple, can create a brownish, "muddy-looking" section in the middle of the blend.

Applying Line Attributes

You can change the color and thickness of lines. A line can be the outline surrounding a closed shape or just a simple straight line. You can format lines to create a thick outline around a triangle, or build a thin line to underline the company name. As with fill colors, remember to consider printing methods when adding color to lines. Use only colors your selected printing process can print.

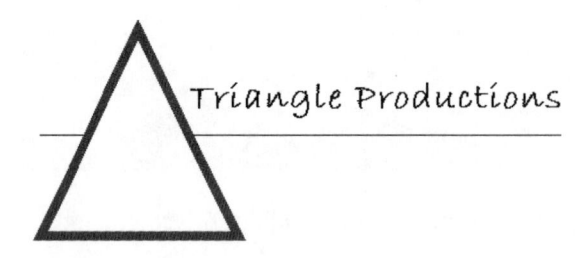

Line thickness is measured in points, as is type size. There are 72 points per inch. Points are actually easier to work with than inches. For example, to get a thin line, you can use 2 points as opposed to .02778 inch.

 **NOTE:** *BorderArt, discussed in Chapter 7, can only be applied to frames, not to graphics created with Publisher's drawing tools.*

Publisher uses the Line dialog box to format lines, and the Border dialog box to format the outline of graphic shapes. They are basically the same dialog boxes, except the Line dialog box provides an option for adding arrowheads (discussed next). The following steps illustrate use of the Border dialog box to adjust line color and thickness:

1. Select the line or graphic whose outline you want to modify. If a line is selected, choose Line from the Format menu. If another type of graphic is selected, such as a circle, choose Border from the Format menu. This example uses the Border dialog box.

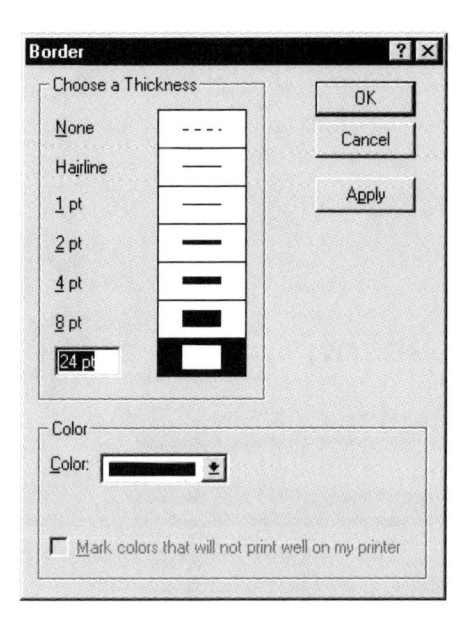

2. Several preset line thickness are available; click one to select it. To set a custom line thickness, click in the white box and enter the desired thickness. For instance, enter **24** to create a 24 point line.

3. To select a line color, click on the down arrow by Color. Select a color from the palette, or click on the More Colors option to see a wider range of colors. Click on the Patterns & Shading option to apply tints and shades of colors to lines.

4. Click OK to apply the selected attributes to the line or graphic.

You can also click on the Border tool in the Formatting toolbar to adjust line thickness and color. Click on the More option to display the Border Or Line dialog box. For more information about the colors available, refer to the previous section, "Applying Fills to Graphics," in this chapter. You cannot apply patterns and gradient fills to lines and the outlines around graphics.

NOTE: *Hairlines and outlines around graphics often don't print well on laser printers. You might try the 1 or 2 point line instead.*

Adding Arrowheads

Publisher also allows you to add arrowheads to lines. The arrowheads help express direction in flowcharts and time lines. Publisher provides a wide variety of arrowheads that can be applied to the beginning and ending point of lines.

Use the following steps to add arrowheads to lines:

1. Select the line or lines where you want arrowheads. From the Format menu, choose Line.

2. In the Arrowheads section of the Line dialog box, click on Right, Left, or Both to add the desired arrowheads.

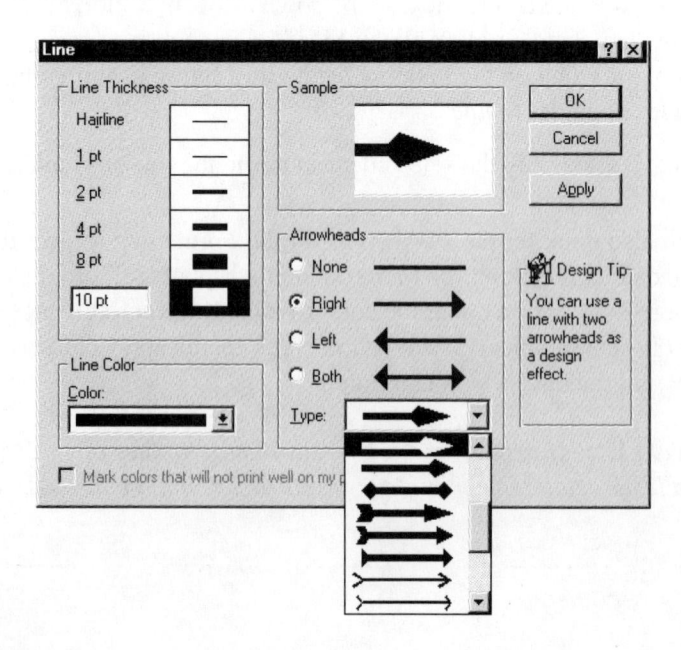

3. Click on the down arrow by Type to select the style of arrowhead. The sample at the top of the dialog box previews the line attributes.

4. Click OK to apply the selected attributes.

The size of the arrowhead is determined by the line thickness, so for larger arrowheads, you might want to increase the line width. You cannot add arrowheads to closed shapes, such as circles and rectangles.

Adding Shadows to Frames

Shadows add depth and dimension to graphics. In Figure 11-11, the shadows on the star bursts add emphasis to the page elements. You can add a shadow to one or several graphics at a time. Simply select the graphic(s) and click on the Add/Remove Shadow tool in the Formatting toolbar.

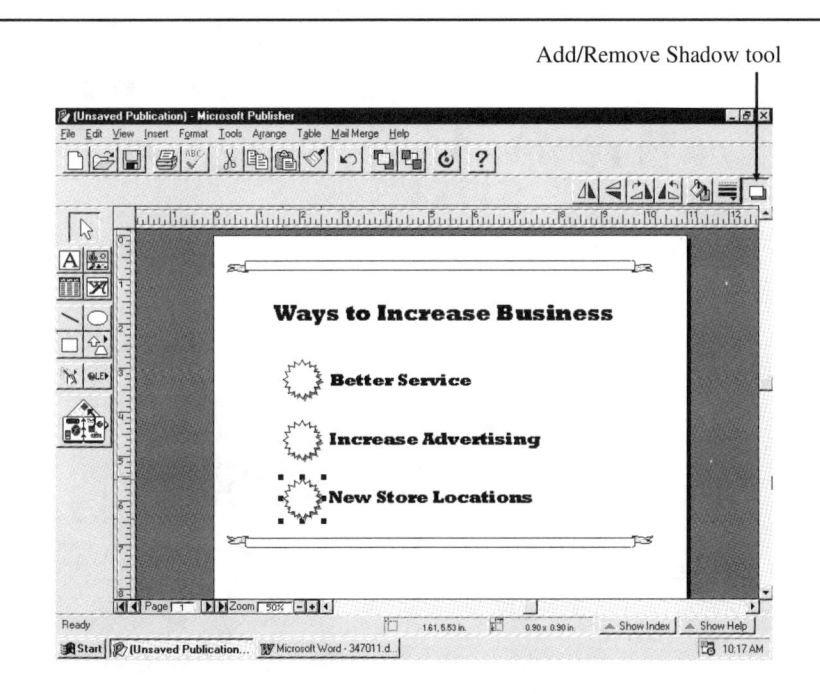

Use shadows to draw attention to objects in a publication

FIGURE 11-11

Creating Logos in Publisher

With a little creative thinking and Publisher's drawing tools, you can create logos for business cards, postcards—even menus. The logos on this page represent two distinct styles of graphic design. The first, a formal, timeless design, is ideal for professional business cards and letterheads. The second is a trendier, contemporary style with a warm, welcoming personality.

Timeless

The first logo was created entirely with text, boxes, and lines. For starters, a box was drawn and duplicated twice. Ruler guidelines were used to align and separate the boxes. The boxes were then filled with increasingly dark shades of gray to lead the eye from left to right. Text was added below the boxes. An elegant typeface was selected, and the spacing between the letters was increased to spread out (and draw attention to) the text. A fourth box was added to unify the design—it cut horizontally through the gray boxes and the descending letter J in the name. The box was then sent to the back, placing it under the gray boxes. The white fill of the text frame blocked the line of the box, so the text frame was made clear. However, once the line under the text was visible, it intersected with the lower part of the letter J. To eliminate the problem, a small box was drawn where the line ran into the letter J (see inset). A white fill with no border was applied to the box. The white box was then sent behind the text but in front of the large box. In effect, the white box blocks out the line behind the letter J.

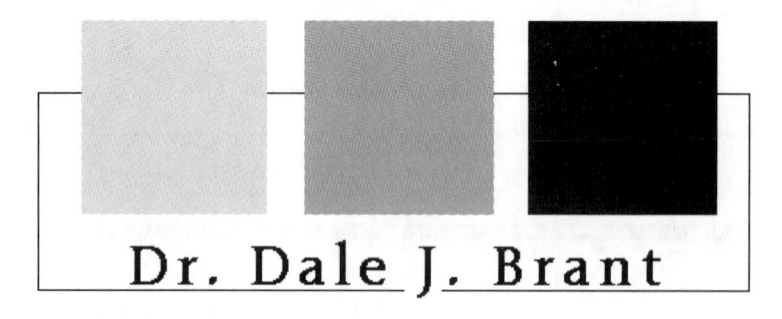

Timeless
logo

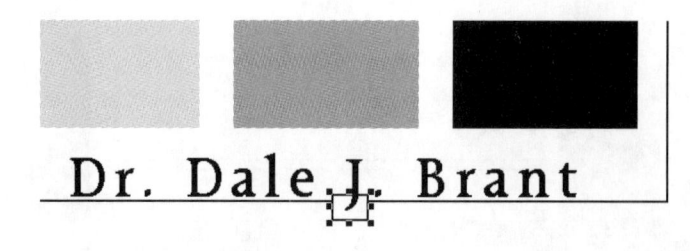

Inset showing
box used to
cover up line
through J

Trendy

The second logo took advantage of Publisher's clip art, decorative typefaces, and Custom Shapes tool. First, the clip art. By use of the Find feature in the Clip Gallery, several variations of coffee cups were quickly found. A casual, uncomplicated style of coffee cup was selected. The colors in the clip art were changed to shades of gray by use of Publisher's Recolor Object feature. The "roof" of the house was created with the Custom Shapes tool. Actually, the shape was drawn as shown in the inset. The shape was then rotated to point up like a roof. A light gray fill was applied to the shape and the border was removed. The shape was placed over the top half of the cup, and then sent to the back behind the cup. The text was entered and centered in a text frame. A decorative, almost handwritten-looking typeface was selected. The spacing between the letters was adjusted to tighten up the typeface, which enhances the graphic appeal of the letters.

Trendy
logo

Inset for
trendy
logo
illustrating
custom
shape used
to create
roof

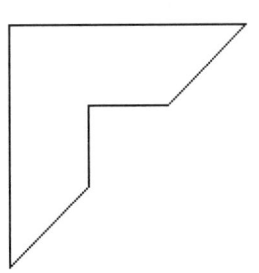

Summary

Publisher provides some nice tools for designing simple graphics. Use the drawing tools in Publisher to add lines, circles, boxes, and other shapes to publications. These tools are great for creating flow charts, organization charts, and basic logos. As discussed in this chapter, you can move, size, flip, and rotate graphics created with Publisher's drawing tools. There are also many options for controlling the color and borders around graphics.

Take some time to experiment with the drawing tools described in this chapter. The possibilities are endless.

12

Adding Tables to Publications

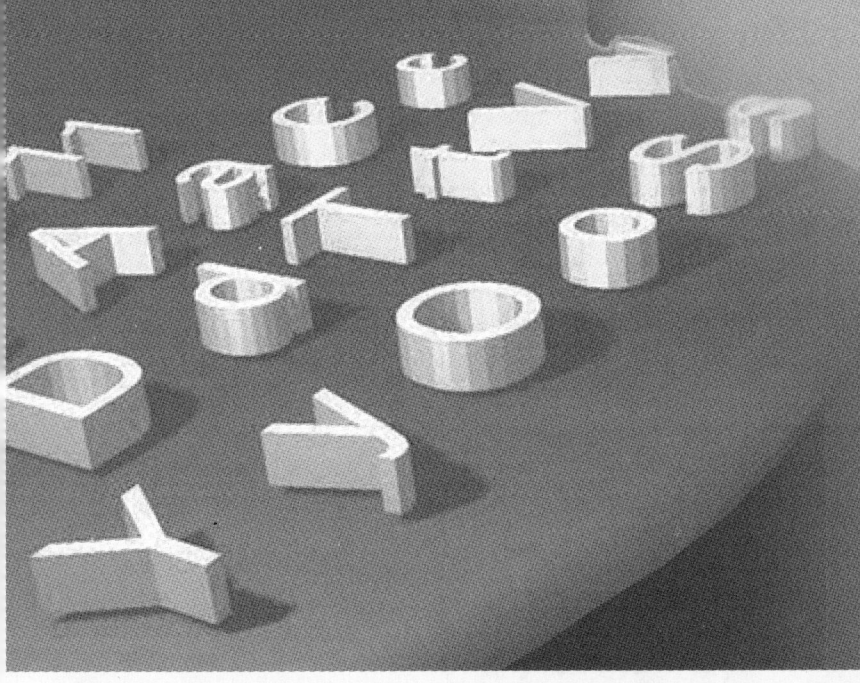

Numerical and technical data such as statistics, price lists, and sales figures are much easier to digest when presented in a table. After you begin to work with tables, their uses become evident. You'll find schedules, calendars, and even forms can be quickly generated using Publisher's table features.

Publisher makes it easy to add tables to publications. You simply draw a table frame and begin entering data. You can format tables to include shading, lines, and borders.

This chapter focuses on creating and formatting tables in Publisher. First, you will learn about the elements that compose a table—rows, columns, and cells. Entering and editing data in tables is covered next. Inserting columns and rows, sizing columns and rows, and merging cells is also discussed. The chapter ends with a look at the many ways you can enhance tables by adding color and table borders.

Understanding Table Structure

A table consists of columns and rows in a grid format that displays data in side-by-side columns. The intersection of a column and a row is called a *cell*. As shown in Figure 12-1, the table text and cells can be formatted to make the data more enticing to read.

When to Use Tables

Tables help you present a lot of information in a concise and orderly way. If you look through publications using tables, you'll see tables have more visual impact on a page than a block of text. In fact, a table can often replace several sentences of text. Use tables in proposals, reports, and brochures to make a point, to support a statement, and to help your reader draw conclusions.

Numerical data can be effectively presented in tables. People in the "number-crunching" business frequently use tables on slides and overheads to help others assimilate the information. Whereas charts and diagrams show trends and comparisons, use a table when you need to focus the reader's attention on the actual numbers and text. The reader can easily read down or across to compare information in the rows and columns.

TIP: *Don't go overboard with tables—too many on the page is intimidating and lessens the impact of the tables on the page.*

Cell   Rows

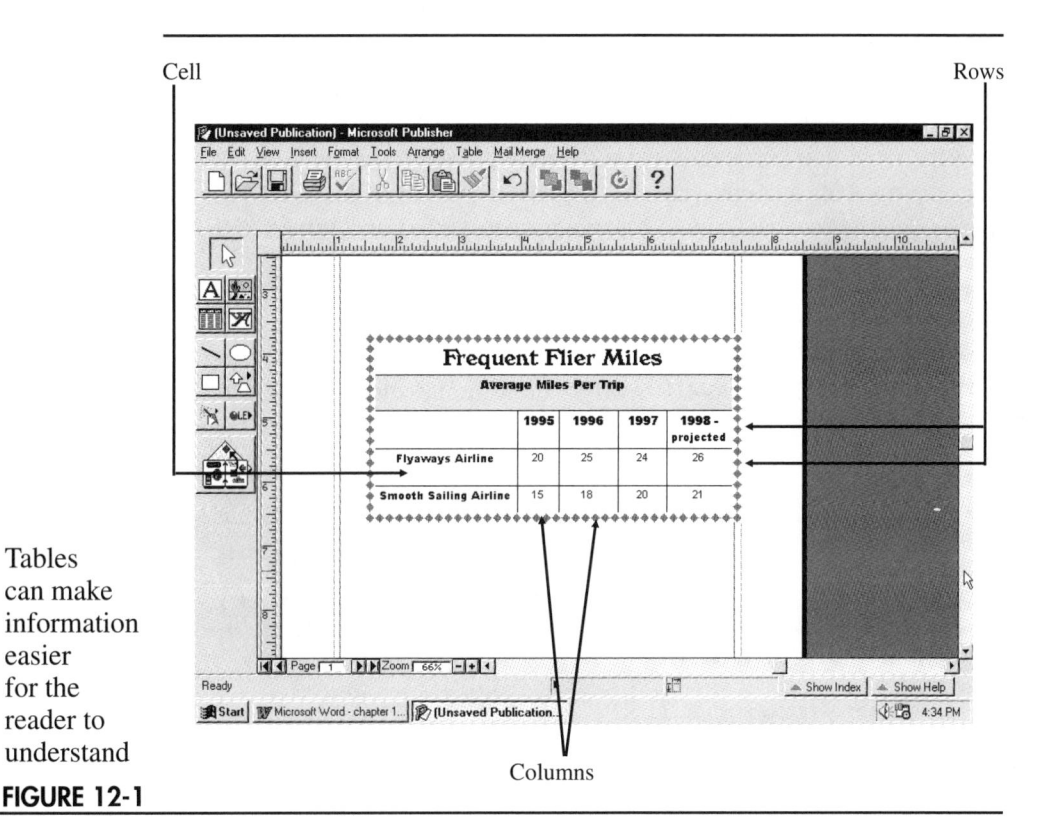

Tables can make information easier for the reader to understand

Columns

FIGURE 12-1

Many users still use TAB or SPACEBAR to line up data in columns and rows. In this chapter, you will discover how much easier and more powerful it is to use the table feature.

Working with Table Frames

As discussed in Chapter 7, Publisher uses table frames to hold and position tables on a page. The frame surrounding a table can be moved, sized, and rotated. BorderArt and fill colors can also be applied to table frames. As with text frames, you can format text in a table by selecting typefaces and sizes. You can also format the columns, rows, and cells in a table. They can all be formatted identically or with different attributes in each cell.

When PageWizards are used to build publications, table frames may already be included on the page. For instance, the newsletter PageWizard places tables on many of the newsletter page designs. The table frames hold sample data that you replace with your data. The tables are already formatted, but you can adjust the formatting to meet your needs.

When you draw table frames on the page yourself, they will be empty until you enter the numbers and other table text. Chapter 7 covered the basics of working with frames, such as drawing frames. Refer to that chapter for more information if necessary.

Creating Tables

Publisher's Table frame tool is used to draw frames that will hold the new table. Immediately after a table frame is drawn, Publisher displays the Create Table dialog box.

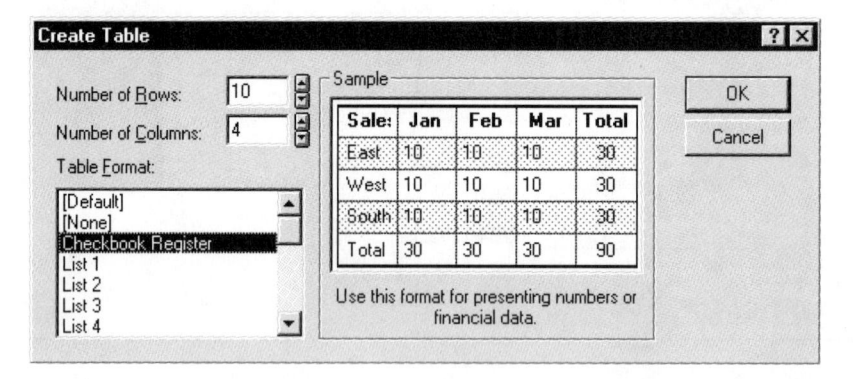

Here, you specify the number of columns and rows you want in the table. Don't worry if you're not sure of the exact number, you can always add or delete columns and rows later.

Click in the Number Of Rows box to enter the desired number of rows for the new table. Click in the Number Of Columns box to enter the desired number of columns. You can also use the default numbers appearing in the boxes. The default numbers are based on the size of the table frame. For instance, if you draw a wide table frame, the number of suggested columns is higher than it would be for a narrower table frame. The number of rows is determined by the height of the table frame.

Saving Time with Automatic Table Formats

The Create Table dialog box also allows you to select a format for the table. Scroll through the choices under Table Format—when you click on a format, a sample appears of the selected formatting. Table formats can save you tons of time by automatically applying lines, shading, and text alignment. If you want to format the table yourself, select the None option. Click OK to create the table.

Examining a Table

Gray buttons appear at the top of each column and to the left of each row after a table is created. The gray buttons indicate the table frame is selected. As with other frames, click away from the frame to deselect it. Click again on the table frame to select it. If formatting was applied to the table, the shading and lines are visible in the new table. If no formatting was applied, nonprinting lines appear around the cells in the table, creating the grid structure. The section "Formatting Tables" later in this chapter examines how to add lines and shading to tables.

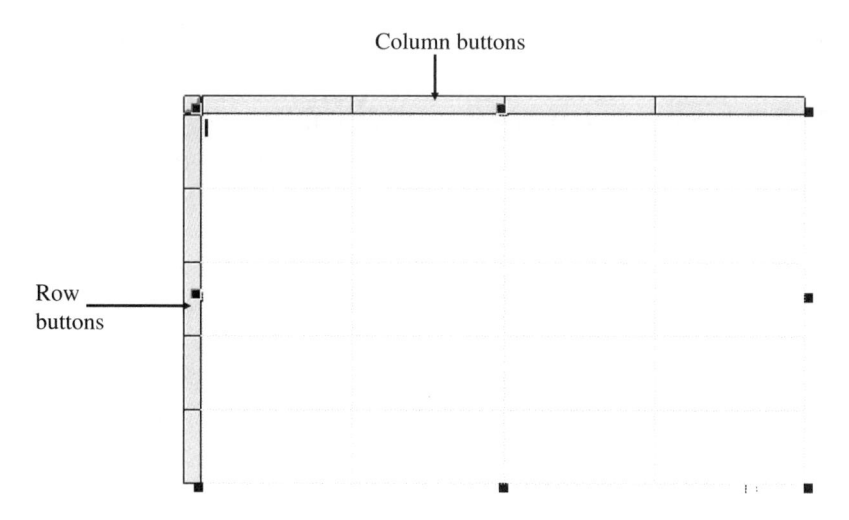

Column buttons

Row buttons

The mouse cursor changes to the I-beam when placed inside the table—this is similar to working with text. The mouse cursor displays as an arrow when placed outside the table.

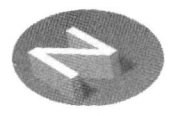 **NOTE:** *Adjusting the size of the table frame will not increase or decrease the number of columns or rows. It only affects the width and height of the columns and rows.*

Moving Through a Table

The insertion point appears in the first cell after a table is created. The cell containing the insertion point is the *active cell.* A cell must be active before you can enter text

12

and numbers into it. One way to make a cell active is to click in it with the mouse. With the keyboard, you can use the arrow keys to move the insertion point through the cells in a table:

- Press UP ARROW or DOWN ARROW to move up or down through the cells in a table.

- Press LEFT ARROW or RIGHT ARROW to move to the left or right. You can also press TAB to move to the next right cell.

- Press SHIFT-TAB to move to the next left cell.

The keys for moving around a table do not circle through the table. For instance, when you press DOWN ARROW to move to the bottom a column, you will need to press RIGHT ARROW and then UP ARROW to move through the next column.

Selecting Cells, Columns, and Rows

As with formatting text, you need to select or highlight cells before modifying the typeface or type size of the text in the cells. You also need to select cells, columns, and rows before adding shading and lines.

To select a cell, place your mouse cursor just left of the cell. Press and hold the mouse button and drag across the cell. It's easy to select two cells accidentally—if this happens, keep pressing the mouse button and drag to the left to select only one cell. The cell turns black, indicating it is selected. To select several cells, use the same steps but just drag across all of the cells you want to select.

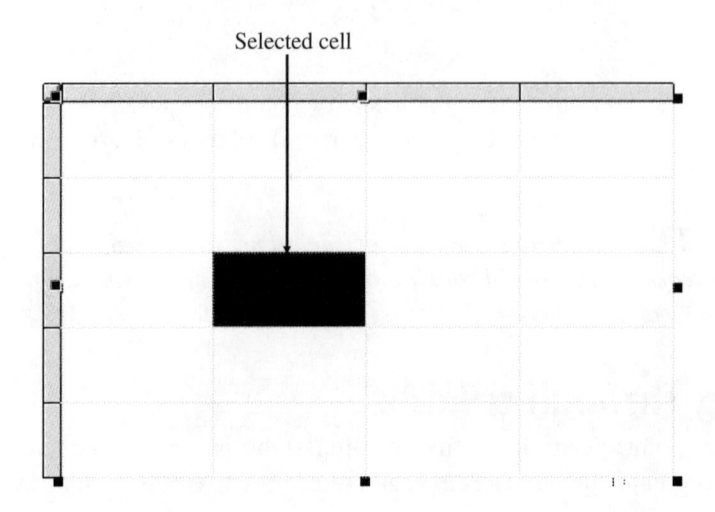

Selected cell

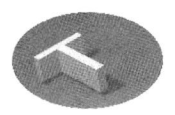 **TIP:** *If you'd rather use the keyboard to select cells, hold SHIFT and press the arrow keys to select several cells at one time.*

Selecting Columns and Rows

To select a whole column, place the mouse on the *column button* (the gray button at the top of the column). When the mouse shape changes to a hand, click to select the column. Drag across several column buttons to select several columns at one time. To select a whole row, place the mouse on the *row button* (the gray button to the left of the row). Again, when the mouse shape changes to a hand, click to select the row. You can also drag across several row buttons to select several rows at once.

Before applying formatting to a whole table, you need to select it. To select an entire table, click on the gray button at the top left corner of the table. You can also click on the Highlight Entire Table command in the Table menu.

Select Entire Table button

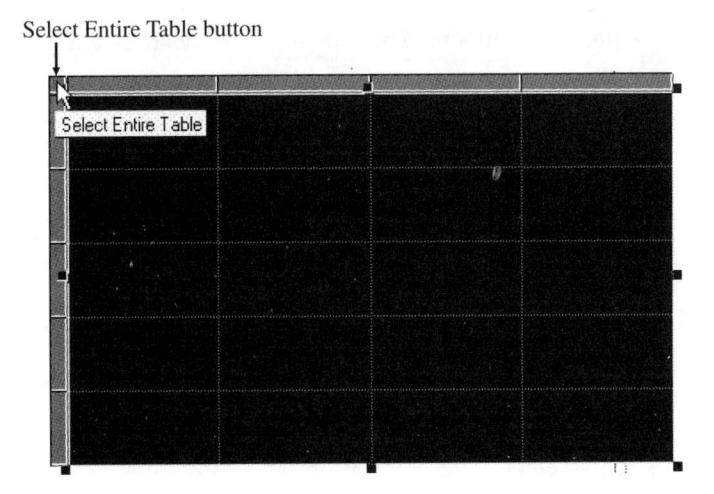

Entering Text and Numbers in a Table

To enter text and numbers in a table, move to a cell and begin typing. By default, text and numbers are aligned to the left side of the cell. Longer text strings may wrap around, creating a second line of text within the cell. As discussed later in this chapter ("Adjusting Column Width and Row Height"), you can adjust the width of columns. You can also press ENTER to start a new line within a cell.

12

	Jan - Mar	April - June	July - Sept	Oct - Dec
Salespeople				
Cason Reeder	2,000	3,000	4,000	4,500
Callan Reeder	2,225	3,225	4,500	3,750
Bryce Reeder	1,980	2,050	3,990	4,000

Avoid including more detail than necessary when entering table data. Too much text in a table lessens the table's visual appeal. Instead of including all digits in large numbers, try rounding off numbers. You can also abbreviate headings for months and days of the week.

NOTE: *You will need to enter commas, and currency and percentage symbols for numbers. Publisher does not have a feature for automatically adding these.*

Copying Table Data from Other Applications

Tables created in applications such as Microsoft Word or Microsoft Excel can be copied and pasted as a table into Publisher. For instance, suppose you prepared a table in Word and now want to place it in a brochure you're designing in Publisher. You simply select the table in Word and copy it (select Copy from the Edit menu, or click on the Copy tool). Then switch to Publisher and select Paste from the Edit menu, or click on the Paste tool. The table is placed in a table frame that you can move, size, and format as desired. Use the same steps to copy data from an Excel spreadsheet.

If the data is not in a table, but is separated by tabs (pressing TAB), select the data and copy it. To place it as a table in Publisher, choose Paste Special from the Edit menu. In the Paste Special dialog box, select New Table and click OK. The data is pasted as a table in a table frame.

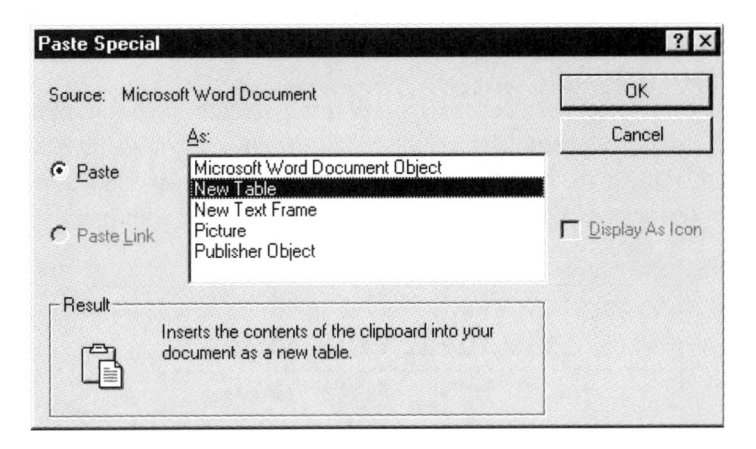

You can also use the Insert Text File command to place a table created in another application, such as Excel, into a Publisher publication. Refer to the section "Importing Text from Other Applications" in Chapter 8.

Using Fill Down and Fill Right

The Fill Right and Fill Down features allow you to copy data from one cell and place or *fill* it in selected adjacent cells.

Use the following steps to fill data:

1. Click in the cell containing the data you want to fill or copy.

2. Drag down to select the cells below the active cell where you want to fill the data, or drag right to select the cells to the right of the active cell where you want to fill the data.

3. From the Table menu, choose Fill Down to fill the data down through selected cells, or choose Fill Right to fill data to the right in selected cells.

CAUTION: *When using the Fill commands, be careful to select only cells where you want to fill the data. If there is any data in the selected cells, it will be replaced by the new data filling the cells.*

Deleting Cell Contents

Text in a table can be edited the same way you edit text in a text frame. For instance, you can use DELETE and BACKSPACE to delete text and numerical characters. If you want to delete a word in a cell, you can double-click on it with the mouse to highlight it and then press DELETE.

To delete the contents of a cell, row, or column: select the cell, row, or column, and then press DELETE. For example, selecting the fourth row, as shown here, and pressing DELETE would remove the data from all cells in the row. The row is not deleted, just the text. Refer to the next section to learn how to delete rows and columns.

Frequent Flier Miles

Average Miles Per Trip				
	1995	1996	1997	1998 - projected
Flyaways Airline	20	25	24	26
Smooth Sailing Airline	15	18	20	21

 **NOTE:** *The steps for moving and copying table text are the same as those discussed in Chapter 8, which covers adding text to publications. Refer to the section "Moving and Copying Text" in Chapter 8 for more information.*

Adding and Deleting Columns and Rows

It's hard to know the exact size you will need for a table when you first create it, so Publisher makes it easy to add or remove columns and rows.

Adding Columns and Rows

If you need to add data to a table, you may need to add columns and rows. You can add one or several new columns or rows at a time. Publisher allows you to add columns before or after another column. For instance, if a column is added before the third column, the new column becomes the third column—the original third column becomes the fourth column. If a column is added after the third column, the new column becomes the fourth column. This also applies to rows. For instance, if a row is added before the fourth row, the new row becomes the fourth row. If a row is added after the fourth row, the new row becomes the fifth row.

The following steps illustrate adding a column or row:

1. Select the column or row where you want the new column or row to appear. You can also just click in a cell in the column or row.

2. From the Table menu, choose Insert Rows Or Columns. The Insert dialog box appears.

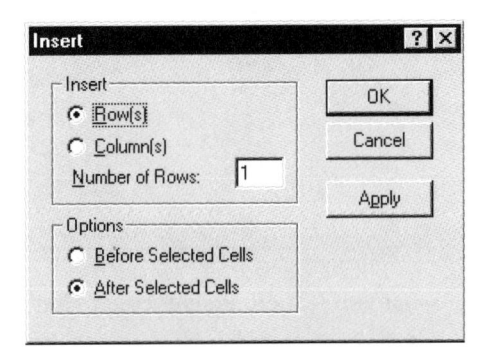

3. Make sure that what you want to add, either Column(s) or Row(s), is selected.

4. To enter more than one row or column, enter a new number in the Number Of box.

5. Under Options, specify whether the new row or column should be added before or after the selected cells. Click OK.

Newly added columns and rows use the same width and height as the selected column or row. Adjusting column width is covered later in this chapter.

 **TIP:** *Adding a new row at the end of a table is simple. Move to the last cell in the table, press TAB, and a new row appears.*

Deleting Columns and Rows

When you delete a column or row, any text in the cells is also deleted. For instance, if your table headings appear in row 1 and you delete row 1, the table headings are also gone.

The following steps outline deleting a column or row:

1. Click in a cell in the column or row you want to delete.

2. From the Table menu, choose Delete Rows Or Columns. The Delete dialog box appears.

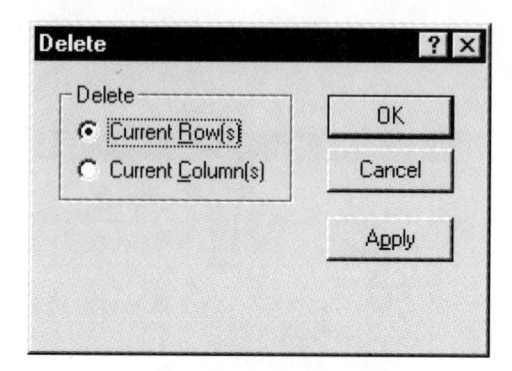

3. Make sure that what you want to delete, either Current Column(s) or Current Row(s), is selected. Click OK.

If you select an entire column or row, the Table menu will offer the command Delete Column(s) or Delete Row(s). These commands delete the selected column(s) or row(s) without displaying a dialog box. If you accidentally delete a row or column, remember you can choose the Undo command in the Edit menu to bring it back.

Adjusting Column Width and Row Height

Initially, all columns in a table are the same width, and all rows are the same height. However, you can adjust the width of columns and height of rows to accommodate different types of data. For instance, you may need a wider column for sales representatives' names and a narrower column for sales figures. You also may want to increase the height of a row to provide more emphasis to the table title.

Widget Sales, Inc.	
Sales Figures for 1988 (in millions)	
Yvonne Howington	90
Jana Bugatto	95
Mary Corban	100
Carrie Guest	110
Annette Bain	125

The black lines separating the gray column and row buttons around the edge of a table are used to adjust the column width and row height. First, make sure the table is selected, so the gray buttons are visible. To adjust the width of a column, place the mouse cursor on the black line (in the gray buttons) to the right of the column you want to adjust. The mouse cursor changes to the Adjust icon. Drag left to decrease the width of the column, drag right to increase the column width.

To change the height of a row, place the mouse cursor on the black line below the row you want to adjust. Again, the mouse cursor changes to the Adjust icon. Drag up to decrease the height of the column, drag down to increase the row height.

Merging and Splitting Cells

You can merge several cells into one cell. Merging all of the cells in a row allows you to center a title above a table. You can also merge several cells in a row as opposed to the whole row. Only cells in the same row can be merged. You cannot merge a column into one cell. However, you can select several columns and merge them into one column, as shown here:

12

Texas Oil				
	Jan - Mar	April - June	July - Sept	Oct - Dec
Salespeople				
Cason Reeder	2,000	3,000	4,000	4,500
Callan Reeder	2,225	3,225	4,500	3,750
Bryce Reeder	1,980	2,050	3,990	4,000

The following steps illustrate merging cells:

1. Select the rows, columns, or individual cells you want to merge.

2. From the Table menu, select Merge Cells. The cells in the rows are merged into one cell.

After merging cells, you can separate or split them again. Select the merged cell, and then choose Split Cells from the Table menu. This command is not available unless the selected cells had been previously merged.

TIP: *To create a title above a table after merging cells in a row, click on the Center Alignment tool to center the title above all of the columns.*

Formatting Tables

Selecting the right typeface, type size, and type style for the text in a table adds a touch of style and makes the information easier to understand and interpret. You can change the appearance of text in table cells just as you would other text in a publication. First, you select the table text, and then you choose the desired formatting options. You can format a single cell or format several cells at one time. You can also select a row, column, or even the entire table before applying formatting.

When formatting information in tables, be sure to leave enough "breathing room" around the text or numbers. For instance, select a type size that lets the table text fit comfortably in the cell, not jammed in. Row and column headings should be significantly larger, or bolder, than the information they introduce (see Figure 12-2). Lines are often placed around the outside of a table to separate it from other elements of the page. You can also use shades of black or another color to set off title information.

Choosing a Typeface, Type Size, and Type Style

Stick with clean, readable typefaces, such as Times New Roman and Arial, for information in tables. Script and decorative fonts can make data, especially numbers,

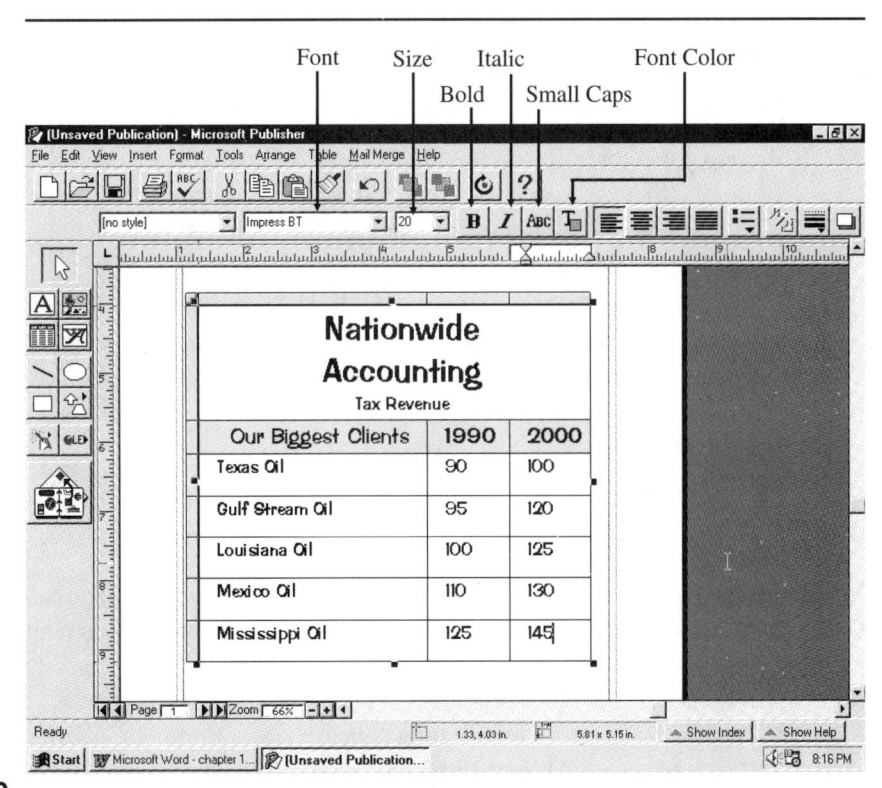

The design of a table greatly affects its readability

FIGURE 12-2

hard to read. Formatting table text by applying typefaces, sizes, and styles is exactly the same as formatting other text in Publisher. You can use the Character command in the Tools menu, or as discussed in this section, you can use the tools on the Formatting toolbar. Refer to Chapter 8 for more information on formatting text.

Color can be added to table text; however, keep in mind the printing process selected for the publication, and stick with colors that work with that process.

The following steps illustrate selecting a typeface, size, and style for table text. The steps for adding color are also covered.

1. Select the cell(s), row(s), or column(s) containing the text you want to format.

2. To apply a new typeface, click on the down arrow by the Font list in the Formatting toolbar. Select the desired typeface.

3. To apply a new type size, click on the down arrow by the Size list, and select the desired size.

4. To apply a new type style, click on the Bold, Italic, or Small Caps tool.

5. To apply a color, click on the Font Color tool to display a drop-down list of colors. Select the desired color. Click on the More Colors button to see a wider range of color choices. Click on the Patterns And Shading button to use a color tint or shade for table text.

For additional type style choices, such as superscript, subscript, and underlining, choose Character from the Text menu. For more information about color options, refer to the section "Adding Color to Frames" in Chapter 7. As with other text, you cannot apply patterns and gradients to table text.

Adjusting Table Text Alignment

When you enter text, it is automatically aligned to the left side of a cell. You can position the text in the center or right side of a cell by changing the alignment (see Figure 12-3). First, select the cell, row, or column containing the text you want to align. Then click on the Left, Center, Right, or Justified tool in the Formatting toolbar.

Here are some suggestions for aligning data in a table. Numbers are often aligned to the right side of a cell. Title information, including columns and row titles, are often centered. Other table text is generally left-aligned. Justified alignment spreads

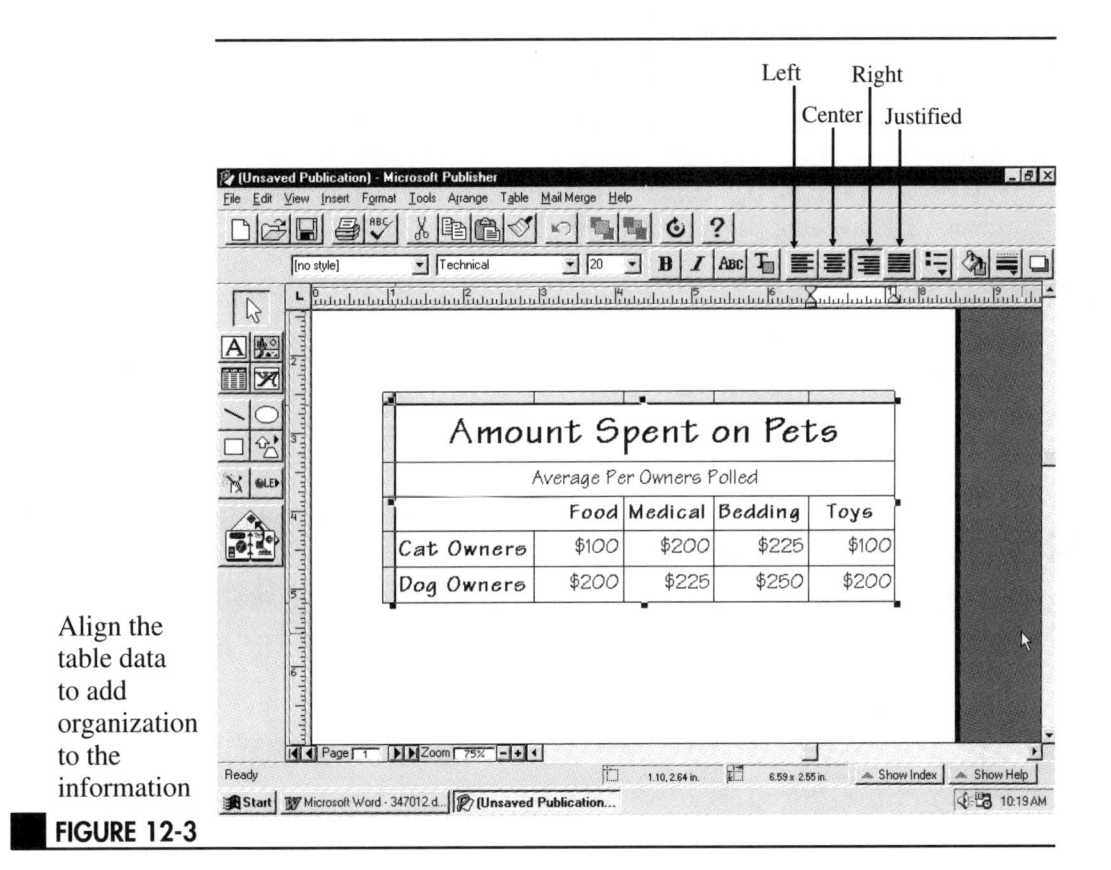

Align the table data to add organization to the information

FIGURE 12-3

the text out within the cell, making the left and right sides of the text even. Because justified text spreads out, it can be hard to read.

Adding Lines and Color to Tables

Borders (including Publisher's BorderArt) can be added around the entire table to separate it from other elements on the page. Borders or lines can also be added around the individual cells to separate data into sections, making it easier to read.

When available, color adds a nice touch to tables, making them even more prominent on the page. You can add color to the cell background, or to borders surrounding the table and cells.

Bordering the Whole Table

Borders can be applied to the outside edge of the table frame. You can pick a border from Publisher's BorderArt or add a simple line border. Basically, the steps are the same as those for applying borders to frames. Refer to Chapter 7 for more information about adding BorderArt and line borders to frames.

 **NOTE:** *BorderArt is predesigned borders including everything from balloons to diamonds to ladybugs.*

Use the following steps to apply a border around the table:

1. Click anywhere in the table, and click on the Borders tool. From the drop-down list click on the More option.

2. To apply BorderArt around the table, click on the BorderArt tab at the top of the dialog box. Scroll through the selections and click on the desired border. When finished, click OK.

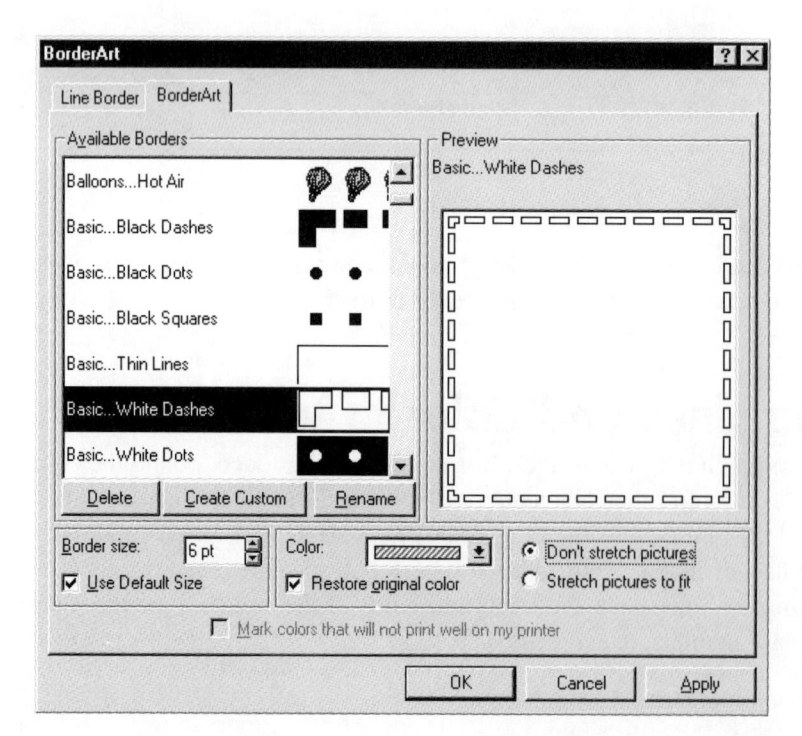

3. To apply a line border around the table, click on the Line Border tab at the top of the dialog box. Click on the desired line thickness, or enter a custom thickness in the last box. Click on the down arrow by Color, and pick another line color if desired.

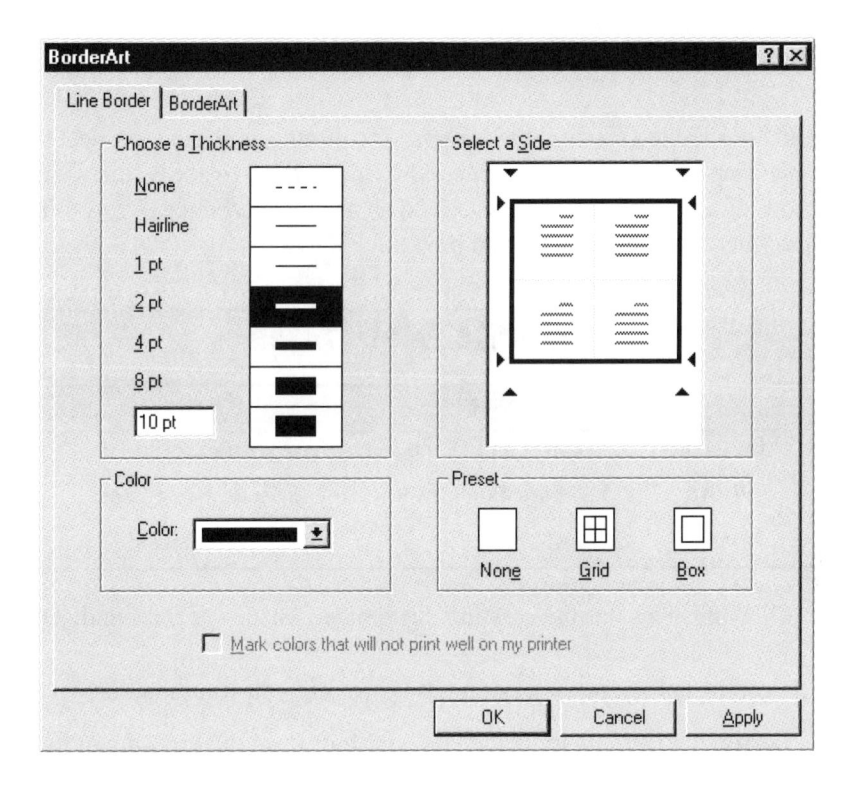

4. On the right side of the dialog box, click on the Box option. The preview displays the border around the table. When finished, click OK.

Bordering the Cells

You can add lines around the cells, columns, and rows in a table to organize the information. The lines can all be one thickness, creating a grid effect.

The following steps illustrate adding lines in the same thickness around all of the cells in a table:

1. Click anywhere in the table, and click on the Borders tool. From the drop-down list click on the More option.

2. Click on the Line Border tab at the top of the dialog box. Click on the desired line thickness, or enter a custom thickness in the last box. Click on the down arrow by Color, and pick another line color if desired.

3. On the right side of the dialog box, click on the Grid option. The preview displays the lines surrounding the cells in the table. When finished, click OK.

To add lines around specific cells, rows, or columns, you need to select that part of the table. For instance, select the second row of a table to apply lines only to the second row of the table (as shown here with the "Male/Female" row). You can customize where the lines appear and how thick they are.

Favorite Web Sites		
	Male	Female
Under 18	Calvin and Hobbes	Dilbert
19-40	X-Files Home Page	Friends Home Page
41-65	FBI	White House

The following steps outline creating customized line borders around cells:

1. Select the cell(s), row(s), or column(s) where you want the lines to appear.

2. Click on the Borders tool, and choose More from the drop-down list. Click on the Line Border tab at the top of the dialog box.

3. Click on the desired line thickness, or enter a custom thickness in the last box. Click on the down arrow by Color, and pick another line color if desired.

4. Move to the preview area in the dialog box, and click on the gridline where you want a border to appear. For instance, click on the top gridline to add a line above the selected cells.

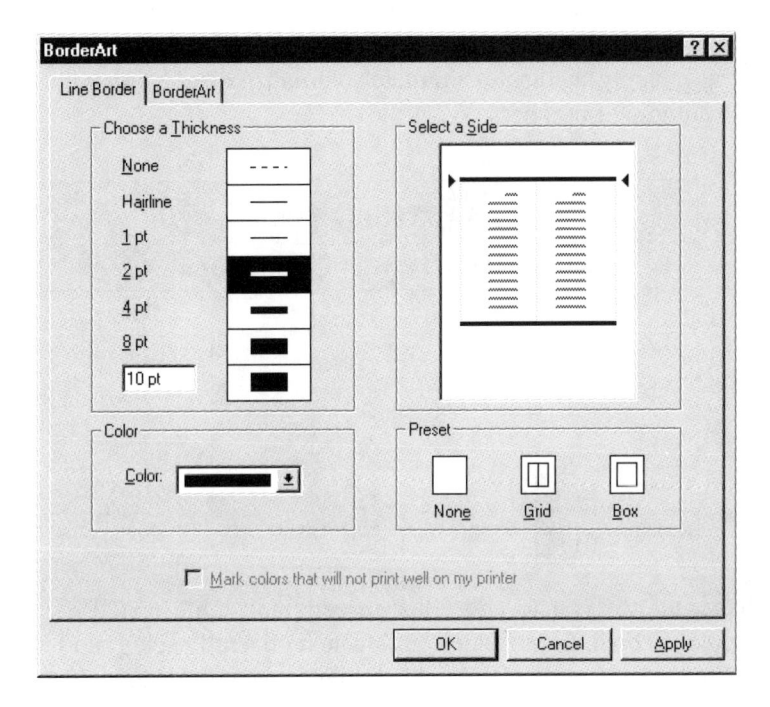

5. Click another line thickness if desired, and click on another gridline in the preview to add another line in the specified thickness. For instance, you might add a thick line above the selected cells, and a thin line below the selected cells.

6. When finished, click OK to apply the lines to the selected cells.

You can create many appealing effects by customizing the lines around table cells. As a general rule, however, avoid using thick rules that darken a table and overwhelm the information inside. Stick with thin lines, especially in the lines separating data such as numbers.

Adding Color

In addition to coloring the borders and lines around tables, as discussed in the previous section, you can add color to the cell background. For instance, you might want to apply a light shade of gray to the cells containing title information. Another alternative is to apply shading to alternate columns of data, guiding the reader's eye down each column of numbers.

Textiles, Inc			
Percentage of Growth in Textile Industry			
	1980	1990	2000
Africa	10%	20%	25%
China	12%	15%	25%
Brazil	13%	12%	20%
Europe	16%	12%	18%
Russia	20%	28%	25%

Publisher allows you to add color to cells and table text. Be careful when applying color to both. For instance, yellow text on a red background would not be readable. For the most part, it's probably best to place text, whether black or another color, against a white or light background.

The following steps illustrate adding color to cell backgrounds in a table:

1. Select the cell(s), row(s), or column(s) where you want to add color.

2. Click on the Object Color tool in the Formatting toolbar.

3. Select a color from the palette, or click on the More button to see a wider range of colors. Click on the Patterns And Shading button to add tints, shades, patterns, and gradient fills to cell backgrounds.

Refer to Chapter 7 for more information on the patterns and shading options.

Converting Text to Tables

With all the power available in tables, you may be thinking, "Gosh, I wish I had used a table to create that list of figures in my last publication." Well, here's some good news. Text separated by tabs or commas can be converted to tables. After you convert the text to a table, you can apply borders and shading.

Remember, as discussed in Chapter 8, that when the Show Special Characters option is turned on in the View menu, you can see arrows where TAB was pressed and paragraph marks where ENTER was pressed. In the top set of data in Figure 12-4, the columns of data were separated by tabs. The tabs tell Publisher when to create a new column. Notice also that ENTER was pressed at the end of each line except the last. The paragraph marks tell Publisher when to create a new row. The bottom set of data represents the text after it was converted to a table.

TIP: *Press CTRL-SHIFT-Y to quickly display the special characters.*

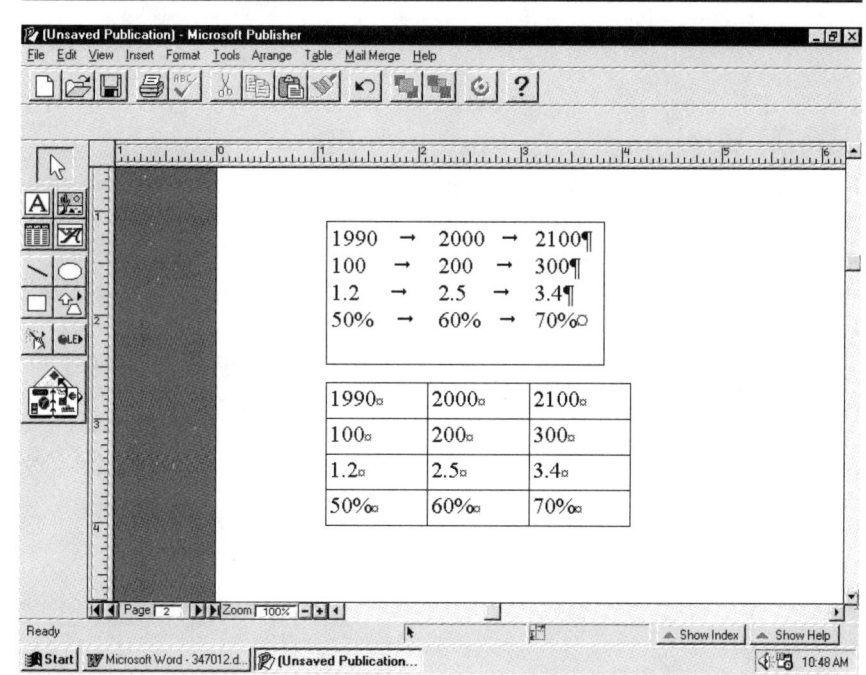

Text aligned with tabs or commas can be converted to a table

FIGURE 12-4

The following steps illustrate converting text to a table. Remember tabs or commas must be separating the data into columns, and a paragraph mark must appear at the end of each row, except the last.

1. Select the text you want placed in the table. Make sure you've selected all paragraph marks.

2. From the Edit menu, choose Cut if you want to remove the existing data, or choose Copy if you want to place a copy somewhere else.

3. Move to the page where you want the table to appear.

4. From the Edit menu, choose Paste Special. In the Paste Special dialog box, choose New Table and click OK.

The text is placed in a table. Check through the text to make sure the data appears in the correct cell and row. Now you're ready to format the new table with the techniques you've just learned.

Summary

Tables are a popular feature for laying out technical and numerical information. You can build and format tables in Publisher or import tables created in other applications, such as Word or Excel. As you discovered in this chapter, there are many tools for formatting tables, such as merging cells, adding shading, and controlling column width and line height.

The next chapter looks at another popular feature—adding WordArt to publications.

13

Adding WordArt to Publications

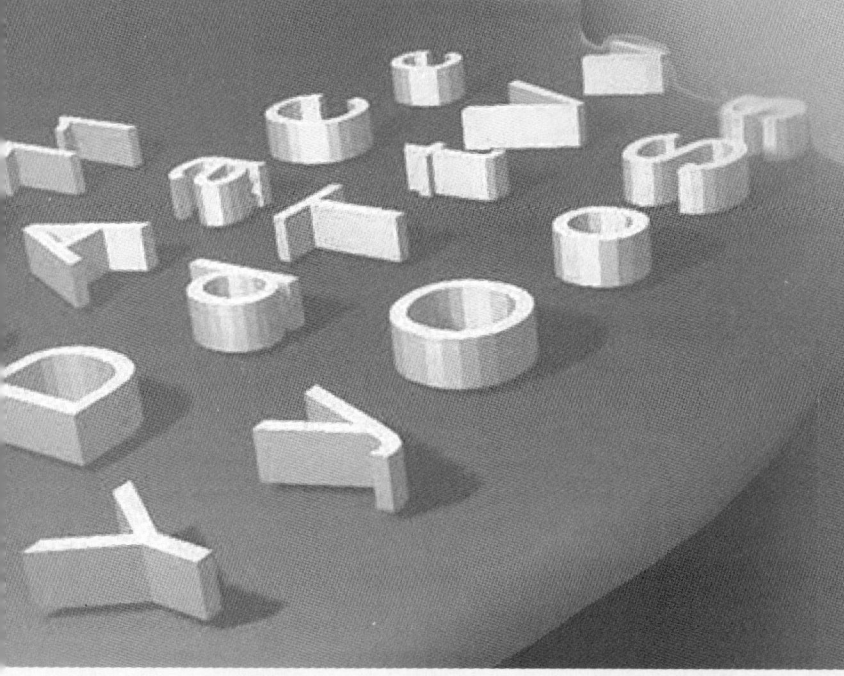

303

WordArt allows you to create flashy text effects such as shaping words into a circle, rotating text at any angle, adding text shadows, and stretching or distorting text. You can use these effects to create a logo for your business, to add emphasis to a heading in a brochure or flyer—basically, anytime you want to attract attention to a text block.

This chapter begins with a look at what WordArt is and how it works. Here, you'll learn the difference between regular text in a text frame and text in a WordArt frame. Next, the chapter discusses creating WordArt in Publisher, and applying a special effect. The chapter then looks at the formatting options in WordArt, such as selecting a typeface and adjusting the type size. You'll also see how to add color and borders to WordArt frames. The chapter ends with the steps for editing WordArt once it has been placed in a Publisher publication.

What Is WordArt?

WordArt is an add-on module included with Microsoft Publisher. Think of WordArt as a small application whose sole purpose is to apply special effects to text blocks. WordArt does not work with graphic shapes—only text. WordArt performs many of the text effects found in more advanced (and more expensive) graphics applications. For instance, the perspective and wave effects found in WordArt can also be accomplished in CorelDRAW. However, with WordArt you don't have to leave your Publisher publication. You create and design the text in WordArt as you design your page in Publisher.

WordArt uses *OLE* or *object linking and embedding*. OLE allows you to add a text effect with WordArt to a publication without ever leaving Publisher. When you edit text created with WordArt, the WordArt menus take over Publisher's menus, letting you edit the text in place. When you've finished editing, you can click anywhere on the page to return to Publisher's normal menus.

 **NOTE:** *WordArt is also included with the Microsoft Office suite. The information you learn about WordArt in this chapter would also apply to using WordArt with Microsoft Word, Excel, and PowerPoint.*

The Difference Between Text and WordArt

Both text frames and WordArt frames work with text. In fact, you'll be working with text frames most of the time, creating headings and other paragraphs of text. It is quicker and easier to edit text in a text frame than in a WordArt frame, so only use WordArt when you want one of the special effects it provides. For instance, in Figure 13-1, the first heading was created in a text frame—even though it is large and decorative, the actual shape of the text has not been altered. The shape of the text in the second heading has been changed. This heading was created in a WordArt frame to add this special effect.

Generally, you can recognize a text frame or a WordArt frame by looking for a special effect. However, some of the page designs created with PageWizards use WordArt frames for text without special effects. You can tell the difference by clicking in the frame—if an insertion point appears in the frame, it is a text frame;

Only use WordArt to add special effects to text (as in the example of the second heading)

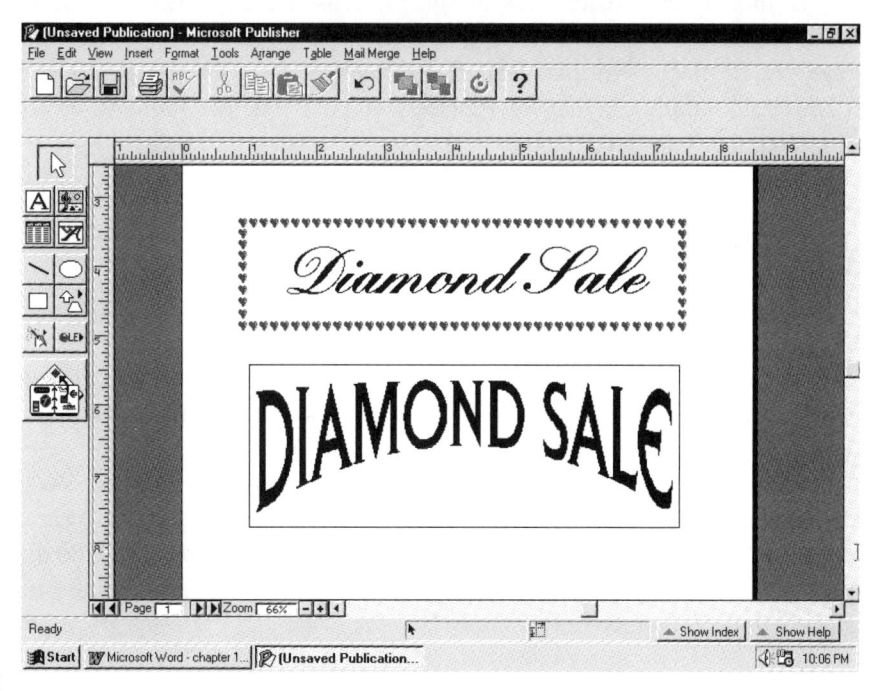

FIGURE 13-1

if no insertion point appears, it is a WordArt frame. As you will learn later, you need to double-click on a WordArt frame to edit its contents.

Working with WordArt Frames

As discussed in Chapter 7, Publisher uses WordArt frames to hold and position WordArt text elements. As with other frames, WordArt frames can be moved, sized, and rotated. You can also add margins, color, and borders to WordArt frames. Refer to Chapter 7 for more information on working with frames, such as drawing, moving, and sizing them.

Adjusting the size of a WordArt frame adjusts the size of the WordArt text. For example, if you increase the size of a WordArt frame, the WordArt text in the frame also gets larger. This is different from text frames, where the size of the frame determines how much text appears in the frame. The size of a text frame does not affect the size of the text.

As mentioned earlier, when PageWizards are used to build publications, WordArt frames may already be included on the page. For instance, the Postcard PageWizard places WordArt frames on many of the page designs. The WordArt frames hold sample text that you replace with your text. The WordArt text is already formatted, but you can adjust the formatting to meet your needs.

Creating WordArt Text

Publisher's WordArt frame tool is used to draw frames that will hold WordArt text. Immediately after a WordArt frame is drawn, the WordArt module takes over. As you can see in Figure 13-2, the publication remains displayed, but the menus and toolbar change to reflect WordArt commands. The WordArt module also takes over the screen when you double-click on an existing WordArt frame.

Notice the Enter Your Text Here dialog box appears below the WordArt text, and a gray border surrounds the WordArt frame. These are all indications you are creating or editing WordArt text. If you have just drawn the WordArt frame, the dialog box displays "Your Text Here." If you are editing existing WordArt text, the actual text appears in the dialog box.

WordArt menus   WordArt toolbar

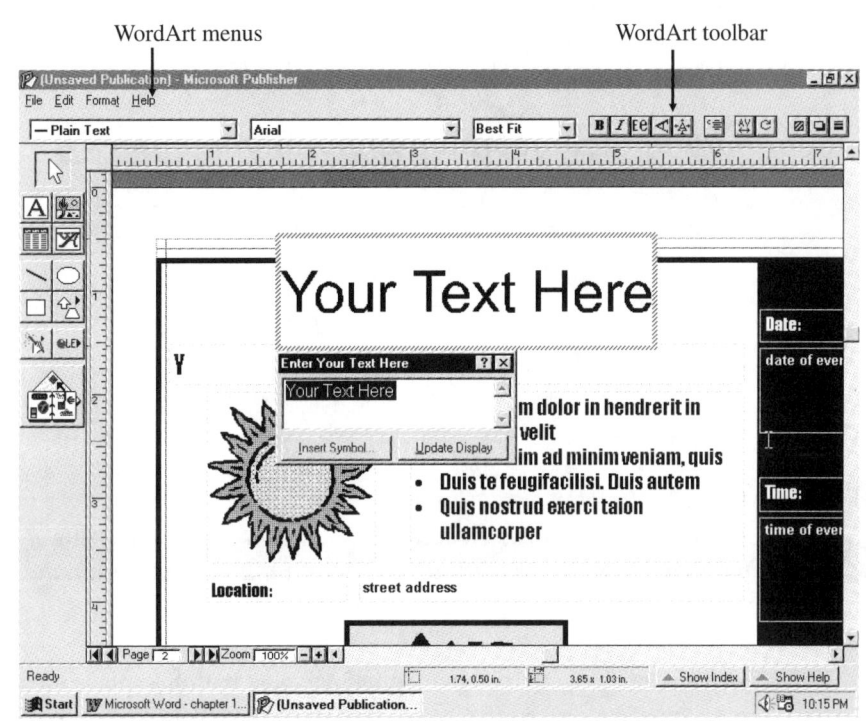

WordArt's menus and tools replace the Publisher menus and tools when you work with WordArt text

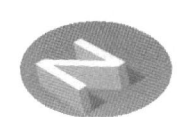
FIGURE 13-2

NOTE: *As you work with WordArt text, do not click outside of the gray box surrounding the frame until you are finished with the WordArt. If you do so, double-click on the WordArt frame to return to the WordArt module.*

Entering Text and Symbols

The text in the dialog box is selected, so to enter new text, simply begin typing to replace the old text. The text you type does not have to be on one line. You can press ENTER to add another line. In fact, some of the special effects require more than one line for the effect.

13

When you need symbols for copyright marks, accented letters, or fractions, click on the Insert Symbol button to display the Insert Symbol dialog box. Click on the symbol you want to add and click OK. The symbol is placed in the dialog box.

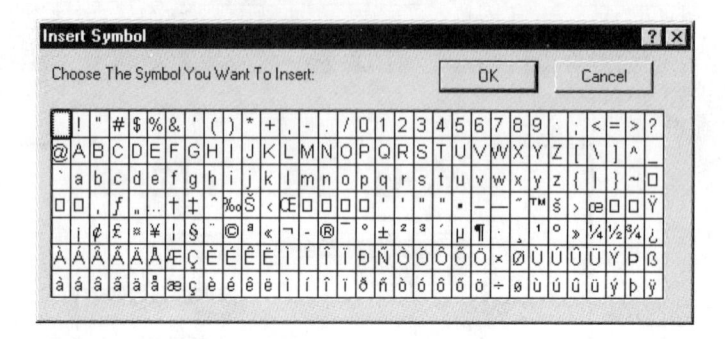

NOTE: *If you want to insert a symbol from Wingdings or some other symbol font, you will need to select that font before inserting a symbol. Changing typefaces is discussed later in this chapter in the section "Selecting a Typeface, Size, and Style."*

After entering the text, click on the Update Display button to place the new text in the WordArt frame. As with other text, you can format WordArt text by selecting another typeface or type size, and by applying type styles, such as bold and italics. You can also add shadows and patterns to WordArt text. The formatting can be done before or after a special effect is applied. However, you may find it more practical to select a special effect and then apply typefaces and other formatting to enhance the look of the selected effect.

Selecting a Special Effect

WordArt's special effects change the shape and direction of text. To apply a special effect, click on the first drop-down list box in the toolbar. A menu appears, as shown here, displaying all the shapes that can be applied to WordArt text. Click on a shape and your text is modified to match that shape. Feel free to experiment—continue clicking on shapes until you find one that works with your text and publication.

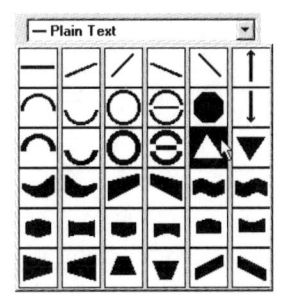

Tips for Finding the Right Effect

 Not all text will look good with all the shape choices. For instance, a short line of text may not look good in a circle shape. A long line of text may become unreadable when the cascade down shape is applied. Look at the examples shown here, and take time to play with the options. Here are a few tips on working with certain shapes.

 **NOTE:** *Each special effect or shape has a name. To see the name, you must apply the special effect to your text. The name of the selected effect then appears on the toolbar.*

 ■ The Slant Up and Slant Down shapes are nice when you need to rotate text but not the frame. Remember, you can rotate a frame, which also rotates the text inside. But when you don't want to rotate the frame, just the text in the frame, use these shapes.

13

- The Arch and Circle shapes will look better with at least four or five words. With one or two words, the letters get all spread out.

- The Button shapes require three lines of text, each separated by pressing ENTER. The first line is the top of the button, the second line is the middle, and the third line is the bottom.

- Many of the shapes, including the Stop Sign, Triangle, Curves, Cascades, Waves, Inflate, and Deflate shapes, work with one or multiple lines of text. The effect is more pronounced with one line of text.

- In general, try using all uppercase or all lowercase for the special effects. When the letters are all the same height, they do not interfere with the shape of the special effect.

Most important of all, avoid using special effects that compromise the readability of the text. For instance, you don't want people to have trouble reading your company name in the logo! If none of the shapes work for you, remember, you can always dress up the text with typefaces and color.

Formatting WordArt Text

You must use the tools in the WordArt module to format WordArt text. You cannot format WordArt text with the tools in Publisher. However, formatting text in WordArt is very similar to formatting text in Publisher. They both use drop-down lists and tools for applying typefaces and more. Although WordArt text cannot be edited in Publisher, a WordArt frame can be. You can move, size, and rotate it. You can add a frame background color and borders.

You will find that WordArt text is like a graphic in many ways. For instance, you can add shadows, and apply patterns and borders to WordArt text. This section examines the options for formatting WordArt text. Many of the commands can be done by use of a menu command or tool in the toolbar—the steps in this section will focus on using the tools.

Unfortunately, WordArt does not use "tooltips," those helpful little pop-up notes that display the tool name. In fact, WordArt does not even name the tools. Because of this, it can be difficult to identify them. Table 13-1 shows the tools on the WordArt toolbar and offers brief descriptions of what each does.

Tool	Description
Impact	Select a new font for WordArt text
Best Fit	Select a new type size for WordArt text
 B	Applies bold to WordArt text
 I	Applies italic to WordArt text
 Ee	Make all letters same height
 ◁	Flips letters
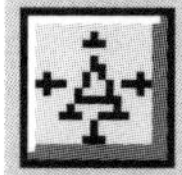 ⊹A⊹	Stretches letters to edge of frame
 ⊂≣	Controls alignment of WordArt text
 AV	Controls spacing between characters
 C	Adjusts rotation and angle of special effect
 ▨	Applies color and shading to WordArt text
 ◻	Applies shadow effects to WordArt text
 ≡	Applies borders to WordArt text

Tools on
the
WordArt
Toolbar

TABLE 13-1

13

Selecting a Typeface, Size, and Style

As with all text, the typeface you choose for WordArt text reflects the mood of your publication. Formal typefaces create more professional-looking effects, casual typefaces add an easygoing look to a publication. Whether you're going formal or funky, stick with a fairly simple typeface (see Figure 13-3). Script and many decorative typefaces are too much when combined with a special effect in WordArt.

The following steps illustrate selecting a typeface and type size for WordArt text. The steps also cover adding bold and italic. Before following the steps, make sure you are in the WordArt module. Remember, the dialog box and gray border appear around the WordArt frame.

1. To apply a new typeface, click on the down arrow by the Font list in the toolbar. Select the desired typeface. The WordArt text is displayed in the selected typeface.

2. By default, the text is sized to best fit the frame area. (In many cases, it works best to leave the type size at the Best Fit option.) To adjust the size of the text, click on the down arrow by the Size list, and select the desired size. The WordArt text is displayed in the selected type size.

3. To apply a new type style, click on the Bold or Italic tool. Again, the WordArt text is displayed in the selected type style.

You cannot use more than one typeface, size, or style in WordArt text. For instance, you cannot have one word display in Times New Roman and another in Arial. If you need to create an effect with two different typefaces or sizes, consider creating two WordArt frames with different text formatting. You can then position the WordArt frames on the page so the text elements read as one.

NOTE: *If you've changed the type size, but want to return to the Best Fit option, select Best Fit from the Size drop-down list.*

Aligning WordArt Text

The WordArt text can be aligned to the left, center, or right edges of the WordArt frame. However, if the text completely fills the frame, as it does when the Best Fit option is selected for the size, any changes in alignment aren't really noticeable. You

Font   Size   Bold
Italic

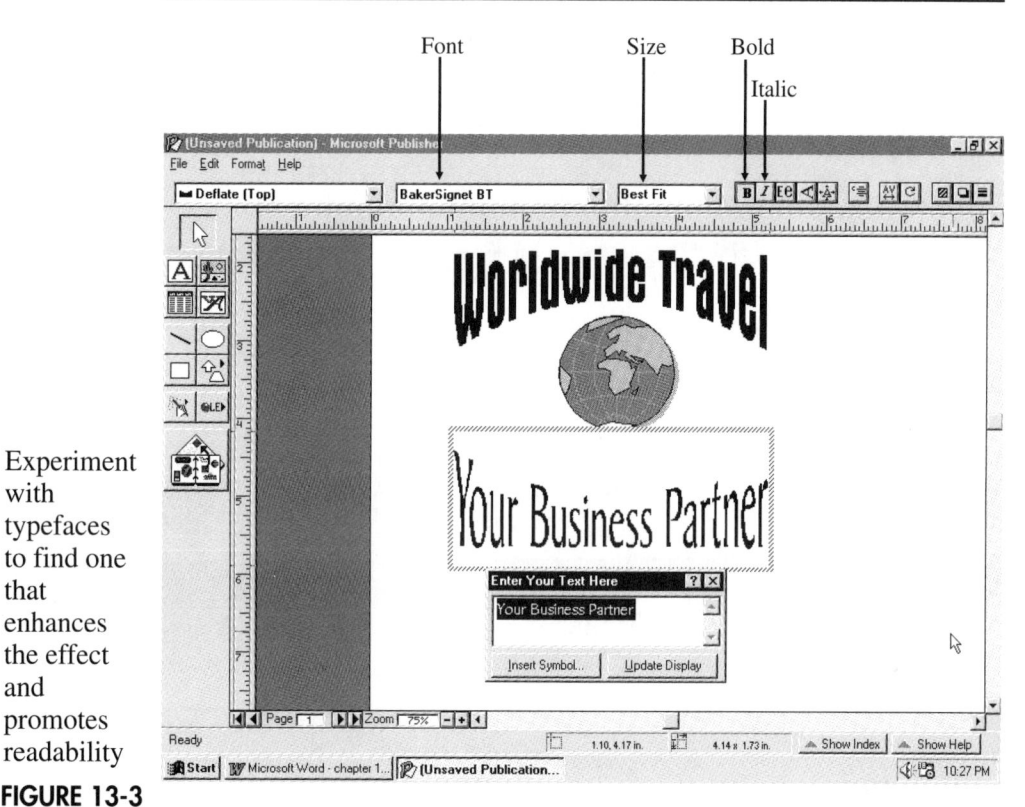

Experiment with typefaces to find one that enhances the effect and promotes readability

FIGURE 13-3

will notice the changes if you have reduced the size of the text and it no longer completely fills the frame.

 To change the text alignment, click on the Alignment button to display a list of alignment choices. Figure 13-4 shows the different alignment options. The type size is the same for all of the WordArt. As you can see, the justified options can distort the look of the text.

Adding Color and Patterns

By default, WordArt text is black. You can select another color with WordArt's shading options. Patterns can also be applied to WordArt text. The ability to apply patterns is another reason to create WordArt text instead of regular text, because you cannot apply patterns to regular text. Be careful with patterns, though; they diminish the readability of text.

13

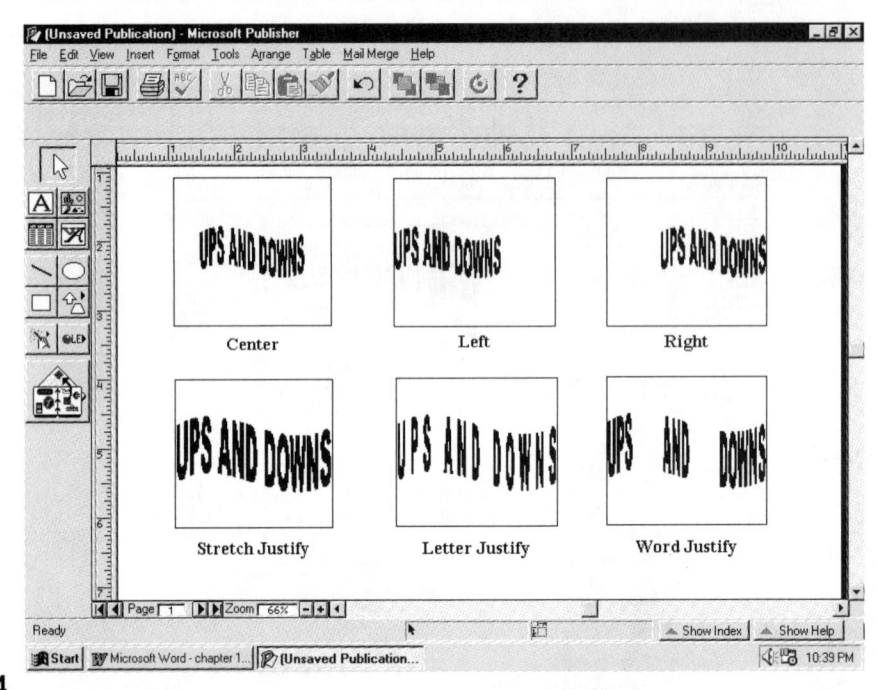

When
WordArt
text is
smaller
than the
frame, you
can control
the
alignment

FIGURE 13-4

The following steps illustrate selecting colors and applying patterns to WordArt text. As always, make sure you are in the WordArt module before editing WordArt text.

1. To apply color, click on the tool for colors and shading (the third button from the right). As shown in Figure 13-5, the Shading dialog box appears.

2. To select another color, click on the down arrow by Foreground and select a color. The sample provides a preview of the color.

3. To select a pattern, click on one of the patterns on the left side of the dialog box. Use the Foreground and Background options to select the colors for the pattern. The sample provides a preview of the pattern in the selected colors.

4. Click OK to apply the pattern to the WordArt text.

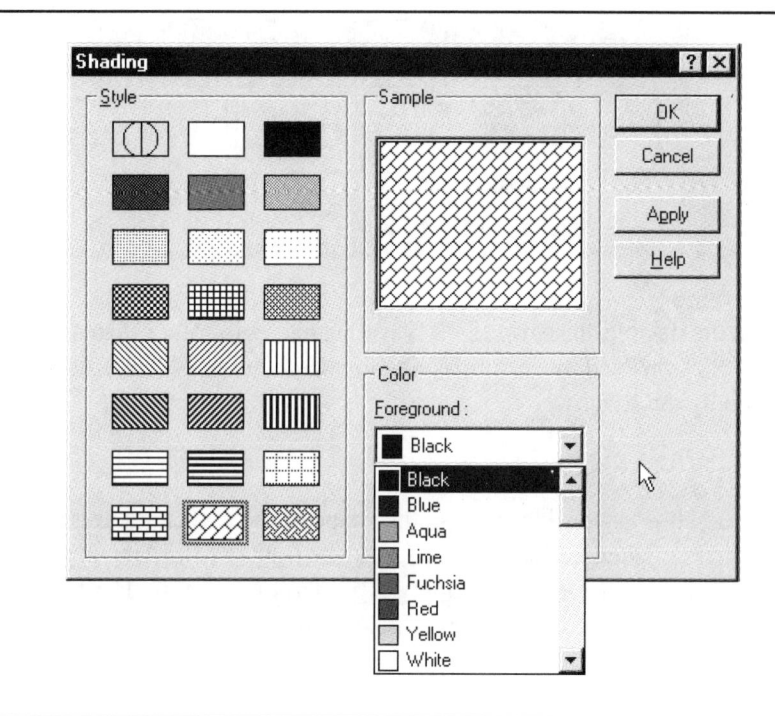

Use the Shading dialog box to select patterns and colors for WordArt text

FIGURE 13-5

The colors in the WordArt color palette do not match those in the Publisher color palette. When printed, they will not necessarily match a color applied in Publisher. Consider how the publication will be printed as you select colors in WordArt. If you are printing in full color, you can probably use any colors. If you are printing with one spot color, the spot color you are working with in Publisher will not match the color in WordArt. In this case, it might be best to leave the WordArt text black. If necessary, talk with your printing representative to find a way to work around the problem. With black-and-white printing, stick with white, black, or shades of gray.

Adding Shadows

WordArt provides some great options for adding shadows to WordArt text. To apply a shadow, click on the tool for applying shadows (the second button from the right). The Shadow dialog box is displayed.

13

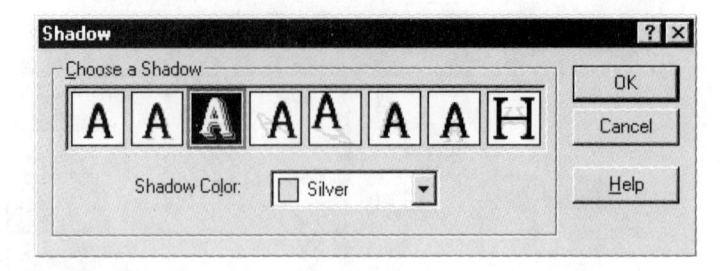

Click on the desired shadow effect. If you want a color other than silver used in the shadow, click on the down arrow by Shadow Color and select a different color. Click OK to apply the shadow.

Adding Borders

You can add borders or lines around the shape of the text characters with the border options. In Publisher you can add borders to the frame; WordArt lets you add a border to the actual text characters. To apply a border, click on the last tool on the right. The Border dialog box is displayed. Click on the desired border thickness. To select a border color other than black, click on the down arrow by Color and select a different color. Click OK to apply the border.

Additional Formatting Options

Because WordArt text is similar to a graphic, you'll find some unique options for modifying the text. Since WordArt does not provide tooltips indicating the purpose of a tool, refer to Figure 13-6 (and back to Table 13-1) for help on selecting the right tool.

Makes all letters same height   Stretches letters to edge of frame
Flips letters

Unique formatting tools provide many options for designing WordArt text

FIGURE 13-6

Adjusting Height of Characters

Many of the effects look better when all of the letters are the same height. WordArt provides a tool that automatically makes the letters the same height, regardless of their capitalization. Click on the tool (it's to the right of the Italic button) to see how the effect looks when all letters are the same height. Click again on the tool to turn off the feature. As mentioned, you can also manually enter all of the letters in uppercase or lowercase.

Letters Adjusted to be
Same Height

Flipping Text

Click on the tool with the sideways *A* to flip letters. It's worth experimenting with this option, since flipping drastically changes the look of the special effect. Click again on the flipping tool to "unflip" the letters.

Flipped WordArt Text

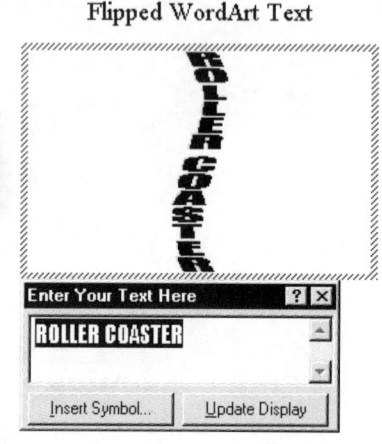

Stretching Text to Fit the Frame

To enlarge the text so it touches the edges of the WordArt frame, click on the tool with the *A* surrounded by four arrows. This distorts the shape of the characters to meet the edges of the frame. Click again on the tool to remove the stretching.

Text Stretched
to fit frame

Controlling Spacing Between Letters

You can increase or decrease the spacing between letters in WordArt text. When designing with WordArt text, you may want to scrunch up the letters for a logo, or spread them apart for an easy-to-read heading.

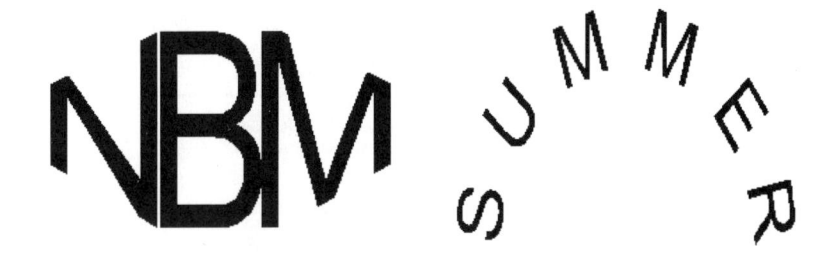

Click on the tool for tracking—it shows the letters *AV*—to display the Spacing Between Characters dialog box. Click on the desired spacing option, such as Very Loose, and click OK. You can also enter custom spacing in percentages. For instance, entering **200%** would double the amount of space between the letters.

Exiting WordArt and Returning to Publisher

To exit WordArt, click outside the gray border surrounding the WordArt frame. The Publisher menus and toolbars appear, and the WordArt text is placed on the page. As discussed, you can edit the WordArt frame, but not the WordArt text in Publisher. To edit WordArt text, you must return to the WordArt module.

Editing WordArt Text

Whenever you need to tweak WordArt text—for instance, maybe you need to fix a misspelling or select another typeface—simply double-click on the WordArt frame. The WordArt module is started, and the WordArt menus and toolbar are displayed. The Enter Your Text Here dialog box and the gray border surrounding the WordArt frame are also visible.

13

Creating a Price List

The Business Form PageWizard was used as a starting point for designing a contemporary price list. The "before" and "after" pictures illustrate how the initial price list created by the PageWizard was jazzed up with graphics and casual typefaces. After the price list was developed, the look and style of the publication was used to develop invoices, expense reports, and purchase orders. The result was a set of nicely designed, casual, yet professional business publications.

Before

After

Step 1: Modifying the Table

The price list created by the PageWizard included a large table. To keep it simple, the basic structure of the PageWizard table was used for the new price list. Each item on the price list was given three rows—one for the product name, one for sales information, and one for customers to write in their order. The cells in the first row of each category were merged, and the product name was typed in. A less formal typeface was selected for the product names. The second row for each category was shaded. The text in this row was bold, so it could be easily read against the shaded background. The third row for each category was left blank.

Step 2: Adding Clip Art

Clip art was inserted by the product names to add visual appeal. A small picture frame was drawn near the product name on the first row. This picture frame was copied to the other rows so the size of the clip art would be relatively the same. Ruler guides were used to align the picture frames. The clip art of the fruit was then placed in the frames. Notice how each piece of clip art has a similar look, almost as if it were drawn with colored pencils. The similar style of clip art is important—it wouldn't work to mix rigidly designed clip art with this freestyle clip art.

Step 3: Adding WordArt

The text block at the top was rather plain, so it was deleted and replaced by WordArt. After the company name was entered, the Wave special effect and a shadow were applied. A gray rectangular box was drawn behind the WordArt to help anchor it to the page. The gray box also ties in with the gray rows in the table.

Publisher in action

Once WordArt is activated, you can apply special effects and add type styles and the other options discussed in this chapter. When finished editing, click outside of the gray border surrounding the frame to return to Publisher.

Summary

WordArt is great for those times when you want to shape, slant, or rotate text. The preceding chapters of this book have focused on placing text, graphics, tables, and WordArt into frames. As discussed in the next chapter, you can also place video and sound in frames.

14

Lights, Camera, Action: Adding Sound and Video

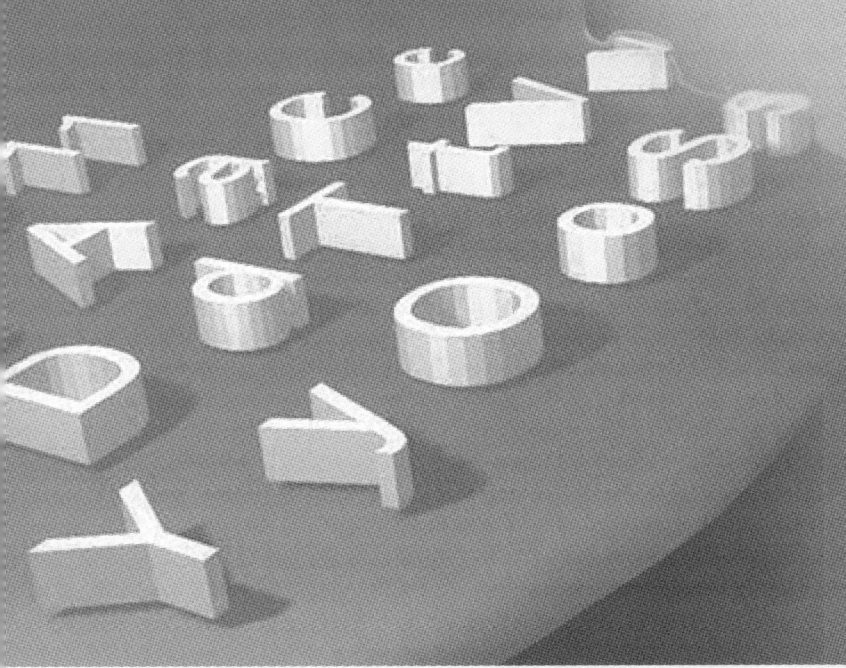

Just five years ago, everyone was excited about adding color to desktop publications. Now, the newest rage is adding sound and video. Obviously, you can't "print" sound and video on a postcard; but when you are designing a web page, sound and video are powerful design elements. Imagine a web page for a television show where you can hear the theme music and catch a short scene from the show, or a real estate agent's web page with video of new homes.

This chapter focuses on working with sound and video so you'll be familiar with the options when you begin designing web pages. The actual steps used to build web pages are covered in Chapter 15.

First, this chapter discusses sound clips. You'll discover how to place sound clips in a publication, and how to play them. Use of the Sound Recorder to adjust the volume and speed of sound clips is also discussed. Next, the chapter examines working with video clips. Again, you'll discover how to add video to a publication, and how to play it. Use of the Media Player to play only a section of a video clip is included in this section.

Working with Sound and Video

Adding sound and video to publications is very similar to adding clip art. You simply draw a picture frame, and then place the sound or video file. You can delete and move the frames holding the sound and video just as you would any other type of frame. However, as you will see, there are some unique options for modifying sound and video clips.

NOTE: *This chapter assumes you understand the basics about working with frames and placing clip-art graphics into the frames. Refer to Chapters 7 and 9 for a quick review if necessary.*

Working with Sound Clips

If you have ever tried watching your favorite movie or television show without sound, you know how important sound can be. Imagine seeing *Jaws* without that ominous thumping soundtrack—it just wouldn't be the same.

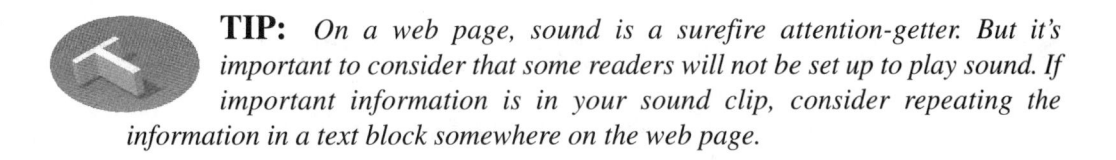

TIP: *On a web page, sound is a surefire attention-getter. But it's important to consider that some readers will not be set up to play sound. If important information is in your sound clip, consider repeating the information in a text block somewhere on the web page.*

Where to Get Sound Clips

You can download sound clips from the Microsoft Clip Gallery web site on the World Wide Web. As discussed in Chapter 9, Clip Gallery Live is a web site provided by Microsoft containing clip-art drawings, photographs, as well as sound clips that you can preview and download. To use Clip Gallery Live, you must have access to the World Wide Web (for example, through a provider such as Microsoft Network, Prodigy, or CompuServe), and a web browser (such as Netscape Navigator or Microsoft Internet Explorer).

The URL for the Microsoft Clip Gallery is **http://www.microsoft.com/ clipgallerylive**. At the web site, you can preview some sound clips, and then download the ones you want to keep. If you download a clip file, it is added to your hard disk and automatically added to the Clip Gallery. Keep in mind that sound files can be large, so if you're tight on hard disk space, you may want to download a few sound files at a time. You can always go back for more.

NOTE: *There are no sound or video files included on the Microsoft Publisher CD-ROM.*

Sound files can also be bought at computer stores—they are generally sold with other photographic and video images. You can also find a few sound files (with the .WAV filename extension) in the Windows/Media directory. These are short sound clips that are great for experimenting. If you own any graphics or animation software applications, you may find sound files on CD-ROMs included with the software. For instance, CorelDRAW provides lots of sound files, such as drums, rocket ships, and people yawning.

With the right hardware, such as a microphone and a sound card, you can record your own sound clips. There are several software applications for recording sounds. In fact, the Sound Recorder, which is discussed later in this chapter in the section "Editing Sound Clips," can be used to record sounds. Refer to the Sound Recorder online help files for information on recording sound.

14

Sound Clip Formats Accepted by Publisher

Publisher can recognize sound files with filename extensions such as .WAV and .MID. Sound files in the .WAV format (which is short for "Windows Audio Visual") are the most common for Windows applications.

Importing Sound Clips into the Clip Gallery

This section starts with the steps for importing a sound file into the Clip Gallery. The main reason for adding sound clips to the Clip Gallery is to make them more accessible. For instance, if you plan on using a sound clip of the company's theme music frequently, you might want to add the clip to the Clip Gallery.

In the following steps, a sound clip from a CD-ROM is placed in the Clip Gallery:

1. From the Insert menu, select Clip Art. The Microsoft Clip Gallery is displayed. Click on the Sounds tab at the top of the dialog box.

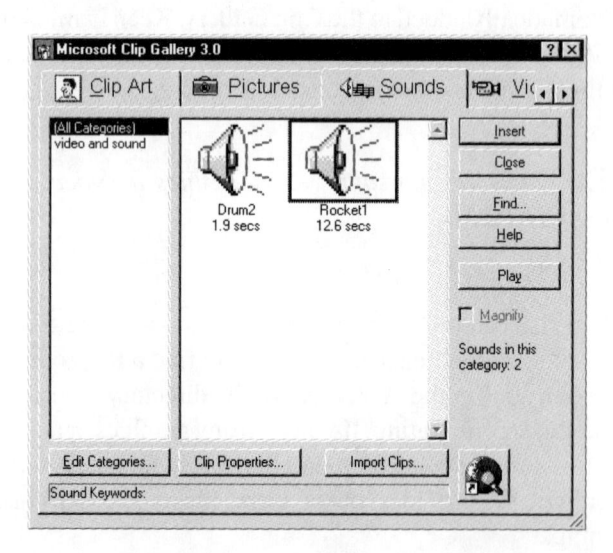

2. To import a sound, click on the Import Clips button. The Add Sounds To Clip Gallery dialog box is displayed.

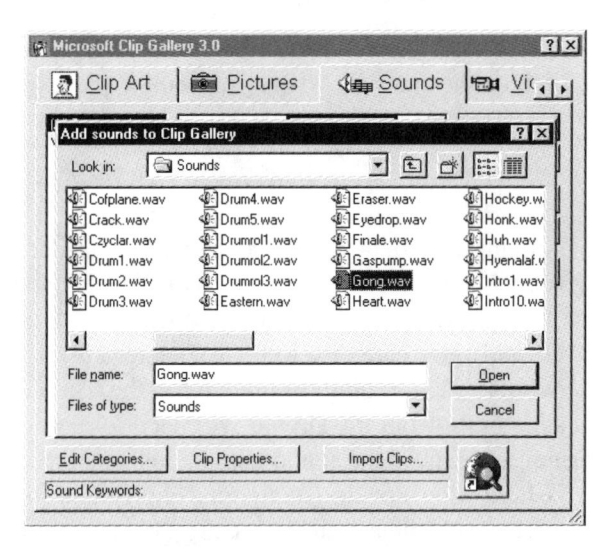

3. At the top of the dialog box, change to the drive and folder where the sound file is located. For instance, you might select E:\ for a CD-ROM drive.

4. Select the sound file you want to place in the gallery and click Open.

5. The Clip Properties dialog box appears. Notice the file size and the length of the sound file listed at the top. To hear the sound clip, click on the Play button. It will stop automatically when finished, or you can press ESC to stop it sooner.

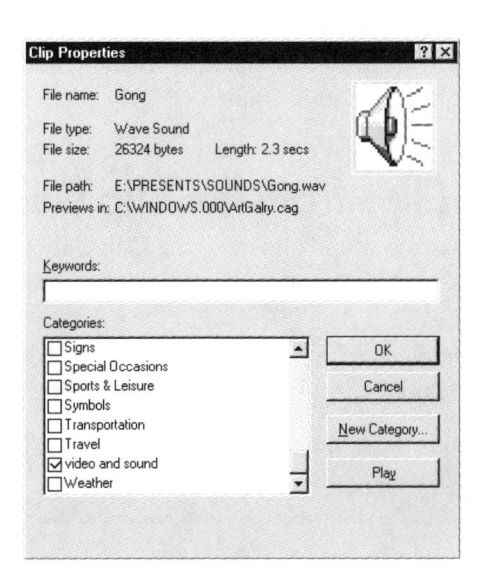

6. The Clip Gallery uses categories to store the various types of clips. Under Categories, click on the category where you want to place the sound file.

7. Click OK to return to the Clip Gallery. The sound, represented by a Speaker icon, appears in the Clip Gallery. Click on Close.

When you are assigning the sound clip to a category, consider making a new category for storing your sound files. This way they will all be together when you're ready to add one to a publication. Click on the New Category button in the Clip Properties dialog box to add a new category. Refer to Chapter 9 for more information on working with keywords and searching for graphics in the Clip Gallery.

If you import a sound clip from a CD, you will need to place that CD in the CD-ROM drive whenever you need the sound clip. Publisher stores only a preview of the sound clip on the hard drive, not the actual sound clip. Sound clips downloaded from the Clip Gallery Live web site are automatically saved on your hard drive.

Placing Sound in Publications

Picture frames are used to store sound clips in a publication. As mentioned, when a frame contains a sound, a Speaker icon appears in the frame to visually represent the sound. The Speaker icon will print. Keep this in mind when placing and sizing the sound frame. For instance, on some web page designs, you may want the icon to be visible—perhaps you include a note for the user to click on the icon to hear the sound. You might instead want the sound to play automatically in the background—in this case, users would not need to see the sound frame, so you could make it small and hide it under another frame.

Placing Sound Clips from the Clip Gallery

Once you have imported some sound clips into the Clip Gallery, you can add them to the page by using steps similar to those for adding photographs and clip art:

1. Draw or select the picture frame where you want to add the sound. From the Insert menu, choose Clip Art. The Microsoft Clip Gallery is displayed.

2. Click on the Sounds tab at the top of the dialog box. Click on the desired sound. To hear the sound, click on the Play button.

3. Click Insert to place the sound in your publication. The Speaker icon appears in the frame.

If you do not draw a frame before inserting a sound clip, Publisher will add a new one for you. The frame Publisher adds will be very small, so be sure you can locate it.

Placing Sound Clips Not from the Clip Gallery

Placing sound clips in the Clip Gallery takes up space on your hard drive. Not much, but if you're only going to use a sound clip one time, there's no need to add it to the Clip Gallery. Use the following steps to place a sound file that's not in the Clip Gallery:

1. Draw or select the picture frame where you want to add the sound. From the Insert menu, choose Object. The Insert Object dialog box appears. Since you are adding an existing sound file, click on the Create From File option on the left.

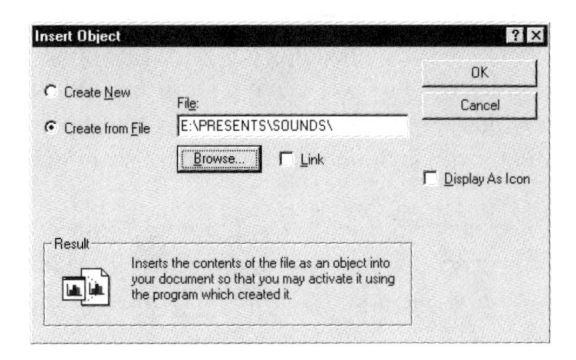

2. Click on the Browse button to display a dialog box for locating the sound file. Change to the drive and directory where the sound file is located.

3. Select the desired sound file, and click on the Insert button.

4. The path and filename of the sound file appear in the Insert Object dialog box. Click OK to place the sound.

There's no need to turn on the Display As Icon option in the Insert Object dialog box. Whether the option is on or not, the sound file works the same once placed in a publication. Turning on this option does affect the look of the icon; instead of just a speaker, the icon reads "Wave Sound" and displays a speaker.

Playing Sound Clips

As mentioned in the previous steps, you can play a sound clip in the Clip Gallery. Once a sound clip is placed on the page, you simply need to double-click on the sound (the Speaker icon) to hear it. If you want to stop the sound, press ESC.

If you prefer to use a menu command, select the frame containing the sound, and click on the Edit menu. At the bottom of the menu, choose Wave Sound Object. From the submenu, choose Play.

Editing Sound Clips

You can perform some basic sound editing right in Publisher. For instance, suppose you want to crank up the volume or speed up the tempo in a sound clip.

Publisher uses the Sound Recorder add-on module to edit the sound clip. Sound Recorder is a small application that provides tools for editing sound clips. Sound Recorder uses object linking and embedding (OLE). OLE allows you to edit a sound clip with Sound Recorder without ever leaving Publisher. When you edit a sound, the Sound Recorder window appears on top of your publication in Publisher. When you've finished editing, exit the Sound Recorder to return to Publisher.

 **NOTE:** *For more information on the Sound Recorder, Media Player, and other multimedia accessories, refer to* Windows 95 Made Easy: The Basics & Beyond!, *by Tom Sheldon (Osborne/McGraw-Hill).*

Using the Sound Recorder

The Sound Recorder provides tools to modify sound clips to fit your needs. To start the Sound Recorder, select the frame containing the sound you want to edit. From the Edit menu, click on Wave Sound Object. From the submenu, choose Edit. The Sound Recorder window appears.

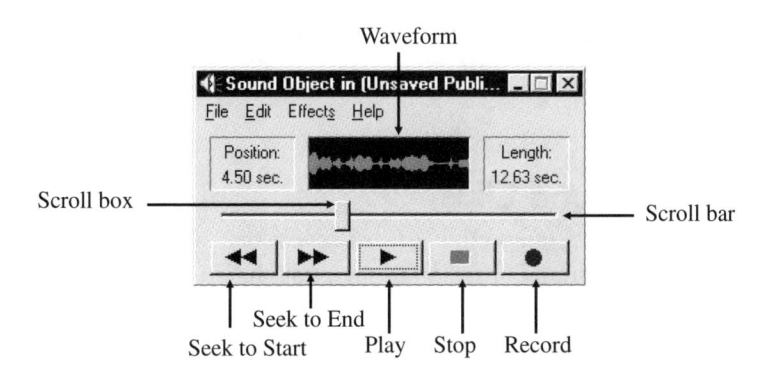

The buttons on the bottom of the Sound Recorder window work like those on a tape recorder. Click on the Play button to play the selected sound clip. When you play a sound file, the Sound Recorder displays a graphic representation of the sound, called a *waveform*. Click on the Stop button to stop playing the sound. Click on the Seek To Start (works like rewind) button to return to the beginning of the sound clip. Click on the Seek To End (works like fast forward) button to go to the end of the sound clip.

Adjusting the Volume

You may want to adjust the volume of a sound clip. For instance, if the sound is meant to be background music, you'll want the volume low. To change the volume of a sound file, choose Increase Volume (25%) or Decrease Volume from the Effects menu in the Sound Recorder. As the name implies, the volume is increased or decreased by 25 percent. Play the sound again to hear the adjusted volume. Repeat the steps if you need to continue increasing or decreasing the volume.

Adjusting the Speed

To increase or decrease the speed of the sound, choose Increase Speed (100%) or Decrease Speed. Play the sound again to hear the adjusted speed. Repeat the steps if you need to continue increasing or decreasing the speed.

 **NOTE:** *Publisher's online help doesn't say much about the Sound Recorder. For more information about it, click on the Help menu in the Sound Recorder window.*

Adding Other Sound Clips

You can combine several sound clips, or just repeat one sound clip several times. For instance, if a music sound clip is not long enough, you can insert more copies of the sound clip so it plays longer.

1. Drag the scroll box on the Sound Recorder where you want to insert the new sound. For instance, drag it to the end (you could also click on the Seek To End button) if you want the sound to play right after the current sound.

2. From the Edit menu, choose Insert File. Select the sound file you want to add and click OK.

3. Now click the Play button to hear the current and newly added sound.

Exiting Sound Recorder and Returning to Publisher

When you're finished editing a sound clip, select Exit And Return To *Name Of Your Publisher File* from the File menu in the Sound Recorder. The Sound Recorder module is closed, and you're ready to continue working in Publisher.

Working with Video Clips

Video adds instant motion and drama to web pages. You can add video footage of the company sales conference, or a short clip from the company president. Although video can be compelling, keep in mind that watching video on a web page can be painfully slow. In addition, viewers hate to wait for dull, uninteresting video clips. For best results, keep your video clips short and entertaining.

Video images are stored on frames, which when played quickly create the sense of movement. Your computer system will probably not be able to match the video (or frame) speed you are accustomed to seeing on your VCR. On many systems, video clips have a tendency to be rather jumpy. Overall, keep in mind that working with video clips on personal computers is still relatively new, and some of the kinks have not been worked out.

Where to Get Video Clips

As with sound clips, the Clip Gallery Live includes video files. As mentioned earlier, the URL is **http://www.microsoft.com/clipgallerylive**. Refer to the previous section on getting sound clips for more information on working with Clip Gallery Live. Keep in mind that when you download a video clip from the Clip Gallery Live, the video file is automatically loaded on your hard drive. Video files can be really large, so don't load your hard disk with video files you won't use.

Search the Internet for other video clip resources. Enter "clip art" or "video clips" as the search string in a search engine, such as Yahoo! or Web Crawler.

You can also find video clips on CDs at computer stores. As with sound, graphics and animation software applications frequently include video files on the CD-ROMs included with the software. CorelDRAW provides several video files with scenes of a fire, buses, and airplanes.

With the right hardware and software, you can also record your own video clips. Recording video can be expensive. For help, check out some books on desktop video, or find a user group that specializes in multimedia. You might find a friend to guide you through the process.

Video Clip Formats Accepted by Publisher

Publisher can recognize video files with the filename extension .AVI. This is a popular video format that works with the Windows 95 Media Player.

Importing Video Clips into the Clip Gallery

As with sound, you can add video clips to the Clip Gallery. The steps are similar to adding sound files.

In the following steps, an .AVI file from a CD-ROM is placed in the Clip Gallery:

1. From the Insert menu, select Clip Art. The Microsoft Clip Gallery is displayed. Click on the Videos tab at the top of the dialog box.

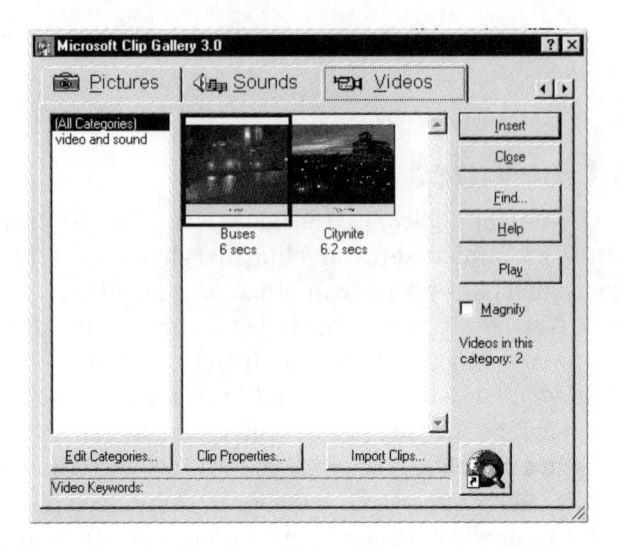

2. To import a video clip, click on the Import Clips button. The Add Videos To Clip Gallery dialog box is displayed.

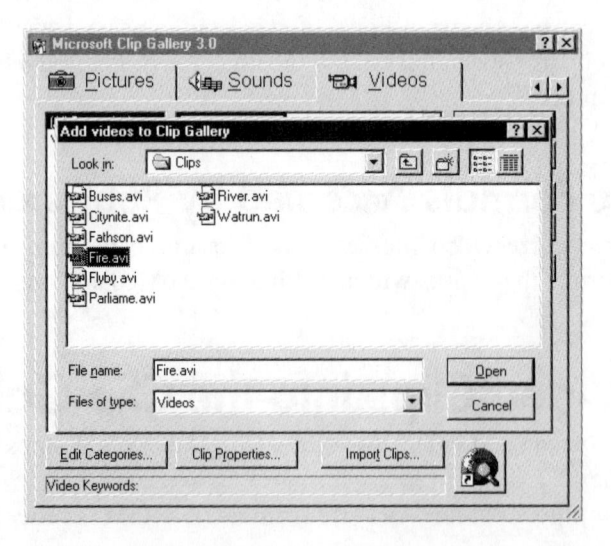

3. Change to the drive and folder where the video file is located. For instance, you might select *E:* for a CD-ROM drive.

4. Select the video file you want to place in the Gallery and click Open.

5. The Clip Properties dialog box appears. Notice the file size and the length of the video file listed at the top. The Clip Gallery uses categories to store the various types of clips. Under Categories, click on the category where you want to place the video file.

6. To see the video clip, click on the Play button. The video is show at its *optimal size*—more on this in the following section. It will stop automatically when finished, or you can press ESC to stop it sooner.

7. Click OK to return to the Clip Gallery. The first frame of the video appears in the Clip Gallery. Click on Close.

Placing Video in Publications

Picture frames hold video clips in a publication. In general, you can move and format frames containing video clips just like other picture frames. However, there is a difference—frames containing video clips should not be sized. Video clips look best when displayed in the size in which they were recorded—this is their optimal size. For instance, a clip recorded using the dimensions 4 inches by 5 inches should be placed in a frame that is 4 inches by 5 inches. To make sure a video clip is placed in a frame in the optimal size, insert the clip without drawing or selecting a picture frame first. That way, Publisher adds a new frame for the video clip in the optimal size.

If you adjust the size of a video clip, you will distort the image quality. Try adjusting the size of other page elements to work with the optimal size of the video clip.

Placing from the Clip Gallery

Once you have imported some video clips into the Clip Gallery, you're ready to add them to a publication. As suggested, in the following steps a picture frame is not selected before adding the video:

1. From the Insert menu, choose Clip Art. The Microsoft Clip Gallery is displayed.

2. Click on the Videos tab at the top of the dialog box. Click on the desired video clip. To see the video, click on the Play button.

3. Click Insert to place the video in your publication. A new frame is placed in your publication displaying the first frame of the video.

A gray bar displaying the video filename appears at the bottom of the frame. The text in the gray bar is called a *caption*—you will learn more about captions in the section "Editing the Caption," later in this chapter.

Placing Video Clips Not from the Clip Gallery

You can also place video files that are not from the Clip Gallery:

1. From the Insert menu, choose Object. The Insert Object dialog box appears. Since you are adding an existing video file, click on the Create From File option on the left.

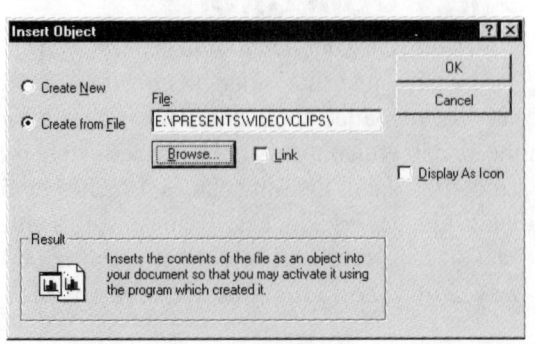

2. Click on the Browse button to display a dialog box for locating the video file. Change to the drive and directory where the video file is located.

3. Select the desired video file, and click on the Insert button.

4. The path and filename of the video file appear in the Insert Object dialog box. Click OK to place the video. A new frame is placed in your publication displaying the first frame of the video.

As mentioned, a caption is placed in the newly inserted video clip frame. You will see how to change the text in the caption later in this chapter.

Playing Video Clips

Video clips can be played in the Clip Gallery. To play a video clip that has been placed in a publication, double-click on the video clip. A control panel appears at the bottom of the video clip with a scroll bar indicating the progress of the video. Buttons for playing and stopping the video are also displayed.

 **NOTE:** *Don't be surprised if it takes a few seconds for the video to begin playing. Long clips, especially, can take some time to get going.*

You can also play a video by selecting the frame containing the video, and clicking on the Edit menu. At the bottom of the menu, choose Video Clip Object. From the submenu, choose Play. Click the right mouse button on the video clip to display another menu with the same commands.

Editing Video Clips

The Windows 95 Media Player can be used to perform basic video editing right in Publisher. For instance, suppose you want to use only a section of a video clip rather than the whole thing. The Media Player is an add-on module included with Windows 95. You can think of Media Player as a small application designed specifically for editing video clips.

Media Player uses object linking and embedding (OLE). OLE allows you to edit a video clip without ever leaving Publisher. When you edit video in Media Player, the Media Player menus take over Publisher's menus, letting you edit the video in place. When you've finished editing, you can click anywhere on the page to return to Publisher's normal menus.

NOTE: *The Media Player and Sound Recorder also work with other Windows applications such as Microsoft Word, Excel, and PowerPoint. The information covered in this chapter would also apply to editing video and sound in those applications.*

Using the Media Player

The Media Player provides tools to customize video clips for your needs. To start the Media Player, select the frame containing the video you want to edit. From the Edit menu, click on Video Clip Object. From the submenu, choose Edit. The Media Player's menus and toolbar replace Publisher's menus and toolbars. As you can see in Figure 14-1, the publication remains and a gray border surrounds the frame containing the video clip.

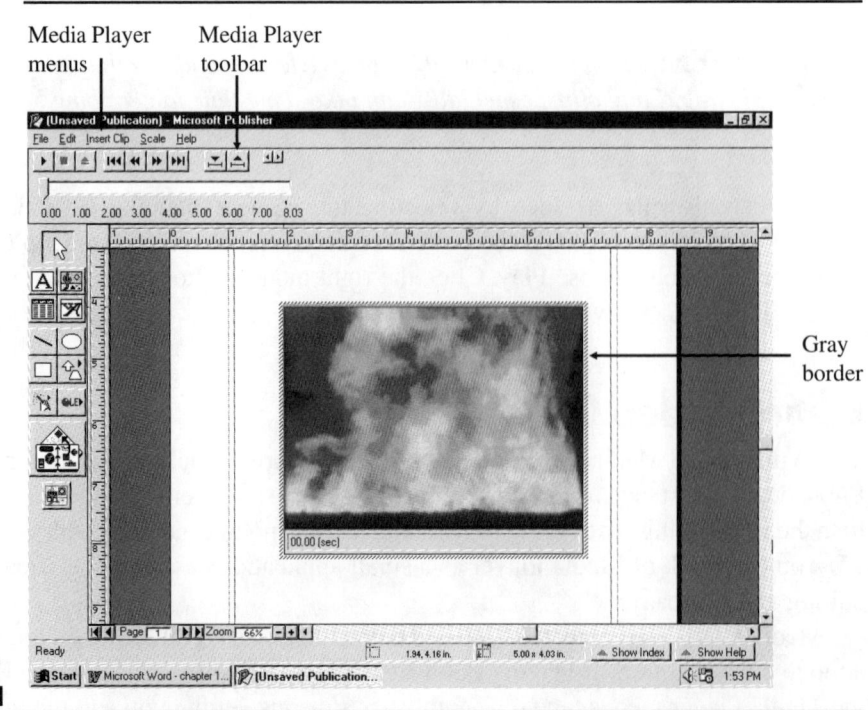

The Media Player's menus and tools replace Publisher's menus and tools when you edit a video clip

FIGURE 14-1

 **NOTE:** *As you work with the Media Player, do not click outside of the gray box surrounding the frame until you are finished editing the video clip. If you do so, repeat the steps for starting the Media Player.*

 **TIP:** *You can also click the right mouse button on a video clip to reveal a menu with the Video Clip | Edit commands.*

Just as the buttons on the Sound Recorder are similar to a tape recorder, the buttons on the Media Player are similar to those on a VCR. Click on the Play button to play the selected video clip. Click on the Stop button to stop playing the video. Click on the Rewind button to rewind the video clip in small increments. Click on the Fast Forward button to move forward through the video clip in small increments. These last two options are useful when you are focusing on a particular section of the clip and need to watch it over and over without watching the whole clip.

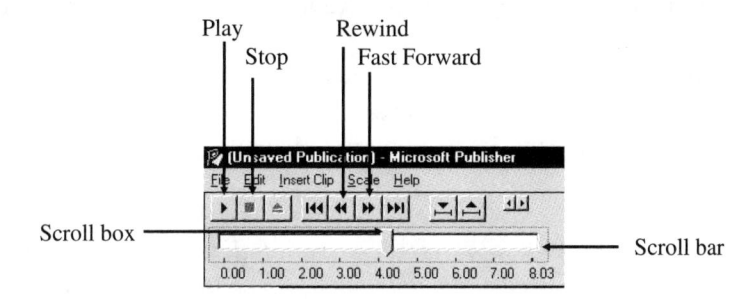

The scroll bar in the Media Player represents the length of the video clip in seconds. You can drag the scroll box to move to a specific time in the video. For instance, to move to the middle of a clip, drag the scroll box to the middle of the scroll bar. The gray box at the bottom of the video clip displays the time (in seconds).

Using Auto Rewind

Rather than clicking on the Rewind button each time you finish playing a video clip, turn on the Auto Rewind option. From the Edit menu, select Options. In the Options dialog box, click to place a check mark by Auto Rewind.

NOTE: *Click on the Help menu in the Media Player menu bar to access online help files for more information.*

Using Auto Repeat

Once a video clip has been started, you may want to have it play continuously. When a clip plays continuously, it automatically rewinds itself and begins playing again. The clip continues to play until the user clicks the Stop button or presses ESC. To play a video clip continuously, select Options from the Edit menu. In the Options dialog box, click on the Auto Repeat option to have the clip automatically repeat when it reaches the end.

NOTE: *Generally, it is recommended that you not run a clip continuously on a web page. Running a clip continuously consumes a lot of a computer's resources and can significantly slow down the system.*

Editing the Caption

The caption identifies the contents of the video clip. Captions are useful in letting viewers know a little about what they are going to see when they play the clip. By default, the video filename is placed in the caption area. To enter new text for the caption, select Options from the Edit menu. In the Options dialog box, enter new text in the Caption box. You can enter up to 80 characters. For example, on a web page for your local fire department, you could enter "Double-click here to see footage of an actual fire." This informs viewers of what to do and what they will see.

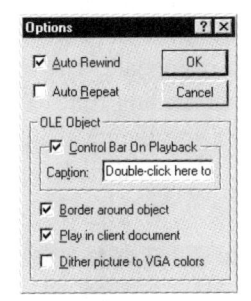

Viewing a Section of a Clip

Imagine you have a clip about 20 seconds long, but you only need about 10 seconds of the footage. Media Player allows you to select the part of the clip you want to see, and to edit out the rest.

First, drag the scroll box to the location on the scroll bar where you want the clip to begin. In the example shown here, the clip begins at one second.

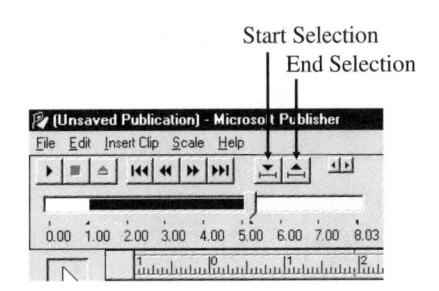

To mark the beginning, click on the Start Selection button. A small black triangle is placed at that point on the scroll bar. To mark the ending, drag the scroll box to the spot where you want the clip to end, and click on the End Selection button. A small black triangle marks the ending point. A blue bar appears in the scroll bar, indicating the selected portion. Now, when you play the video clip, only the selected portion is played.

> **NOTE:**   *The scroll bar can also display frame numbers instead of seconds that compose the video clip. From the Scale menu, select Frames to see the length of the video clip depicted in frames. You may wish to work with frames instead of seconds when selecting a section of a video clip.*

If you need to edit the selection, choose Selection from the Edit menu. The Set Selection—Time Mode dialog box appears. The From box indicates the beginning time, and the To box indicates the ending time. You can modify these numbers if needed. The Size box represents the length of the selected area. To remove the selection, click None. Click OK when finished.

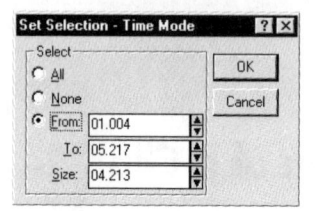

Exiting Media Player and Returning to Publisher

When you're finished editing the video clip, click outside the gray border surrounding the video clip frame. The Publisher menus and toolbars reappear, and you're ready to continue working in Publisher.

Summary

Sound and video are the latest hot items to place in web pages. However, you can certainly design great-looking and informative web pages without sound and video. The elements discussed so far in this book—text, graphics (pictures), tables, WordArt, as well as sound and video—all play a role in designing web pages. Now that you're familiar with adding these elements to a publication, the next chapter looks at the steps for building and publishing a web page.

15

Designing Web Pages

If you spent the last couple of years on Mars, you may not have heard about the Internet. If you've been here on Earth, you couldn't help but notice the lingo ("surfing the Web"), the URLs (web page addresses), and the general buzz about the Internet. The Internet is revolutionizing the way people communicate, the way people look for information, and the way people buy products and services. The fastest growing and one of the most exciting parts of the Internet is the *World Wide Web.* Publisher can help you make your own mark in the World Wide Web by designing a web page.

This chapter provides an introduction to designing web pages in Publisher. First, you'll find an overview of the Internet and the World Wide Web. The structure of web sites and how hyperlinks connect web pages are also discussed. In the next section you'll find tips for designing effective web pages. The rest of the chapter focuses on using Publisher's Web Site PageWizard to create web sites. Here you will see how to assign hyperlinks to text and objects. The chapter ends with the steps for previewing and publishing your web site.

What Is the Internet?

The Internet is a worldwide network of computers. Because the Internet connects millions of people and enables users like you to share ideas, documents, and files, the Internet has been referred to as an "Information Superhighway." As with many highways, the Information Superhighway is constantly under construction, with new users and new information being added continually.

 **NOTE:** *The Internet was started in 1969 by the United States Department of Defense as a way to ensure that military communications could continue in the event of war.*

Anyone with a computer, modem, phone line, and Internet service provider can access the Internet. There are many components to the Internet—e-mail, FTP (file transfer protocol), and especially popular, the World Wide Web (more on this later).

You can also create web pages for an *intranet*. An intranet is a small network of computers within a company or organization. Corporate phone directories, personnel policies, and corporate news are just a few of the items placed on intranets. The steps for creating a web page in Publisher are the same, whether it's for the Internet or an intranet.

NOTE: *This chapter assumes you have some idea of what the Internet is and why you would want to create a web page. If you need more basic information about the Internet and World Wide Web, refer to* The Internet for Busy People, Second Edition *(1997) and* The World Wide Web for Busy People *(1996), both published by Osborne/McGraw-Hill.*

What Is the World Wide Web?

A popular portion of the Internet is the World Wide Web (WWW). The WWW displays *web pages* of information enhanced with text, graphics, and (in some cases) sound and video. A *web site* is a collection of web pages. As an example, the web site for American Airlines consists of web pages displaying information on flight arrivals, departures, and schedules. Publisher can help you create a web site with multiple web pages or just a single web page.

Each web page has a unique address, called the *uniform resource locator* (URL). Web page URLs begin with *http://* followed by the web page address. For instance, the URL for Microsoft is **http://www.microsoft.com**, and the URL for CNN is **http://www.cnn.com**. You can access any web page by entering the URL in your web browser software.

Understanding the Structure of a Web Site

As mentioned earlier, a web site consists of multiple web pages. The first page in a web site is called a *home page*. The home page is usually the first page viewers see when they visit your web site. From the home page users can connect to other web pages.

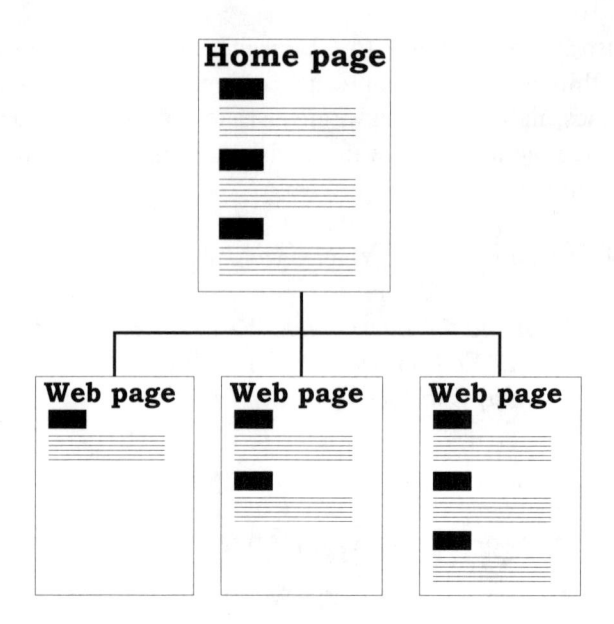

Understanding Hyperlinks

Web pages contain *hyperlinks,* which allow readers to quickly move from one web page to another. A hyperlink "points" to an address or URL of another web page in the Internet—when you click on a hyperlink, your screen then displays the web page with that address. In Publisher, you can assign hyperlinks to graphics such as a photograph or text. When text is linked, it is generally called *hypertext.*

If you've ever used online help in a Windows application, you've already had experience dealing with linked text. For instance, in Publisher's online help, if the mouse pointer changes to a pointing finger when placed on text or a graphic, you can click on the text or graphic to move to another page of help information. The same is true on a web page; the pointing finger indicates when text or a graphic has a hyperlink. In addition to the pointing finger, hypertext links are usually in color and often underlined.

Browsing through web pages (also called "surfing the Web") is made simple because of hyperlinks. Readers click on hyperlinks to quickly navigate through information found in the Web. In many cases, hyperlinks connect web pages within the same web site. However, some hyperlinks take the viewer to another web site altogether. For instance, the web pages in *USA Today*'s web site are loaded with hyperlinks to soft drink companies, clothing retailers, airlines—the same companies that advertise in the newspaper every day.

Effectively placing hyperlinks is one of the keys to successful web page design. It should be easy for the reader to spot text and graphics with hyperlinks. The text and graphics should also give the viewer a good idea of where the hyperlink will take them. For instance, on an airline web page, the hypertext link might read, "Flight Arrivals." Following are more tips for good web page design.

Tips for Successful Web Page Design

As with printed publications, creating professional web pages requires a little prep work. Before you begin designing, decide what you want to accomplish with your web pages. For instance, is the purpose of your web page to inform the public about products and services you offer? Or are you designing a web page to share information about a specific topic?

Web page design is different from other types of publication design. For instance, in newsletters, several articles are frequently placed on one page, whereas in a web site, each article would be placed on a different web page. The following are a few things to consider when building web pages:

- Outline the contents of your web pages on the home page. This allows readers to quickly find the information they want without having to read pages that do not interest them.

- Each web page should contain a different concept or idea, and should have enough content to fill a single screen.

- Web pages should not be too short or too long. If a web page is shorter than half a screen of information, try to combine the information with another page. If a web page is longer than five screens of information, try to break up the information into separate web pages.

- Always display the most important information at the top of each web page. Some readers will not scroll through a web page. These readers will miss important information if it is not displayed at the top.

- Carefully check the spelling and grammar in your web pages. A spelling mistake will make readers think you are careless and your web pages are inaccurate.

- Use headings to indicate your main topics. Headings make it easier for readers to glance through a web page and find specific information without having to read through all the content.

■ If you are going to use information or an image from another source, make sure the information or image is not copyrighted or that you have obtained written permission for its use.

■ Images increase the time it takes for a web page to appear on screen. Use small images rather than large images, since large images take longer to transfer.

A good way to get started is to take a close look at some of your favorite web pages. Determine what you like about these pages, and consider how you can use these ideas in your pages. *USA Today* offers a listing of new web pages daily in the Home Tech section. In addition, visit the web site at **http://www.pointcom.com** for a daily listing of new web sites.

Creating Web Sites

Creating web pages in Publisher is very similar to creating printed publications. There's a Web Site PageWizard to help you build the initial publication. As with other publications, text, graphics, sound, and video are placed in frames. Much of what you have learned so far will apply to building and designing web pages.

Web pages differ from printed publications in that hyperlinks are assigned to text and graphic elements on the web pages. After the web site is complete, the site is *published,* or made available on the Internet or on your intranet.

 **NOTE:** *Hypertext Markup Language (HTML) is the language used to develop web pages. Fortunately, you don't have to learn HTML, because Publisher automatically generates the HTML commands to build your web page.*

This chapter focuses on using the Web Site PageWizard to design a web site. You can, however, create a web site from scratch by using the Blank Page option discussed in Chapter 5. You can also turn a previously existing publication into a web page. (Refer to Publisher's online help for more information.) However, since designing a web page is a little more complex than designing a normal printed publication, this is a good time to take advantage of the predesigned page layouts supplied by Publisher's PageWizards. You can modify the page design as much as you need, but starting out with the Web Site PageWizard provides a good base for creating a web site.

Using the Web Site PageWizard

The Web Site PageWizard provides assistance by asking questions specific to web site design. You are asked whether you want a single- or multiple-page web site. You can select the style of web page you prefer, as well as enter address information on your web site.

The following steps illustrate using the Web Site PageWizard to create a web site. After the site is created, the chapter discusses placing your own text and graphics on the pages and then assigning hyperlinks to connect the pages.

1. From the File menu, select Create New Publication. Make sure the PageWizard tab is selected, and then double-click on the Web Site PageWizard.

2. The first screen in the Web Site PageWizard lets you specify what type of web site you are creating. You can choose from Business, Community, or Personal. After making a selection, click on the Next button.

3. The next screen asks if you want a one-page or multiple-page web site. By default, a multiple-page web site includes four pages. After making a selection, click on the Next button.

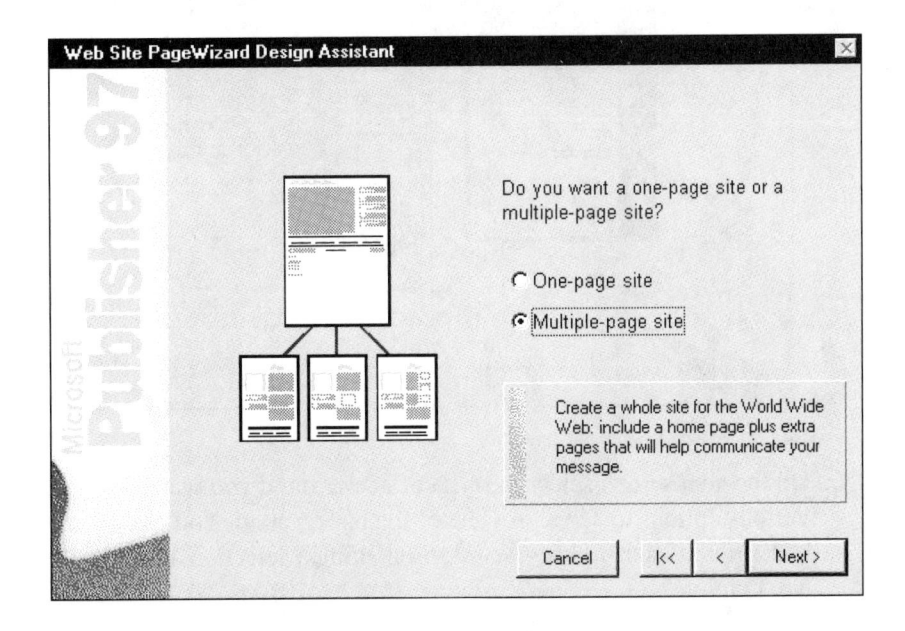

4. The next screen allows you to specify topics for your web pages. You can add more topics to increase the number of pages in your web site, or remove topics to delete pages from your web site. The topic names will appear on the web pages; however, you can edit the topic names if desired. After making your selections, click on the Next button.

 **NOTE:** *If you're unsure if you want a specific topic for your web site, add it. It's easier to delete a designed web page than to manually build a new one.*

5. The next screen displays several web page designs to choose from. Remember, the style you choose is just a starting point for your design. You can modify it to fit your exact needs. After making a selection, click on the Next button.

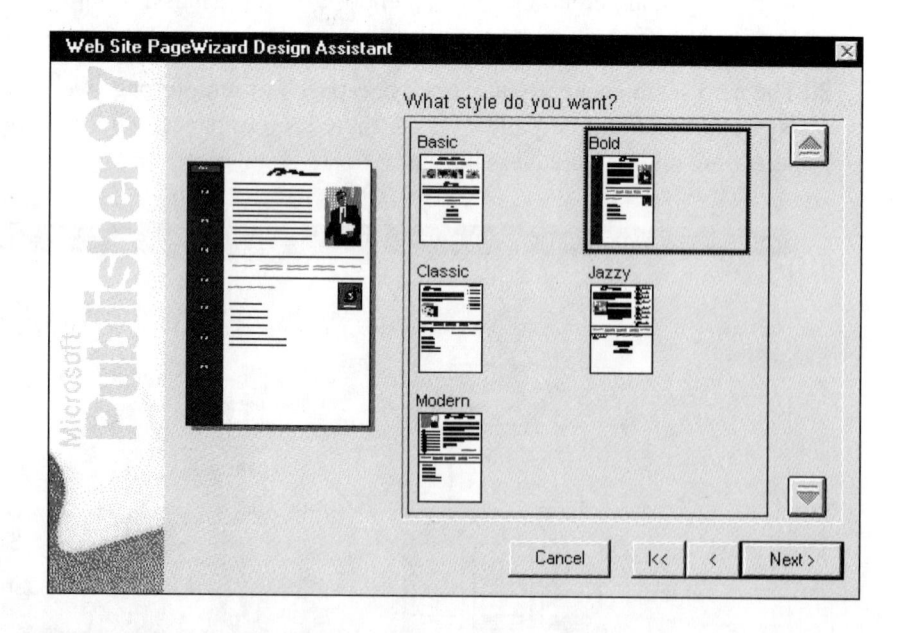

6. On the next screen select the type of background you want. Click on the various options to see a preview of the background. You can change the background later if necessary. After making a selection, click on the Next button.

7. Depending on which web page design you selected, another screen appears asking you to select the style of navigation buttons. For instance, the Classic web page design lets you select the button style, while the Basic web page design does not. Select Text Only to assign hyperlinks to text only. Select Buttons And Text to create buttons (with text on them) that can be assigned a hyperlink. Select Icons And Text to create graphic cues with text that can be assigned a hyperlink. Click on each option to see a preview. After making a selection, click on the Next button.

8. On the next screen enter the title for your home page. For instance, you might enter the name of your business or organization here. Click on the Next button when finished.

9. The next screen asks if you want to include a postal address on the web site. Click Yes, Please! to include an address or No, Thanks to skip it. After making a selection, click on the Next button.

10. If you opted to include your postal address, another screen asks for the address information. Enter the appropriate information and click on the Next button.

11. The next screen asks if you want to include a phone number, fax number, or e-mail address. Click on the option's check box, and then enter the information in the box below. If you add your e-mail address, a hyperlink will be added to your e-mail address. After making your selections, click on the Next button.

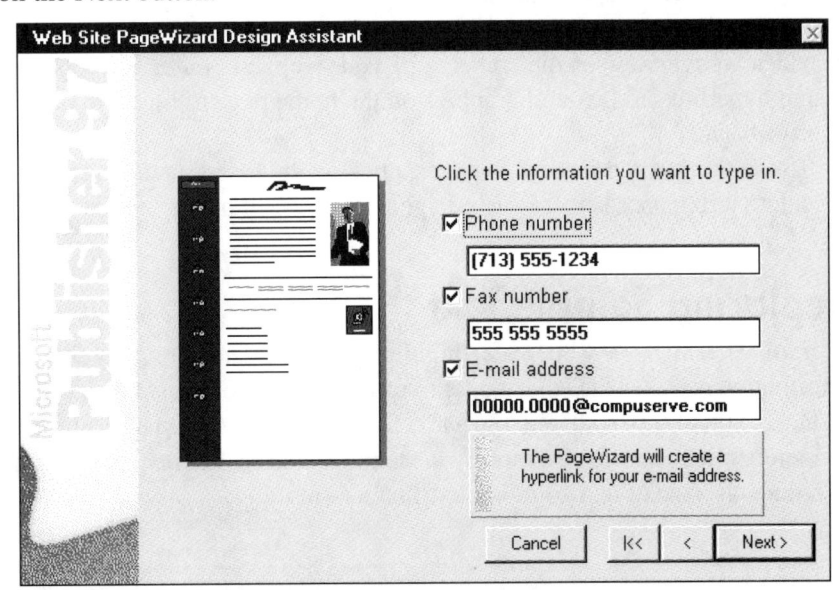

 **NOTE:** *Including your address, phone number, fax number, and e-mail address is imperative if you want readers to be able to contact you easily!*

12. On the next screen, click on the Create It! button to begin creating your web site. A message box appears indicating the progress of the web site production.

13. On the final screen of the Web Site PageWizard, select Yes to display help information as you build the web page, or No to not display help information. (If you're new to designing in Publisher, click Yes—it certainly can't hurt!) After making a selection, click OK.

The first page of the web site is displayed. As with other publications, use the Page Counter to move between the pages in your web site. Use the Zoom indicator to zoom into the page for close-ups and to zoom out for an overall view of the page.

Customizing the Page Design

The Web Site PageWizard automatically adds sample text and graphics to the page design. The text and graphics are in frames. As with other publications, you can move, size, and delete the frames. You can also add borders and backgrounds to the frames.

The first page, page 1, is the home page of your web site. Remember, this is generally the first page readers see when visiting your site. The home page usually provides an overview of the contents of your web site. Later you will see how to assign hyperlinks to text and graphics on the home page to link it to other pages in your web site.

If you need to add more web pages, click on the Insert menu and choose Pages. To delete web pages, select Delete Page from the Edit menu.

Replacing Sample Text

To replace text on a web page, highlight the text and begin typing. The new information replaces the selected text. You may need to adjust the text frames. For instance, you may need to enlarge a text frame when entering large amounts of text. Remember that you can also modify the text formatting. For instance, you may want to reduce the size of text so more text fits in a frame.

In many cases, the sample text on a web page can provide helpful tips on content and writing style for web pages. For instance, on the home page shown here, the sample text block reads, "This is a good spot to let readers know the purpose of this Web site. The home page gives readers their impressions of your site's style. Use energetic language to hold readers' attention."

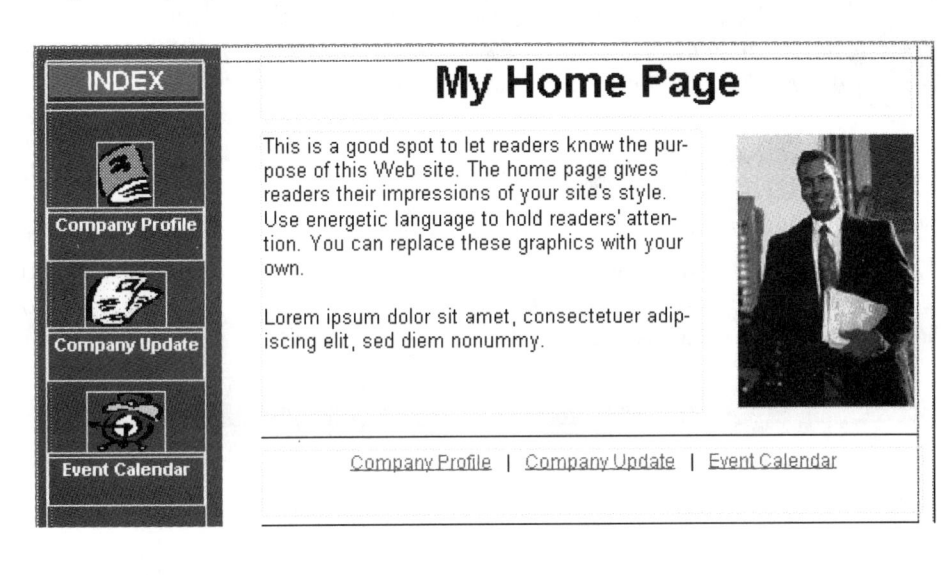

 **NOTE:** *Refer to Chapter 8 for more information about editing and formatting text, and to Chapter 9 for more information on working with graphics.*

Replacing Sample Graphics

To replace graphics on a web page, double-click on the graphic to display the Clip Gallery. You can also select the graphic and choose Insert | Picture File to place a graphic created in a drawing application.

Sound and video are also placed in picture frames. It's best not to put important information in a sound clip, since many users will not be set up for sound. Video clips increase the time it takes for a web page to appear on screen. Rather than placing a video clip on the home page, consider creating a hyperlink that takes readers to another web page where they can view a video clip. Chapter 14 discussed working with video and sound.

Finally, remember you can always add or delete frames to change the layout of the web page. For instance, the Basic web page design shows four images at the top of the home page—you may wish to cut this to two images, and make those two images larger.

 **NOTE:** *Don't forget about running the spell checker and the Design Checker to find any errors in spelling and page layout. With so many potential readers you certainly don't need any mistakes!*

Background Choices

Publisher provides many choices for the background of your web pages. To see the background options, select Background And Text Colors from the Format menu. In the dialog box, make sure the Standard tab is selected to display a list of background choices. Click on a choice to preview it.

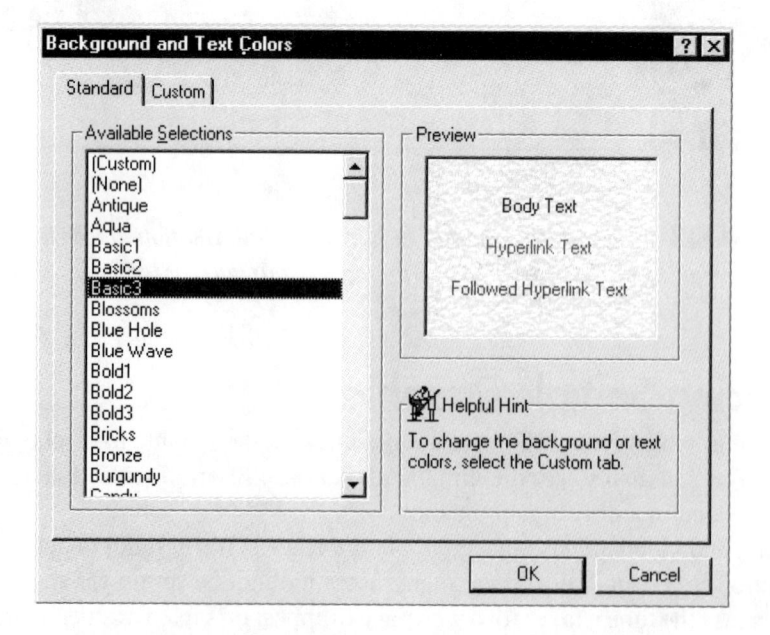

15

To customize a background, click on the Custom tab at the top of the dialog box. To select a background color, click on the down arrow by Color. (If a texture was previously selected, click on the No Texture button to remove the texture.) The preview will display the selected background color. You can also change the color of text on web pages. Click on the down arrow by Body Text, Hyperlink, and Followed Hyperlink (text hyperlinks the reader has already read) to select another color for these text strings. Watch the preview to see if the text colors are attractive and easy to read against the background.

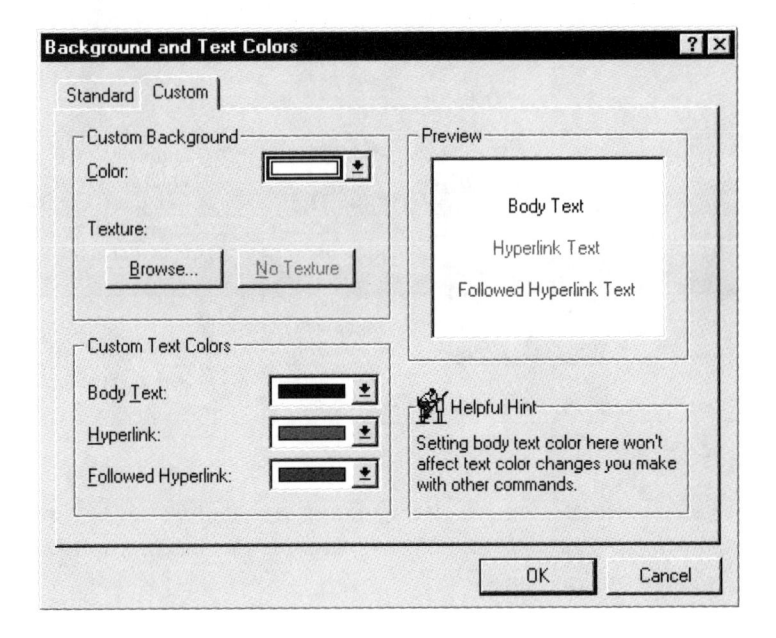

You can create a custom background texture with a photograph or other type of graphic. For instance, you could use a photo of your house as a background for a personal web page. Any graphic file format recognized by Publisher can be used as a background for a web page. (Chapter 9 includes a complete listing of these file formats.) To select the file you want to use as the background, click on the Browse button. Change to the drive and directory where the graphic file is located and select the file. The graphic file will be *tiled,* which means repeated across the background—kind of like floor tile—on the web page.

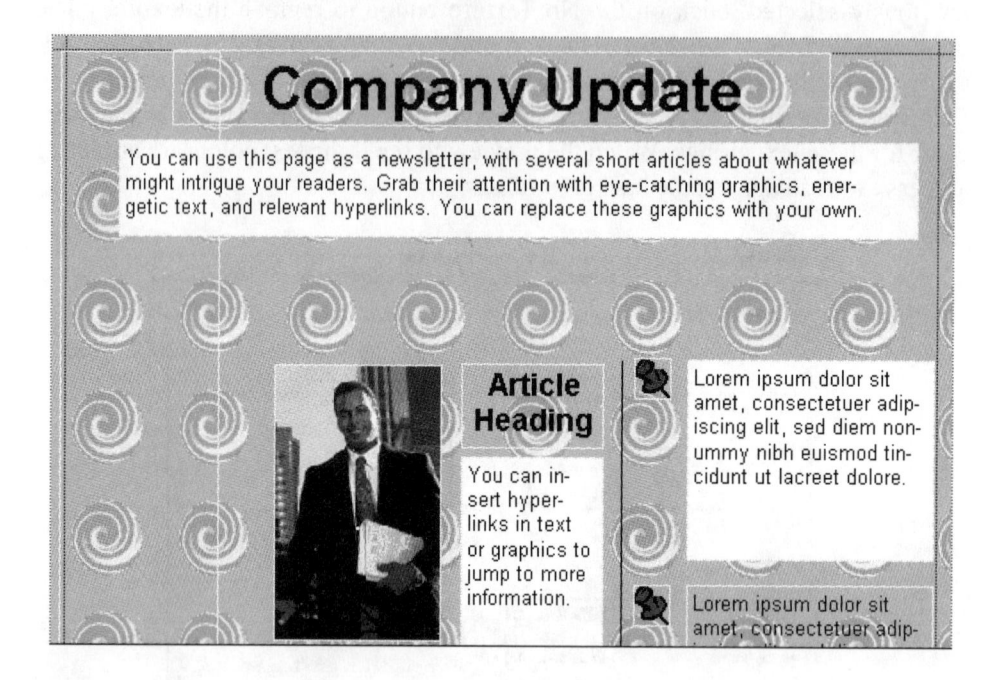

NOTE: *Make sure the background you choose does not affect the readability of your web page. There's nothing like a clean, solid background to enhance text and graphics.*

Assigning Hyperlinks

Hyperlinks allow readers to quickly jump from one page of your web site to another. As mentioned earlier, hyperlinks contain an address or URL to another page in the Web. You can assign hyperlinks to text or graphics in your web pages.

If you used the Web Site PageWizard to create your web site, the PageWizard automatically added hyperlinks to certain text headings and graphics. The web page in Figure 15-1 was designed with the Web Site PageWizard. Hyperlinks were automatically assigned to the text heading "Company Profile" and the top graphic on the left. These hyperlinks connect the reader to the second page in the web site. The heading "Company Update" and the second graphic on the left contain

Hyperlink tool   Preview Web Site tool

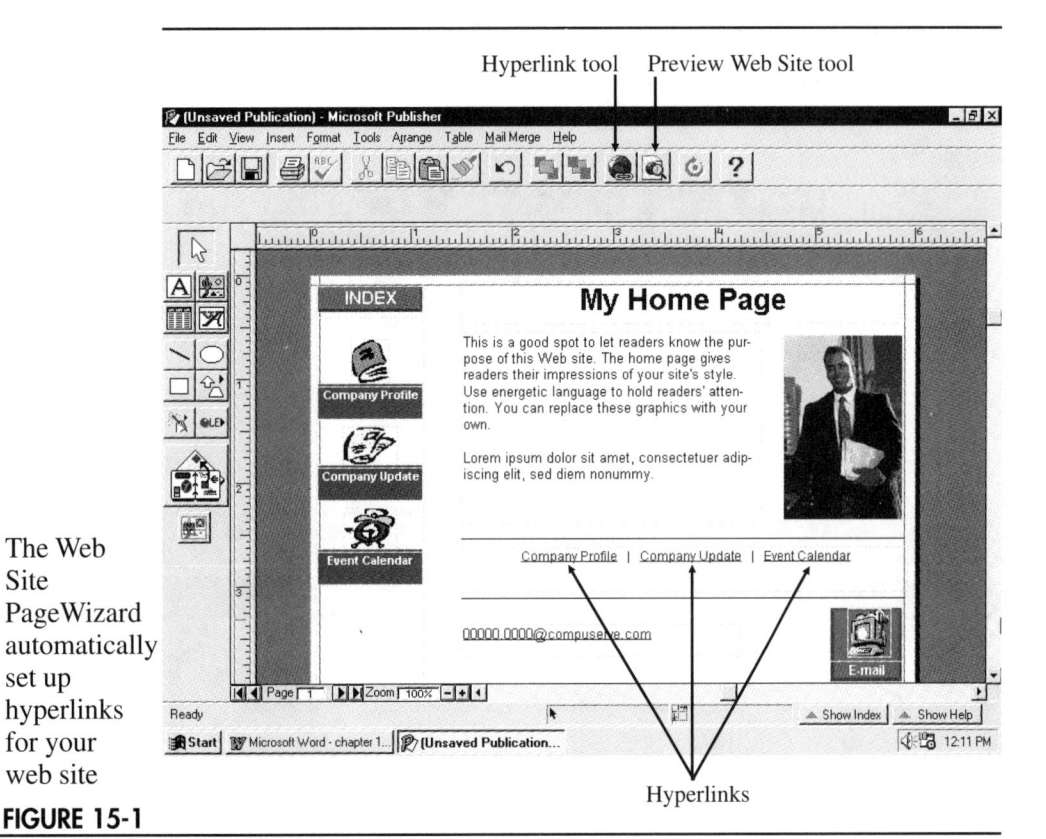

The Web Site PageWizard automatically set up hyperlinks for your web site

Hyperlinks

FIGURE 15-1

hyperlinks connecting to the third page in the web site. As the designer, you can add new hyperlinks or modify existing hyperlinks to meet the needs of your web site.

If you built the page without the PageWizard, you will have to assign the hyperlinks manually. Publisher will automatically apply color and an underline to hyperlink text, which is common in web page design. You can make it easy for readers to identify graphics with hyperlinks by adding instructional text. For instance, below a small photograph of the new company building, you could place a text block that reads, "Preview photos of the new company building."

The following steps illustrate assigning hyperlinks to text or graphic objects:

1. Select the graphic or text where you want to assign a hyperlink. With text, you will have to highlight the text by dragging across it. You cannot just select the text frame.

2. Choose Hyperlink from the Insert menu, or click on the Hyperlink tool in the Standard toolbar (shown in Figure 15-1). The Hyperlink dialog box is displayed. You have four options for creating hyperlinks:

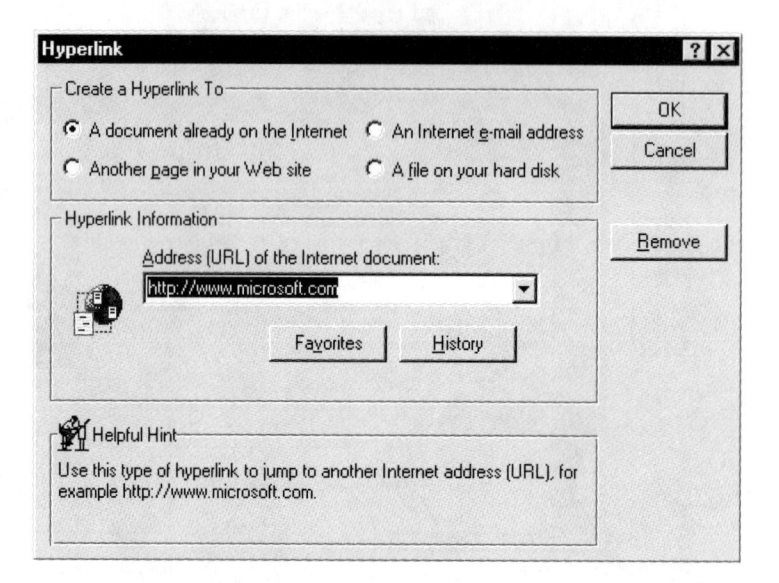

- Click on the first option, A Document Already On The Internet, to create a hyperlink that takes the reader to another web site on the Internet. For instance, a web site about minivans may include hyperlinks to car dealerships where minivans are sold. Enter the URL of the web site you want to link to in the Address (URL) Of The Internet Document box.

NOTE: *When creating hyperlinks that take readers to another web site, place the hyperlink at the bottom of a page, so they find it* after *they've read your information.*

- Click on the second option, Another Page In Your Web Site, to create a hyperlink that connects readers to other pages in your web site. You can choose to link to the first page, next page, or previous page. Click on the down arrow by Specific Page to specify the number of the page you want to link to.

15

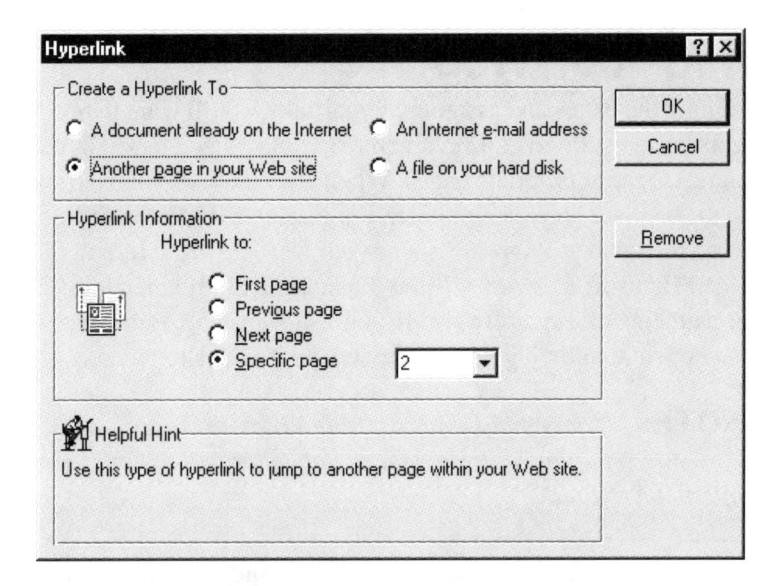

- Click on the third option, An Internet E-Mail Address, to create a hyperlink to an e-mail address anywhere on the Internet. If you enter your own e-mail address, readers can reply to you just by clicking this hyperlink. Enter the address in the Internet e-mail address box.

- Click on the fourth option, A File On Your Hard Disk, to create a hyperlink that connects to a file on your computer or network. This type of link could be used when creating intranet web pages—readers could access information from the network by clicking on a hyperlink. Enter the location and name of the file in the Path Of The File box. Click on the Browse button to search for the file if necessary.

3. After selecting the type of hyperlink, click on the OK button.

The hyperlink is added to the highlighted text or selected graphic. However, the hyperlinks will not work, meaning you cannot move from page to page by clicking on the hyperlinks, until you preview or publish the web site as discussed in the following sections.

TIP: *To remove a hyperlink from text or graphics, select the text or graphic, and click on the Remove button in the Hyperlink dialog box.*

Previewing Your Web Site

After designing the pages and assigning hyperlinks, you'll want to preview how the site will appear on the Internet. Previewing also allows you to test hyperlinks to see if they connect to the appropriate pages. When you preview your web site, Publisher opens it in the browser on your computer. For instance, if Microsoft Network is your Internet service provider, Publisher opens your web site in the Internet Explorer (the browser for Microsoft Network). Many business and organizations use Netscape Navigator as their browser software. If you use Netscape, Publisher will find this browser and open it, allowing you to preview your web site.

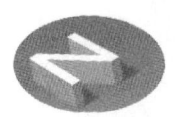 **NOTE:** *If you have Microsoft Internet Explorer and several other browsers set up on your computer, Publisher will default to the Microsoft Internet Explorer.*

To preview your web site, select Preview Web Site from the File menu. You can also click on the Preview Web Site tool in the Standard toolbar (shown in Figure 15-1). A message appears indicating the progress as Publisher generates your pages for the Web. Once your web site appears in the browser windows, you can click on the hyperlinks to make sure they work correctly.

When you are through previewing and testing, exit your browser software. For instance, in Microsoft Internet Explorer, select Exit from the File menu. After exiting the browser, return to Publisher to make any necessary changes.

Using the Preview Troubleshooter

The Preview Troubleshooter can help you identify and fix previewing problems. When you return to Publisher after previewing your web site, the Preview Troubleshooter appears in the Help window at the right of your screen. Click on a problem to display additional Help screens with information about solving that type of problem. For instance, click on the topic "The layout is wrong" to locate specific information about problems with the page design.

15

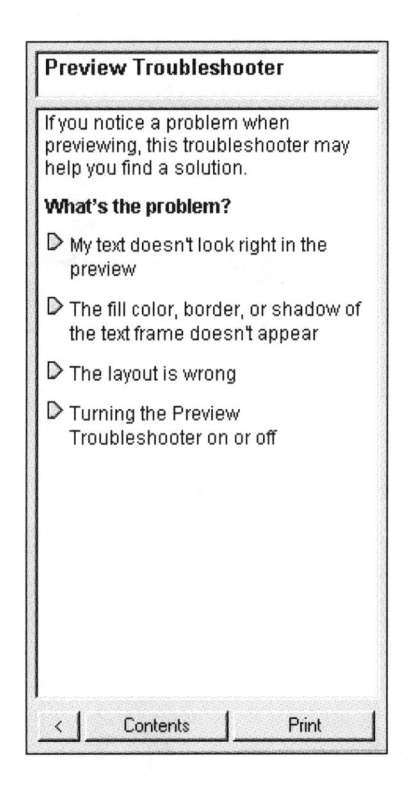

A Note About Browsers

You web pages will look different when viewed with different web browsers. If possible, check your pages on different browsers to make sure the pages look the way you planned. Test your pages with Netscape Navigator and Internet Explorer, two of the most popular browsers.

Some browsers, especially older versions, may not display your web pages as you designed them. For instance, typefaces and sizes can get switched, graphics can be repositioned, and colors may change. Because of this, you might want to include a message informing readers they will need a new browser such as

Netscape 3.0 or Internet Explorer to see your web site as it was originally designed. In fact, as shown next, many of the web page designs created with the Web Site PageWizard already include a tag line telling the reader that it's best to visit the web site with Internet Explorer.

Microsoft is a registered trademark and the Microsoft Internet Explorer Logo is a trademark of Microsoft.

Publishing Your Web Site

After previewing and testing your web site, you're ready to publish it. Making your web site available on the Internet or an intranet is called *publishing*. You must publish your pages before anyone can view them.

As discussed in the following sections, you can publish your web site to the Internet, or more specifically, to the World Wide Web. You can also publish to a folder for use in your organization's intranet. Publishing to a folder is useful when you want to generate and save the web pages and then transfer them to the Internet later.

Publishing to the Web

Publisher uses the Web Publishing Wizard to publish web sites to the Internet. The Web Publishing Wizard supports Internet providers such as CompuServe, Sprynet, and America Online (AOL). Basically, the Web Publishing Wizard connects to the Internet provider, determines the protocol needed to copy the files, and uploads the files to the appropriate directory on the Internet provider's computer.

The Web Publishing Wizard is not installed with the Publisher software, so you will have to download a copy of the Web Publishing Wizard from the Microsoft web site. The URL is **http://www.microsoft.com/windows/software/webpost**. At this web site, you will be asked a few basic questions, and then you can download the Web Publishing Wizard. Give yourself plenty of time—it can take awhile to download the file.

After downloading the Web Publishing Wizard, open the web site publication in Publisher. From the File menu, select Publish To The Web. The Web Publishing Wizard appears—answer the questions and follow the instructions to publish your web site.

Additional Notes About Publishing

When you publish your web site, the web pages are converted to Hypertext Markup Language (HTML) documents. The name of your web publication file becomes the title of your web site when you publish it. For example, if your publication is named "Texas Oil Web," your web site will be titled "Texas Oil Web." Web site titles are displayed in the title bar at the top of the browser window.

Before transferring files, you may want to contact your Internet service provider to get more information on how you must name and organize web page files. As an example, Publisher assigns the filename index.html to the home page—this is standard for most Internet service providers. If your Internet service provider requires a different home page filename, you can change it by selecting Web Site Properties from the File menu. In the Web Site Properties dialog box, enter a new filename and filename extension for the home page.

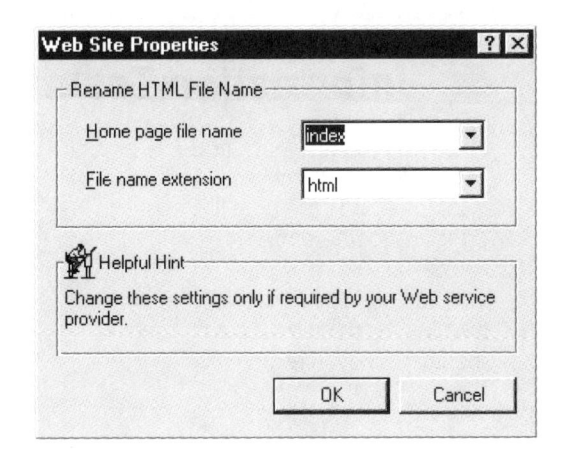

Publishing to a Folder

If you want to make your web site available on your organization's intranet, you can publish it to a folder on a network drive. When publishing to an intranet, contact the person responsible for the intranet to make sure you are placing the web page on the right network drive.

Publishing to a folder also enables you to generate the HTML documents for your web site and store them in a folder on your computer's hard drive. When you're ready, you can transfer the files to the service that will make your pages available on the World Wide Web.

Designing an Intranet Web Site

Why go through the hassle of learning and working with HTML (Hypertext Markup Language) to design web pages when Publisher can create them quickly and easily? This example shows a web site created for the Information Technology training department within Texas Oil, Inc. After completion, the site was published to the company's intranet.

Publisher's Web Site PageWizard was used to quickly develop the web pages. Three web pages were created by use of the Bold style. The Bold style includes a colored bar on the left that contains text and graphic hyperlinks to the other pages. To tie the site together, the graphic used on one web page is used as the hyperlink on the colored bar on the other pages. For instance, the globe image on the home page appears on the colored bar on pages 2 and 3. The globe is set up as a hyperlink to quickly take the viewer back to page 1—the home page. This creates visual continuity between the pages in the site. Here are some highlights on laying out each page.

Step One: Designing the Home Page

The text on the home page welcomes the reader to the web site and provides a brief overview of the contents. A clip-art image of a globe was placed on the home page and was added as a hyperlink in the colored bar on the other pages. The two hyperlinked text blocks created by the PageWizard were replaced with two new text blocks—"Course Schedule" and "Register On-Line!" The hyperlinks had to be reassigned since the original text was replaced. Course Schedule was linked to page 2, and Register On-Line was linked to page 3.

INDEX

Course Schedule

Register On-Line!

Information Technology

Welcome to the Information Technology web site. We work hard to provide the best training possible for the employees of Texas Oil, Inc.
You can use this web site to view the class schedule for the current month, and even register for a class on-line!

Course Schedules | Register On-LIne

Step Two: Designing the Second Page

The title text on page 2 was replaced with "Course Schedule." All of the text and picture frames on page 2 were deleted and replaced by a new clip-art image and a text frame, positioned similarly to those on page 1. The clip-art image was also placed in the colored bar on pages 1 and 3 as a hyperlink. A calendar created by the Design Gallery was added below the text and clip art. The calendar dates had to be modified to fit the current month. Class titles were entered into the calendar.

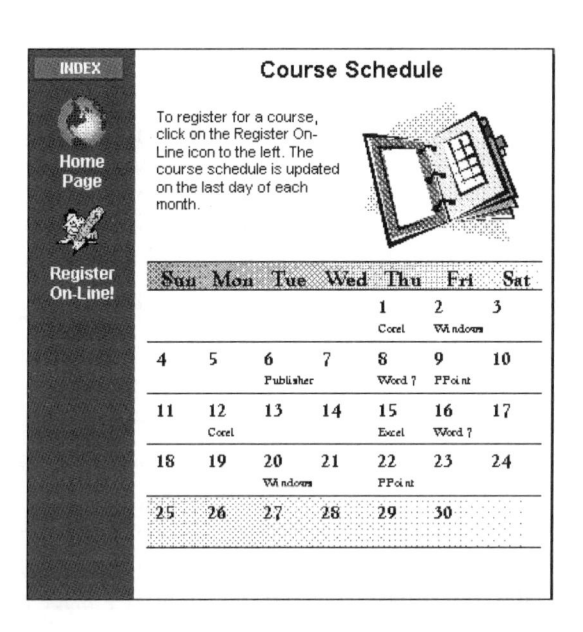

Step Three: Designing the Third Page

The title on page 3 was changed to "Register On-Line!" The text and picture frames were deleted. To continue the look from the previous pages, a text and picture frame were added to the top. The clip-art image was placed in the colored bar on pages 1 and 2 as a hyperlink. Another text frame was added that contained a hyperlink to an e-mail address where the viewers could register for a course. For visual appeal, an arrow and another clip-art image were added.

Use the following steps to publish your web site to a folder:

1. From the File menu, select Publish Web Site To Folder. The Select A Folder dialog box appears.

2. Change to the drive and folder (directory) where you want to publish your web site. Publisher defaults to the Publisher/Publish folder.

3. Click OK. A message box appears indicating Publisher is saving the web site to the folder.

You can publish only one web site to a folder. If you attempt to publish another web site to the same folder, you will be asked if you want to replace the current contents of the folder. In Figure 15-2, the Windows Explorer is used to display the contents of the folder after a web site is published to it. The .GIF files are the graphics in your web site, and the .HTML files are the text and other page information.

You can then transfer all of these files to your Internet service provider to make your web site available on the Internet. Contact your Internet service provider to find out how you should transfer files to them. You can use the Web Publishing Wizard to transfer the files, or your Internet service provider may provide an FTP (file transfer protocol) program to transfer the web page files.

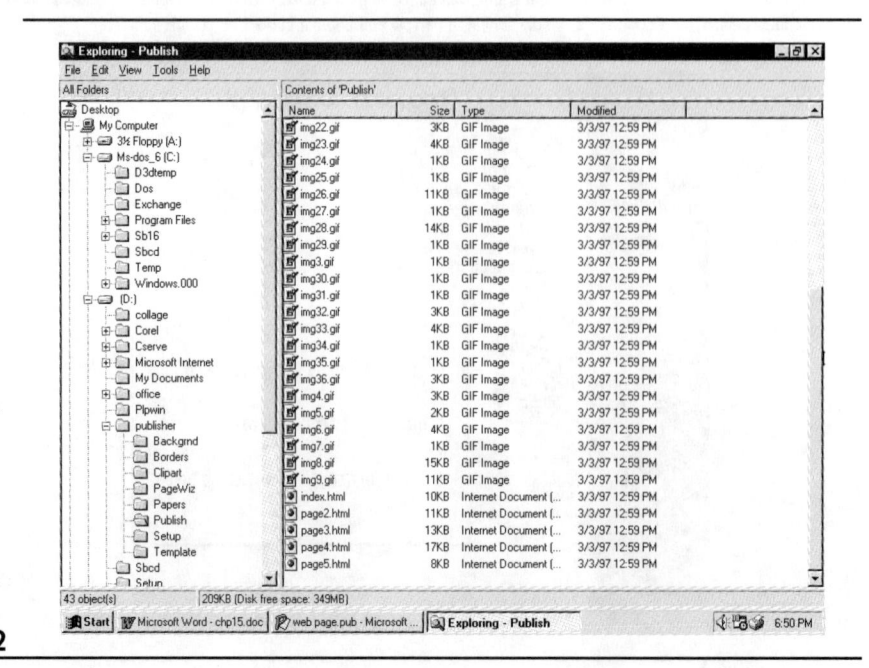

Publish to a folder to generate the files used to build web pages

FIGURE 15-2

Summary

This chapter focused on using Publisher to design and publish web sites. As you learned, the actual creation and design of a web site publication is similar to creating printed publications. This chapter examined how to assign hyperlinks to text and graphics, as well as how to preview and publish the web site to the Internet or an intranet.

The next chapter discusses working with background pages to add repeating elements, such as header and footer text, throughout your publications.

16

Working with Background Pages

Continuity is an important element of page design. Repeating certain graphic elements, such as logos or lines, on each page ties a publication together, creating a cohesive, organized look. Certain text elements repeated on every page are also important to help the reader maneuver through a publication. For instance, placing the page number and section title on every page lets your reader thumb through a publication quickly to find desired information. As discussed in this chapter, Publisher provides background pages to help you quickly add elements to every page in a publication.

This chapter begins with an overview of how background pages work and when to use them. Here you'll learn to view background pages. Creating and working with two background pages is also examined. The next section focuses on adding graphics and text to background pages, with special emphasis on creating headers and footers. The chapter ends with options for hiding and deleting background elements.

Background Information

To understand how background pages work, imagine that the regular pages you've been working with are transparent. Now imagine that behind every regular page is a background page. The same background page is used for all of the regular pages. Since the regular pages are transparent, you can see through them to the background page. Because there is only one (maybe two) background page, the elements on the background appear on every page of the publication.

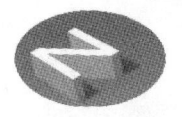 **NOTE:** *You'll notice no difference in printing when you use background pages. Objects on the background pages print just like objects on regular pages.*

The major benefit of working with background pages is the time you'll save by not having to place repetitive elements on every single page. You place an element once on the background page, and every other page displays the element automatically.

In most cases, you will probably need just one background page. Anything placed on it is repeated on every page of your publication. However, you can also create a second background page. In this case, one background page is used as the background for all left pages in the publication, and the other is used for the background of all right pages. Creating a second background page is discussed later in this chapter.

 **TIP:** *Background pages are important tools in ensuring design consistency throughout a publication.*

Any changes made to the background page affect all regular pages using that background page. For instance, if you change the color of a red line on a background page to green, all regular pages using that background now show the green line.

When to Use Background Pages

Look through newsletters, slide presentations, and brochures to see what types of elements are generally repeated throughout a publication. Following are some ideas for using background pages:

- Use background pages to add background color to every page. For instance, when creating an overhead presentation, you could draw a frame that completely covers the background page, and then fill the frame with blue. Then every overhead transparency in the presentation would have a blue background.

- Draw thin lines across the top and bottom margins of the background page. The repetition of the lines on every page helps tie the publication together. Look around—you'll notice many reports and brochures use this simple design effect.

- Place your company logo on a background page to have it automatically display on every page in the publication. This is great for sales materials and web sites where you want the readers to keep your company name foremost in their mind.

- Place important text information, such as names, phone numbers, and e-mail addresses, on background pages of presentations to make yourself readily accessible.

- Help your reader navigate through longer publications by placing page numbers, dates, and section titles at the top and bottom of background pages.

Don't shy away from using background pages if you aren't sure you want the element on every page. Although the purpose of background pages is to place something on every page of a publication, you can hide the background elements on certain pages. Hiding background elements is discussed at the end of this chapter.

Viewing Background Pages

Every publication has at least one, maybe two, background pages. To view background pages, select Go To Background from the View menu. Don't be surprised if the background pages are blank—you haven't added anything to them yet. If your margin and column guides are displayed, you will see them on the background pages. Use the shortcut CTRL-SHIFT-O to display the guides if desired.

Publications designed by PageWizards may include a few elements on the background pages. Many of the newsletters designed by the Newsletter PageWizard use background pages for page numbering and other graphic effects. For instance, as displayed in Figure 16-1, the Classic newsletter style adds a gray rectangular box with a pound sign (representing the page number) to the background. You can see how the element appears on the regular page in Figure 16-2.

Using the Background Buttons

When you switch to the background pages, Publisher displays the background buttons in the bottom left corner of the screen (as opposed to the page controls). If you see only one background button, your publication has only one background page. If you see two background buttons, as in Figure 16-1, your publication has two background pages. Click on the left button to see the background page for all left pages. Click on the right button to see the background page for all right pages.

When you're viewing a publication in Two-Page Spread view (select Two-Page Spread from the View menu), both of the background buttons are pushed in, indicating you are looking at both background pages.

TIP: *Press CTRL-M to quickly toggle between the background and regular (foreground) pages.*

16

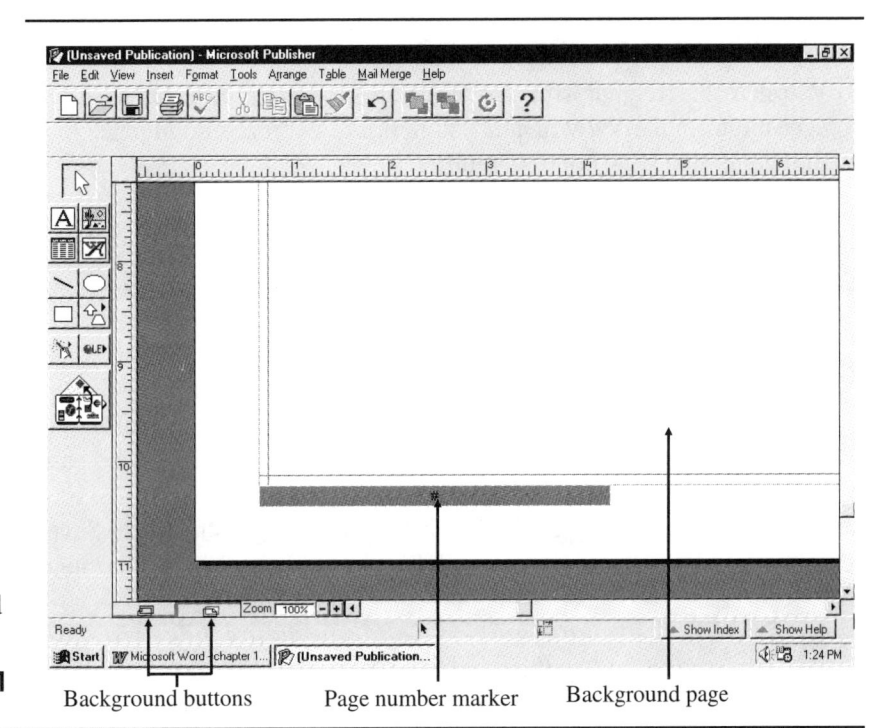

Some of Publisher's background elements

FIGURE 16-1

Background buttons   Page number marker   Background page

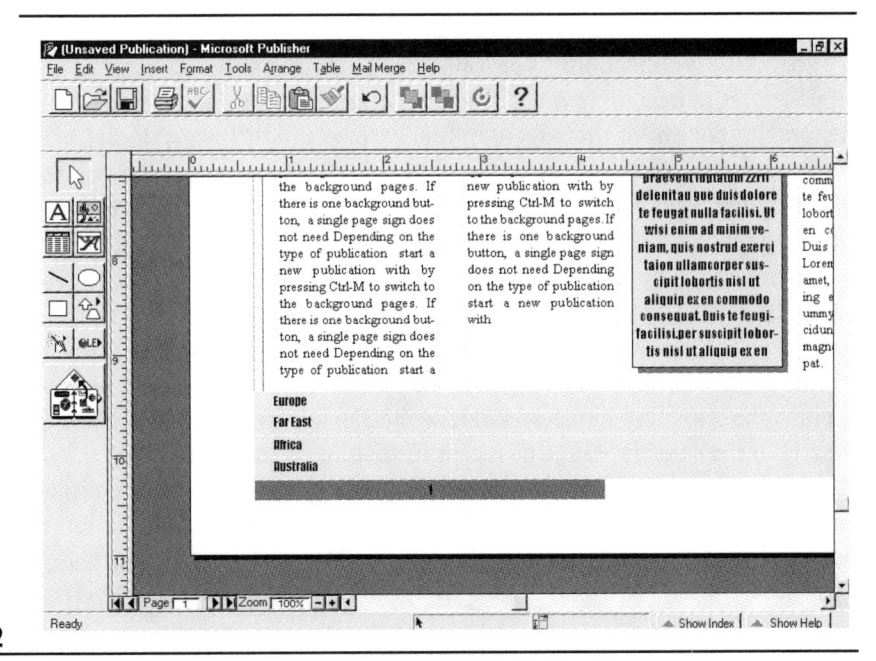

Page numbers are often placed on background pages

FIGURE 16-2

Viewing the Foreground

To return to the regular (foreground) pages of your publication, select Go To Foreground from the View menu. You return to the foreground page you were last in, and the normal page controls return.

Working with One or Two Background Pages

When you start a new publication with the Blank Page option, only one background page is created. This background will be used for every page in the publication. When you build a publication with the PageWizards, two background pages may be created—it depends on the type of publication. For instance, postcards, signs, and web sites created with PageWizards have one background page. Several of the newsletters and brochures created with PageWizards use two background pages.

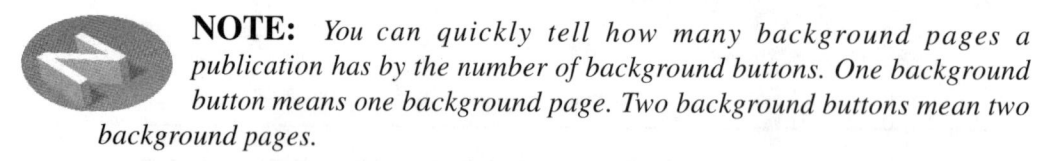 **NOTE:** *You can quickly tell how many background pages a publication has by the number of background buttons. One background button means one background page. Two background buttons mean two background pages.*

For many publications, you only need one background page. For instance, suppose you're designing a four-page brochure, and you want to add a thin line at the top and bottom of the pages. In this case, you don't want the left pages of the brochure to look different from the right pages, so you only need one background page. Another example might be web pages. There are no left and right pages on the Web, so you could place all repetitive elements on one background page.

However, if you are producing facing-page publications, where you have left and right pages, you might want the added flexibility of having two background pages. Two background pages enable you to set up different background elements for the left and right pages. For instance, in a lengthy sales report, you might want to place the company name and date as header information on the left pages, and the title of the sales report as header information on the right pages.

Placing different information on the left and right pages is quite common in long, facing-page publications. This book is another example; notice the information at the top of the left page is different from the information at the top of the right page.

Creating Two Background Pages

When you create a second background page, the original background page becomes the right background page, and the new one becomes the left background page. To create a second background page, select Layout Guides from the Arrange menu. The Layout Guides dialog box is also where you can adjust margin spacing, and set up columns and rows on the page.

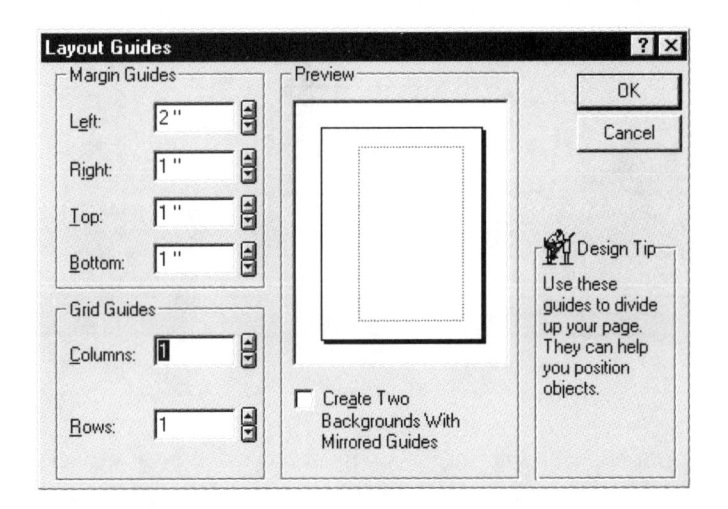

The Layout Guides dialog box shows a preview of one background page. To create another, click on the Create Two Backgrounds With Mirrored Guides option. The preview changes to show two background pages. Click OK to create the second background page. Now when you view the background pages, there will be two background buttons.

TIP: *Having two backgrounds also means double the work for you in setting them up. Consider whether you need a different look on the left and right pages before adding a second background. (If the publication already has two backgrounds, you can delete one as discussed later in this section.)*

When you create a second background page, margins and column guides are flipped or "mirrored" to the new left background page. Mirrored guides are common in publications with facing pages. For instance, when creating a sales report, you may want a wide margin in the middle of the pages to leave room for binding. You could increase the left margin on the original background page. When you add a second background, the wider margin is mirrored and becomes the right margin on the new background. As the preview shows, this creates a wide margin in the middle of the facing pages.

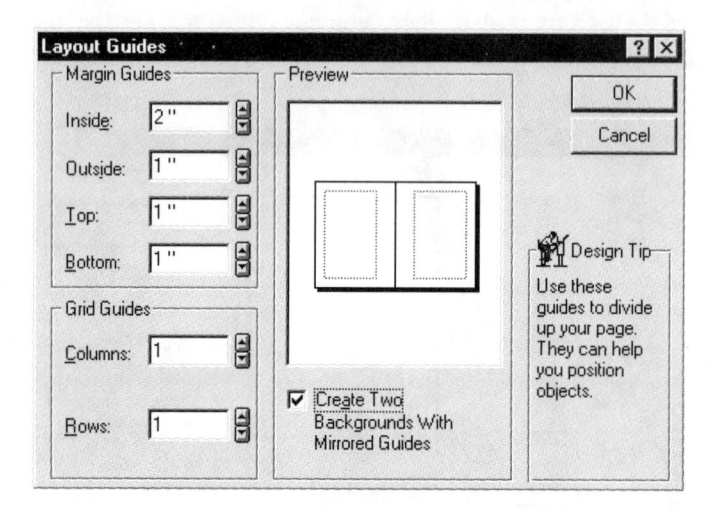

Text and graphic elements are also mirrored on the new background. For instance, suppose you placed a small copy of your company logo in the bottom right corner of the original background page. When you create a second background page, the logo is mirrored to the bottom left corner of the new background page. Graphic and text information is generally placed to the outside edges of facing pages, making it easy for readers to locate. Later in this chapter you will learn how to build header and footer information that mirrors on the left and right pages.

Deleting the Second Background

You can delete the second background if your publication has two backgrounds and you only need one. When you delete the second background, the left background page is deleted, and the right background page remains (you can't delete it). If you used a PageWizard to design the publication, make sure you understand how deleting one of the backgrounds will affect the publication. For instance, in the Classic newsletter style, page numbers appear in the bottom left corner of the left background page, and in the bottom right corner of the right background page. If you delete the second (left) background, all pages will then show page numbers on the bottom right corner.

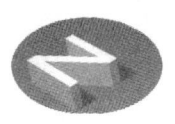

NOTE: *Remember, to switch views, choose Single Page or Two-Page Spread from the View menu.*

To delete the second background, select Layout Guides from the Arrange menu. Remove the check mark by the Create Two Backgrounds With Mirrored Guides option, and click OK. However, it's important to note that when you're deleting the second background, the outcome depends on what view you're in at the time. If you are in *Single Page* view, any objects on the left background page are hidden, not deleted. If you later decide to use two backgrounds again, and are still in *Single Page* view, the hidden objects are redisplayed.

If you are in *Two-Page Spread* view when the second background is deleted, any objects on the left background page are *permanently* deleted. (You do get a message warning you of this first.) If you later decide to use two backgrounds again, objects on the first (right) background are mirrored to the new left background.

Adding Text and Graphics to Background Pages

Adding text and graphics to background pages is just like adding these objects to the regular foreground pages. For instance, to add text, draw a text frame and then enter and format the text. To add a graphic, draw a picture frame and then place the graphic.

Elements placed on background pages are generally small, subtle, and close to the edges of the page. This is mainly because you do not want background elements to compete with elements on the regular page. As a general rule, design the background pages first. This way you can see the background objects as you design the foreground pages, and you can work around them. If you do add background objects after designing the foreground pages, glance through each foreground page to make sure nothing on the foreground collides or competes with something on the background.

TIP: *When placing frames on the foreground pages, remember they can be transparent or opaque. An opaque frame on a foreground page will hide any underlying background objects, whereas a transparent frame allows the underlying object to show through. Refer to Chapter 7 for more information.*

Editing Text and Graphics on Background Pages

Elements added to background pages can only be edited when you are viewing the background pages. For instance, if you add the date to a background page and then want to change the date, you must switch to the background pages view before editing the date. You cannot select background objects on the foreground pages.

If you make a change to a background page, all foreground pages using that background will also be affected. Keep this in mind when working with two background pages. Changes made to the left background page affect all left pages in the publication. Changes made to the right background page affect all right pages in the publication. If your publication uses two background pages, try working in Two-Page Spread view for a visual reminder that you have two background pages to design.

Building Headers and Footers

Headers and *footers* contain information that refers to the body text and are located at the top and bottom of the page, respectively. The text in headers and footers typically consists of section titles, company names, and page numbers. This information serves as a road map to help the reader locate information quickly.

 **TIP:** *To set header and footer text apart from other text on the page, use a smaller point size or add bold or italics.*

Placing header and footer text on background pages makes it easy to add information to every page. It also keeps the information consistent—if you change the header or footer text on the background page, every page using that background page also gets changed.

Typically, header and footer information is mirrored in facing-page publications (see Figure 16-3). When you're designing two background pages, work in Two-Page Spread view so you can see how both the left and right pages will look. If you are placing the same elements on the left and right pages, you can create the element once and then copy and paste it to the other background page.

To create headers and footers, move to the background page and draw a text frame. As shown, keep the frame small and place it outside the margin guides, so it won't interfere with text on the regular pages. Keep in mind that many printers can't print all the way to the edge of the page, so allow for the printer margin when placing header and footer text frames. In fact, it's probably a good

16

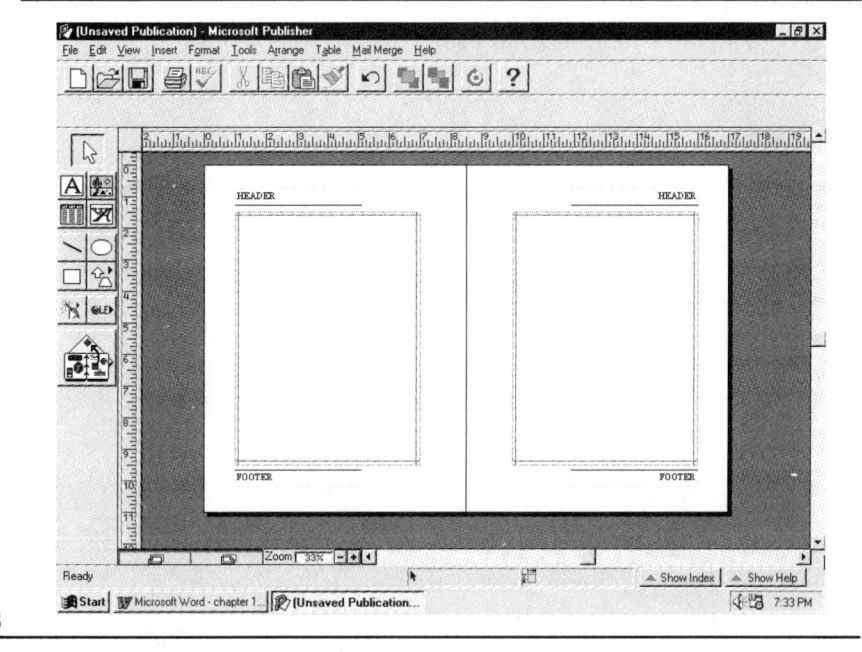

Place header and footer information along the outside edges in facing-page publications

FIGURE 16-3

idea to increase the top and bottom margins, so you'll have plenty of room for the header and footer text.

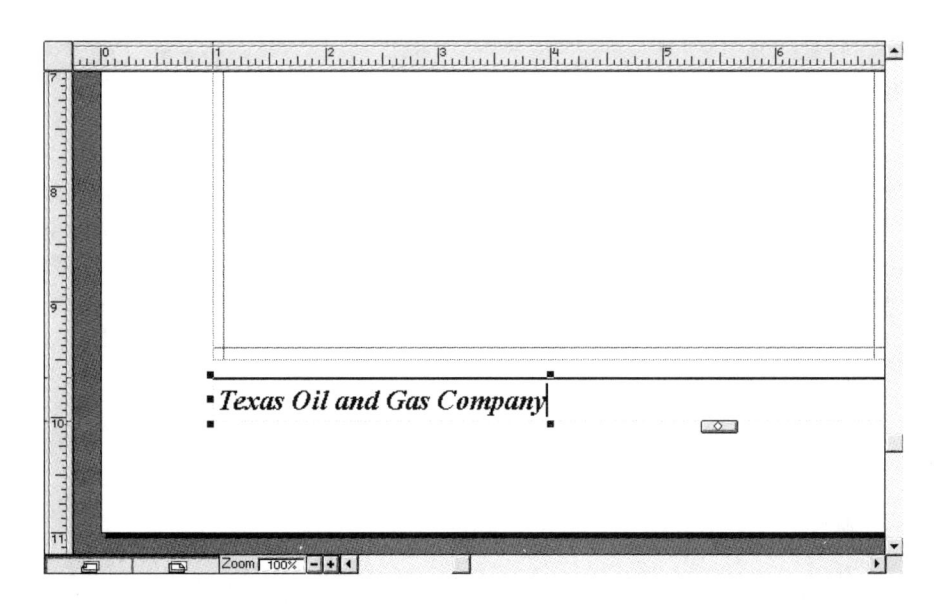

 **TIP:**   *Embellish headers and footers with thin lines below header text and above footer text to separate the information from text on foreground pages.*

After drawing the text frame, simply type in the header or footer text. Remember, if you're working with two background pages, you will need to create headers and footers for both pages. With two background pages, you can enter one type of header and footer information for the left pages, and another type of header and footer information for the right pages.

When the information is the same on the left and right pages, but just mirrored, you can place all of the header and footer text (and any other graphics) on the original background page and then create a second background page that will automatically copy and mirror the elements to the new background.

Adding Page Numbers to Headers and Footers

Perhaps the most common information placed in headers and footers is page numbers. To create page numbers, you insert a page-number code in the header or footer frame. If your publication has two background pages, and you want page numbers on both the left and right pages, you need to insert a page-number code on *both* background pages.

 **TIP:**   *If you want, add the word "Page" and press SPACEBAR before the page number. This is not mandatory though, because readers know what the number means.*

To add a page-number code, click in the text frame where you want the code. From the Insert menu, choose Page Numbers. Publisher inserts a pound sign (#), which will automatically display the correct page numbers on the foreground pages. You can control where the code is placed in the frame by changing the alignment. For instance, click on the Right Alignment tool in the Standard toolbar to position the code on the right edge of the frame.

16

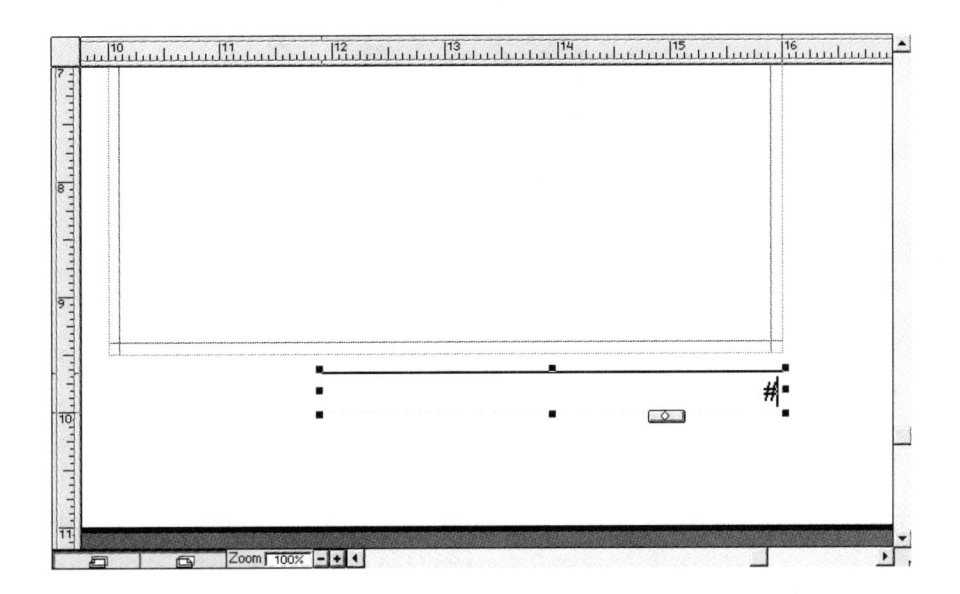

NOTE: *You can insert page numbers, dates, and times on the foreground pages, too. However, those elements are discussed in this section because they are most commonly used in header and footer text.*

You can apply text formatting to the page-number code. For instance, add bold or italics to emphasize the number.

Adding the Date and Time to Background Pages

In publications that are constantly updated, placing the date and time in headers or footers can be an important way to let readers know if they are viewing a recent copy. Inserting the date and time on the background pages works pretty much like inserting page numbers. First, you click in the text frame where you want the date or time to appear. From the Insert menu, choose Date And Time to display the Date And Time dialog box.

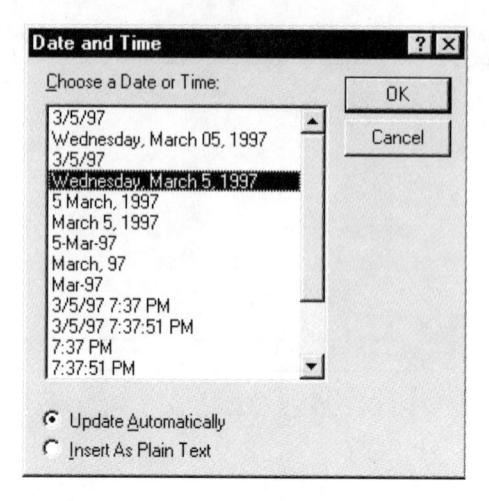

The dialog box provides several styles of dates and times (or both). Select the one that works for your publication. If you want the date or time to be automatically updated every time you open the publication file, make sure the Update Automatically option is selected. For instance, if you insert the date on March 5, and then open the file the next day, the date will read "March 6." If you do not want the date to be updated, click on the Insert As Plain Text option. Click OK to insert the current date or time.

As with page numbers, use the alignment tools and text formatting options to customize the look of the date and time. To delete the date or time, you simply need to click in front of it and press DELETE. The entire date or time is removed.

Hiding Background Elements

When designing publications, you may have one or two pages where you do not want the elements on the background pages to be displayed. For instance, headers and footers are usually left off of the first page in a publication. You might also want the company logo to appear on every overhead transparency in your publication, except one or two where the logo conflicts with something on the foreground.

Publisher makes it easy to hide background objects on a specific page. First, display the foreground page where you want to hide the background. From the View menu, choose Ignore Background. All elements on the background page are no longer visible on the specified page. If you are in Two-Page Spread view when you select the Ignore Background command, a dialog box appears asking which background page you want to ignore—the Left, Right, or both. Make your selection and click OK.

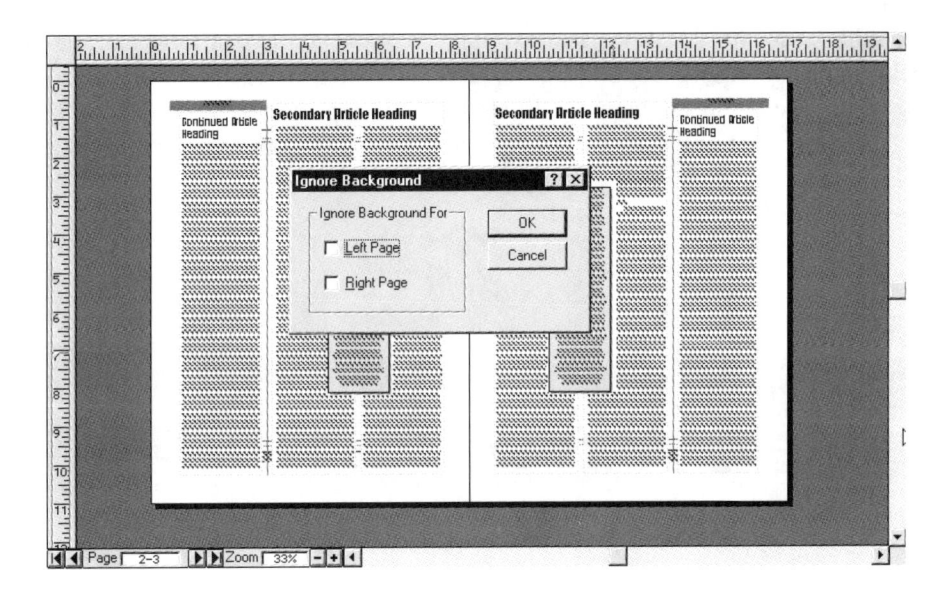

To redisplay background objects on a page, choose Ignore Background again from the View menu. This command toggles between hiding and displaying background objects.

Hiding Specific Objects on the Background Pages

The Ignore Background command hides every background object. However, you can employ a graphic designer's trick to hide some but not all of the background objects. Remember that text frames by default are opaque, meaning you cannot see through them. First, move to the foreground page where you want to hide an object showing through from the background page. Now simply draw a text frame over the object you want to hide. Voilà—the object is hidden. You might need to send the text frame to the back if it is in front of another element (press SHIFT-F6 to send a selected object to the back). When you send an object to the back, it goes to the back layer of the foreground page, which makes it perfect for covering up background objects.

Summary

In multipage publications, background pages can help you quickly place text and graphics on all of the pages. The repetition of graphics and text adds cohesiveness to publications. As discussed in this chapter, publications can have one or two background pages. Steps for building headers and footers on background pages, with dates and page numbers, were highlighted in this chapter.

The next chapter discusses advanced text formatting options, such as creating bulleted lists and adding fancy first-letter effects.

Advanced
Text-Formatting Options

There is much more to formatting text than simply selecting fonts and adding bold to important words. To produce good-looking publications, you must consider details, such as spacing between words and where a line of text begins and ends. Consider the use of bulleted and numbered lists to organize text into easy-to-read sections. The difference between an amateur- and a professional-quality publication lies in the attention paid to details.

This chapter focuses on advanced text-formatting options, beginning with an examination of the special effects available in Publisher. Here you will learn how to create fancy first letters, and how to wrap text around frames. Adding bullets and numbers to text is also discussed. The chapter then looks at spacing between characters, lines, and paragraphs. The steps for setting, moving, and aligning tab stops, as well as adding tab leaders are also examined. The chapter ends with a look at using the Word story editor as another tool to help you format and prepare text.

Adding Fancy First Letters

The first letter in a paragraph can be enlarged to create a fancy first-letter special effect. The effect is even further enhanced when the letter is set in a different typeface. Fancy first letters placed at the beginning of an article provide a visual transition between the headline and the text. Fancy first letters also help to cue the reader to the start of major sections in publications. As shown, the letter can be dropped or can be set into the paragraph it introduces, as you'll soon see. Fancy first letters can also be raised so the letter sits on the first line of text, extending into the white space above the text it introduces.

Digital Cafe

Our agenda today is to discuss how software applications work together to create graphic documents such as brochures, posters and slides. We will also examine file formats - such as which formats are accepted at Chroma Copy. We will take a look at working with fonts, one of the most important aspects of any job. Next,

When you're considering fancy first-letter effects, think about what else will be on the page. If you already have a lot of drawings, charts, and tables, skip the fancy first letter. However, if the publication is mostly text, fancy first letters are a great way to liven up the page. You don't need a fancy first letter at the beginning of every paragraph—save them for the first paragraph in a newsletter article, or the first text block in a brochure.

TIP: *Avoid creating a duel between the headline and fancy first-letter effect, by making one significantly larger than the other.*

Inserting Fancy First Letters

Publisher provides a wide selection of preset fancy first-letter effects. Select a style that works with other elements on the page. For instance, if you already have several typefaces on a page, don't throw in a new typeface for the fancy first letter. Select a style that uses a typeface already on your page. Consider colors, too—unless you want the fancy first letter to really pop out on the page, keep it black.

You can modify the preset fancy first-letter styles. For instance, you can change the font, choose another color, and adjust the line position. The following steps illustrate adding a fancy first letter:

1. Click inside the text paragraph where you want to add the fancy first letter. The insertion point appears in the text.

2. From the Format menu, select Fancy First Letter. Make sure the Fancy First Letter tab is selected at the top of the dialog box. Scroll through to see all of the available styles.

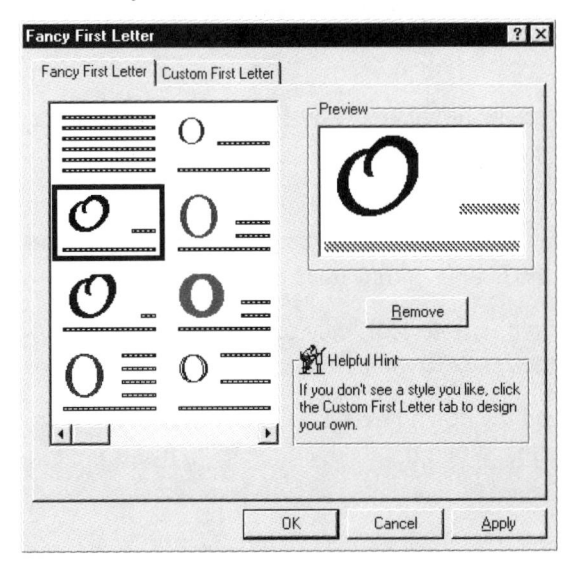

3. Select a style and click OK to insert the fancy first letter into your paragraph. If the style is close to what you want, but not exactly what you want, click on the Custom First Letter tab.

4. Here you can choose the letter position. Choose Dropped to set the letter into the paragraph. Choose Up to sit the letter on the first line of the paragraph. In the third option, Lines, enter the number of lines you want the fancy first letter to extend up or down. Click on the up and down arrows and watch the preview to get an idea of how the letter will appear.

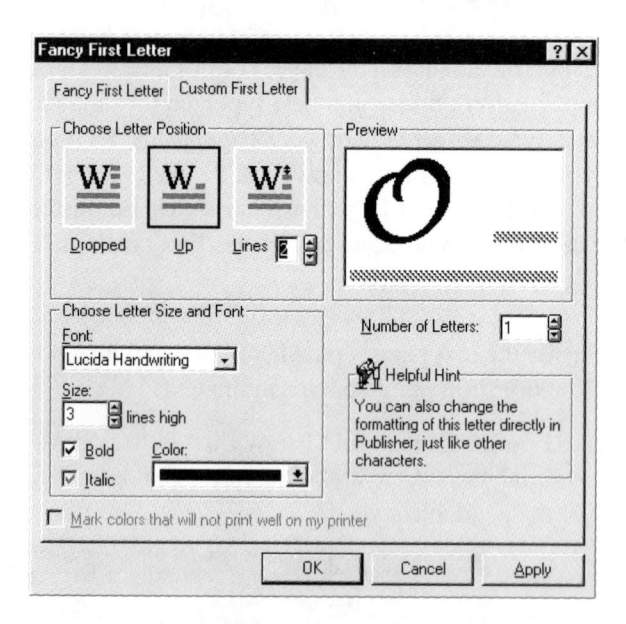

5. Click on the down arrow by Font to select another typeface for the fancy first letter.

6. In the Size box, type the height you want the fancy first letter to be in number of lines. For instance, enter **4** to create a fancy first letter that is the same height as four lines of text.

7. Click by the Bold and Italic options to add or remove bold and italics from the fancy first letter.

8. Click on the down arrow by Color to select another color for the fancy first letter. When finished, click OK to insert the fancy first letter.

After placing the fancy first letter in a paragraph, you can highlight it and change its formatting just as you would regular text characters.

Creating Fancy First Words

For a new look, apply the fancy first-letter effect to the first word in a text paragraph. To do this, click in the paragraph where you want the fancy first word, and select Fancy First Letter from the Format menu. In the dialog box, select the desired Fancy First Letter style, and click on the Custom First Letter tab. Below the preview, enter the number of letters in the word in the Number Of Letters box. For instance, for the word "first," enter **5**.

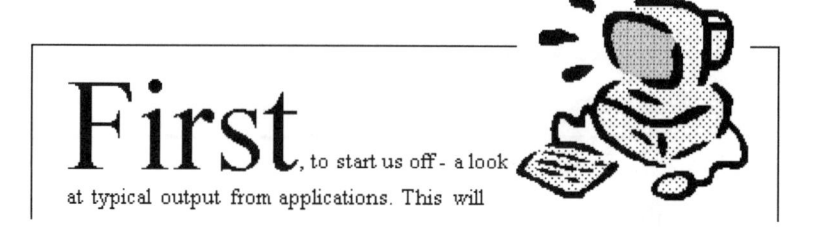

Wrapping Text Around Graphics

To add visual variety to your page layouts, Publisher provides an option for wrapping text around the shape of graphics. By default, when you place a picture frame on top of text, the text wraps around the picture frame, creating a rectangle of blank space around the picture. For a different look, wrap the text around the shape of the graphic instead of the frame. As you can see in Figure 17-1, the text wraps around the *frame* of the first picture and around the *graphic* in the second picture.

To make the text wrap around the graphic, select the picture frame and click on the Wrap Text To Picture tool on the Formatting toolbar. The lines of text are conformed to the shape of the graphic. Click on the Wrap Text To Frame tool to return to the default text wrap.

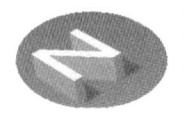 **NOTE:**   *You can also wrap text around text objects created in WordArt. Refer to Chapter 13 for more information on working with WordArt.*

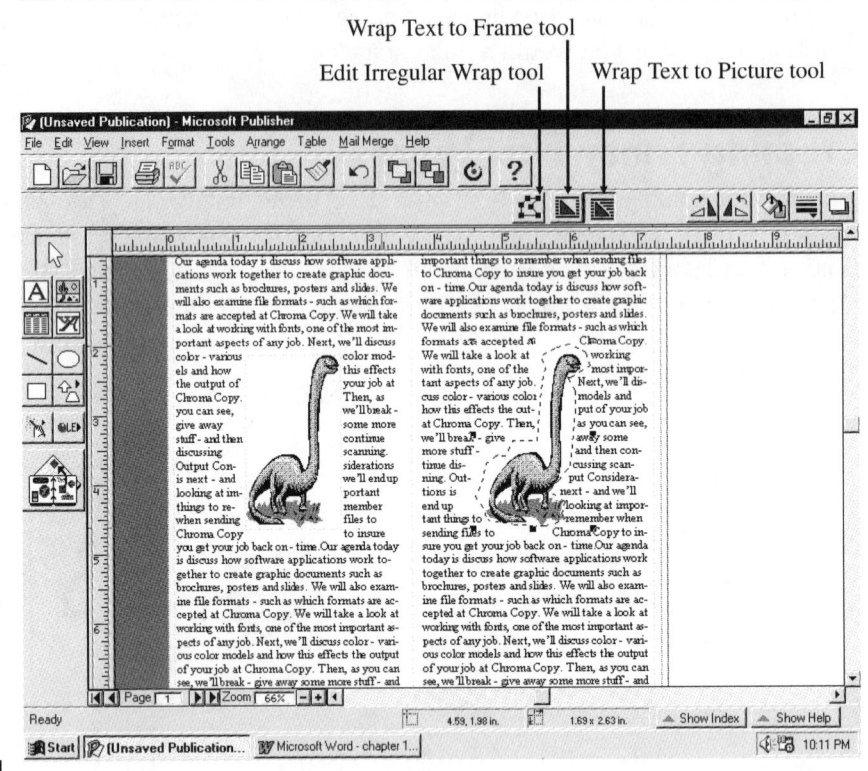

Wrap Text to Frame tool

Edit Irregular Wrap tool

Wrap Text to Picture tool

Publisher's text wrap feature enables you to conform text to the shape of pictures

FIGURE 17-1

Editing Irregular Text Wraps

After the text has been wrapped around the picture, you can manipulate *how* the text wraps. For instance, the text might be a little too close to the picture; in this case, you could increase the amount of space between the picture and the text. To edit how the text wraps around the picture, make sure the picture is selected, and click on the Edit Irregular Wrap tool in the Formatting toolbar. An outline appears around the picture with a series of handles (black dots) used to adjust the outline. Place the mouse cursor over one of the handles—the shape of the cursor changes to the Adjust icon—and drag the handle to change the outline of the picture. Keep adjusting the handles until you have the desired spacing around the picture.

The photos and images created in photo manipulation or bitmap edit-ing pack-ages (we're going to use bitmap editing today) such as Pho- toshop or Photo Styler are imported in page layout programs. Therefore, the output is **not** directly from the photo manipu-lation pro- gram. First, to start us off - a look at typi-cal output from applications. This will help us make sure ev-eryone knows what we're talking when spe- cific applications

If you need a new handle to help you adjust the text wrap around a picture, hold the CTRL key and click on the outline. A new handle is added. You can also delete handles by holding CTRL and SHIFT and clicking on the handle you want removed.

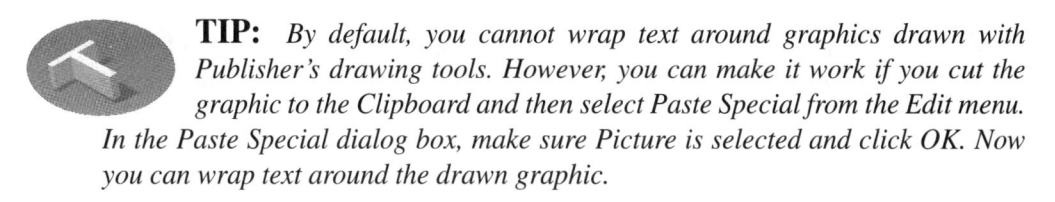

TIP: *By default, you cannot wrap text around graphics drawn with Publisher's drawing tools. However, you can make it work if you cut the graphic to the Clipboard and then select Paste Special from the Edit menu. In the Paste Special dialog box, make sure Picture is selected and click OK. Now you can wrap text around the drawn graphic.*

Inserting Line Breaks

As you type, text automatically wraps to the next line when it reaches the edge of the text frame. When you finish typing a paragraph, pressing ENTER ends the current paragraph and begins another. If you want to end a line before it reaches the guide, without creating a new paragraph, you need to insert a *line break*. For instance, in the example, line breaks were used to stack the headline into three lines. Without the line breaks, the headline would have flowed into two lines instead of three, and lost some of its visual impact.

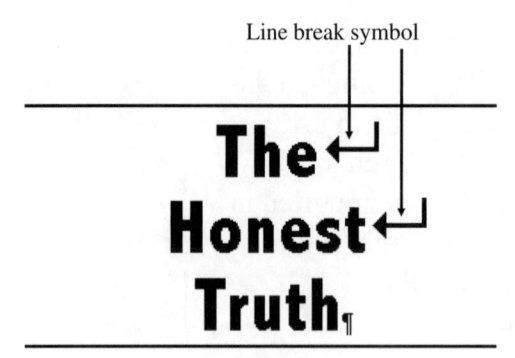

To insert a line break, position the insertion point before the character you want wrapped to the next line. Press SHIFT-ENTER to create a line break. If the Show Special Characters command is turned on, a line-break symbol appears indicating the presence of the line break.

Indenting Paragraphs

Indenting paragraphs of text enables you to add space to the left or right side of a paragraph. As shown in Figure 17-2, Publisher provides four basic options for indenting paragraphs.

- Use the Flush Left option to align all lines evenly on the left side of the paragraph. This is the default setting for paragraphs.

- Use the First Line option to indent the first line in a paragraph. Generally used in text-intensive publications, this type of indent helps readers identify the beginning of a new paragraph. Rather than pressing TAB to indent the first line of text in every paragraph, you could select the First Line indent option to automatically add the indent spacing.

- Use the Hanging Indent option to indent all lines except the first line. This indent style is used when creating bulleted and numbered lists, which is discussed later in this chapter.

- Use the Quotation option to indent all lines from both the left and right. As the name implies, use this style when formatting quotations or any other text you want to call to someone's attention.

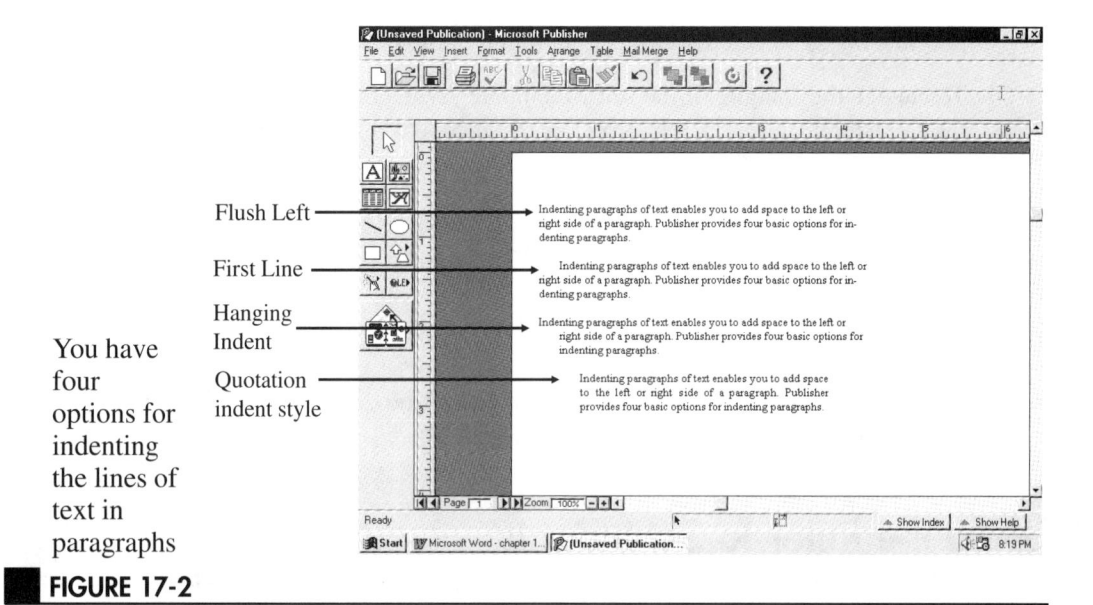

Flush Left

First Line

Hanging Indent

Quotation indent style

You have four options for indenting the lines of text in paragraphs

FIGURE 17-2

The following steps illustrate indenting a paragraph and adjusting the indent spacing:

1. Click in the paragraph you want to indent. To apply the same indenting to several paragraphs at once, highlight all of the paragraphs.

2. From the Format menu, select Indents And Lists. Under Indent Settings at the top of the dialog box, make sure Normal is selected.

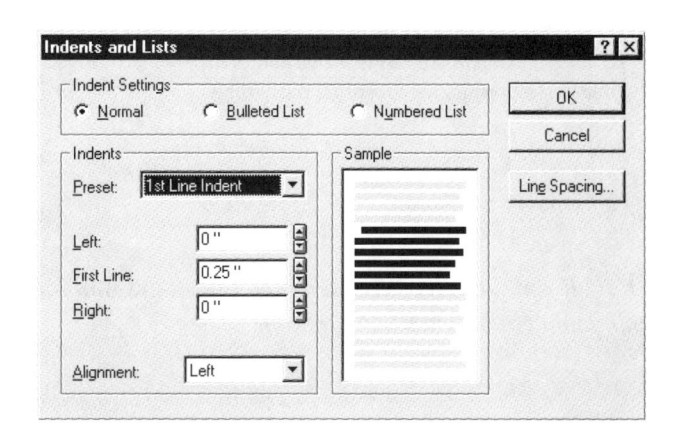

3. Click on the down arrow by Preset, and choose the desired indent style. A preview of the selected style appears in the Sample box.

4. To change the spacing of the selected indent style, enter a new amount in the Left, First Line, or Right box. For instance, 0.25" appears in the First Line box when the First Line indent style is selected. You could enter **.5** to increase the spacing.

5. Click on the down arrow by Alignment to change the paragraph alignment to centered or flush right. Click OK to apply the indenting.

When you change the spacing or alignment of a preset style, you are actually creating a Custom indent style. Notice how the Preset box changes to "Custom" when changes are made to the spacing and alignment.

Using the Ruler to Set Indents

The ruler provides another quick and easy way to set indents. When you click in a paragraph, *indent markers* appear in the ruler, representing the first-line, left, and right indents of the paragraph. You can adjust the indents by dragging the indent markers along the measurements of the ruler.

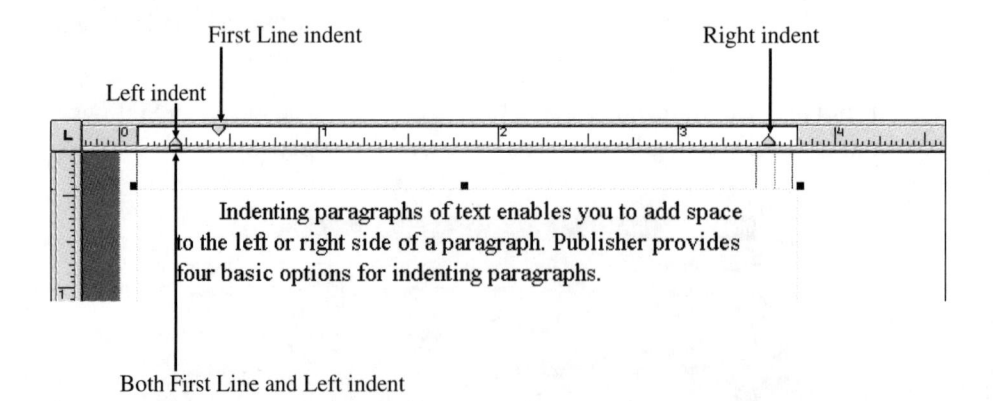

First Line indent   Right indent

Left indent

Indenting paragraphs of text enables you to add space to the left or right side of a paragraph. Publisher provides four basic options for indenting paragraphs.

Both First Line and Left indent

TIP: *If you don't see the ruler, select Toolbars And Rulers from the View menu, and turn on the Rulers option.*

To create a first-line indent, click in the paragraph and drag the First Line indent marker to the desired measurement on the ruler. For instance, drag it to the $\frac{1}{2}$-inch tick mark to indent the first line of the paragraph by 0.5 inch. To create a hanging indent, drag the Left indent marker to the desired measurement. All of the lines except the first line are indented by the specified amount.

To indent all lines on the left side of a paragraph, including the first line, drag the Both First Line And Left indent marker to the desired mark on the ruler. (The Both First Line And Left indent marker is the small rectangle below the Left indent marker. Watch out—it can be tricky to get!) To indent lines on the right side of a paragraph, drag the Right indent marker to the desired mark on the ruler.

17

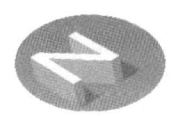 **NOTE:** *It can be easy to accidentally add tab stops to the ruler while trying to drag the indent markers. Refer to the section "Working with Tabs" to learn more about setting and deleting tab stops.*

Creating Bulleted and Numbered Lists

Creating bulleted and numbered lists is a great way to call attention to information. Placing graphic symbols or bullets in front of paragraphs adds a decorative flair to the page while emphasizing information. Numbering paragraphs indicates the information is broken into steps, as with the exercises in this book.

Creating Bulleted Lists

You can use any character from any installed font as a bullet character. Several fonts, such as Wingdings and Symbol, are loaded with graphic symbols that make great bullets.

The following steps illustrate adding bullets to text:

1. Click in the paragraph where you want to add a bullet. To add bullet characters to several paragraphs at once, highlight all of the paragraphs.

2. From the Format menu, select Indents And Lists. At the top of the dialog box, make sure Bulleted List is selected.

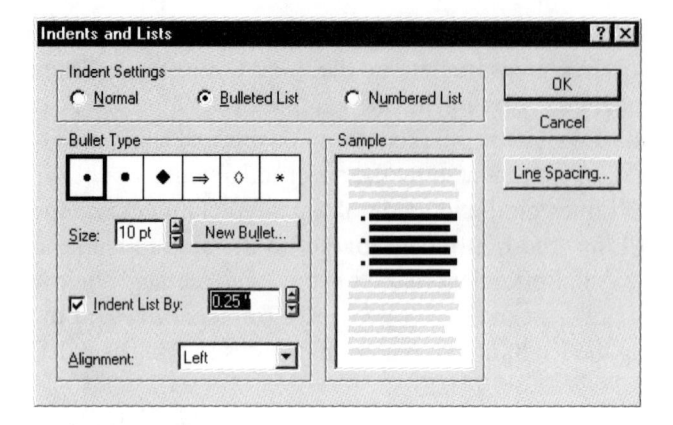

3. Select the desired bullet type. If you don't see the bullet character you want to use, click on the New Bullet button. In this dialog box, click on the down arrow by Show Symbols From and select a font. Click on the desired bullet character, and click OK to return to the Indents And Lists dialog box. The new bullet is displayed here.

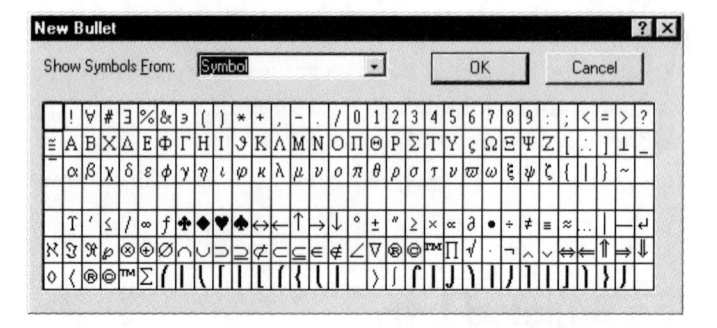

4. Enter a new value in the Size box if you wish to change the size of the bullet character. Use the Indent List By box to control how much space there is between the bullet and the text. For instance, with large bullets, you may need to increase the spacing between the bullet and text.

5. Click on the down arrow by Alignment to change the alignment of the bulleted paragraphs. Left is the default and most frequently used alignment for bulleted lists. When finished, click OK.

Click on the Bulleted Or Numbered List tool in the Formatting toolbar to quickly add bullets to highlighted paragraphs. The More option on the tool takes you to the Indents And Lists dialog box described in this section.

TIP: *Use the line and paragraph spacing options discussed later in this chapter to space out bulleted and numbered paragraphs. If you instead press ENTER to add extra spacing between your bulleted or numbered paragraphs, a bullet character or number appears on those blank paragraphs.*

17

Creating Numbered Lists

With Publisher you can create numbered lists that use Arabic numbers, or lower- or uppercase alpha characters. You can choose what type of characters appear with the number or letter. For instance, you may want a period after the numbers, or you may want parentheses around the letters.

The following steps illustrate adding numbers to text:

1. Click in the paragraph where you want to add a number. To add numbers to several paragraphs at once, highlight all of the paragraphs.

2. From the Format menu, select Indents And Lists. At the top of the dialog box, make sure Numbered List is selected.

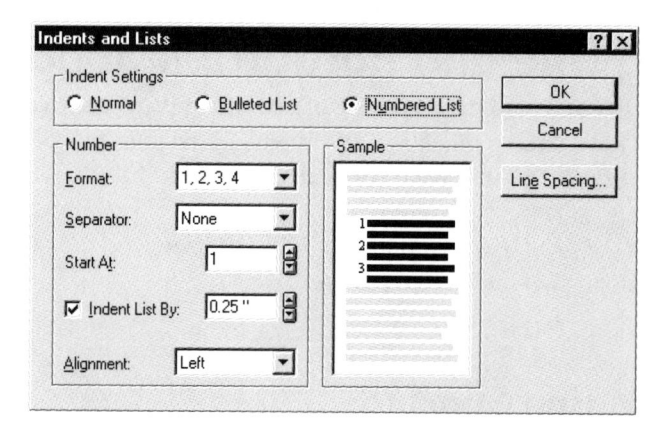

3. Click on the down arrow by Format, and select the desired numbering scheme. Click on the down arrow by Separator, and choose what

characters you want added to the numbers or letters. The preview displays your selections.

4. Enter a new value in the Start At box if you want the numbering to start at a number or letter other than 1 or A (keep reading for more information on this option). Use the Indent List By box to control how much space there is between the numbers and the text.

5. Click on the down arrow by Alignment to change the alignment of the numbered paragraphs. When finished, click OK.

The Start At option is handy when you want to place a paragraph without numbering in the middle of a numbered list. For instance, suppose you have steps 1–3, and then a paragraph without numbering, followed by steps 4–7. By default, your step 4 would display the number 1 since it follows a paragraph with no number. You could enter **4** in the Start At box to adjust the numbering of the steps.

NOTE: *The steps in these sections illustrate adding bullets and numbers to text that has already been entered. You can also add bullets and numbers before entering the text. Click in the blank line where you want the bullet or number, and use the steps for adding bullets or numbers. Now when you press ENTER to end the paragraph, a new bullet or number automatically appears at the start of the next paragraph.*

Controlling Line and Paragraph Spacing

Adjusting the line and paragraph spacing of text can improve the overall appearance and readability of your publication. With Publisher you can control the space between lines of text and the space between paragraphs.

TIP: *For a professional look, keep line and paragraph spacing consistent throughout a publication.*

Adjusting Line Spacing

Lines of text that are too close together or too far apart are harder to read. As a general rule, line spacing should be proportionate to the length of the lines of text. For example, you might use single-line spacing for short lines of text and double-line spacing as the line length increases. By default, Publisher uses single-line spacing.

Use the following steps to adjust line spacing:

1. Click in the paragraph where you want to adjust the line spacing. To adjust several paragraphs at once, highlight all of the paragraphs.

2. From the Format menu, select Line Spacing. In the Line Spacing dialog box, click on the up and down arrows by Between Lines to adjust the line spacing. You can also enter a new value. For instance, enter **2** to set up double-line spacing. A preview of the line spacing appears to the right.

17

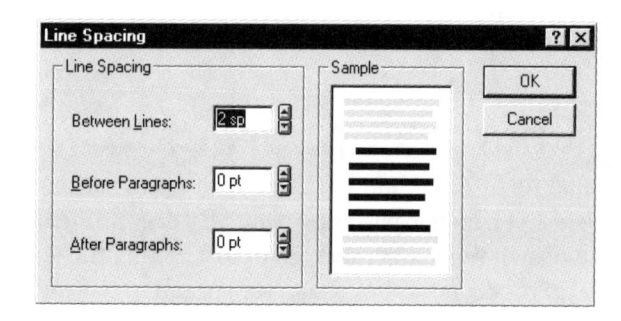

3. Click OK to apply the line spacing.

Adjusting Paragraph Spacing

In addition to setting line spacing, you can adjust the spacing before and after paragraphs. For instance, you can increase the spacing above headings to separate the sections of text. Rather than pressing ENTER to add space above or below paragraphs, use the paragraph-spacing options for more control over the exact amount of space.

Use the following steps to adjust paragraph spacing:

1. Click in the paragraph where you want to adjust the paragraph spacing. To adjust several paragraphs at once, highlight all of the paragraphs.

2. From the Format menu, select Line Spacing. To adjust the spacing before the selected paragraphs, click on the up and down arrows by Before Paragraphs. To adjust the spacing after the selected paragraphs, click on the up and down arrows by After Paragraphs. A preview of the spacing appears to the right.

3. Click OK to apply the paragraph spacing.

You may have noticed that Publisher uses points to measure the space before and after paragraphs. Points are a measurement system used in publishing and printing. There are 72 points per inch. Picas are another measurement system used in publishing and printing. There are 6 picas per inch. You can enter measurements in inches (in), centimeters (cm), picas (pi), and points (pt). Enter the value followed by the appropriate two-letter code. For instance, enter **.5 in** to specify $\frac{1}{2}$ inch as the paragraph spacing. This also works in the line-spacing option.

TIP: *Use paragraph spacing to separate items in a bulleted or number list. The extra spacing can make them easier to read.*

Controlling Character Spacing

If you've ever had to fit three and a half pages of text on three pages, you will appreciate Publisher's character-spacing feature. By decreasing the amount of space between letters, you can tighten paragraphs of text, fitting the text on fewer pages.

It's best to *slightly* decrease the character spacing—too much makes the text hard to read. In addition, if you're working with small text, such as 10 or 12 point type, it might be best to leave the word spacing alone for readability purposes. In this case, try adjusting the line and paragraph spacing, or modifying the page margins and column widths to make more room for the text.

Tightening the word spacing in large titles and headings (text over 48 points), can often enhance the look of the text. Look at magazines to see how large text blocks use tight spacing—sometimes the letters even touch. The close spacing brings the words together and makes the text a more dominant design element.

Ideas to Images

Indenting paragraphs of text enables you to add space to the left or right side of a paragraph. Publisher provides four basic options for indenting paragraphs. Indenting paragraphs of text enables you to add space to the left or right side of a paragraph.

As shown in figure 16-2, Publisher provides four basic options for indenting paragraphs. Indenting paragraphs of text enables you to add space to the left or right side of a paragraph. As shown in figure 16-2, Publisher provides four basic options for indenting paragraphs. Indenting paragraphs of text enables you to add space to the left or right side of a paragraph.

Publisher provides four basic options for indenting paragraphs. Indenting paragraphs of text enables you to add space to the left or right side of a paragraph.

 **TIP:** *When decreasing word spacing, you will find that some typefaces can handle tighter word spacing without affecting readability. For instance, Avant Garde and Century Gothic can withstand tighter spacing.*

Increasing the space between characters is used to create an effect called *spread heads,* where the letters in a headline are spread across the top of a page or column of text. This effect generally works best with one-word headings.

17

Controlling Spacing for the Entire Paragraph

With Publisher, the amount of space between words can be increased or decreased. You can modify the spacing for the whole paragraph, or just the highlighted text (more on this later). The following steps illustrate modifying the word spacing for a whole paragraph:

1. Click in the paragraph where you want to adjust the word spacing. To adjust several paragraphs at once, highlight all of the paragraphs.

2. From the Format menu, select Spacing Between Characters. At the top of the dialog box, make sure the Entire Paragraph option is selected.

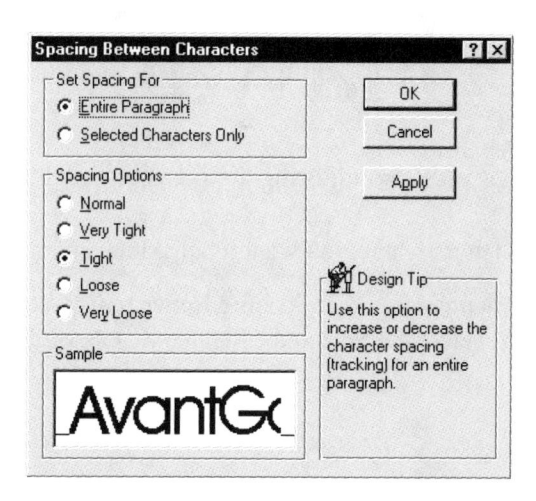

3. To decrease the spacing between characters, click on either the Tight or Very Tight option. To increase the spacing, click on either the Loose or Very Loose option. A preview appears at the bottom of the dialog box.

4. Click OK to apply the selected spacing.

 **NOTE:** *Adjusting word spacing is also referred to as* tracking. *Adjusting the spacing between specific letter pairs is also referred to as* kerning.

Controlling Spacing for Highlighted Text Only

Sometimes, certain pairs of letters appear to be separated by too much space. The effect is especially apparent in larger titles and headings. If the text is large, 36 points and above, and you notice extra or uneven spacing between characters, you can adjust the spacing for just those characters. For instance, look at the extra spacing between the *a*'s and *w* in the word "Hawaii" (it is especially noticeable in large text). In the second example, the letters have been tightened.

Hawaii
Hawaii

The following steps illustrate adjusting the spacing of highlighted text:

1. Highlight the letters where you want to adjust the character spacing.

2. From the Format menu, select Spacing Between Characters. At the top of the dialog box, select the Selected Characters Only option.

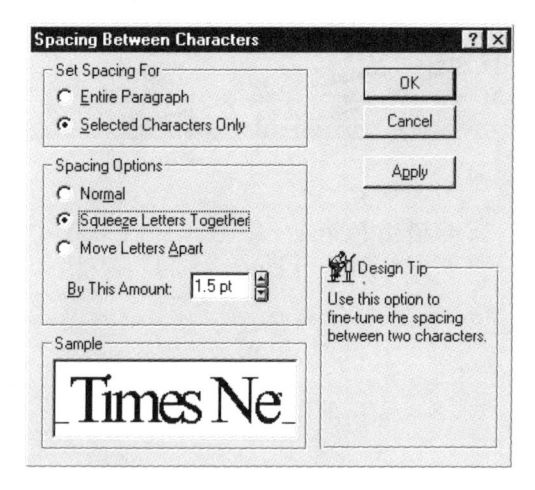

3. To decrease the spacing between the highlighted letters, click on the Squeeze Letters Together option. To increase the spacing, click on the Move Letters Apart option. You can accept the default amount, or enter a new value in points. A sample appears at the bottom of the dialog box.

4. Click OK to apply the selected spacing.

Working with Tabs

Tab stops are fixed positions that run horizontally within a text frame. When you press TAB, the insertion point moves to the next tab stop. With tabs you can create columns or tables of text. For example, in the following table, the tab stops are set at 1, 2.5, and 4 inches. When you click in a paragraph, the ruler displays the tab stops set up in that paragraph. The ruler provides the quickest and easiest way to add, move, and delete tabs.

Tab markers

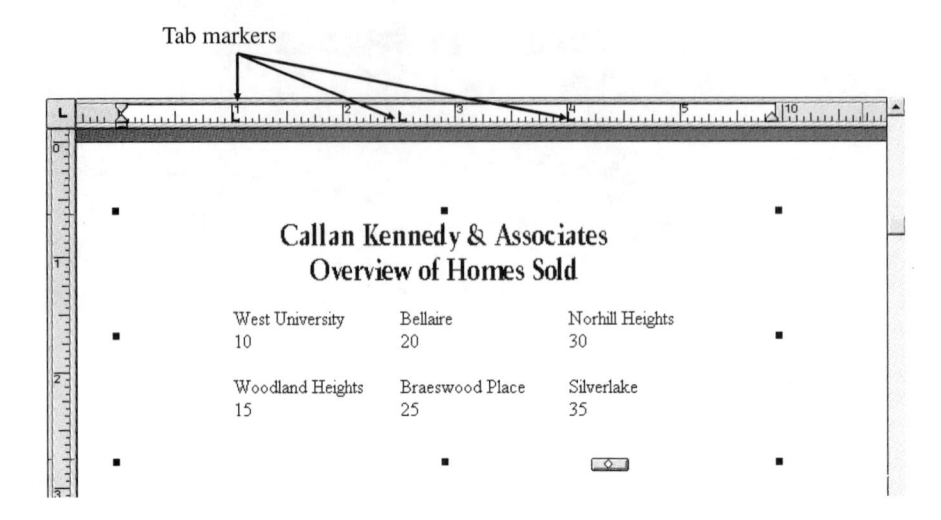

NOTE: *Although you can use tabs to create tables of information, you may find it easier to use Publisher's table feature. Refer to Chapter 12 for more information.*

Understanding Tab Types

There are four types of tabs: left-, center-, right-, and decimal-aligned. In Figure 17-3, the five lines of text are aligned to 3-inch tab stops. In the left tab, the text is aligned to the left of the 3-inch tab stop. The center tag is centered over the 3-inch point. The right tab is aligned to the right of the tab stop. The numbers are aligned by use of a decimal-aligned tab so the decimal point sits precisely at the 3-inch point on the ruler.

Publisher sets left tabs until you specify otherwise. As you will learn, the Tab Alignment button is used to select another tab type. As shown in the following table, each tab type is represented by a tab marker.

	Tab Marker	Tab Type
L	(Left tab symbol)	Left-aligned tab
⊥	(Center tab symbol)	Center-aligned tab
⌐	(Right tab symbol)	Right-aligned tab
⊥.	(Decimal tab symbol)	Decimal-aligned tab

Tab Markers

TABLE 17-1

Tab Alignment button

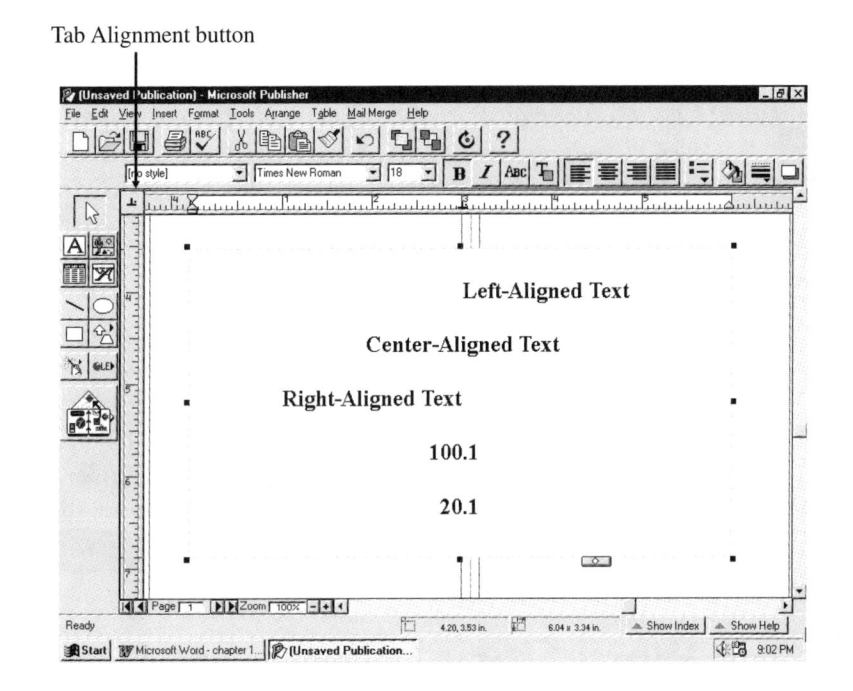

Use the Tab Alignment button to select the tab type before setting a tab stop

FIGURE 17-3

Setting Tab Stops

Tab stops are measured from the left edge of the text frame. By default, Publisher places tab stops every 0.5 inch on the ruler. This means when you press TAB, the insertion point moves 0.5 inch to the right unless you have set a different tab stop.

The following steps illustrate setting tab stops with the ruler:

1. Click in the paragraph where you want to set tab stops. To set several tabs for several paragraphs at once, highlight all of the paragraphs.

2. To select the tab types, click on the Tab Alignment button until you see the marker representing the desired tab type.

3. Now click on the ruler where you want to place a new tab stop. The tab marker appears at that point on the ruler.

4. Continue selecting tab types and setting tab stops as needed.

When aligning text with tabs, you only need to press TAB once between the columns of data. You can then set your own tab stops to spread and align the text.

 **NOTE:** *You can also use the Format | Tabs command to set tab stops. However, the ruler provides a much more visual way of setting tabs, letting you see the results immediately as you add, move, or delete tabs.*

Moving and Deleting Tab Stops

After setting a tab, you can adjust its placement by dragging the tab stop to a new location on the ruler. For example, suppose you set a tab at 2 inches and then wanted to move the tab to 4 inches. Using the ruler, simply drag the 2-inch tab stop to 4 inches. A dotted vertical line appears on screen as you drag the tab marker.

To delete a tab, position the mouse on the tab marker on the ruler and drag the tab marker down into the page area. When you release the mouse, the tab marker disappears and the tab stop is deleted from the ruler.

Using the Word Story Editor

As discussed in this chapter and others, you can edit and format text in Publisher. You can also edit text in the word processing application Microsoft Word 6.0 if you have it installed on your computer. For instance, you may want to use Word if you're big on the thesaurus in Word—since there's not one in Publisher. Another good example is if you're editing text that appears on different pages in Publisher; it might be easier to edit it in Word, where you could see all of the text at one time.

You must have Microsoft Word 6.0 installed on your computer. To edit Publisher text in Word, select the text frame containing the text you want to edit. If you want to create the text in Word, select a blank text frame in your publication. From the Edit menu, choose Edit Story In Microsoft Word. This command launches Word and opens the program with your text in the document window, as shown in Figure 17-4. When you are finished editing and close the Word window, you are automatically returned to Publisher.

Summary

This chapter began with a look at adding special effects to text, such as fancy first letters and wrapping text around graphics. The rest of the chapter focused on

Publisher's
Edit
Story In
Microsoft
Word
feature
automatically
opens
Word and
displays
your text in
the Word
document
window

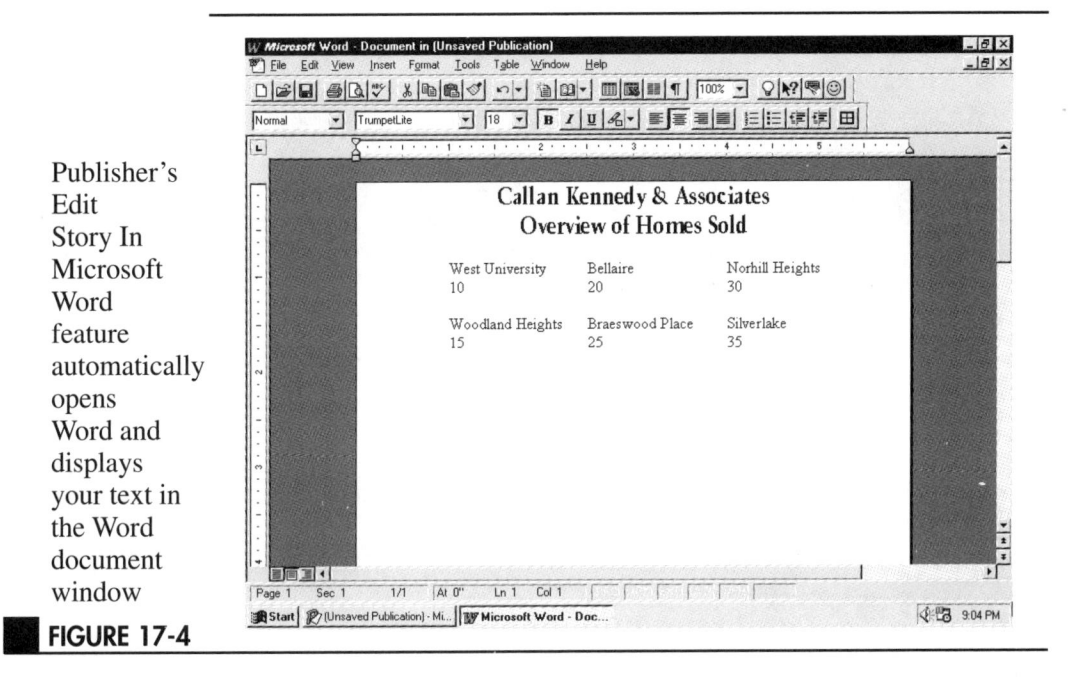

FIGURE 17-4

advanced text-formatting options, such as adding bullets and numbers, working with text spacing, and setting tab stops. These advanced formatting options are often what sets a professional-looking publication apart from the rest.

So far, this book has focused on the many options and features available for building publications in Publisher. The next three chapters give you a chance to practice what you've learned by providing real-life examples or "case studies" using Publisher. These chapters are designed as tutorials to provide actual hands-on training using Publisher. The first, Chapter 18, guides you through the process of creating a newsletter from start to finish.

PART

IV

Case Studies

18

Designing a Newsletter

This is the first of three case-study chapters designed to show you how Microsoft Publisher can be used in the real world. This chapter focuses on issues involved in designing and producing a newsletter.

The chapter begins by examining the goals for the newsletter—this is essential for any design process. Next it discusses how the publication will be printed, and how the printing process affects the design and production of the newsletter. Finally, the chapter walks you through the actual steps for designing the newsletter with Publisher. Here you will find step-by-step instructions for using the Newsletter PageWizard, working with background pages, adjusting the length of text columns, replacing clip art, wrapping text around pictures, and creating print files.

The steps were designed so you can follow along using the case study as a tutorial. However, it is assumed you have read through the rest of the book and have a basic understanding of how Publisher works.

The Scenario

Peabody's Paints is a small paint-supply store that prides itself on helping customers select the perfect colors for their home and providing top-notch painting supplies. The owners of Peabody's are preparing for an upcoming interior design show where they hope to attract new clients. They want to put together a two-sided newsletter filled with tips for selecting paint colors and information on trends in paint to hand out at the show.

Peabody's clientele is generally upper-class professionals, so the owners need a stylish, well-designed publication. Because color is such a big part of their business, the owners decide to print the publication in full color on glossy paper. They also estimate they will need about 500 newsletters. There isn't much time or money to produce the piece. To save time, the owners of Peabody's decide to use Publisher's Newsletter PageWizard to quickly lay out the newsletter. The PageWizard will also save them money, because they won't have to hire a professional graphic designer.

Publication Goals

To help them determine the content of the newsletter, the owners hold a meeting to outline the goals of the publication. Of course, the owners want the people attending the show to become familiar with Peabody's services. They want people to hang on to the publication, so they plan on filling it with informative tips and suggestions about interior design.

Discussions with the Outside Printing Company

The owners of Peabody's know they have to work with an outside printing company to print the newsletter. For one thing, Peabody's only has a black-and-white laser printer, not a color printer. A lack of color output is important to consider, because they will not be able to print color rough draft copies of the newsletter. The rough drafts will have to be in black and white.

Several friends and business acquaintances recommend One-Stop Print Shop, a printing service specializing in printing and copying services, for their prices and quality work. Peabody's owners call One-Stop Print Shop before beginning work on the newsletter. The sales representative has two great suggestions. The first is to get a color rough draft of the newsletter before the final printing process. As discussed in Chapter 10, designing and printing in color can be rather imprecise—the colors you see on the screen will not exactly match the colors on the printed page. With the color rough draft Peabody's owners can proof the color and make changes. The second idea is to print one high-quality newsletter and use it as the master for making color copies for the 500 newsletters. Copying the master newsletter rather than actually printing each newsletter is considerably more cost-effective. The representative assures Peabody's the color would show well on the glossy paper stock. Color copying is also a speedy process—one that fits in well with Peabody's time constraints.

However, One-Stop Print Shop does not output directly from Microsoft Publisher, so the people at Peabody's have to create a print file. This file will contain all the information needed to print the newsletter created in Publisher.

 **NOTE:**   *Refer to Chapter 10 for information on creating print files and installing printers.*

Working with Printer Drivers

To get the best print quality, Peabody's needs to install the printer driver of the printer that will be used to output the master newsletter. The representative of One-Stop

Print Shop tells Peabody's to install the QMS ColorScript 100 printer driver. This printer driver is available on the Windows 95 installation disks, so they are able to quickly install it.

Ironing Out Some Specifics

The newsletter is to be printed on the front and back. The representative of One-Stop Print Shop notifies Peabody's that the color printer has a 0.5-inch margin, meaning all elements in the newsletter must be placed at least this far from the edge of the page. Because the newsletter will be printed in full color, Peabody's can use any color in the design process. Since the piece will be handed to potential customers, there is no need to leave room for a mailing address. However, if the newsletter is a success, they can always modify the design to add a mailing label.

Time to Design:
Using the Newsletter PageWizard

With the printing process determined, the people at Peabody's are ready to begin designing the newsletter. The Newsletter PageWizard offers several designs for different types of newsletters. In addition to basic business style newsletters, Publisher provides community, family, holiday, and school newsletter designs.

 **NOTE:** *See page 196 of the* Microsoft Publisher Companion *for an overview of the available newsletter styles.*

Use the following steps to create a newsletter with the Newsletter PageWizard:

1. From the File menu, select Create New Publication. Make sure the PageWizard tab is selected at the top of the dialog box. Double-click on Newsletter to start the PageWizard.

2. The first screen of the Newsletter PageWizard asks you to select the style of newsletter you want to create. Peabody's owners want a basic newsletter style that would be easy to edit. They decide on the Bold style. Select Bold, and click on the Next button.

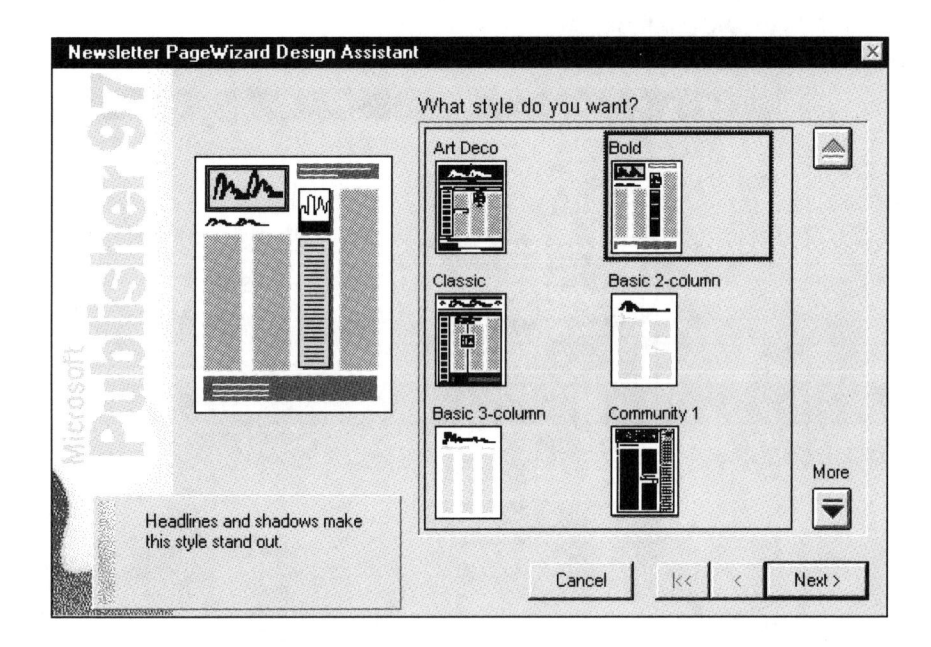

3. The next screen asks how many columns (one, two, three, or four) you want to use in the newsletter design. The preview displays the selected column style. Select Three Columns and click on the Next button.

4. The next screen asks how many stories (one, two, or three) you want on the first page of the newsletter. Select Two and click on the Next button.

5. At the top of the next screen, enter **Color News** as the title of the newsletter, and click on the Next button.

6. The next screen asks if you want to include a Table Of Contents, Date, and Volume And Issue number on the newsletter. Since this will be a short newsletter, turn off the Table Of Contents option. In addition, since this newsletter is not part of a series of newsletters, turn off the Volume And Issue option. The date will be added to the newsletter. Click on the Next button.

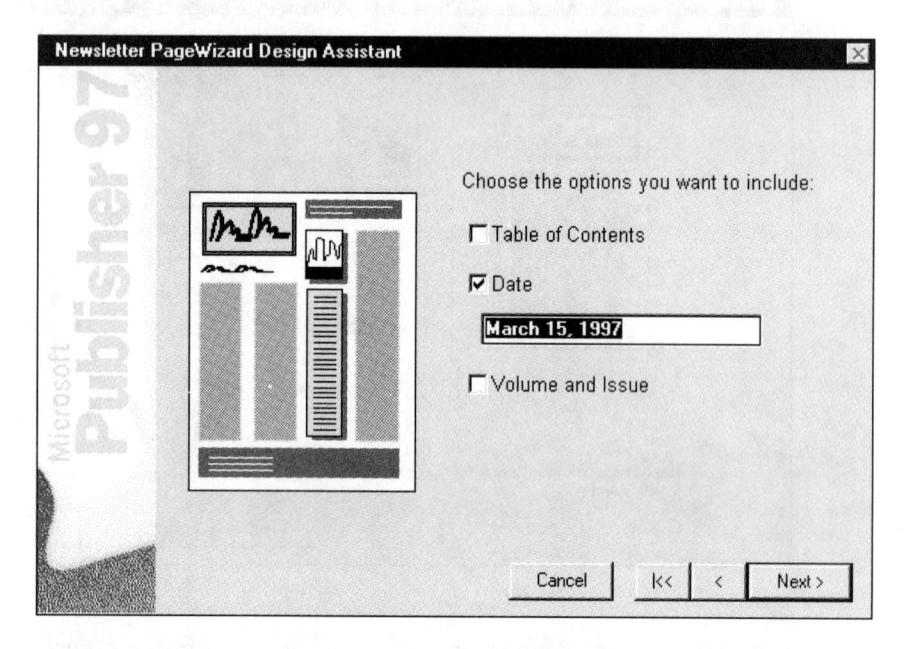

7. The next screen asks how many pages should be in the newsletter. This will be a two-page newsletter printed on the front and back of one piece of paper. Enter **2** for the number of pages, and click on the Next button.

8. The next screen asks if you want to leave room for a mailing label on the back of the newsletter. As mentioned, this newsletter will be handed out, so select No, and click on the Next button.

9. The next screen asks if the newsletter will be printed on both sides of the paper. Make sure Yes is selected, and click on the Next button. (This step refers to output from the commercial printer, not the desktop printer.)

10. The final screen tells you to sit back and relax while Publisher goes to work. Click on the Create It! button. A status bar appears indicating the progress of the job.

11. After the PageWizard is finished, another screen appears asking if you want step-by-step help as you add your own text and pictures. For the purposes of this exercise choose No, and click on the OK button.

As shown in Figure 18-1, the first page of the newsletter is displayed. Notice the newsletter title, "Color News," and date appear in the top left corner. Before beginning customization of the newsletter, Peabody's owners want to set up the newsletter for full-color printing.

Setting up the Printer

Before designing, Peabody's owners need to set up the newsletter for full-color printing by an outside printing service. The procedure helps them select the right printer driver and other options for the specific printing process. The QMS ColorScript 100 printer driver is installed, but still needs to be selected as the output device for the newsletter.

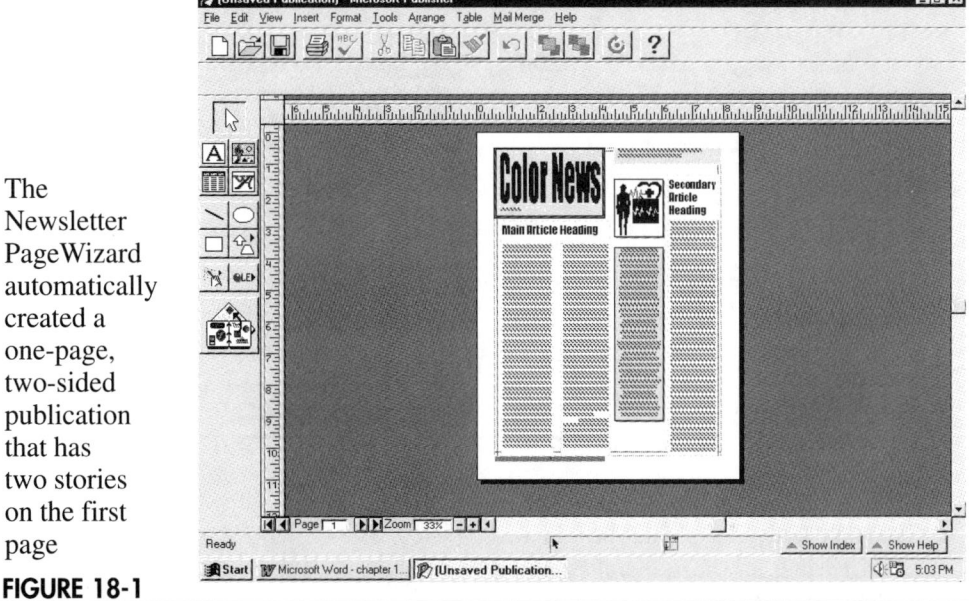

The Newsletter PageWizard automatically created a one-page, two-sided publication that has two stories on the first page

FIGURE 18-1

The following steps illustrate setting up the newsletter for printing by an outside company:

1. From the File menu, select Outside Print Setup. If this is the first time you've used this command, a message appears asking if you wish to see a quick overview of the outside printing process or get step-by-step instructions as you work. If desired, run through the demo. If not, click on the Continue button.

2. The Outside Print Setup dialog box appears asking about the type of printing you will be using for the publication. Select the third option, Full Color, On A Color Printer At Less Than 1200 Dpi Resolution. Click on the Next button.

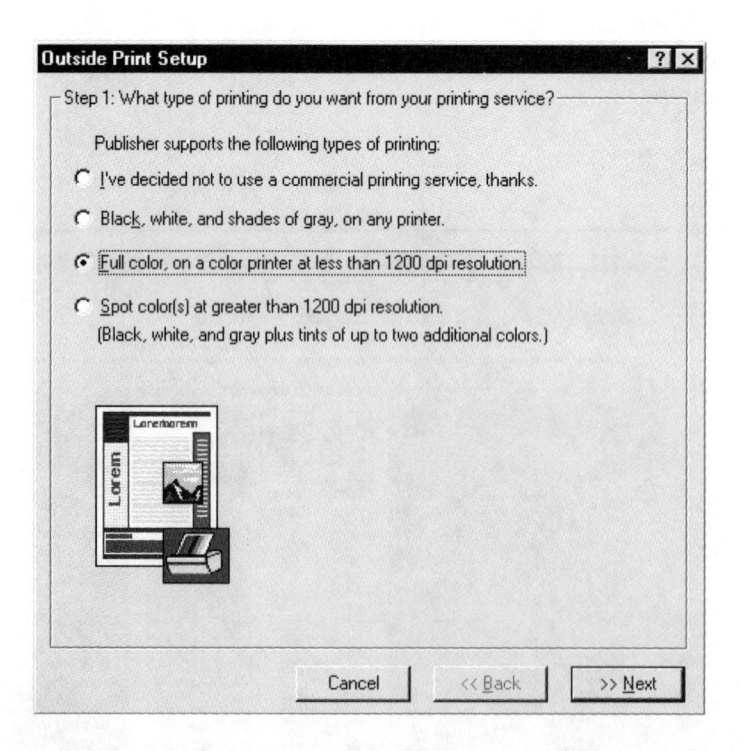

3. The next screen asks what printer will be used. The QMS ColorScript 100 printer driver has been installed, but needs to be selected. Click on the option Select A Specific Printer.

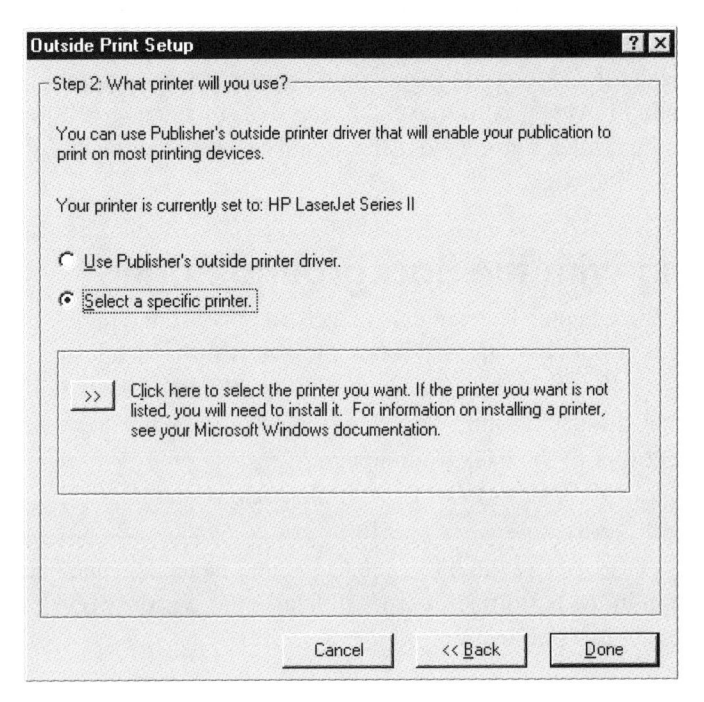

4. Click on the >> button to select a new printer. In the Print Setup dialog box, click on the down arrow by Name, and choose the QMS ColorScript 100 printer driver—if you don't have it, just select one of your available printers. Click OK to return to the Outside Print Setup dialog box, and then click on the Done button.

5. Publisher displays a message asking to update embedded objects. Basically, Publisher wants to check the settings used in the newsletter design now that a new printer has been selected. Click Yes.

6. After starting the newsletter and selecting the printer, it's time to save the publication. From the File menu, select Save As. Enter **Color News** for the filename and save the file. After the initial save, the keyboard shortcut CTRL-S can be used for future saving.

Now it's time to add the text and pictures that will make the newsletter unique to Peabody's Paints.

Designing the Newsletter

Using the Zoom tools, the people at Peabody's take a close look at the newsletter. There is room for two stories and some sidebar text on the first page. The stories are continued on the second page. The graphic on page 1 needs to be replaced, and they decide to delete the sidebar on page 2 and replace it with a graphic. The first item on the agenda, however, is to make sure the margin spacing is at least 0.5 inch as required by the printer. Setting the margins and several other tasks will be performed on the background page.

Working with the Background Page

As discussed in Chapter 16, elements placed on background pages are displayed on every page of a publication. Peabody's owners want to delete the page numbers, since there's really no need for them on a short publication. They will also add color to the box on the background page, and place a company logo and name in the lower-right corner of the background page.

Use the following steps to work with the background page:

1. Press CTRL-M to switch to the background page. The one background button in the bottom left corner indicates there is only one background page for this publication.

2. Select the gray box in the bottom left corner, and click on the Zoom indicator. From the pop-up menu, choose Zoom To Selection. The gray bar with the page number is displayed. Press DELETE to delete the page number (the pound sign).

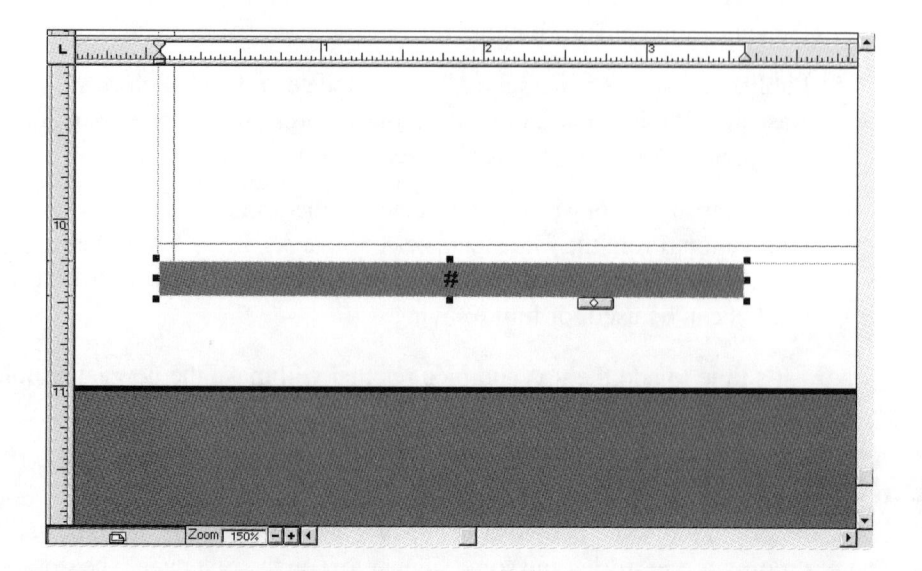

3. To change the color of the box, click on the Object Color tool on the Formatting toolbar. From the drop-down menu, choose the color Red.

4. Use the Zoom indicator to return to Full Page view.

5. To check the margin spacing, select Layout Guides from the Arrange menu. The margins are set at 0.5 inch or higher, so they will work fine with the printing process. However, to make room for the logo, enter **1.5** as the spacing for the bottom margin.

Adding Text and a Logo to the Background

To make the company name prominent on the newsletter, it will be added to the bottom of the background page along with clip art of a paintbrush.

Use the following steps to add text and a logo:

 **NOTE:** *Watch the rulers to determine ruler guide placement and height and width of frames.*

1. Zoom in for a close look at the bottom of the background page. Hold SHIFT and drag a ruler guide from the horizontal ruler so it sits at 10 $\frac{1}{4}$ inches—this is $\frac{3}{4}$ inch from the bottom of the page.

2. Drag the red box up until it sits on the ruler guide.

3. To the immediate right of the red box, draw a text frame about 2 $\frac{1}{2}$ inches wide by $\frac{1}{2}$ inch high. Enter **Peabody's Paints** in the text frame.

4. Highlight the text and click on the down arrow by the Font tool on the Standard toolbar. Select Impact as the typeface. Click on the down arrow by the Size tool (also on the Standard toolbar), and select 24 as the point size for the text. The results should look like the following:

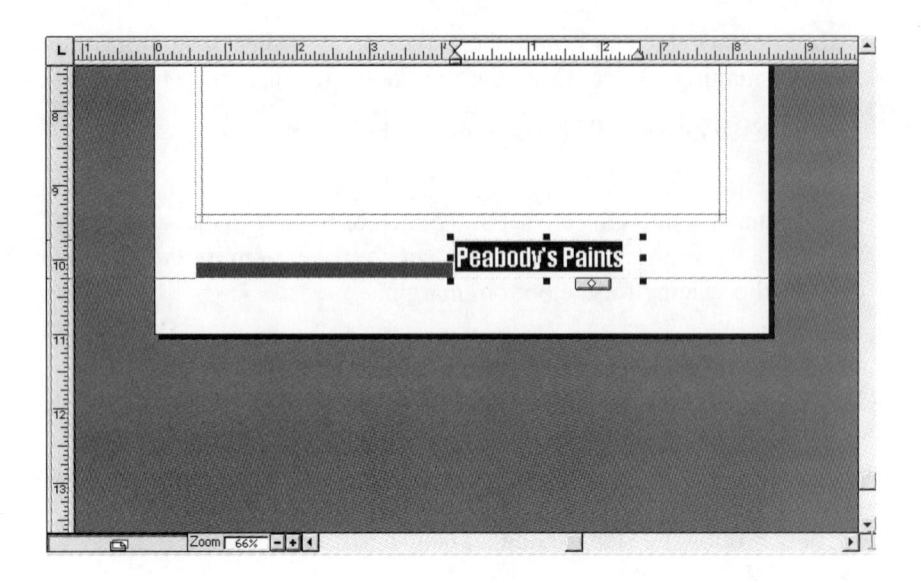

5. To the immediate right of the text frame, draw a picture frame about 1 inch wide and $\frac{1}{2}$ inch high.

6. From the Insert menu, select Clip Art. In the Clip Gallery, select Industry as the category. (You will need the CD-ROM to get this clip art.) Select the clip art of a paintbrush and hand, and click on the Insert button.

7. Click OK to instruct Publisher to size the frame to meet the dimensions of the clip art.

8. Drag the text frame down until the baseline (bottom) of the text sits on the ruler guide, as shown here:

**TIP:**   *Press* CTRL-T *to make the text frame transparent—this makes it easier to position the text. Drag the picture frame down until the bottom of the paintbrush sits on the ruler guide.*

9. Press CTRL-M to return to the foreground pages. Click on the Zoom indicator to return to Full Page view. Press CTRL-S to save the newsletter file.

Working with Page 1

The most obvious thing that needs to be done to page 1 is to shorten the text columns so they do not cover up the logo added to the background page. The text and graphics also need to be replaced.

Use the following steps to shorten the text columns:

1. Click on the first column of text—the Connect and Flow icons appear, indicating this column flows into the next column. Place the mouse at the bottom middle of the selected column. When you see the Resize icon, drag up until the bottom of the frame lines up with the pink margin guide.

2. Repeat this procedure with the second and third columns on the page.

 **NOTE:** *If the Snap To Guides feature is turned on, the text columns should snap to the pink margin guide. If this is not happening, select Snap To Guides from the Tools menu.*

Replacing the Graphic

The picture on page 1 needs to be replaced with an image more in tune with painting supplies. A graphic with a similar shape would be best, so the frame size will not have to be adjusted too dramatically. The color of the box containing the pull-quote will also be changed.

1. Double-click on the frame containing the graphic on page 1.

2. In the Clip Gallery, select Industry as the category. (You will need the CD-ROM to get this clip art.) Select the clip art shown here, and click on the Insert button.

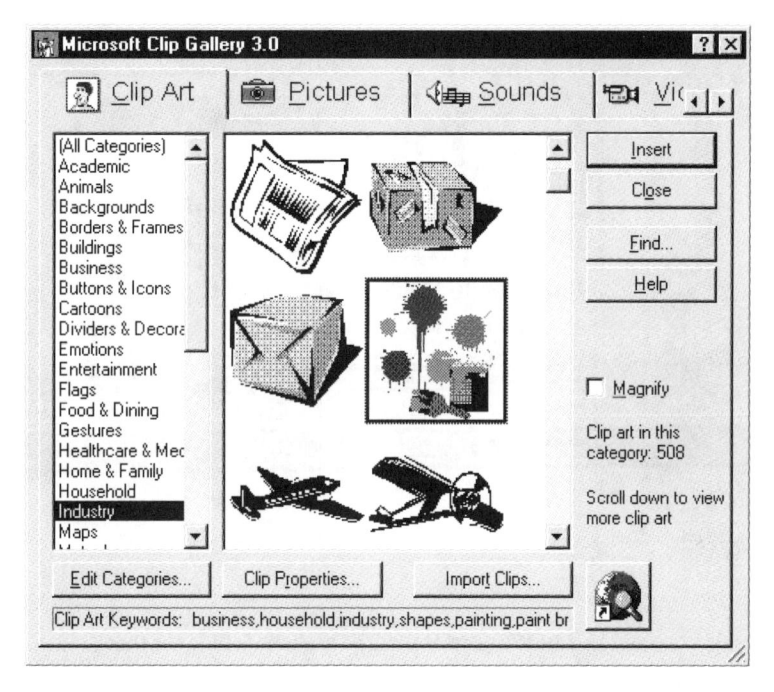

3. Click OK to instruct Publisher to size the frame to meet the dimensions of the clip art.

4. Select the gray box in the top right corner of the page. Click on the Object Color tool, and choose Red at the top of the dialog under Recent Colors.

Replacing the Text Headings and the Pull-Quote

The text for the headings and the pull-quote in the top right corner needs to be entered. For the purposes of this tutorial, the body text will not be replaced. As you may recall, to enter body text, just click inside the frame and begin typing. Refer to Chapter 8 for more information on entering and editing text.

Use the following steps to replace the heading and pull-quote text:

1. Zoom in closer to the top of the page. Click on the text "Main Article Heading," and enter **Color For Your Home** as the new heading. As displayed in the toolbar, this heading uses the same font as the company name on the background page.

2. Click on the text "Secondary Article Heading." Type in the text **Tips**, and then press ENTER. On the next line, type in **From** and press ENTER again. On the third line, type **the Pros**.

3. Click on the red box in the top right corner. Click on the Zoom indicator, and choose Zoom To Selection to get a close-up view of the pull-quote box.

4. Enter **Before painting, always put down a primer coat!** as pull-quote text. Click on the Center align tool to center-align the text. Highlight the quote and click on the Size tool—change the size to 12 points. Return to Full Page view.

5. Press CTRL-SHIFT-O to see how page 1 looks without the guides and frame boundaries. Press the keys again to redisplay the guides and boundaries. Press CTRL-S to save the file.

Page 1 is complete—now it's time to design page 2.

Working with Page 2

As with page 1, the text columns on page 2 need to be shortened so the background objects can be seen. There is also a line between the second and third columns that needs to be adjusted. In addition to replacing the text headings, the gray sidebar will be deleted and replaced with a picture. Another picture will also be added to the third column.

Use the following steps to shorten the line and text columns:

1. Click on the right-pointing arrow in the Page Counter to view page 2.

2. Click on the first column of text—the Connect and Flow icons appear, indicating this column flows into the next column. Place the mouse at the bottom middle of the selected column. When you see the Resize icon, drag up until the bottom of the frame lines up with the pink margin guide.

3. Repeat this procedure with the second and third columns on the page.

4. Click on the line separating the second and third columns. Place the mouse cursor at the bottom of the line. When you see the Resize icon, drag the line up until the end of the line touches the pink margin guide.

5. While the line is selected, click on the Border tool, and choose More from the drop-down list. In the dialog box, click on the down arrow by Color and choose Red.

 **TIP:** *Once you select a color, Publisher puts it under the heading Recent Colors. By always selecting this color from Recent Colors, you can be sure you are getting the same shade you selected before.*

Wrapping Text Around Graphics

The gray sidebar will be replaced by a graphic. The text wrap will be modified to wrap around the picture, not the frame.

Use the following steps to add a graphic and to wrap text around the picture:

1. Click on the gray sidebar, and press CTRL-DELETE to delete the text frame.

2. In about the same position as the deleted sidebar, draw a picture frame about 3 inches wide by 3 inches high.

3. From the Insert menu, choose Clip Art. In the Clip Gallery, click on the All Categories option, and select the clip art shown here. Click on the Insert button.

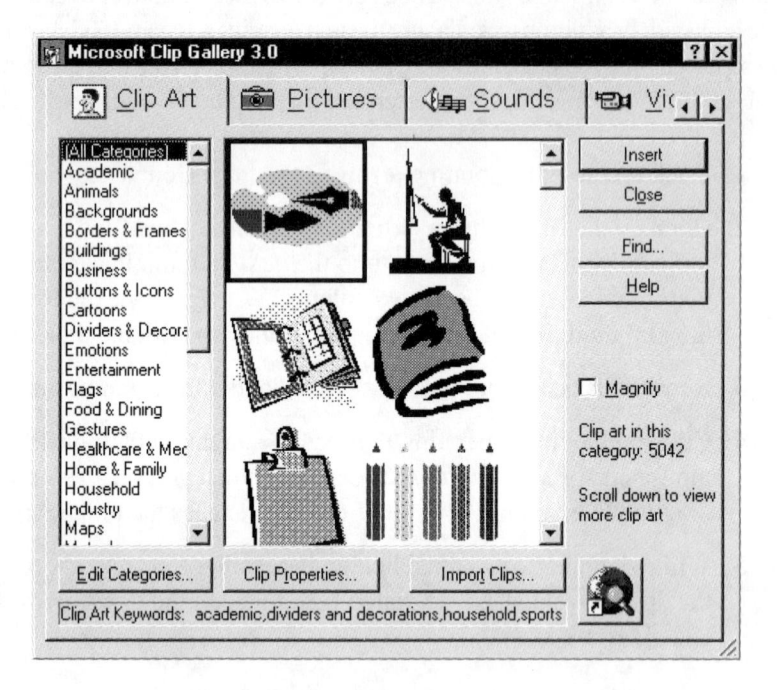

4. Click OK to instruct Publisher to size the frame to meet the dimensions of the clip art.

5. Zoom in for a closer look at the graphic. Make sure the graphic is still selected, and click on the Wrap Text To Picture tool.

6. To adjust how the text wraps around the edges of the picture, click on the Edit Irregular Wrap tool. Drag the black dots in the outline about $\frac{1}{4}$ inch from the edges of the picture.

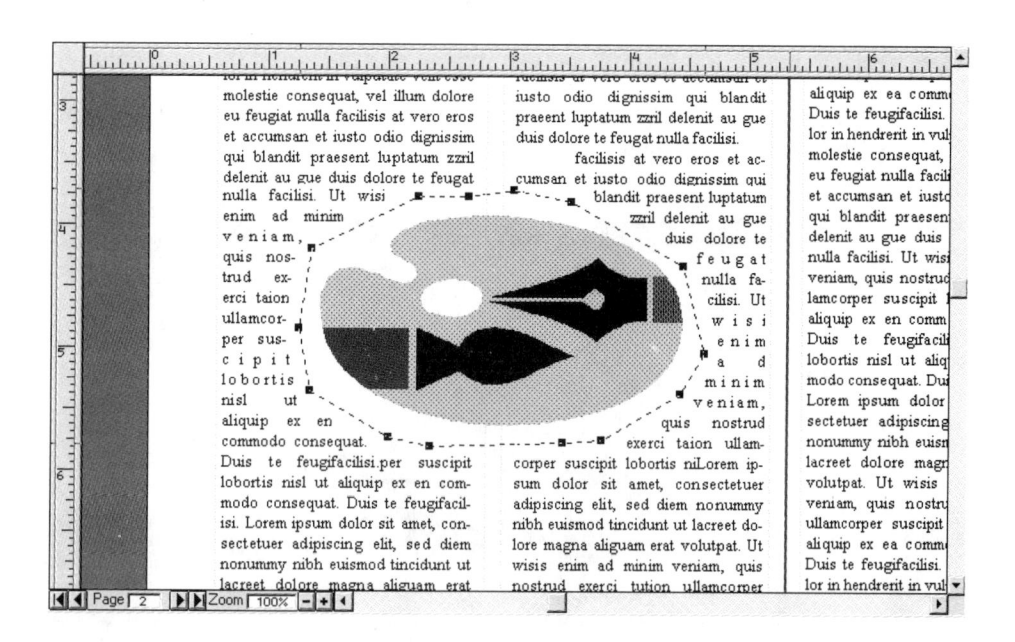

Adding a New Graphic

A new graphic will be placed at the top of the third column. The heading and body text frames will have to be moved down to make room for the new graphic.

1. Return to Full Page view, and select the gray box in the top left corner. Click on the Object Color tool and select Red.

2. Click in the third column of text. Place the mouse at the top middle of the selected column. When you see the Resize icon, drag down until the top of the frame lines up at 4 inches on the vertical ruler.

3. Move the heading text frame down so it sits directly above the third column of text.

4. Draw a picture frame in the now-empty spot at the top of the third column.

5. From the Insert menu, choose Clip Art. In the Clip Gallery, select the clip art shown here, and click on the Insert button.

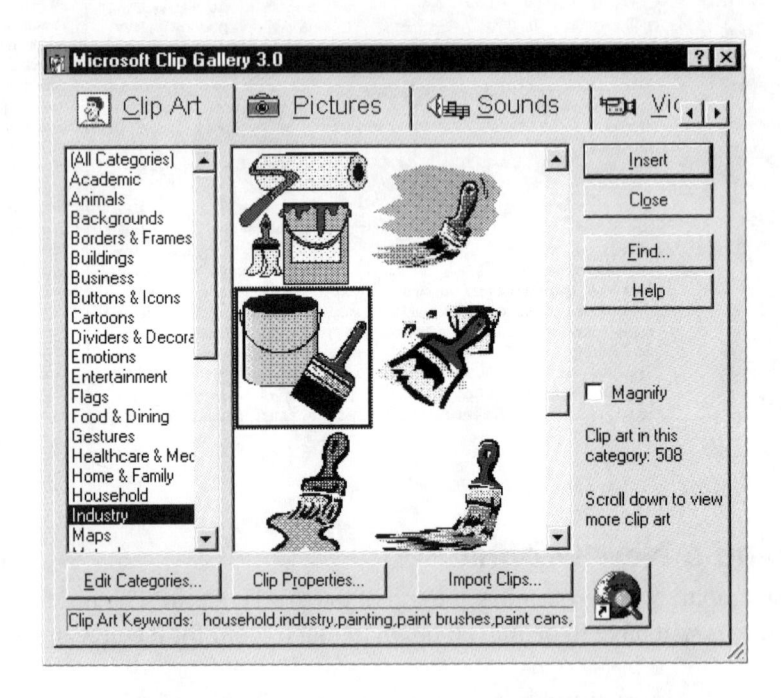

6. Click OK to instruct Publisher to size the frame to meet the dimensions of the clip art.

NOTE: *When selecting clip art, consider how the colors and style of the clip art work with your publication.*

Replacing Text Headings

The text for the headings needs to be replaced. For the purposes of this tutorial, the body text will not be replaced.

Use the following steps to replace the heading text:

1. Click on the text "Secondary Article Heading," and enter **Work with Comfortable Colors** as the new heading. Notice the same font is used for all the headings.

2. Click on the text "Continued Article Heading," type **Hire Painting**, press
ENTER, and type **Professionals**.

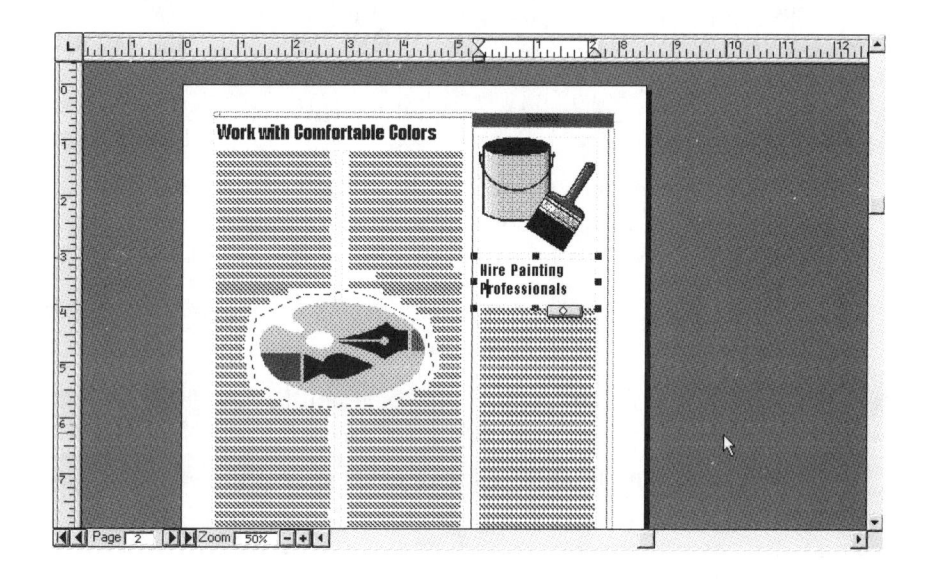

3. Press CTRL-SHIFT-O to see how page 2 looks without the guides and frame
boundaries. Press the keys again to redisplay the guides and boundaries.
Press CTRL-S to save the file.

Page 2 is complete. With Publisher, the newsletter was created quickly and easily.
The newsletter is bright, colorful, and will make a great first impression at the interior
design showcase.

Printing the Newsletter

With the newsletter design finished, Peabody's owners are ready to do some printing.
First, they want to print a proof on their black-and-white laser printer. Next, they
have to prepare a print file for One-Stop Print Shop. From the print file, One-Stop
Print Shop will output another color proof. Peabody's will check the proof to make
sure the colors look as intended. When the color proof looks good, the copies of the
newsletter can be made.

Printing a Proof

A proof is a sample copy of the publication. Because the newsletter has been set up for outside printing, the black-and-white laser printer at Peabody's can be used as the proof printer. Although the printer cannot print color, the proof can help Peabody's check the placement of elements and text formatting.

Use the following steps to set up a proof printer:

1. From the File menu, choose Print Proof. As discussed in Chapter 10, the Print Proof command is not available unless you set up the publication for outside printing.

2. In the Print Proof dialog box, click on the down arrow by Name, and select a printer (your in-house printer).

3. Click OK to print one copy of both pages of the newsletter.

The black-and-white proof of the newsletter is carefully examined by several people at Peabody's. No mistakes are found, so Peabody's owners are ready to create a print file and transport it to One-Stop Print Shop.

 **TIP:** *Ask people not involved in the production of a publication to proof it. They might find mistakes those close to the project have missed.*

Creating a Print File

The systems at One-Stop Print Shop do not have Publisher installed, so the people at Peabody's need to send them a print file. Before creating the print file, it's important to make sure the printer used by the printing service is selected. Peabody's owners selected the QMS ColorScript 100 printer in the Outside Print Setup commands performed before the newsletter was designed. Since Peabody's owners do not have a QMS ColorScript printer, they connected the printer to the File option instead of a computer port.

Use the following steps to create a print file:

1. Open the publication file you want to print. Choose Print To Outside Printer from the File menu. The Print To Outside Printer dialog box appears.

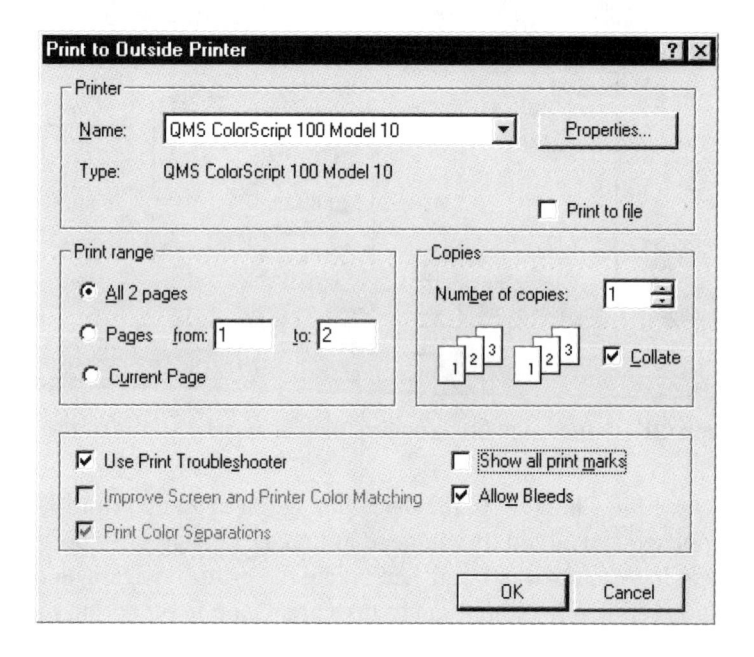

18

2. Make sure the QMS ColorScript 100 printer is selected. Since the printer uses the File connection instead of a port, the Print To File option does not need to be turned on.

3. Make sure the Print Range is set to All 2 Pages, and the Number of Copies is set at 1.

4. Turn off the Show All Print Marks option. Because the newsletter is printed on the whole page area, there is no room for the crop marks.

5. Click OK. The Print To File dialog box appears. Enter **newslett** as the print filename. Publisher will add the filename extension .PRN. If necessary, change to the drive and directory where you want to save the print file.

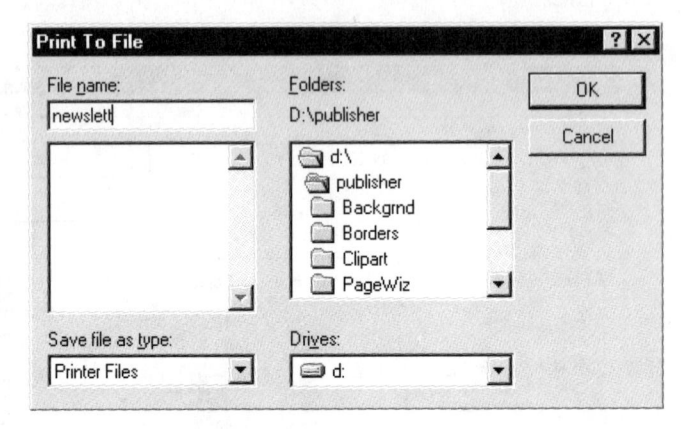

6. Click OK. A message box appears displaying the status of the print job.

As discussed in Chapter 10, the disadvantage of sending print files is that they cannot be opened and edited. If you need to make a change or if the service finds a problem, you have to fix it in Publisher, create the print file again, and send it back to the printing service. It's important to take great care in preparing the publication file *before* creating the print file.

Now the print file can be copied to disk and delivered to One-Stop Print Shop. Since the print file is large, you may need to compress the file using a program such as WinZip. If you plan on working frequently with a printing service, it might be worth the money to invest in a large removable drive such as a SyQuest or Iomega.

Summary

From start to finish, it takes just three days to design and produce the newsletter. The people at Peabody's have the newsletter in plenty of time for the interior design showcase. They also save big bucks by not hiring an advertising agency or graphic designer to produce the newsletter. Based on the ease of creating the newsletter, Peabody's owners decide to use Publisher to redo their business cards, update some brochures, and redesign their entire set of business documents. Now that everybody at Peabody's is familiar with Publisher, all future publications should be produced quickly and easily. Already being planned is a new web site—designed and published to the World Wide Web by Publisher!

19

Designing a Postcard

This is the second of three chapters set up as real-life case studies using Microsoft Publisher to create and design publications. Read through the chapter to gain an understanding of the issues involved when it comes to producing postcards. First, you are given an outline of the needs and goals of the publication. Next, the chapter discusses specifics about printing the publication. The actual steps for designing the postcard with Publisher complete the chapter. Here you will find step-by-step instructions on selecting a PageWizard, recoloring clip art, editing WordArt, and entering text. The steps were designed so you can follow along using the case study as a tutorial.

 **NOTE:**   *Company names are fictitious.*

The Scenario

Technology Trainers is a training company specializing in helping people access the Internet, set up intranets, and design web pages. With the addition of two new instructors, they are eager to offer more classes. The owners of Technology Trainers want to design a postcard announcing new Internet training-class dates. Not willing to hire a graphic designer and certainly not page-design gurus themselves, they decide to use Publisher's Postcard PageWizard to quickly set up and design the postcard.

When finished, the postcard will be sent through bulk mail to a list of 2,000 people. The owners also want several hundred extra copies that they can pass out to other customers and leave at related businesses. The total number of postcards to be printed is 2,500.

Publication Goals

With only a few seconds to grab the reader's attention, the owners know the postcard needs to quickly publicize the Internet training classes. The information on the postcard also needs to clearly announce class dates, locations, fees, and how to register.

Discussions with the Outside Printing Company

Printing such a large number of postcards is beyond the capability of the in-house printers at Technology Trainers. They do have a desktop color printer that can be used for rough drafts of the postcard, but they need help for the final output. Before beginning work on the postcard, the owners consult Chroma Colors, a company specializing in color printing jobs under 5,000.

The representative at Chroma Colors informs the owners that the most cost-effective process for 2,500 postcards is *offset printing*. Offset printing involves creating a separate piece of film (like the negatives you get back with your snapshots) for each ink color used in the publication. The film is used to create a printing plate, which is then used to print the inks on paper. For a low-run printing job of 2,500 copies, paper (instead of metal) printing plates could be used to reduce the cost.

 **NOTE:** *There are all kinds of books and brochures that explain printing processes in detail. Check out a bookstore or ask a printer to recommend some publications.*

Working with the Postcard Size

The size of the postcard is also an issue. The owners decide to produce the postcards at 5 ½ by 4 ¼ inches. However, postcards are not printed one at a time. Depending on the size of the paper, several postcards can be printed at one time. For instance, with a large piece of paper you can print six or eight postcards at a time. This is frequently referred to as "6 up" or "8 up." After some discussion, the owners decide to design the postcard "1 up," or one postcard per page. Then in the printing process, Chroma Colors will arrange six postcards on the printing plates to print "6 up."

Working with Printer Drivers

Chroma Colors gives the owners of Technology Trainers a copy of a PostScript printer driver. They recommend installing this printer driver to ensure that the film for the postcard will print correctly on their output devices. The printer driver could be used with all future print jobs done at Chroma Colors. The printer is installed through the Control Panel in Windows 95. Refer to Chapter 10 for steps on installing printers.

Selecting Colors

After analyzing printing costs, the owners of Technology Trainers decide to use one spot color on the postcard. This means printing the postcard will involve two inks—the spot color and black. The spot color Teal 288 is selected from a Pantone spot-color swatch book. Teal and black are the only colors that can be used when designing the postcard. The Chroma Colors representative tells them to pick a color that resembles their teal spot color when designing in Publisher. When the postcard is printed, the teal selected from the Pantone book will be used. The teal color selected in Publisher will not exactly match the teal when it is printed, but it will indicate what elements of the page design are to be printed in teal and black.

NOTE: *Refer to Chapter 10 for more information on spot-color printing.*

Ready to Work: Using the Postcard PageWizard

With the printing process in mind, the spot color selected, and some tips from the printer, the owners are ready to produce the postcard. Publisher's Postcard PageWizard will be used to streamline the production process.

The Postcard PageWizard offers designs for all types of postcards. They are divided into three categories: Business, Community, and Personal. After completing the tutorial and designing the postcard for Technology Trainers, thumb through the choices to see what kinds of postcards are available.

Use the following steps to start the postcard:

1. From the File menu, select Create New Publication. Make sure the PageWizard tab is selected at the top of the dialog box. Double-click on Postcard to start the PageWizard.

2. The first screen of the Postcard PageWizard asks you to select the type of postcard to be created. In this case, select Business, and click on the Next button.

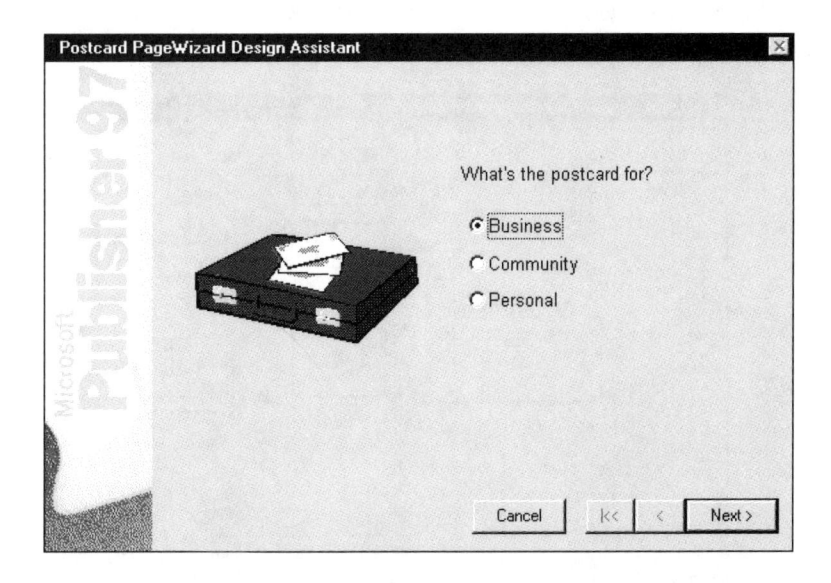

3. The next screen asks you to select the kind of postcard you want. Select Event Announcement and click on the Next button.

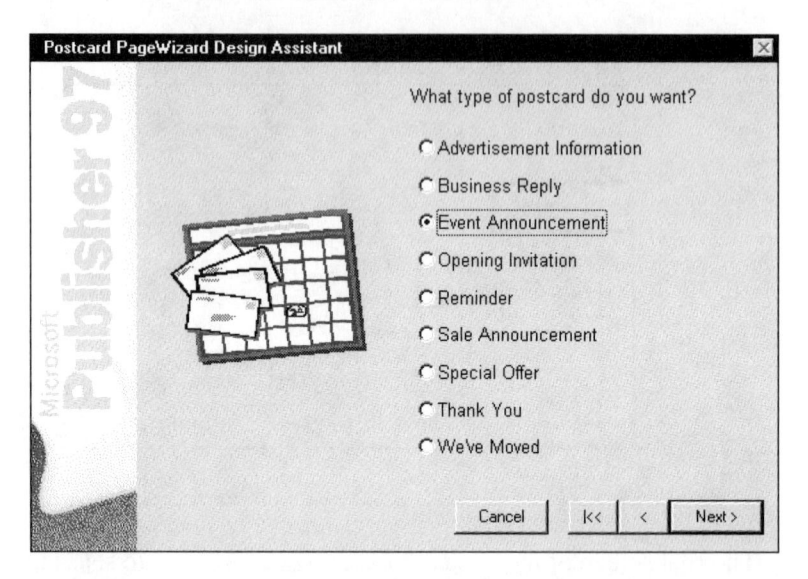

4. The next screen offers four styles of postcards. Click on a style to see a preview on the left. Wanting something a little different, the owners consider Jazzy, but decide it uses too many colors and would be hard to edit. Instead, they choose Modern. Select Modern and click on the Next button.

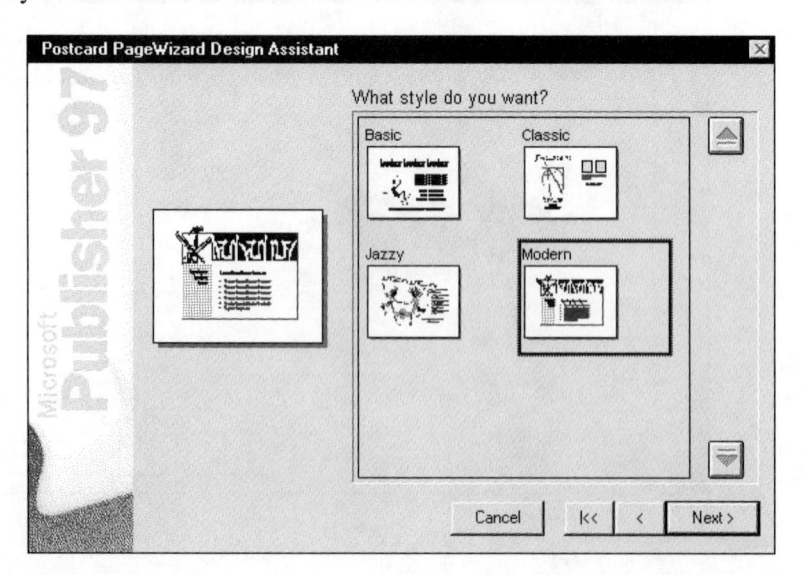

5. The next screen asks you to select the postcard size. It had been determined in discussions with the printer that the postcard would be 4 $\frac{1}{4}$ by 5 $\frac{1}{2}$ inches. Select the 1/4 Page (4 $\frac{1}{4}$" x 5 $\frac{1}{2}$") option, and click on the Next button.

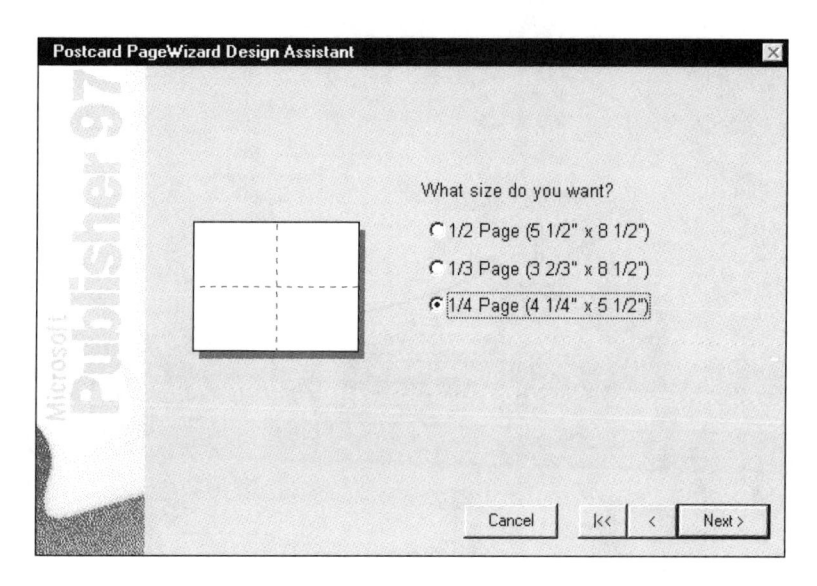

6. The next screen is for the return address of the postcard. Select My Business Address at the top of the screen. Enter **Technology Trainers** as the name and **123 Main Street, Suite 123, Houston, TX 77009** as the address. Click on the Next button.

7. The next screen asks how many copies of the postcard should be printed on a page. As discussed with the printer, one copy will be placed per page. Choose One In The Center, and click on the Next button.

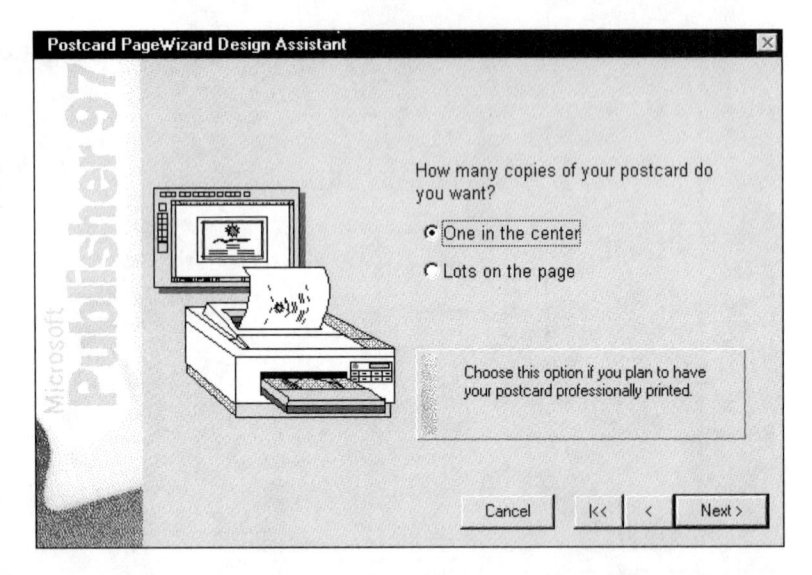

8. The next screen informs you that postcards have two sides. You will be working with two pages of information. Click on the Next button.

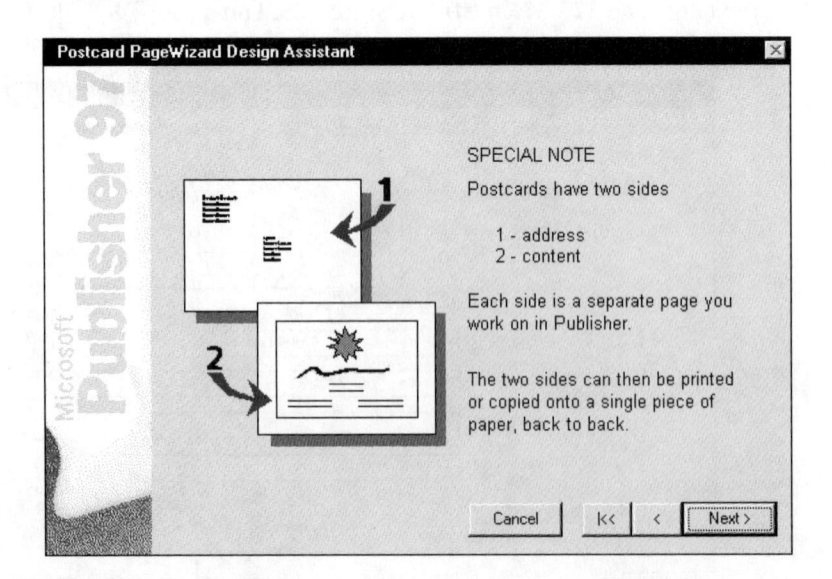

9. The final screen tells you to sit back and relax while Publisher goes to work. Click on the Create It! button. A status bar appears indicating the progress of the job.

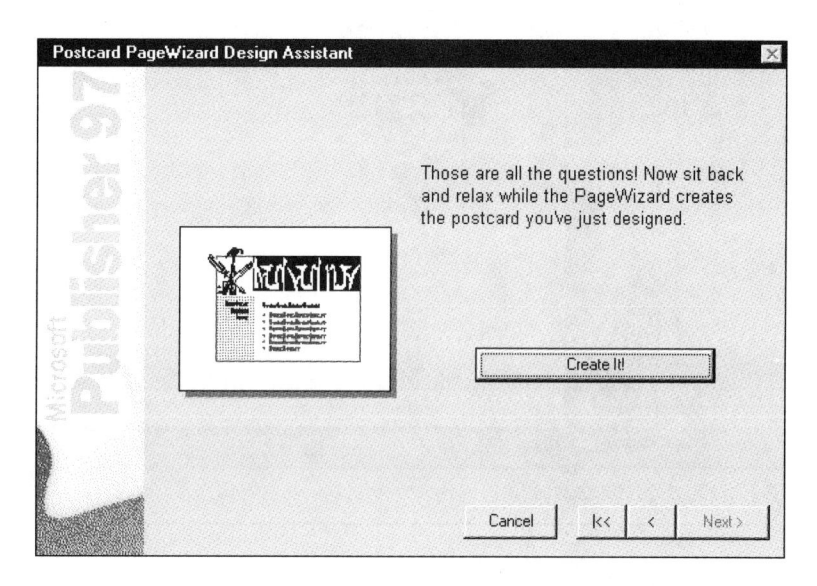

10. After the PageWizard is finished, another screen appears asking if you want step-by-step help as you add your own text and pictures. For the purposes of this exercise choose No, and click on the OK button.

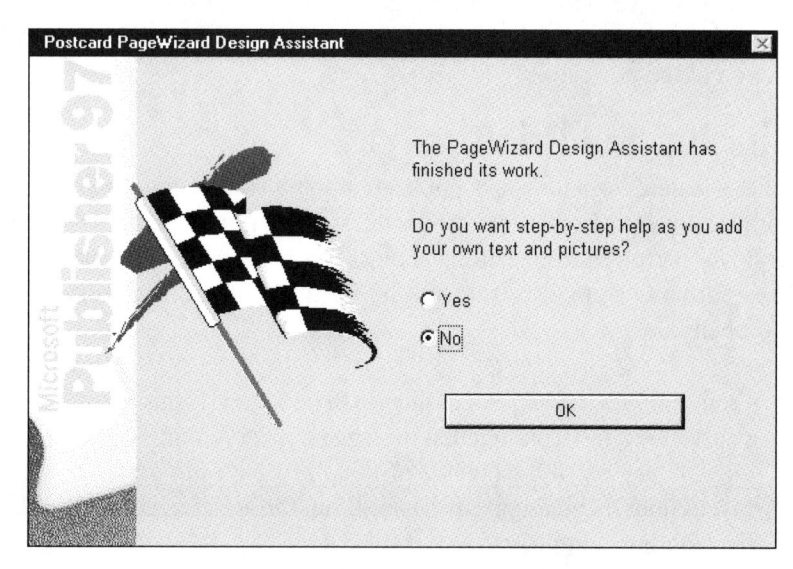

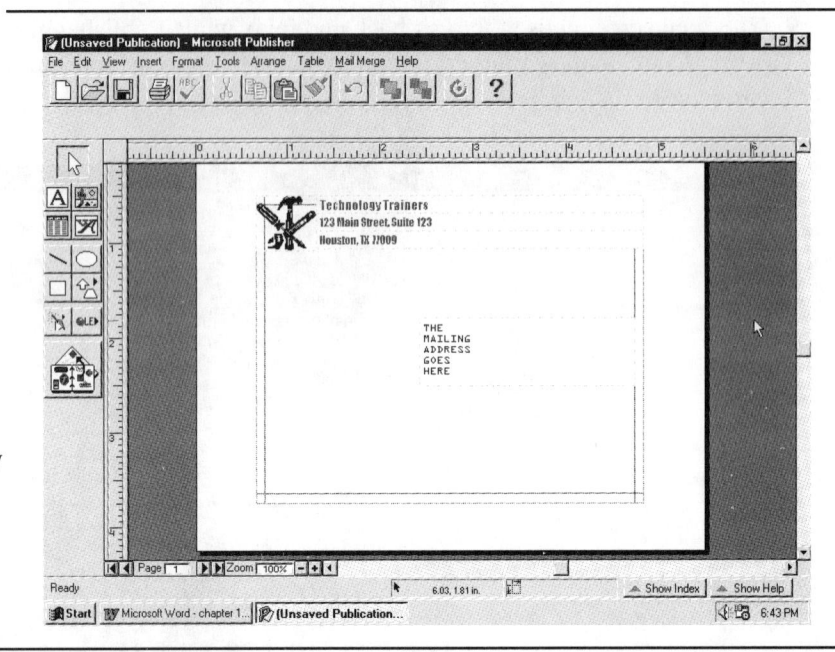

The Postcard PageWizard automatically created a two-sided (two-page) postcard

FIGURE 19-1

As shown in Figure 19-1, the first page of the postcard is displayed. Notice the company name and address appear in green in the top left corner. Before making any editing changes, the owners want to set up the postcard for printing by an outside company. They can still do rough drafts on the in-house color printer, but determining certain printing information before designing will help with the production of the postcard.

Setting up the Printer

Publisher's feature for setting up a publication for outside printing helps you select the right printer driver and other options for the specific printing process. The PostScript printer driver borrowed from Chroma Colors was installed but not selected.

The following steps illustrate setting up the postcard for printing by an outside company:

1. From the File menu, select Outside Print Setup. If this is the first time you've used this command, a message appears asking if you wish to see a quick overview of the outside printing process or to get step-by-step instructions as you work. If desired, run through the demo. If not, click on the Continue button.

2. The Outside Print Setup dialog box appears asking about the type of printing you will be using for the publication.

3. Select the last option, Spot Colors At Greater Than 1200 Dpi Resolution. The dialog box changes to let you select the spot colors you'll be using. Click on the down arrow by Spot color 1 and choose the color Teal. Remember this is just a representation of the spot color; the Pantone swatch book displays the actual ink color that will be used in the printing process. Click on the Next button.

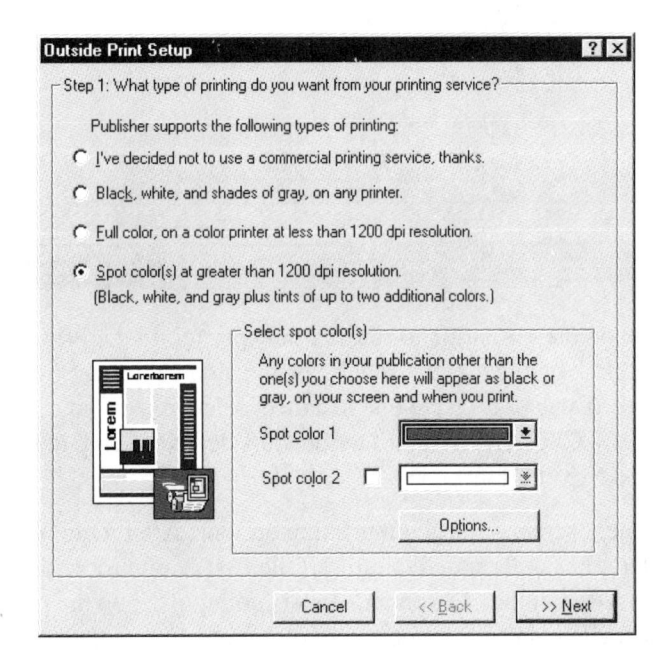

4. The next screen asks what printer will be used. The PostScript printer driver has been installed, but needs to be selected. Click on the option Select A Specific Printer.

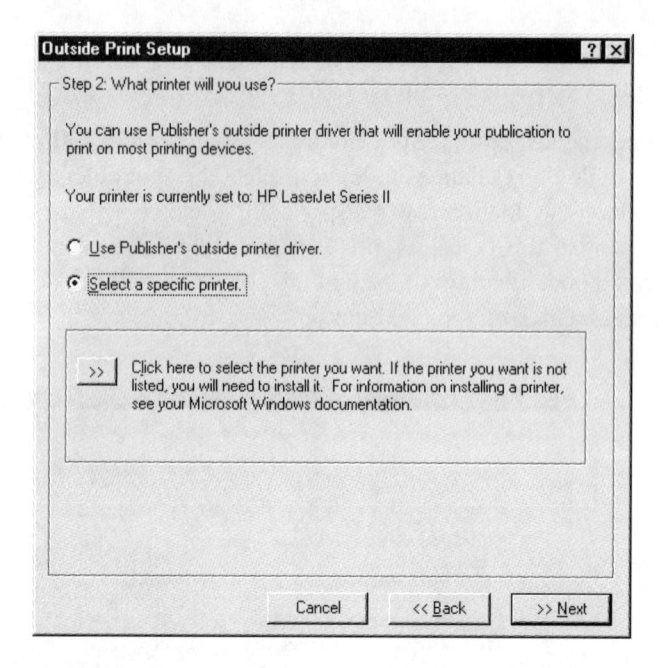

5. Click on the >> button to select a new printer. In the Print Setup dialog box, click on the down arrow by Name, and choose a PostScript printer driver. If you don't have one installed, select one of your available printers. Click OK to return to the Outside Print Setup dialog box. Click on the Next button.

6. The next screen asks about printing options. After a quick call to Chroma Colors, it is determined to turn off the first option for adding extra paper sizes. (Remember, Chroma Colors is going to set up the postcard to print 6 up.) Click on the first option to turn it off. The second option will be left on so crop marks will be printed, making it easy to trim the edges. Click on the Done button.

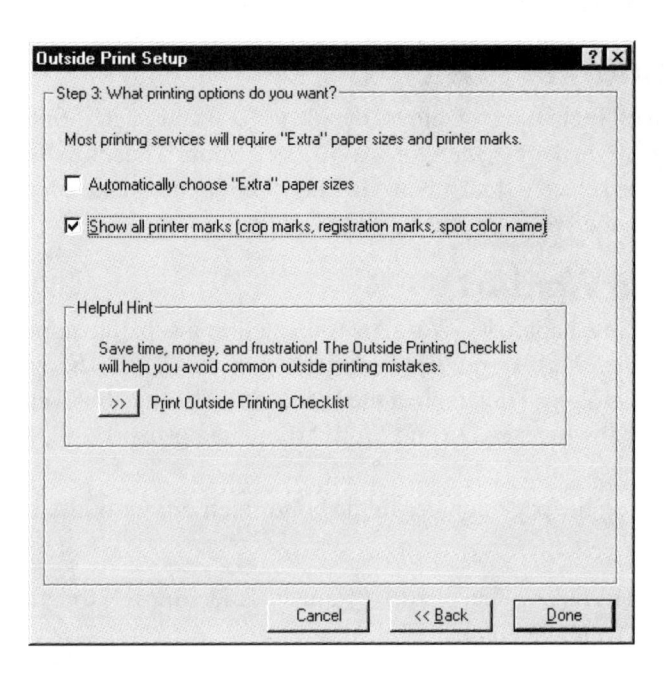

7. Publisher displays a message asking to update embedded objects. Basically, Publisher wants to check the settings used in the postcard design now that a new printer has been selected. Click Yes.

8. A yellow pop-up message appears informing you that since Publisher is now in spot-color mode, the color dialog boxes will only offer shades of black and the selected spot color. Other colors cannot be used. Notice how the company name and address are now gray.

9. After you start the postcard and select the printer, it's time to save the publication. From the File menu, select Save As. Enter **Internet class postcard** for the filename and save the file. After the initial save, the keyboard shortcut CTRL-S can be used for future saving.

Now it's time to begin customizing the postcard to meet the needs of Technology Trainers.

Designing the Postcard

The owners of Technology Trainers decide to focus on page 2 first, and then come back to page 1. On page 2, the WordArt ("Trade Show") needs to be edited, new clip art needs to be selected, and a new "tag line," bullet text, and directions need to be entered. First, the WordArt will be edited.

Editing the WordArt

As discussed in Chapter 13, WordArt is created in a separate application that runs within Publisher. WordArt provides a variety of effects that can be applied to text. The owners of Technology Trainers feel the WordArt looks fine, but want to edit the text.

Use the following steps to edit WordArt on the postcard:

1. Click on the page counter in the bottom left corner of the screen to view page 2.

2. Double-click on the WordArt frame ("Trade Show") to launch the WordArt application.

3. In the dialog box, enter **Surf the Web**, and click on the Update Display button.

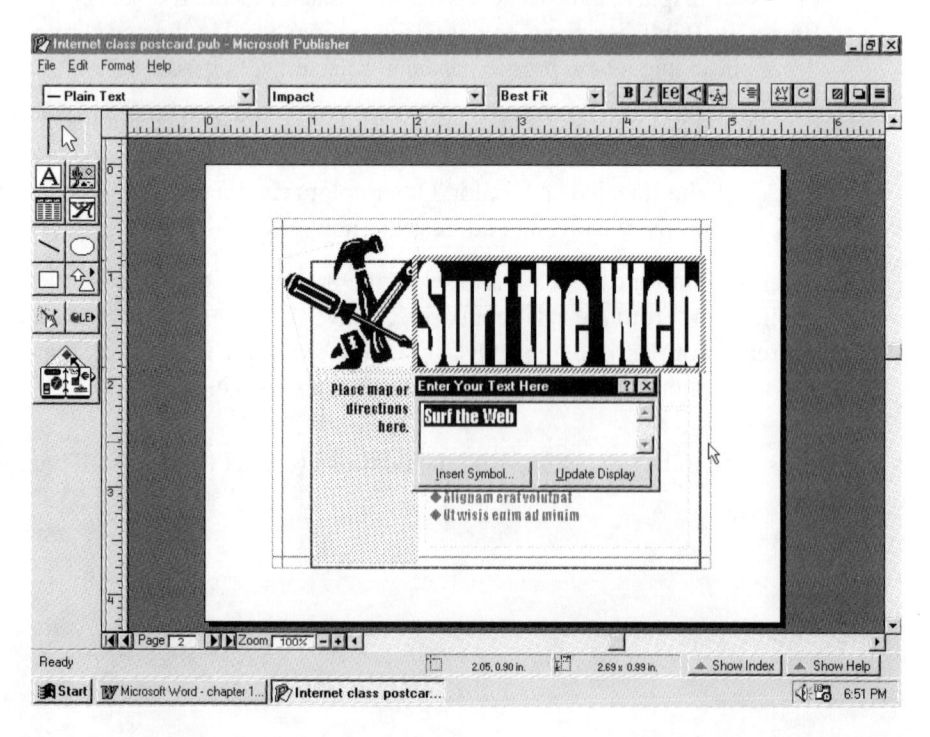

4. Click outside the dialog box to exit WordArt. The new text appears in the WordArt frame.

Now the clip art will be adjusted.

Selecting and Recoloring Clip Art

The owners want to replace the clip art of the hammer and other tools with clip art of a computer. They also want to use the teal spot color on the clip art, so the clip art will be recolored.

The following steps illustrate replacing the old clip art with new clip art and changing its color:

1. Double-click on the clip art to display the Microsoft Clip Gallery 3.0 dialog box.

2. Change the category to **Science & Technology**, and select the computer clip art shown in the illustration. Click on the Insert button.

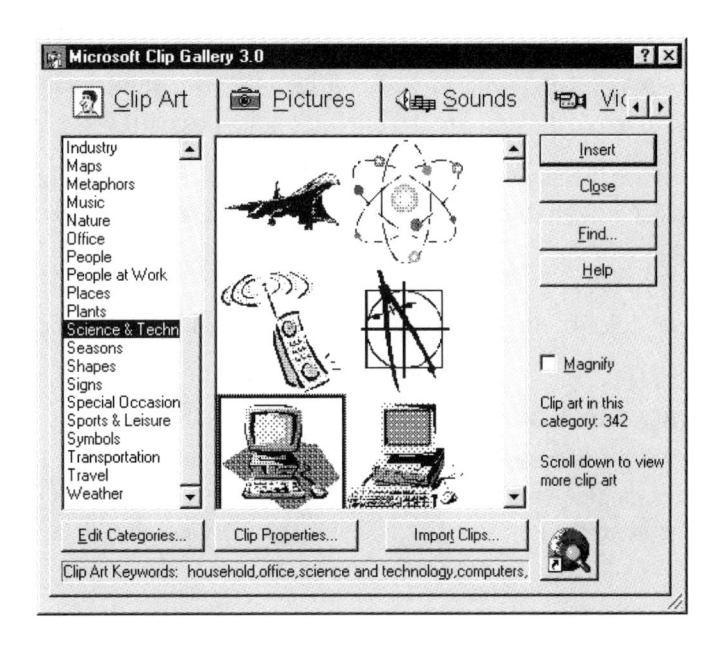

3. The Import Picture dialog box appears. To avoid distorting the clip art, stick with the default option, Change The Frame To Fit The Picture, and click OK.

4. Make sure the clip art is selected, and choose Recolor Object from the Format menu. Only shades of teal and black—the colors that will be used to print the postcard—are available in the dialog box.

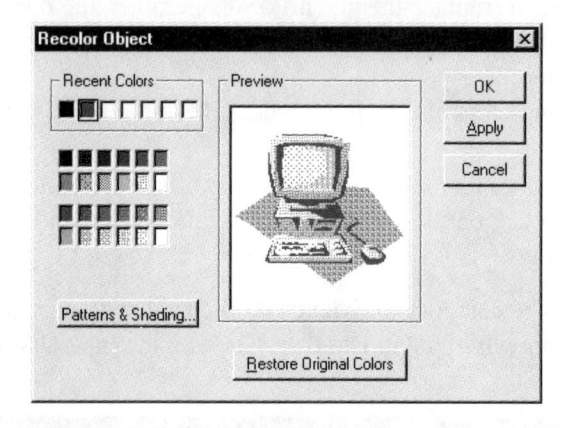

5. Select Teal—the preview displays the clip art in the selected color. Click OK to apply the color to the clip art on the postcard.

6. Click on the page counter to return to page 1. Select the clip art and replace it with the same clip art used on page 2. It also needs to be recolored.

Next, the color of the border surrounding the postcard will be changed.

Changing the Border Color

The border of a square surrounds the WordArt, clip art, and text. The border helps to tie the design elements together. The spot color teal will be applied to the border color. Remember, the *border* color is being changed, not the *fill* color.

Use the following steps to change the border color of the square around the page:

1. Return to page 2. Click on the outside edge of the square to select it.

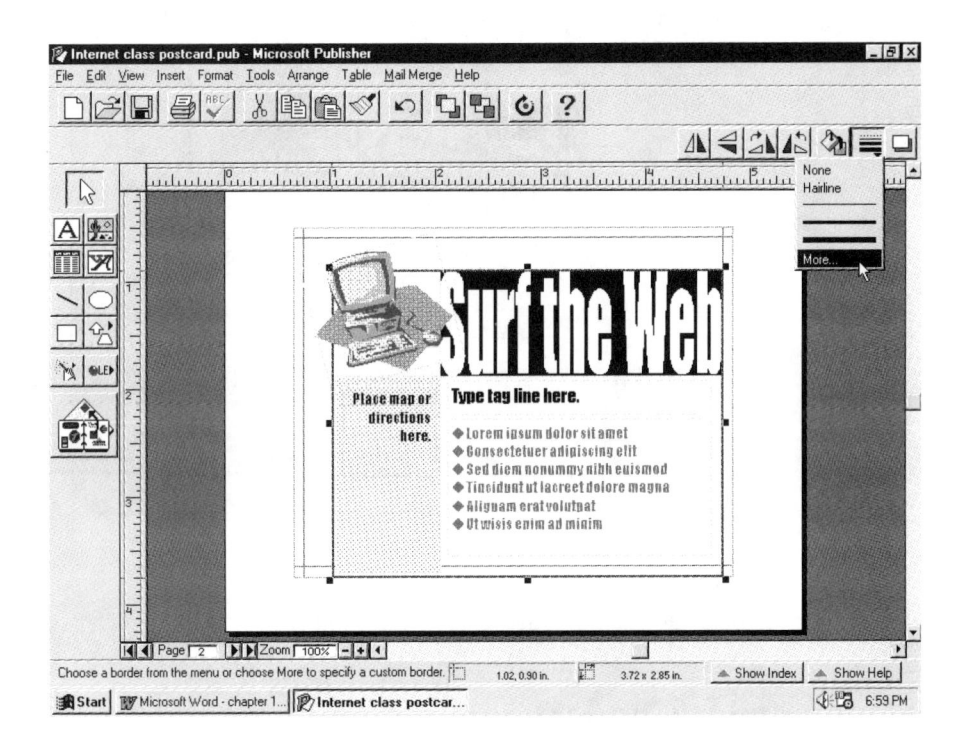

2. Click on the Border tool in the Formatting toolbar and select More.

3. In the BorderArt dialog box, click on the down arrow by Color and choose Teal. Again, notice that only shades of black and teal are available. Click OK to apply the color to the border.

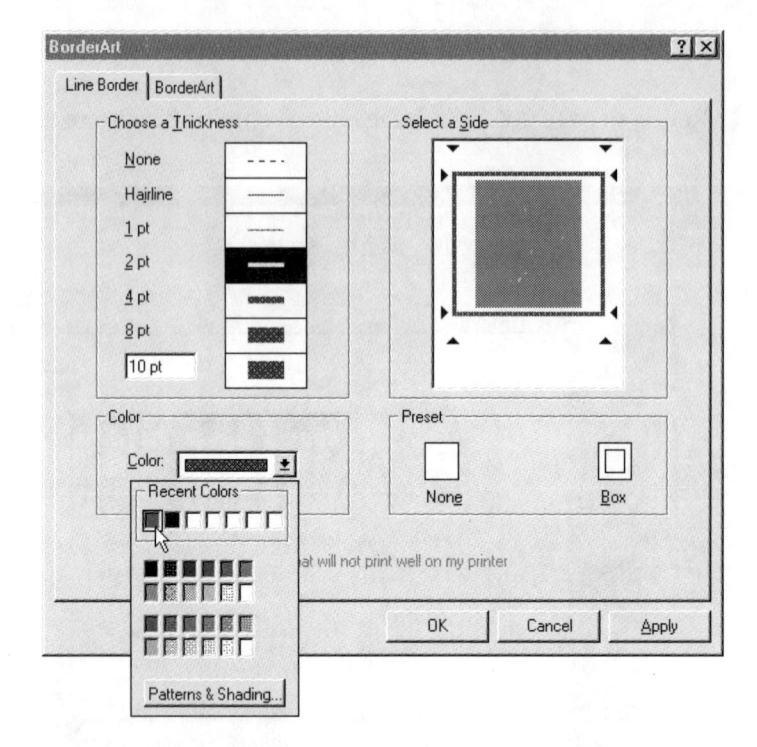

The next step is to add text about the Internet training classes.

Entering and Editing Text

The tag line and the bulleted text need to be replaced. The line spacing of the bullet text will be changed as well as its color. A spell check will also be run to detect errors.

1. Click once on the text "Type tag line here." The text is highlighted. Type **Internet Training—April 2, 18 and 24** to replace the old text.

2. Click on the bulleted text. Type in the following lines of text. Press ENTER after each line.

Course Materials Provided
30 Days Free Telephone Support
Convenient Location
Full Day of Training
$100 per participant

3. After entering all the bulleted text, select it. From the Format menu, choose Line Spacing. In the Line Spacing dialog box, click once on the up arrow by Between Lines to increase the spacing to **1.25**. Click OK.

4. Make sure all of the text is still selected, and click on the Font Color tool in the Formatting toolbar. Choose Teal.

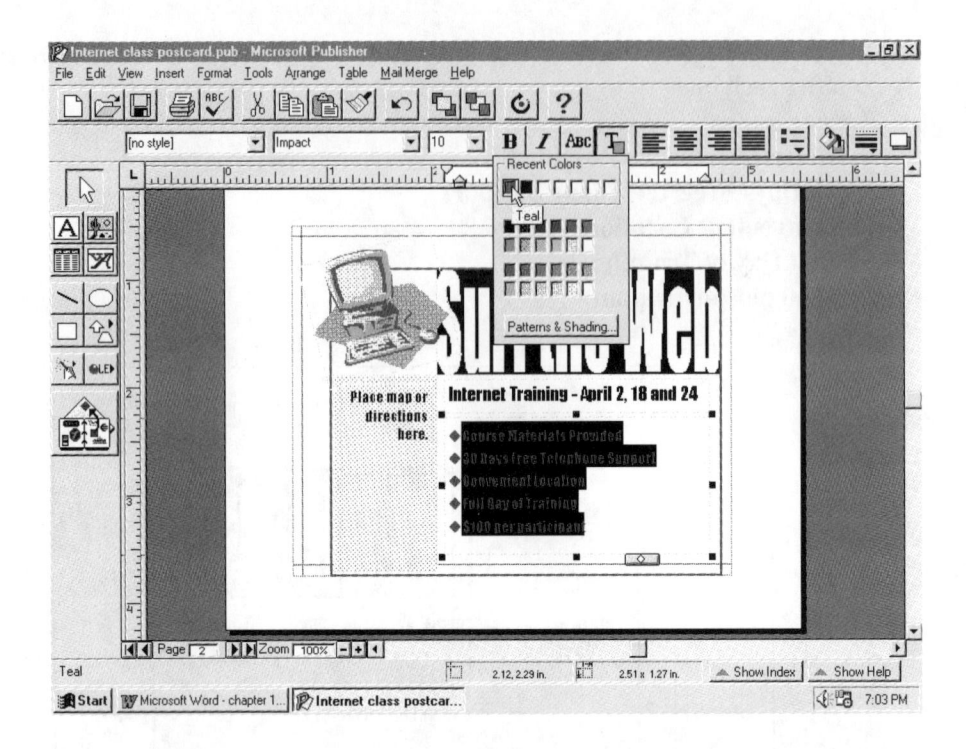

5. Click on the text "Place map or directions here," and enter **You'll find us at the Loop. Call 555-1234 to register.**

6. Press CTRL-SHIFT-O to hide the margin and column guides. This is how the publication will look when printed. Press CTRL-SHIFT-O again to redisplay the guides.

7. Display page 1. Drag across the company name in the return address to select it. Select black for the text color by using the Font Color tool. Repeat the steps for the rest of the return address.

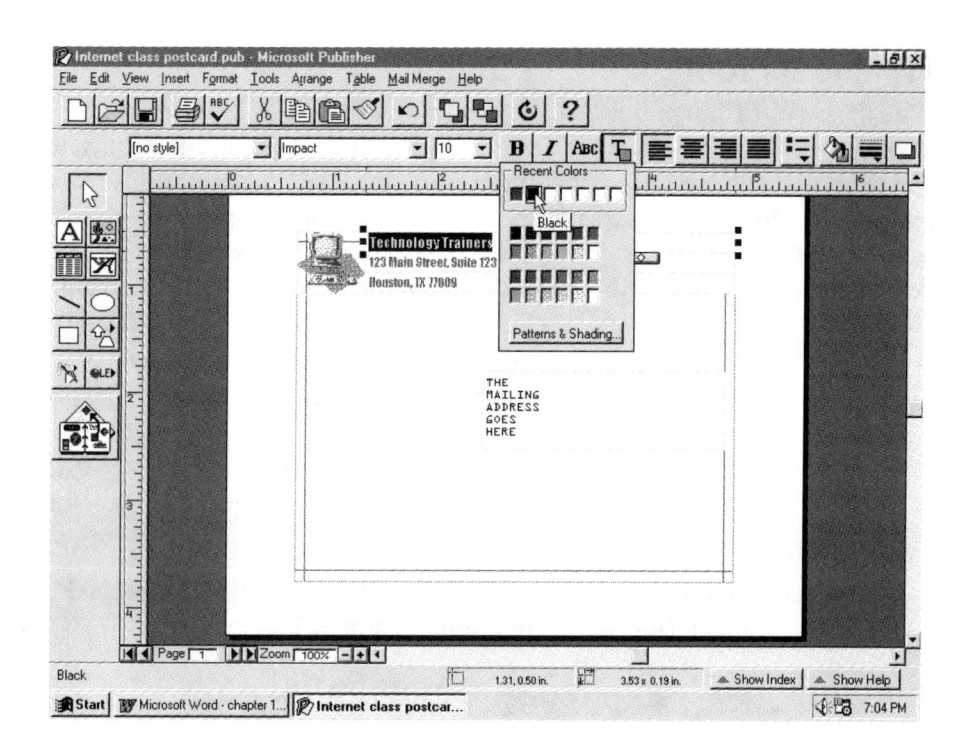

8. Since no more text will be added, it's time to run a spell check. Select one of the text frames, and click on the Spelling tool in the Standard toolbar. Correct any mistakes. The spell checker checks the whole publication. Remember, if no dialog box appears, no misspellings were found.

9. Hide the margin and column guides again if desired. Press CTRL-S to save the postcard publication.

A mailing label will be placed on the postcard to cover the "The Mailing Address Goes Here" text block. This text frame could also be deleted if desired.

With Publisher, the postcard was created quickly and easily. Pretty good, for a couple of novice page-layout artists!

Printing a Proof

With the postcard design finished, the owners of Technology Trainers want to print a *proof* of the postcard. A proof is a sample copy of the publication. Publisher allows you to select another printer just for printing proofs. Once the postcard is set up for outside printing, the in-house color printer at Technology Trainers can be selected as the proof printer. Although the postcard is composed for a PostScript output device, the proof printer will print a close approximation of the final output. The spot color will not match the output they will get from Chroma Colors, but the proof will help them check the placement of elements and the text formatting.

Use the following steps to set up a proof printer:

1. From the File menu, choose Print Proof. As discussed in Chapter 10, the Print Proof command is available only if you set up the publication for outside printing.

2. In the Print Proof dialog box, click on the down arrow by Name, and select a printer (just select your in-house printer).

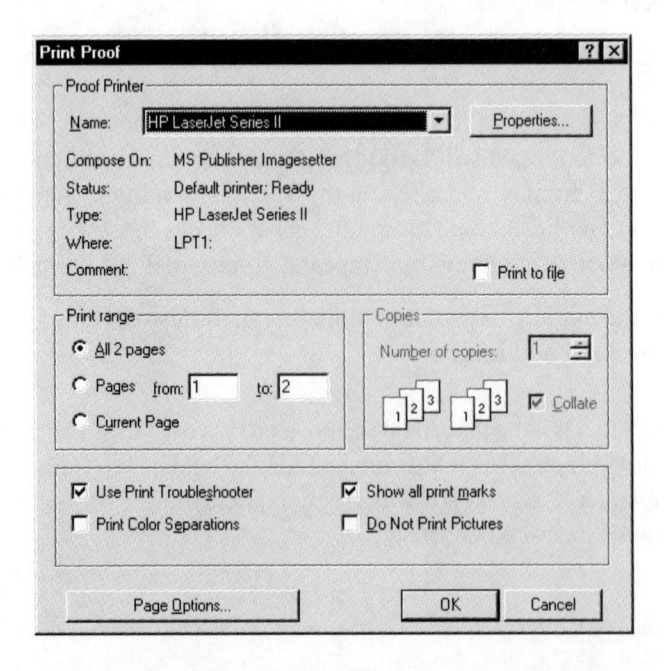

3. Click OK to print one copy of both pages of the postcard.

Now the owners can run the Publisher file over to Chroma Colors for output. Since this postcard has turned out so well, they decide to save it as a template for future use.

Saving a Template

A template will make it easy to start a new postcard with all of the text and clip art used in this postcard already in place. Refer to Chapter 5 for more information on saving and using templates.

1. From the File menu, choose Save As. Click on the Template option at the bottom of the Save As dialog box.

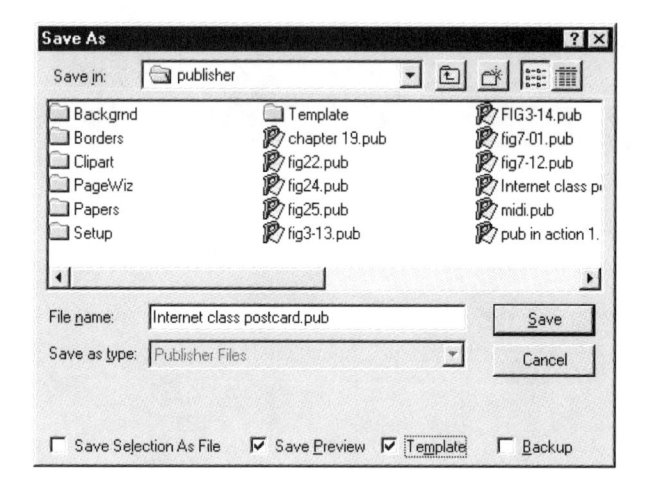

2. By default, Publisher saves templates in the Publisher\Template folder. Click on the Save button to save the file as a template.

You may not see a "Template" folder until you save a template. Publisher creates a folder with the name "Template" the first time you save a template.

Summary

Aside from deliberations on what text to add and what clip art to use, it took the owners of Technology Trainers less than 30 minutes to produce the postcard. The

Postcard PageWizard helped them create a professional-looking postcard without hiring a professional. In addition, they got acquainted with an outside printing service and acquired a copy of the printer driver the service wants them to use. The next time they produce a postcard it should go even quicker. All they have to do is start a new postcard using the old one as a template and tada!—much of the work is already done for them.

20

Producing Labels with Mail Merge

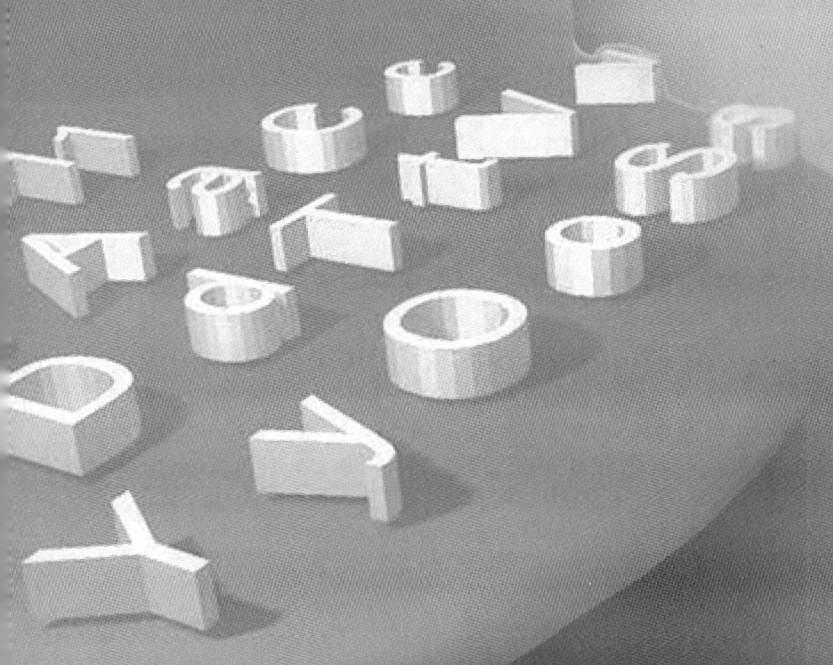

This is the last of three case-study chapters designed to show you how Microsoft Publisher can be used in the real world. This chapter focuses on producing mailing labels by use of Publisher's merge feature.

The chapter begins with a quick overview of the mail-merge process. Next it discusses the specifics about this case study—how the mailing labels will be used, where the mailing list comes from, and the mailing process used. Finally, it walks you through the actual steps for producing and printing the mailing labels in Publisher. Here you will find step-by-step instructions for using the Label PageWizard, creating and customizing an address list, inserting field codes, merging, and sorting the data. The steps were designed so you can follow along using the case study as a tutorial.

 **NOTE:** *See page 165 in the* Microsoft Publisher Companion *for information on creating successful mailings, building address lists, and deciding what class of mail to use.*

What Is Mail Merge?

Merging refers to the process of combining information from two sources to produce an entirely new document. One source is the data—in the case of mailing labels, the data source is the *address list.* As the name implies, the address list is composed of names and addresses. The other source is a label containing *field codes,* which show Publisher where to insert information from the address list. For instance, with the field codes you specify whether you want the company name to appear before or after the person's name. When the two sources of information are merged, the labels with the correct name and address are created.

 **NOTE:** *Merging is sometimes referred to as "mail-merge" because it is often used to mass-produce personalized form letters and mailing labels.*

Merging is handy for tasks that require the repetitive use of text. For example, you might create a merge document that contains the text of a letter you frequently send to clients. The text of the letter would always be the same, but the client information contained in the address list would vary for each letter. When you perform the merge, a document will be created with a letter for each client.

The Scenario

In Chapter 19, a postcard was created for Technology Trainers, a training company specializing in helping people access the Internet, set up intranets, and design web pages. The postcard announced dates for new Internet training classes.

Technology Trainers has a mailing list of 2,000 people. The list is composed of previous clients and other business acquaintances. Mailing labels need to be generated from this list and attached to the postcards. Rather than creating each label individually, the owners at Technology Trainers decide to use Publisher's mail-merge feature. Although it will take some time to enter all 2,000 names (you won't do that in the tutorial), once the list is created, it can be used again for future mailings.

The postcard will be sent through bulk mail, which requires that the pieces be sorted by ZIP code. Publisher's ability to sort the labels will be a great help here. The labels will be printed on a black-and-white laser printer.

Ready to Work: Using the Label PageWizard

20

The address list at Technology Trainers has never been entered into a software application before, so Publisher will be used to create the electronic address list. The Label PageWizard provides the easiest and quickest way to create labels and to set up for mail merge.

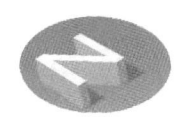

NOTE: *With the Label PageWizard you can create labels for audio and videocassettes, CD cases, and computer disks. You can even design labels for jars, bottles, and gift boxes! Thumb through the choices to see what is available.*

Publisher uses label styles from Avery to set up label sizes and dimensions. Technology Trainers will be using Avery label style 5061 for the mailing. If Avery labels are not used, you will have to set up the label size with the Custom page size option in the Page Setup dialog box. Refer to Chapter 5 for information on creating custom page sizes.

Use the following steps to start the postcard:

1. From the File menu, select Create New Publication. Make sure the PageWizard tab is selected at the top of the dialog box. Double-click on Label to start the PageWizard.

2. The first screen of the Label PageWizard asks what type of label will be created. Make sure Address Bulk Mailing is selected, and click on the Next button.

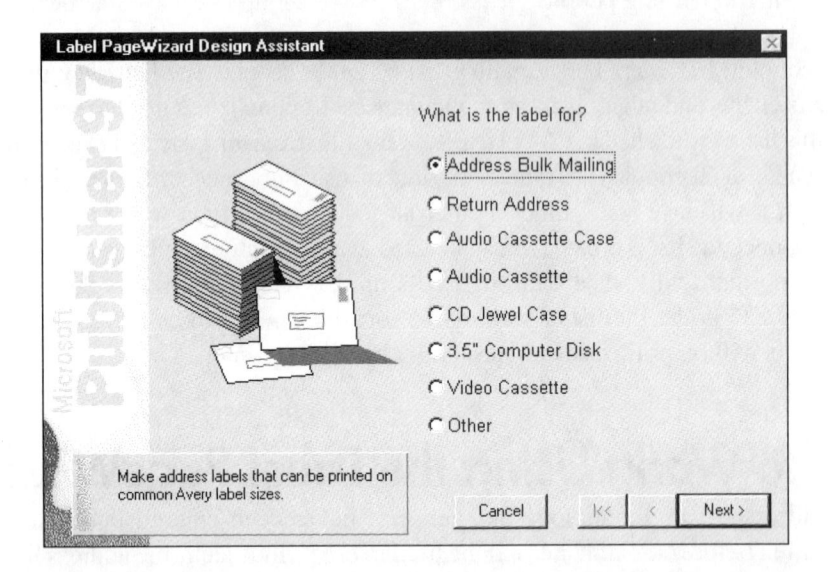

3. The next screen asks which style of Avery label will be used. For this tutorial, make sure Basic #5160 is selected, and click on the Next button.

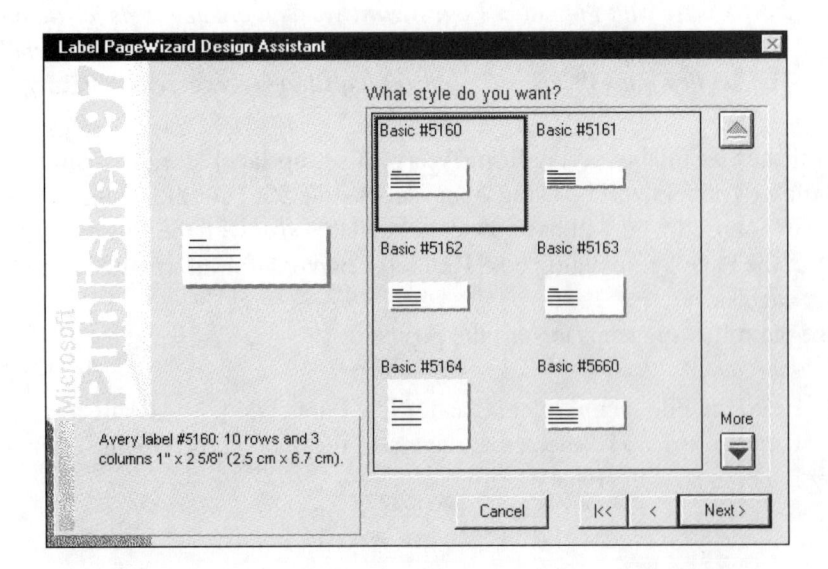

NOTE: *If you are using an Avery label style that is not listed, pick a basic style, such as Basic #5160. When the Label PageWizard is finished, select File | Page Setup. In the Page Setup dialog box, click on Labels—you will find a broader range of Avery label styles here. Just pick your label style and click OK. You may have to adjust the size of the text frame after selecting the new label style. Refer to Chapter 5 for more information on the Page Setup dialog box.*

4. The next screen asks if Publisher should set up for mail merge after the PageWizard creates the mailing labels. This is the easiest method, so click Yes and then click on the Next button.

5. The final screen warns that the label designs may exceed the printable region of the printer. The screen recommends a test sheet be printed first. Click on the Create It! button.

TIP: *Print a test sheet. It can save you time and headaches later if you know how your printer handles your labels. If the labels don't work with your printer, try another label size—there are many to choose from.*

6. After the PageWizard is finished, another screen appears asking if you want step-by-step help as you build the labels. For the purposes of this exercise choose No, and click on the OK button.

A label is displayed. You will replace the information on the label with field codes from your address list.

Creating an Address List

In the previous step 4, Publisher was instructed to set up for mail merge after creating the label, so it automatically continues with the mail-merge process. (If you see a message asking if you want to see a quick demonstration of mail merge or receive step-by-step instructions as you work, click on the Continue button. If you wish to view the demo later, select Help | Demos and choose Mail Merge from the Demos dialog box.)

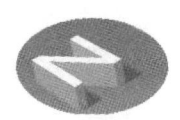

NOTE: *If you selected No in step 4 when the Label PageWizard asked to set up for mail merge, choose the Open Data Source command from the Mail Merge menu to begin creating an address list.*

As mentioned, the people at Technology Trainers have not entered the list into a software application, so the data source needs to be created. The following steps illustrate creating a data source:

1. After the PageWizard is complete, the next screen asks you to identify the data source (the address list). Click on the Create An Address List In Publisher option.

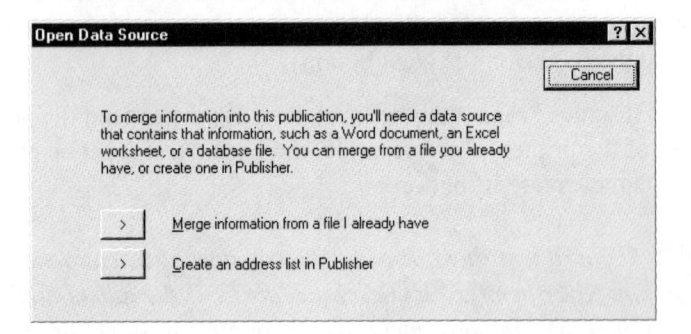

 **NOTE:** *Since many users will already have their data source in electronic format, the steps for importing a data source are covered in the section "Importing a Data Source."*

2. The New Address List dialog box appears. Information about each person on the mailing list is entered here.

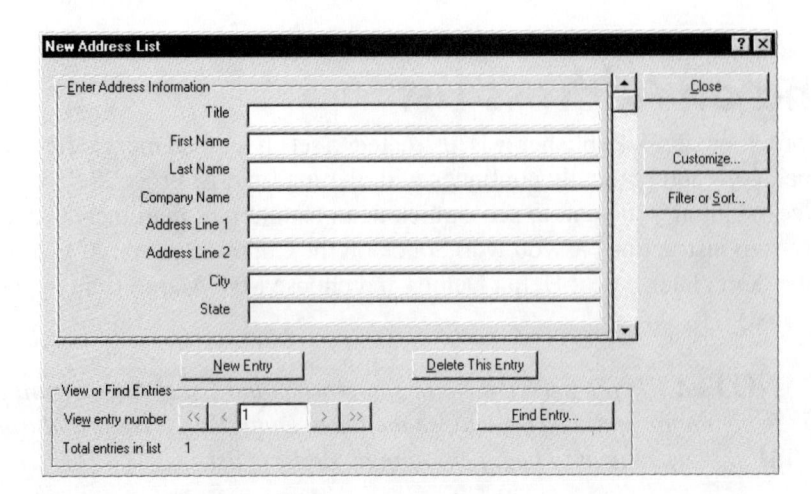

Each piece of information is called a *field*. For instance, City is a field and State is another field. A set of fields for one person is called a *record* or *entry*. Before information is entered, the field names will be customized to fit the needs of Technology Trainers.

Customizing an Address List

Publisher provides a default set of fields for creating address lists. You can add to the list, delete fields from the list, move the fields up and down in the list, and rename fields.

Use the following steps to customize an address list:

1. Click on the Customize button to display the Customize Address List dialog box. The owners of Technology Trainers do not want several of the fields to appear on the mailing labels, so they will be deleted.

20

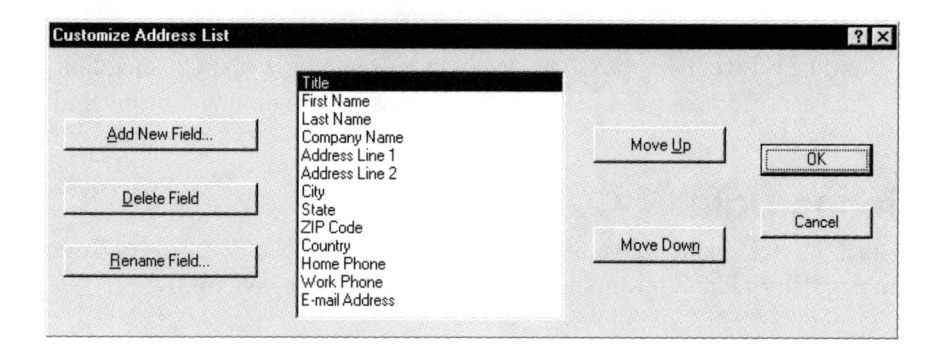

2. Make sure Title is selected, and click on the Delete Field button. A message appears to verify that you want to delete the field. The message also informs you that any information entered into this field will be deleted. For example, if you enter some Title information and then delete the Title field, the information is also deleted. Click Yes to delete the Title field. Repeat this step to delete the Country and Home Phone fields.

TIP: *Even if you don't plan on using a particular field in your mailing labels, you can still enter information in the field—you just won't add the field to the label. For instance, you may want to enter your clients' work phone number for reference purposes. However, the phone number wouldn't be placed on a mailing label.*

3. The people at Technology Trainers also want to rename the Company Name field. Select Company Name and then click on the Rename Field button. Enter **Organization** in the Rename Field dialog box and click OK.

NOTE: *Use the Add New Field button to add new information to the data source. For instance, you might add a field called Salesperson so you could enter the name of the salesperson responsible for the client.*

4. Click OK in the Customize Address List dialog box to return to the New Address List dialog box. The deleted fields are gone, and Organization replaces Company Name. Now the address information will be entered.

Entering Data

Now that the field names have been customized for the specific needs of Training Technology, the address information for each person can be entered.

1. At the top of the New Address List dialog box, enter **Bryce** in the First Name box. Press TAB and enter **Benjamin** in the Last Name box. Press TAB and enter **Benjamin Construction** in the Organization box. Continue entering the following information in the appropriate boxes:
   1234 Main Street
   Suite 100
   Baton Rouge
   LA
   66007
   (509) 555-1212
   benjamin@xxx.com

2. When you finish entering the data, click on the New Entry button. The entry is added to the address list. Notice in the bottom left corner that the

Total Entries In List is 2. In addition, the field boxes are cleared out, waiting for the next set of data.

3. Enter the following information to create two more entries. (Some information is purposely left blank—you can tell Publisher not to print a line of information if the field is blank. This is discussed in the "Printing Merged Labels" section.)

First Name	**Callan**	Cason
Last Name	**Kennedy**	Kanai
Organization	**Texas Oil**	Children's Hospital
Address Line 1	**1108 Fugate**	1700 Willowbrook
Address Line 2		**Suite 700**
City	**Houston**	Blue Springs
State	**TX**	MO
ZIP Code	**77009**	64063
Work Phone	**(713)555-1212**	(816)555-1212
E-mail Address	**ckennedy@xxx.com**	

4. After the last entry, click on the Close button to add it to the list. Do not click on the New Entry button—this makes a new entry with no information. Blank entries or records just add extra work later when merged and printed, because you have to delete them.

5. Publisher displays the Save As dialog box to save the data source (the address list). Enter **address list** as the filename. Don't worry about a filename extension; Publisher automatically adds .MDB as the extension. Change to the drive and folder where you want to save the file and click OK.

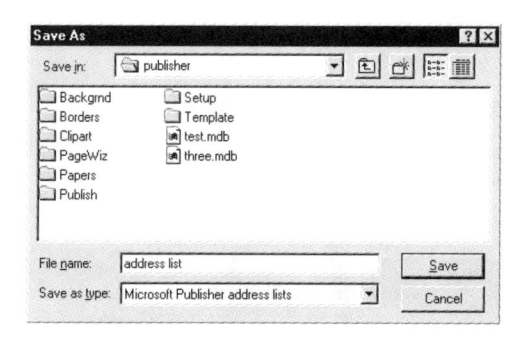

After the file for the list you have created is saved, a message appears asking if you want to merge information from the address list into your publication—click Yes. Publisher continues the mail-merge process by displaying the Insert Fields dialog box. But before you learn how to insert fields, the next section, "Importing a Data Source," shows how to import data already created in another program. If you have been performing the steps thus far on your computer, just read through the next section. You can resume following the steps in the "Inserting Fields" section.

Importing a Data Source

If you've already created an address list in another program, such as dBASE, or Microsoft Word, Excel, Access, Works, or FoxPro, you can import the data into Publisher. As discussed earlier, the Open Data Source dialog box is automatically displayed if you select Yes on step 4 while the PageWizard is creating the labels. If you selected No, choose Open Data Source from the Mail Merge menu to display the Open Data Source dialog box.

Use the following steps to import a data source for mail merge:

1. In the Open Data Source dialog box, click on the Merge Information From A File I Already Have option.

2. A dialog box appears where you can select the data source (address list) file. Click on the down arrow by Files Of Type and choose the appropriate format. For instance, if the data file was created in FoxPro, select Microsoft FoxPro (*.dbf).

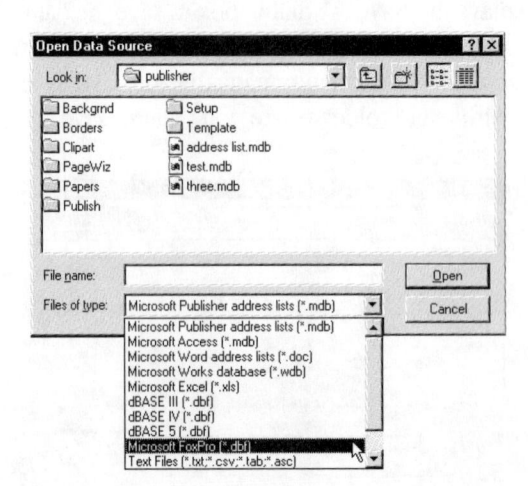

3. Select the file containing the data and click OK. The Insert Fields dialog box appears.

Inserting Fields

Once the data file has been created or imported, the next step for Technology Trainers is to specify where the names, addresses, and other information should be printed on the labels. This is done by inserting field codes on the label. There are several fields in the data source that the people at Technology Trainers do not want to appear on the mailing labels.

1. The Insert Fields dialog box is used to add fields to the label. To add the First Name field to the label, make sure it is selected, and click on the Insert button.

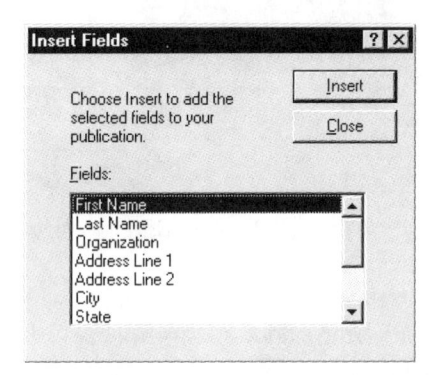

2. The field code for First Name is added to the label. (You will probably have to move the dialog box to get a good view of the label—just drag on the dialog box title bar.) The << and >> added around the field name are part of the code and should not be deleted. Notice that the insertion point appears after the field. Press SPACEBAR to add a space between the first name and last name.

3. Select Last Name in the dialog box and click on Insert. Press ENTER to start a new line.

4. Select Organization and click on Insert. Press ENTER to start a new line. Select Address Line 1, click on Insert, and press ENTER. Select Address Line 2, click on Insert, and press ENTER.

5. Select City and click on Insert. Now, enter a comma and press SPACEBAR. Select State and click Insert. Press SPACEBAR twice. Select ZIP Code and click on Insert. When finished, click on Close in the Insert Fields dialog box.

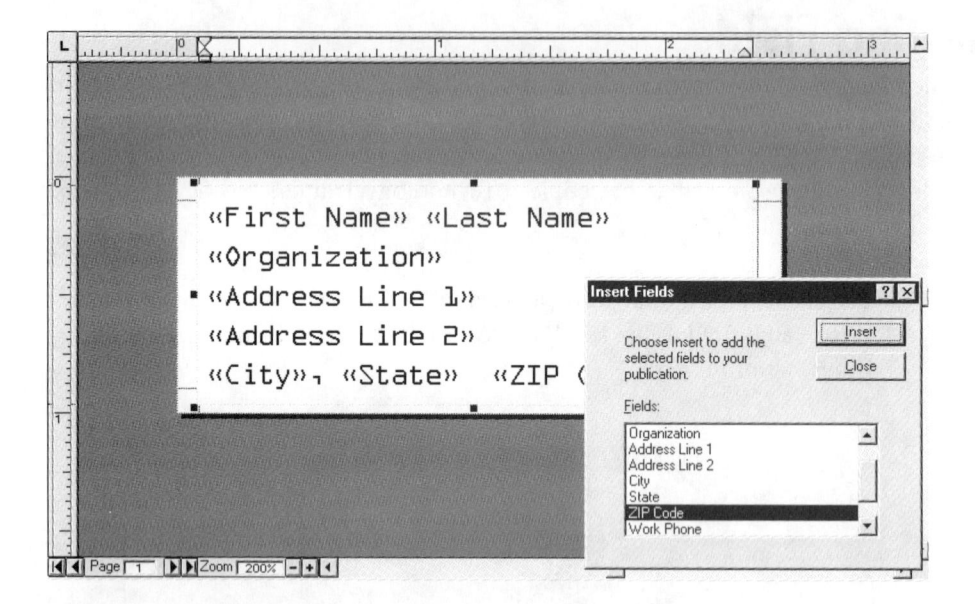

The field codes appear on the label. The address list will be merged with this label document to create the mailing labels.

Before continuing with the merge process, save the label with the field codes. (Remember the data source—the address list—was saved earlier.) From the File menu, select Save As. Change to the drive and directory where you want to save the file and enter the filename **mailing labels**. Publisher will add the .PUB filename extension. Click on the Save button to save the file.

Editing the Data Source

After creating the address list and inserting the fields, the owners of Technology Trainers discover mistakes in the data source. In this case, only the address information will be changed. However, if the actual field *names* were changed, the process of inserting fields onto the label might have to be redone. For instance, suppose you changed the field name Address Line 1 to Street Address. In this case, you would have to insert Street Address onto the label, and delete the reference to Address Line 1, since that field name no longer exists.

NOTE: *Once you've created or imported an address list, you can use Publisher as a basic database program. For instance, when you need to find a client's phone number, just select Edit Publisher Address List from the Mail Merge menu and locate the phone number.*

Editing the data source is also a way to view the contents of an imported data source. The following steps illustrate editing the data source:

1. From the Mail Merge menu, select Edit Publisher Address List. The Open Address List dialog box appears. Select address list.mdb—this is the name of the data file created by Technology Trainers. Click on the Open button.

2. A dialog box appears showing the information in the address list. The first entry is displayed—to view the next entry, click on the > button in the bottom left corner of the dialog box. Click on the >> button to view the last entry in the address list. Click on the < button to view the previous entry in the list. Click on the << button to view the first entry in the list.

3. Use the just-described navigation buttons to display the second entry. Click after "Texas Oil" in the Organization box, and add **Incorporated**. Display the third entry. Highlight the information in the City box (Blue Springs), and replace it with **Kansas City**. Click on the Close button.

NOTE: *To delete the displayed entry, just click on the Delete This Entry button in the Address List dialog box.*

Formatting Label Text

The people at Technology Trainers want to use another typeface on the mailing labels. Readability is an important issue when selecting typefaces and sizes for labels. If you decide to make formatting changes, do so *before* merging, so the changes affect all the new labels. You certainly don't want to format all 2,000 labels individually. Formatting the label text can be integral in getting the information to fit on the label. For instance, you can squeeze more information on the label if you reduce the type size and decrease the line spacing. Notice that the field names are placed in a text frame just like regular text in Publisher. You can also adjust the size of the text frame to control how the text appears on the label.

The following steps illustrate selecting a new typeface, modifying the line spacing, and adjusting the text frame size:

1. Make sure the insertion point appears in the text and press CTRL-A. This keyboard shortcut selects all of the text in the frame.

2. Click on the down arrow by the Font tool in the Formatting toolbar and select Times New Roman.

3. From the Format menu, select Line Spacing. In the Between Lines box, enter **1**, and click OK.

4. Click on the down arrow by the Size tool in the Formatting toolbar and select 10.

5. From the left side of the text frame, drag the sizing handle to the right about $\frac{1}{4}$ inch to decrease the frame size. This helps to center the text on the label.

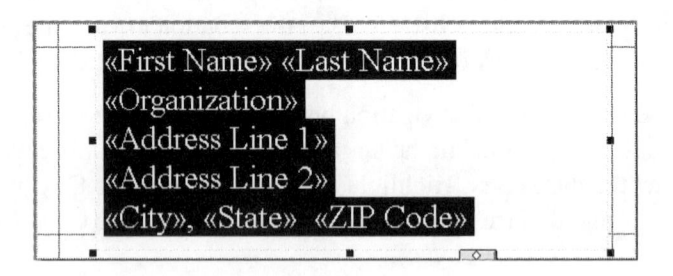

6. Press CTRL-S to save the formatting changes to the label.

When formatting text on labels, make sure all of the text is visible. If part of a field code is hidden, text on the labels might not be printed. You may find that after printing a test run of the labels, you need to tweak the formatting even more to get all of the address information to fit on the label.

Merging

The two sources of information—the data source and the label (complete with field codes)—have been created and saved. Now, Technology Trainers is ready to merge.

1. From the Mail Merge menu, select Merge. The field codes are replaced with information from the first entry in the data source.

2. Publisher displays the Preview Data dialog box to help you view the other labels. (You will probably have to move the dialog box to get a good view of the labels—just drag on the dialog box title bar.)

3. To view the second entry, click on the > button. Click again to view the third entry. Click on the |<< button to view the first entry.

4. When finished, click on the Close button. The field codes reappear on the label.

The files are merged; you do not need to use the Merge command again. If you wish to see the labels with the address information, select Show Merge Results from the Mail Merge menu. The Preview Data dialog box returns, and you can use it to view the labels.

If you wish to disconnect the label from the data source (the address list) and cancel the mail merge, select Cancel Merge from the Mail Merge menu. The publication is disconnected from its data source, and the field codes are converted to regular text.

Sorting the Merged Labels

After viewing the merged labels, the owners of Technology Trainers remember the bulk-mail process requires mail to be sorted by ZIP code. Rather than sorting by hand, they decide to have Publisher sort the labels by ZIP code. The people at Technology Trainers can then sort the postcards as they apply the labels.

Use the following steps to sort the merged labels by ZIP code:

1. From the Mail Merge menu, select Filter Or Sort. The Filtering And Sorting dialog box appears. Click on the Sort (Change Order Of Entries) tab.

2. Click on the down arrow under the heading Sort By This Field, and select ZIP Code. Make sure Ascending order is selected. Click OK.

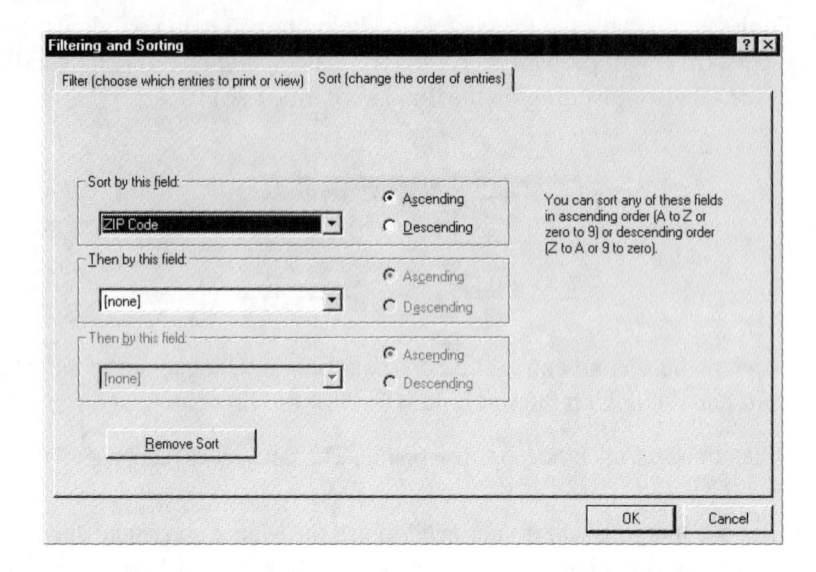

3. To see the sorted labels, select Show Merge Results from the Mail Merge menu. Use the buttons in the Preview Data dialog box to move through the labels.

4. When finished, click on the Close button.

With the information merged and sorted, Technology Trainers is ready to print the labels!

Printing Merged Labels

Technology Trainers will do a test print first to make sure the address information fits properly on the labels. After the testing, all of the labels will be printed.

 **NOTE:** *Refer to Chapter 10 for more information on selecting printers, using the Print Troubleshooter, and printing to file.*

Use the following steps to print a test of the mailing labels:

1. From the File menu, choose Print Merge—you can also press CTRL-P. The Print Merge dialog box is displayed.

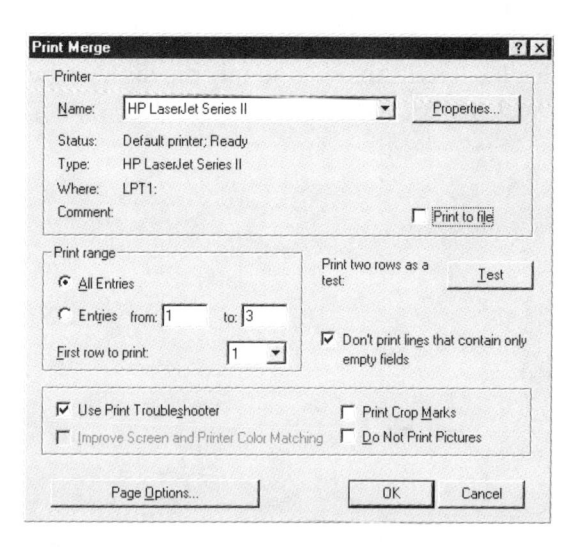

2. Recall that several fields were left blank in the address list. However, the people at Technology Trainers do not want these to appear as blank lines on the labels. Make sure the Don't Print Lines That Contain Only Empty Fields option is turned on, so blank lines do not appear on the labels.

3. Click on the Test button by Print Two Rows As A Test. A message appears indicating the progress of the print job. The selected printer prints the first two rows. The Print Merge dialog box stays on screen.

4. The test looks good, so Technology Trainers is ready to print all the labels. Under Print Range, make sure All Entries is selected, and click OK.

The people at Technology Trainers can now apply the labels (and stamps) to the postcards.

Summary

The most time-consuming task of generating mailing labels is entering address information—it takes time to enter 2,000 names. However, now that the address list is created, Technology Trainers can use it again and again to quickly produce mailing labels for future postcards and newsletters. If the owners of Technology Trainers use the same size of labels and the same address list, they can just repeat the printing steps whenever they need some labels. To add new clients to the address list, they can use the Edit Publisher Address List commands discussed in this tutorial. If they choose to use another label style, they can simply run through the Label PageWizard to set up another label source, and connect it with the existing data source—their address list.

Installing Microsoft Publisher

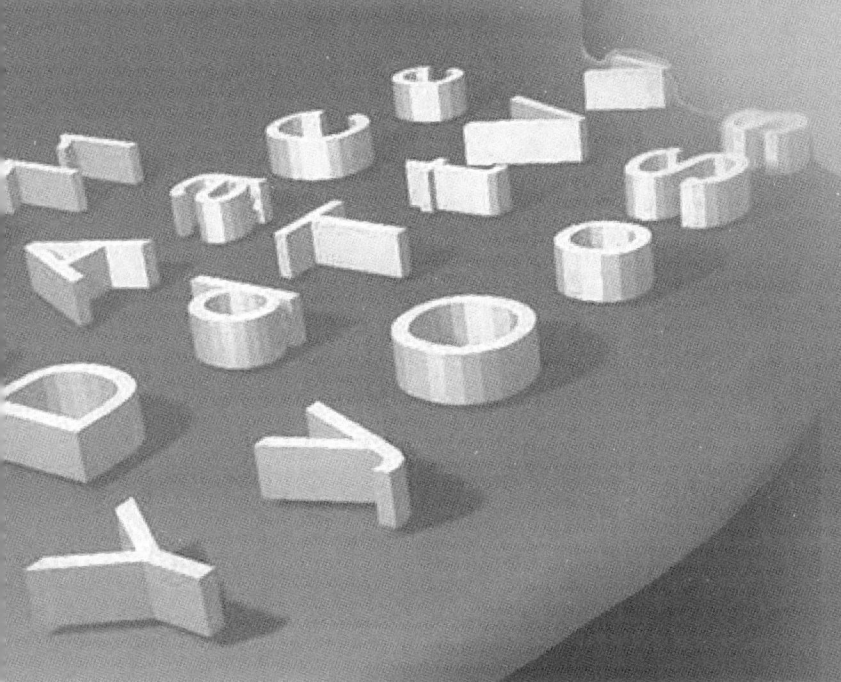

Before you can join in the fun of producing publications with Microsoft Publisher, you'll need to install the software on your computer's hard disk. Publisher uses a Setup program that prompts you for information as the software is being installed. If you've never installed software, don't fret—it's a relatively painless procedure.

Before You Begin

Microsoft Publisher 97 is designed to run under the Windows 95 operating environment. You can also run it with Windows NT. (Publisher will not run under Windows 3.1.) Windows 95 or Windows NT must already be installed on your computer before you can install Publisher.

If you have a previous version of Publisher, the Setup program will detect the earlier version and suggest that you install Publisher 97 in the same drive and folder as the earlier version. The Setup program updates the program files and removes any files that are no longer needed. You don't need to worry about losing any publication files—the Setup program does not overwrite existing publication files.

NOTE: *Publications created in Publisher 97 cannot be opened in earlier versions of Publisher. However, publications created in earlier versions can be opened in Publisher 97.*

At any time you can go through Publisher's Setup program again to install new items or reinstall the whole program if you accidentally delete files or need to overwrite corrupt files.

Hard Disk Space Requirements

You will need 117 MB of available hard disk space for a typical installation of Microsoft Publisher. You will need at least 9.5 MB of available space on the drive that contains Windows 95 for the Setup program to install *all* of the Publisher utility and system files. You'll need less if you don't want to install the text converters, fonts, graphic filters, speller, Setup files, mail-merge components, or

Microsoft Draw. (Refer to the section "Custom Installation Options" for information on not installing certain components.) If there is not enough space on the drive where you want Publisher installed, you'll need to make room on that drive before installing Publisher.

Skip the Virus Detection

Publisher's Setup program will not install Publisher to a machine with virus protection turned on. To successfully install Publisher, you need to remove the virus protection software from memory. To remove the virus protection software from memory, disable your virus protection software (see your virus protection software manual for instructions). Then restart your computer. Run Publisher's Setup program. After Setup is complete, turn on your virus protection software again.

Your Publisher floppy disks have already been checked for viruses by Microsoft. Do not check them for viruses yourself. Virus-checking software can corrupt the disks and prevent you from successfully installing Publisher.

Preparing to Install

First, make sure that Windows 95 or Windows NT is running. Close any open programs (except Windows)—if you don't, the Setup program will recommend that you exit the programs before continuing the installation.

TIP: *If you get error messages while trying to install Publisher from the CD, try gently cleaning the disc. Any marks or smudges may prevent the laser from correctly reading your disc. If this doesn't solve the problem, call the Microsoft Order Desk at 800-360-7561 between 7:00 A.M. and midnight Eastern time, Monday through Friday, to order another CD. You could also try exhanging the disc at the store where you purchased it.*

Starting the Setup Program

1. Insert the Publisher CD-ROM or Setup Disk 1 into the appropriate drive. Depending on your computer, if you're installing from a CD-ROM for the first time, the Setup program may start automatically. If that happens, skip to the next section, "Installing Publisher."

2. Click on the Start button on the taskbar. (You can also press CTRL-ESC to display the Start menu.) From the menu, select Settings and then click Control Panel.

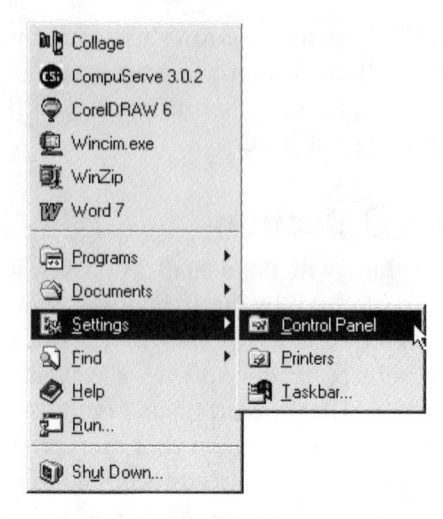

3. Double-click on the Add/Remove Programs icon in the Control Panel.

4. In the Add/Remove Programs Properties dialog box, make sure the Install/Uninstall tab is selected at the top. Click on the Install button.

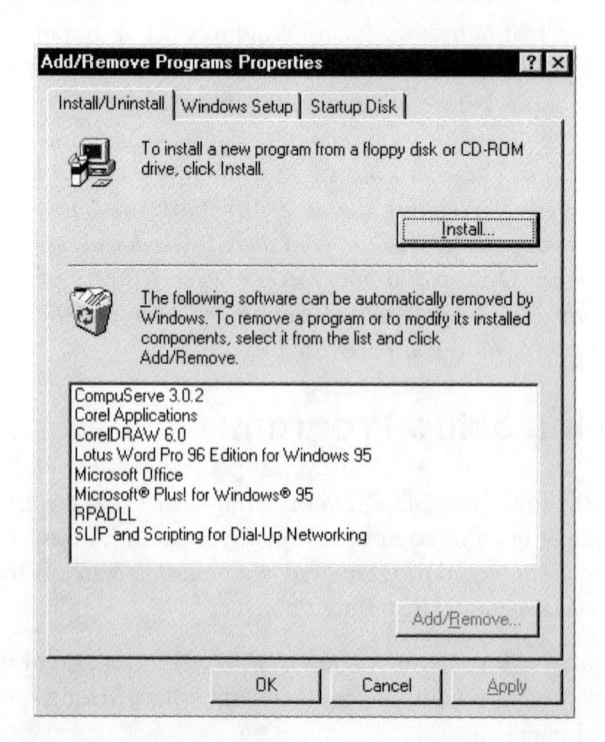

5. The next screen asks you to install the first installation floppy disk or the CD-ROM. This was already done in step 1, so click on the Next button.

6. Windows searches the disk drives for installation files. The screen displays the path and filename of the Setup program—setup.exe. If you are installing from floppy drives, the path might read "A:\setup.exe." If you are installing from a CD-ROM drive, the path might read "D:\setup.exe." If the search did not locate the right file, click on the Browse button, change to the drive where the Publisher disk is, and select the setup.exe file.

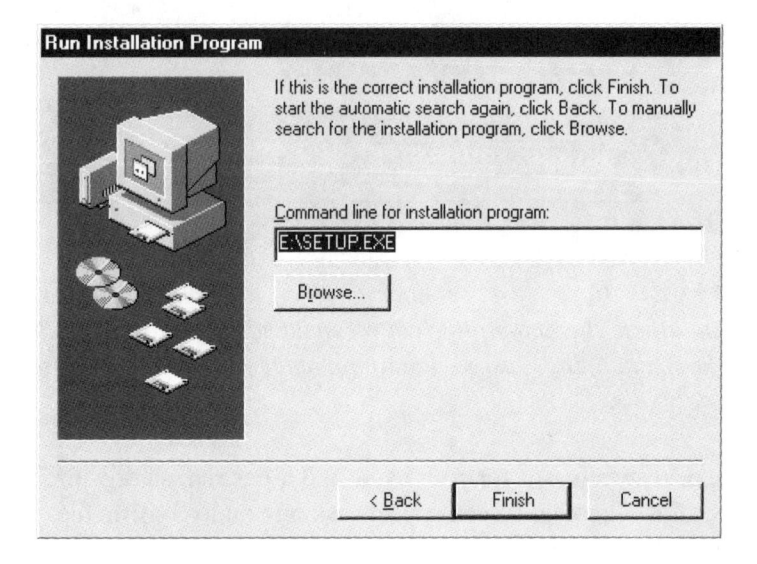

7. Click on the Finish button.

Installing Publisher

Before you begin installing, keep in mind that the setup process is complex. The large number of files in the Publisher package, including font and clip-art files, may require 15 minutes or longer to install, depending on the type of computer. Although the setup process takes a relatively long time, that doesn't mean there is a problem. As long as the setup progress bar moves occasionally, Setup is probably working correctly.

1. After a few seconds, the Microsoft Publisher 97 Setup begins. The opening screen welcomes you to the installation program and recommends you read the License Agreement. Click on the Continue button.

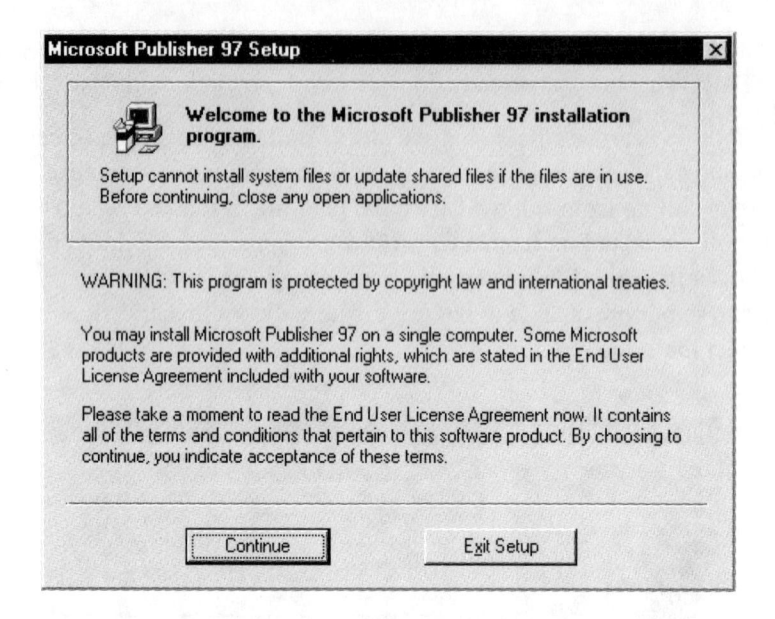

NOTE: *If you are running another program when you begin the installation, the Setup program recommends you close the other program before continuing. Just switch to the other program, and close it down as you would normally.*

2. The next screen asks for your name and if desired, an organization name. Click OK—another screen appears asking you to confirm the information. Click Change to redo the information, or click OK to continue the installation.

3. The next screen asks for your 10-digit CD key number. This number is on the back of your CD case. You will need this number every time you install Publisher or one of its components. After entering the number, click OK.

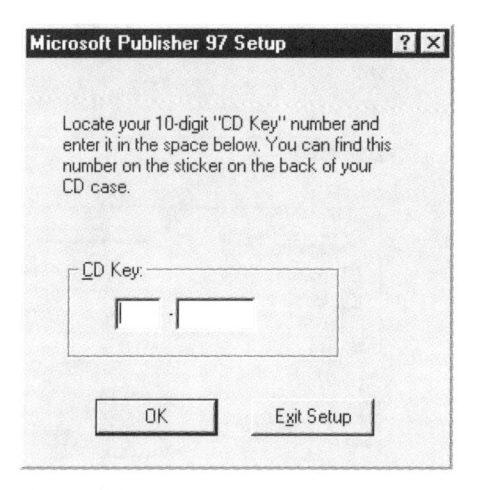

4. The next screen displays your product information number. You will be asked for this number when you call Microsoft Technical Support about Publisher. Once Publisher is installed, you can access this number from the About command in the Help menu. Click OK to continue.

NOTE: *At any time, you can click on the Exit Setup button to halt the installation.*

5. The next screen lets you specify where to install Publisher. If the drive and folder displayed in the path line is where you want Publisher installed, click OK. If not, click on the Change Folder button. In the Change Folder dialog box, select the drive and folder where you want to install Publisher. You can create a new folder by selecting the desired drive and then entering the new folder name in the Path box. Click OK to return to the previous dialog box. If the specified folder is correct, click OK.

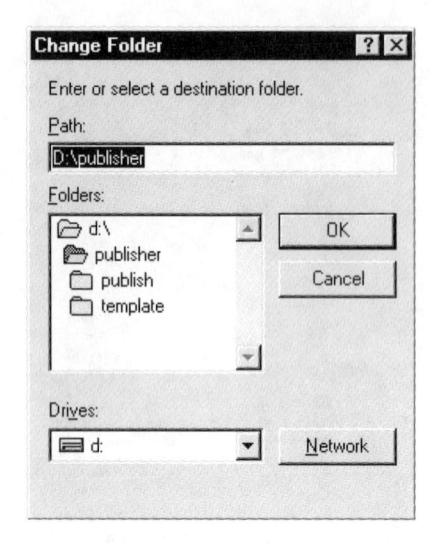

 **NOTE:** *Microsoft Publisher will not install to the root directory of a hard disk (for example, C:\ or D:\). Publisher must be installed in a subdirectory, such as C:\Publisher.*

6. At this point you have two options for installing Publisher. Click on the Complete Installation button to install the files necessary to run Publisher.

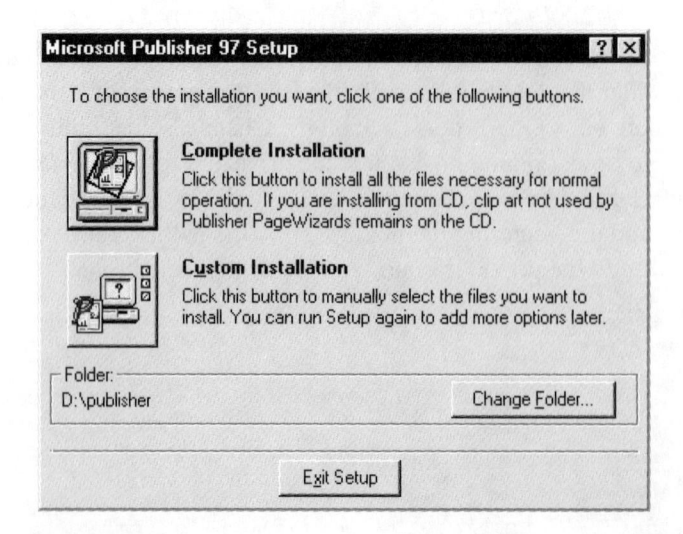

7. A message appears indicating the Setup program is checking for the necessary disk space. If there is enough space, the installation begins. A status bar shows the progress of the installation.

8. When the installation is complete, a dialog box appears announcing the successful installation of Publisher. Click OK to return to the Windows desktop. You can now run Publisher. You do not have to restart your computer before launching Publisher.

Complete Installation is the best option if you have enough room on your hard disk. You will be installing the PageWizards, fonts, and clip art used in the PageWizards. Complete installation also installs the mail-merge tools and Microsoft Draw, a drawing application discussed in the section on recoloring clip art in Chapter 9. Graphic filters and text converters, which enable Publisher to read pictures and text created in other programs, are also installed.

NOTE: *Screen-saver software can interfere with the setup process, so Setup automatically turns off your screen saver while installing Microsoft Publisher. Setup will restart your screen saver after installing Publisher. If your screen saver does not start automatically, you can restart it manually after Setup is finished.*

Custom Installation Options

If you are low on hard disk space, or want to limit the options that are installed, use the Custom Installation option. Custom Installation is also handy to copy all of the clip art from the CD onto your hard drive. The following steps discuss the options available.

NOTE: *The fonts, PageWizards, and demo files are stored on the same drive as Windows. For example, you might specify the D:\ drive for the Publisher program files, but the fonts, PageWizards, and demos are stored on the C:\ drive where Windows is loaded.*

1. Click on the Custom Installation button to show a screen displaying an Options list. By default, all of the options will be installed. If you do not want an option installed, click on the check box to the left of the option to remove the check mark.

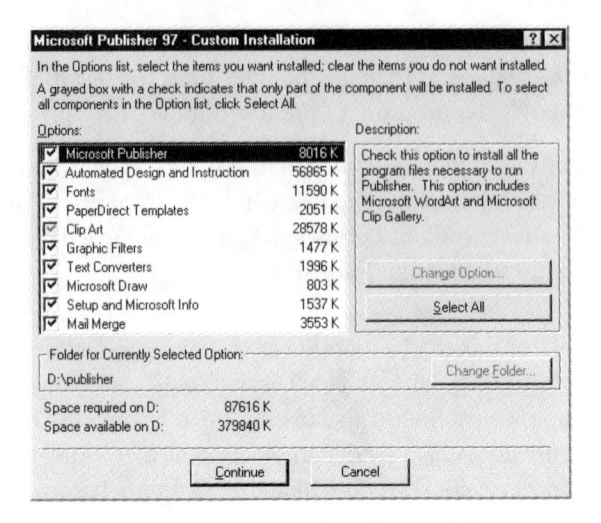

2. The dialog box includes three important pieces of information. First, the amount of space required to install each option appears to the right of the option name. For instance, the PaperDirect templates use 2051K of hard disk space. Second, when you click on the option name, a description of the option appears on the right. Third, the hard disk space required to install the selected options, as well as the space available, appears in the bottom left. Use the following information to help you determine whether you need to install an option:

■ The *Microsoft Publisher* option installs the files necessary to run the program. If you are installing Publisher for the first time, make sure this option is selected. However, if you have already installed Publisher and just want to add some other options, turn off this option.

■ The *Automated Design and Instruction* option installs Publisher's PageWizards and demonstrations. You must install this option to take advantage of the predesigned PageWizards, which make Publisher so easy to use.

■ The *Fonts* option installs Publisher's collection of fonts. If you do not install the fonts, a substitute font will be used on the PageWizard designs. The substitute fonts may not look as good as the Publisher fonts. However, if you are low on disk space and have fonts installed through other applications, you could turn off this option. If you later discover you need the fonts, run through the Setup program again and install the fonts.

- The *PaperDirect Templates* option installs paper templates to use with special PaperDirect paper choices. You might elect not to install this option if you are trying to conserve disk space.

- By default, the *Clip Art* option installs clip art used in the PageWizard publication designs. For additional choices, select the Clip Art option, and click on the Change Option button. In the Clip Art dialog box, the first option, View Clip Art In Clip Gallery, should be selected if you want to be able to preview all of the available clip art, whether it is on your hard drive or on the Publisher CD. If this option is not selected, you will only see previews of clip art loaded on your hard drive. The next option, Copy All Clip Art, copies all of the clip art on the CD to your hard drive. This takes a considerable amount of hard disk space (174,144 K), so make sure you have the room. After making your selections, click OK to return to the Custom Installation dialog box.

- The *Graphic Filters* option installs filters for importing graphics or pictures created in other applications. To specify which filters are installed, click on the Change Option button. In the Graphic Filters dialog box you can remove the check mark by the graphic formats you will not be using. For instance, you might choose not to install the filter for the WPG WordPerfect Graphic. Again, remember you can always come back and install the filters if necessary. After making your selections, click OK to return to the Custom Installation dialog box.

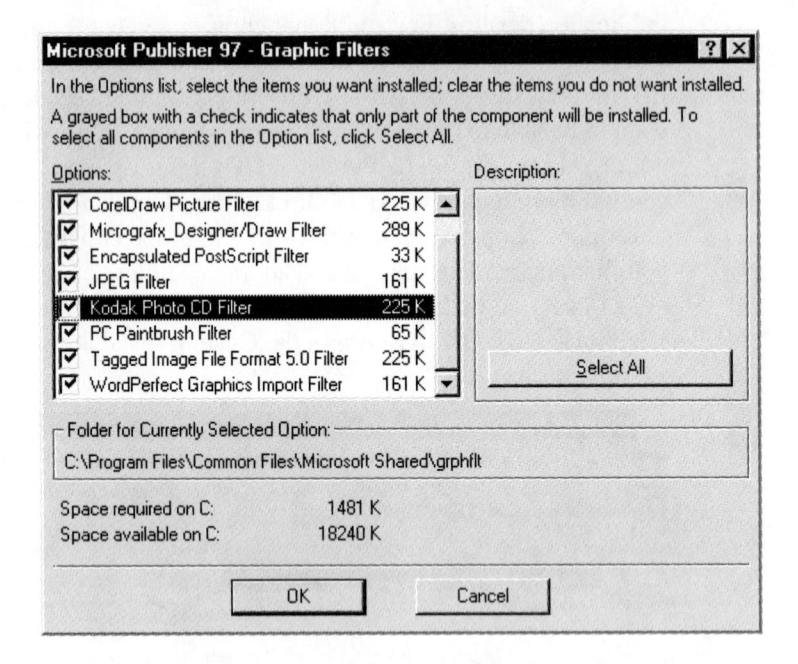

- The *Text Converters* option installs filters for importing text created in other applications. To specify which text filters are installed, click on the Change Option button. In the Text Converters dialog box you can remove the check mark by the text formats you will not be using. As with the graphic filters, you can install the filters later if necessary. After making your selections, click OK to return to the Custom Installation dialog box.

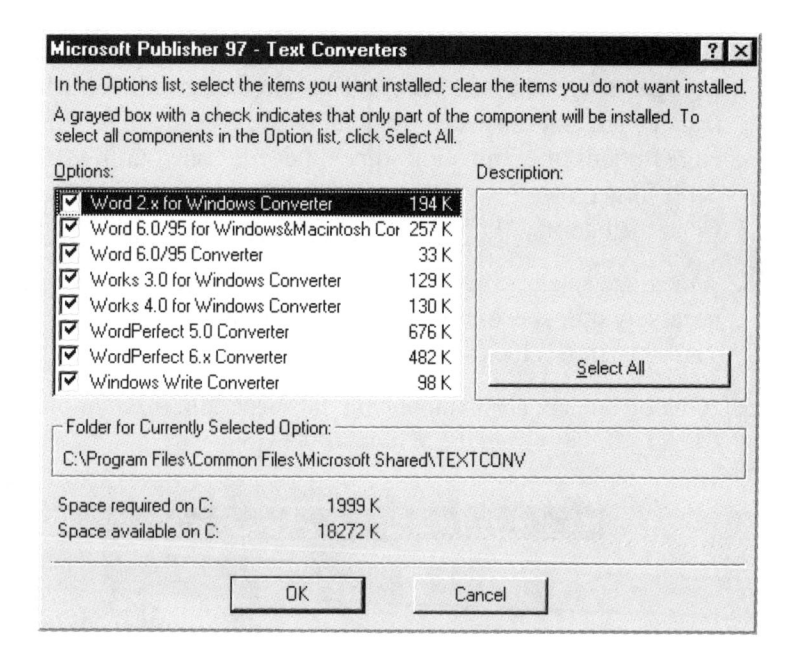

The *Microsoft Draw* option installs the Microsoft Drawing add-on module used to create basic drawings and edit the colors in Publisher's clip art. You might elect not to install this option if you are trying to conserve disk space or have another drawing program, such as CorelDRAW, that can edit clip art.

The *Setup and Microsoft Info* option installs the Setup program on the drive where Windows is stored. This makes it easy to install other options later. You might elect not to install this option if you are trying to conserve disk space.

The *Mail Merge* option installs the files necessary so you can use Publisher to merge and print address information from other programs. You might elect not to install this option if you have another program, such as Microsoft Word, which also does mail merge.

3. When you have finished making selections, check the bottom of the dialog box to make sure the space required to install Publisher is less than the amount of space available. If not, consider removing a few more options or eliminating some other files on your hard drive(s). (Also don't forget to empty the Recycle Bin.) When ready, click on the Continue button.

4. A message appears indicating the Setup program is checking for necessary disk space. If there is enough space, the installation begins. A status bar shows the progress of the installation.

5. A dialog box appears announcing the successful installation of Publisher. Click OK to return to the Windows desktop.

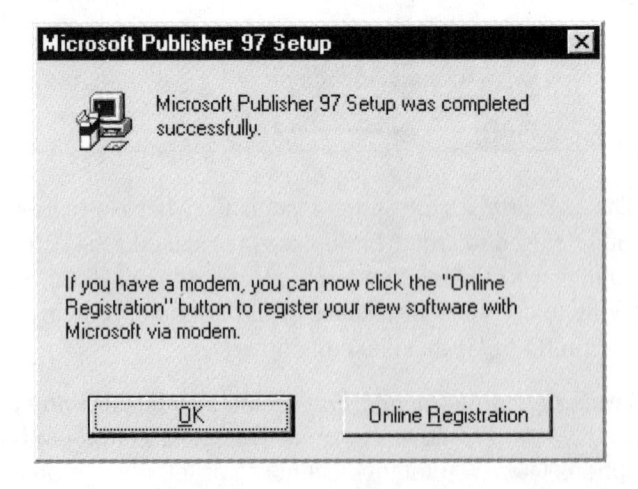

After installing Publisher, you're now ready to return to the front of the book and begin learning how to create publications. You do not have to restart your computer before launching Publisher.

Installing Printer Drivers

While running the Setup program for Microsoft Publisher 97, you may see the following message:

"Publisher 97's Outside Printing feature helps you create publications that will print well at commercial printers and service bureaus. In order to install this feature, Setup requires files from your Microsoft Windows disks or network installation share. Do you want Publisher Setup to install this feature?"

If you choose Yes, Publisher will ask you to insert one of your Windows disks or the Windows compact disc. Publisher then installs two PostScript printer drivers that you may need if you want to use a commercial printing service. As discussed in Chapter 10, you can install the PostScript printers at a later time.

Uninstalling Publisher

If you need to remove Publisher or any components from your computer, take advantage of the installation maintenance program.

NOTE: *The installation maintenance program will not work if you did not install the Setup And Microsoft Info option as described in the section on custom installation options. In this case, you will need to use your CD or floppy disks to launch the Setup program; then select the options to uninstall Publisher.*

Use the following steps to start the installation maintenance program:

1. Click on the Start button on the taskbar. (You can also press CTRL-ESC to display the Start menu.) From the menu, select Settings and then click Control Panel.

2. Double-click on the Add/Remove Programs icon in the Control Panel.

3. In the Add/Remove Programs Properties dialog box, make sure the Install/Uninstall tab is selected at the top. Microsoft Publisher 97 should appear in the list of programs that can be automatically removed by Windows. Select Microsoft Publisher 97 in the list, and click on the Add/Remove button.

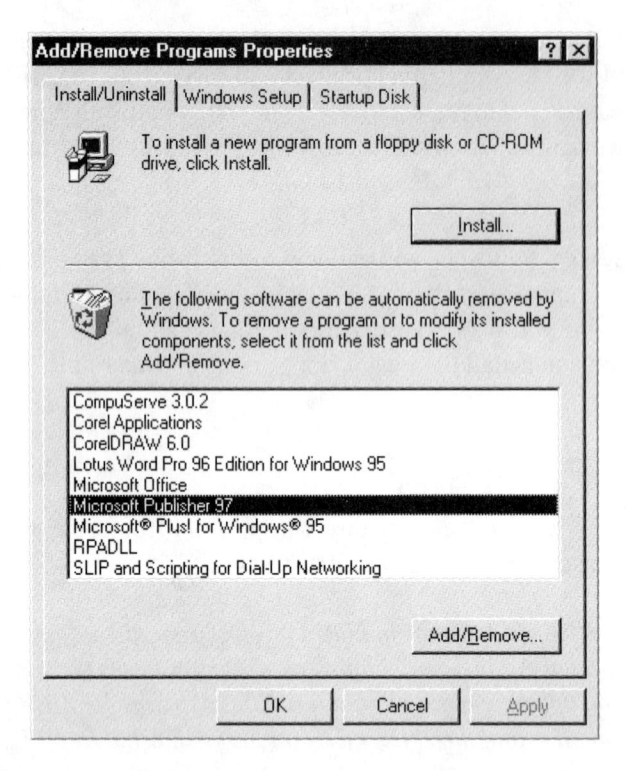

4. The Microsoft Publisher Installation Maintenance dialog box appears. Click on the Add/Remove button to add or remove installed components. This takes you to another dialog box listing the options you can add or remove. Refer to the section "Custom Installation Options" for information on each option.

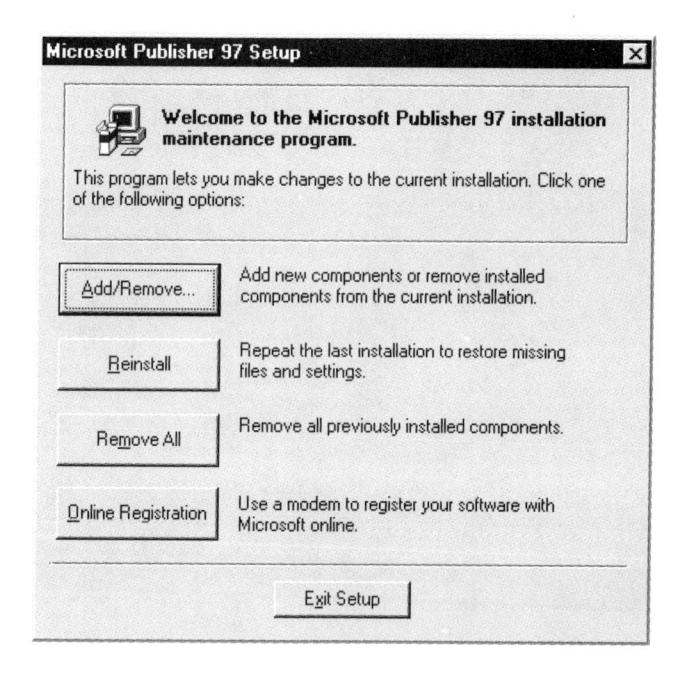

5. Click on the Remove All button to remove all previously installed components. A message appears asking you to confirm this step—click Yes. A status bar indicates the progress as the files are removed.

6. When finished, a message may appear asking you to restart Windows—click on the Restart Windows button.

After restarting your system, the Setup program will have successfully uninstalled Publisher.

INDEX

N